The Gulf War and the New World Order

The Gulf War
and the
New World Order

International Relations of the Middle East

EDITED BY

Tareq Y. Ismael and
Jacqueline S. Ismael

University Press of Florida

GAINESVILLE □ TALLAHASSEE □ TAMPA □ BOCA RATON
PENSACOLA □ ORLANDO □ MIAMI □ JACKSONVILLE

Library of Congress Cataloging-in-Publication Data

The Gulf War and the new world order: international relations of the
Middle East / edited by Tareq Y. Ismael and Jacqueline S. Ismael.
    p. cm.
  Includes bibliographical references (p.   ) and index.
  ISBN 0-8130-1264-3. — ISBN 0-8130-1265-1 (pbk.)
  1. Middle East—Politics and government—1979-   2. World
politics—1989-   3. Persian Gulf War, 1991- —Diplomatic history.
I. Ismael, Tareq Y.   II. Ismael, Jacqueline S.
DS63.1.G86   1994   93-37415
327.56—dc20   CIP

PS
63.1
.G86
1994

The University Press of Florida is the scholarly publishing agency for the State University
System of Florida, comprised of Florida A&M University, Florida Atlantic University, Florida
International University, Florida State University, University of Central Florida, University
of Florida, University of North Florida, University of South Florida, and University of West
Florida.

b157446 44
43.96

University Press of Florida
15 Northwest 15th Street
Gainesville, FL 32611

In Memory of Hajia Um Tareq

born Nazzi Haji Nabi Sherwani at Arbil in 1927 and
died in Baghdad 8 October 1991

Sleep, sleep, my son
Your enemy is feeble
and dwells in the wilderness

(from a traditional Baghdadi lullaby)

CONTENTS

Preface

This endeavor was initiated as a deeply personal reaction to the Gulf War. It began in April 1991, when I sent the following open letter to the Sixteenth Annual Symposium of the Center for Contemporary Arab Studies, Georgetown University:

On February 26, I withdrew from participation in this symposium as an expression of my sense of intellectual impotency in the face of the Gulf crisis. Nothing in my intellectual or professional experience had prepared me for the sheer savagery of unfolding events. And speculation about its consequences seemed well beyond the pale of any scientific theory I know. Now, six weeks later, as you initiate the symposium, the situation in the Middle East is even more savage and precarious, and I feel compelled to share with you my professional concerns as they relate to this enterprise.

Six weeks ago, I felt the discipline of political science generally, and the field of Middle East studies specifically, to be intellectually bankrupt and irrelevant. Now I fear it may have been implicated all along in the trajectory toward genocide by contributing to the obfuscations, mystifications, and, ultimately, falsifications that mask the making of tyrants and warmongers, and sanction their profiteering handmaidens; that mask the perpetration of genocide behind humanitarian handmaidens.

For twenty years, while the Iraqi people suffered the brutality of Saddam Hussein's dictatorship, the world flirted with his regime. In this period, the same nations that participated in Operation Desert Storm conducted business with his government, sold him arms, supported his territorial aggressions, and ignored his human rights record. Saudi Arabia and other Gulf states, in fact, financed his war with Iran and heralded him as a great Arab leader and hero, even while thousands of Iraqis languished in his prisons and died in his torture chambers.

The war to liberate Kuwait destroyed the Iraqi people but

salvaged Saddam Hussein's regime, preserving its power base, the Republican Guard. The Iraqi nation is hemorrhaging: Arabs, Kurds, Turcomans, Assyrians, Shi'is, Sunnis, Christians—all fleeing the bloody wrath of the Republican Guard, all facing the ravages of disease and starvation unleashed by the war to liberate Kuwait.

Iraq's community infrastructure was destroyed in the name of some obscene conception of military strategy. The Republican Guard, with all their arms, was salvaged in the name of some obscene conception of regional stability. The Iraqi people were enticed into open rebellion in the name of some obscene conception of psychological warfare. The Republican Guard's subsequent rampage against them was unchecked in the name of some obscene conception of national sovereignty. And in the name of some obscene conception of objectivity, the experts and specialists are immobilized in the quagmire of debate over the conceptual obscurities of these obscenities.

We are trapped somewhere between Saddam Hussein's 1984 and Henry Kissinger's Brave New World *on the road to President George Bush's new world order. On a trail of destruction that leads from Palestine through Baghdad, this road has all the signposts of the future. We can all read them. What do we do with our knowledge? Add to the jingoism and benefit our careers? Ignore it and protect our careers? Challenge it and risk our careers? As experts and specialists, what role do we play in history?*

Since the beginning of this disaster, I have had calls and letters from academic colleagues all over the world expressing the kind of intellectual anguish that I am experiencing. This symposium is the first major meeting of scholars of Middle East studies since this crisis began. Therefore, I raise this issue before you in the hope that it will initiate serious debate over the question of whether we have abandoned the responsibilities of academic freedom to guide rather than legitimate policy.

The symposium organizers did not release the letter, and the issues were not addressed. As a result, we (Jackie and I) organized a plenary session on the issues raised by the letter at the Fifth Congress of the International Association of Middle Eastern Studies (IAMES), held in Tunis, Tunisia, 20–24 September 1991. This project is one result of the intense discussions and concerns expressed at that conference.

We wish to express our gratitude to the Executive Committee of IAMES for accommodating our organization of the plenary session well after the conference program was finalized, the contributors to this volume for their participation in this endeavor and patience throughout the many revisions, and the Ford Foundation for providing a grant that facilitated the attendance of scholars from the Arab world at the conference and the publication of this volume. We would be amiss if we did not acknowledge the assistance of Elsie Johnson and Doreen Neville in getting the manuscript formatted and typed, and keeping a cheerful disposition throughout; and Siren Fisekci in coordinating the project and keeping it on track. Finally, we want to thank Walda Metcalf of the University Press of Florida for her enthusiasm for this project and her confidence in us.

Tareq Y. Ismael

Introduction

The concept of a new world order, introduced into the lexicon of international politics with the collapse of communism in Eastern Europe, was strongly invoked by President George Bush in response to the Gulf crisis. Thus, the end of the cold war and Iraq's invasion of Kuwait in August 1991 constitute the historical reference points for the concept. This suggests at least two dimensions in its meaning: the end of an international order determined by the struggle for hegemony between the United States and the Soviet Union; and the initiation of a U.S. foreign policy doctrine based on U.S. hegemony in the international order.

This volume seeks to explore the impact of the Gulf War on the fashioning of a new world order, with particular reference to the role of the Middle East region. It is divided into four parts, each addressing a different facet. The purpose is to develop a holistic perspective of the new world order and to explore its external and internal dynamics. What is revealed is that the processes of policy articulation, formulation, and impact are interactively interrelated rather than sequentially related and dynamic rather than static vis-à-vis the relationship between objectives and outcomes. In a linear model, the new world order and the Gulf War are viewed as independent and dependent variables. In a nonlinear model—the focus demanded by a holistic perspective—they are dynamically interrelated and interdependent simultaneously on a number of planes rather than sequentially related in space-time.

Part I, "The Gulf War and the International Order," examines central principles of international relations inherent in the articulation of the new world order and the power dynamic among protagonists of world order. The first chapter, "Reflections on the Gulf War Experience: Force and War in the UN System" by Richard Falk, initiates this section with an examination of the failure of the United Nations to abide by international law and to forestall the trajectory toward war.

The aim of progressive international law has been to outlaw war. Resort to force in foreign policy is unconditionally prohibited in modern international law except in situations of self-defense. This legalist undertaking, however, has remained unfulfilled. The Iraqi invasion of Kuwait challenged and tested the willingness and capacity of the UN to mount an effective response by way of collective security. The results are mixed.

Prior to the Gulf crisis, collective security had been generally discredited by a combination of failures of capacity and consensus, first during the period of the League of Nations and next during the UN period. The Gulf crisis generated an early response that appeared encouraging. In the aftermath of the Gulf War, however, few would argue that collective security as an approach to international aggression had been vindicated or even tested. Instead, it appears that the UN authorized a resort to war as a result of pressure exerted by the U.S. government, thereby neglecting to be guided by the conception of collective security specified in Chapter VII of the UN Charter.

Falk concludes that the UN's failure in relation to the Gulf War is tragic and far-reaching. The war was improperly initiated, and carried well beyond the basic UN mandate. Then, having been so dubiously extended, it was perversely terminated in a highly disruptive fashion that caused severe and massive additional suffering and devastation.

In Chapter 2, "The United Nations in the Gulf Crisis," Robert Springborg examines the process by which the United States recruited the United Nations to its cause to crush Iraq while simultaneously ensuring that the international organization did not intrude into the Israeli-Palestinian conflict. Washington invoked the name and authority of the UN for its unilateral naval blockade two weeks prior to the passing of Security Council Resolution 665 that authorized such action. Resolution 678, which authorized the use of force against Iraq, was a masterpiece of obfuscation intended to avoid UN control over U.S. military actions. The deployment of U.S. troops to Saudi Arabia was predicated on the spurious claim that an Iraqi invasion was imminent. The General Assembly was essentially excluded from playing any role during the crisis, while the Security Council was prevented by the United States even from meeting during the most intensive phase of military action. The secretary-general was similarly prevented by Washington from using his good offices to avert war. From the onset of the crisis, the United States was intent on maintaining control of events and on legitimating its intervention through the UN. That it succeeded is testimony to the status of the United States as the sole surviving superpower and to the inability of the UN to defend its organizational interests and integrity.

Together, these two chapters identify the extent to which the notion of a new world order is a U.S.-imposed design on a unipolar world rather than a higher stage in the evolution of international affairs toward conflict management. In Chapter 3, "Bush's New World Order: A Structural Analysis of Instability and Conflict in the Gulf," Yasumasa Kuroda examines the *new* elements in President Bush's new world order, how European colonial powers structured the Gulf, as well as the whole of West Asia and North Africa, to suit their interests rather than to foster democracy, and how the United States has dealt with the region to maintain the status quo rather than to promote democracy, not differing significantly from its European allies. From this perspective, it is argued that instability and conflict in the Gulf are the product of colonial design rather than any indigenous systemic process. Structurally, the new world order simply represents the continuation of the colonial design under U.S. tutelage.

In addition to the structural elements of the Gulf's instability, actors who contributed to increasing hostility against Iraq are presented to provide a wider picture of why and how the Gulf War occurred. The history of anti-Arab sentiment in the West in general and the United States in particular has been manipulated to legitimate imperialistic policies and reveals the pattern of vilification that provided popular legitimation for the Gulf War. The media campaign of half truths and misinformation mustered support for a righteous campaign. Bush told an audience of soldiers departing for the Gulf that the United States was going to war so that "what we say goes" in the Gulf. Secretary of State James Baker said repeatedly that the war created a window of opportunity to work toward peace and security in the region.

What kind of peace and security are sought by a superpower with little sympathy for the peoples of the area? One can be optimistic only if this moment is used by hegemonic powers to rekindle "the better angels of our nature," as another Republican president, Abraham Lincoln, said. Of course, better elements of our ideals are to promote political and economic freedom in the region, as the superpowers profess for Eastern Europe, so that security and stability are founded on a sound legitimate base rather than brute force. The forces that are likely to challenge the prevailing institutions and geographic boundaries in the region to establish a new order call for restructuring the entire region.

The dominant role played by the United States in orchestrating the international response to Iraq's invasion of Kuwait and the Gulf War begs the question of the role of other powers in the international arena. The international consensus supporting U.S. policy was both impressive and surprising. The United States, after all, may be a military superpower, but it is no longer an economic superpower. The European Community (EC) and Japan are ascendant powers in the global economy. And unlike the United States, both are heavily dependent on Middle East oil and would ostensibly appear to have a strong vested interest in distancing themselves from U.S. geostrategic policy in the region. Yet both acquiesced to the uncompromising U.S. agenda of restoration of the status quo ante in Kuwait and destruction of Iraq. The last three chapters in this section examine the cases of the roles played by these powers.

In Chapter 4, "The European Community's Middle Eastern Policy: the New Order of Europe and the Gulf Crisis" Friedemann Buettner and Martin Landgraf examine the European Community's failure to assert an independent policy in the Gulf crisis in terms of the changes in Europe at the end of the cold war, and the position of the EC and of individual European states during the crisis. When Iraqi troops invaded Kuwait on 2 August 1990, the EC acted swiftly and in concord to condemn the invasion and impose economic sanctions. The activities out of Brussels seemed to indicate that the Europeans were determined to play a leading role in the crisis. Such a role would have been fully in consonance with Europe's new potentials after the end of the cold war.

In a way, the Gulf crisis came to the Europeans as a test case for their ability to coordinate their individual foreign policies in a situation of crisis and to design new structures for a joint European security policy. The crisis found the Europeans in disarray at a time when a joint European stand might have been of some consequence for the course of events. Verbally the Europeans continued to support all Security Council resolutions in perfect unison. But there followed no successful effort to implement a joint European policy beyond making declarations. By the time the aerial bombardment of Iraq started in mid-January 1991, it had become clear that the Europeans obviously had missed an opportunity to effect the course of the crisis.

In spite of many bitter comments on European disunity, most Middle Eastern states did expect an active European role in the peace process and in endeavors to frame a new regional order in the Middle East. In order to make the prospects for and limits to such a

European role assessable, the problems of coordinating European foreign policies and the emergence of the European Political Cooperation as an institutional framework are outlined, with special reference to European Middle Eastern policy.

In Chapter 5, "Regional Cooperation and Security in the Middle East: The Role of the European Community," Timothy Niblock offers another perspective on the rather undistinguished role of the EC during the Gulf crisis. There have been two distinctive aspects to the EC's approach to the Middle East: an emphasis on promoting regional integration in the area, and a belief in the need to establish an overall framework within which the region's problems could achieve resolution. The overall framework sought is one in which the EC itself has a direct role, by virtue both of its proximity to the Middle East and of there being a "Mediterranean region" of which the Community forms part.

The effect of the crisis has been to create a more concerted EC policy on matters that relate to both "distinctive aspects." As regards the promotion of regional integration in the region, new policies are now being developed that involve supporting integration through technical cooperation, infrastructure projects, and educational and research activities. Some of the projects which are under consideration—such as the creation of infrastructures that link together water, gas and electricity networks—suggest a major undertaking.

As regards the pursuit of an overall approach to the area, the proposals for a cooperation and security framework in the Mediterranean are now much more concrete than they were before. The concern is to create a stable system of regional cooperation, where all the states accept a set of principles and roles (similar to the Conference on Security and Cooperation in Europe). The basis would be laid for peace conferences for the resolution of specific disputes: security structures grounded on local support and involvement; the treatment of some of the socioeconomic problems of the region; and the promotion of some general principles promoting tolerance and the respect for human rights. Thus, the crisis did bring about some significant developments in EC policy. These developments may prove of particular importance to the EC's future role in the Middle East.

Chapter 6, "Japan: An Economic Superpower in Search of Its Proper Political Role in the Post-Cold War Era" by Yasumasa Kuroda explains why Japan acted as it did in dealing with the Gulf War. It examines how the government, the public, the media, and area specialists responded to the war. It shows how peace-oriented Japan's constitution is, how well the public accepted its pacifist constitution over the years, and, in relation to the West, how untainted it is by a history of colonial ambitions in West Asia and North Africa. Historically, Japan has taken somewhat different policies toward the region with respect to its foreign policy, which is often accused of simply following the U.S. lead. Who controls the oil makes little difference to Japan, which relies on oil from the region. The Japan-U.S. relationship is important and vital to Japan, however, and it constrains Japan from making its own independent foreign policy rather than following the U.S. lead in world politics. Japan finds it a Herculean challenge to play an active role in world politics while it proved its ability in a few decades to become an undisputed economic superpower after its economy was almost totally ruined in World War II.

As a U.S. model for world affairs, the meanings of both the new world order and the Gulf War are embedded in the lexicon of U.S. politics. Part II, "The United States and the New World Order," explores the scope and range of this lexicon as it relates to U.S. policy in the Middle East. The purpose is to examine the relationship between President Bush's concept of a new world order and his orchestration of the Gulf War. The first chapter in the section (Chapter 7), "Between Theory and Fact: Explaining U.S. Behavior in the Gulf Crisis" by Shibley Telhami, considers the conventional interpretations of U.S. policy in the Gulf crisis, from its initial reaction to Iraq's invasion of Kuwait to its culmination in military action against Iraq.

Three categories of theoretically significant but logically flawed explanations are critiqued: oil, Israel, and the end of the cold war. A fourth category, other, examines some of the theoretically insignificant types of explanation. Although an interesting case can be made for each of the interpretations, none can ultimately stand up to the facts.

An alternative explanation—one that addresses the decision-making process rather than motives—provides a framework for examining policy as a product not only of objectives but also of the changing exigencies and contingencies of time and space in a course of action. Viewed from this perspective, the author argues that the early U.S. decision to deploy forces in the Gulf was almost "automatic"; no matter who sat in the White House, or who had access to it, the decision would have been the same. The decision to escalate U.S. deployment in October 1990 made war inevitable. It is argued that this decision was ultimately caused by the inherent tension between the domestic and international context of U.S. policy in the Middle East. The tension was exacerbated by the major Israeli-Palestinian crisis during that month.

In Chapter 8, "The New World Order and the Gulf War: Rhetoric, Policy, and Politics in the United States," Enid Hill examines the speeches and other statements issued by President Bush and Secretary Baker during and immediately following the Gulf crisis and war to deconstruct the notion of a new world order. The concept was invoked repeatedly as both an objective of the war and as the antecedent condition that the war was being fought to restore. The formulations of the Bush administration enthusiastically embraced the Gulf War as the "first test" of enforcing security in the new world order. Although the overwhelming majority of senators supported the administration's Gulf policy, there were several senators who expressed serious reservations. Initially dismissed as isolationists, journal commentaries pointed up various contradictions to explain away their reservations; however, the debates reflected serious substantive concerns in the emerging critique of the new world order.

The rhetoric of the Bush administration during the Gulf crisis is contrasted with pre- and post-Gulf crisis rhetoric. The movement of the Bush administration's foreign policy from one extreme to another is revealed. Schizophrenic tendencies in U.S. policy are not limited to pre- or post-war Iraq, however. The author contends that although policy in the Gulf seems to lack rationality, coherence, or common sense, it is symptomatic of U.S. policy toward the Middle East in general.

The next chapter (9), "The Making of the New World Order: The Role of the Media" by Malcolm Hayward, broadens the rhetorical lens from a focus on the rhetoric of policymakers to the narration of war as a cultural phenomenon. To view the Gulf War from this perspective, attention is given to the roles of audience, narrative, and mode of presentation. Three factors influence events and ideas about these events: "interpretative situations," which encompass both the series of events that constitute the Gulf War and the vision of the new world order; the narratives participants use to relate those events; and the mode of presentation and its effect on the audience.

The interpretative situation of the United States esteems rationality, codified fairness, consensual democracy, and a dependence on technology. U.S. understanding of the Arab world was measured by these qualities. During the Gulf crisis, the media, influenced by area specialists and politicians, perpetuated a number of stereotypes that found the Arab world to lack these four qualities. These stereotypes were encased in political narratives drawn from U.S. popular culture, casting Iraq in the role of the villain. The media of presentation—television, video, and new photographs—were also designed to elicit negative emotional responses to the Iraqis. As Bush's new world order was a contingent response to specific events during the Gulf crisis, the shape that this agenda for U.S. foreign policy has taken was markedly influenced by the emergent realities of the conflict and by the rhetorical terms in which the conflict was cast. The result is a vision of U.S. values instituted on a global scale, with the sanctioned use of force to implement these designs.

The final chapter in this section (10), "Defeating the Vietnam Syndrome: The Military, the Media, and the Gulf War" by Andrew T. Parasiliti, examines the special role played by U.S. media in developing and presenting the narrative. Although the Bush administration hailed a new world order in orchestrating the UN coalition forces against Iraq in the Gulf War, U.S. policy was in many ways characteristic of traditional U.S. cold war foreign policy. On 16 January 1991, the day the air war against Iraq began, President Bush promised the American people that "this will not be another Vietnam."

During the Gulf War, the Bush administration fell prey to a common misperception stemming from the Vietnam War—that the U.S. media played an oppositional role to government policies. According to this view, the media's critical reporting of that conflict, especially television's coverage of combat, undercut U.S. policy and undermined faith in the U.S. presidency. Operating on this assumption, the Bush administration placed controls on the media during the Gulf War in order to avoid "another Vietnam." The media, also influenced by criticism of its alleged role as an oppositional force during the Vietnam conflict, in fact performed as an establishment institution, generally supportive of the president's policies. The result was a public relations landslide for the Bush administration and a limited and relatively uncritical view of U.S. participation in the Gulf War presented by the media to the U.S. people.

Part III, "The Gulf War and the Middle East Order," turns attention to significant actors in the Middle East drama. For reasons of space, only the core participants of the Middle East political system are included. These are the actors whose policies—domestic, regional, and international—have essentially defined the nature and scope of the Middle East political system in the twentieth century.

Hence, these are the core actors of the system. Although the Middle East includes many other states, generally they have been more or less peripheral to the systemic patterns of Middle East politics. In other words, their participation in regional politics may have been intense at various times, but neither their active participation nor their withdrawal to peripheral participation significantly altered the nature of the system.

On this basis, neither the North African nor the Gulf states are included. Though they were participants in the Gulf War (directly in the case of the Gulf states but only indirectly for those of North Africa), they really played only a peripheral or passive role in the orchestration of the new world order that was a central factor in the waging of the war.

Part III begins with Chapter 11, "Iraq and the New World Order" by Marion Farouk-Sluglett and Peter Sluglett. How Iraq came to be the object of a U.S.-led war in the Middle East is a central issue in understanding the nature of a world order premised on the destruction of the country. Although Parts I and II focused on the international and U.S. political arenas in addressing this issue, part of the answer lies in the dynamics of Iraqi politics as well. In this chapter, the Slugletts analyze recent developments in Iraq through an interpretation of Iraqi history since the foundation of the state in 1920.

In spite of the artificiality of Iraq as a political entity, some progress toward national integration was visible by the 1950s and 1960s; during the 1970s and 1980s much of this was dissipated, although perhaps not irrevocably, by the brutality and arbitrariness of the present regime.

In part, the current situation in Iraq has come about as a result of the absence of democratic and other checks to the rise of one particular individual to a position of absolute authority and in part because of the support given to him at crucial moments by an eclectic assortment of foreign powers. Saddam Hussein has ruined the Iraqi economy and destroyed much of civil society by constructing a monstrous machine of internal repression and a military leviathan that has taken the country into two disastrous military adventures.

National reconciliation will be possible only if all sectors of society—Sunnis, Shi'is, Kurds—can feel confident that any new government is truly representative of their interests. To have moral authority, the new world order requires that all possible support be given to those forces struggling to introduce democracy and the rule of law into Iraq. The temptation on the part of the West, prompted largely by the more conservative Arab states, simply to maintain the status quo in Iraq and elsewhere in the region because it is familiar and thus in some sense manageable must be resisted. If the present situation persists, there is a real danger of the rise of religio-political movements that may threaten the fragile peace and security of the region as a whole, as well as impeding processes of national reconciliation.

Iraq and Iran are the major regional powers in the Gulf. With organized central governments since ancient times, these states (known in the past as Persia and Mesopotamia) have always functioned as gatekeepers to the Gulf—a perennially important waterway in the history of world affairs in general and East-West relations in particular. Since Britain sought hegemony over the Gulf in the eighteenth century, pacification of Iraq and Iran has been a strategic imperative of imperial policy. Although the local tribes and tribal principalities of the Gulf never constituted a political or strategic obstacle to external penetration of the area, the central powers in Iraq and Iran (or Mesopotamia and Persia in the past) have always been a bane to Western policy in the Middle East.

In the modern era, oil replaced trade routes in the Middle East's geopolitical significance in international politics. And with oil resources concentrated in the Gulf states, Iraq and Iran have been pivotal points in Western strategies to secure control over these resources. With the stability of the fragile Gulf sheikhdoms securely tied to Britain or the United States, Iraq and Iran remained strategic gadflies in the Gulf's security. Iran's 1979 revolution demonstrated not only the frailty of a security system dependent on anachronistic regimes but also the pivotal role of Iraq and Iran in the whole system. Although the Iran-Iraq War temporarily staved off threats to the weak Gulf sheikhdoms, it also opened the door to direct military intervention by the West to preserve the status quo. Maintenance and protection of the status quo ante in the Gulf were unqualified and unambiguous objectives of Bush's call for a new world order. Viewed from this perspective, the destruction of Iraq and preservation of the status quo ante there after the war is a means of immobilizing a gadfly. What about Iran?

Chapter 12, "Iran and the New World Order," by Scheherazade Daneshkhu examines Iran's reaction to the new world order and notes that it has been relatively subdued for a state not given to diffidence in its foreign policy. Whenever the phrase is mentioned at the official level, it is invariably with a sense of mistrust and cynicism. But the more pragmatic faction in Iran's leadership, led by President

Hashemi Rafsanjani, has not gone out of its way to condemn the new world order. There are a number of reasons for this uncharacteristic ambivalence.

On the international level, the Iranian government, like many others, is unsure of what is meant by a new world order. If it means that the United States is willing to forgo some of its powers to allow the UN to play a greater role in world affairs, Iran would welcome it. The collapse of communism as an ideological doctrine was certainly a positive development for Iran's Islamic rulers, but they view the logical extension of this with less equanimity. Does it follow that the United States will have increased power and that it will be able to impose a Pax Americana unchallenged? Or does it mean that a United States no longer threatened by the Soviet Union will become inward looking and feel less need to intervene in the domestic affairs of other states? Obviously, Iran would feel threatened by the first development but would welcome the new world order if it resulted in the second.

In regional terms, the Iranian government is anxious to know how the new world order translates itself into a new regional security structure for the Gulf and specifically for its own role within that structure. The outcome of the first major international crisis to occur after the collapse of communism—the Iraqi invasion of Kuwait—ended in Iran's favor. Its old enemy was humiliated by the coalition forces. Yet the first indications for a new regional security structure, the Gulf Cooperation Council (GCC) countries and Syria and Egypt, excluded Iran, giving rise again to Iran's mistrust of what the United States is hoping to achieve. The Damascus Declaration has all but collapsed, and Iran's view of the new world order will be tempered by the U.S. response to the size of its role in the region.

Domestically, moves toward a new world order have come at a time of change in Iran. Even when Ayatollah Khomeini was alive, Iran began to break through its isolationism. Iran's hand to the world was first extended through the Soviet Union when a delegation visited Mikhail Gorbachev in January 1989, carrying a message of praise for the Soviet leader and his reforms from Ayatollah Khomeini.

Since Khomeini's death in June 1989, President Rafsanjani has been regarded as trying to institute his own form of perestroika in Iran by relaxing the stricter conditions, a position for which he gets increasingly vocal criticism from harder line Iranian opponents. These opponents view the new world order with less ambivalence than does

Rafsanjani. It is taken to mean that the United States will now be able to rule the roost without hindrance from the Soviet Union. Under these circumstances, they argue, it is even more important for Iran to assert Islam as a political and ideological force to challenge the hegemony of U.S. rule. Hardline idealogues argue that Islam was the third force in international relations (after capitalism and communism), and it should now be the second force.

The systemic patterns of Middle East politics have revolved around two poles of interaction: oil and the Palestinian problem. Oil is the primary pole of attraction for external actors, and its center of gravity is the Gulf. The Palestinian problem, on the other hand, has been the primary pole of interaction for regional actors, and its center of gravity is the Fertile Crescent. Although the U.S. doctrine of a new world order clearly translates into preservation of the status quo in the Gulf, what does it indicate vis-à-vis the Palestinian problem?

The question of U.S. credibility as the leader of the new world order would seem to be a factor working in favor of a resolution of the Palestinian problem. How, it might be asked, after marshaling the entire UN to redress Iraq's invasion and occupation of Kuwait, can Washington ignore those very issues in regard to the Palestinians? Will it not be necessary for the United States to act consistently and principally, in accordance with UN resolutions, to bring about a just resolution of the Palestine issue?

In Chapter 13, "The Gulf War, the Palestinians, and the New World Order," Cheryl A. Rubenberg examines the prospects facing the Palestinians in the new world order. In the aftermath of the Gulf War, no actor (except, of course, Iraq) is in a weaker or more vulnerable position than the Palestinians. They have lost the financial support of their major Arab state backers and the political support of a significant number of other states, their bargaining power has been significantly diminished, the Intifada has come to a virtual halt, and there is a leadership crisis as well as a new exodus of Palestinians, this time from Kuwait. To a considerable extent, this situation is a consequence of the Palestinians having sided with the "wrong" party in the Gulf conflict, though there has been a great deal of distortion concerning their positions. In addition, the transformation of the international system into a unipolar structure with a hegemonic U.S. purposefully promoting its design for a new world order does not bode well for Palestinians. The United States has been historically consistent in its rejection of fundamental Palestinian rights, and there is nothing to suggest that it will change significantly.

Even before the Gulf War, the collapse of communism in the Soviet Union and Eastern Europe had a negative impact on Palestinian interests. Although the Soviet Union had never been a strong supporter of the Palestinians or the Palestine Liberation Organization (PLO), its position on an international conference, its relationship with Syria and Iraq, and its general counterpoint to the United States provided the Palestinians with some hope that the U.S.-Israeli behemoth might be contained and Palestinian interests realized. But the Soviet Union's eagerness for trade, aid, investment, and loans from the U.S. led Moscow to acquiesce readily to U.S.-backed Israeli interests, the most important being the immigration of Soviet Jews to Israel.

Palestinian interests have also suffered a significant setback as a consequence of the shifting positions of actors in the aftermath of the Gulf War. Traditional U.S. allies such as Kuwait, Saudi Arabia, Egypt, and Jordan (despite a less than "correct" position during the war) have more openly than ever embraced the United States, even having an evident willingness to formalize relations with Israel and in effect negate Palestinian rights. Moreover, with the Soviet Union in partnership with the United States, Syria, a traditional U.S. foe, was quick to side with Washington (in exchange for control over Lebanon) and to do "business" with Israel, also apparently at the expense of the Palestinians.

Indeed, in the aftermath of the war against Iraq the Middle East will never be the same. Even the idea of Arab nationalism or pan-Arabism, with its Palestinian cornerstone, seems moot. While in the past the Arab states felt constrained by the strength of mass sentiment regarding the Palestinians at least to give lip service to the Palestinian cause, with the new world order—especially the promise of U.S. force to maintain the status quo should disgruntled masses try to make their voices heard—no major Arab state seems either willing or able to demand rights for Palestinians.

In Chapter 14, "Israel and the New World Order," Meir Porat examines the impact of the Gulf War and the doctrine of a new world order on Israel. Although the discussion is organized in terms of global, regional, and domestic spheres of Israeli politics, a determinant factor across all spheres is Israel's diplomatic, military, and economic dependence on the United States, a dependence fostered by the buildup of Israel's regional military hegemony. This factor has served both U.S. objectives of global hegemony and allied containment and Israel's domestic objectives of immigration absorption and territorial expansion. In other words, the creation of Israel as a regional military superpower has served the U.S. strategy of destabilizing pan-Arab politics and increasing U.S. influence in the oil-producing states; as a correlative, Israel, as a military superpower in the region, has pursued Zionism's more extreme messianic and xenophobic ambitions.

The combination of military means and ideological ends resulted in Israel's diplomatic isolation, especially after the 1967 war. This further increased dependence on the U.S. internationally and on military means regionally. The end of the cold war witnessed a reduction of diplomatic isolation with an improvement in Soviet-Israeli relations, but the removal of obstacles to the immigration of Soviet Jews to Israel intensified domestic economic and social problems and hardened messianic policies. The Gulf War and the breakup of the Soviet Union strengthened the alignment between the United States and Israel in the regional sphere. In the domestic sphere, Israeli politics have polarized around issues of war and peace.

In Chapter 15 "Jordan and the Gulf War," Kamel S. Abu Jaber examines the complex and intertwined international, regional, and domestic factors that influenced Jordan's course of action in the Gulf crisis. Diminishing U.S. aid to Jordan following the peace treaty between Egypt and Israel, the growth of Jordan's economic ties with Iraq as a result, Israel's arms buildup and pressure on Jordan, the popularity of Saddam Hussein in Jordan—all were factors influencing Jordan's efforts to de-escalate and de-internationalize the crisis. This course of action was in contradiction with the U.S. response to Iraq's invasion of Kuwait. As a result of its pursuit of an Arab solution to the crisis, Jordan raised the ire of the United States and suffered manifold consequences, including diplomatic isolation and the curtailment of aid. The impact on Jordan has been profound.

Thus, as the cold war subsided and official declarations of its death were repeated almost ritually by politicians in East and West, international cooperation and the peaceful resolution of conflicts appeared to be the hallmarks of a new order in international affairs. It was becoming readily apparent that in the Middle East this new world order of harmony and peace was only the surface of an order that consecrated the hegemony of the winners of the cold war.

In Chapter 16, "Syria, the Kuwait War, and the New World Order," Eberhard Kienle observes that, unlike its counterpart in Baghdad, the Assad regime of Syria understood the implications of the end of the cold war. Since the late 1980s, this understanding, together with a number of other considerations (foremost among them the need for foreign capital), led Syria to seek closer relations with the West. Prior to the Kuwait crisis, however, there were limits to such a rapprochement as the Western powers continued to suspect Damascus of sponsoring or protecting international terrorists. In the United States, moreover, the less conciliant features of Syrian policy toward Israel continued to be exaggerated, while little attention was paid to more accommodating stances.

The invasion of Kuwait fundamentally changed Western attitudes toward Syria. The Assad regime all of a sudden emerged as a centerpiece of any strategy against the Iraqi regime that disrupted the new world order (in the sense that it pursued policies that were not endorsed by the victors of the cold war). Hence, the crisis enabled Damascus to demonstrate its willingness to play the new game. It provided an opportunity, but not the excuse, for Syria to support the new world order openly.

Though strengthened by the outcome of the Kuwait crisis, the position of the Syrian regime remains precarious in a number of ways. The need for Western capital particularly narrows its policy choices and may result in a formal arrangement with Israel. Combined with the relative decline of Soviet support and assistance, itself an expression of the new order, it will reinforce tendencies in Syria toward the acceptance of rules laid down in the cabinets and boardrooms of the West.

The cases included in this section thus far as core members of the Middle East's systemic patterns of politics are all active participants in at least one of the two poles of interaction. In contrast, the remaining two chapters in this section—on Egypt and Turkey—represent cases that had withdrawn from active participation well before the Gulf crisis. They are included here for the opposite reason as some states have been excluded: namely, changes in the nature of their participation significantly alter the Middle East order, and this played a key role in the orchestration of the Gulf War.

Chapter 17, "Imagining Egypt in the New Age: Civil Society and the Leftist Critique," by Raymond Baker examines Egypt's relationship to the Gulf crisis through the prism of the critique of policy within the Egyptian arena. To assess the impact of the crisis on civil society in Egypt, first the promise and reality offered Egypt in a new world order are contrasted; then Egypt's domestic debate on the Gulf War is considered.

The promise of a new world order is a large and generous role for a prosperous Egypt, at peace with Israel and playing a regional leadership role. The reality is the persistence of the old system with changed conditions that make the global environment even less favorable to Egypt. The possibility for progressive change was blocked by the U.S.-led military action in which Egypt played a supporting role. To make the point, a sketch is made of the alternative world order that was scuttled by the military action against Iraq. That alternative did emerge as a possibility, however dimly, in the truncated U.S. domestic debate on Gulf policy—only to be overwhelmed by the victory in the war. Instead, the war resulted in a reassertion of the old order. U.S. hegemony was asserted against the new challenges from Europe and Japan. Consequently, Egypt's room for maneuver was sharply circumscribed.

A detailed analysis of the Egyptian domestic debate on the Gulf crisis indicates the state of Egypt's civil society. Social and structural constraints on the debates limited their scope and terms of reference, yet they exposed the views of the regime and secular left opposition. Official restrictions and repression combined with all manner of internal disabilities to deny the left a coherent and unified institutional presence on the political scene. Despite these handicaps, however, the Egyptian left did manage to develop and bring before public opinion a coherent alternative to the official policy.

The Gulf War and the Egyptian reaction to it has brought important though partial clarifications on some key aspects of Egyptian and international political life. Realities of fundamental power and policy direction remain unchanged. Egypt is an authoritarian regime originating and sustained by the military that relies ultimately on the police and security apparatus to preserve an effective monopoly on policy making. Despite divisions and opposition, the regime can sustain a commitment to force to pursue its policy objectives, even though those objectives are questioned by a substantial portion of the population.

In Chapter 18, "Turkey, the Gulf Crisis, and the New World Order," Tozun Bahcheli examines the important role played by the Turkish government in the imposition of sanctions against Iraq following its invasion of Kuwait in August 1990 by shutting off the pipeline that carries half of Iraq's petroleum exports through Turkey. It also helped the military effort of the U.S.-led coalition by massing a substantial military force on its border with Iraq, thus raising the possibility of a second front, and by allowing the United States to use the Incirlik base to bomb targets in northern Iraq.

In taking an unequivocal position on Kuwait, Turkey was showing a commitment to the protection of the existing state system in the Middle East. Further, Iraq's absorption of Kuwait threatened to change the existing balance of power in the region. Although Turkey's relations with Iraq were not marred by deep-seated animosities, in recent years relations between the two neighbors were strained principally because of the water issue. Against this background, Turkish President Turgut Ozal saw the crisis as offering opportunities to Turkey to garner both short- and long-term diplomatic and military advantages; in particular, Ozal wanted to capitalize on Turkey's activist role in the coalition to improve Turkey's case for membership in the EC.

What has been stressed thus far in this introduction is that there has been a significant reordering of power relations between external and regional actors and among regional actors in Middle East politics. This reordering is largely a product of structural changes in the international system that include, in addition to the Gulf War, the decline of communism and collapse of the Soviet Union. Although the structural patterns and dynamics of a new world order as it relates to the Middle East have been identified in the preceding chapters, the normative patterns underlying this new age in international relations remain obfuscated. Part IV, "Political Trends and Cultural Patterns," explores the relationship between politics and culture emerging in the post-Gulf War world order.

The first chapter in this section (Chapter 19), "The Middle East in the New World Order: Political Trends" by Louis J. Cantori, examines the political trends in the Middle East in the aftermath of the Gulf War from three perspectives: the international system, the regional subordinate system, and the dynamics of internal politics. Not only have the global changes in the international system been more dramatic, but their impacts upon the Middle Eastern regional subordinate system have been profound and significantly determining of its politics.

The end of the cold war in 1989 has seen the international system make the transition from competitive bipolarity to hegemonic unipolarity. This has enormous implications for Middle Eastern international relations in terms of a presumed U.S. hegemony there as well, but the Middle East is illustrative of an additional point in this regard, and that is the potential emergence of worldwide regional areas of conflict. In the Middle East, the question of the ability of the United States to be a hegemonic power needs to be examined in light of the Gulf War and its impact.

In the future, can the United States do what neither it nor anyone else has been able to do, namely, prevent the outbreak of future conflict in the region? Or can it repeat what it has just done and did before in 1956, namely, reverse the consequences of aggression? Finally, what impact will U.S. hegemony have on the regional balance of power? Prior to the invasion, a multipolar system existed, with Iraq pressing to become the hegemon of the Gulf subregion and Egypt attempting to do the same in the Eastern Mediterranean via an active policy on the Palestinian question. Syria was preoccupied in Lebanon.

In the aftermath of the war, Saudi Arabia has striven to exclude Egypt and Syria from the Gulf even as Egypt continues its activist policy on the Palestinian question and harbors ambitions to dominate the entire Middle East. Thus the prewar pattern of the Gulf-Eastern Mediterranean separation continues. Just as the 1989 date of the end of the cold war indicates, so, too, the forces at work in the internal politics of Middle Eastern states originated prior to the Gulf War. The years after 1970 have seen a remarkable pattern of relative domestic stability in the Middle East, but just prior to and during the Gulf War, economic grievances and Islamic revivalist sentiments came to a head in all of North Africa and Jordan. These grievances appear to have been further provoked by the Iraqi invasion of Kuwait, but, more important, by the absence of an Arab solution to the crisis and the Western power intervention. These pent-up domestic forces need to be analyzed in these anticoalition countries and in the coalition partnership states of Egypt, Syria, and the Gulf states as well. Finally, the medium-term stability of the region will be determined by the interaction of the U.S. hegemonic rule, the resolution of the remaining crises of Lebanon and the Palestinians, attaining a security regime in the Gulf, and achieving greater domestic stability possibly via a mechanism for the redistribution of wealth in the region.

In Chapter 20, "Islam, Democracy, and the Arab Future: Contested Islam in the Gulf Crisis," Raymond Baker examines political trends in the Middle East from a cultural perspective, focusing on the powerful stamp of Islam on politics in the region. Mass demonstrations against the Gulf War in Jordan, Morocco, Tunisia, Algeria, Egypt, and the West Bank reflected the fact that throughout the Arab world today oppositional political thought often expresses itself most effectively in the universalistic language of Islam, pronounced everywhere with strong local accents that reflect the circumstances and imperatives of particular groups and agendas.

Faced with the powerful imprint of Islam on politics in the Middle

East, how does the West understand the world in which Islam and politics interplay so powerfully? The understandings of Islam that dominate the Western media and academia take shape in the context of the U.S. strategic vision, codified by the Bush administration under the rubric of a new world order and a new Middle East. The official U.S. strategic vision provides the broad intellectual context for mainstream understandings of Islam, generating two alternative but ultimately related definitions of Islam. The first is *Islam as terrorist ideology*. This dominant definition reflects the primary strategic concern that sees Islam as a disruptive and destabilizing force that challenges the U.S. hegemonic position. This conception impels the use of force to contain or destroy the Islamic threat when it is directed against U.S. interests or, less frequently, to exploit it when directed against a perceived enemy of those interests. The second is *Islam as benign cultural sensibility*. This subordinate definition allows accommodation with Muslim regimes in the Western sphere, such as Saudi Arabia, the Gulf states, and Egypt. Despite the contrasting policy implications of these two available understandings of Islam, both have certain important shared characteristics. Islam in both conceptions is understood as ahistorical, unitary, apolitical, and essentialist.

Such definitions of the subject matter of Islam suggest commonsense guidelines for the best means to understand (for policy and mass publics) or to study (for media and the academic community) Islamic subjects. Though they implicitly claim general applicability, these prevailing definitions and guidelines are of little use in making sense of Islam in contexts other than that of the dominant U.S. strategic vision and for purposes other than those of furthering U.S. interests so understood.

Although the first two chapters of this section addressed systemic and cultural dimensions of regional politics in terms of the pattern of U.S. hegemony established by the Gulf War, the remaining chapters broaden the focus to address underlying global patterns and trends in the new world order. In Chapter 21, "Islam at War and Communism in Retreat: What Is the Connection?," Ali A. Mazrui explores the topography of international relations in terms of the Muslim-Christian dichotomy historically rooted in the weltanschauung of the Crusades, rather than the standard East-West dichotomy of the cold war paradigm or the North-South dichotomy of economic development. Viewed from this perspective, a causal relationship between the resurgence of Islam and the decline of communism is examined.

On a normative level, this causal relationship is interrelated by two distinct historical processes: the de-Leninization of Marxism and the dis-royalization of Islam. The impact of three explosive events in the Muslim world reveal the linkage between these processes—the Iranian revolution, the war in Afghanistan, and the Gulf crisis. Their impact has ranged from undermining the Soviet empire to the slow erosion of royalist Islam.

The resurgence of Islam in Iran and Afghanistan was a major contributory factor to the Soviet decision to intervene militarily in Afghanistan in December 1979. Soviet military losses and political setbacks in Afghanistan helped to erode Moscow's imperial will to intervene anywhere else. On the other hand, U.S. humiliation in Iran under the Carter administration resulted in the triumph of Ronald Reagan's militarism in his first years in office. It was this combination of the humbling of the USSR and the emboldening of Reagan's United States that helped Gorbachev in his quest to end the cold war. But although resurgent Islam was thus among the causes of East-West reconciliation, that reconciliation has itself exacted a price—from the Muslim world—ranging from large-scale emigration of Soviet Jews to Israel to the decline of the strategic value of Pakistan and Turkey in international politics.

The third most momentous Muslim crisis is the Gulf War. Its aftermath exhibits many contradictions, including the dialectic between monarchies and republics, between wealth and power, between piety and worldliness. The Gulf crisis and its aftermath completed the triad of dramatic Muslim experiences of the last quarter of the twentieth century. As a result, the nature of the twenty-first century has been remarkably altered.

Although a Muslim-Christian dichotomy in international affairs has historic roots in the Crusades, religion is not the only dimension of polarization in world affairs. A racial division is emerging that is at least as profound and much uglier in its implications. In Chapter 22, "Global Apartheid? Race and Religion in the New World Order," Ali A. Mazrui examines the impact of the end of the cold war on international stratification. The cold war prevented the global caste system from becoming global apartheid because it divided the white world ideologically. Rivalry between the two white power blocs averted the risk of racial solidarity among the more prosperous whites.

But there is now a closing of the ranks among the white peoples of the world. Pan-Europeanism is reaching levels greater than anything experienced since the Holy Roman Empire. The question that has arisen is whether this new Pan-European force, combined with the economic trend toward a mega–North America, will produce a human race more than ever divided between prosperous whites and poverty-stricken non-whites. Is a global apartheid in the making?

Race and religion remain potent forces in global affairs. Historically, race has been the fundamental divisive factor between Westerners and people of African descent almost everywhere. Religion has been the fundamental divisive factor between Westerners and people of Muslim culture almost everywhere. Was the collapse of the Berlin Wall in 1989 the beginning of the racial reunification of the white world? Is the twentieth century getting ready to hand over to the twenty-first century a new legacy of global apartheid? The trends are ominous.

The final chapter of the volume (23), "Democracy Died at the Gulf" by Richard Falk, places the foregoing in normative perspective by examining the nature of the new world order revealed by the Gulf War. It is an order based fundamentally on a technology gap between North and South that makes the modern industrial states of the Northern Hemisphere the primary beneficiaries of economic development, and the underdeveloped countries of the Southern Hemisphere the primary victims. The War revealed the racist and militaristic traditions embedded in the West's liberal democracies and the imperialistic relationship between North and South represented by the technology gap. The Gulf War not only unmasked the configuration of militaristic forces operating within the framework of democratic systems to forestall the realization of any democratic substance; it also revealed the hostility inherent in the West, especially in the United States, toward democratization in the Third World.

The Gulf War reflects the nature of modern warfare within the framework of the North-South polarity. Called Nintendo war, it is warfare in which money inserted at one end generates a technopower that inflicts one-sided destruction at the other end, and depends for its reality on denying the weaker side the technological and political means to fight back. More accurately portrayed as a massacre, Nintendo war represents a new stage in the evolution of warfare from the Crusades. It is a product of the inner logic of modernity where democracy, capitalism, and technology combine to create the momentum for a racist perception of world order and a militarist concept of security.

Part I
The Gulf War and the
International Order

1
Reflections on the Gulf War Experience

Force and War in the UN System

Richard Falk

The most ambitious aim of progressive international law is to outlaw war as an instrument of policy available to sovereign states. Resort to force in foreign policy is unconditionally prohibited in modern international law except in situations of self-defense. This legalist undertaking remains unfulfilled, existing in a domain of jurisprudential traction: It is neither repudiated nor implemented. Implementation would require several fundamental political adjustments: a real shift in the practice of powerful states with respect to force as an international policy option; a limitation of expenditures and deployments to accord with a purely defensive role for weaponry; and a commitment of resources to establish a collective security system to protect weak countries against aggression.

Iraq's invasion of Kuwait on 2 August 1990 challenged and tested[7]* the willingness and capacity of the United Nations to mount an effective response through collective security. The results were definitely mixed, and the reality is too recent and unresolved to yield anything as definitive as "the lessons of the Gulf War." Nevertheless, it is time to reflect upon the experience: to identify strengths and weaknesses, and to offer some preliminary appraisal from the perspective of international law.

At the outset, it seems clear that if the UN Security Council's response had achieved unconditional Iraqi withdrawal without recourse to counterwar, it would have greatly strengthened tendencies toward the renunciation of force and increased overall confidence in the potential role of the UN in the war-peace area. Such a result would encourage the view that the political situation after the cold war was open to a collective security approach to combat aggression.

Prior to the Gulf crisis, collective security was generally discredited. During the period of the League of Nations, there was neither requisite will nor capacity to act on behalf of victims of aggression. The crucial failure for the League came in 1935 when it was unable to protect Ethiopia effectively against outright aggression by Italy. Despite sanctions, Italy successfully annexed Ethiopia, and two years later these results were acknowledged and the ineffectual sanctions quietly dropped. During the UN period, it was evident that the East-West split prevented collective action at the global level, except in the special circumstances of the Korean War (1950-1952) and in marginal situations where superpower interests happened to converge.

Thus, in crucial respects, the Gulf crisis generated an early response that appeared encouraging from the perspective of both capabilities and consensus: The United States displayed the initiative and muscle to confront Iraq with a formidable response and mobilize a common front within the Security Council behind the demand that Iraq withdraw unconditionally from Kuwait. The erosion of this positive image of the UN's role was a serious concern from the outset; however, it gained a decisive character on 29 November—the day that Security Council Resolution 678 was adopted—when the deadline of 15 January was imposed on Iraq, after which date resort to war would be authorized.

In the aftermath of the Gulf War, few would argue that collective security as an approach to the problems of international aggression was vindicated, or indeed, even properly tested. Closer to the bloody reality of what transpired during the early months of 1991 in the desert of Arabia is the impression that the UN gave its official blessings to a war that it could not control. The war's objectives far exceeded the mandated mission to restore Kuwaiti sovereignty, and the military action of the coalition forces generated a series of security and legal problems as serious and dangerous as those the UN response were supposed to correct. Partly, this criticism reflects the strong conviction that the UN was induced to authorize recourse to war as a result of pressure exerted by the U.S. government, thereby giving up on sanctions prematurely and inappropriately, as well as evidencing a disinclination to find a diplomatic solution. At root, the Security Council seemed overwhelmed by President Bush's call for "a new world order," the opportunistic phrase invented by the White House to mobilize public support, and in the process the UN failed to be guided by the proper conception of collective security as specified in Chapter VII of the UN Charter.

The UN Framework

The Gulf War reversed, at least temporarily, concerns about the relation between the prevention of war and the existence of the UN. For decades, peace-oriented social forces had hoped to strengthen the role of the UN, particularly the capacity of the Security Council to respond effectively to war-threatening situations. The UN's path to global security was regarded as both distinct from, and preferable to, the superpower path. In the climate of the cold war, the latter path consisted of the familiar structures of bipolarity, the bloc system, and the logic of mutual deterrence. Most significant conflicts in international life were entangled in this bipolar encounter, making it impossible for the UN to play a role. If necessary, the main antagonists relied upon their veto in the Security Council to prevent a significant UN initiative in relation to a contested major use of force. Thus, long wars in Vietnam and Afghanistan and between Iraq and Iran continued for years without generating any significant response from the UN; the organization consistently failed to challenge frequent military intervention by the two superpowers in the internal affairs of a series of countries.

The disappointing performance of the UN was regarded as an inevitable casualty of the cold war. Its formal structure in the areas of peace and security reflected the judgment that an effective Security Council depended decisively on the capacity of the five permanent members to cooperate in relation to major threats directed against international peace. The veto gave these countries the assurance that the UN Security Council could not be turned against their vital national interests. The idea that the UN's effectiveness was built upon the fragile foundation of keeping the World War II alliance against fascism alive in the period after 1945 was a prospect that was completely eliminated by 1947, if it ever existed.

The implementation of the UN Charter was dependent upon the cooperation of the great powers, especially with regard to the Security Council playing a central role. The Charter was drafted on the assumption, based on false optimism, that such cooperation would be forthcoming after 1945. The basic commitment of the organization was expressed in the Preamble: "to save succeeding generations from the scourge of war." The centrality of this complex undertaking was stated more carefully at the start of the operative part of the Charter in which the purposes of the UN were specified. Article 1(1) reads:

To maintain international peace and security, and to that end:
to take effective collective measures for the prevention and
removal of threats to the peace, and for the suppression of acts
of aggression or other breaches of the peace, and to bring
about by peaceful means, and in conformity with the principles
of justice and international law, adjustment or settlement of
disputes or situations which might lead to a breach of the
peace.

This central purpose was expressed in Article 2 under guiding principles. Members were obliged in Article 2(4) to renounce the use of
force as an instrument of foreign policy and in Article 2(3), to settle
all disputes by peaceful means. The sole exception to the Charter's
outlawry of war was the preservation, in Article 5(1) of the right of
individual and collective self-defense against a prior armed attack,
and then only until the Security Council could act. According to the
Charter, even the rights of self-defense validly asserted by a victim
of aggression were provisional and subordinate to the primary responsibility of the Security Council to arrange for an appropriate response. In the language of Article 51, "Measures taken by Members
in the exercise of this right of self-defense shall be immediately reported to the Security Council and shall not in any way affect the
authority and responsibility of the Security Council under the present
Charter to take at any time such action as it deems necessary in
order to maintain peace and security." Such a legal relationship
prompted a recent study to comment on "the UN's almost total monopoly of the lawful use of force on the international plane."[1] Even
regional organizations were legally precluded from entering conflict
situations unless expressly authorized to do so, within the terms of
Article 53, by the Security Council.

The UN's scheme was ambitious and potentially far reaching. The
Security Council, according to Article 39, was empowered to make
recommendations to parties in any war threatening situation. Its primary mandate was, of course, one of war prevention, which suggested a responsibility for addressing grievances that endangered
international peace and paving the way for negotiation and peaceful
resolution of disputes that could lead to war if unaddressed. In addition, the Charter granted the Security Council more extensive competence to engage, as a last resort, in enforcement activities. Articles
40 and 41 authorized the Security Council to make recommendations
and decisions with respect to nonmilitary measures against a state

that engaged in aggression, and to authorize provisional measures to prevent a war-threatening situation. Such action could include sanctions and an embargo. If the Security Council considered these undertakings inadequate, Article 42 authorized military measures. A key element in the Security Council's conception was collective and institutional responsibility for enforcement activity. Article 46 reads: "Plans for the application of armed forces shall be made by the Security Council with the assistance of the Military Staff Committee." Further, in Article 47, conditions were specified for establishing the Military Staff Committee and according it full responsibility "on all questions relating to the Security Council's military requirements" including "the employment and command of forces placed at its disposal" and "the strategic direction" of these forces. Finally, Article 45 obliged members of the UN to identify and earmark, in advance, contingents of their armed forces for participation in such UN enforcement measures.

The UN conception of collective security rested on three key elements: (1) avoiding war, while protecting countries against wrongful uses of force; (2) according the Security Council broad authority to fulfill the objectives of (1); and (3) ensuring that enforcement action undertaken on behalf of the Security Council was genuinely collective at all stages of implementation.

This envisaged scheme for collective security was never implemented. As one respected specialist concluded "enforcement action under Chapter VII . . . was a dead letter in 1945 and . . . likely to remain so for the foreseeable future."[2] The cold war, centering upon rivalry between the two superpowers, not only stalemated political action requiring their assent, but completely frustrated any effort to bring into being the collective mechanisms contemplated by the Charter to confer upon UN enforcement actions a global community character. For different reasons, and to different degrees, in variance with political leadership and the issue posed, neither the United States nor the Soviet Union wanted to move very far away from traditional geopolitics, that is, unilateral policy-making and capabilities supplemented by alliances and bloc arrangements. In this regard, although it is difficult to assess the extent, the cold war provided leading governments with a pretext to keep diplomacy within the familiar parameters of statecraft, expressed by traditional preoccupations with alliances, balances, and military preparedness.

What did evolve, through practice and the innovative initiatives of Dag Hammarskjöld during his period as secretary-general in the 1950s, was the notion of peacekeeping, informally identified as "Chapter VI 1/2," to emphasize its creative relation to the Charter as drafted and to locate its reality between Chapter VI (pacific settlement) and Chapter VII (enforcement action). Brian Urquhart, former UN undersecretary-general and the UN's official most closely involved with devising this pattern of "innovation," defined peacekeeping in the following language: "the use by the UN of military personnel and formations not in a fighting or enforcement role but interposed as a mechanism to bring an end to hostilities and as a buffer between hostile forces. In effect, it serves as an internationally constituted pretext for the parties to a conflict to stop fighting and as a mechanism to maintain a cease-fire."[3] UN peacekeeping arose as a practical set of responses within a political climate of fundamental conflict, and to take advantage of the periodic willingness by both superpowers to contain and terminate outbreaks of warfare, especially those in which neither superpower was a direct participant, such as several of the wars in the Middle East and Africa. The Congo crisis of 1960 illustrated the tenuous boundary between peacekeeping and enforcement, and disclosed the inability of the UN to function in a cold war setting whenever one superpower perceived that the organization was, in effect, aligned with the foreign policy of the other superpower. The UN was badly strained by this experience, and the membership never again tried to press so hard against the modest limits of superpower consensus. In a sense, even the Gulf mandate accepted the necessity of acting on the basis of superpower consensus, but the political conditions had shifted markedly making enforcement an option, although a legally dubious one.

The problematic character of enforcement actions by the UN in the cold war period was clearly manifested in relation to the Korean War. In a series of Security Council resolutions, the UN condemned North Korea's attack on South Korea, encouraged states to assist South Korea and refrain from helping North Korea, and established a unified UN command under U.S. leadership.[4] The condemnation of North Korea and the authorization of a UN response were formally possible only because of a Soviet decision some months earlier to boycott Security Council proceedings on a quite unrelated matter, as a protest against the UN's unwillingness to resolve the question of Chinese representation in favor of the Beijing government. The Soviet delegation had walked out of the Security Council in January 1950, long before the North Korean surprise attack in June. The Soviets returned on 1 August 1950, apparently deciding that their global interests required participation in Security Council activity, including the opportunity to cast a veto and block adverse UN action.

The Korean precedent was important in relation to the Gulf War in at least two respects. First, the validation of the Security Council votes, despite the absence of Soviet participation, initiated constitutional opportunism as a tendency with respect to the UN Charter, specifically in relation to Article 27(3); it was an extremely strained reading of the Charter language that treated the Soviet absence as enabling the Security Council to reach decisions supported by "the concurring votes of the permanent members."[5]

Second, the Korean operations were notable for the displacement of any UN influence upon military operations supposedly undertaken on its authority and, in the Korean instance, even under its banner. The military undertaking was shaped in Washington and became, in every substantive sense, a U.S. operation, including the definition of the scope and tactics of the mission. Indeed, the United States used the war to march north of the demilitarized zone with the objective of unifying Korea under the control of the south. This move brought the People's Republic of China into the war, prolonging the fighting until, evidently, China and North Korea submitted to the infamous, secretly conveyed threats by President Dwight Eisenhower to use atomic bombs. This unilateralism is analogous to the Gulf experience where the United States expanded the mission beyond the restoration of Kuwaiti sovereignty, redirecting enforcement against Iraq in a manner that greatly increased the orbit of devastation and suffering, and determined on its own the scope, scale, and tactics of warfare.

There were also important differences between the Korean and Gulf contexts: In Korea, the Soviet absence explained the avoidance of a Soviet veto; in the Gulf, there was a genuine agreement, especially during the early stages of response among the permanent members and the rest of the Security Council, on the unacceptability of the Iraqi invasion of Kuwait. China's abstention on Security Council's Resolution 678 was not intended to block enforcement action, but to distance China in a political sense from a likely subsequent recourse by the anti-Iraq coalition to forcible means.[6] It should be noted, however, that China's willingness to allow its abstention to be treated as if the requirement of concurring votes had been satisfied (Article 27(3)) does not resolve the question of legality under the Charter, particularly since those members who were not represented permanently on the Security Council had a right to have the Charter interpreted as drafted in relation to the voting rules of major UN members.

The UN's role in the Korean War should have aroused concern by members in relation to the Gulf crisis, particularly because military phases of any "UN response" could so easily become indistinguishable from U.S. foreign policy undertaken quite independently of the organization.

Where does this survey of background issues lead with respect to the central issues of UN enforcement? As a primary consequence of the cold war, although not exclusively a result of East-West tensions, the Security Council never established the machinery contemplated under Chapter VII to give enforcement its collective, UN character. There was reason to doubt that the machinery to implement collective security could have been created even if the victorious alliance in World War II had lasted longer. It entailed an ambitious set of encroachments on sovereign discretion that seemed to go beyond the "realist" attitudes prevalent in the foreign policy establishments of all leading countries during the past several decades. The Charter's conception of collective security seemed too idealistic to be realized without a prior drastic shift in policy-making and societal attitudes toward national security issues. Many leading countries were reluctant to institutionalize the authority of the UN in relation to peace and security in this post-cold war period. Later, in the 1980s, Soviet proposals set forth by Gorbachev to establish standby forces and implement the framework referred to in Chapter VII never elicited serious support.

At the same time, this constitutional framework of the Charter remains on the books and provides the only legally valid basis for UN enforcement action in situations where pacific settlement and nonmilitary measures fail. Consequently, it is necessary to assess any UN enforcement operation by referring to these Charter provisions, which contain the ingredients of the most fundamental international treaty governing political relations among sovereign states. It would undermine confidence in the UN if the extent of its authority could be shaped arbitrarily and on a case-to-case basis by the political will of its most powerful members, particularly if done in flagrant disregard of the letter and spirit of the Charter.

It must be acknowledged that any formal undertaking by the UN needs to be validated by reference to the Charter, the basic constitutive instrument of the organization. It is also the case that formal modifications by way of amendment depend on a cumbersome procedure. A path of creative interpretation of the Charter often seemed especially justified given the urgency of the UN tasks: The avoidance of war and the protection of states against aggression as overriding priorities in relation to peace and security. The practical contributions of the UN depend on a flexible capacity for response in light of shifts in the political climate and given the nature of war-threatening dangers.

This flexibility is consistent with the Charter framework. Although such interpretative discretion is general and incomplete, it allows considerable room for innovation in the manner of Chapter VI 1/2, but also places limits and imposes guidelines on any undertaking that entails the use of force under a UN mandate. The Korean and Gulf experiences confirmed the wisdom of some degree of constitutionalism while the peacekeeping undertakings sustained the wisdom of flexibility.

The Gulf War and the UN's Framework for Enforcement

Without doubt, the Iraqi conquest of Kuwait was a violation of Article 2(4) and, to the extent that it was the outcome of a dispute between the two countries, a flagrant violation of Article 33, which required members to settle disputes by peaceful means. Iraq's subsequent annexation of Kuwait, attempting by unilateral fiat to extinguish the existence of a UN member, confirmed Baghdad's aggressive intention. Although there have been many acts of aggression by various countries since 1945, no prior attempt to annex a member of the UN had ever been made.[7] These developments were further aggravated by gross crimes of humanity committed by the Iraqi occupying armies against the civilian population of Kuwait and, later in the crisis, by the seizure as hostages of hundreds of foreign nationals in Iraq, with their subsequent use as "human shields" to discourage attacks upon potential military targets.

The aggression against Kuwait on 2 August was so rapidly consummated that Kuwait could not invoke its rights of self-defense under Article 51, although its government immediately appealed to the UN for help. During the early stages of the crisis, the United States and the United Kingdom insisted that they could act in collective self-defense outside the UN framework if the Security Council's response fell short of what they regarded as an acceptable mandate.

In the euphemistic language one might expect from a former high-level diplomat associated with the UN Secretariat, Urquhart described this claim as a "tendency to diverge from the procedures of Article [sic; Chapter] VII," a tendency which, he asserted, was "inherent from the beginning of the crisis." He described the British-U.S. backup plan as "a parallel operation" to the one the Security Council "mounted under the leadership of the United States to protect Saudi Arabia." Urquhart noted that "it was accepted wisdom" that this deployment was supplemental to a reliance on sanctions that, in the early weeks of the crisis, "were to be the means of securing Iraq's withdrawal." He acknowledged that such an interpretation of the UN intentions lost plausibility after 8 November when troop deployments were deliberately and unilaterally doubled by the U.S. government thereby enabling offensive action against Iraq, and making it costly and politically difficult to let the crisis drag on.[8]

The main point, obscured by Urquhart's neutral designation of this process as "a parallel development," was that the Charter preempted action in self-defense under Article 51 once the Security Council was aware of and seized the situation. This was crucial, as the process of U.S.-led deployment was never critically reviewed or approved by the Security Council, and the UN never attempted to retain appropriate and comprehensive control over the response that was legitimated largely by reference to UN authority. At all stages after the invasion, the United States insisted on discretion to initiate military action against Iraq and it possessed the means to abandon sanctions and diplomacy and opt for war. The Security Council never asserted any claim in support of its supervisory role in relation to anti-Iraqi military forces deployed in the region and thus, without even proper discussion, the Council improperly relinquished its primary responsibility to achieve Iraqi withdrawal from Kuwait without war. Such a failure by the Security Council to maintain control was, in many respects, a fundamental constitutional defect. In the end, the defects of Resolution 678 were a formalization and extension of this overriding failure, which was unchallenged on these grounds by any member of the Security Council, not even Cuba or Yemen.

The practical problem of containing Iraq, thus preventing the threat or use of further force by Iraq, could have been properly addressed through a reliance on U.S. forces, but in a mode *explicitly subordinate to the Security Council and its resolve to secure Iraqi withdrawal by sanctions and diplomacy,* thereby upholding the fundamental imperative of the Charter to avert war. Such subordination would have entailed a strict limit on the function and scale of foreign military forces introduced into the region during the period of reliance on sanctions and diplomacy. This, in turn, would have precluded "the war of nerves" that ensued after 8 November when an offensive option became the result of decisions made in Washington apparently without prior consultation within the UN. Arguably, such an authorization would not have entirely satisfied the literal requirements of Chapter VII, which seemed to call for a more direct Security Council role as specified in Articles 46 and 47. The position taken here was that so long as the spirit of the Charter was upheld, that is, adherence to the purposes and respect for explicit requirements (for example, voting rules), a degree of flexibility in relation to mechanisms of implementation would be acceptable for the sake of achieving UN effectiveness in this critical area of peace and security. In peacekeeping, the UN often needs to rely on the independent military capabilities of its members, but in doing so it must ensure, in all respects, that such forces are used in a manner compatible with the Security Council definition of its enforcement mission.

The Security Council responded to the Iraqi invasion on 2 August with a series of resolutions that received the concurring votes of five permanent members and support from the overwhelming majority of the Council as a whole: Resolution 660 on 2 August, which demanded that Iraq withdraw from Kuwait, was approved by a vote of 14-0, Yemen not participating; Resolution 661 on 6 August, which imposed comprehensive sanctions on trade to and from Iraq except for medicine and, in humanitarian circumstances, food, was approved 13-0, with Cuba and Yemen abstaining; Resolution 662 on 9 August, which declared that the annexation of Kuwait was null and void, was approved by a 15-0 vote; Resolution 664 on 18 August, which demanded that Iraq permit foreign nationals to leave Iraq and Kuwait and rescind its order closing Kuwaiti diplomatic missions, was approved by 15-0; and Resolution 665 on 25 August, which permitted the use of naval force to uphold economic sanctions, was approved by 13-0, with Cuba and Yemen abstaining. This level of consensus in the Security Council, in relation to a major use of force in a strategically sensitive area of the world, was unprecedented in the history of the UN. During this early flurry of resolutions, many observers believed that a new era of internationalism was in evidence and that the UN Security Council might at last live up to its role as set forth in the Charter. The collaborative relationship maintained between the superpowers was particularly impressive, as was the degree to which the Third World supported the attempt to coerce the withdrawal of Iraq from Kuwait, despite Saddam Hussein's attempt to cast himself in an anti-imperialist role and despite Kuwait's dynastic and repressive internal rule that appropriated the largest portion of oil revenues for the personal benefit of the royal family.

Initially, the UN seemed to uphold the purposes of the Charter with a single, although major, exception: the failure to curtail and gain authority over the U.S.-led deployment of coalition forces in the region. It was also questionable from the outset to include food within the purview of sanctions; the UN should never support coercive policies designed to withhold necessities from civilians.

The second phase of the UN's response commenced on 8 November, the date of offensive deployment of U.S. forces, and ended on 15 January (or 17 January), the date of the expiry of the withdrawal deadline (or alternatively, on the date of the initial coalition attacks on Iraq), with the whole period centering upon the adoption of Resolution 678 on 29 November, thereby ratifying the shift from sanctions to war. Once this shift was made the UN's role was fundamentally flawed from the viewpoint of international law. The guidelines for coordination and supervision of military measures (Chapter VII) were not followed, nor was any improvised functional equivalent relied upon that would sustain the Security Council's constitutional responsibilities. The Security Council violated its own constitutional framework to the extent that it allowed the coalition to operate independently and, more blatantly, by allowing the shift from sanctions to military measures without the finding contemplated by Article 42, namely, an explicit conclusion that nonmilitary measures had failed. Although there was controversy surrounding the effectiveness of sanctions and the extent to which the interests in liberation of the abused occupied population in Kuwait should be deferred, there was little doubt that the Security Council invalidly aligned itself with the refusal by United States and the United Kingdom to allow any reasonable negotiating space that might have produced a diplomatic solution. Also, Resolution 678 invalidly delegated authority to the coalition to wage unrestricted war after 15 January. In this regard, the Gulf War was fought on the basis of a formal UN authorization that was of a doubtful constitutional character.

The third phase of the UN's response encompassed the war itself. Despite the delegation of authority in Resolution 678, the Security

Council was responsible and accountable in relation to international law, as were the countries participating in the coalition, especially the United States, which dominated war-making policy. There were several issues posed: the expansion of the mission beyond securing Iraq's withdrawal; the use of air supremacy to destroy the civilian infrastructure of Iraq; the deliberate continuation of "the duck shoot" against Iraqi troops withdrawing from Kuwait and no longer in a combat posture; the reliance on napalm, cluster bombs, and near-nuclear "Daisy Cutter" bombs; and the failure to accede to a cease-fire prior to the ground campaign, despite Iraq's substantial acceptance of UN demands in the form of the Soviet peace initiative and the adverse human, political, and environmental consequences of continuing the war. These features of the Gulf War, carried out in the name of the UN, raised serious questions about violations of the law of war and the refusal to limit coalition objectives and minimize reliance on force.

The fourth phase of the UN's response involved the aftermath of the war, including the imposition of a punitive cease-fire and the constraint of Saddam Hussein's regime from committing crimes of humanity against the Kurdish people and other segments of the Iraqi population. Having continued the war to the point of provoking a breakdown of internal order, partly encouraged by President George Bush's call to insurrection, a distinct set of responsibilities ensued for coalition forces to remove the criminal regime in Baghdad from power and uphold the human rights and the right of self-determination of the Iraqi people. In essence, the war was improperly initiated and was continued well beyond the basic UN mandate; however, after being so dubiously extended, it was perversely and prematurely terminated in a highly disruptive fashion that caused severe and massive suffering and devastation.

Some Conclusions

The UN's failure in relation to the Gulf War was tragic and far reaching. The essence of this failure was the refusal of the Security Council to control the United States and the coalition, allowing the UN to become formally associated with waging unrestricted warfare in a manner that, according to a UN report, reduced Iraq to preindustrial conditions, resulting in "near apocalyptic" devastation.[9] If the UN is to learn from this experience and overcome its deficiencies, it must respond effectively in several broad areas of concern:

1. the establishment of a viable constitutional framework to ensure that future undertakings of an enforcement character are kept within the scope of Chapter VII;
2. the reaffirmation of a fundamental commitment of the organization to preclude the UN's recourse to military measures if any peaceful path exists;
3. the confirmation of an autonomous negotiating and diplomatic role for the secretary-general in line with the primary objective of the office to resolve all disputes by peaceful methods;
4. a requirement that the Security Council not allow independent initiatives beyond its purview and be responsible for extending its authority over all aspects of response to any war-threatening situation once its jurisdiction has been successfully established;[10]
5. the necessity to conduct military operations under UN auspices in strict conformity with the laws of war, including a full acceptance of individual and institutional responsibility for violations;
6. the overriding duty to take diplomatic initiatives that will moderate war-threatening situations, including the commitment to avoid "double standards" and selective application of UN decisions;
7. the essential requirement that the UN resort to forcible tactics be confined to "military measures," carefully delimited, and never extended, directly or indirectly, to unrestricted war-making; and further, that the effects of military measures be fully and continuously assessed by the Security Council, including the probable scale of devastation, impacts on civilian population, and likely aftereffects; and
8. the obvious need for careful monitoring of all future Security Council activity by nongovernment organizations and citizen initiatives dedicated to safeguarding the Charter imperative to protect the peoples of the world from war, including UN-mandated war, and thereby to exert a continuous pressure upon the Security Council to operate within its constitutional boundaries.

Notes

1. Belatchew Asratt, *Prohibition of Force Under the UN Charter: A Study of Art* 2(4) (Uppsala, Sweden: Iustus Forlag, 1991): 13.

2. John Gerard Ruggie, "The United States and the United Nations: A New Realism," in *The Politics of International Organizations*, ed. Paul F. Diehl (Chicago: Dorsey Press, 1989): 396–410, quote on p. 400.

3. Brian Urquhart, "International Peace and Security: Thoughts of the Twentieth Anniversary of Dag Hammarskjöld's Death," *Foreign Affairs* 60 (1981): 6.

4. For a convenient summary of the UN response to the Korean crisis see Ahiaed M. Rifaat, *International Aggression* (Stockholm: Almquist & Wiksell, 1979): 208–10.

5. The passage of the Uniting for Peace Resolution (General Assembly Resolution 498 [V]) on 2 November 1950 was an acknowledgment that in the future the Security Council could not be expected to carry out its role to safeguard victims of armed attack, and purported to shift the locus of authority for collective action to the General Assembly. This shift was later challenged by the Soviet Union in relation to its financial obligations for peacekeeping operations of which it disapproved. The Soviet challenge was unsuccessful in an international law sense, but it was politically effective. By the 1960s, the increased influence of the Third World in the General Assembly led the United States to back away from this earlier attempt to pursue its political objectives within a UN framework. The record of this period reveals a series of opportunistic attempts to avoid the burdens of the Soviet veto without resorting to the formal amending procedure set forth in Articles 108 and 109 of the Charter.

6. It is notable that the key postinvasion resolutions, including the establishment of sanctions, enjoyed unanimous council support.

7. It is notable that although the term "aggression" is not used in the Charter itself, the idea of aggression underlies the condemnation of non-defensive use of force.

8. For quotations see Brian Urquhart, "Learning from the Gulf," *NY Review of Books* 38 (March 7, 1991): 34–37, quotes on p. 34.

9. Ahtisaari Report to the UN Secretary General, S/22366, 20 March 1991.

10. It is possible to complicate the issue by arguing that the Gulf War started on 2 August, not on 17 January. For purposes of my analysis, I have assumed that the Iraqi war of conquest was completed and that the Security Council was faced with what to do to uphold its authority in relation to the restoration of Kuwaiti sovereignty, which included the war option that eventually was selected.

2

The United Nations in the Gulf War

Robert Springborg

Beginning with the Nixon administration, the United Nations, which since 1947 had been more actively involved in the Middle East than in any other region, was gradually excluded from high level diplomatic activity related to the Arab-Israeli conflict. The United States, for example, did not work through the UN when it formulated the Sinai observer force to monitor the Egyptian-Israeli peace agreement, nor was the UN involved in intense, U.S.-dominated diplomatic activity surrounding the 1982 invasion of Lebanon. Yet less than a decade later, the UN had become the principal arena within which the United States pursued a major foreign policy objective in the Middle East. As a result, the UN authorized an embargo and the use of force against Iraq; it dispatched police to protect Iraqi Kurds from their own government; and it legalized its own seizure of 100 percent of Iraq's future oil earnings, earmarking some of those funds for confiscation of Iraqi weaponry and redrawing the border between Iraq and Kuwait.

The vastly different levels of UN involvement in Middle Eastern events resulted from the dramatic increase in U.S. influence within the organization as a result of the collapse of the Soviet Union. Whereas the United States could not muster sufficient support in the UN for the Multinational Force and Observer Mission to the Sinai, it had little difficulty a decade later in steering resolutions through the Security Council that, as cited by President George Bush, were proof that the Gulf crisis "is not a matter between Iraq and the United States of America. It is between Iraq and the entire world community."[1]

The UN's acquiescence to Washington's diplomatic and military initiatives brought praise from precisely those U.S. circles that for years had berated the international body as an agent of various Third World excesses and radicalisms, especially of the Arab variant. The *New York Times*, whose coverage of UN involvement in Middle

Eastern affairs has been noted for its cynicism, distortion, and pre-
dilection for condemnation, suddenly discovered that real virtue
lurked in the UN precincts in East Manhattan.[2] More independent
opinion in middle America, less enamored of the Gulf operation
than the *Times*, concurred with the assessment that the UN had
emerged from the crisis as the big winner. The *Minneapolis Tribune*,
for example, wrote that "the war's rancid aftertaste does not extend
to the United Nations. . . . Beginning last August, member states
let the United Nations be the force for good its founders envisioned."[3]
Even noted commentators on the Middle East found little to fault in
the UN's volte-face. Robin Wright, for example, despite her worries
about destabilizing consequences of the Gulf crisis, noted that "most
of the good news . . . centers around the spirit of the renewal at
the United Nations. . . . [T]he unprecedented unity in the UN Security Council on a host of resolutions on the Gulf . . . carried the
potential to establish a framework for a 'new world order'."[4]

Academics of the U.S. establishment joined the chorus of praise
for the UN. Writing in *Foreign Affairs*, Bruce Russett and James
Sutterlin proclaimed that "the new world order envisioned by Bush
and Gorbachev would be founded on . . . the possibility of military enforcement measures by the United Nations." Such measures,
according to them, were "improvised" during the Gulf crisis in a
creative fashion that, although not provided for in the UN Charter,
helped to achieve "international peace and security."[5] Russett and
Sutterlin conceded that this "improvisation" may have resulted in the
Security Council's insufficient control over military operations. In
practice, however, this did not matter because, unlike the Korean
War, when U.S. troops (exceeding the terms of the Security Council
resolution under which they were operating) crossed the thirty-eighth
parallel, thereby bringing China into the war, the United States, in
this case, did not engage in military actions "beyond the Kuwaiti
theater of operations."[6]

This is patent nonsense, unless the "Kuwaiti theater of operations"
extended throughout the length and breadth of Iraq, in which case it
should have been termed the Iraqi theater of operations. That terminology, however, would strip the fig leaf away from the military onslaught, embarrassing the United States and UN in the process.
Russett and Sutterlin, unconcerned about local sensitivities, except
as they affected Western interests, forecast that Kuwait would likely
be targeted again by Iraq's quest for revenge, or by "one or more of
its neighbors." They therefore recommended "a substantial UN pres-

ence in the Gulf in the future."[7] That Kuwait required protection in perpetuity from surrounding countries did not cause Russett and Sutterlin to ponder the reasons for this profound hostility. Those reasons concerned the ill fit of the nation-state system to the Middle East, a system imposed to serve Western interests, which, not coincidentally, would continue to be served by Russett and Sutterlin's remedy.

The chief reservation among those who viewed the new UN role as the "good news" of the Gulf crisis was that its assertiveness would be short lived. They feared that the convergence of events, including Iraqi audacity and clumsy disregard for the etiquette of international affairs, coupled with Soviet and Chinese submissiveness, would prove unique.

These staunch advocates of UN interventionism, at least when serving a cause they supported, were not resigned to a diminished UN role in the future. Indeed, the *New York Times* in its lead editorial on 7 August 1991 urged the UN to "Keep the heat on Iraq to disarm" and warned the organization that it "dare not let him [Saddam Hussein] manipulate his people's misery to escape pressure to comply." Two days later, the *Times*, delighted that the Security Council was about to approve the confiscation of Iraq's oil revenues, quoted a Western diplomat's remarks that "the UN has Iraq spread-eagled against the car and is going through its pockets." It then observed, "that's as it should be. . . . Only after Baghdad unequivocally complies with its cease-fire responsibilities will it be entitled to ask for the rights normally available to law-abiding members of the international community, like free access to oil markets and sovereign control of its cash receipts. Until then, the UN does right to treat it like the outlaw state it is, keeping it spread-eagled and under surveillance."

The *Times* editors, chiding the UN and the United States to "keep the heat on Iraq," and then revealing smug self-satisfaction when they did so, need not have been so concerned that the activist phase of the UN behavior was going to pass quickly. The U.S. administration, confronting virtually no opposition in the Security Council, continued to orchestrate its pressure on Iraq through the UN more than a year after the war ended. With one exception—a disagreement between the United States and various other member states as to whether 30 or 50 percent of Iraq's future oil earnings should be allocated for reparations and compensation—the United States obtained all that it wanted in the Security Council, including perpetuation of the embargo and unrelenting pressure to strip Iraq of its chemical weapons and most missiles, as well as its nuclear research capability. Thus, the UN legitimated the unilateral disarmament of the sole Arab military threat to Israel, without insisting on any countervailing arms reductions by Israel, Iran, or other Arab states.

On other fronts, however, the UN behaved in the timid and bumbling manner that previously had earned it the derision of its U.S. critics. After the Security Council agreed to send a police force to northern Iraq to protect the Kurds, it had difficulty in cajoling member states to donate sufficient personnel and other resources to make the operation viable. Of greater significance was the UN's abnegation of its responsibilities in the Arab-Israeli conflict. Simultaneous with the campaign of pressure against postwar Iraq, the UN acquiesced to the joint U.S.-Israeli demand that the "international" conference planned for October 1991 should not be convened under UN auspices. The UN further suffered the indignity of being permitted (by the United States and Israel) only observer status at that conference, with no right to comment on or otherwise participate in the proceedings. The UN meekly agreed to these conditions after passing more General Assembly and Security Council resolutions on the Arab-Israeli conflict than on any other aspect of international affairs; after approving on 24 May 1991 its sixty-fourth resolution condemning Israeli violations of Arab rights; after defining the terms upon which the U.S.-endorsed "international" conference was to be convened (Security Council Resolutions 242 and 338); and after passing Security Council Resolution 681 on 20 December 1990, which, in conjunction with the accompanying statement by the chairman of the council, pledged UN support for and involvement in an international conference on the Arab-Israeli conflict "at an appropriate time." Needless to say, the *Times*, given its pro-Israeli record, did not find this evasion of responsibility worthy of comment. Sauce for the Iraqi goose was not meant for the Israeli gander.

Those who viewed the UN's performance in the Gulf crisis as a new departure, and who bemoaned the lost opportunities of previous years when the Security Council was paralyzed by Soviet-U.S. rivalry, ignored the pattern of consistency that had characterized the UN's behavior toward the Arab-Israeli conflict. That pattern can be summed up as acquiescence to pressure from the United States. The Partition Resolution (181) of 29 November 1947, dividing Palestine into Arab and Jewish states, was developed as a result of enormous leverage applied by the U.S. government on recalcitrant member states. Any UN delegates present in 1990 who had been in attendance in 1947 would have had a strong sense of déjà vu. The carrots and sticks waved by the U.S. delegation in the faces of recalcitrant representatives were more or less the same as those wielded forty-three years earlier, although in the current round more attention was concentrated on the two vulnerable Security Council members, China and the USSR, than on run-of-the-mill states in the General Assembly, which this time were rendered impotent by the concentration of activity in the council. Of those members, only Cuba and Yemen remained immune to U.S. blandishments and threats. Cuba abstained on three and voted no on three of the twelve Gulf resolutions passed between 2 August and 29 November 1990, while Yemen absented itself on one vote, abstained on three, and voted against two of those resolutions. This required particular courage and sacrifice by this newly united country, which paid for its independence with an immediate reduction in aid from the United States.

Since 1947, the United States had consistently supported Israel in the UN and vetoed any Security Council resolutions deemed to be critical of that country. Other manifestations of this support included threats to withdraw from UN agencies that demonstrated sympathy for the Palestinian national movement (for example, the World Health Organization); funds withheld from the UN on the grounds of an alleged anti-Israeli bias, and threats to withdraw entirely from the UN if the organization treated Israel in a fashion analogous to South Africa. The United States remained steadfast in its support of the Jewish state except in instances where Israel clearly violated international law, such as its annexation of the Golan Heights and East Jerusalem, or its deportation of Palestinians from Occupied Territories, in which case the United States supported condemnations of Israel while stripping resolutions of appropriate penalties during negotiations prior to their formulation. The United States exercised its veto in support of Israel more times than the Soviet Union vetoed resolutions. This suggests that the biggest impediment to the proper functioning of the UN between 1950 and 1990 was the United States, not the USSR.

The process by which the United States recruited the UN to crush Iraq, while simultaneously ensuring that the international organization did not intrude into the Israeli-Palestinian conflict, illustrated diplomatic duplicity and purposeful misinterpretation of the UN Charter. Sir Anthony Parsons, permanent representative of the United Kingdom at the UN from 1979 to 1982, characterized the claim made by the United States that it had UN authorization for its naval enforcement of sanctions "as sailing close to the wind."[8]

Of greater concern than the United States's bending of the rules to achieve its objectives, or the UN's acquiescence in apparent violation of its charter, was the stark hypocrisy and moral outrage, real or feigned, of the U.S. administration. The premise upon which the United States based its case for action was that Iraq could not be allowed to invade and annex Kuwait lest a terrible precedent be established, plunging the world into chaos. Yet, since the formation of the UN, the United States had opposed mildly, or not at all, several annexations through aggression. Indonesia's annexation of East Timor, India's annexation of Goa, and Israel's annexation of the Golan Heights and East Jerusalem are cases in point. Other instances included South Africa's aggression against Namibia, Syria's and Israel's actions in Lebanon, Turkey's presence in Cyprus, and Morocco's actions in the Sahara. In fact, shortly before the United States launched its campaign to crush Iraq, it invaded Grenada and Panama on the flimsiest of justifications.

The hypocrisy of the U.S. appeal to international law was further revealed by the chicanery of its methods in the UN during the Gulf crisis. It invoked the name and authority of the UN to use warships unilaterally to intercept vessels suspected of violating the sanctions imposed by Security Council Resolution 661 of 6 August 1992. A statement issued by Washington immediately following the passage of that resolution warned that "in response to requests from the legitimate government of Kuwait, and in exercising the inherent right of collective self-defense recognized under Article 51 of the UN Charter, United States forces will . . . intercept the import and export of commodities and products to and from Iraq and Kuwait that are prohibited by UN Security Council Resolution 661."

An international lawyer, strongly supportive of the U.S. and UN actions against Iraq, commented that "this came close to a claim . . . to assume a police role on behalf of the international community."[9] The UN, left with a choice of renouncing U.S. unilateralism or endorsing it, chose the second course of action two weeks later, when it passed Security Council Resolution 665, which extended the authority of the council to the naval blockade. In that interim, however, the blockade had no official UN sanction, despite attempts by the United States to make it appear otherwise.

A similar arrogation of UN authority was later attempted by the United States in its claim that no Security Council resolution was required to legitimate the use of force to expel Iraqi troops from Kuwait. The United States argued that the liberation of Kuwait by military means was justified by Article 51 of the UN Charter, which provided for "the inherent right of individual or collective self-defense if an armed attack occurs against a member of the UN." That article, however, also limited the use of self-defense "until the Security Council has taken measures necessary to maintain international peace and security." The Security Council had already done this by imposing economic sanctions (Resolution 661). The United States was therefore forced to seek specific authorization (Resolution 678, 29 November 1992) to convince key states in the anti-Iraq coalition of the justification of Kuwait's liberation.

Resolution 678 was itself a masterpiece of obfuscation. Because Article 51 could no longer serve as justification for military action, only Article 42 remained; however, it required UN control of military operations through the Military Staff Committee, an agency of the Security Council. It also required an evaluation of the effectiveness of sanctions before military intervention could be launched. The framing of Resolution 678 thus necessitated "constructive ambiguity," as the U.S. ambassador to the UN, Thomas Pickering, characterized this probable violation of the UN Charter. Resolution 678 did not refer to either Article 51 or Article 42, but was worded in such a way as to invoke their authority. Thus the reference in 678 to the need to "restore international peace and security in the area" was a paraphrase of Article 42 and was included to convey a sense of legality. In fact, Resolution 678 was a free-floating initiative not anchored to any article of the UN Charter and thus, as the Yemeni and Iraqi UN delegates argued, was probably in violation of it.

The initial deployment of U.S. troops to Saudi Arabia was also dubious legally. It was predicated on the claim that an Iraqi invasion of that country was imminent, thus invoking the right of collective self-defense under Article 51. No substantial evidence of Iraq's alleged intention was ever produced to support this premise in the UN or any other public forum. What was presented as evidence resembled a disinformation campaign, probably orchestrated in the White House. No satellite reconnaissance photographs were released showing Iraqi troop and armored concentrations in pre-invasion deployments, despite claims that they existed.[10] Soviet satellite reconnaissance photography, obtained by a U.S. professor of engineering at George Washington University, revealed that on 13 September 1992, the date on which the Pentagon estimated that over 250,000 Iraqi troops were in Kuwait with 2,000 tanks and thousands of support vehicles, the roads and airfields were deserted. Another independent analyst with access to these photographs stated that "the KFA-1000 [satellite] images implied a defensive rather than offensive Iraqi posture, and that Saddam had no intention of attacking Saudi Arabia."[11] Ground observations, including those broadcast on CNN and other U.S. networks, revealed the movement of earthmoving equipment into place by Iraq immediately following the fall of Kuwait City. This equipment was moved so that Iraq could prepare defensive fortifications.

By 23 September, there was insufficient substantiation for the allegation that Iraq intended to invade Saudi Arabia. "U.S. officials" associated with "the U.S. intelligence community" leaked (through Douglas Jehl of the *Los Angeles Times*) information intended to bolster the case against Hussein; namely, that in 1985 Iraq had drafted a plan to attack Kuwait "under a war plan designed ultimately to conquer the oil fields of eastern Saudi Arabia." Why the Iraqis should draw up such a contingency plan while mired in a war with Iran, why the plan did not alert the United States to Iraqi intentions vis-à-vis Kuwait, and why its existence was revealed at this particular time, were not explained. The fact that the UN did not seek independent confirmation of Iraq's alleged intentions and that member states of the Security Council did not evaluate that evidence constituted gross derelictions of duty.

In the UN, the United States confined deliberations on the crisis to the Security Council. If its objective had, in fact, been to underscore the role of the UN as the major enforcer of a new world order, two courses of action were open. One was to invoke the principle embodied in Chapter 8 of the UN Charter, which deemed that disputes be settled by regional arrangements. In this case, the Arab League was the relevant body to settle such a dispute. But the United States, working with its dependent client Egypt, ensured that the Arab League could not resolve the issue in a manner likely to bring about a negotiated settlement.

The alternative approach was to encourage the General Assembly's participation in the crisis, possibly by invoking the peace resolution used for the first UN peacekeeping operation in the Middle East, the Suez debacle. Although the United States would have exercised less direct control over the course of events if they had centered the issue in the General Assembly, there was evidence that the "parliament" of the UN was prepared to deal with the matter in a responsible fashion, thereby establishing a valuable precedent. On 18 December 1990, it adopted Resolution 45/170 on the "Situation of Human Rights in Kuwait" (the vote was 144 to 1, the dissenting vote being Iraq's). This resolution condemned the Iraqi invasion of Kuwait and Iraq's "serious violation of human rights against the Kuwaiti people and third-state nationals," affirmed the applicability of the Geneva Convention, and demanded that Iraq facilitate Red Cross activities in Kuwait. This was the General Assembly's sole contribution during the crisis; it was not in session during the actual hostilities.

Nor did the Security Council meet during the first three weeks of the bombing campaign, despite its obligation under the UN Charter (Article 46) to ensure that the Military Staff Committee "be responsible for the strategic direction of any armed forces placed at the disposal of the Security Council." This abnegation of responsibility was not a violation of Article 46, because the United States refused to place its forces "at the disposal of the Security Council" and, instead, agreed only (by Resolution 678) to "inform" (not report to) the council on the progress of the military campaign. But the Security Council's complete inactivity at this critical time constituted a serious blow to the UN as the enforcer of the new world order; instead it appeared to become merely a willing accomplice to U.S. interventionism.

Not only did the United States ensure by this maneuver that UN consideration of the crisis was confined to the Security Council, it also hobbled the council. Resolution 678 carefully excluded the council's control over military operations and impeded access to information about them. After several days of the most intensive aerial bombardment in history, Third World members of the Security Council sought to convene a meeting to discuss the war being waged in the UN's name. The United States successfully blocked that move for three weeks, giving way only when the motion to convene included the proviso that it be done in camera, the fourth time in history that the council agreed to meet behind closed doors. Security Council Resolution 686, which set out the terms of the cease-fire, extended the time during which Resolution 678 remained in effect, thereby precluding any independent initiatives by the council. The surrender outlined in Resolution 687 authorized the United States to recommence military activities if Iraq violated its terms, including a rigorous 120-day timetable for implementation of wide-ranging demands and unilateral disarmament by Iraq. Having authorized the war (but not supervised its conduct), the Security Council now authorized (but did not control) some of the harshest surrender terms ever imposed on a defeated nation. In the summer of 1992, President Bush cited these terms as legitimating U.S. initiatives.

Concomitant with the hobbling of Security Council, the secretary-general's ability to use his office to avert war was undermined. Javier Pérez de Cuéllar, never a strong figure and further weakened at the time of the Gulf crisis by his desire to secure nomination for a second term, made a few cautious moves but they were quickly neutralized by the United States. Early in the crisis, he announced plans to travel to Amman and meet with the Iraqi foreign minister. President Bush immediately commented that he "did not see any hope for a diplomatic solution" and ruled out these initiatives to stimulate negotiations. The secretary-general responded meekly on 25 August, saying that he would only seek to induce Iraq to accept the five resolutions, by then passed, which virtually precluded the possibility of a negotiated settlement. On 1 November, Pérez de Cuéllar suggested that Israel should abide by the 1949 Fourth Geneva Convention Relative to the Protection of Civilians in Time of War. This was clearly intended as a face-saving initiative to provide grounds on which Iraq could claim victory vis-à-vis Israel and thus justify withdrawal from Kuwait. The United States chose to ignore this move, and it immediately became a dead issue.

On the eve of war (13 January 1991), the secretary-general traveled to Baghdad and met with Saddam Hussein. Following his departure, the Iraqi government released a transcript of the meeting, quoting Pérez de Cuéllar as saying that the Security Council resolutions represented U.S. domination of the UN. The office of the secretary-general did not confirm or deny the remarks. Two months previously, Brigadier Michael Harbottle, former chief of staff of the UN peacekeeping force in Cyprus, noted that "it was a matter of concern" that President Bush ensured that "the good offices of the secretary general have not been used."[12] That observation was an accurate description throughout the remainder of the crisis. Pérez de Cuéllar suffered the indignity of learning about the impending commencement of the U.S. bombing campaign only one hour before it was launched, by a courtesy telephone call from George Bush.

From start to finish, the United States was intent on maintaining control of events and legitimating its intervention through the UN. That it succeeded on both counts was testimony to the diplomatic skills of President Bush and Secretary of State James Baker, to the status of the United States as the sole surviving superpower, and to the inability of the UN to defend its interests and integrity.

The UN's failure was due in part to the global distribution of power that conditions the world in which it operates and in part to its own organizational deficiencies, which benefit the United States Although the UN could do little or nothing about global inequities of power and access to resources, it should tackle some of its short-comings, including the balance of power between the General Assembly and the Security Council. If any changes occur, they could be claimed as the "good news" of the Gulf crisis. Otherwise the "bad news" surrounding the crisis must also be deemed applicable to the UN and its performance. The UN, however, cannot be blamed for the war itself. As President Bush replied when asked what he would have done if the UN had refused to accede to U.S. demands: "I might have said, 'To hell with them, it's right and wrong, it's good and evil; he [Saddam Hussein] is evil, our cause is right, and—without the UN—sent a considerable force to help'."[13]

Notes

1. *New York Times*, 23 August 1990.

2. Norman Finkelstein, "Israel and Iraq: A Double Standard," *Journal of Palestine Studies* 20 (Winter 1991): 43–56.

3. *Minneapolis Tribune*, 4 August 1991.

4. Robin Wright, "Unexplored Realities of the Persian Gulf Crisis," *The Middle East Journal* 45 (Winter 1991): 28–29.

5. Bruce Russett and James E. Sutterlin, "The UN in a New World Order," *Foreign Affairs* (Spring 1991): 69.

6. *Ibid.*, 76.

7. *Ibid.*, 71.

8. Anthony Parsons, "The United Nations Comes into Its Own," *Middle East International* 382 (31 August 1990): 29.

9. Christopher Greenwood, "Iraq's Invasion of Kuwait: Some Legal Issues," *The World Today* 47 (March 1991): 41.

10. It has been claimed that Secretary of Defense Richard Cheney used such photographs to convince King Fahd that an invasion was imminent. See Bob Woodward, *The Commanders* (New York: Simon & Schuster, 1991): 263–74. A former U.S. ambassador to Saudi Arabia, James Akins, believes those photographs may have been purposely misinterpreted by the U.S. administration in order to dupe Fahd. Speech given by Akins at the Annual Conference of the Australasian Middle East Studies Association, Sydney, 26 July 1991.

11. Vipin Gupta of the Verification Technology Information Center, cited in Jon Trux, "Desert Storm: A Space-Age War," *New Scientist* (27 July 1991): 26–30.

12. Michael Harbottle, "Avoiding the Worst Case Scenario," *Middle East International* 387 (9 November 1991): 17.

13. Cited in Christopher Layne, "Why the Gulf War Was Not in the National Interest," *The Atlantic* 268 (July 1991): 77.

3

Bush's New World Order

A Structural Analysis of
Instability and Conflict in the Gulf

Yasumasa Kuroda

*President Bush told the families of soldiers at Fort
Stewart, Georgia, that one result of the war would
be "what we say goes" in the Gulf.*
James McCarney, 1991

President George Bush's masterful orchestration of the war was a
remarkable demonstration of his political skill, which only a few
knew he possessed. This chapter examines his concept of the new
world order, analyzes the possible structural causes of the Gulf War,
and looks at the region's possible and preferred futures in the aftermath of the war.

Johan Galtung, long known for his peace studies and activities,
stated that causes of war can be answered only "in terms of a model
of the world" (Galtung 1980:179–253). There are two basic models
of the world, he justly claims: first, an *actor-oriented model* that
looks for violence carried out by actors including groups and nations, and second, a *structure-oriented model* that focuses on systemic conditions that are responsible for the occurrence of direct
military violence. These two models are not mutually exclusive but
can be viewed as complimentary to each other in answering fully
the question of causes of any war.

Similarly A. J. Taylor, a British historian, divided causes of war
into basic and particular, or immediate (Khalidi 1991). (Taylor's basic
causes are equivalent to Galtung's structure-oriented model and immediate causes of the actor-oriented model, except that Taylor approaches the subject less systematically than Galtung.) On the other

hand, such efforts as the one based on *ad hoc* case studies by John G. Stoessinger (1990) lack the strength of systemic efforts.

This chapter first examines the new elements in President Bush's new world order. Second, it attempts to explain how the British and French established boundaries and institutions to assure their future hegemony over the region. Third, U.S. policy toward the region is reviewed in a historical perspective. Fourth, the chapter presents the forces that could challenge the prevailing institutions and geographic boundaries in the region to establish a new world order and call for restructuring of the entire region.

Bush's New World Order

In 1990, as President Bush waged a war of words with Saddam Hussein and demonized him, he termed his efforts as an attempt to establish a new world order. Initially, some were excited and elated by what he might have meant by the term in light of what he wanted to achieve in Eastern Europe. Gradually, however, we realized that Bush's main objective in the Gulf region was not to promote democracy as he had in Eastern Europe, but to re-establish hegemony in the region, or, as was stated at the outset of this chapter, to promote conditions of "what we say goes" in the Gulf.

This was a far cry from what those in the region who desired democracy wanted to hear; they wanted to unite the Arab world by establishing democratic rules everywhere for Kurds, Shiites, and other minorities. What happened to the Kurds, Shiites, Palestinians, and Kuwaiti nationalists following the Gulf War in Kuwait and Iraq was indicative of President Bush's policy emphasizing the restoration of the old political order as designed and structured by the Anglo-French colonial powers instead of bringing democracy to the region.

What was new about his policy? President Bush was correct in describing it as an effort to bring about a new world order in the following senses:

1. The demise of Soviet influence eliminated the U.S.-Soviet rivalry in the region. There were no longer any superpowers to which Iraq or Syria could turn for military hardware or assistance.
2. The policy was new in the sense that the United States alone could not financially wage war against Iraq, a Third World

power, without damaging its own economy. This required that Bush ask Great Britain, France, Japan, Germany, and other nations (including the Soviet Union and China) for their assistance through the United Nations to achieve his objectives. In the past, world superpowers did not ask other nations for financial or military assistance; they carried out their military plans unassisted.

3. The United States, which brought victory for the Allied Forces during World War II, established the UN in 1945. Since then, U.S. influence has gradually waned as smaller nations multiplied. The Gulf War marked a departure from this historical trend and demonstrated to the world that the United States was again a superpower to be reckoned with at the UN.

4. The policy was a new order in the sense that, for the first time in history, President Bush placed Israel and its Arab neighbors on one side against Iraq.

5. Bush demonstrated remarkable skill, enforcing his policy while successfully winning cooperation from many nations and eliminating his image as a "wimp." He was decisive and swift; it was a seemingly new Bush. Looking back at what he did in Panama and Nicaragua, however, we should have guessed what he might do in the world outside Eastern Europe. How much democracy prevails in Panama, Grenada, and Nicaragua today? How much assistance has the United States provided to those countries to establish democracy and political stability?

Not much else is new about his new world order. So why is this vital region, which contains over 60 percent of the oil reserves, so unstable and subject to so many crises and wars of various magnitude? My response is that it is unstable by design.

Structural Instability by Design: Colonial Subjugation

There is agreement among many who discuss West Asia or the Middle East that these are regions of the world characterized by instability, and that these regions experience periodic war and revolution. There are several built-in sources of instability that have existed for many centuries, such as ethnic and religious diversity and maldistribution of natural resources prior to the development of nation states in the region. Great Britain and France, which dominated much of the region following the end of World War I, drew national boundaries and placed kings in certain areas to ensure that the Arab world would forever be divided. It was then easy for the European nations to continue their hegemonic rule in the region even after the Arab nations became independent. The request of the General Syrian Congress to accept assistance from the United States while the country prepared for total independence, rather than be ruled by the British or French, was disregarded by the superpowers that dominated the League of Nations.[1]

Although individual and group alienation based on ethnicity, class, religion, region, and history cannot be underestimated, the focus here is on colonial domination of the region, due to the nature of national boundary disputes involved in the Gulf War.[2]

The Arab world is united by language. Although the spoken language varies by region, the written language remains constant throughout the Arab world. There are nearly 200 million Arabs in twenty-one Arabic-speaking nations of West Asia and North Africa. The combined size of the Arab world is 5.4 million square miles (71 percent of which is desert), representing a land area about 50 percent larger than the United States. Gulf states such as Kuwait and the United Arab Emirates (UAE) are 100 percent desert or urban, while only 21 percent of Syria is so classified. Arab countries such as Sudan and Algeria are large, while others such as Bahrain are very small (230 square miles).

The Arab world is richly endowed with such natural resources as oil and gas. It is remembered for its glorious history as the ancient Orient, and its Islamic teaching spread from Spain in the West to Indonesia in the East. It is a potentially dynamic power that could rank equally with the United States, Western Europe, and Japan. Its inherent strength of unity was demonstrated clearly and loudly by King Faisal of Saudi Arabia when he successfully orchestrated the 1973 Arab oil embargo. Never in the history of international relations had such a sudden shift in the distribution of money and power been made possible so swiftly without armed conflict. (Faisal's life came to a quick end when he was killed under unusual circumstances.) Although the unity did not last long, it showed the world its potential strength. An earlier effort by Gamal Abdel Nasser to challenge the British and French by nationalizing the Suez Canal led the colonial West to call him a Hitler who must be stopped before it was too late. He was no match militarily for the combined assault of the British, French, and Israeli forces, but Nasser won the hearts of millions of Arabs.

Divide and Rule

As the Ottoman Empire finally collapsed in World War I, the British and French carved out protectorates in West Asia and North Africa (Sykes-Picot Agreement of 1917). The British promise to grant independence of the Arab countries to Faisal and Abdullah of the Hashemite family in Hijaz if the Arabs sided with the Allies was never kept. Similarly, President Franklin D. Roosevelt's words of 5 April 1945 in his letter to King Ibn Saud stating that the U.S. government would make no decision on Palestine "without full consultation with both Arabs and Jews" were disregarded after World War II (*Foreign Relations of the United States* 1945:698). King Ibn Saud was further assured that Roosevelt would "do nothing to assist the Jews against the Arabs and would make no move hostile to the Arab people."

All Arabs were subjugated to new Western colonial masters after 400 years of Turkish rule. Remnants of colonialism remained in West Asia and North Africa even after the end of the cold war. The tradition of Western intervention in Arab affairs was dramatically confirmed in the 1991 Gulf War. The old world order was very much alive and well. President Bush's prediction of what would happen after the Gulf War revealed one of his objectives in going to war. As he said to the families of soldiers at Fort Stewart, Georgia, one consequence of the war will be "what we say goes" in the Gulf region (McCarney 1991:14).

After the Arabs were divided and national boundaries drawn by colonial powers, the new countries naturally developed their own national interests and agenda that were antithetical to Arab unity and independence.

Iraq and Kuwait   In 1899, Mubarak Al-Sabah "the Great" of Kuwait signed an agreement with the United Kingdom, to stop German influence in the Gulf region. The Berlin-Baghdad railroad did not extend to the Gulf as a result. Thus began the development of Kuwait as a nascent state—a British "protection."[3] The development of Kuwait, which blocked Iraq's outlet to the Arabian Gulf, certainly contributed to the weakening of Iraq and caused potential conflicts between Iraq and Kuwait.

Iraq, Palestine, and Transjordan   Faisal of Iraq and Abdullah of Jordan were brothers, members of the Hashemite family, which is descendent from the Prophet Muhammed from Mecca, the king of Hijaz. Both opposed the establishment of the British Mandate in Palestine and Transjordan because the British promised independence to the Arabs if they sided with the Allies against the Turks during World War I, which the Arabs did. Their objections were disregarded by the League of Nations, and the League ordered Great Britain to maintain its mandate over Iraq, Palestine, and Transjordan. In 1921, Faisal was given Iraq in which to establish a kingdom, and Abdullah was given Transjordan.

Saudi Arabia derives its name from the Saud family of the Najd. In 1902, Ibn Saud set out to build his country by first defeating the Rashidis and subsequently the Hashemites, his major rivals, thereby uniting the three provinces of Hijaz, Majd, and al-Hasa into one. Ibn Saud announced himself as king of the Arabian peninsula and named Saudi Arabia after his family. Ibn Saud's conquest of Saudi Arabia was made possible through assistance from Wahhabi Muslims. He too, succumbed to British pressure and the area became a protectorate in 1915.

In 1926, Ibn Saud successfully ousted Hashemite leader Sherif Hussein from the Hijaz in the Great Hall of Mecca, thereby eliminating his principal rival. The seeds of animosity between the Hashemites, who traced their ancestry to the Prophet Muhammed, and the Saud, the region's most powerful family, were planted.

In a declaration of 1917 announced by Arthur Balfour, British secretary of foreign affairs, the British promised that the Jews would have a "national home" in Palestine without jeopardizing the civil rights of non-Jews. Eventually, the U.S.-led UN General Assembly passed a resolution to partition Palestine into Arab and Jewish states. Jews, who had previously owned 6 percent of the land, were to receive 56 percent of the land under the new arrangement, the Arabs were to receive 43 percent, and the remaining 1 percent—Jerusalem—was to be classified under the international zone. The Palestinians' rights to self-determination and property were totally disregarded by the West.

The colonial practice of drawing national boundaries to suit the West's needs continued even after World War II when Western hegemony over West Asia and North Africa was achieved through the allegiance of "moderate" Arab states and Israel, the bastion of "democracy." In fact, these states owed their existence to the Western powers in terms of financial assistance from the United States (Israel) and military assistance to some of the states. The West's interests in the region were both financial and political. For example, Western Asia and North Africa attracted more weapons than any other part of the world; witness the number weapons purchased by Iraq before the outbreak of the Gulf crisis.

Keeping the Countries in Line

Those who challenged Western hegemony were punished by Western powers. The democratically elected prime minister of Iran, Dr. Muhammed Mossadegh, was overthrown in a coup backed by the Central Intelligence Agency (CIA) in 1953 (*Congressional Quarterly* 1990:151). His "crime" was the nationalization of the oil industry in Iran. The Shah then allowed the return of Western oil companies. Saddam Hussein of Iraq challenged the West when his forces invaded Kuwait and occupied it on 2 August 1990. Backed by the UN, the U.S.-led multinational forces started military actions against Iraq.

Although there is no evidence to prove a conspiracy, Iraqi rulers who claimed Kuwait to be part of Iraq did not stay in power long. Ibn Rachid, backed by the Turks, attempted to gain control of Kuwait in 1901 but was repelled by shelling from British fleets in the Gulf. In April 1939, when King Ghazi of Iraq died in an automobile accident, shortly after he refused to give up Iraq's claim to Kuwait even after a warning from British Ambassador Peterson, it was widely believed that he was assassinated by British agents. In 1961, when Kuwait declared itself independent, Iraqi ruler General Abdul Karim Kassim renewed Iraq's claim on Kuwait and threatened to advance Iraqi forces into Kuwait. British troops prevented the invasion, and in 1963 Kassim was ousted in a coup reportedly through assistance from outside forces. These events are strikingly similar to those of the Gulf crisis of 1990–1991. Iraq's attempts to claim its rights to Kuwait have been repeatedly crushed in one way or another by the West.

King Hussein of Jordan, whose economic ties with Iraq were considerable, refused to join the Allied Multinational Forces during the Gulf War. He disapproved of the Iraqi invasion of Kuwait, to be sure, but he did not side with the other "moderate" Arab states. For this he paid a high price: The U.S. Congress cut $50 million out of $80 million aid given to Jordan at a time when Jordan's economy was adversely affected by the Gulf War. In contrast, moderate nations including Syria received financial assistance either directly from the West or from oil rich countries of the Gulf. It is ironic that this shift in U.S. policy occurred when Jordan was probably the most open and democratic nation in the Arab world.

The Role of the United States in the Gulf

The U.S. interest in the Gulf was initiated by a businessman from New Hampshire, Edmund Roberts, who went to Oman in 1827. Critical U.S. economic interest in the region did not start until nearly a hundred years later, however, when U.S. oil companies discovered oil in Bahrain and Kuwait in the early 1930s (Long 1976:133). During that 100-year period, U.S. involvement in the Gulf was limited to action in the area during World War I.

U.S. involvement in World War I led President Wilson to send the King-Crane Commission to assess the public pulse in Syria and Palestine. The commission's report, which spoke for the self-determination of the region, was in basic agreement with the "General Syrian Congress," which proclaimed Sherif Faisal of the Hashemite in Hijaz as king of Syria and expressed its desire to receive assistance from the United States rather than succumb to the colonization of the region by the British and French colonial powers (Rustow 1982:65). The report warned against the Western powers (including the United States) and the danger of establishing a Zionist state in Palestine. Both the General Syrian Congress and the King-Crane Commission were totally disregarded by the European colonial powers. Faisal, whose father was betrayed by the British, was named King of Iraq in 1921 and the British Mandate was established over Palestine.

Great Britain continued to maintain supremacy in the Gulf by controlling 73 percent of the oil reserves as of 1939. Following World War II, its share declined to 49 percent while the U.S. share climbed to 44 percent. It was not until the successful, CIA-engineered overthrow of the democratically elected Mossadegh government in Iran in 1953 that the United States surpassed Great Britain; its share had declined to 20 percent while the U.S. share rose to 54 percent by 1954 (Yokoyama 1989:183).

President Roosevelt's request to allow Jewish refugees to settle in Palestine was firmly rebuffed by King Abd al-Aziz Ibn Saud of Saudi Arabia in 1945.[4] President Roosevelt promised him that the United States would not make any decision with respect to Palestine without consulting both Arabs and Jews. Despite repeated pleas by Saudi Arabia's foreign minister, Crown Prince Faisal, the United States pushed for the partitioning of Palestine and helped establish Israel, against the will of the indigenous population. Saudi Arabia, along with the Palestinians, was betrayed by the United States.

With the birth of the cold war in 1947, the United States added two more objectives to the Gulf policy in addition to control of oil and support for Israel. The first was the containment of the Soviet influence in the entire region. This new policy, known as the Truman Doctrine, was proclaimed on 12 March 1947.[5]

In 1956, the United States joined others in the UN to force the invading colonial powers of Great Britain, France, and Israel to withdraw their troops from Egypt when Nasser nationalized the Suez Canal.

The Eisenhower Doctrine, a 1957 congressional resolution, contained the second objective. Eisenhower promoted the establishment of a security agreement among Britain, Iraq, Iran, Pakistan, and Turkey known as the Baghdad Pact. The Hashemite kingdom of Iraq was overthrown by Brigadier General Abdul Karim Kassim in 1958, and Iraq withdrew from the Baghdad Pact following the military coup. This led to the United States effectively joining the remaining Baghdad Pact nations by renaming the alliance as the Central Treaty Organization (CENTO). Despite Muslim opposition, President Camille Chamoun of Lebanon accepted the Eisenhower Doctrine. It called for the United States "to use armed forces to assist . . . any nation or groups of nations requesting assistance against armed aggression from any country controlled by international communism" (Congressional Quarterly 1990:187). To illustrate, some 15,000 U.S. marines landed in Lebanon briefly and peacefully on 15 July 1958 at the request of Chamoun, who feared the United Arab Republic's interference in domestic Lebanese politics.

In the 1960s, Kennedy's brief tenure made it impossible to leave much impact on the region, although he showed sympathy for the Arab struggle to be free of colonial powers. In 1964, British imperial strength, which had lasted three centuries, was greatly reduced as Prime Minister Harold Wilson attempted to significantly cut his country's military presence in the Gulf.

Using information obtained by invoking the Freedom of Information Act, Stephen Green (1984) was able to determine that the U.S. Air Force directly participated in the June 1967 war against the

Arabs. The United States, with infrared cameras designed for night vision, helped Israel by providing reconnaissance flights at the outset of the spectacular preemptive attack that annihilated the Egyptian Air Force. Green speculated that President Lyndon Johnson ordered the U.S. Air Force to take part in the war to destroy as many MIGs as possible so that the Soviets would be busy supplying new MIGs and weapons to Egypt rather than to North Vietnam. Following this, the Nixon Doctrine, issued on 9 July 1969, urged nations to defend themselves, although the United States would continue to honor its treaties and agreements with other nations. The United States would continue to ship arms but should not be expected to send its troops to defend other countries. As part of his doctrine, Richard Nixon provided more arms to Iran and Saudi Arabia, and he visited Teheran in 1972.

King Faisal, mobilizing all oil-producing Arab countries, used oil as a weapon against anti-Arab forces led by the United States in the 1973 October War. Abdulsalam Massarweh claims that President Nixon, in cooperation with Secretary of State Henry Kissinger, planned to occupy oil fields by force primarily in Saudi Arabia to maintain the free flow of oil to the world (Mussarweh 1990:34). Henry Kissinger did ask the Congressional Research Service to develop such a plan in 1975 (reported by John Collins and Clyde Marks of the Congressional Research Service's Middle East specialists). This idea became the foundation upon which President Jimmy Carter established the "Rapid Deployment Force" (RDF), which called for the deployment of a combined force of 228,900 soldiers. This new policy, announced on 23 January 1980, was precipitated by the Soviet entry into Afghanistan a few weeks before. Another factor was the loss of Iran as a U.S. ally in 1979.

Then, the Carter Doctrine was born: "Any attempt by an outside force to gain control of the Persian Gulf region will be regarded as an assault on the vital interests of the United States of America, and such an assault will be repelled by any means necessary, including military force" (Johnson 1991:88).[6] In April 1980, President Carter's efforts to use special forces to rescue U.S. hostages failed. Carter's attempts to obtain U.S. bases in the region also met with little success. The United States gained access agreements with Somalia and Oman but nowhere else in the region.

President Ronald Reagan's efforts to achieve a "strategic consensus" among "moderate" states in the Gulf had no success, as leaders in the moderate states informed Secretary of State Alexander Haig and Undersecretary for Near Eastern Affairs Richard Murphy, that they were primarily concerned with Israeli threats to their security rather than possible Soviet entry into the Gulf region.[7] On 1 January 1983, the RDF was transformed into the U.S. Central Command (US CENTCOM), headquartered in Tampa, Florida. Its responsibility encompassed all of the Gulf nations including Afghanistan, Iran, Jordan, Egypt, Sudan, Djibouti, Somalia, and two non-Arab states in Africa, Ethiopia, and Kenya.

It is within the framework of the U.S. CENTCOM that the United States responded positively in 1987 to the Kuwaiti request for reflagging its oil tankers to protect them from Iranian attacks in the Gulf region. President Reagan also decided to strengthen Kuwaiti defenses by selling them forty F-18 fighter-bombers, several varieties of missiles, and cluster bombs (*Congressional Quarterly* 1990:30). Relations between Iraq and the United States were rocky but friendly enough, as evidenced in the U.S. acceptance of Iraq's explanation for mistakenly attacking the USS *Stark*, resulting in the death of thirty-seven crew members in 1987.

It was after Iran accepted a cease-fire on 18 July 1988 that the United States started its campaign to criticize the use of chemical weapons by Iraqis, particularly on the Kurds. Television viewers were repeatedly shown Kurdish children, women, and men lying on the ground, presumably killed by chemical weapons used by Iraqis. This was the beginning of the United States' hate-Iraqi campaign. Iraq's usefulness as a force against Islamic fundamentalists in Iran (who called the United States the Great Satan) ended with the end of the Iran-Iraq War. The hate campaign reached a high point when, in 1990, President Bush referred to President Hussein as a Hitler whose advancement must be stopped before it was too late. The tone was reminiscent of British Prime Minister Anthony Eden's demonization of Gamal Abdel Nasser when the Egyptian hero nationalized the Suez Canal in 1956.

On 28 February 1989, General H. Norman Schwarzkopf, the now famous commander in chief of US CENTCOM, reported to the Defense Subcommittee of the U.S. Senate Appropriations Committee that, although Soviet influence in the region was growing, the United States maintained the confidence of its friendly nations in the region— U.S. CENTCOM's objective did not focus on Israel's threat to the security of the Arab Gulf region. It is in this historical context that the following events took place.

Incidents that Led to the War[8]

During the 1967 Arab-Israeli War, Iraq severed diplomatic relations with the United States because of its support for Israel. Relations were resumed in 1984 when Saddam Hussein announced a change in policy.

The United States sided with Iraq in the Iran-Iraq War. The United States extended credits for its export of agricultural products, supplied needed information to Iraq in its war against Iran, and sold the country many items including arms. The Reagan administration's earlier flirtation with moderate forces in Iran, as revealed in the Iran-Contra affair, was a failure.

Then, on 1 September 1988, the *New York Times*, citing unnamed U.S. State Department officials, claimed that Iraq had deployed some 60,000 troops against the Kurds. Their leader, Jalal Talabani, accused Iraq of using chemical weapons since 25 August against some twenty-five Kurdish villages. An official study was conducted by the U.S. Army War College to address this issue (Pelletiere et al. 1990:52–53).[9] The report noted that when the United States accused Iraq of the alleged use of chemical weapons against its Kurdish population the action signalled a radical shift in the United States' pro-Iraq policy during the last half of the Iran-Iraq War. According to Pelletiere et al. (1990:51, 90), in early September 1988, about two hours before Secretary of State George Shultz was to meet with Iraqi Foreign Minister Tareq Aziz, Shultz publicly accused Iraq of using chemical weapons against innocent civilian Kurds. The report by the U.S. Army War College could not verify the State Department's allegation that poison gas was employed, and, in fact, concluded that there was no evidence to prove Iraq's guilt.[10]

On 3 September, Foreign Minister Tareq Aziz denied the use of chemical weapons while admitting that the Kurds were being relocated to government housing developments near the Iranian border (*The Washington Post* 9/4, 1988:A-33). Not to be outdone by the State Department, the U.S. Senate passed an economic sanction bill against Iraq for its "gross violation of international law" with respect to its alleged use of chemical weapons against an innocent Kurdish population. Some Kurds sought refuge in Turkey. A day after the U.S. Senate approved economic sanctions, the government of Turkey responded by saying that it could not find any evidence of the alleged use of chemical weapons by Iraq (*New York Times* 9/10, A-4, 9/15, A-12, 1988).

This was a departure from the days when Iraq was accused by Iran of using chemical weapons on its citizens during the Iran-Iraq War. Then the United States remained mute over the Iranian allegations. Why did Shultz choose to use the shaky allegation to insult Aziz just before the scheduled meeting? Does it relate to an increased concern shown by Israel about the same time as the victory of Iraq over Iran? For the first time since 1979, Israel faced a potential enemy capable of developing nuclear weapons and directing missile attacks on its soil.

The actions taken by the U.S. State Department and Senate were likely welcomed by Israel but predictably angered Iraq. The first mass demonstration against the United States in Iraqi history took place in Baghdad on 11 September 1988. An estimated 150,000 Iraqis took to the streets of the capital (*The Washington Post* 9/12, 1988: A-14). This was the beginning of the U.S. campaign against Iraq, which prompted the three Army War College researchers to conclude that "The United States seems to be on a collision course with the Ba'athists. This is unfortunate and unnecessary. The root of the problem appears to be Washington's inability to appreciate the intensity of Iraq's determination to overcome its present economic crisis" (Pelletiere et al. 1990:69). There was little doubt that Iraq's decision to invade Kuwait was based on economic concerns. This prompts the question, was it Washington's inability or Washington's concern for regional security, including that of Israel, that put the two nations on a collision course? Certainly President Bush acted as a leader who knew what he was doing, as did Secretary of State George Shultz.

What disturbs the author as a consumer of U.S. mass media is that the media joined in a vicious anti-Iraq campaign initiated by Shultz to make us believe that Iraqis used poison gas on its people, when, in fact, the U.S. Army War College's research team, with access to intelligence reports, could not find a witness or evidence to support that claim, nor could the Turkish government authorities who received Kurdish refugees.

We saw pictures of the victims of chemical weapons on television and in many publications, however, those victims were from Halabjah, a city gassed in March 1988 during the Iran-Iraq War. There is no hard evidence that Iraqis used chemical weapons on the Kurds in Halabjah. According to the U.S. Army War College's report, Iranian chemical bombardment was most likely responsible for the deaths of many Kurds in Halabjah, and not the Iraqis, who denied the use of any chemical weapons inside Iraq.[11] When these pictures were televised, we believed that the Iraqis caused those deaths, but we should have demanded at least some witnesses to this tragedy before we believed anyone's allegation, because no television stations showed Iraqis actually using chemical weapons. We, the naive and gullible consumers of U.S. media, were deceived by Washington, who had its own agenda, and the mass media, which also was fooled.

Unifying Forces

What forces challenged Western efforts to maintain a firm grip of hegemony in the region through its military supremacy? The answer to this question becomes apparent when we review how the Arab masses reacted to the Gulf War. Although all Arab governments, including the Palestinian Liberation Organization (PLO), denounced the Iraqi invasion of Kuwait, not all Arab nations and their people sided with Kuwait and Saudi Arabia.

The divide-and-rule method used by Western colonial powers to maintain their hegemony over the region has been discussed. Naturally, any force that unified and challenged the divided nature of the Arab states presented a threat to the West. Forces that united the Arabic speaking world in West Asia and North Africa can be divided into three categories: (1) secular pluralistic democracy, (2) Islamic fundamentalism, and (3) anti-colonial and anti-Zionist sentiments.

Secular Pluralistic Democracy

There were two major ideological attempts to promote pan-Arabism. Nasser's pan-Arabism of 1958 as well as the Ba'ath party (founded on the philosophy of Michel Aflaq) posit Arab unity, which is to be achieved through the development of national strength. Pan-Arabism was to promote an Arab unity in which wealth and resources were shared more evenly among all Arab peoples. In so doing, Nasser's pan-Arabism appeared to be more pragmatic while the Ba'athist philosophy was more ideological. Nasser's pan-Arabism was constrained by his Egyptian nationalism. The Ba'ath, as its name (meaning resurrection or renaissance) suggests, emphasized the awakening of past Arab greatness. Despite lofty ideals of Arab unity, neither of the pan-Arabist theories succeeded in capturing the imagination of all

Arabs. It is an extremely difficult task to rise above Egyptian, Syrian, or Iraqi nationalism to pursue the welfare of the Arab world at large.

If the improvements under the Iraqi Ba'athist regime in the past twenty years could be measured in terms of the advancement of women's rights in Iraq, the following statistics from the Iraqi women's federation in 1985 are impressive in comparison with women's status among its Gulf neighbors. "Nearly one-third of university students are female. Women compose 70 percent of pharmacists, 46 percent of teachers, 46 percent of dentists, 45 percent of the voters, 37 percent of petroleum designing project engineers and 30 percent of construction supervisors in the Ministry of Petroleum, 29 percent of physicians, 21 percent of civil servants, and 15 percent of accountants" (Freedman 1989:42–46).

Both Nasser and Aflaq emphasized the common heritage of Islam as a base upon which to work toward Arab unity, although both of their ideologies remained secular. In contrast to these secular forces, there was a rising force of Islamic fundamentalists who were gaining power and influence in the Islamic world.

Islamic Fundamentalism

The number of militant Islamic fundamentalists has increased noticeably over the last two decades, probably aided by an Islamic revival. Islamic fundamentalists offered an alternative to secular democratic nationalists. They wish to revive the fundamentals of the Islamic religion and strengthen Islamic influence on society. The failure of nationalists to achieve their objectives has contributed to the rise of militant Islamic fundamentalism. Furthermore, the failures of modernization and pan-Arabism, defeats in wars against the West with the notable exception of the Algerian war of independence, and the paucity of social justice and legitimate and responsible political leadership have all added to the frustration of the Arabs. To restore the dignity of people who have long been subjugated to Western colonialism, some forum or thought system was needed through which they could articulate pride in who they were. For many, the forum resided in Islamic fundamentalism.

Anti-colonialism and Anti-Zionism

There are few examples to illustrate Arab supremacy in the struggle against colonial Western powers. The only war won by Arabs in the twentieth century was the Algerian revolution. It took eight long years, from 1954, when the Front de Liberation National (FLN) declared war on France, to its successful conclusion in 1962.

Another example of victory was the Suez crisis of 1956. Abba Eban wrote that Dwight Eisenhower "would not permit France and Britain to renew their colonial hegemony. The United States joins with the Soviet Union in a UN resolution condemning the invasion" (Eban 1983:36). Prime Minister Eden equated President Nasser's nationalization of the Suez Canal with the Nazi blitz on world order in the late 1930s and called Nasser "Hitler" exactly as President Bush referred to Saddam Hussein in 1990 (Carlton 1981:298-309, 327-30, 428-30). Nasser lost military battles but won the hearts of millions of Arabs. Colonial powers did not think Egyptians could run the canal but they learned to do it.

In 1956, in cooperation with the Soviet Union, President Eisenhower forced his European allies and Israel to withdraw from Sinai and Gaza. Eden resigned. It was a remarkable moment in U.S. history when a superpower acted in the name of a principle—a traditional belief in self-determination against colonialism upon which the nation was founded—rather than its own strategic self interests. Is President Bush following the footsteps of Anthony Eden and Dwight Eisenhower?

In 1973, anti-Zionism was the uniting factor in King Faisal's orchestration of the oil embargo by the Organization of Arab Petroleum Exporting Countries (OAPEC). An earlier oil embargo during the 1967 War failed to achieve its purpose because at that time anti-Arab Western nations did not depend enough on Arab oil. The situation had changed by 1973, when Faisal succeeded in using oil as a political weapon against Israel and its supporters. Anti-colonialism could be a unifying force if channelled into building unity in the Arab world—an important but difficult task to achieve.

Reactions from the Arab World

It should be noted that support for Saddam Hussein was felt not only in the Arab world but also among the 800 million people in the Muslim world. Hundreds of babies born in Pakistan were named Saddam after the Gulf War broke out. Of course, others sided with Saudi Arabia and Kuwait, which have been generous in their financial assistance to less privileged Muslim nations. Although some argued, justifiably, that the rich oil nations did not give enough, they were at least more generous than Western nations in providing foreign aid.

The extent of mass support given to Iraq in the Gulf War varied from one country to another in the Arab and Islamic regions. Palestinians, Jordanians, and Yemeni topped the list of Iraqi supporters, while Saudis and Gulf nationals were least likely to support Iraq. The rest of the Arab world was somewhere between.

No countries condoned the Iraqi invasion of Kuwait. Why, then was President Hussein viewed as an Arab hero? Although many did not approve of the ruthlessness by which Hussein governs Iraq, many supported Iraq at the start of the Gulf War on 16 January 1991. The massive demonstration of support by 300,000 people that took place in Morocco on 3 February 1991 was indicative of the support Arab masses gave to Iraq. It is more significant when one considers that Morocco was a U.S. ally in the Gulf War, sending 5,000 of its troops to the war theater. In the words of Ramy Khouri, editor of *The Jordan Times*, in his response to Charlayne Hunter-Gault of the MacNeil, Lehrer News Hour, "the West has pushed the button that released a collective Arab anger which has been building for centuries" (Hunter-Gault 1990:27).

It appears that the Gulf crisis, as it escalated under the masterful orchestration of President Bush, was transformed from a direct confrontation between Iraq and Kuwait to a dichotomy between Arab aspirations for independence and unity, and traditional Western imperialism under the guise of the UN. The United States initially sent troops to Saudi Arabia to defend it from Iraqi aggression, not to force the withdrawal of Iraqi troops from Kuwait. To the Arab masses, history was repeated with the advent of Western imperialist armies coming to the Arab world to draw national boundaries and dictate their will upon the Arabs.

Linkage

It is in this context that Israel was viewed as part and parcel of the problem facing the Arabs. To the Arabs, Israel was the latest illustration of Western imperialists drawing new national boundaries with total disregard for the aspirations and property rights of indigenous Christians and Muslim Arabs in order to carve out a European settler state in the Arab world. In this regard, the Iraqi invasion of Kuwait was seen as an Arab challenge to Western imperialism.

Israel was perceived as the U.S. client state that could maintain the colonial world order in West Asia, although at times it has been difficult to tell which country is being manipulated. It certainly was in Israel's interest to destroy Iraq's offensive capabilities, particularly its weapons of mass destruction. This is a step the United States took under the guise of the UN's resolution to force Iraqi troops to withdraw from Kuwait. The resolution, however, called for Iraq's withdrawal of its troops from Kuwait, but not for the destruction of Iraq's weapons of mass destruction. This departure from the original intent of the UN resolution angered the Arabs because all Arab states approved of the resolution. Furthermore, successful efforts made by Chairman Yassir Arafat and King Hussein to release all foreigners in Iraq, which finally led Saddam Hussein to release them in December 1990, did not receive any recognition from the West.

Standing Up to the West

The popularity of President Hussein in the Arab world was based on Arab frustrations that have accumulated over the years, which Arabs largely attributed to Western imperialism. To them, Hussein was a hero strong enough to squarely confront the United States—the superpower of the West and the symbol of Western imperialism. He offered them a long-denied opportunity to stand up for their independence and dignity.

In the 1956 Suez Canal crisis, Nasser lost the war but won in peace as Egypt was assisted by Eisenhower and backed by the Soviet Union. In the Algerian war of independence, French Prime Minister Guy Mollet did not think the Algerians could win without a leader like Nasser, but they eventually did.

Iraq has not been as successful as Egypt or Algeria in its long-term efforts to control Kuwait and stand up to the West. In 1901, Iraq was forced to withdraw after the British shelled that country from the Gulf when Iraq attempted to claim Kuwait as a part of Basra Province. In 1939, King Ghazi of Iraq made a demand on the Sabah family to stop the persecution of those who took part in the Free Kuwait Movement. He was told by British Ambassador Sir Maurice Peterson to keep his hands off Kuwait. Shortly after this incident he died in a car accident. And in 1961, when Iraqi President Kassim tried to lay a claim on Kuwait by sending his troops after Kuwait proclaimed its independence, Iraqi forces were repulsed by the British military.

Western Hypocrisy and Double Standards

If maintaining the territorial integrity of nations was so important to the United States, why did the United States not protest Israel's continuing military occupation of South Lebanon and Palestine? Why did the United States not protest Israel's annexation of Jerusalem and the Golan Heights but, instead, even encouraged its expansion by providing massive foreign aid? If the development of weapons of mass destruction is so undesirable, then the United States should apply the same credo to Israel and South Africa as it did to Iraq and Pakistan. Saddam Hussein agreed to disarm the mass destruction weapons in his region if Israel took part in such a conference. If human rights' violations in occupied Kuwait were so important to the United States, why did the United States not do anything to reduce the incidence of human rights' violations in occupied Palestine? If Saddam Hussein was a terrorist, why did the United States accord such respect and financial assistance to Prime Minister Yitzhak Shamir, who was reportedly responsible for killing, among others, a fellow Zionist Jew, UN envoy Count Folke Bernadotte, and Walter Edward Guiness (Lord Moyne)? Shamir also flirted with Adolf Hitler in an effort to gain cooperation in sending Jews to Palestine. His underground organization joined the Irgun in the massacre of Dayr Yasin. Why was the United States so concerned with human and property rights in Kuwait while it deprived and continues to work against the restoration of civil and property rights to Palestinian Christians and Muslims? And what about Syrian President Hafez Assad's record on human rights violations in Syria? The list is long (see Finkelstein 1991).

Concluding Remarks

Structural factors that gave rise to the Gulf War include Western colonialism, the lack of political legitimacy in Arab governments, the lack of Arab unity, and the balance of power threatening the supremacy of Israeli military forces. We documented the consistent historical pattern of actions taken by the Western superpowers to maintain hegemony over the region since the turn of the century. The last three factors cited are largely a corollary to the first; hence, the emphasis in this chapter.[12]

The Western colonial powers used everything from secret agents to the outright use of the military to maintain the territory drawn on maps in 1899. Perhaps, in part, because of this colonial heritage many existing governments in the region lacked political legitimacy, which kept them unstable. Arab unity was achieved rarely and only momentarily. If more unity and cooperation existed among Arab countries, they could have solved the problem of the Iraqi invasion through the Arab League. Unfortunately, in 1990, there was no Nasser or King Faisal to provide leadership.

Where do we go from here? The United States said that it would like to see President Hussein go but also would like to see Iraq maintain its territorial integrity. Now, that is clearly beyond what the UN resolutions called for in dealing with Iraq. Be that as it may, if Saddam Hussein falls, the most likely alternatives for leadership are religious fundamentalists in the south and Kurds in the north. Such possibilities are not welcomed by either the Gulf Arab countries (in the south) or Turkey (in the north), which were the allies of the United States in the Gulf War. If the United States and its allies have a common formula for the post-war Arab world, they certainly are not disclosing its contents. Undersecretary of Defense Paul Wolfowitz conceded that the U.S. authorities lack a clear vision of the future for Iraq.

Many government officials in much of the world would like to restore political stability in the region. In the words of President Bush on 8 August 1990 when he ordered U.S. troops to the Arabian Gulf, a principal objective of the United States was to achieve "security and stability in the Persian Gulf." What many in the Arab world disagreed on, however, was the kind of political stability. Should it be based on the legacy of colonialism left by the West, which continues to maintain hegemony there? I am reminded of President Bush's statement concerning the objective of the Gulf War as explained to the families of soldiers at Fort Stewart, Georgia. He said a result of the war would be "what we say goes" in the Gulf region. If this is not a manifestation of his interest in maintaining U.S. hegemony in the region, what is? If this is what he meant by a new world order, it certainly is not new to the region. It is precisely what Arabs, who are striving to develop democracy, independence, and Arab unity, tried to eradicate.

It is difficult to imagine how political stability can prevail in the Arab world in which fifteen million oil-rich Arabs in the Gulf are investing over $600 billion abroad while 185 million Arabs are suffering from a foreign debt of $200 billion (Khouri 1991:6). Political stability based on an authoritarian system has its limits. Just as Eastern Europe is moving toward democracy, there are nascent forms of democracy on the rise in such Arab states as Algeria, Jordan, Lebanon, Tunisia, and Yemen where there is freedom of choice in political parties.[13] In many of these states, religious fundamentalists are gaining power as they become the first beneficiaries of democracy.[14] In this sense, moves by the U.S. Congress to eliminate aid to Jordan is counterproductive to efforts to promote democracy abroad.

Just as the departure of communism was necessary for democracy to commence in Eastern Europe, lingering imperialism, along with its client states and compradors in the Arab world, must be eliminated for democracy to be nurtured. A majority of Arabs, I am certain, would welcome the United States if it treated Arab countries the same way it does Eastern European countries, such as Poland, by encouraging economic and political freedom and independence. By so doing, the United States would win not only the Gulf War, but also the hearts and minds of the Arab people.

Political leaders do what they must to achieve their objectives, but the media's role should be different from their government's role and should not indiscriminately become a tool for government propaganda as evidenced in the alleged use of chemical weapons by Iraq. The use of Kurdish victims' pictures not connected with Iraq's alleged attack on the Kurds in August 1988 to convince the public that Iraq used chemical weapons against its own people is unconscionable. In the words of Crown Prince Hassan of Jordan, "Arabs and Muslims deserve far better treatment on the front pages and telecasts of the global media than what they have received to date" (Hassan 1991:10).

Perhaps I am an optimist, but I hope that when President Bush said "what we say goes," he intended to promote economic and political freedom in the Gulf so that "security and stability" based on a sound foundation would prevail rather than control the price of oil.

In searching for causes of the war, we need to look at the social structure as a possible indirect cause of the war. If the structure built by British and French colonial powers was an unhealthy basis from which security and stability could rise, what will secure the stability everyone seeks? Such a structure should be economically productive and equitable, regionally and nationally integrated, socially communitarian, psychologically secured, politically dynamic and democratic, religiously and ideologically tolerant, militarily secured through collective security, and culturally exhilarating.[15]

This is the moment that Thomas Paine referred to when he said: "We have it in our power to begin the world over again." The United States is in a unique position to encourage the region to move toward this preferred future, not only in the Arab world, but in the entire region including Iran, Israel, and Turkey. Such a vision—a new regional order—would move the globe toward a new world order in the post-cold war era. It could, in Abraham Lincoln's words, kindle "the better angels of our nature."

Notes

1. Syria's request was echoed by the King-Crane Commission, which went to Palestine to assess Palestinian public opinion at the request of President Woodrow Wilson. Their report, likewise, was ignored by the League of Nations.

2. See, for example, Lenczowski (1968): 97–118.

3. Khodduri (1990) successfully argues that Kuwait should be referred to as a "protection and not as a protectorate." Shaykh Mubarak gave up not only an external sovereignty but certain domestic sovereignty as well. Kuwait raised the Ottoman flags and paid yearly tributes, among other concessions.

4. "Give the Jews and their descendants the choice lands and homes of the Germans. . . . Amends should be made by the criminal, not by the innocent bystander" (Eddy 1954:34).

5. Harry Truman said: "Totalitarian regimes imposed on free people, by direct or indirect aggression, undermine the foundation of international peace and hence the security of the United States." He urged the "support [of] free people who are resisting attempted subjugation by armed minorities or by outside pressure" (*Congressional Quarterly* 1986:42). To an outside observer, Truman's action to create Israel certainly contradicts his own doctrine by disregarding the majority inhabitants of Palestine and giving away their land to armed minorities. It was clearly outside colonial forces led by the United States under the guise of the UN General Assembly resolution that made Christians and Muslims into stateless refugees.

6. For more detail of the doctrine's development see Gold (1988).

7. For Reagan Doctrine, see Lakoff (1988).

8. Unless otherwise noted, this section draws heavily from the "Chronology" section of recent issues of *The Middle East Journal.* Major sources of

the "Chronology" are: *Foreign Broadcast Information Service Daily Report—Middle East & North Africa and South Asia; Western Europe, Financial Times, The Jerusalem Post, The New York Times, The Washington Post, and The Wall Street Journal.*

9. This paragraph draws heavily from Pelletiere et al. (1990), as reported by Neff (1991).

10. "Having looked at all of the evidence that was available to us, we find it impossible to confirm the State Department's claim that gas was used in this instance. To begin with, there were never any victims produced. International relief organizations who examined the Kurds—in Turkey where they had gone for asylum—failed to discover any. Nor were there ever any found inside Iraq. The claim rests solely on testimony of the Kurds who had crossed the border into Turkey, where they were interviewed by staffers of the Senate Foreign Relations Committee" (Pelletiere et al. 1990:52). They cite the following as the source: "Chemical Weapons Use in Kurdistan: Iraq's Final Offensive," a Staff Report to the Senate Committee on Foreign Relations, 21 September 1988.

11. "Photographs of the Kurdish victims were widely disseminated in the international media. Iraq was blamed for the Halabjah attack, even though it was subsequently brought out that Iran too had used chemicals in this operation, and it seemed likely that it was the Iranian bombardment that had actually killed the Kurds" (Pelletiere et al. 1990:52).

12. This is not to state that Arabs could not have achieved unity or developed one nation, however Herculean the task may have been, but the West certainly has done everything possible to make sure that unity did not happen. Political instability has been built into the region.

13. Ironically, or perhaps logically, these nations tended to take positions contrary to that of the United States's Arab allies in the Gulf War.

14. We should note here that religious fundamentalists in Jordan who publicly advocated a holy war against the U.S.-led coalition forces in defense of Iraq during the Gulf War lost their popularity and trust in Jordan by the end of the war. The reason was that they talked profusely but failed to take any action, while King Hussein was applauded for his role in the war.

15. This characterization of the preferred future for the Arab world is similar to what Rami G. Khouri (1991) envisions, which I suspect is shared by many in the Arab world.

References

Carlton, David. *Anthony Eden, a Biography.* London: Penguin, 1981.
Congressional Quarterly. *The Middle East.* 7th ed. Washington, DC: Congressional Quarterly, 1990.

Eban, Abba. *The New Diplomacy: International Affairs in the Modern Age.* New York: Random House, 1983.

Eddy, William A. *F. D. R. Meets Ibn Saud.* New York: American Friends of the Middle East, 1954.

El-Hassan bin Talal, Crown Prince. "New World Order of Understanding of the Arab Muslim World." Prepared for delivery at the IPS Council on Information and Communication for International Development, Rome, 30 May 1991.

Finkelstein, Norman. "Israel and Iraq: A Double Standard," *Journal of Palestine Studies* 20(2) (Winter 1991): 43–56.

Foreign Relations of the United States (1945): 8.

Freedman, Jennifer. "Women in Iraq," *American Arab Affairs* (Summer 1989): 42–46.

Galtung, Johan. *The True Worlds: A Transnational Perspective.* New York: Free Press, 1980.

Gold, Dore. "Toward the Carter Doctrine: The Evolution of American Power Projection Policies in the Middle East, 1947–1980." In *The Soviet-American Competition on the Middle East*, edited by Steven L. Spiegel, Mark A. Heller, and Jacob Goldberg, 113–25. Lexington, MA: D. C. Heath, 1988.

Green, Stephen. *Taking Sides: America's Secret Relations with a Militant Israel.* Brattleboro, VT: Amana Books, 1988.

Hunter-Gault, Charlayne. "The View from Amman," *The Return.* MacNeil, Lehrer News Hour 2(12 & 13) (Oct.–Nov. 1990): 27–29, 48.

Johnson, Lock K. *America as a World Power: Foreign Policy in a Constitutional Framework.* New York: McGraw-Hill, 1991.

Khadduri, Majid. "Iraq's Claim to the Sovereignty of Kuwait," *Journal of International Law and Politics* 23(1) (Fall 1990): 5–34.

Khalidi, Walid. "The Gulf Crisis: Origins and Consequences," *Journal of Palestine Studies* 20(2) (1991): 5–28.

Khouri, Rami G. "The Post-War Middle East," *The Link* 24(1) (Jan.–Mar. 1991): 1–13.

Lakoff, Sanford. "The 'Reagan Doctrine' and U.S. Policy in the Middle East." In *The Soviet-American Competition in the Middle East*, ed. Steven L. Spiegel, Mark A. Heller, and Jacob Goldberg, 125–44. Lexington, MA: D. C. Heath, 1988.

Lenczowski, George, ed. *United States Interests in the Middle East.* Washington, DC: American Enterprise Institute for Policy Research, 1968.

Long, David E. *The Persian Gulf.* Boulder, CO: Westview Press, 1976.

McCarney, James. "Saddam May Win by Losing." *The Honolulu Advertiser* (9 February 1991: 14).

Massarweh, Abdulsalam. "Setting the Stage for War: The Gulf Script Was and the Players Cast a Decade Ago," *Return* (October/November, 1990): 34–36.

Neff, Donald. "How and Why the US Turned Against Iraq." *Middle East International* 394 (2-7 February 1991): 19-21.

New York Times, 10 Sept. 1988: A-4 and 15 Sept. 1988: A-12.

Pelletiere, Stephen C., Douglas V. Johnson, and Leif R. Rosenberger. *Iraqi Power and U.S. Security in the Middle East.* Carlisle Barracks, PA: Strategic Studies Institute, U.S. Army War College, 1990.

Rustow, Dankward A. *Oil and Turmoil.* New York: W. W. Norton, 1982.

Stoessinger, John G. *Why Nations Go to War*, 5th ed. New York: St. Martin's Press, 1990.

Washington Post, 4 Sept. 1988: A-33 and 12 Sept. 1988: A-14.

Yokoyama, Sanshiro. *Perushawan.* Tokyo: Shinchosha, 1989.

4
The European Community's Middle Eastern Policy

The New Order of Europe and the Gulf Crisis

Friedemann Buettner and Martin Landgraf

When presidents Mikhail Gorbachev and George Bush proclaimed the end of the cold war at their December 1989 Malta summit, many thought that the European Community (EC) would become an international actor of first-rate importance. At a time when military power was seemingly losing its significance, the EC as an economic superpower was winning more room to maneuver to pursue specific Western European interests within the international system. European integration gained momentum toward the end of the 1980s as the Soviet Union was on the brink of disintegration and the United States was feeling the heavy economic burden of the arms race of preceding decades. The prospect of completing the Internal European Market by the end of 1992 and the progress toward economic and monetary, as well as political, union made it seem likely that the EC would be involved in restructuring the international system as an equal partner of the United States.

In a way, the Gulf crisis was a test case for the possible new role of the EC, for its ability to pursue a common foreign and security policy in a crisis. The EC's activities immediately following the Iraqi invasion of Kuwait seemed to indicate its determination to play a leading role in the crisis: The EC immediately censured the Iraqi invasion, imposed economic sanctions, decided to give extensive humanitarian and financial aid to the refugees from Kuwait and Iraq and to countries negatively affected by the UN embargo, and threatened to impose sanctions against any country that did not respect the embargo. Furthermore, by early October more than thirty warships from EC member states were operating in the Gulf.

But despite this swift action in the early days of the crisis and the continuous assurances by the Italian EC Presidency on the "consequent and constructive cohesiveness" of the EC and its readiness to play a "central role,"[1] the Gulf crisis clearly demonstrated the EC's difficulties in pursuing an active common foreign and security policy that went beyond declarations. The general picture is well known: Britain, France, and, to a lesser extent, Italy were actively involved in the military buildup and later in the fighting. The Netherlands and, to a lesser extent, Luxembourg fully supported the U.S. position, while the other EC members kept a low profile—none of them contributed more than token forces. Rich Germany, hampered by its constitution and primarily occupied with the process of unification, limited itself to checkbook diplomacy.

Obviously, the EC missed its chance; it was in disarray at a time when a joint Western European stance could have been of some consequence. But at no time in the course of the crisis did the Community offer a viable alternative to the policy almost exclusively formulated in Washington and New York.

In spite of bitter comments about the EC's disunity, most Middle Eastern states still expect Europe to play an active role in the peace process and in endeavors to frame a new regional order in the Middle East. In order assess the prospects for and the limits to such a European role, this chapter attempts to analyze and explain the EC's policy during the Gulf crisis in four steps: First, it outlines the EC's Middle Eastern policy with special reference to the Community's foreign policy-making structures; second, it explains the impact of the end of the cold war on European integration; third, it analyzes the positions of the Community and of individual EC member states during the Gulf crisis; and fourth, it reflects on a possible future role for the EC in the Middle East.

The EC's Middle Eastern Policy and its Restraints

When six European states—Belgium, France, West Germany, Italy, Luxembourg, and the Netherlands—founded the European Community in 1957, a common foreign policy was not their immediate aim. Nevertheless, the EC's founding fathers hoped that the established integration in well-defined, limited policy areas would spill over to others and would eventually lead to integration in those areas where the nation-states were most reluctant to give up decision-making power; these included the areas of monetary policy and internal security, as well as foreign and security policy.[2]

Although this basic assumption seemed to hold true in the 1950s and 1960s when the EC became a success story, early ambitious designs for a viable framework of a common West European foreign policy failed. The establishment of the customs union by the end of the 1960s, however, made a common external economic policy more and more indispensable, to protect the attainments of the integration process, and to cope with the increasing integration in and thus dependence on the world economy. Although the EC's common commercial policy became an exclusive matter of the EC institutions in the early 1970s, the EC members also decided in 1969 to found the European Political Cooperation (EPC) to coordinate traditional foreign policy matters. This decision was made because the members were convinced that economic integration had to be accompanied by political integration and that such an organization was needed to cope with world politics in the post-colonial era and to handle the ever denser network of the Community's external economic relations.

The EPC is probably the most vivid example of a basic dilemma of European integration: The specific structures of the EPC and its development demonstrate the insight of the EC members into the need for cooperation, even in the field of foreign policy, but they were and still are reluctant to give up their ultimate control. The EPC was founded as a confidential, purely intergovernmental forum outside the established EC institutions. The EPC did not have a budget, nor was it equipped with any operational mechanisms, and its selective, nonbinding character did allow different national foreign policies to be pursued simultaneously. But with these specific structures of the EPC, the EC members not only created an *additional* framework for their national foreign policies, they introduced an utterly artificial division between the EC's integrated external economic policy and the traditional foreign policy that was dealt with in the nonobligatory, intergovernmental forum of the EPC.[3]

The momentousness of this artificial division was obvious from the beginning. Therefore, the EC Commission was soon admitted into the EPC where today it plays an important role.[4] But the intergovernmental character of the EPC remains unchanged. "From the gunboats to the embassies," as the British foreign minister Douglas Hurd once put it, everything remains under the ultimate control of the nation state. Also unchanged is the division between external economic and traditional foreign policy, which explains much of the somewhat ambivalent role the Community played during the Gulf crisis.

The emergence and development of the EC's Middle Eastern policy must be seen in context with the 'composed' nature of the EC's complex foreign policy-making structures. In its common commercial policy, the EC acknowledged the increasing importance of the Middle East by developing the Global Mediterranean Policy in the early 1970s, a policy that basically upgraded to preferential agreements some of the trade and other agreements which the EC had concluded in the fifties and sixties with several states bordering the Mediterranean.[5]

Although the EC created a roughly balanced network of agreements with all the riparian states of the Mediterranean (with the exception of Libya and Albania), the ambitious attempt to create a uniform structure of economic cooperation and an integrated management of regional relations failed. This was mainly because there was no basic understanding among the EC members about a political concept that would serve as a framework for a common policy toward the region beyond mere economic agreements. Such a basic understanding was missing, a main reason being that the member-states displayed differing attitudes toward the Arab-Israeli conflict, which dominated the EC's Middle Eastern policy agenda throughout the 1970s.

The Middle East War of 1967, which threatened Europe with an Arab oil embargo, and the precarious situation along the Suez Canal in the early 1970s, caused the EC members to face a future situation in which the Arab-Israeli conflict could seriously affect their economic and political interests. Thus, from the beginning, the Middle East—together with the Conference on Security and Cooperation in Europe (CSCE)—was the main subject under discussion within the EPC. Despite an obvious convergence of basic interests, the affair surrounding the Schumann Paper of 1971 revealed the difficulties involved in taking a common stand. In this policy paper, "the Six" (the original founders of the EC) outlined principles for a solution to the Middle Eastern conflict that went beyond Security Council Resolution 242 of 22 November 1967 on three major points, or at least beyond Israel's reading of it. These points were an Israeli withdrawal from all Occupied Territories, the right of Palestinian refugees to return to their homes, and an international administration for Jerusalem. Although the Arab states welcomed the new policy, Israel strictly rejected the paper and pressured Germany, Italy, and the Netherlands to revoke their consent, or at least express reservations about the policy paper.[6]

The affair revealed a structural dilemma in the Community's Middle Eastern policy: In its efforts to find a common position, the EC had to start from the basically pro-Israeli position of most of its members, and then had to face the critical reactions of both sides because any shift in the status quo extended beyond what Israel would accept, but did not extend far enough for the Arab states. Moreover, the member states held quite different positions: while France and to a lesser extent Italy were basically "pro-Arab," the Benelux countries, particularly Germany with its historical responsibility for the Holocaust, took a more pro-Israeli stance. The fact that the United States and Israel strongly resented any involvement by the EC in the Middle East also played an important role. From the beginning, France regarded the EPC rather as an instrument to push its own foreign policy interests and its position vis-à-vis the United States and it wanted to use the EPC as a framework for an independent European role in world politics, while any deterioration of the strategic alliance with the United States was unacceptable for the Netherlands and West Germany. The same was true for Great Britain which joined the EC in 1973, along with Denmark and Ireland.[7]

This deadlock was partially resolved during the first oil crisis. Under threat of an Arab oil embargo, the EC issued a joint declaration in November 1973 that, like the policy paper of 1971, moved closer to the Arab view of the Arab-Israeli conflict without impinging upon Israel's rights.[8] Although Israel again rejected the declaration, the Arabs warmly welcomed it and suggested the creation of a common forum for the EC and the Arab League, the Euro-Arab Dialogue (EAD). Although the EC accepted the offer and the EAD was officially established in 1974, it never really got off the ground. Not only was it difficult to coordinate thirty different states, but the two sides in the EAD were pursuing incompatible aims. Although the Arab side wished to secure EC support for political objectives following the 1973 October war, the EC members bowed to the heavy pressure from the United States and Israel and insisted on excluding the two most burning issues—the Arab-Israeli conflict and oil—from the agenda. They successfully kept the EAD at the level of expert meetings dealing with economic and technical cooperation.[9]

In subsequent years, the EC members used the additional scope that the EPC offered to them to skillfully maneuver among Arab demands, Israeli protests, and U.S. misgivings. The potential of the EPC as a foreign policy framework in addition to national policies becomes clear when considering the example of West Germany which, within the EPC, took a more 'pro-Arab' stand while, at the national level, claimed that its position toward Israel was unchanged. Germany—so it was officially argued—still stood firmly behind its responsibilities for the Holocaust, but could not obstruct a common stance within the EPC without endangering European integration.[10]

As reflected in the EPC declarations of the mid-1970s, the EC eventually developed a specifically European position toward the Arab-Israeli conflict. From a refugee problem that was subordinate to the problems of recognition, sovereignty, and border protection, the Palestinian issue emerged as the focal point of any confllict solution. The terminology of the EC declarations shifted from "the Palestinians" to "the Palestinian people," who had "legitimate rights," a "national identity," and "the need for a homeland."[11] But in spite of these changes, the EC's joint policy remained merely declaratory throughout the 1970s.

At the beginning of 1980, however, the EC prepared its own Middle Eastern peace initiative. This was due to a number of interrelated factors: The U.S.-led peace process had come to an obvious standstill in the months after the Egyptian-Israeli peace treaty of March 1979, and the Arab side, whose voice gained added weight because oil prices spiralled upward, pressed the EC to influence U.S. policy. In addition, the Soviet invasion of Afghanistan reinforced concern about the security situation in the Gulf, which was already under pressure from the Islamic revolution in Iran. A halt to the peace process, so the Community thought, would strengthen radical anti-Western tendencies in the Arab world, and as the United States was increasingly preoccupied with the presidential elections, the Community could not stand aloof.

Hectic European activism in early 1980 resulted in the Venice declaration on the Middle East in June 1980 which is often identified as the starting point of the EC's 1980 Middle Eastern initiative. Close scrutiny, however, reveals that the initiative was practically dead before it was conceived. Strong pressure from the United States and Israel divided the EC members over the issue on the eve of the Venice summit and, due to the need for consensus of all members, the original plans for the EC initiative were changed beyond recognition. Thus, from the outset the EC's "peace missions" in the wake of the declaration had little chance of success.[12]

But the weakness of the EC's foreign policy-making structure to counteract external pressure was not the only deficiency in the EC initiative. After the split in the Arab world caused by the Camp

David Accords, there was no strong Arab counterpart for a European initiative. The ongoing civil war in Lebanon deepened the cleavages in the Arab world, and in the Iran-Iraq War the two belligerents were supported by different Arab states so that cross-cutting alliances emerged in the various theaters of conflict. Furthermore, because of the reduced threat of an all-out Arab-Israeli war and the precarious situation in the Gulf, attention shifted eastward away from the Mashriq. As the EAD had, for all intents and purposes, been put on ice after the expulsion of Egypt from the Arab League, the EC tried unsuccessfully to initiate closer relations with the oil-rich countries of the Arabian peninsula.[13]

The EC maintained a low profile in the Middle East throughout much of the 1980s. Aspirations for an independent political role in the resolution of major conflicts were abandoned, and the individual interests and bilateral relations of the various Community members preceded common efforts. Instead of pursuing Venice-style autonomous initiatives, the EC opted—although not unconditionally or without criticism—for supporting U.S. initiatives in the Middle East. The most visible expression of this support was the military participation of major European countries in the various multinational forces in Sinai in 1981, Lebanon from 1982 to 1984, the Red Sea in 1984, and the Gulf from 1987 to 1988. Less visible and more complex, although no less important, was the political and economical support that EC member states gave to U.S. initiatives in the form of sanctions, embargoes, and condemnatory statements against regional actors but also in the form of credits, trade benefits, and increased cooperation.[14]

It was only during the second half of the 1980s that the Middle Eastern policy of the Community gained some momentum: East-West tensions eased and the deep institutional crisis in the EC of the early 1980s ("Eurosclerosis") was resolved by the Fontainebleau summit of 1984, which led to signing the Single European Act (SEA) in 1986. With the SEA, some progress was made to integrate foreign policy matters. The EPC was given a legal base and officially accepted as the "second pillar" of European integration.[15]

Furthermore, the situation in the Gulf was again disquieting. Partly due to specific regional developments, and partly because of rapidly falling oil prices and the EC's successful policy of diminishing its dependence on Middle Eastern oil, the Gulf was not prominent on the Community's agenda from 1982 onward. But when Iran captured the Iraqi Fao Peninsula in early 1986, directly threatening to invade Kuwait, and when the ensuing "tanker war" menaced the freedom of shipping in the Gulf, the EC members once again became concerned about the situation in the Middle East. Moreover, the second enlargement of the EC, which brought Spain and Portugal into the EC in 1986, threatened vital export outlets for the Mashriq and, in particular, the Maghreb, a problem that could not be pushed aside.[16]

Although the Community tried to readjust its Global Mediterranean Policy,[17] it also made a fresh attempt to re-introduce itself into the Middle Eastern peace process. The EC continued to see a peaceful solution to the Arab-Israeli conflict as central to the stability of the entire region. Indicative of the new start was the Brussels declaration of February 1987 in which the Twelve (the enlarged Community of the original six plus Denmark, Great Britain, Ireland, Greece, Portugal, and Spain), declared renewed interest in making "an active contribution" to a settlement of the conflict.[18]

There are some interesting parallels between the Venice episode and renewed Community activism from 1987 onward. Both EC peace initiatives occurred when the United States was anything but well-placed to keep the Middle East peace process going. During the first initiative, there were negative Arab reactions to Camp David, there were presidential elections, the Iranian hostage crisis, and Afghanistan; during the second, there was the Iran-Contra Affair and the changes in the Soviet Union, which required a new policy. During both occasions it was feared in Western Europe that a lack of progress toward some prospect of peace would strengthen radical trends on its southern periphery.

Contrary to its Venice predecessor, however, the Brussels declaration of 1987 was preceded by careful consultations with the parties concerned; it was more attentive to the requirements of the various actors and therefore promptly welcomed by all sides. The Community no longer prejudged the outcome of the peace process but, rather, threw its weight behind a certain framework for negotiations, namely a UN-sponsored international peace conference.[19]

Despite the failure of the initiative, the Community subsequently distanced itself more clearly from endeavors by Israel and the United States to find bilateral solutions. One of the main reasons for a hardening of the Community's attitude was the sharp decline in Europe of sympathy for Israel after the beginning of the Intifada in December 1987.

In their Madrid declaration of June 1989, the Twelve pointedly challenged key elements of the "Shamir plan," which countered the Palestinian National Council's proclamation of a Palestinian state by offering limited local elections in the Occupied Territories.[20] In addition to restating the need for a comprehensive and balanced approach that would effectively equate Israeli security needs and Palestinian rights as parallel objectives of the peace process,[21] the Madrid declaration also called for PLO participation in the negotiations, inclusion of Jerusalem in the proposed elections, and a formulation of negotiations based on "land for peace."[22]

None of these initiatives, however, had a visible impact on the Middle Eastern peace process, let alone on the overall stability of the region. Bilateral accords between some EC members and some regional actors even obstructed the efforts of the EC institutions, or were at odds with supposedly common positions taken within the EPC.[23] When the situation in Eastern Europe and the Soviet Union changed in 1989, the EC became increasingly preoccupied with European affairs. Although the EC expressed concern when the U.S.-PLO dialogue dissolved in June 1989, and although the EAD was revived by the EC in late 1989, it was essentially concerned with different matters.[24]

European Integration and the End of the Cold War

The disintegration of the Eastern bloc and the virtual abdication of the Soviet Union as a superpower removed the residual risks of the cold war from Europe. The long and cumbersome process of the Conference on Security and Cooperation in Europe (CSCE) had already changed the atmosphere and culminated in the adoption of the extensive Concluding Document of Vienna that cleared the way for successful negotiations on Confidence and Security-Building Measures (CSBM), and on Conventional Armed Forces in Europe (CFE).[25]

The end of bipolarity could mean the emergence of a new multipolar international order in which the Community plays a pivotal role together with the United States, Russia, Japan, and possibly China. Furthermore, new challenges lie ahead in Europe. Suddenly, the Community is the anchor for European stability and the Eastern European states look toward it for political guidance, substantive help for restructuring their economies, and, ultimately, membership.

At the end of the 1980s, the Community was all but ready to develop political concepts that could serve as a framework for common action to meet the challenges ahead. At the time of the "Eurosclerosis," there had been enormous pressure to reform the Community institutions, including the somewhat unwieldy foreign policy-making structures. This debate found an outlet in the form of the Single European Act (SEA). But as the EC members could not agree on further political integration, the SEA did not represent substantial progress in this field. As a matter of fact, by adopting the SEA— which focused on the establishment of the Internal Market—the EC members responded to the pressures for reform by "suspending" politics. Having put the "1992 train" on the rails, the heads of state and government could now lean back, leave the initiative to the Commission, and postpone the debate about political reform until 1993.[26]

What the EC members had tried to contain with the SEA was put back on the agenda with renewed urgency by the profound changes in 1989. The new challenges upset the EC members' leisurely drive toward the completion of the Internal Market and stirred discussion about the need for political integration. The unification of Germany caused a tremendous shift within the EC. France and Britain had misgivings about a united Germany. British commentaries warned of a new German nationalism and militarism, while France was especially concerned about an even stronger German economic hegemony. The breakthrough came with the Strasbourg summit in December 1989. In one of the package deals so typical of the history of European integration, France's "yes" to German unification was traded for the German promise to push for the European Economic and Monetary Union (EMU), which the West German government previously had been reluctant to concede.[27]

Although most EC member states were interested in EMU, they were confronted with a major problem: Germany linked EMU to the parallel establishment of the European Political Union, but apart from Italy and the Benelux countries, none were ready to follow Germany's open call for a federal Europe. As Germany continued to insist on substantial progress toward integration in the political field as a quid pro quo for giving up its national control of the Deutschmark, however, the development of a common foreign and security policy moved into focus.[28]

Given the new international environment, it was clear to all EC members that the EC could not assume more political responsibility without reforming its foreign policy-making machinery. In the twenty years of its existence, the EPC had become a unique system for foreign policy cooperation where different forums allowed coordination and cooperation at all levels, from the heads of state down to the lower ranks of civil servants. The *communauté d'information* had long since been realized and through the socialization process of the actors involved, the Twelve had gone a long way towards the *communauté de vue*.[29]

The basic structural deficiencies of the EPC, however, had resisted all attempts at real reform. One of these deficiencies, its selective character, now became more visible. Security and defense matters had always been strictly excluded from its agenda, and there was no other European forum where all EC members could coordinate, or at least discuss, the security and defense dimensions of their common foreign policy actions.[30] These subjects were reserved for the North Atlantic Treaty Organization (NATO), but France had withdrawn its armed forces from NATO command in 1966 and Ireland had never been a member. And anyway, could NATO with its outdated doctrine meet the new challenges ahead? Conflicts over the "out-of-area" competence of NATO in the 1980s pointed out the limits of the Atlantic alliance. NATO did not seem to be a very useful tool for dealing with the growing instability in Eastern Europe and the disintegrating Soviet Union.[31]

The only purely European forum for the discussion of security matters was the West European Union (WEU). The WEU, founded in 1954, soon ceded its original objectives (economic, political, and cultural cooperation in addition to collective self-defense) to NATO and to the Council of Europe and was unimportant by the end of the 1960s. In 1984, however, the WEU was revitalized, one of the main reasons being the obvious limitations of the EPC responses to the Soviet invasion of Afghanistan a few years earlier. In 1987, against the background of the European participation in the reflagging of tankers and other merchant ships in the Gulf, the WEU members adopted the "Platform on European Security Interests," which specified some institutional reforms, intensifying cooperation in and coordination of "out-of-area" activities by its members. But dusting off the WEU did not mean that a ready-made forum was at hand for a prospective EC security policy: Portugal and Spain only became members in 1989; Denmark, Greece, and Ireland still remained outside; and the WEU had renounced its own defense structures in favor of NATO.[32]

Even more significant was that the development of a common foreign and security policy had implications for more than the existing Western security architecture; sovereignty over external affairs was also central to the legitimacy of the nation states. Great Britain in particular—always suspicious of any integrational step going beyond economic integration—strongly opposed the introduction of majority decisions in the EPC, let alone giving the Community a security and defense dimension. For Britain, NATO was the only viable forum for European security and defense coordination. The development of a proper Community policy in these fields, so it was argued, would not be feasible and the endeavor would strain relations with the United States. Equally important for the British preference for NATO was, of course, its determination to keep its freedom of action and, through the "special relationship" with the United States, counterbalance the close cooperation between France and Germany (manifested in the Franco-German Brigade, which first held maneuvers in 1987).[33]

But other EC members also had their difficulties with the proposal for a new defense dimension to the Community: The Netherlands, still fearful of being dominated by its powerful European neighbors, was, like Portugal, a staunch supporter of NATO. Denmark did not want to abandon the concept of the EC as a "civilian power" for fear of the possible hegemonic ambitions of a new superpower, and Ireland continued to cling to its neutrality.

Thus in June 1990, when the European Council gave the green light to convene an intergovernmental conference to discuss possible steps toward political union, the discrepancies between the EC member states were all too obvious: Political union was as yet a "fuzzy objective" as the concrete forms of the union were still unclear.[34] The Iraqi invasion was to change this view.

The Community's Response to the Gulf Crisis

Although the EC, with its Global Mediterranean Policy, had developed a framework for its relations with the Mediterranean countries in the 1970s, there was no serious attempt to design an overall concept for the Gulf region. With the exception of Britain, all EC members had closer historical and economic ties with the Arab states of the Mediterranean than with the Gulf states. Because even France and Britain had long lost the capability to cope with a medium or high intensity military conflict out-of-area, protection of the oil supplies from the Gulf was ultimately left to the United States.[35]

Nevertheless, EC member states were heavily involved in the spiralling arms race in the Gulf during the 1980s. Between 1983 and 1987, France, Britain, Germany, and Italy exported some U.S. $17 billion worth of weapons to the Gulf countries (Iran, Iraq, and the Arabian Peninsula) representing almost one third of these countries' arms imports. With arms deliveries of more than U.S. $12 billion, France alone exported almost twice as many weapons to the region as the United States and was the second largest arms supplier to the Gulf after the Soviet Union.[36] Great Britain and France, and to a minor extent West Germany and Italy, profited in particular from the wish of Saudi Arabia and the smaller Gulf states to reduce dependence on the United States for arms deliveries. There were two reasons for this diversion strategy: first, because it seemed generally advisable to make the close security alliance with the United States not too visible, and second, because arms imports from Europe helped to counteract the restrictions the U.S. Congress set for the sale of advanced technology weapons to Arab states. Britain's most spectacular arms deal in the 1980s, for example, the 1985 sale of seventy-two Tornado combat aircraft to Saudi Arabia, was struck after the U.S. Congress—with reference to Israel's security—voted against the delivery of F-15s.[37]

The Twelve's efforts to end the Iraq-Iran War were in sharp contrast to these activities. And in fact, although the offices of German Foreign Minister Hans-Dietrich Genscher were crucial in bringing about the cease-fire in 1988, during the eight preceding years the Twelve hardly did anything more than call for a cease-fire. In 1987, they responded very reluctantly to the heavy pressure of the United States to dispatch warships into the Gulf. Even the United Kingdom, with its "Armilla-Patrol" that shadowed British merchant vessels in the Gulf without much public noise since 1980, did not trust the U.S. strategy in the area.[38] How little the Community actually was ready to contribute to stability in the Gulf was demonstrated by its reluctance to create closer ties with the Gulf Cooperation Council (GCC). Although the GCC had pressed for the conclusion of a cooperation agreement since 1982, the EC gave clear preference to protecting its own petrochemical industry over encouraging economic diversification in the GCC states.[39]

Typical of the reactive character of the EC's foreign policy was that, at the height of the tanker war in September 1987, the EC finally agreed to reopen negotiations with the GCC after stalling them for years. A limited agreement was concluded in "record time" by the summer of 1988.[40] By this time, however, the cease-fire in the Iraq-Iran war had eased tensions in the Gulf. Further negotiations already agreed upon by the EC and the GCC about the establishment of a free-trade zone promptly came to a halt. In July 1990, even the European Parliament, contrary to its earlier position, called for a tougher stand toward the GCC.[41] Obviously, the joint statement of the Twelve of 2 August 1990, that they had followed the growing tension between Iraq and Kuwait prior to the invasion "with concern," was little more than rhetoric. In the summer of 1990, the EC discussed European matters—Gulf security was not on the agenda.[42]

The swift and cohesive reaction of the Twelve after the invasion does not mean that the Community had closely watched the deployment of Iraqi troops on the Kuwaiti border.[43] It should be seen rather as a remarkable example of how smoothly the integrated parts of the Community's established foreign policy machinery worked. In a joint statement on 2 August 1990, only hours after the UN Security Council passed Resolution 660, the Twelve strongly censured the invasion, demanded complete restoration of Kuwait's territorial integrity and sovereignty, and declared unconditional support for the Security Council resolution. On 4 August 1990, two days before the Security Council imposed such measures in Resolution 661, the EC imposed economic sanctions against Iraq, including an oil and arms embargo, and froze Iraqi assets in the member states. Six days later, the Twelve pledged economic and financial aid to the countries most effected by the embargo against Iraq.[44] On 7 September 1990, they declared readiness to give extensive humanitarian aid to refugees from Kuwait and Iraq; the majority of them were labor migrants stranded in Jordan and Turkey. At the same time, the Twelve threatened to impose sanctions against any country that did not respect the UN embargo against Iraq.[45]

The extensive humanitarian and financial aid granted by the EC was part of the Community's strategy to isolate Iraq and prevent the crisis expanding to an all-out confrontation between the Arab-Islamic world and the West. With the same aim, the Twelve tried to improve relations with Iran and Syria, which had been somewhat strained since the early 1980s. By late August 1990, the EC Commission started to negotiate with some Arab Mediterranean countries to intensify relations. And in September 1990, the Twelve called for an EAD ministerial meeting to discuss joint efforts in the search for a peaceful solution to the Gulf crisis. Moreover, the EC tried to establish closer links to the Arab Maghreb Union (AMU) and agreed to revive negotiations with the GCC about the establishment of a free-trade zone.

From the outset, the Twelve clearly indicated to the Arab states that siding with the West against Iraq would positively influence their relations with the EC, their most important trading partner. Prospects for peace and economic development in the Arab world were given added substance by the proposal of a Conference on Security and Cooperation in the Mediterranean (CSCM)—an idea that had been discussed before the Gulf crisis and which Spain and Italy officially proposed in September 1990.[46]

Pointing to these measures and initiatives, the EC was reluctant to respond to U.S. demands for direct participation in Operation Desert Shield. The Twelve warmly welcomed President George Bush's "line in the sand" but were anxious not to be seen as too closely aligned with the United States. In a press conference on 7 September 1990, the Italian EC Presidency declared: "The U.S. alone have decided on the operation. We will engage ourselves with other activities, which will supplement those of Washington."[47]

That the Europeans attempted to maintain an independent position was evident after Saddam Hussein tried to link the withdrawal from Kuwait with the Palestinian issue, proposing the immediate withdrawal of all occupation forces in the Middle East and the implementation of all respective Security Council resolutions. This proposal highlighted the double standard of the United States, as for years it had used its veto in the Security Council to block all initiatives intended to pressure Israel. But although the proposal was rejected by the United States, Israel, and Saudi Arabia, Saddam Hussein succeeded in opening a debate that continued throughout the crisis.

The Twelve did not accept Saddam Hussein's proposal as a basis for a solution either, but did discuss the link between the Gulf crisis and the Palestine question. In contrast to the United States, the EC member states had always regarded the unsettled Palestine issue as one of the main threats to the stability in the Gulf so that the call for a comprehensive solution of the problems of the Middle East found much approval in Western Europe. In his speech to the UN General Assembly, for example, the EC Presidency deliberated on the linkage and told the assembly how vital a political solution to the Gulf crisis was in the eyes of the Twelve, and that the Community would continue to support "Arab initiatives" to resolve the crisis. A later joint EC-Soviet declaration had the same tenor.[48]

This clearly was in contradistinction to the position of the U.S. government, which insisted on the "unconditionality" of an Iraqi withdrawal from Kuwait and tried to orient its allies toward a military solution. Such a military commitment was highly unpopular in much of Western Europe, but despite its preference for a peaceful solution, the Community could not offer a clear alternative to the use of force.

Nowhere in any of the numerous common declarations by the Twelve during the crisis can one discern a clear line on how they were to achieve the proclaimed "political solution"; nowhere did the EC members indicate which of the various Arab peace plans and compromise proposals were feasible. It remained equally unclear how the Palestinian issue could reasonably be linked to the Gulf crisis. The Twelve were unable to reach a consensus on how their declared aims could be achieved. A feasible forum to coordinate the divergent national interests and to develop an independent Community response to the crisis, as an alternative to the U.S. position, was not at hand. By October 1990, it became clear that individual reactions and national policies took precedence over common actions.

National Responses to the Gulf Crisis

British Prime Minister Margaret Thatcher was in the United States at the time of the Iraqi invasion of Kuwait. Thatcher was said to have urged President Bush from the beginning to take a tough stand against Saddam Hussein;[49] and throughout the crisis, the United Kingdom sided unconditionally with the United States. This was not only, as was officially argued, because the violation of international law could not be tolerated on principle. Equally important were Britain's close historical and economic ties to its former protectorate, Kuwait, and the GCC states in general as well as the extensive Kuwaiti investments in the United Kingdom.[50] Moreover, as was revealed in early 1991, the British government had pledged in a secret protocol at the time of Kuwait's independence in 1961 to defend Kuwait militarily to avoid its oil falling into other hands.[51]

Also, more subtle considerations were important. By demonstrating its "special relationship" with the United States, the United Kingdom could emphasize its importance as a still strong, independent, international power and as a reliable partner to the United States in the changing international system. After all, the British economy faced a severe crisis, while German unification seemed to strengthen German economic supremacy in the new Europe. Not for naught was it Bonn, not London, to which President Bush offered a "partnership in leadership" in 1989. An intensive commitment also enabled Britain to emphasize its sovereignty and independence to the Community—and its mistrust of political union and the "Franco-German axis."

Without hesitation, Britain thus took up President Bush's concept of the "New World Order" that depended on Iraq's unconditional compliance with the UN resolutions. The Iraqi invasion was quickly renounced by Thatcher as "going back to the law of the jungle;" Saddam Hussein was likened to Hitler and Stalin, and any mediation effort to "Munich 1938."[52]

The British position was underlined by the reinforcement of its naval forces in the Gulf immediately after the Iraqi invasion. Sizeable contingents of naval and air forces were sent to Saudi Arabia just a day after President Bush announced Operation Desert Shield on 8 August. In September 1990, some 8,000 soldiers arrived in Saudi Arabia and were immediately put under U.S. command. Close association with the United States was also demonstrated by the extensive interpretation of Security Council Resolution 661. When in early November the United States announced that they would double their troops in Saudi Arabia, the British government promptly followed suit. And in early December, when U.S. Defense Secretary Richard Cheney questioned the effectiveness of the sanctions publicly, his British counterpart, Tom King, followed suit some days later (although he had stated the opposite earlier).

With some 40,000 soldiers, sixty aircraft, and twenty warships, Britain was the second largest contributor to the allied forces in the Gulf and, together with the U.S. Air Force, British fighter-bombers started the aerial attacks on Iraq on 17 January 1991. Borne on a wave of widespread public and parliamentary support,[53] Thatcher—and her successor, John Major—strongly criticized the other Community members, Germany in particular, for its lack of determination and support for the United States.

Besides Luxembourg, only the Netherlands, a small country that had experienced invasion and occupation by a larger neighbor more than once in its history, openly supported the British position and sent three warships to the Gulf in mid-August 1990. From the outset, however, the government in the Hague favored a UN command to coordinate all military activity in the Gulf, and the Dutch ships did not participate in the later fighting.[54]

In preference for a strong UN role, the Netherlands was backed by France. The motives of the French government, however, were quite different. The outbreak of the Gulf crisis confronted France with a major dilemma: Considering the U.S. and British commitments in the Gulf, France could not remain aloof if it wanted to be part of any redistribution of economic and political power in the area. France's position in the Gulf had been weakened by the Bush administration's more aggressive arms export policy since 1989. The breakdown of relations with Iraq, with whom France had developed particularly close trade relations, meant an additional blow to its ambitions in the region. Moreover, the smaller Arab Gulf states pushed for a French commitment.[55] And as it had done for Britain, unified Germany's increased weight played a role in France's considerations: its seat and vote in the UN Security Council were vestiges of French "grandeur" and for a long time a psychological counterweight to German economic supremacy. But in recent years, some EC members (Italy in particular) demanded the "communitarization" of France's and Britain's UN seats with increasing determination.[56] In such a situation, France could hardly stay behind in the enforcement of the UN resolutions.

On the other hand, France lacked the means to play an independent military role in the crisis, while a role as a junior partner to the United States (as the French saw the British role) was at odds with the Gaullist self-perception. In addition, the French parliament and the general public, in particular the large Arab community in France, were less supportive of an all-out military engagement. France also had to consider its strong historical and economic ties with the Arab world, especially the Maghreb, but also with the Arab "radicals"— Algeria, Libya, Yemen, and the PLO.[57] From the outset, President François Mitterrand, therefore, adopted a double strategy. With 15,600 soldiers, aircraft, and warships, France contributed the third-largest Western contingent of troops to the allied forces. France argued that it could not allow a "second Munich," and had to uphold its "international standing" as a "soldier of the law."[58]

At the same time, the French government emphasized the role of the UN and stressed its independent position. The French government called Operation Desert Storm a defensive action and its participation in it as the only alternative in the absence of an "Arab solution." Also, French troops were not put under U.S. command until the last moment before the fighting started. And France generally advocated a more restrictive interpretation of the Security Council resolutions.[59]

To demonstrate its independence and counter the domestic and external criticism of France's military commitment in the Gulf, Mitterrand sought to distinguish himself as an advocate of a peaceful solution. Without consulting his EC partners, he presented a four-point peace plan to the UN General Assembly on 24 September 1990. In it, he rejected any direct link between the Gulf crisis and the Palestinian conflict, but did suggest that the other regional conflicts in the Middle East should be resolved after Iraq had withdrawn.[60] The outright opposition of the United States to this "hidden" linkage did not prevent Mitterrand from repeatedly putting the proposal forward in different guises, until 16 January 1991 when he tried to halt the imminent allied attack with a last-minute initiative in the Security Council.

With his demonstrated willingness to negotiate, Mitterrand almost automatically assumed the role as mediator of the peace initiatives for both the Arabs and the Soviet Union. Telling in this respect was the fact that the UN Secretary General, Javier Pérez de Cuéllar, returning from his last mission to Baghdad on 14 January 1991, met with Mitterrand before contacting the representatives of the Community.

To gain support for its policy, France tried to mobilize the Community. Mitterrand was the driving force behind the immediate imposition of sanctions; with Germany, he initiated the joint declaration with the Soviet Union in September 1990; and in December 1990 he advocated a meeting of EC representatives with the Iraqi foreign minister. France was also instrumental in convening the WEU ministerial meeting on 21 August 1990 when an ad-hoc-group was appointed to coordinate the naval activities in the Gulf.[61]

From the outset, however, efforts to unite the Community behind the French position had little chance of success. This was partly due to Britain's unconditional support for the U.S. position, which made the unanimity required for any common EC foreign policy action impossible. In addition, the other EC members, opposed to the Iraqi invasion but unable to formulate a viable solution, tried to keep as low a profile as possible.

Ireland withdrew into its neutrality and the smaller EC countries such as Denmark, Belgium, and Portugal succeeded for a while in taking little notice of the crisis.[62] The other EC members faced the problem of how to demonstrate at least a minimum show of loyalty to the United States without becoming too closely associated with its policy. After all, they had hardly any influence on U.S. policy and the consequences of the crisis for Euro-Arab relations were unforeseeable. Confronted with this dilemma, the Community offered a perfect framework for the anonymization of national measures.

One example of this was Greece: On the one hand, the Greek government had to consider its strong economic interests and the large Greek communities in many Arab states as well as its population's particularly strong aversion to toeing the U.S. line. On the other hand, Greece did not want to be put at a disadvantage vis-à-vis its traditional rival Turkey, which was receiving substantial financial and military aid from the United States for its active role in the crisis. Greece thus sent a frigate to the Gulf in mid-August but only announced it officially after the WEU meeting of 21 August.[63]

Taking part in the naval blockade within the framework of the WEU, Spain also satisfied U.S. demands but kept its distance from the United States. This not only seemed advisable because of the strong antipathies in the Spanish population against the United States in general (stemming largely from the U.S. support for the Franco regime), but Spain also saw pro-Iraqi sentiments in neighboring Arab countries as a direct threat to its security, especially for Ceuta and Melilla, Spain's last enclaves in Morocco. So the Spanish government repeatedly stressed that it was only participating in the allied effort to ensure that it did not become a "new crusade." The Spanish drive for a Conference on Security and Cooperation in the Mediterranean (CSCM), suggested in September 1990, must also be seen in this light.

Moreover, the massive Spanish logistical support for the United States was kept top secret. It was only through an indiscretion by British Foreign Minister Douglas Hurd that it became known that the Spanish and German air forces were transporting large quantities of ammunition to the Morón Air base where it was reloaded into American B52 bombers, which flew their sorties over Iraq and Kuwait directly from Spanish territory. And only after the end of the war did the Spanish government admit that more than one-third of all U.S. transports to the Gulf was carried out via Spanish territory.[64] The U.S. agreement to convene the first round table Middle East peace talks after the Gulf War in Madrid could be seen as an acknowledgment of Spain's contribution and an attempt to restore its somewhat tarnished image in the Arab world.

Spain's proposal to convene a CSCM was supported by Italy for whom Mediterranean security is also a major determinant of foreign policy. There was, however, a heated debate in the governing multi-party coalition as well as in the population about the Gulf crisis.[65] But the opinion eventually prevailed that Italy could not stand aloof. Italy thus played an important supporting role during the Gulf crisis and sent ten Tornado aircraft to Saudi Arabia, which later took part in the fighting. As with most of the other EC members, the Community played a central role in the case of Italy, too, by providing a cloak of legitimacy for the Italian actions during the crisis. It is interesting to note that this represented a departure from the Italian tradition of anchoring its security policy in NATO. Instead, the Italian government publicly put forward plans for developing a common European security and defense policy.[66]

Of all the EC members, Germany had the greatest difficulty maintaining a low profile and anonymizing actions that might have upset its relations with the Arab world. As the strongest economic power in Europe, Germany was the main target for harsh British-U.S. accusations about the EC members' lack of determination to support the United States. The pressure on Germany increased, particularly when more evidence was revealed on how German industry had supplied Iraq with vital parts for its nonconventional arms industries.[67] As the latter included chemical weapons, Saddam Hussein's threat to use gas against Israel was particularly abhorrent. How, it was argued, could the Germans stand aside while Jews were threatened by German-made gas?[68]

Although it was argued that Germany should change its constitution and shoulder more responsibility in international politics, the German government had to consider not only its economic interests in the Arab countries, but also the strong public opposition to any German involvement in the Gulf crisis as expressed in Europe's largest peace demonstrations. Foreign Minister Genscher's strategy for maneuvering between the divergent pressures on German policy was to make a visible contribution to the allied effort, but keep all activities as far as possible within the EC framework.

Genscher became France's partner in the search for a European role in the crisis. He personally went to Tehran and Damascus to improve EC relations with Iran and Syria. And the attempt to involve the EAD in the search for a peaceful solution to the crisis was born out of a joint German-Egyptian initiative. Moreover, Germany contributed the lion's share of the Community's aid as well as the bilateral financial transfers by individual EC members to countries effected by the embargo. Germany demonstrated its willingness to participate in future military operations when Genscher informed his European partners at the WEU meeting of 21 August that his government intended to change the respective articles in the German constitution.[69]

Due to pressure from the United States, however, Germany could not ultimately avoid making public its vast direct contribution to Desert Shield. Initially, the German government argued that Desert Shield was a bilateral agreement between the United States and Saudi Arabia, and tried to downplay its vast contributions to Desert Shield. Apart from large quantities of munitions, including highly sophisticated hardware, Germany provided massive logistical support and also agreed to make direct payments to the United States (some U.S. $6 billion!), the United Kingdom, France, and NATO. Including this aid, the overall German contribution amounted to some U.S. $12 billion—after Japan, the second-largest financial burden of any Western ally. The Supreme Commander of NATO, General John R. Galvin, was later to tell the U.S. Senate's Armed Services Committee that the allies' momentous buildup would not have been possible without the logistical support of Germany and Spain.[70] Eventually, Germany also made a direct military contribution: after dispatching minesweepers to the Mediterranean in mid-August 1990 to replace American vessels sent to the Gulf, Germany sent eighteen AlphaJet aircraft and eleven air defense units with some 700 men to Turkey in January 1991 after Turkey had demanded NATO protection against a possible Iraqi attack.[71]

Contrary to most of the EC members, however, Germany's low profile policy was equally determined by its domestic situation. Although the German government spent some time discussing the Gulf crisis, its invested energy was minimal when compared with the administrations of the United States, Britain, and France. German politicians, as well as the German media and the German public, had another agenda: when Saddam Hussein threatened Israel in April 1990, Germans in the East and West were excitedly preparing for unification and anxiously awaiting the results of the negotiations between the four World War II allies and the two Germanies. When Iraq invaded Kuwait, the two Germanies had just established their

Economic and Monetary Union. When the allies escalated their forces to offensive strength, the Germans were preparing for the "great day" of unification on 3 October. And when the Security Council issued its ultimatum to Iraq, Germany was completely preoccupied with the first all-German elections in fifty-eight years. In Germany, the whole process of unification produced an all-pervasive feeling of elation, even unreality, which made one sometimes wonder whether Kant's essay "On Eternal Peace" (1795) might not have been a recent contribution to a leading intellectual weekly.

The EC and the Gulf Crisis: A Balance Sheet

Given the lack of consensus among the EC members about an independent role for the Community in the crisis, the ultimate dependence on the United States in security matters, and the absence of a mandatory framework for a common foreign and security policy, the chances for an autonomous initiative by the Twelve were slim from the beginning. Attempts to mobilize the Arab League, the Islamic Conference Organization, the Arab Maghreb Union, or the nonaligned countries could not produce any result as long as the Twelve did not develop a political concept around which they could rally. True, there was a basic convergence of positions among the EC members. In the words of the German foreign minister: "We agree that the occupation of Kuwait has to be brought to an end. We agree that everything must be done to ensure that there is no reward for aggression, and that we bring this about by peaceful means."[72]

The very problem, however, was that in the final analysis, these aims proved to be contradictory. How little they could serve as a rallying point for joint action became clear in connection with the political burlesque over the proposed talks with the Iraqi foreign minister, Tariq Aziz, staged during December 1990 and January 1991 in Brussels. While the other EC members favored such talks, Britain, the Netherlands, and Luxembourg were strongly opposed. The compromise finally agreed upon was to meet Aziz but not to obstruct the U.S. position: just to "talk" and not to "negotiate." Not surprisingly, Aziz refused to meet EC representatives on such a basis, regretting that the Europeans had their policy dictated by the United States. Even less diplomatic, though more telling in respect of the impression which the EC made on the outside world, was a remark of the Iraqi ambassador to Spain: "We only talk with Bush, with the boss, not with his underlings."[73]

If the Community could not influenced the responses of Western governments to the crisis, the United States was at all times dependent on its European allies. Without the EC members' massive logistical and financial contribution, the rapid and smooth deployment of U.S. troops in Saudi Arabia—and indeed the war itself—would have encountered difficulties; the political support for the United States, moreover, was an important psychological factor for the U.S. public. Likewise, one cannot overestimate the importance of the Community's successful policy of isolating Iraq in the Arab world.

The Community's performance during the crisis is often viewed negatively because of its failure to provide a viable alternative to U.S. policy. Most of these assessments ultimately presume, however, that the U.S.-led action was "wrong" and that a possible alternative provided by the Twelve might have been "right." Putting a final evaluation aside for the moment, this assumption is a weak basis for an academic analysis. Instead of "eternal peace" or "structural stability in the Middle East," a better key to understanding the Twelve's action can be found in the interests of the various EC members in the light of the results of Desert Shield and Desert Storm.

True, none of the problems of the region are solved. The Iraqi invasion of Kuwait was only a visible outbreak of a continuing crisis situation. The deceptive calm in the Gulf, maintained by U.S. commitment to Saudi Arabia and Kuwait, and the openly demonstrated readiness of the United States to intervene again should Western interests be threatened, does not signify more stability in the region, let alone a structural improvement of the situation. In the long run, the visible U.S. presence on the Arabian Peninsula, as well as the boldness with which Western countries so obviously applied double standards of "international law" to the Middle East will have negative effects on the stability of the region and the relations of the Arab or Islamic world with the West in general. Moreover, the manipulation of the UN Security Council as a forum for legitimizing the enforcement of Western interests has discredited the UN in the Middle East and will have negative consequences if another major crisis erupts in the near future.

The more immediate results of the Gulf War for the EC member states are anything but disastrous. The uneasy threat of a powerful Iraq, dominating the region and commanding substantial parts of the oil reserves that are still so important for keeping the Western economies going, was effectively countered. With the Gulf War, the West proved its willingness and its ability to defend its interests, a fact that might make a potential aggressor think twice. But although most EC members profit from this deterrent effect, the United States and to a lesser extent Britain are reproached for their imperialistic attitudes and hegemonic ambitions. All other EC members' reputations, and in particular their vast trade interests in the Middle East, hardly suffered—business as usual, including arms trade, resumed almost without restriction.

As has often occurred during the last twenty years, the EC and the specific foreign policy-making structures of the EPC provided an effective framework within which the EC members could cope with the divergent demands on their foreign policies. The loss of this additional framework for formulating foreign policy parallel to the national level will be regretted by national foreign policymakers if the EC will ever develop into a fully fledged federal state. The convenience of the present system is one of the main reasons for resistance by some member states to developing a common foreign and security policy deserving of the name. But as was pointed out earlier, without progress in this direction, the Community—as is clear to all member states—will be unable to assume the new political responsibilities thrust upon it in the changing international system.

Although the Gulf War was used by Italy in particular and by the EC Commission to actively promote a European Common Foreign and Security Policy (CFSP), the situation in the Middle East was not and will not be decisive in bringing about more integration in this field. As long as the United States ultimately guarantees Western oil supplies, the need to respond effectively to the developments in the countries of the former Eastern bloc will be far more important for the EC, at least in the 1990s.

Nevertheless, the outbreak of the Gulf crisis had an enormous effect on the Twelve's ongoing discussions about political union. When the European Council decided in June 1990 to convene an Intergovernmental Conference on Political Union, it was still unclear what shape this political union should take. But under the impact of the crisis, a *deus ex machina* was found:. The proclaimed political union would be constructed around an EC security pillar.[74] And when the EC members signed the "Treaty on European Union" in Maastricht in December 1991, the acknowledgment of the WEU as an "integral part of the development of the European Union" was the most important step on the way to a common European foreign and security policy. This decision also reflected the effective coordination by the WEU for the EC during the naval blockade of Iraq.[75]

Perspectives

The future role of the Community in the Middle East will be largely determined by the Community's ability to develop an effective common foreign and security policy. In economic terms, the EC already acquired the status of a superpower, and will enhance its influence in the international system throughout the 1990s and beyond. Once the Community's foreign policy-making structures enable the EC to directly translate its economic weight into political power, the EC might become the most influential external actor in the Middle East. This, however, is very unlikely to happen within the next decade.

The Maastricht Treaty was the latest step in the development of the EC's foreign policy. By the relevant provisions, European Political Cooperation (EPC) was replaced by the Common Foreign and Security Policy (CFSP), but this does not mean that the Community has now assumed full external sovereignty on behalf of its members. Far from it. Insofar as the Maastricht Treaty only implies a further step toward European integration and not its completion, it provides a marginal improvement in respect of the EC's common foreign policy-making capabilities. On the one hand, the artificial division between external economic policy and foreign policy in the traditional sense was largely abolished. EC and CFSP are still separate "pillars" of the European Union, but, due to institutional reform, the full association of the Commission, and, indirectly, a greater say for the European Parliament, the policies followed in the two forums will be more complementary. In addition, all areas of foreign, security, and defense policy, including military aspects, might now be subjects of debate.

On the other hand, the CFSP remains a nonobligatory forum. The member states committed themselves to support the objectives of the European Union "actively and unreservedly in a spirit of loyalty and mutual solidarity" but there are no sanctions foreseen in case they do not.

In addition, the main obstacle to an effective common foreign policy, the need for unanimity for all policy decisions, was not removed. Majority decisions are only foreseen for the implementation of joint action; and it requires a unanimous vote by the member states to decide which matters concerning joint action may be decided by majority vote. As past experiences (such as with the EC's environmental policy) show the reluctance of member states to use the *possibility* of majority voting, we can expect the consensus principle to remain largely intact for the foreseeable future.[76]

Moreover, neither the provision of the Maastricht Treaty that the WEU will now "elaborate and implement decisions and actions of the Union which have defense implications," nor the much applauded Petersberg Declaration of June 1992 that strengthened the operational role of the WEU and set criteria for peace-enforcing activities, do mean that the EC now has a fully developed "defense arm." The WEU will continue to have a separate institutional structure for some time to come. The admission of Greece into the WEU and the early granting of an observer status to Denmark and Ireland, as well as the move of the WEU secretariat from London to Brussels do not alter this fact.

As the relations between EC-CFSP and WEU remain unclear, so do the relations between EC-CFSP-WEU and NATO. Although the decision to set up a multinational Eurocorps by 1995, as well as the upcoming integration of Eurogroup and the Independent European Program Group (IEPG) into the WEU, point to the development of a European pillar inside the Atlantic Alliance, the development of an overall structure for the future European security system will be the subject of much debate for the foreseeable future.[77]

Given these perspectives of the structural prerequisites for a common foreign policy by the Community, the prospects for an independent role of the EC in the Middle East are rather dim. It is not that the situation in the Middle East is of no concern to the EC. On the contrary, EC member states not only import more than half of their crude oil from the Middle East and North Africa, the countries between the Atlantic and the Gulf are also important export markets (4 to 5 percent of extra-community exports), and their loss would be very disruptive. Finally, the demographic pressure, especially in North Africa, the emigration caused by economic failure, and fundamentalist tendencies are of grave concern, in particular to the southern EC members of Spain, France, Italy, and Greece.

European problems are, however, of much more immediate concern to the Community. The EC and its member states are facing a serious economic crisis, accompanied by a disastrous loss of credibility concerning Community as well as national policymakers and policy-making structures. While the enlargement of the EC and the difficult task of democratization of the integration process are on the Community's agenda, the Twelve, under heavy budget constraints, are simultaneously confronted with the difficult situation in Eastern Europe and the former Soviet Union. Coping with these tasks and problems, shaping a new order in Europe, and defining the role the EC should play in European and world affairs will absorb much of the Community's financial resources as well as political and administrative attentions in the coming years. Therefore, it seems highly unlikely that the Community will seriously engage in the much needed economic reconstruction of the countries of the southern Mediterranean in the short- to medium-term.

Besides, the discussions and activities in the defense sector (in particular the drive for effective Western out-of-area capabilities) do not indicate that structural improvements in the Middle East and the developing countries in general are of high priority. Despite all solemn declarations at the 1992 UNCED conference (the Rio summit), they rather indicate the firm will to maintain and enhance a supremacy of the Western developed countries, and—preferably in "security partnership" with Russia and the Eastern European countries—to intervene militarily should *this* New World Order be threatened.

In contrast to the time invested in future European intervention schemes, the Community seemed little concerned about the development of new security arrangements for the Middle East after the Gulf War. The proposed Conference on Security and Cooperation in the Mediterranean (CSCM) was formally buried at the informal European Council meeting in April 1991. Germany and the United Kingdom were opposed to the conference from the very beginning, and even France rejected the idea because it prefers to keep the United States out of the Mediterranean. Instead, France opted for an intensification of the "5+5 dialogue," and on the Community level, the southern EC members are pushing for a closer association of the Maghreb through the establishment of an EC-Maghreb free-trade zone. The current preliminary talks of the EC Commission with Morocco and Tunisia cannot, however, conceal the difficulties involved. On one side, the EC does not want to open its market to Mediterranean agricultural products, and on the other side, the Maghreb countries cannot open their markets to European industrial products. An agreement is very unlikely in the foreseeable future.[78]

Concerning the settlement of the Palestine question, the Twelve were, initially, very eager to play an active role in the convening of an international peace conference after the Gulf War, but as there was no consensus on an alternative concept, they opted for the support of the U.S. initiative. In the end, it did not take too much U.S. and Israeli pressure to exclude the Community from the main negotiations in the Arab-Israeli peace talks following the Madrid conference in October 1991.

As for the Gulf, the Twelve could not agree on a specific security arrangement. France openly stated its opposition to a Pax Americana and supported the proposed security pact between the GCC states, Syria, and Egypt (the "Cairo group"). Germany opted for an inclusion of Iran into the Cairo group, but stressed that this would be the decision of the countries of the region. Besides, Germany was opposed to any Community activities in the Gulf without close cooperation with the United States. Finally, the United Kingdom generally doubted the Twelve's ability to play a useful role in the Gulf. Enhancing stability in the region, so the British government argued, required first and foremost, measures in the field of security policy, a policy area where the Community was not ready to act.

In 1992, the United Kingdom followed the example of the United States and concluded a defense agreement with Kuwait. Concern about the stability in the Gulf was not the only motive. Britain's defense minister, Tom King, declared that the agreement should "produce valuable orders for British industry."[79]

King was soon proven correct. Besides the United States, the United Kingdom not only earned a lion's share of the rebuilding contracts in Kuwait, it also maintained a top position in the race for fueling the newly spiraling armament in the region after the Gulf War. The sale of forty-eight Tornado combat aircraft to Saudi Arabia as part of a U.S. $4.5 billion arms package, announced in January 1993, is expected to presage a stepped up effort by Britain to expand its arms sales. All of this is unaffected by the international arms export guidelines adopted in September 1991 by the five permanent members of the UN Security Council, which call for avoidance of destabilizing arms sales to the Middle East.[80]

Other EC members, in particular France and Germany, are following suit. A common EC policy for the control of arms, nuclear materials, and dual-use goods is not in sight.[81]

These activities already indicate that, in spite of the numerous statements and activities of the Community during the Gulf War and its aftermath, the EC's policy toward the Mediterranean and the Gulf region cannot be expected to experience fundamental changes in the 1990s. As in the case of the dysfunctional economies of the southern Mediterranean countries and the proliferation of sophisticated weaponry in the Middle East, the Community did not find an answer to the other challenges ahead, such as the dynamics of Islamic resurgence or the enlargement of the "arc of crisis" through the independence of the Muslim republics of the former Soviet Union. Even already obvious developments, such as Iran's muscle-flexing in the Gulf, are not the subject of serious debate.

Rather, the Community will continue its policy of focusing on specific development projects and the sponsorship of regional organizations such as the Arab League, the Gulf Cooperation Council, the Arab Maghreb Union, and, once the current difficulties are overcome, the Arab Cooperation Council or an equivalent structure. Given the experience of European integration, these attempts at regional cooperation hold promise in the eyes of many Western European policymakers.

Instead of pushing for independent peace plans or participation in comprehensive enterprises that require funds and administrative attention in great demand elsewhere, the Community will likely continue to support U.S.-sponsored initiatives, although not without criticism or different accentuation. After all, any successful step toward peace in the region has always been welcomed by the EC in the past, and any new attempt in this direction will find the support of the EC again, diplomatically and, more importantly, financially— even if this new order turns out to be a Pax Americana, which does not necessarily create more structural stability.

Despite its preoccupation with European affairs, the EC's Middle Eastern policy will have considerable influence on events in the region. Since the disintegration of the Soviet Union, the EC has for some Middle Eastern countries become more important as a political counterweight to the United States. Also, the Community is by far the most important trading partner of the countries in the region between the Atlantic and the Gulf, including Turkey and Iran.[82] The economic development of these countries will depend to a considerable extent on the EC's financial aid programs and the ease of access to the Community's market. In this connection, the completion of the Internal Market is of particular importance to the countries of the Middle East. Despite all the solemn declarations by the EC Commission as well as the member states, the Internal Market might well lead to the creation of the much feared "Fortress Europe" with unforeseeable repercussions for the Middle Eastern economies.

In this respect, in 1996 a moment of truth will come: By that time, Portugal and Spain will complete their transition to full membership in the EC, further aggravating agricultural exports of the southern Mediterranean countries, provided no new ruling comes into force. Current developments leave room for doubts that this will be the case. Although the Maastricht Treaty includes a new chapter on a common EC development policy, major changes in the EC's trade relations with the southern Mediterranean countries cannot be expected as long as development aid is understood by the member states as being similar to export promotion, and as long as it is counteracted by other measures, in particular the EC's restrictive agricultural policy.[83]

At their June 1992 Lisbon meeting, the Twelve heads of state agreed, inter alia, that the Maghreb and Mashriq would be priority areas of future common foreign policy for the Community. This was mainly due to the pressure of the southern EC members who intended to balance the overall eastward orientation of the EC, which will increase when Austria, Sweden, Finland, and perhaps Norway join the Community by the mid-1990s.

Although the Gulf region was not mentioned in this connection, it is very likely that this part of the Middle East will increasingly move into the focus of the EC's attention in the following years. Oil remains the Achilles heel of the Community, and the significance of oil from the Gulf region for the EC will increase steadily throughout the decade. Other oil exporters will, because of growing domestic needs or the depletion of resources, be less willing and able to meet the EC's demand which is expected to remain stable throughout the decade.[84] Although this fact is well known, the member states could not agree on the long envisaged establishment of a free-trade zone with the GCC. After the expulsion of Iraqi troops from Kuwait, the negotiations, in a striking parallel to the events after the 1988 cease-fire in the Iran-Iraq War, slowly lost momentum. In the spring of 1992, high Community officials had already warned that, if no agreement could be reached in 1992, a unique opportunity could perhaps be lost forever, as long as, one is tempted to add, no major crisis erupts in the Middle East.

Notes

1. Quoted from *le Monde*, 11 August 1990. See also the UN speech by the Italian Presidency of 25 September 1990. Text in *Bulletin of the European Communities* 9 (September 1990).

2. On the concept of the "spillover," see the work of Ernst B. Haas, in

particular *The Uniting of Europe, Political, Social and Economic Forces 1950-1957* (London: Stevens, 1958). For an example of the new prominence of neo-functionalist theory see Robert O. Keohane and Stanley Hoffman, eds., *The New European Community, Decision-making and Institutional Change* (Boulder, CO: Westview Press, 1991).

3. On the EPC, see Phillipe de Shoutheete, *La Coopération Politique Européenne*, 2d edition (Brussels: Editions Labor, 1986); Panayiotis Ifestos, *European Political Cooperation. Towards a Framework of Supranational Diplomacy?* (Avebury: Aldershot, 1987); Alfred Pijpers, Elfriede Regelsberger and Wolfgang Wessels, eds., *European Political Cooperation in the 1980s. A Common Foreign Policy for Western Europe?* (Dordrecht: Martinus Nijhoff, 1988); Martin Holland, ed., *The Future of European Political Cooperation: Essays on Theory and Practice* (London: Macmillan, 1991); Simon Nuttall, *European Political Cooperation* (Oxford: Clarendon Press, 1992).

4. For an insider's account of the role of the Commission in the EPC and the interaction between EC and EPC see Simon Nuttall, "Where the Commission Comes In." In Pijpers et al., *European Political Cooperation*, 104-17; idem "Interaction between European Political Cooperation and the European Community," in *Yearbook of European Law 1987*, ed. F.G. Jacobs (Oxford: Clarendon Press, 1988): 211-49; idem "The Institutional Network and the Instruments of Action, in *Toward Political Union: Planning a Common Foreign and Security Policy in the European Community*, ed. Reinhardt Rummel (Baden-Baden: Nomos, 1992): 61-62; see also Charles Reich, "La role de la Commission des Communautés Européennes dans la Coopération Politique Européenne," *Revue du Marché Commun* 331 (November 1989): 560-63.

5. For details, see Timothy Niblock in Chapter 5 of this volume.

6. For details about the affair around the "Schumann Paper" see Ifestos, *European Political Cooperation*, 420-21.

7. On the Community's Middle Eastern policy in the 1970s and at the beginning of the 1980s, see Dominique Moisi, "Europe and the Middle East," in *The Middle East and the Western Alliance*, ed. Steven L. Spiegel (London: George Allen & Unwin, 1982): 18-32; Harvey Sicherman, "Europe's Role in the Middle East: Illusions and Realities," *Orbis* 28 (4) (Winter 1985): 803-28; Ifestos, *European Political Cooperation*; Ilan Greilsammer and Joseph Weiler, eds., *Europe and Israel: Troubled Neighbors* (Berlin: de Gruyter, 1988). Particularly helpful is David Allan and Alfred Pijpers, eds., *European Foreign Policy-Making and the Arab-Israeli Conflict* (The Hague: Martinus Nijhoff, 1984).

8. Text of the declaration in *Bulletin of the European Communities* 11 (November 1973).

9. On the EAD see Jacques Bourrinet, ed., *Le dialogue euro-arabe* (Paris: Economica, 1979); David Allan, "Political Cooperation and the

Euro-Arab Dialogue," in *European Political Cooperation: The Historical and Contemporary Background*, ed. David Allan, Reinhardt Rummel, and Wolfgang Wessels (London: Butterworths, 1982): 69–82; Bishara Khader, ed., *Coopération euro-arabe: Diagnostic et prospective* (vols. 1–3) (Louvain-la-Neuve: Centre d'Etude et de Recherche sur le Monde Arabe contemporain de l'Université Catholique de Louvain, 1982); Hubert Dobers and Ulrich Haarmann, eds., *The Euro-Arab Dialogue. Le dialogue euro-arabe* (St. Augustin: Institut für Internationale Solidarität der Konrad-Adenauer-Stiftung, 1983).

10. On the German position see Lily Gardner Feldman, *The Special Relationship between West Germany and Israel* (Boston: George Allen & Unwin, 1984); Karl Kaiser and Udo Steinbach, eds., *Deutsch-arabische Beziehungen* (Munich: R. Oldenbourg, 1981); Friedemann Buettner and Thomas Scheffler, "Die Nahostpolitik der sozial-liberalen Koalition" in *Hilfe + Handel = Frieden? Die Bundesrepublik in der Dritten Welt*, ed. Reiner Steinweg (Frankfurt: Suhrkamp, 1982): 139–75; Udo Steinbach, "Germany," in Allen et al., *European Foreign Policy Making*, 91–106; Sharam Chubin, ed., *Germany and the Middle East: Patterns and Prospects* (London: Pinter Publishers, 1992). The most detailed account of German policy in the European context is given by Amnon Neustadt, *Die deutsch-israelischen Beziehungen im Schatten der EG-Nahostpolitik* (Frankfurt: Haag und Herchen, 1983).

11. See, in particular, the European Council's London Declaration of 29 June 1977; text in *Bulletin of the European Communities* 6 (June 1977).

12. Text of the Venice declaration in *Bulletin of the European Communities* 6 (June 1980). For the most detailed account of the period preceding the Venice initiative see Martin Landgraf, *Die Europäische Politische Zusammenarbeit—eine gemeinsame europäische Außenpolitik? Nahostdiplomatie der Europäischen Gemeinschaft vom ägyptisch-israelischen Friedensvertrag bis zur Erklärung von Venedig.* Dipl. pol. thesis, Free University of Berlin, 1991.

13. For details see Martin Landgraf, *The European Community and the Gulf Cooperation Council. A Case Study in Interregional Cooperation* (Research paper, College of Europe, Bruges, 1992), 9–11.

14. Laura Guazzone, "The Mediterranean Basin," *The International Spectator* 25, no. 4 (October–December 1990): 303.

15. On the SEA see in particular Jean de Ruyt, *L'Acte Unique Européenne*, 2d edition (Brussels: Institut d'etudes européennes, 1989); for the changes in the EPC see Renaud Dehausse and Joseph Weiler, "EPC and Single Act: From Soft Law to Hard Law?" in Holland, *European Political Cooperation*, 121–42; Text of the SEA in *Bulletin of the European Communities*, supplement no.2 (1986).

16. On the impact of the second EC enlargement cf. the special issue "The Enlarged European Community and the Mediterranean," of the *Jeru-*

salem Journal of International Relations 10(3) (September 1988); George Yannopoulos, "Trade Effects from the Extension of Customs Union to Third Countries: A Case Study of the Spanish Accession to the EEC," *Applied Economics* 19(2) (April 1987): 39–50; Fathallah Oualalou, "La problematique de la coopération maghrebine et l'élargissement de la C.E.E.," in *Études Internationales* (Tunis) 28(3) (October 1988): 75–86; Alfred Tovias, *Foreign Economic Relations of the EC. The Impact of Spain and Portugal* (Boulder, CO: Lynne Rienner Publishers, 1990).

17. For a very detailed account see Agence Europe and Promethee, eds., *Les nouveaux accords méditerranéens de la C.E.E. à partir de 1988* (Brussels 1988). For an overview see Roberto Alibioni, "The Mediterranean Scenario. Economy and Security in the Regions South of the EC," *The International Spectator* 25(2) (April–June 1990): 138–54; Commission of the European Communities, ed., *Vers une politique méditerranéenne rénové* (Brussels 1989).

18. Text of the declaration in *Bulletin of the European Communities* 2 (February 1987). For an analysis of the events following the declaration cf. Raymond Cohen, "Twice Bitten? The European Community's 1987 Middle East Initiative," *Middle East Review* 20(3) (Spring 1988): 33–40.

19. *Ibid.*, 33–34.

20. Friedemann Buettner, " 'Frieden für Land' oder 'Frieden für Frieden'. Nahostkonflikt und Palästinafrage nach dem Zweiten Golfkrieg," *Vereinte Nationen* 39(4) (August 1991): 139–43.

21. Ellen Laipson, "Europe's Role in the Middle East. Enduring Ties, Emerging Opportunities," *Middle East Journal* 44(1) (Winter 1990): 11.

22. Text of the declaration in *Bulletin of the European Communities* 6 (June 1989).

23. *The Middle East* 186 (April 1990): 35.

24. *The Middle East* 188 (June 1990): 21–22; the Dublin declaration of the European Council, text in *Bulletin of the European Communities* 4 (April 1990).

25. For an overview of the CSCE process and all relevant documents see Arie Bloed, *From Helsinki to Vienna. Basic documents of the Helsinki Process* (Dordrecht: Martinus Nijhoff, 1990). On the new dynamics of the CSCE see Ian Cuthbertson, ed., *Redefining the CSCE: Challenges and Opportunities in the New Europe* (Boulder, CO: Westview Press, 1992); Michael Staack, ed., *Aufbruch nach Gesamteuropa: Die KSZE nach der Wende im Osten* (Münster: Lit-Verlag, 1992).

26. For a very telling account of these circumstances as well as an analysis of the debate about political reform within the EC in 1989/1990 see Panos Tsakaloyannis, "The Acceleration of History and the Reopening of the Political Debate in the European Community," *Journal of European Integration* 14(2/3) (Winter/Spring 1991): 84–102.

27. *Ibid.*, 85–87.

28. *Ibid.*, 89.

29. For the terms see de Shoutheete *Coopération Politique.*

30. The SEA stipulated that only "political and economic aspects" of security matters were to be discussed within the EPC; see *ibid.*.

31. On the "out-of-area" discussion in the 1980s see Joseph Coffey and Gianni Bonvicini, eds., *The Atlantic Alliance and the Middle East* (Houndsmills: Macmillan, 1989); for an overview see Marc Bentinck, *NATO's Out-of-Area Problem* (London: IISS, 1986).

32. Text of the WEU Platform on European Security Interests in Reinhardt Rummel, ed., *The Evolution of an International Actor: Western Europe's New Assertiveness* (Boulder, CO: Westview Press, 1990), 310-15. On the WEU in great detail see Peter Schell, *Bündnis im Schatten. Die Westeuropäische Union in den 80er Jahren* (Bonn: Bouvier, 1991); see also Matthias Jopp, Reinhardt Rummel, and Peter Schmid, eds., *Integration and Security in Western Europe: Inside the European Pillar* (Boulder, CO: Westview Press, 1991); Werner Ruf, ed., *Vom Kalten Krieg zur heißen Ordnung: Der Golfkrieg—Hintergründe und Perspektiven* (Münster: Lit-Verlag, 1991): 86-96.

33. On Franco-German defense cooperation see the chapters of David Garnham and Peter Schmidt in Rummel, *Evolution of an International Actor*, Urs Leimbacher, *Deutsch-französische sicherheitspolitische Zusammenarbeit 1982-1989* (Baden-Baden: Nomos, 1992).

34. Tsakaloyannis, "Acceleration of History," 90.

35. On the "out-of-area" capabilities of France and Britain see Anthony Cordesman, *The Gulf and the West. Strategic Relations and Military Realities* (Boulder, CO: Westview Press, 1987): 118-20.

36. Anthony Cordesman, "The Changing Military Balance in the Gulf. Iraq's Invasion of Kuwait and its Aftermath," *RUSI and Brassey's Defence Yearbook 1991* (London: Brassey's, 1991): 228.

37. Helmut Hubel, "Non-regional Powers in the Middle East: New Trends in the 1980s?" *The Jerusalem Journal of International Relations* 10(4) (June 1988): 63.

38. On this point see the respective chapters in Cordesman, *The Gulf and the West*; and John Chipman, "Europe and the Iran-Iraq War," in *The Iran-Iraq War*, ed. Efraim Kaish (London: Macmillan, 1989): 215-28.

39. On this point see Achim von Heynitz, *Industrialisierung in den Mitgliedsstaaten des Gulf Cooperation Council (GCC): Die wirtschaftlichen Folgen für die Industrieländer* (Ebenhausen: Stiftung Wissenschaft und Politik, 1985).

40. According to the EC Commission's chief negotiator, Eberhardt Rhein. See his "Agreement with the Gulf Cooperation Council: A Promising but Difficult Beginning," in Edwards and Regelsberger, *Europe's Global Links*, 114. For a detailed analysis of the agreement see C. P. Lucron, "Communauté Européenne et Pays du Golfe. Accord de Circonstance ou

Rapprochement Durable?" *Revue du Marché* Commun 331 (November 1989): 527–35.

41. For details of the EC-GCC negotiations cf. Landgraf, *Gulf Cooperation Council*, 14–34. On EC-GCC relations in general see Rummel and Reinhardt "On EC-GCC Cooperation," *Außenpolitik* 37(1) (1st Quarter 1986): 84–99; Salah A. Al-Mani, "The Politics of the GCC Dialogue with the European Community," *Journal of South Asian and Middle Eastern Studies* 12(4) (Summer 1989): 57–71; Rhein, "Agreement with the Gulf Cooperation Council," 112–18; Achim von Heynitz, *Die Beziehungen zwischen dem Gulf Cooperation Council und der Europäischen Gemeinschaft* (Ebenhausen: Stiftung Wissenschaft und Politik, 1990).

42. Text of the declaration in *Bulletin of the European Communities* 7/8 (July/August 1990).

43. On the Community's responses to the crisis see Martin Landgraf, "Die Europäische Gemeinschaft und die Kuwait-Krise," in *Die Kuwait-Krise und das regionale Umfeld. Hintergründe, Interessen, Ziele*, ed. Ferhad Ibrahim and Mir A. Ferdowsi (Berlin: Das Arabische Buch, 1992): 47–73, and references quoted there; Helmut Hubel, *Der zweite Golfkrieg in der Internationalen Politik* (Bonn: Europa Union Verlag, 1991): 44–64.

44. Text of the declarations in *Bulletin of the European Communities* 7/8 (July/August 1990).

45. *Ibid.* 9 (September 1990).

46. On Spain's and Italy's drive for a CSCM see Francisco Fernández Ordoñz, "The Mediterranean: Devising a Security Structure," in *NATO-Brief* 38(5) (October 1990): 7–13; Italian Ministry of Foreign Affairs, ed., *The Mediterranean and the Middle East after the War in the Gulf: The CSCM* (Rome 1991); Carlos Zaldivar and Andrés Ortega, "The Gulf Crisis and European Cooperation on Security Issues. Spanish Reactions and the European Framework," in *Western Europe and the Gulf*, ed. Nicole Gnesotto and John Roper (Paris: The Institute for Security Studies, Western European Union, 1992): 138.

47. Quoted from *Le Monde*, 10 September 1990.

48. Text of speech and declaration in *Bulletin of the European Communities* 9 (September 1990).

49. See Pierre Salinger and Eric Laurent, *Krieg am Golf. Das Geheimdossier* (München: Carl Hanser, 1991): 102, 106.

50. Paul de la Gorce, "L'eclatante démission de la diplomatie europénne," *Le Monde Diplomatique* (February 1991): 6–7.

51. See Norbert Ropers, "Schulterschluß: Die britisch-amerikanische Allianz," in *Krieg und Frieden am Golf. Ursachen und Perspektiven*, ed. Gert Krell and Bernd W. Kubbig (Frankfurt: Fischer Taschenbuch Verlag, 1991): 98, 103.

52. Louise Fawcett and Robert O'Neill, "Britain, the Gulf Crisis and Eu-

ropean Security," in Gnesotto and Ropers, *Western Europe and the Gulf*, 143.

53. See Ropers, "Schulterschluß," 98; Fawcett and O'Neill, "Britain," 143.

54. On the positions of Luxembourg and the Netherlands see the respective chapters in Gnesotto and Ropers, *Western Europe and the Gulf.*

55. *Le Monde*, 10 October 1990.

56. E.g., the UN speech of the Italian Presidency of 25 September 1990, *Bulletin of the European Communities* 9.

57. On the internal political debate in France see François Heisbourg, "France and the Gulf Crisis," in Gnesotto and Ropers, *Western Europe and the Gulf*, 29–31.

58. See, e.g., the press conference of Mitterrand of 20 December 1990 in *Le Monde*, 21 December 1990.

59. Particularly with respect to Security Council Resolutions 661 and 678.

60. *UN-Doc. A/45/PV 4* of 27 September 1990, 37–45.

61. On the WEU activities during crisis see Arnaud Jacomet, "The Role of the WEU in the Gulf Crisis," in Gnesotto and Ropers, *Western Europe and the Gulf*, 159–80.

62. On Belgium and Portugal see the respective chapters in Gnesotto and Ropers, *Western Europe and the Gulf.* On Denmark see Nicolaj Petersen, "La politique de defense au Denmark," *Ares* 12(3) (1990): 40–54.

63. John Cooley, "Pre-war Gulf Diplomacy," *Survival* 33(2) (March/April 1991): 137. On Greek policy during the crisis see Heinz-Jürgen Axt, *Die Golfkrise und Griechenland: Front gegen den befreundeten Irak* (Ebenhausen: Stiftung Wissenschaft und Politik, 1990).

64. *Süddeutsche Zeitung*, 4 February 1991, and 7 March 1991.

65. Laura Guazzone, "Italy and the Gulf Crisis," in Gnesotto and Ropers, *Western Europe and the Gulf*, 82–83.

66. *Ibid.*, 71, 74–76.

67. For a good overview see Hans Leyendecker and Richard Rickelmann, *Exporteure des Todes. Deutscher Rüstungsskandal in Nahost* (Göttingen: Steidl 1990).

68. On the difficulties of Germany with its history in respect to the Gulf crisis see Sylvie Lemasson, "L'Allemagne et la crise du Golfe," *Documents politique* 5 (December 1990): 18–26; Dan Diner, *Der Krieg der Erinnerungen und die Ordnung der Welt* (Berlin: Rotbuch Verlag, 1991); "Der Golfkrieg, Israel und die deutsche Friedensbewegung," *israel & palästina. Zeitschrift für Dialog*, Special issue (April 1991).

69. *Europe*, 22 August 1990.

70. For details on payments see Karl Kaiser and Klaus Becher, *Deutschland und der Irak-Konflikt. Internationale Sicherheitsverantwortung Deutschlands nach der deutschen Vereinigung* (Bonn: Europa-Union Verlag, 1992): 114–26.

71. Apart from Kaiser and Becher, *ibid.*, the most complete listing of differing accounts about Germany's contribution to the allied efforts seems to be Michael J. Inacker, *Unter Ausschluß der Öffentlichkeit. Die Deutschen in der Golfallianz* (Bonn/Berlin: Bouvier-Verlag, 1991).

72. From *Das Parlament*, 30 November 1990.

73. For details of the EC's attempt to arrange talks with Aziz see Landgraf, *Kuwait-Krise*, 67-70.

74. Tsakaloyannis, "Acceleration of History," 90. See also Finn Laursen and Sophie Vanhoonacker, eds., *The Intergovernmental Conference on Political Union: Institutional Reforms, New Policies and International Identity of the European Community* (Maastricht: Nijhoff, 1992).

75. See Jacomet, "The Role of the WEU"; Jacob de Hoop Scheffer, "The Gulf Crisis. Lessons for Western European Union (Report submitted on behalf of the Defense Committee, 13th May 1991)," *Assembly of the WEU. Proceedings*, 37th Ordinary Session, 1st Part. Paris: WEU, 1991: 181-208.

76. For the full text of the Maastricht Treaty see Agence Europe, ed., *Europe Documents* no. 1759/60 (7 February 1992). For an analysis of the chapter concerning the CFSP see Elfriede Regelsberger, *The Common Foreign and Security Policy of the European Union: An Assessment of the New Treaty Provision and the Follow-up Debate since Maastricht* (Bonn: Institut für Europäische Politik, 1992). For the actual discussion about the CFSP see Reinhardt Rummel, ed., *Toward Political Union? Planning a Common Foreign and Security Policy in the European Community* (Baden-Baden: Nomos, 1992).

77. On this discussion see Robin Laird, *The Europeanization of the Atlantic Alliance* (Boulder, CO: Westview Press, 1991); Wolfgang Danspeckgruber, ed., *Emerging Dimensions of European Security Policy* (Boulder, CO: Westview Press, 1991); Reimund Seidelmann, "Zur Neuordnung der westeuropäischen Sicherheitspolitik," in *Die Integration Europas*, ed. Michael Kreile (Opladen: Westdeutscher Verlag, 1992): 335-61; Erhard Fondran and Hartmut Pohlmann, eds., *Europäische Sicherheit nach dem Ende des Warschauer Paktes* (Baden-Baden: Nomos, 1993).

78. See Eva Weidnitzer, *Regionale Kooperation im Rahmen der 'Union du Maghreb Arabe' und Perspektiven der Zusammenarbeit mit der EG* (Berlin: Deutsches Institut für Wirtschaftsforschung, 1991); Bishara Khader *Le Grand Maghreb et l'Europe: Enjeux et perspectives* (Paris, 1992).

79. Quoted from *The Middle East* 209 (March 1992): 9.

80. *Arms Control Today* 23(2) (March 1993): 23. On the new arms race in the Gulf see in particular Anthony Cordesman, "No End of a Lesson? Iraq and the Issue of Arms Transfer," *The RUSI Journal* 136(1) (Spring 1991): 1-131; Mark Kramer, "The Global Arms Trade after the Persian Gulf War," *Security Studies* 2(2) (Winter 1992): 260-309; Martin Navias, "Arms Trade and Arms Control in the Middle East and North Africa since

Operation Desert Storm," in *The Middle East and North Africa 1993* (London: Europa Publications, 1992): 128-34.

81. See Harald Mueller, "The Export Control Debate in the 'New' European Community," *Arms Control Today* 23(2) (March 1993): 10-14. On the basic problems in this domain see Harad Bauer et al., eds., *Arms and Dual-Use Exports from the E.C.: A Common Policy for Regulation and Control* (London: Saferworld Foundation, 1992).

82. The only exception is Bahrain where the EC is in second place behind Saudi Arabia.

83. For perspectives on the EC's development policy in the 1990s, see Franz Nuscheler and Otto Schmuck, eds., *Die Südpolitik der EG: Europas entwicklungspolitische Verantwortung in der veränderten Weltordnung* (Bonn: Europa Union Verlag, 1992).

84. On this point see the analysis of the EC Commission in *Energy in Europe: A View to the Future* (Brussels, 1992).

5
Regional Cooperation and Security in the Middle East

The Role of the European Community

Timothy Niblock

Perspective

A recent article by Fred Halliday warns that European perceptions of Europe's role in the Middle East are encumbered by myths. Among these, Halliday states, is the myth that a special relationship exists between Europe and the Arab states—the belief that the Europeans "have a better understanding of the region than do the Americans, by dint of history, proximity, diplomatic sophistication, and so forth."[1] He contends that to retreat into the "transcendental world of the Euro-Arab dialogue" ignores the realities. The relationship between Europe and Arab states, he says, is not a function of anything "special"—historic, cultural, or geographical—but exists because of a "trade and diplomatic position." It is necessary to be mindful of this to avoid unrealistic notions and misleading concepts when conducting political analysis.

It must also be recognized that many policies pursued by European governments during the Gulf War provided little evidence of the latter's sagacity or insight. This paper will contend, however, that there is a distinctive European Community (EC) approach to the problems of the Middle East, that the community has begun to shape and implement policies reflective of that approach; and that the Gulf War has accelerated the development of these policies. The writer's view is that the community's contribution to (or impact on) the peace and security of the Middle East will be of increasing significance over the last decade of the twentieth century. Difficulties over the Maastricht Treaty will affect the scope and effectiveness of community policy in the region, but even without Maastricht this policy is likely to become more coordinated and coherent.

The Background to European Community Policy on the Middle East

Prior to 1990, the involvement of the community (as distinct from that of individual European states) in the Middle East was largely restricted to two fields: trade or cooperation agreements with particular Middle Eastern states, and the conduct of the Euro-Arab dialogue.[2]

Trade and Cooperation Agreements with Southern Mediterranean Countries

From its inception, the European Economic Community (EEC) had to develop appropriate arrangements for the conduct of trade with those countries that had enjoyed preferential access to the French market—the Maghreb countries, in the case of the Arab world. A protocol annexed to the Treaty of Rome (1957) authorized France to maintain preferential trading arrangements with Tunisia and Morocco (Algeria was not yet independent). There was also the more general problem of how to regularize trade with non-EEC Mediterranean states with which many EEC states had traditionally maintained strong economic relations. The treaty empowered the EEC Council of Ministers to conclude trade or cooperation agreements with outside countries and, in the course of the 1960s and early 1970s, a number of such agreements with Middle Eastern states were concluded: a nonpreferential trade agreement with Israel in 1963, followed by a preferential agreement in 1970; a non-preferential agreement with Lebanon in 1965, followed by a preferential agreement in 1972; cooperation agreements with Tunisia and Morocco in 1969; and a preferential trade agreement with Egypt in 1972.[3]

Even in the 1960s, the community was uneasy about the piecemeal manner in which its relations with Mediterranean states were being handled. In May 1964, the Italian government (so often at the forefront in pressing for an EEC Mediterranean policy) presented a memorandum to the EEC Council of Ministers suggesting a "global" approach to the region. Three elements of such an approach were proposed: the establishment of a free trade area for industrial goods between the community and the Mediterranean countries; the provision of financial aid by the community to the poorer states of the Mediterranean; and the offer of some limited concessions on agricultural imports to the community from non-EEC Mediterranean countries. The council of ministers did not accept the Italian proposals, but the latter did encourage the community to give more thought to overall policy in the Mediterranean region.[4]

From the early 1970s, the community developed an overall policy for the Mediterranean to provide a framework for future trade and cooperation arrangements. In 1971, the EC Commission initiated and presented a memorandum to the council of ministers evaluating the record of the community's economic relations with the southern Mediterranean countries. The memorandum stated that "the considerable overlap of political and economic interests, and the influence that Mediterranean could have in this region make it possible to see the development of the European basin as a natural extension of European integration."[5] The council of ministers responded positively to the initiative and instructed the EC Commission to outline some specific proposals for mutual cooperation with non-EEC Mediterranean countries, not just on trade, but also on general economic and technical relations and social concerns. The development of a clear policy received impetus from the summit meeting of European heads-of-state and governments that convened in Paris on 19 October 1972. The summit resolutions referred to the "vital importance" that the community attached to the implementation of its commitments to the countries of the Mediterranean basin, with which agreements had been or would be concluded. It was stressed that these agreements would be subject to an "overall and balanced approach."[6] Seven Arab countries—Egypt, Libya, Tunisia, Algeria, Morocco, Lebanon, and Jordan—and Israel were specified as being within the scope of the community's Mediterranean policy.

The EC Commission's recommendations on an overall Mediterranean policy were passed by the council of ministers in November 1972, and in June 1973 the council issued directives to the commission instructing it to open negotiations with the non-community Mediterranean countries. Agreements were to include not only trading arrangements (free access to the European market for all industrial goods except for refined petroleum products and certain textiles; and limited tariff concessions on specified agricultural products), but also financial and technical cooperation, joint institutions (cooperation councils composed of representatives from both sides, sometimes aided by specialist committees), and, where appropriate, social affairs (such as concerned the conditions of Maghrebi workers in Europe). The community concluded wide-ranging cooperation agreements with

Israel in 1975, with Tunisia, Algeria, and Morocco in 1976, and with Lebanon, Syria, Jordan, and Egypt in 1977.[7]

A further development in the community's Mediterranean policy occurred in the mid-1980s when it expanded to include Spain, Portugal, and Greece. The states of the southern Mediterranean feared, with some justification, that the new members would damage their own export markets in Europe. Some adaptation to Mediterranean policy, therefore, was necessary. The non-community Mediterranean countries had become dissatisfied with the existing relationship: They complained that the advantages they had hoped to gain from their agreements with the EEC had not been realized, and that the community's approach to the region was still not truly "global."[8]

In June 1982, the EC Commission presented a report to the council of ministers, outlining the implications that the enlargement of the community would have for Mediterranean policy. The report predicted that the problems already being encountered in the Mediterranean would be aggravated and recommended that the community adopt new measures to promote intra-Mediterranean cooperation, to develop "traditional trade flows," and to ensure better community participation in the development of the southern Mediterranean countries.[9]

In March 1985, the community announced a new Mediterranean policy. A statement issued by the council of ministers stressed the importance that the community attached to cooperation with the southern Mediterranean countries and expressed the community's determination to make an appropriate contribution to the economic and social development of these countries. The existing cooperation agreements were adapted to account for the expansion. The traditional export trade of the non-community Mediterranean countries was maintained to ensure "significant and stable results in the medium term."[10]

The guidelines for the community's "contribution to the economic and social development" of the southern Mediterranean countries, adopted by the council in November 1985, specified three main areas for community action: support for domestic food production (aimed at reducing the dependence of southern Mediterranean countries on food imports); the broadening of industrial, scientific, and technical cooperation (intended to achieve greater complementarity between the economies of the community and those of the southern Mediterranean); and support for stronger cooperation and integration among the southern Mediterranean countries (giving priority to regional undertakings). New financial protocols between the EEC and the non-community Mediterranean countries were to be concluded.[11]

Negotiations with the non-community Mediterranean countries to adapt the existing cooperation agreements, giving expression to the new objectives and guidelines, opened in December 1985. Adapted cooperation agreements were reached and financial protocols were expanded and renewed with Egypt, Lebanon, Jordan, Algeria, Tunisia, and Morocco. An agreement was also concluded with Syria in 1988, but no financial protocol was offered due to the position taken by the British government after the Hindawi affair in 1987.[12]

The Cooperation Agreement with the Gulf Cooperation Council

In addition to, and separate from, the relationship that the community had established with the Mediterranean countries was its more recent relationship with the Gulf states. This was initiated by the West German government in 1980, when Foreign Minister Hans-Dietrich Genscher proposed to the EC Council of Ministers the conclusion of bilateral cooperation agreements with the seven Arab countries of the Gulf.[13] The initiative was premature. The Gulf states (especially Iraq, Kuwait, and Saudi Arabia) were suspicious that the initiative was motivated solely by short-term commercial objectives. During a visit by representatives of the seven Arab countries to Brussels in June 1980, the Gulf representatives argued that the initiative stemmed from "the EEC countries' present uncertainty about their oil supplies" and that the proposals "totally disregarded the other aspects of cooperation."[14] There were also misgivings on the European side: The French government, for example, feared that Arab governments would see the initiative as an instrument to divide Arab opinion. After the outbreak of the Iran-Iraq War in September 1980, the council of ministers formally suspended consideration of the issue, on the grounds that such consideration would be "inopportune and premature."[15]

The creation of the Gulf Cooperation Council (GCC) in May 1981 created new possibilities for the development of an EEC-Gulf relationship. In September 1981, the council of ministers decided to initiate informal preliminary contacts with the secretariat of the GCC to determine the scope for cooperation.[16] The secretary-general of the GCC, Abdallah Bishara, visited Brussels for talks in June 1982, and an EC Commission delegation visited the headquarters of the GCC in al-Riyadh in March 1983. Over the following two years, further visits were exchanged to "explore the possibility and make preparations with a view to launching negotiations to conclude a cooperation agreement."[17] Exploratory discussions held in March 1985 were followed by a joint communique, which stated that the two sides had "agreed that it was in their mutual interest to conclude a comprehensive, mutually beneficial, all-embracing agreement to foster the broadest possible commercial and economic cooperation between the GCC and the European Community."[18]

The actual conclusion of an EEC-GCC cooperation agreement, however, was beset with difficulties. The major issue that impeded progress concerned the access of GCC exports into the community. The GCC sought preferential treatment for Gulf industrial products (especially petrochemicals) in the Community market, which the EEC was not prepared to grant.

The agreement signed in June 1988 (and in effect by 1990) provided for cooperation in economic affairs, agriculture and fisheries, industry, energy, science, technology, investment, the environment, and trade. The transfer of technology through joint ventures would also be encouraged. Despite the long list of fields in which cooperation would be promoted, however, the community did not concede to the GCC's main demand; imports of Gulf petrochemicals would continue to be subject to tariffs.

The GCC's attempt to obtain a cooperation agreement which encompassed a free trade area arrangement, similar to the agreements the EEC had concluded with the Arab Mediterranean countries, failed. The EC-GCC agreement was more akin to one that the community had concluded with the Association of South East Asian Nations (ASEAN) in 1980, where the scope of concern was limited to the strengthening and diversification of economic relations. The June 1988 agreement envisaged that further talks would be held on GCC industrial imports into the Community, and the close coordination between some EEC and GCC states during the Gulf War provided the stimulus for the re-opening of negotiations in 1991. At the time of writing, however, no new arrangements had been made.

The Euro-Arab Dialogue

The Euro-Arab dialogue was largely the product of the 1973 war and the use of oil as a weapon by the Organization of Arab Petroleum Exporting Countries (OAPEC). The community needed to develop a new relationship with the Arab world wherein oil supplies (at reasonable prices) could be secured and Arab petrodollars could be recycled into European industry. The delicate interweaving of political and economic factors was, therefore, evident from the outset. On the side of the community, the main objectives were economic, yet the means used to attain those objectives were political. The Arab states demanded a political dimension; it was a condition for their participation. Once engaged in a political forum, the community found it necessary to develop and define more clearly its political objectives and concerns in the area.

Between 1973 and 1978 the Euro-Arab dialogue was intense. After numerous meetings, a framework of cooperation between the community and the states of the Arab League was established.[19] Although it is difficult to identify any concrete achievements from these meetings, it was nonetheless significant that the community sought to achieve a collective understanding with the Arab world. The Venice Declaration of June 1980, defining community policy on Arab-Israeli matters (in terms that explicitly recognized the right of Palestinians to self-determination), was a natural outcome of the dialogue, however unwilling the community may have been to give practical effect to the policy that it had espoused.

The "intensive" phase of the Euro-Arab dialogue was ended by political developments in the Middle East, not by any change in community policy. As a result of the Camp David agreement and the Egyptian-Israeli peace treaty, the Arab governments were no longer able to act together. Subsequent attempts to resurrect the dialogue (the convening of the fifth general committee meeting in 1983 and the sixth general committee meeting in 1990) did not further the process.[20]

Distinctive Characteristics of the European Community's Approach

Two aspects of the community's approach to the Middle East were distinctive. The first was its emphasis on promoting regional integration in the area. This, of course, constituted the local application of a policy that was generally typical of community external policies. The policy was adopted in 1974, when a special meeting of the EEC Council of Ministers (convened to undertake an overall review of development cooperation policies) adopted a resolution on "regional integration among developing countries." The council indicated that the community would in the future respond favorably to requests from developing countries seeking to establish or to consolidate mechanisms of regional cooperation or integration.[21] This position was repeated regularly over subsequent years, and it now forms an important element in the guidelines for the community's financial and technical cooperation programs.[22]

Despite the community's adoption of this general principle in 1974, it was not promoted in a concerted manner in the Middle East until the mid-1980s. In a document issued in 1985, the commission identified regional cooperation as a priority and designated community financial assistance to promote development in non-EC Mediterranean countries. A multilateral framework was deemed necessary if the region was to undergo any far-reaching industrialization. Among the schemes of regional cooperation that the commission was eager for the community to support were cross-border connections, regional research centers, chambers of commerce, a common program for the fight against drought, and a common program for the use of solar energy.[23] A "regional facility" was written into the financial protocols that were agreed upon by the southern Mediterranean countries in 1987. Notwithstanding the commission's stated priorities, no community financial assistance went to projects involving two or more regional states in the second half of the 1980s, mainly because regional states showed little interest in submitting project proposals.

The limited effects of this policy led to the development of a stronger one in 1991—a development that was probably also shaped by the Gulf crisis. Arrangements for the provision of financial assistance to non-community Mediterranean countries over the period 1992 to 1996 specifically reserved funds for regional projects. In addition to the established protocols with individual states covering bilateral financial arrangements, additional funds were allocated to "those measures whose scope extends beyond the context of a single country and those which concern the environment."[24] Of particular interest to the community were projects that involved collective action to reduce pollution of the Mediterranean. The community would promote cooperation in the area through technical cooperation, feasibility studies of regional infrastructure projects, and educational and research activities.

The second distinctive aspect in the community's approach was the emphasis placed on an overall framework within which the region's problems could be solved. The community wanted a direct role in the "overall framework," justified both by its proximity to the Middle East and its inclusion in the "Mediterranean region." The Euro-Arab dialogue fits within the perspective of an overall framework as did the proposal to establish a Conference on Security and Cooperation in the Mediterranean (CSCM). The latter initiative has been pursued most diligently in the period since Iraq invaded Kuwait and is discussed in the next section.

The Development of Community Policy During and After the Gulf War

The Trend Toward a New Mediterranean Policy

The Gulf War, not unnaturally, led to a substantial deepening and widening in the community's consideration of a Middle Eastern policy. It should be stressed, however, that this "deepening and widening" had already begun before Iraqi troops moved into Kuwait. The process was initiated in the Conferences on Security and Cooperation in Europe (CSCE). From the outset, some community countries (Italy in particular) insisted on the indivisibility of the interests of Europe and the Mediterranean. A chapter on "Issues Relating to Cooperation in the Mediterranean" was inserted into the Final Act at the Helsinki conference in 1975. After the 1984 CSCE, a workshop on cooperation in the Mediterranean was held in Venice. The final document of the 1986 Stockholm CSCE stressed the close linkage between the security of Europe and the Mediterranean, while the 1989 Vienna CSCE committed participating states to the promotion of security and cooperation in the Mediterranean.[25] In September 1990, a CSCE meeting specifically devoted to the Mediterranean area was held in Palma de Mallorca.

At the end of the 1980s, moreover, a trend toward developing and defining EC policy on the Middle East was set in motion by political events within the community. By 1992, it was obvious that a more coherent external policy was needed for the Community; therefore plans were made to hold a Conference on Security and Cooperation in the Mediterranean and the Middle East (CSCM). This was verbalized in December 1989 by the Italian foreign minister, Gianni de Michelis:

Why . . . should we not think of applying the same rationale (ed: as the CSCE) to solving the problems of the Mediterranean area? And what prevents us from considering the CSCE model as suitable to be tailored to the peculiar features and heterogeneous nature of all the Mediterranean and Middle Eastern countries as a whole?

I am becoming increasingly convinced of the paramount need to make concrete and positive proposals to boost cooperation with the Arab world. And this can only be done by taking a global approach to the problems which have long hampered the development of the less advanced countries in the area, and dialogue and cooperation between our countries.

For I believe that the time has now come to extend the spirit and the rationale of Helsinki to the Mediterranean and the Middle East and thereby foster democracy and economic development in its most objective and practical forms.[26]

The Italian foreign minister's initiative came at a time when the community's commissioner for Mediterranean policy, Mr. Matutes, had circulated ideas on a "renewed Mediterranean Policy." The EEC General Affairs Council in July 1990 discussed a proposal for the establishment of a financial institution for the developing countries of the Mediterranean, where the provision of finance would be linked to structural reforms.

Proposal for a Conference on Security and Cooperation in the Mediterranean and the Middle East

Despite earlier developments, it was only after the Gulf crisis had begun that concrete proposals for the convening of a CSCM were made. Although the detailed proposals on the CSCM have emanated from individual EC states, rather than the Commission or council of the community, a strong link does exist with overall community policies. The lead was taken by Italy, which at that time held the presidency of the EC Council of Ministers. The EC Commission produced documents that emphasized the same general objectives as those found in the detailed Italian/Spanish/French/Portuguese proposals, and the council of ministers issued declarations that stressed similar objectives. Among the former was a paper presented by Mr. Matutes to the EEC General Affairs Council in February 1991, entitled "Security and Cooperation in the Middle East and in the Mediterranean: Action by the Community and the Member States after the Gulf Crisis." Among the latter was the council's declaration on 15 December 1990:

the European Council remains convinced that relations of mutual confidence and cooperation must be encouraged among the countries of the region, with a view to establishing a situation of stability, security, economic and social well-being, and respect for civil and political rights, to forestalling the recurrence of crises, and to preventing the spread of weapons of mass destruction. The European Community and its Member States remain ready actively to cooperate with the concerned countries and to achieve these goals.[27]

The proposals for the CSCM emerged gradually, through a series of meetings and conferences held in late 1990 and early 1991. Of particular importance were the speeches delivered by the Italian and Spanish foreign ministers to the CSCE meeting (together with the joint Italian-Spanish "nonpaper") held on 24 September 1990; submissions made to the meeting on regional cooperation in the western Mediterranean on 10 October 1990, which brought together the foreign ministers of France, Spain, Portugal, Italy, Libya, Morocco, Mauritania, Malta, Tunisia, and Algeria (when a "Declaration on the CSCM" was issued); the press communique that followed the December 1990 meeting on security and cooperation in the Mediterranean held in Cairo and attended by high officials from Algeria, Egypt, France, Italy, Malta, Portugal, Spain, and Yugoslavia; and the joint document on the CSCM issued by the governments of France, Italy, Portugal, and Spain following a meeting in Lisbon on 17 January 1991.[28]

The account of the CSCM proposals that follows is based on points gathered from the above-mentioned statements and documents.[29] The focus of the CSCM proposals (as was the case with the CSCE) was on creating a stable system of regional cooperation, where all the participant states accepted certain principles and rules. Also comparable to the CSCE was the emphasis placed on adopting a global approach, deemed necessary because the issue of security should not be separated from economic development and mutual tolerance.

Flexibility was an important aspect of the CSCM framework. Just as the CSCE process took fifteen years to move from the preparatory conference in Helsinki to the "Charter of Paris for a New Europe" (November 1990), so also could the CSCM process take time—time to remove the distrust and misunderstanding on minor issues before dealing with the more substantial questions. Diplomatic and political initiatives to achieve the resolution of Mediterranean and Middle Eastern problems that take place outside of the specific context of the CSCM would not conflict with it. If successful, they could either be included within the CSCM framework, or be regarded as complementary to it.

The principle of universality determined which states should participate in the CSCM. Any state with a substantial interest in the region was to be extended an invitation. The definition of "substantial interest" was a broad one and included twelve member states of the EC, seventeen non-community states bordering, or almost bordering, the Mediterranean (Albania, Algeria, Bulgaria, Cyprus, Egypt, Israel, Jordan, Lebanon, Libya, Malta, Mauritania, Morocco, Romania, Syria, Tunisia, Turkey, and Yugoslavia), nine Gulf and Arabian peninsula states (including Iran and Iraq), three other states involved in the CSCE (Canada, the Soviet Union, and the United States), and one other UN-recognized entity, Palestine.

The UN was deemed an integral part of the CSCM process. Indeed, it was intended that the legal and diplomatic basis for convening the CSCM would be defined in UN resolutions, particularly with that passed by the General Assembly on 12 December 1990. The latter was concerned with strengthening security and cooperation in the Mediterranean region and noted "the widespread support among Mediterranean countries for the proposal to convene a conference on Security and Cooperation in the Mediterranean and their willingness to open regional consultations with a view to creating the appropriate conditions for the initiation of such a process."[30] The UN could, on this basis, be directly involved in convening and organizing the CSCM.

The immediate objectives pursed by the CSCM in the aftermath of the Gulf War, were to prevent new imbalances from emerging in the region (possibly arising from the attempt by some states to benefit from Iraq's weakness); to control the acquisition of arms and avoid the re-emergence of an arms race; to create a system of security for the region that would not be dependent on the presence of troops from outside; and to prevent the defeat of Saddam Hussein from being perceived within the Arab world as a humiliation inflicted on the Arabs by the West. The last required a demonstration of evenhandedness over the implementation of international law, that is, ensuring that violations of international law in Palestine and elsewhere were given attention.

The longer-term objectives and principles would be similar to those found in the CSCE, with the same baskets of security, economic cooperation, and human rights. The basis would be laid for the peaceful negotiations for the resolution of specific disputes; international peace conferences for the resolution of wider-ranging problems; the establishment of security structures grounded on local support and local involvement; the treatment of some of the socio-economic problems of the region through the use of not only European and Western resources but also those of oil-producing states; and the acceptance of some general principles promoting tolerance and a respect for human rights.

With regard to developing principles of governmental conduct, however, it was recognized that the framing of such principles (similar to those drawn up by the CSCE) would take time. Meanwhile, a more limited set of principles could be used as an "entry ticket" into the CSCE. The latter could include respect for the territorial integrity of states and the inviolability of borders; responsibility of the richer states to provide economic support for the poorer; rejection of the use of force to settle disputes; tolerance and dialogue in all fields (political, cultural, and religious); and support for ending the arms race.

Conclusion

Despite the subservient role that the EC countries played during the Gulf crisis, the divisions among them on both strategy and objectives during the crisis,[31] and the narrow national interests that some community countries continued to pursue in the area, there does exist a distinctive community approach to the Middle East. The Gulf crisis fostered the further development of that approach.

The emphasis on creating frameworks of cooperation (whether by coordinative arrangements suitable for the CSCM or integrative schemes among Arab states) represented the beginning. The future will likely see a refinement of strategies for promoting cooperative frameworks, with care taken to ensure that the political prerequisites for integrative efforts are not neglected. A simplistic assumption that cooperation under existing conditions is inevitably good would aggravate problems and probably fail to resolve crucial problems such as that of Palestinian dispossession. Hence the need to develop a strategy that recognizes the full range of the region's problems and the responsibility that external powers have had in the creation of some of them.

Whether community policy will prove effective seems likely to depend on two factors. The first is the determination with which it is pursued. Already there are some grounds for pessimism on this score. The community's external policies tend to be crisis-driven; they develop when the community is confronted by an immediate crisis and lose their impetus when the crisis subsides. The urgency for a resolution has already diminished since the ending of the Gulf War. Paradoxically, the coherent development and pursuit of community policies in the Middle East may thus be dependent on the continuation of crisis conditions in the region.

The second factor impinging on the policy's success concerns its realism: whether the promotion of integration and coordination is in fact a viable means through which the region's divisions and rivalries can be managed, and whether there exists within the region the desire and the political will to pursue this option. There was a widespread assumption at the time of the Gulf War that the confrontation would give rise to new political forces committed to finding more effective ways of resolving the region's problems. The validity of the community's approach may well depend on whether this assumption is justified.

Notes

1. F. Halliday, "The War and its Aftermath: Three Myths on Europe and the Middle East." (Paper delivered at the Round-Table Debate on "After the Gulf War: Europe and the Middle East," European University, Florence, February 1991).

2. The most thorough account of the development of relations between the European Community and the Arab countries is that given in H. Jawad, "Euro-Arab Relations: A Study in Collective Diplomacy" (Ph.D. diss., University of Exeter, 1989). Considerable use is made of H. Jawad's excellent work in the second section of this paper.

3. Commission of the European Communities, *The European Community and the Arab World* (Brussels: Directorate-General for Information, 1982): 1.

4. C. Pirzio-Biroli, "Foreign Policy Formation within the European Community with Special Regard to the Developing Countries," in *Contemporary Perspectives on European Integration*, ed. L. Hurewitz, (London: Aldwych Press, 1980): 237.

5. Commission of the European Communities, *Europe-South Dialogue,* (Brussels: Commission of the European Communities, 1984): 10.

6. Commission of the European Communities, *The Mediterranean Policy: Thirty Years of Community Law,* (Luxembourg: Office for Official Publications of the European Communities, 1983): 391.

7. Jawad, "Euro-Arab Relations," 51.

8. D. Buysse, *The Effects of Enlargement on Other Mediterranean Countries* (Brussels: Europe News Agency, 1984): 4-5.

9. Jawad, "Euro-Arab Relations," 67-68.

10. Commission of the European Communities, *Bulletin of the European Communities* 9 (1985): 18.

11. Commission of the European Communities, *Nineteenth General Report on the Activities of the European Communities, 1985* (Luxembourg: Office for Official Publications of the European Communities, 1986): 300.

12. Commission of the European Communities, *Twenty-Second General Report on the Activities of the European Communities, 1987* (Luxembourg: Office for Official Publications of the European Communities, 1988): 366.

13. A. Wiexzorek, *Trade Relations Between The EEC and the Gulf States* (Luxembourg: European Parliament, 1981): 9-10.

14. *Ibid.,* 8.

15. C. Cova, *The Arab Policy of the EEC* (Brussels: Bureau d'Information European, 1983): 109.

16. Commission of the European Communities, *Twenty-Ninth Review of the Council's Work, 1981* (Luxembourg: Office for Official Publications of the European Communities, 1982): 167.

17. Commission of the European Communities, *Thirty-Second Review of the Council's Work, 1984* (Luxembourg: Office for Official Publications of the European Communities, 1985): 174.

18. Commission of the European Communities, *The European Community and the Gulf Cooperation Council* (Brussels: Directorate of Information of the European Communities, 1985): 3.

19. Jawad, "Euro-Arab Relations," ch. 4.

20. *Ibid.,* 347-48; and Commission of the European Communities, *Bulletin of the European Communities* (June 1990): paragraph 1.4.16.

21. Council of the European Community, "Cooperation Technique: Integration Regional Entre les Pays on Voie de Developpement (resolution)," *Releve des Decisions Prises par le Conseil lors de sa 284eme Session Tenue le 30 Avril 1974 a Luxembourg—Cooperation et Developpement,* R/1310/74, Brussels, 10 May 1974, Annex VII.

22. Commission of the European Communities, "Proposal for a Council Decision Concerning General Guidelines for Financial and Technical Cooperation with the Developing Countries in Latin America and Asia during the Period 1991-96," COM (85) 517 final, 11-12.

23. Commission of the European Communities, "La Communaute et la

Mediterrancee: Orientations pour la Cooperation Economique," COM (85) 517 final, 11–12.

24. Commission of the European Communities, "Proposal for a Council Regulation Concerning Financial Cooperation in Respect of all the Mediterranean Non-Member Countries," COM (91) 48 final. 19 February 1991.

25. Italian Ministry of Foreign Affairs, *The Mediterranean and the Middle East After the War in the Gulf: The CSCM* (Rome: Ministry of Foreign Affairs, 1991): 2.

26. Gianni de Michelis, (Address given at the Ministerial Summit Meeting of the Euro-Arab Dialogue, December 1989). Reproduced in Italian Ministry of Foreign Affairs, *Mediterranean and the Middle East*, 13.

27. "Declaration on the Middle East," Annex II of the European Council conclusions, 14–15 December 1989.

28. The text of all the relevant statements and documents can be found in Italian Ministry of Foreign Affairs, *Mediterannean and the Middle East.*

29. A useful resume of the main arguments can be found in "Conclusions," in Italian Ministry of Foreign Affairs, *Mediterranean and the Middle East*, 141–45.

30. Resolution adopted on the reports of the First Committee, Report A/45/790, General Assembly of the United Nations 12 December 1990.

31. A clear indication of this was Margaret Thatcher's criticism of her European allies at a press conference on 30 August, when she described the European military contribution so far as "patchy and disappointing." Employing her customary hectoring tone, she compared the European response ungenerously with that of the United States. She ended with the peroration "it is sad that at this critical time Europe has not measured up to its expectations."

6
Japan

An Economic Superpower in Search of Its Proper Political Role in the Post-Cold War Era

Yasumasa Kuroda

In Search of Self: Beyond Economic Power

On 19 August 1991, as the first Japan-U.S. Hawaii Conference of Legislators, Scholars, and Journalists began at the Maui Prince Hotel on the island of Maui, we learned of a coup in the Soviet Union.[1] At the conference, former Prime Minister Noboru Takeshita remarked that he was glad not to be in Tokyo as leaders there would be busily consulting with each other as to what the government should do. This revelation, among others, pointed to the absence of an established Japanese foreign policy to deal with key issues of the 1990s. The Gulf crisis was more difficult for Japan to deal with because of its constitutional constraint on the use of military forces abroad.

There are some generalizations that can be made about Japanese foreign policy that were illustrated by the Gulf crisis, in particular, and conditions in West Asia and North Africa, in general. First, Japan had not established a basic policy to deal with emerging world problems, particularly in the post-cold war era, even though it wished to play a greater role commensurate with its economic prowess. This prompted the question: Should Japan send its self-defense forces abroad? Article 9 of its constitution clearly and unambiguously renounced war as a policy instrument; therefore Japan maintained no military forces. The Gulf crisis was the first situation that called for possible military action from Japan. In the past, Japanese policy-making toward the Gulf and West Asia did not include a military component.

Second, the Japanese, because of their language and culture, were structurally nonselection-oriented in relation to Semites and Westerners.[2] Hence, Japan was less likely to take decisive and extreme positions. Certainly, this was the case in its reaction to the Tiananmen Square incident, the Gulf crisis, and the recent Soviet changes. This cultural proclivity translated itself into a policy similar to the one taken by Japan toward the Iran-Iraq War—evenhanded diplomatic ties (Murata 1990; Oki 1990; Orr 1990; Takahashi 1990). Japan's less decisive and ambiguous reactions frustrated Americans who were trying to improve relations with Japan.

Third, unlike other areas of Japanese foreign policy, Japan traditionally had taken an independent policy toward West Asia and the Middle East. In fact, West Asia was the only region in the world where Japanese foreign policy often differed from U.S. policy. Japan's *Idemitsu* imported oil from Muhammed Mossadegh's Iran in the early 1950s while the Seven Sisters—Exxon, Shell, British Petroleum, Mobile, Standard Oil of California, Texaco, and Gulf Oil—refused to deal with Iran during his regime. Japan sided with the Arabs during the first energy crisis in 1973 despite Henry Kissinger's entreaties to conform to U.S. policy (see Katakura 1986; Kuroda 1986b). Likewise, Japan was instructed by the Carter administration not to trade with the Iranian revolutionaries. Japan, however, managed to maintain friendly relations with both Iraq and Iran during the Iraq-Iran War while the United States sided with Iraq. This was in accordance with the nondirectional orientation of Japan.

Fourth, unlike Britain, France, the United States, and others who played the role of colonizers, particularly after the fall of the Ottoman Empire, Japan's association with Western colonial subjugation of people in West Asia and North Africa was limited to signing the San Remo Treaty in 1920. In fact, to Arabs and Jews, the Japanese were a model, for they had struggled against Western imperialism and racism and had been victorious over Tzarist Russia.[3] Japan was not a member of the United Nations on 29 November 1947 when the UN passed a partition plan that deprived Palestinians of their land, ignoring the national aspiration and property rights of the Christians and Muslims who constituted a majority in Palestine. West Asia was not East Asia or Southeast Asia, where Japan had been a colonizer prior to the end of World War II.

Fifth, unlike Western and Communist countries that had sold weapons to Iraq for profit, Japan had not. Hence, Japan was not responsible for Iraq's rise as a significant military power in the region as were the United States and other countries.

Sixth, one still must be cognizant of the role that the Japan-U.S.

bilateral relationship played in the development of Japanese foreign policy, including that toward West Asia. Japan always formulated foreign policy in respect to its effect on the United States, its largest trading partner. The Japanese-U.S. bilateral relationship was the most important external factor upon which all of Japan's foreign policies were based.

The Gulf crisis was no exception; Japan announced its U.S. $4 billion aid program for countries adversely affected by the Gulf crisis and a U.S. $9 billion package for the Desert Storm military operation. Probably in response to prodding by the U.S. Ambassador Michael H. Armacost, Liberal Democratic Party Secretary General Ichiro Ozawa, in cooperation with Prime Minister Toshiki Kaifu, proposed the "United Nations Peace Cooperation Bill" on 16 October so that Japan could send Japan's Self Defense Forces (SDF) abroad. Reportedly, the bill had an approval rate of only 13 percent of the Japanese public as of the end of October (Itoh 1991:279–80); it was withdrawn on 8 November due to heated arguments.

Finally, Japan sent minesweepers to clean up the Gulf after the war.[4] Other efforts to send the SDF did not materialize. The U.S. reaction to these efforts was less than enthusiastic;[5] Japan's response was too "fuzzy" for Americans. The Japanese contribution to the Gulf War was not appreciated.

The absence of an established foreign policy created a forum for various leaders to suggest what course of action Japan should follow in the Gulf crisis. Opinions expressed in print media and public opinion polls indicated Japan's views. Area specialists on West Asia and foreign policy scholars also expressed their views on the subject during the crisis. The following section attempts to analyze Japan's response to the Gulf War.

Who Started the Gulf Crisis?

> The U.S. seems to be on a collision course with the
> Ba'athists. This is unfortunate and unnecessary.
> The root of the problem appears to be Washing-
> ton's inability to appreciate the intensity of Iraq's
> determination to overcome its present economic
> crisis.
>
> Pelletiere, Johnson, and Rosenberger 1990:69

Iraq's invasion of Kuwait on 2 August 1990 appeared to surprise the Japanese government and others.[6] It did not take long for the three researchers at the U.S. Army War College in Pennsylvania to conclude that the United States and Iraq were heading toward a collision (Pelletier et al. 1990). The invasion should not have come as a surprise to anyone in Japan, for there, at least one week before it happened, the papers were reporting Saddam Hussein's plot to regain control of Kuwait under the guise of raising oil prices and sending troops to the Kuwait border.[7] Iraqis repeatedly showed interest in gaining control of Kuwait from King Ghazi in the 1930s and from General Abdul Karim Kassim in the 1960s. It is true that the United States gave mixed signals to Iraq, but, at the same time, it is impossible to deny that the State Department, headed by George Schultz, intensified its hate-Iraq campaign. This occurred exactly one month after the end of the Iraq-Iran War when Schultz blasted Iraq for its alleged use of chemical weapons against the Kurds. Pelletiere and his associates could find no evidence to support Schultz's allegation (1990:51–52). The mass media succeeded in convincing the public, not only in the United States but in much of the rest of the world, that Iraq used chemical weapons against its own people, the Kurds. It is sad and regrettable that we were so susceptible to government propaganda. The so called "free press" also failed to question the validity of Schultz's claim.[8]

This incident definitely signalled the end of U.S. support of Iraq, which was no longer needed to keep Iranian influence out of the Gulf region. Schultz feared that the security of the Gulf and Israel would be threatened if Iraq's power continued to increase. This fear became a salient element in U.S. Gulf policy. Then came President George Bush's swift and decisive action in reaction to Iraq's invasion of Kuwait. He demonstrated remarkable diplomatic skill in orchestrating the mobilization of multinational forces through the UN and other diplomatic channels. How did the Japanese react to this? Why did their reactions produce such disappointment to the Americans?

Japan's Reactions

Japan's new mood, pitted against a souring American attitude toward Japan, has produced the deepest split between the two countries since World War II.

Fortune (16 May 1991): 38.

Although *Fortune* magazine may have exaggerated Japan-U.S. relations in the aftermath of the Gulf War, no one can deny the disappointment of Americans who expected the full and swift cooperation of its allies, including Japan. In turn, the Japanese were disappointed as they had contributed a total sum of U.S. $13 billion by raising taxes—not an easy task in any democratic country.

The U.S. taxpayers picked up U.S. $7.4 billion of the conflict's U.S. $61.1 billion estimated costs. The rest of the money came from contributions U.S. officials successfully sought from Japan, Kuwait and other allies (*The Honolulu Advertiser* 29 July 1992:D-1).

In response to Washington's prodding, the Japanese government announced on 24 January 1991 that it would provide an additional U.S. $9 billion to support the multinational forces in the Gulf. Taxes were increased to about $74.00 per citizen to fulfill the promise. As it turned out, the Japanese government thought its payment was $9 billion in the current yen while the Americans thought of it in terms of dollars. As a result of the increased value of the dollar by the time the payment was made later that spring, the United States complained that it fell short by approximately U.S. $1 billion. After negotiation, the Japanese government promised to provide an additional amount close to U.S. $1 billion in aid to various agencies and organizations adversely affected by the war. The differences in expectations stemmed from public sentiment toward peace and war, and Article 9 (cited herein) of the Japanese constitution. The Japanese government interpreted the constitution to mean that "the exercise of the collective right of self-defense is not permitted" (Ito 1991:278).[9]

Renunciation of War

Article 9. Aspiring sincerely to an international peace based on justice and order, the Japanese people forever renounce war as a sovereign right of the nation and the threat or use of force as means of settling international disputes.

In order to accomplish the aim of the preceding paragraph, land, sea, and air forces as well as other war potential, will never be maintained. The right of belligerence of the state will not be recognized.

At the start of the Korean War, the United States asked Japan to develop what was to become the SDF, which was financed by the world's third largest budget of U.S. $30 billion per year to maintain 300,000 uniformed soldiers. The government's interpretation of Article 9 was that the SDF did not constitute a war potential because it was strictly designed for defensive purposes. Furthermore, it did not recognize military action as part of collective security while Japan maintained a collective security treaty with the United States.

In addition to this formal constitutional constraint in the use of military personnel abroad, Japan was concerned with its Asian neighbors' justifiable fears as well as strong pacifist sentiment that was ever present in the Japanese public.

Any efforts to amend the constitution in the foreseeable future appears extremely unlikely. Thus, Japan legally cannot employ any extensive use of its military forces even if it wishes to cooperate with the UN or the United States.

Area Specialists: West Asian and Islamic Scholars

Although the Gulf is vitally important to Japan as the supplier of 70 percent of its oil, Japanese knowledge of the Middle East remains scant, in spite of great strides made since the 1973 energy crisis (see Kuroda 1986a; Kuroda and Asai 1990). There are an increasing number of area specialists on West Asia in Japan whose reactions are interesting to note.

Many area specialists and Islamic scholars expressed their views on the crisis as it unfolded. By and large they were critical of Saddam Hussein but remained reluctant to go along with the United States' determination to use military force to resolve the crisis (see, e.g., Mutaguchi 1990). Most of them expressed optimism that the use of force could be avoided; perhaps the area specialists who knew the region did not want to see its destruction. Furthermore, the Japanese passion for pacifism made them hopeful for a peaceful solution rather than prompting any professional analyses.

Over two dozen specialists' views were expressed in a book entitled, *Chuto Wangan-senso to Nihon* (The Middle East: The Gulf War and Japan) edited by Japan's foremost scholar on the region, Yuzo Itagaki of the University of Tokyo (1991). In the book, several specialists (Takeshi Hayashi, Yoshiro Mutaguchi, and Masatake Matsubara) lamented the scant attention paid to Asian workers affected by the Gulf War. Yoshiko Kurita's comments deserve attention. She said that reactions to the Gulf War could be divided into two categories. First, Iraq invaded Kuwait in clear violation of international law and should be punished accordingly, even if that entailed the use of military force—the prevailing view in the West. Second, Kurita questioned who made the international laws and drew the national boundaries of countries in the region without regard for the inhabitants' right to self-determination.[10] What Saddam Hussein attempted to do could be interpreted as an anti-colonial rebellion against Western imperialist forces and their compradors. Kurita correctly generalized that most area specialists belonged to the second group. Then, she proposed that we should explore a third option. We must not forget that Saddam Hussein's government maintained oppressive policies against his people despite his stated objective to liberate the entire Arab world from Western domination. Kurita reminded her colleagues that one should not forget that any new order must be based on respect for the people of the Arab world (Itagaki 1991:25–29).

Asai and others expressed opposition to sending Japanese troops abroad. Twelve area specialists and Yuzo Itagaki, who emceed a gathering on the Gulf crisis on 3 November 1990, were unable to develop any specific joint statement upon which all could agree. Specialists noted that Japan had not sold arms to the Gulf region and made an analogy between Iraq's occupation of Kuwait and Israel's occupation of Arab lands. Islamic scholars such as Toshiro Kuroda disapproved of Saddam Hussein's aggression, as well as U.S. efforts to maintain the existing structure in the Gulf. Kuroda also strongly opposed Japan's positive response to the U.S. request to back war efforts in the Gulf. The views of these area specialists were largely based on their knowledge of the region, which separated them from the rest of the Japanese public who remained relatively uninformed about the region.

Mass Media

The Japanese media were unanimous in denouncing the Iraqi invasion of Kuwait. Japan supported the freeze imposed on Iraqi assets abroad and the enactment of economic sanctions. The press appealed for all nations to unite and end the occupation of Kuwait. The annexation of Kuwait by Iraq on 8 August 1990 was also condemned by all. Conflicting views appeared as President Bush mobilized multinational forces to first defend Saudi Arabia and later force the withdrawal of Iraqi troops from Kuwait.

At the outset, the press was uniform in its condemnation of Iraq's invasion of Kuwait. Later, however, the press became divided on the basic issue of how Japan should respond and Japan's role in dealing with the Gulf crisis. The *Asahi Shimbun* and *Mainichi Shimbun*, the nation's second and third largest papers took the pacifist view that Japan should not alter its constitution and should contribute to and cooperate with the UN within existing constraints.[11] The *Asahi Shimbun*, in its editorial of 23 August expressed opposition to the deployment of Japan's SDF to the Gulf. It did, however, support the provision of nonmilitary assistance including the dispatch of civilians to the region for noncombat duties.

The *Yomiuri Shimbun* and *Sankei Shimbun* disagreed with the position taken by *Asahi Shumbun* and *Mainichi Shumbun*. The *Yomiuri* is the largest paper in the nation with a nine-million plus circulation, while the *Sankei* is the second largest paper among the business and financial sectors. On 24 August (a day after the *Asahi's* editorial), *Yomiuri* suggested that the SDF be sent to the Gulf within the framework of Article 9. The *Sankei* was more forceful in arguing for the deployment of the SDF.

The *Asahi* maintained its basic position of nonmilitary contribution to the Gulf War efforts and urged economic sanctions as a means to resolve the conflict. Should the United States use military means, however, it recommended that Japan should not fully support the United States. Even after the war started on 18 January, the *Asahi* editorial questioned the need for military force. The United States did not exhaust all possible means to resolve the conflict peacefully as far as the *Asahi* was concerned. It questioned the validity of using armed forces to restore peace and stability in the region after the war was over (18 January 1991). The concern expressed in *Asahi Shimbun* was warranted as far as we can ascertain at the time of this writing in the fall of 1991. The region is anything but peaceful and stable. In its editorial on 18 January, *Yomiuri* admitted the premature use of military action while supporting the U.S. position in general. The press, in agreement with the area specialists, also urged the government to extend its assistance to refugees in the region.

On 4 March 1991, after the war ended, *Asahi* carried an editorial questioning the U.S. call for justice in the Gulf. If justice is what we are after, then Israel should be questioned for its occupation of the West Bank, the Gaza Strip, the Golan Heights, and Southern Lebanon, in direct violation of UN Security Council Resolution 242. The United States should also be questioned on its invasion of Grenada and Panama in violation of international law. It asked that the United States be more flexible, sensitive, and thoughtful in view of these related issues.

This contrasted with the *Yomiuri*'s praise for the United States, especially President Bush, on its decisive actions immediately after the war on 1 March. The *Yomiuri* did, however, note that some were critical of the use of military force. The paper questioned the public for its continuing belief in lonely pacifism. Michisada Hirose, an editorial writer for the *Asahi*, opined that the role of world police should be the responsibility of the UN (1991). The present lack of UN military forces requires the United States to assume the major role in any military action against aggression.

The wide differences in opinions expressed by the two largest newspapers in Japan were similar to some minority opinions in the United States, particularly prior to the outbreak of the war in January 1991. As House Majority Leader Richard Gephardt, who led the opposition to President Bush's efforts to use military means rather than wait for the effect of economic sanctions to prevail, stated: "Once President Bush made the decision the nation was fully behind him."[12] Perhaps this is the difference between American and Japanese views on the Gulf War.

Public Opinion

In a democracy, public opinion plays a dominant role in government policy-making. It is interesting to note what the public thought about the proper role of Japan in the Gulf War. The following are the results of some polls conducted regarding Japan's response to the Gulf War in Japan and the United States:

Poll 1

Kyodo Tsushin-sha, 31 August–1 September, 1990
(*The Hawaii Hochi*, 4 September 1990, 2)

Would it be appropriate for Japan to provide financial assistance to the multinational forces and send medical teams to the Gulf?

Appropriate	59%
No need to go that far	22%
That will not be enough	16%
Sending civilian personnel	27%
Mostly economic assistance	2/3
Against sending the SDF	83%
Help within the framework of the constitution	60%

Poll 2

A poll conducted after the Gulf War by Prime Minister's Research Office as cited by Ando (1991:31-32).

SDF participation in international peace-keeping activities within the constitutional constraints	45%
Opposed [22% for and 47% opposed 2 years ago]	37%
SDF for overseas natural disaster relief activities	54%
Opposed	30%

Poll 3

Kyodo News Agency conducted at the end of October 1990 as cited by Ito (1990).

In what form do you think Japan should contribute in the future to world peace and the resolution of conflicts?

Send not only money but personnel	55%
Send not only money but non-military personnel	45%

Poll 4

The *Asahi*/Harris Poll (June 1991) as cited by Hirose (1991).

Americans

How do you rate the role Japan played in the Gulf War?

highly/somewhat highly	13%
not highly at all	71%

During the Gulf War, Japan did not join in with the multinational forces giving constitutional restrictions as its reason. In the future, should Japan remove such restrictions from its constitution so that it can participate in wars such as the Gulf War?

should be removed	51%
should not be removed	31%
others/no response	18%

Japanese

How do you feel about the overseas deployment of the SDF?

No overseas deployment	21%
Support deployment if for non-military purposes such as disaster relief	46%

Take on a military role if under UN leadership   23%
Participate in such military actions as the
     Multinational Forces   5%
Other/No response   5%

Do you think that the clause in the Japanese constitution that re-
nounces all wars is accepted by the rest of the world or not?

Accepted   46%
Not accepted   41%
Other/No response   13%

Do you feel that the clause to "renounce all wars" should be strictly
adhered to or should it be interpreted flexibly?

Strictly   56%
Flexibly   35%
Other/No Response   9%

Poll 5

Nihon Keizai Shimbun's May 1991 poll as cited by Barbara Warner
(1991:6).

What is your evaluation of the role played by the United States
(Japan)?

	United States	Japan
Highly appreciative	5%	20%
Rather appreciative	27%	41%
Don't appreciate very much	33%	30%
Don't appreciate at all	29%	6%
Can't say	6%	3%

Is the United States (Japan) reliable now, or unreliable, when compared to before the Gulf War?

More reliable than before	22%	16%
No change from before	21%	42%
Less reliable than before	44%	35%
Can't say	13%	7%

Some of the percentages given do not add up to 100 percent for
two reasons: (1) In some reports, such as in the first half of Poll 1,
the percentage of those who have no opinion or have refused to respond are omitted; and (2) in some instances, such as the second
half of Poll 1, multiple answers were allowed.

It is safe to assume that about one-fifth of the Japanese public favored sending the SDF abroad within the framework of the constitution while a clear majority were opposed (Poll 1 and Poll 2). A dramatic change in Japanese public opinion occurred as a result of the Gulf War. The *Asahi/Harris* poll conducted in June 1991 (Poll 4) suggested that three-fourths of the Japanese public supported the deployment of the SDF in one form or another. The ratio of approval for SDF activities abroad increased sharply from one-fifth to three-fourths in less than a year as a result of the Gulf War.

A majority (61 percent) appreciated the role that the United States played in the Gulf War while one-third of the Japanese public (36 percent) did not (Poll 5). In terms of how reliable the United States was after the Gulf War compared to before the war, one-third of the Japanese public believed that the United States was less reliable than before the war (35 percent). Only 16 percent thought the United States was more reliable. These Japanese views appear strange and ungrateful to the Americans; however, there could be some explanations. First, the Japanese were still pacifistic in spite of their changed attitude toward the role of the SDF. The Japanese public, as articulated by the *Asahi* editorials, was opposed to the use of military means to resolve the conflict without first exhausting peaceful means, such as diplomatic and economic sanctions. Second, Japan thought that the United States was selective in its use of military action to punish Iraq while it continued to reward Israel for its occupation of the West Bank, the Gaza strip, the Golan Heights, and South Lebanon by providing U.S. $7 billion in aid annually, in addition to special housing loans for Soviet Jews. After all, UN Resolution 242, drafted by the United States and passed by the UN Security Council, called for the withdrawal of Israeli forces from occupied territories just as the UN resolutions called on Iraq to withdraw. Such two-faced actions appeared totally acceptable to the United States, a staunch supporter of Israel, but not to others.

In addition, what the Japanese and their government thought was a generous financial contribution was unappreciated by the United States (Poll 4). Seventy-two percent of the U.S. public did not appreciate Japan's role in the Gulf War and only one-third indicated its appreciation for Japan's contribution.

It should also be noted that there were a large number of anti-war demonstrations, petition movements, and letter-writing campaigns against the Gulf War in Japan both before and after the war broke out in January 1991. Many letters were from women, students, and ordinary citizens who wanted to express their disapproval of war as a means to settle an international dispute as their constitution stipulates. Some collected money to send Asian and other refugees, who fled Kuwait and were stranded in Jordan, to their home countries.

Whither Japan?

While the leadership in Japan and the United States definitely preferred the continuance of the present U.S.-Japanese security arrangement, the public in both countries thought otherwise as revealed in the *Wall Street Journal/Nikkei* poll of April-May 1990.[13]

Questions asked by the *Wall Street Journal/Nikkei* poll were as follows (Watts 1990):

Do you think Japan should continue to depend on the U.S. military for conventional and nuclear protection or should Japan build its own independent military system?

	U.S.	Japan
Continue dependence	22%	31%
Build own independent system	71%	40%
Neither	3%	18%
Don't know	4%	11%

Do you think Japan should or should not stake out a foreign policy that is independent of the United States?

	U.S.	Japan
Should	50%	44%
Should not	36%	17%
Don't know	14%	39%

A majority of Americans and a large plurality of Japanese believed that Japan should develop its own military system and pursue its own foreign policy objectives.

The reasons that Japan did not develop a foreign policy to meet its national interests are two-fold. First, Japanese leaders realized the bilateral relationship between the United States and Japan was of supreme importance. Second, Japan had a legitimate concern that its Asian neighbors would fear the development of an independent Japanese military system. Although Japan enunciated its independent Arab-Israeli policy in response to Arab demands following the 1973 October war, despite Kissinger's efforts to convince Prime Minister

Kakuei Tanaka to the contrary, Japan leaned more and more toward the U.S. policy of favoring Israel over Arab countries (Kuroda 1990).

As long as Japan continues its strong economic and security relationship with the United States, which thus far has proved beneficial to both parties, Japan is unlikely to develop an independent security policy despite the expressed desire of the public. As noted, area specialists in Japan also urged the public and the government to develop a foreign policy toward the Gulf region. The government was not likely to heed those pleas, at least not any that would seriously damage the U.S.-Japanese bilateral relationship. Because of different interests in the Gulf region, and for reasons cited earlier in this chapter, Japan will likely take policy stands that are independent of U.S. policies from time to time, but not to the extent that Japan jeopardizes its bilateral relationship with the United States.

One cannot deny that the Gulf War changed Japanese public attitude toward the SDF; the Japanese will likely continue their debate over the proper role of the SDF in the years to come. A rather lengthy book published on 23 June 1991 entitled *Sogoanpo to mirai no sentaku* (Comprehensive Security System and Futures Selection) historically traced Japan's security system and recommended some preferred futures for Japan (Eto and Yamamoto 1991:594–606). Among other things, the authors suggested that we think of security comprehensively: to use positive sanctions through nonmilitary and economic means to promote political stability; to develop democracy and the economy; and to amend the constitution to clearly reflect reality as it exists while maintaining the renunciation of war as a sovereign right.[14]

If Japan's aspiration for a greater political role in world politics is to become a reality, Japan should learn to be realistic in upgrading its diplomatic corp as it did earlier in beefing up its Ministry of International Trade and Industry to promote economic development.[15] Furthermore, it will be important for the Diet to encourage strong leaders who can effectively deal with foreign leaders. Japanese political culture makes it well-nigh impossible for any charismatic leader to rise.[16] The rule in the world political arena requires different qualities of political leadership than what is required for Japanese domestic leadership. The prime ministerial position is obviously not as powerful as that of the president. Japan could develop a stronger leadership if it selected a prime minister or a minister who was an effective and influential leader within the Liberal Democratic party.

For example, former minister of finance Noboru Takeshita kept his promise to increase the value of the yen after he made a commitment to do so at the New York Plaza Agreement in 1985. His position in the ruling party made it possible to keep his word. His former faction leader, Kakuei Tanaka, was a powerful prime minister who contributed significantly to the strengthening of the Diet members' position vis-à-vis that of the bureaucrats.

If, in the immediate future, Japan cannot develop an internationally active and effective prime minister, the best Japan can do without changing many structural and cultural constraints is for the ruling party to choose an influential leader who commands respect and who is familiar with Western political culture.

There were great expectations for prime minister Kiichi Miyazawa, who was well-versed in English language and U.S. culture, in addition to being an intelligent leader of a large faction when he first assumed his prime ministership in the fall of 1991. But he proved to be not as apt as many had anticipated.

For the first time since the end of World War II Japan sent its SDF to Cambodia in September 1992 for the purpose of a peace-keeping operation under the UN. This was an unprecedented event precipitated by the Gulf War experience. The fear expressed by concerned Asian neighbors, as well as Japanese in Japan who are worried about where this will lead Japan, is genuine. The Gulf War has forced Japan to think more seriously about its pacifist position and its proper political role in the new world order in the making.

Notes

1. The conference happened to coincide with the coup in the Soviet Union. The objective of the conference, appropriately enough, was to discuss the role of Japan and the United States on security issues in comprehensive perspective. The Japanese delegation was led by former prime minister Takeshita while the United States' delegation was led by House Majority Leader Richard Gephardt and included Senator William V. Roth, Representative Patricia Schroeder, Representative Leon Panetta, and Representative Neil Abercrombie. The conference was organized by Yasumasa Kuroda of the University of Hawaii and Takayoshi Miyagawa of the Center for Political Public Relations in Tokyo.

2. Our study of Arabic, English, and Japanese has revealed that the Japanese language is least direction-oriented while Arabic is most direction-oriented, with English being closer to Arabic. It should be noted that the

language in use seems to account more for this variation than the nationality of respondents. For example, Japanese thinking in English become more decisive while Americans thinking in Japanese become ambiguous. See Kuroda and Suzuki (1989, 1991).

3. A Jewish banker in New York loaned the Japanese government money to purchase ships and arms necessary to wage war against Tzarist Russia in 1904-1905. Jews were certainly happy to see Tzarist Russia defeated. Newspapers and magazines in Beirut and Cairo were filled with admiration for Japan's victory over European power. Nationalists in Asia were encouraged by Japan's victory.

4. It was probably an improper decision to send the SDF even for mine sweeping operations in response to a request from the multinational forces and not from the UN. Will Japan send a similar expedition if other nations make a similar request in the future?

5. According to the *Asahi Shimbun* poll conducted by Harris in early June 1991 among 1,000 Americans, the figures indicated a high level of dissatisfaction with the way Japan responded to the crisis. Those answering "rate highly" or "somewhat highly" accounted for only 13 percent while a high 71 percent rated "not highly" or "not at all" (Hirose 1991:4).

6. For example, Takashi Inoguchi (1991) describes how the Japanese government was taken by surprise. He further states that the U.S. government did not give any consistent indication of its signal to Iraq (see Gup 1991).

7. For example, see *Yomiuri Shimbun* (25 July 1990), Satellite U.S. edition, 4. On 26 July 1990 The *Daily Yomiuri* (p. 1) reported that Iraqi troops were sent to the Kuwait border while the United States launched military exercises with the United Arab Emirates and "pledged to stand by its friends" in the Gulf region.

8. The hypothesis that Iraqis did not use any chemical weapons against the multinational forces makes sense only if one realizes that Iraq did not use chemical weapons against its own people, the Kurds, as alleged by Shultz and U.S. mass media.

9. How such an interpretation can be consistent with the U.S.-Japan Mutual Security Pact signed as an integral part of the 1951 Peace Treaty remains a mystery to anyone who adheres to Western logic.

10. These two categories resemble Takashi Inoguchi's categorization of two lines of thought (1991:270-71): His categories are different from Kurita's in that area specialists tend to side with the position taken by King Hussein, PLO's Yassir Arafat, and others that the Iraqi invasion of Kuwait was illegal but that the problem should be resolved by Arabs. If that is possible, then international economic sanction, but not the use of force, would have been more appropriate.

11. This point has been made by many observers of the Japanese media, Hirose (1991) and Ando (1991). My remarks in this section draw from these

sources and others. Takehiko Kiyohara, chief editorial writer for the *Sankei Shimbun*, in his remarks in opposition to the thesis developed by Hirose, made a similar observation at the First Japan-U.S. Hawaii Conference.

12. This was one of the points Representative Gephardt made the first day of the Japan-U.S. Hawaii Conference.

13. Those gathered at the First Japan-U.S. Hawaii Conference appeared to see no reason to alter the present bilateral security agreement. The central topic of our discussion was the role of Japan and the United States on security issues. Neither House Majority Leader Gephardt nor former Prime Minister Takeshita mentioned any need for change. No one at the conference suggested any changes.

14. Yoshinobu Yamamoto, representing the Japanese scholar delegation, expressed similar views at the First Japan-U.S. Hawaii Conference.

15. Japan's diplomatic corp remains relatively small with a little over 3,000 diplomats, which is equivalent to the Italian diplomatic corp. One might note that the Ministry of Foreign Affairs has been given additional funds to increase the number of its diplomats in recent years. The number still remains pitifully inadequate, however, particularly in view of the lack of military power.

16. The Japanese political system discourages persons of strong personality to rise to the position of leadership for a number of reasons. This explains the paucity of internationally known political leaders in Japan in relation to other Asian countries. For more detail, see Kuroda (1988).

References

Ando, Mitsuru. "Japanese Views of the Gulf War" (English text) prepared for delivery at the joint meeting of the University of Hawaii's Summer Session and the Japan-American Society of Honolulu on 2 August 1991.

Daily Yomiuri, The (26 July 1990).

Eto, Shinkichi, and Yoshinobu Yamamoto. *Sozogoanpo to mirai no sentaku.* Tokyo: Kodansha, 1991. *Fortune* (6 May 1991).

Gup, Ted. "A Man You Could Do Business With." *Time* (27 February 1991): 50–54.

Hawaii Hochi, The (4 September 1990).

Hirose, Michisada. "Sogoanzenhosho no bunyadeno nihon to beikoku no yakuwari ni tsuite" (The Role of Japan and the United States in Security Issues in Comprehensive Perspective). Paper presented at the First Japan-U.S. Hawaii Conference of Legislators, Scholars and Journalists on 19–21 August 1991 at the Makena Resort, Maui Prince Hotel.

Inoguchi, Takashi. "Japan's Response to the Gulf Crisis: An Analytic Overview." *Journal of Japanese Studies* 17(2) (1991): 257–73.

Itagaki, Yuzo. *Chuto Wangansenso to Nihon*. Tokyo: Daisan Shokan, 1991.

Ito, Kenichi. "The Japanese State of Mind: Deliberation on the Gulf Crisis." *Journal of Japanese Studies* 17(2) (1991): 275–90.

Katakura, Kunio. "Narrow Options for a Pro-Arab Shift: Japan's Response to the Arab Oil Strategy in 1973." *Annals of Japan Association for Middle East Studies* 1 (1986): 106–149.

Kuroda, Yasumasa. "Japanese Perception of the Arab World: Their Nature and Scope." In *Japan and the Middle East in Alliance Politics*, edited by Ronald A. Morse, 41–55. Washington, DC: University Press of America (1986a).

————. "The Oil Crisis and Japan's New Middle East Policy, 1973." *Annals of Japan Association for Middle East Studies* 1 (1986b): 150–87.

————. "Leadership Recruitment Patterns in the Japanese House of Representatives: General Elections 1–30 (1890–1963)." *International Political Science Review* 9(2) (1988): 119–30.

————. "Japan and the Arab-Israeli Conflict." In *Japan and the Middle East*, ed. Edward Lincoln, 40–49. Washington, DC: Middle East Institute, 1990.

Kuroda, Yasumasa, and Nobuo Asai. "West Asian Studies in Japan." In *Middle East Studies: International Perspectives of the State of the Art*, ed. Tareq Y. Ismael, 174–99. New York: Praeger, 1990.

Kuroda, Yasumasa, and Tatsuzo Suzuki. "Language and Attitude: A Study in Arabic, English, and Japanese on the Role of Language in Cross-Cultural Thinking." In *Cross Cultural Thinking*, ed. Donald Topping, Doris C. Crowell, and Victor N. Kobayashi, 147–61. Hillsdale, NJ: Lawrence Erlbaum, 1989.

————. "A Comparative Analysis of the Arab Culture: Arabic, English and Japanese Language and Values." Paper presented at the Fifth Congress of the International Middle Eastern Studies, El Mechtel Hotel, Tunis, Tunisia, 1991.

Murata, Ryohei. "Keynote Address." In *Japan and the Middle East*, ed. Edward J. Lincoln, 4–8. Washington, DC: The Middle East Institute, 1990.

Mutaguchi, Yoshiro. "Kuweito kiki to nihon no apuroochi." In *Kuweito kiki o yomitoku*, ed. Yuzo Itagaki, 95–101. Tokyo: Daisan shokan, 1990.

Oki, Masamitsu. "Japanese Middle East Policy: Past, Present, and Future." In *Japan and the Middle East*, ed. Edward J. Lincoln, 60–65. Washington, DC: The Middle East Institute, 1990.

Orr, Robert M., Jr. "Balancing Act: Japanese Foreign Aid Policy in the Middle East." In *Japan and the Middle East*, ed. Edward J. Lincoln, 29–39. Washington, DC: The Middle East Institute, 1990.

Pelletiere, Stephen C., Douglas V. Johnson, II, and Leif R. Rosenberger.

Iraqi Power and U.S. Security in the Middle East. Carlisle Barracks, PA: Strategic Studies Institute, U.S. Army War College, (1990).

Takahashi, Kazuo. "Japan and the Gulf." In *Japan and the Middle East,* ed. Edward J. Lincoln, 50–59. Washington, DC: The Middle East Institute, 1990.

Wanner, Barbara. "American and Japanese Attitudes on Bilateral Relations: A Crisis in the Making?" *Japan Economic Institute Report* 31A (16 August 1991).

Watts, William. *Uneasy Eyes Across the Pacific,* Washington, DC: Commission on U.S.-Japan Relations for the Twenty-First Century, September 1990.

Yomiuri Shimbun, Satellite U.S. edition (25 July 1990).

Part II
The United States and
the New World Order

7
Between Theory and Fact

Explaining U.S. Behavior in the Gulf Crisis

Shibley Telhami

Competing Explanations of U.S. Behavior

The Iraqi invasion of Kuwait and the U.S. reaction to it have provided another occasion to "confirm" various theoretical propositions about U.S. policy. Few people take at face value the official explanation that international principles and the UN Charter were the driving forces behind the intervention of the United States. But just about every other school of thought about U.S. foreign policy found "evidence" in this crisis for its own hypotheses. The only exception is the proposition that U.S. policy was motivated by the advocacy of democracy: The nature of the Kuwaiti government before the invasion and after liberation, and the absence of democracy in many states that joined the U.S.-led coalition, rule out this proposition as a serious explanation. Clearly, it is not possible that all these theories hold.

In this chapter, I consider the conventional interpretations of the decisions of the United States following Iraq's invasion of Kuwait and leading up to the military attack on Iraqi forces. I suggest that a good case can be made for each interpretation, but in the end none stands up to the facts. Instead, I argue that the early U.S. decision to deploy forces in the Gulf was almost automatic; no matter who sat in the White House, or who had access to it, the decision would have been the same. Second, I argue that the decision to escalate the U.S. deployment in October 1990, which made war inevitable if Iraq did not withdraw, was ultimately caused by the inherent tension between the domestic and international context of U.S. policy in the Middle East, which was exacerbated by the major Israeli-Palestinian crisis during that month.

The "Oil" Explanation

What makes an assessment of U.S. motives difficult is that one can find some factual support for each argument, creating what James Kurth once called "a posteriori over-determination," with the problem being "not that there are no answers but that there are too many answers."[1] Consider the argument that oil was the primary motive for U.S. intervention, which seemingly lent support to some version of theories of imperialism that emphasize capitalist need for control of raw materials.[2] There is no need to document Western dependence on Middle East oil.[3] Many believe that had the region been blessed with cotton instead of oil, for example, the United States would not have intervened. Although U.S. leaders could not have been expected to advertise this motive prominently at a time when the United States was rallying regional and global backing for its efforts, U.S. officials did not refrain from referring to oil as an important U.S. motive. President George Bush referred to confronting the threat to Middle East oil reserves,[4] among other objectives, and Secretary of Defense Richard Cheney highlighted the economic importance of the Persian Gulf in testimony to Congress.[5]

This explanation has many things going for it: a theoretical foundation in theories of imperialism; a specifiable and quantifiable interest (Western dependence on oil); an apparent threat to that interest (Iraq's invasion of Kuwait); and evidence of U.S. perception of threat to that interest (in the domestic U.S. debate). Yet, this explanation suffers from serious drawbacks. Although the importance of Middle East oil to the West cannot be denied, the assertion that U.S. political and military dominance in the region is necessary to secure the flow of oil at reasonable prices is open to question. Evidence about patterns of trade in Middle East oil shows that states in the region sell oil and import goods independently of ideology and political-military alliances. The international market is a better predictor of these patterns.[6]

With regard to the supply and price of oil, it is not clear that an Iraqi takeover of the entire Arabian Peninsula, even if that were a serious threat, would have substantially affected the oil market in the long run. One reason that Saudi Arabia has had a commanding position in the international oil market is not so much its control of substantial oil resources, but its high resource to population ratio, which has meant that, most of the time, Saudi Arabia's production capacity exceeded its economic need. This excess has allowed the Saudis considerable leeway in dumping oil or withholding production. A lower resource to population ratio, as would have occurred with an Iraqi takeover, would have diminished that leeway.[7]

The behavior of Japan and some of the United States' European allies, who were considerably more dependent on Middle East oil than the United States, was indicative. With the exception of Britain, the early reluctance of these allies to take initiative against Iraq,[8] and their later reservations about the need to use force to compel Iraqi withdrawal, generated much resentment in the United States.[9] If interest in oil logically entailed Western intervention, how can this behavior be explained? Positing the Western interest in oil as the primary reason for the U.S. intervention is thus problematic. This does not exclude the possibility that, whether logical or not, U.S. officials perceived a need to intervene because of oil, although it is difficult to distinguish evidence for causal perception from evidence for instrumental arguments in the process of decision implementation. Still, oil has been central to the United States' view of the Gulf, and the role of oil must therefore be reconciled with U.S. behavior. I will address this issue in the concluding discussion of the prevailing pre-crisis paradigms regarding U.S. interests in the Gulf.

The "Israel" Explanation

Another prevalent explanation for the U.S. intervention was that Israel and its supporters in the United States were the primary reason for the use of force against Iraq. Commentator Patrick Buchanan's view of the role of Israel and its U.S. supporters was only one example of this view that found many adherents in the Middle East, even among Arab states that joined the U.S.-led alliance.[10]

Proponents of this explanation had many things going their way: A general theory about U.S. policy in the Middle East; substantial Israeli interest in seeing the destruction of Iraq's military machine; and a clearly stated preference by most advocates of a pro-Israel U.S. foreign policy for the use of force against Iraq.

At the theoretical level, many students of U.S. policy in the Middle East have suggested that strategic calculations cannot explain the strong pro-Israeli tilt, which has dominated U.S. foreign policy since the 1960s.[11] Instead, scholars have focused on the domestic component of U.S. foreign policy. Some argue that the pro-Israel inclinations are driven by well organized lobbies,[12] while others highlight the importance of issue-publics for U.S. policy in the Middle East.[13] In these perspectives, when major decisions that relate to Israel arise, the option that the United States chooses generally coincides with Israeli interests.

A review of Israeli statements and policies in the months before Iraq's invasion of Kuwait shows that Israel sought to highlight Iraq as a threat, especially after Iraq boasted of military capabilities and chemical weapons that were capable of reaching Israel. Moreover, Israel's supporters in Congress and the U.S. press were quick to focus attention on the perceived Iraqi threats. In congressional hearings, Representative Thomas Lantos (Democrat from California), among others, strongly criticized Iraq, its leaders, and the administration's policy toward it.[14] Similarly, pro-Israeli columnists such as William Safire, A. M. Rosenthal, and Charles Krauthammer were among the earliest to take the offensive against Iraq.[15] In the domestic debate in the United States, supporters of Israel were almost unanimous in their recommendation that the United States respond militarily to Iraq's invasion of Kuwait, even before most other Americans made up their mind.[16] So clear was the position of this group and so close was its correspondence to Israeli government positions that it prompted one conservative commentator, Patrick Buchanan, to suggest that they were merely reflecting Israeli interests.[17]

It was an important Israeli interest to see Iraq militarily destroyed— the sooner the better.[18] The Israelis also actively sought the intervention of the United States.[19] Moreover, the high correlation between being pro-Israeli and recommending military intervention makes it clear that Israel was an issue in the calculation. Does this not confirm the hypotheses that Israel was the primary reason for U.S. intervention?

There are also serious flaws with this argument; correlations, even strong ones, do not always entail causality. Typically, theories about the influence of the Israeli lobby on U.S. foreign policy imply that the link is stronger in Congress than in the executive branch, and more within the Democratic party than within the Republican. It was the president of the United States who first made the decision about the use of force, however, while Congress was hesitant and reluctant. Indeed, President Bush may have sought a UN decision on this question partly as a way to pressure Congress to support him. Also, Democrats were more inclined to oppose the use of force than Republicans in this case.

During Reagan's tenure, it was possible to ignore these facts and point to the strongly pro-Israel inclinations of the president. Very few analysts believed, however, that President Bush was similarly inclined, and his attitude toward Israel's request for U.S. $10 billion dollars in loan guarantees demonstrates that fact. Even before the Gulf crisis, Israeli officials complained about a new attitude in Washington.[20] By spring 1992, many in Israel and among Israel's supporters in the United States were accusing the president and his secretary of state, James Baker, of being anti-Israel.[21] These flaws in the theory that Israel was the primary motive for the U.S. intervention cannot be ignored.

The End-of-the-Cold-War Explanation

Another common explanation of the U.S. intervention had to do with the end of the cold war. In this view, the Gulf crisis was the perfect occasion to anchor an era of Pax Americana. Some versions of this theory even suggested that the United States may have misled Iraq into invading Kuwait, giving it enough rope to hang itself.

This theory, too, has some apparent merits: Had the crisis occurred during the height of the cold war, the United States would have been considerably less inclined to confront an Iraq fully backed by the Soviet Union. Moreover, the international coalition could not have been forged without Soviet support; and states like Syria would have been unlikely to join the coalition had the Soviets provided an alternative to the United States.

But this explanation merely makes the case that the end of the cold war provided new *opportunities* for U.S. foreign policy, not new *motives*. In the past, adherents of the school linking U.S. policy in the Middle East to the global distribution of power and U.S.-Soviet rivalry, posited the pro-Israel tilt in U.S. policy as a function of Israel's strategic utility against the Soviet Union. It follows that if the decline of the Soviet threat changed U.S. *objectives*, this change should have diminished the need for U.S. involvement and lessened concerns about threats to Israel. The 1980 Carter Doctrine, enunciated in the wake of the Soviet invasion of Afghanistan, which officially defined the Gulf region as vitally important to the United States, was based on the perception of a *Soviet* threat to that region. Many of the most important advocates of "realism" (both theorists and policy advocates) took positions against the U.S. intervention.[22] Others made the case that the end of the cold war called for an isolationist, not an interventionist, U.S. foreign policy.[23] Still other realists suggested that the only serious fear that the United States could have had from Iraq's invasion of Kuwait was the possible threat to

Israel.[24] A necessary and sufficient connection between the end of the cold war and the chosen U.S. policy course cannot thus be made.

Other Explanations

A brief survey of other theories about U.S. motivation shows that they, too, have their flaws. The argument that the U.S. military establishment saw the Gulf crisis as an occasion to fashion a new role for itself after the demise of the Soviet threat sounds eminently reasonable and finds some support in the theoretical literature about the link between the military establishment and imperialism,[25] until one confronts the facts: Many of the most senior generals, including the chairman of the Joint Chiefs of Staff, Colin Powell, were reluctant to use force.[26] The reasoning that the U.S. oil industry, assumed to be influential with a Texan president, was a major factor in the U.S. decision is equally problematic: Since when has the prospect of higher oil prices and diminishing supplies seemed threatening to oil companies?

New, seemingly plausible twists on old arguments of power politics were also presented as an explanation of United States behavior. For example, "Whatever else the Bush Administration is doing in the Gulf, it seems to be staking out a place for an economically declining United States vis-à-vis the economically ascendant but largely demilitarized European Community and Japan. . . . A U.S. victory—whatever that means—would assure the United States a central place at the world's bargaining tables alongside the new great powers, Germany and Japan."[27] Although an argument can be made about the beneficial consequences of the war vis-à-vis Europe and Japan, identifying this link as a primary reason for the United States' intervention is implausible, and it gives U.S. decision makers too much credit. Before the Iraqi invasion of Kuwait, the United States was too busy celebrating the defeat of communism to take serious notice of the economic decline.

Domestic political considerations were also offered to explain the administration's policy. Did Bush's popularity not climb to an unprecedented 90 percent rating immediately after the war? Yet, the decline of the president's popularity to only 39 percent by March 1992 was a reminder of the volatility of U.S. public opinion and the temporary impact of international crises on it—an impact that could always be outweighed by the risks entailed in the decision to go to war.[28] Even less plausible is the argument that it was Bush's character that explains his behavior—his chance to kick his "wimp" image.[29] It is peculiar to argue that a wimp does not behave like a wimp because he is a wimp![30]

Implications of Conventional Explanations

Most of the conventional explanations of U.S. behavior during the Gulf crisis have serious flaws. Yet it is still hard to believe that oil was not a factor, that Israel was not an important issue, or that the military establishment did not play an important role in the process. How does one square these issues with the facts of U.S. decisions? In the next section, I present an alternative explanation, an account of U.S. behavior that is based on some predictable dynamics, and that takes into account the possible role of these issues.

The proposed alternative explanation is not intended as a theoretical solution to the problem of over-determination pointed out by James Kurth.[31] The relative strength of this explanation lies in two areas: It overcomes some of the flaws of other explanations and, more important, it rests on more *minimal* assumptions than the other explanations. Put differently, *even without* any of the motives attributed by conventional explanations to the Bush administration in its handling of the Gulf crisis, few basic assumptions explain the administration's behavior. In addition, evidence presented about the regional sentiments before and during the Gulf crisis supports this explanation and challenges some of the widely accepted assumptions about the Iraqi-U.S. relationship.

U.S. Decisions During the Gulf Crisis

The Setting

It is useful to examine the origins of the tension in the Iraqi-U.S. relationship. The sudden end of the Iran-Iraq War left Iraq victorious and U.S.-Iraqi relations at their best in decades. The administration's policy was to maintain and consolidate economic and political relations with Iraq, but there were always critics of this relationship within Congress. Negative publicity about Iraq's use of chemical weapons against the Kurds contributed to the criticism. In addition, proponents of the "Israel" theory of U.S. foreign policy correctly pointed out that Israel's supporters in the media and Congress took the lead in criticizing U.S. relations with Iraq.[32] Most of this criticism, however, did not seriously affect the basic Iraqi-U.S. relationship until the beginning of 1990.

A series of Iraqi statements at the highest levels caught Washington's attention and generated serious concern about Iraqi policy. Especially troubling to U.S. officials was an important speech given by Saddam Hussein to the Arab Cooperation Council in Amman, Jordan, in February 1990.[33] The speech had its share of the type of rhetoric that usually mobilizes supporters of Israel, but other parts of the speech, echoed by other Iraqi statements, infuriated many U.S. officials, including those to whom Israel was not a central issue. In particular, Saddam Hussein warned his Arab colleagues about what he feared would be U.S. hegemony following the weakening of the Soviet Union. He challenged the presence of the U.S. fleet in the Persian Gulf, warning that "if the Gulf people along with other Arabs are not careful, the Arab Gulf region will be governed by the U.S. will," and suggested that Arab investments in the United States be moved elsewhere. "Just as Israel controls interests to put pressure on the US Administration, hundreds of billions invested by the Arabs in the United States and the West may be similarly deployed. Indeed, for instance, some of these investments may be diverted to the USSR and East European countries."[34]

Israel or not, these statements were bound to raise red flags in Washington and cause some rethinking about the relationship with Iraq. Throughout the spring of 1990 there were additional statements that appeared offensive to the United States, aside from the issue of Israel. Most of the popular media during that period focused on Iraqi utterances pertaining to Israel: the reported Iraqi missile and chemical weapons capabilities, Saddam's reference to his ability to "burn half of Israel," and reports about an Iraqi experiment to launch a satellite into space. Although Israel's supporters sought to generate public opposition to Iraq throughout this period, there was a real U.S. concern about potential Iraqi threats to the broader U.S. policy in the region beyond the question of Israel. By the end of the Arab summit conference in Baghdad at the end of May, it became clear that the Iraqi utterances earlier in the year were not mere aberrations, but were an indication of a broader Iraqi ambition. "No Israeli aggression against the Arab nation can be isolated from the desire of American imperialism in this regard. I use the word 'imperialism' only here. In fact I have not used this word for a long time. But when I saw a memorandum presented by the group working at the U.S. State Department, indicating that we should not use the word imperialism, I decided to use it."[35] Although some in the administration believed that the Iraqi-U.S. relationship was not beyond repair, and others assumed that many of Iraq's hostile remarks emanated from the U.S. position on the Arab-Israeli conflict, most had to be concerned. By then, U.S. congressional criticism of administration policy was growing, with members comparing Saddam Hussein to Hitler, even before Iraq invaded Kuwait.[36]

Although the administration did not move quickly to sever relations with Iraq, the relationship did not remain close and normal. The general perception in Iraq and other Arab states in the spring and summer of 1990 was not that the United States was "appeasing Iraq" but that it was preparing a campaign to destroy Iraq, either directly or through Israel. This perception was shared in many Arab states with many friends of the United States in the region, including Kuwait, who recommended a more conciliatory policy toward Iraq (some of these states later joined the anti-Iraq coalition).[37] In contrast to the current charge of U.S. appeasement, Iraqi newspapers wrote in June 1990 that the United States was "launching an unjust campaign against lofty Iraq."[38] The Baghdad Voice of the Palestinian Liberation Organization (PLO) concluded that "Washington and Tel Aviv are making preparation for new war."[39] Egyptian foreign minister Ismat Abd-al-Majid announced that "Egypt reaffirms its full support for Iraq and President Saddam Hussein against the arbitrary and unjust campaign to which Iraq has been subjected since 1981."[40]

The theory that the United States handed Iraq enough rope to hang itself does not hold even if the conversation between Saddam Hussein and the U.S. envoy to Baghdad, April Glaspie, days before Iraq invaded Kuwait was taken at face value. It is not likely, especially given the mood prevailing for many months, that Saddam Hussein's decision to invade Kuwait could somehow have depended on a single conversation with the U.S. ambassador. It is also not likely that this complex military and political operation could have been fashioned on the spur of the moment. There are many indications that Iraq expected a forceful U.S. response; the Iraqis had been saying for months that the end of the cold war would enable the United States to intervene more effectively in the region, as Saddam said in February 1990: "It has become clear to everyone that the United States has emerged in a superior position in international politics," adding that "the U.S. will continue to depart from the restrictions that govern the rest of the world throughout the next five years until new forces of balance are formed. Moreover, the undisciplined and irresponsible behavior will engender hostility and grudges if it embarks on rejected stupidities." Hussein concluded by warning his colleagues that "there is no place in our midst for those who fail to take note of recent developments that have added to U.S. strength, thus prompting it to the possible commission of follies against the interests and national security of the Arabs."[41]

Iraq's miscalculations, when they occurred, had to do not with the U.S. response but with Arab and Soviet responses. The Iraqis calculated that given the anti-Americanism that swept the region in the spring and summer of 1990 for reasons having to do with the Arab-Israeli conflict,[42] it was unlikely that vulnerable Arab governments would permit Arab cooperation with a U.S. military campaign against another Arab state;[43] and without Arab support a U.S. intervention would not succeed.[44] Moreover, it is plausible that Iraq, perceiving the anti-U.S. sentiment in the Arab world as a deterrent to effective U.S. intervention, devised a strategy to aggravate this sentiment on the eve of the invasion of Kuwait.[45] There is also clear evidence of Iraqi miscalculation about Soviet reaction.[46]

Even aside from the question of Israel, tension between Iraq and the United States was on the rise by the summer of 1990 and the administration was increasingly on the defensive in Congress and in the media over its policy toward Iraq. This mood set the stage for the U.S. reaction following the surprising Iraqi invasion of Kuwait.

The U.S. Reaction to the Iraqi Invasion

There were three different stages of U.S. decision making during the Gulf crisis, each decision resulting from different sets of considerations. The first stage involved the immediate decisions following Iraq's invasion of Kuwait on 2 August; the second stage concerned the decisions in October and November that led to a substantial increase in the U.S. deployment; and the third stage pertained to the final decision to use force. In discussing each of these stages separately, I make the argument that there were some predictable U.S. tendencies: In each case the decision preceded the full articulation of objectives, and each decision made the subsequent one more likely.

Stage I

The White House faced a dilemma following Iraq's invasion of Kuwait. The president had been on the defensive about his relationship with Iraq; he had failed to predict the Iraqi invasion of Kuwait; and he now faced the possibility of an Iraqi push beyond Kuwait, in a region defined by the United States as being vitally important.

Bush had to come up with an effective response; the question that remained was the type of response. Because the immediate problem was military, that is, the designs of Iraq's military forces and the immediate threat to other U.S. allies, the military and intelligence establishments were immediately called upon to provide an assessment. One must therefore consider the likely evaluations of those two communities following 2 August 1990.

The position of the military and intelligence establishments was uncomfortable. They had failed to anticipate the invasion of Kuwait or prepare to counter it. Even if they had not been on the defensive in a Congress that was advocating large cuts in their budget following the decline of the Soviet Union, it is not difficult to guess what their assessment would have been. Regardless of the military facts, military officers could not afford not to have assessed that there was a possibility that the Iraqis would move beyond Kuwait.[47]

Once the president was warned by his military advisors of the possibility of an Iraqi push beyond Kuwait, he could not avoid a decision to deploy U.S. troops. Had he failed to anticipate another Iraqi aggression and take steps to counter it, his presidency would have been in jeopardy. Thus the decision to deploy U.S. forces was almost automatic. It follows that the decision preceded a clear vision of the specific objectives of the deployment, which evolved as the crisis went on.[48] The question that remained was of size and shape.

The nature of the U.S. military deployment was decided quickly through procedural and institutional dynamics. The military establishment had concluded from the Vietnam experience that incremental interventions and extended wars are to be avoided. More recent to the experience of the president and some of his advisors were the conclusions of the Reagan administration about military intervention. Following the failed U.S. deployment of troops in Lebanon in 1982, the Reagan administration adopted a set of principles "to guide America in the application of force abroad." This policy included the following principles: (1) The United States should not commit its forces to military action overseas unless the cause is vital to its interest; and (2) if the decision is made to commit its forces to combat abroad, it must be done with the clear intent and support needed to win. It should not be a halfway or tentative commitment, and there must be clearly defined and realistic objectives.[49]

Once the decision was made for massive military deployment, the immediate problem became political rather than military. First, no matter how uncertain the administration was about actual Iraqi plans and intentions, as soon as a decision was made to intervene, the question became one of *implementation*. To implement as important and difficult a decision as the one that faced the administration required substantial domestic and international efforts; no matter how uncertain the facts may have been, selling the decision effectively entailed projecting certainty and probably involved exaggerations both in the domestic and the international arenas.[50]

Second, aware of the hostility of Arab public opinion to the presence of foreign troops on Arab soil, the Bush administration needed to establish both international and regional legitimacy for this deployment. The efforts to get the support of confused Arab states and other members of the UN were to be expected. The early international consensus was relatively easy to forge: Iraq's invasion of Kuwait was a clear violation of the UN Charter. It was highly unlikely that small states could acquiesce in the swallowing of a weak state by a powerful neighbor, and these states had incentives to agree with the United States. This explains the rapid and unanimous adoption of UN Resolution 660 condemning the Iraqi invasion on the same day the invasion took place, to be followed by Resolution 661 imposing sanctions against Iraq on 6 August.

Arab states such as Egypt, Saudi Arabia, and Syria faced a difficult situation. If they allowed Iraq to prevail they would have had to confront a more powerful Iraq in the region and fewer political restraints on the use of force by a militarily dominant Israel. If they went against the U.S.-led alliance and the United States prevailed, they would be on the losing side and suffer the consequences without an international protector. Thus, despite painful soul-searching and concern about the reaction of Arab public opinion, the U.S. effort in Stage I was likely to work.[51]

Reflections on Stage I

What analytical conclusions can be drawn from the U.S. decisions during Stage I? What variables accounted for those decisions? The implicit proposition of the account I offer, that the Bush administration had to respond forcefully to Iraq's invasion of Kuwait, is predicated on two assumptions: Washington and the U.S. public considered the Gulf region to be vitally important and Iraq was viewed as a threat even before it invaded Kuwait.[52] These two assumptions did involve oil and Israel, but not in the direct way that many imagine.

The United States regards the Gulf region as vital because of oil. When the crisis occurred, the United States acted like governments do in similar situations: It did not suddenly reassess whether the region was vital or not, but acted on the assumption that it was. Oil was the reason for how the United States defined its interest in the region, but not for the specific rational calculations pertaining to the crisis in August 1990.

The military deployment as the instrument of U.S. reaction was linked to actual Iraqi behavior. By surprising the international community, Iraq made it impossible for the U.S. military and political leaders to assume anything but the worst about its future intentions; this made a strong military deployment, as opposed to strictly political initiatives, unavoidable.

This analysis suggests that the early U.S. reaction to the Iraqi invasion of Kuwait was almost predictable even without reference to other objectives that the United States may have had, but it does not preclude the possibility that decision makers explored several possible goals from the outset of the crisis.[53] It does mean, however, that even without additional objectives, the early U.S. deployment of troops was likely.

Stage II

The deployment of U.S. troops in the Gulf during Stage I removed the immediate possibility of an Iraqi push beyond Kuwait. With the additional imposition of international sanctions against Iraq, there was no immediate urgency to use force. The general perception was that time worked against Iraq: The sanctions would take their toll economically, and even if a war had to be fought later, Iraqi forces would be weaker for lack of spare parts. Why then did the administration decide, in October and November 1990, to double U.S. troops in the region? I argue that the Arab-Israeli conflict was the primary reason for the U.S. escalation. That conflict, which was not to be "linked" to the Gulf crisis, did provide the linkage that led to the use of force.

The confrontation with Iraq during the first three months of the crisis was primarily political. Saddam Hussein's biggest weapon in the region was public opinion, and the most important issue in his hands was Palestine, the primary source of popular Arab hostility toward U.S. foreign policy. The Iraqi leader almost immediately attempted to focus regional and international attention on this issue and sought to highlight the U.S. "double standard" in applying UN principles to Israel and the Arab states.[54] Members of the alliance were determined to deprive him of this "linkage," and until October 1990 were successful in their efforts.[55]

But events on the Arab-Israeli front provided a serious challenge to the cohesion of the alliance and created a diversion from the Gulf crisis. Clashes between the Israeli police and Palestinian worshipers resulted in the deaths of seventeen Palestinians and the wounding of over 100 of the Haram al-Sharif (Temple Mount) in Jerusalem on 8 October 1990. These clashes created an unavoidable linkage between the Gulf crisis and the Arab-Israeli conflict, and provided the Iraqi leader with the weapon he sought: the focus of public opinion on U.S. policy toward the Arab-Israeli conflict. For much of October the events in Jerusalem replaced the Gulf crisis as the dominant news story as Arabs carefully watched U.S. behavior.[56]

The passage of the U.S.-endorsed UN Security Council Resolution 672 on 12 October 1990, constituted a diplomatic success for the United States. Even though it condemned "the acts of violence committed by the Israeli security forces" and requested the UN Secretary-General to submit a report to the Security Council before the end of October 1990, this resolution fell far short of the condemnation of the Israel in the resolution proposed by seven members of the Security Council on 9 October 1992, which also had the support of many U.S. allies.

Having averted a major confrontation with its Arab allies, some administration officials may have thought that the worst issue of "linkage" between the Gulf crisis and the Arab-Israeli conflict was now behind them. By 20 October, the United States was pushing through a draft Security Council resolution calling for the collection of evidence that crimes have been committed by Iraq, a move which was "seen by Washington as a way of shifting world attention away from the quarrel over Israel that has erupted in the United Nations."[57] This may explain a less urgent mood in Washington in the next few days. On 22 October, General Colin Powell told General Schwarzkopf that "ten days ago [the mood in Washington] was hawkish; in the past four or five days people have been talking about giving the sanctions time to work."[58]

But the crisis was not about to disappear as the Israeli government rejected UN Security Council Resolution 672. Given that the task pertaining to Iraq concerned the implementation of UN resolutions, Israel's position created tension in the alliance and charges of "double standards" in the Arab world.[59] In the meanwhile, clashes continued in Jerusalem, and on 24 October, UN Security Council Resolution 673 was unanimously passed; it deplored the "refusal of the Israeli government to receive the mission of the secretary-general to the region," and asked the secretary-general to submit his report as scheduled by 31 October. Within days, "Israel stoutly defied two unanimous Security Council resolutions . . . despite a personal appeal for cooperation from Bush."[60]

Although the consequence of the October Palestinian-Israeli crisis for Arab public opinion was hard to predict, several events in the Arab world were especially troubling from the point of view of the administration. The speaker of the Egyptian Parliament, Rifaat al-Mahjoub, was assassinated on 12 October 1990, the day that UN Resolution 672 was passed.[61] Perhaps more troubling was a statement by the Saudi defense minister, Prince Sultan Bin Abd-al Aziz, on 22 October suggesting the possibility of compromise with Iraq by granting it the islands of Warbah an Bubiyan—something that conflicted with U.S. policy.[62] On the same day, columnists Rowland Evans and Robert Novak, in noting the troubles in the U.S.-led alliance that were complicated by the Arab-Israeli conflict, stated that "the CIA is studying credible reports that Syrian President Hafez Assad's decision to send troops to join the coalition is causing serious political repercussions that might even produce an army-led revolt." Evans and Novak concluded: "This suggests that time may not be an ally as the sanctions noose tightens around Saddam. Time may prove to be the opposite as strains within the coalition threaten to pull it apart."[63]

The administration's dilemma was this: It needed to maintain the international consensus on the Gulf crisis, a task made difficult by the fact that the United States had not seen eye to eye with the majority of the members of the UN Security Council on Arab-Israeli issues. The United States used a veto against an international majority on several occasions in order to protect Israeli interests. This time too, most members of the UN Security Council were ready for tough measures against Israel. The United States could not go against the international consensus on this issue while maintaining the consensus on Iraq. The administration, however, faced an equally difficult domestic task in securing the support of a reluctant Congress and a divided nation.[64] This domestic task worked against the international task: Punishing Israel would have received international support, but would have generated congressional difficulties.

Faced with this unexpected crisis, the administration had to muster all of its diplomatic skills to maintain a delicate balance between the domestic and the international arenas as it managed to avoid an immediate breakdown. But U.S. ability to handle another intruding crisis on the Arab-Israeli front was diminished. Moreover, an immediate confrontation with Israel was avoided only through postponement: On 31 October, the UN secretary-general, as requested by UN Resolution 672, submitted his report to the Security Council, which called for the convening of the Geneva Convention to address the question of Israeli treatment of Palestinian civilians; this issue was not about to fade away. On the same day, General Powell telephoned General Schwarzkopf to give him the news: "The President has made a decision. Next weekend Secretary of State James Baker will come to ask King Fahd and our other allies to agree to offensive operations."[65]

In short, the outcome of the Israeli-Palestinian crisis of October 1990 was a clear U.S. conclusion: Time no longer worked against Iraq. The international consensus that was deemed essential for an effective strategy to compel Iraqi withdrawal may not be able to withstand another such crisis. Later, while testifying in the U.S. Senate Armed Services Committee, Secretary of Defense Cheney put it this way: "It's far better to deal with [Saddam] now while the [international] coalition [against Iraq] is intact, while we have the United Nations behind us, while we have 26 other nations assembled with military forces in the Gulf."[66]

As a consequence of these calculations, the timetable for a showdown with Iraq had to be accelerated. Even if a decision had not been made by then to use force, it could have reasonably been argued that additional troop deployments were necessary because the crisis had to be resolved soon, either militarily or politically, and either way, military deployment must be increased. If there was a chance that Iraq would withdraw peacefully, the display of military might would convince it to do so quickly. If the Iraqis did not withdraw peacefully, the coalition would have enough forces for a quick victory. The judgment that time now worked in favor of Iraq because of the political vulnerability of the alliance made the decision to increase troop deployment likely.

The decision to escalate the military deployment and the time table for a showdown with Iraq was thus primarily due to the inherent tension in the U.S. position on the Arab-Israeli conflict between domestic and international considerations. In this sense, the issue of Israel was central in the decision to speed up the confrontation, even as the United States was seeking to avoid any linkage between this issue and the Gulf crisis.

This conclusion does not preclude additional variables such as tactical military considerations that recommended escalation.[67] Because the bureaucracy was divided over the use of force, it is to be expected that those who favored military over political settlement employed additional tactical arguments. The administration could not afford to ignore the threat that the volatile Arab-Israeli conflict posed to the international consensus.

Stage III

Regardless of whether the settlement was to be political or military, there was a need to back the deployment of troops with international and domestic authorization for the use of force in order to project a "credible threat." Legally, the administration's position was that it already had the right to use force without additional UN resolutions. In the U.S. view, Article 51 of the UN Charter provided the necessary authorization. The administration also believed that the president had the authorization to use force without congressional action. The administration, however, needed a new UN Security Council resolution authorizing the use of force for political reasons. The administration hoped that such a resolution would persuade members of Congress to support its position;[68] convince Saddam Hussein that the threat was real; and provide an international cover of legitimacy if force had to be used.

Through diplomatic efforts, the administration secured international legitimacy for the use of force on 29 November 1990 with the passage of UN Resolution 678, which authorized member states cooperating with Kuwait to use all means available if Iraq did not implement Resolution 660 by 15 January 1991. This international consensus, which included the Soviet Union and France, helped make the case for congressional approval, which was obtained, with small and hesitant majorities, on 12 January.

Despite the appearance of more international than domestic support for the use of force, the motives in each case were different. The states that found it difficult to support the use of force against Iraq justified their support for Resolution 678 by arguing that it was the only way to convince Saddam Hussein that the international community was serious, thus making a political solution more likely.[69] There were no doubts about the United States' ability to use force successfully, and these states hoped that Iraq shared this assessment. Domestically, the picture was different. Most of those who opposed the use of force feared the costs of the military operation, and believed the military outcome to be uncertain. Following the successful military operation, many opponents of the use of force were quick to point out that, had they known how effective the military option would be, they would not have hesitated.

To the administration, calculations of uncertainty had to look different. The administration had access to superior tactical and strategic information about the configuration of forces in the Gulf that gave it much optimism about the outcome of military operations. By October, National Security Adviser Brent Scowcroft and Secretary of Defense Cheney became convinced that military operations could expel Iraq from Kuwait without much cost.[70] In making the case for the use of force, administration officials emphasized that a war in the Gulf, unlike in Vietnam, would be quick and decisive. Cheney, for example, argued that the outcome of the sanctions was uncertain, while the military option was certain to work.[71]

Although the military option seemed less risky to the administration, the political risks of extended sanctions and the uncertainty about future Iraqi influence, even if Iraq had withdrawn without war, made this option less desirable. Whether or not the president and his advisers decided that war was the preferred option earlier than January, the momentum must have been in the direction of the military option by November, because of the conclusion that time was on Iraq's side and because of the assessments of risks and uncertainty.

The final U.S. decision on the use of force was not independent from Iraqi behavior. Had Iraq pulled its forces from Kuwait before 15 January 1991, the U.S. calculations would have changed. It is clear that the Iraqis could not have been certain that the international sanctions and U.S. pressure would cease even if they had withdrawn. Perhaps contributing to the Iraqi uncertainty were leaked reports citing administration officials that the sanctions would continue even if Iraq withdrew.[72] Even if these reports were accurate, they did not necessarily indicate that a decision to use force had been made. Because there were proponents of the military option within the bureaucracy from the outset, the unnamed officials could have been acting on their own. Moreover, given the certainty of military victory, the only political option that the administration would entertain was one that made no concessions to Iraq. This explains the Bush administration's adamancy that Saddam Hussein not be given a "face-saving" solution along the lines suggested by Soviet envoy Yevgeni Primakov. Whether or not the administration had already made up its mind to use force, the political strategy would have been the same: It was up to Saddam Hussein to choose between political humiliation or military humiliation, because the administration could live with nothing less.

Whether the leaks about future sanctions were intentional or not, the Bush administration would have likely felt it politically necessary to continue to push for sanctions, with international blessing, even if Iraq had pulled out peacefully. Even after the destruction of much of Iraq's military and industrial capabilities, in addition to the liberation of Kuwait, domestic pressure continued for sanctions against Iraq and international support for sanctions continued as well. Had Iraq's military capabilities remained intact, the domestic political costs for the president would have increased, and Iraq's influence in the region would have remained a menace to U.S. policy. The military option thus appeared less risky than the economic and political options.

Concluding Reflections

My intention in this chapter was not to provide "inside information" that would "prove" specific U.S. motives in intervening in the Gulf. I do not believe that there is such proof. One of the remarkable things for someone who has spent any time in government is the extent of rationalization by policymakers and the prevalence of a posteriori reconstruction of reality that raises doubts even in the minds of the actors about their own original motives.[73] Memoirs by the key players in the Gulf crisis will no doubt shed light on specific facts, but they will be unlikely to resolve questions of motives and causality.

One reason for this reconstruction of reality is that decisions, once taken, create new realities and new realities recreate old realities. Whatever Egyptian president Husni Mubarak believed Saddam Hussein to be, on the basis of Hussein's prior behavior, Hussein became the devil only *after* Mubarak *decided* to join the U.S.-led coalition. Once Hussein became the devil, his prior behavior also became devilish. And no matter how uncertain the administration may have been about Iraq's ambitions beyond Kuwait, once a decision was made to confront him, the need to project certainty to mobilize support, hides one's own uncertainty, and maybe even alters it, as one begins to believe what one preaches. Similarly, whether or not the Saudis wanted Iraq's military capabilities destroyed at the outset of the Iraqi invasion of Kuwait, they came to prefer this outcome as soon as they decided to support the deployment of U.S. troops on their soil. Decisions, once taken, alter both perceptions of prior reality and the objectives that may have given rise to these very decisions.

Some of these alterations of perceptions and objectives take place within. The fact that before the decision one's mind may have been pulled in different directions makes it hard to live with a decision to choose one direction. I would expect that the stronger the "pull" before the decision, the larger the overcompensating reconstruction after the decision. Exacerbating this problem is the need to "sell" the decision to an equally divided outside world. Hesitation does not work, making exaggeration and alteration of perceptions necessary for successful implementation. Thus, what could be said about individuals could also be said about polities: No matter how split Congress and the U.S. people were on the issue of going to war, once the decision was made the vast majority rallied behind the decision.

Many policymakers are aware of the impact of decisions on others. It was clear that however undecided Arab leaders may have been about what to do, as soon as they made a decision to join the anti-Iraqi coalition, they showed no hesitation. Despite the knowledge about hostile Arab public opinion, it was clear that war and victory would create new realities, new perceptions, and new expectations.

The implication of all this for "explaining" U.S. behavior in the Gulf crisis is that analysis of motives and causality cannot be fully answered by reliance on memoirs and on the utterances of policymakers, although these too must be taken into account; one always needs some consistent analytical assumptions—the fewer the better.

My account of U.S. behavior during the Gulf crisis was based on some implicit assumptions. But before I specify and discuss these assumptions, it is useful to summarize my arguments about U.S. behavior. First, I have argued that rational calculations of economic interests during the crisis, the direct influence of the Israeli lobby, and the end of the cold war do not provide a satisfactory explanation of U.S. behavior. Second, I have argued that, although there were three important stages in the Gulf crisis, there were primarily two central decisions before the war: the early decision to deploy U.S. forces in the Gulf, and the decision to double these forces in October. I suggested that the early decision was almost "automatic"; no matter who occupied the White House, or what the ultimate motives of Iraq were, this was a predictable U.S. response. As for the second decision in October 1990, I argued that it was based on the conclusion that time now worked in favor of Iraq; the cause of this conclusion was the Palestinian-Israeli crisis, which accentuated the inherent tension between the domestic realm and the international realm of U.S. policy in the Middle East.

My explanation of the first decision rested on two implicit assumptions. It assumed that the Gulf region was viewed as vitally important because of its oil, and that a powerful Iraq was viewed as a potential threat. These assumptions were out there on the decision making shelves, constituting the de facto articulation of the "national interest." I have argued that the fear for the oil resources may now be exaggerated in light of the demise of the Soviet threat, but, nonetheless, this fear was the one on "the shelf," whether or not it reflected objective calculations.[74] This conclusion about the possible discrepancy between the operational "national interest" and the objective interests of the state suggests that there should be an ongoing debate about how policymakers define national interest, *before* crises erupt; these debates are not mere intellectual exercises. When a crisis erupts, policymakers often have to react quickly before a full debate leads to a new conceptualization of the national interest.

A second implicit assumption in my explanation was that Iraq was viewed as a threat; one wonders, for example, how the United States might have felt if Saudi Arabia had occupied Kuwait. What is the ultimate "basis" for this U.S. perception? Stephen Van Evera suggests that, ultimately, the fear of a powerful Iraq is primarily based on its potential threat to Israel.[75] Presumably, this fear has arisen over time as the United States has tried to reconcile its commitment to Israel with its other interests in the Middle East, and as domestic constituencies have built a case for it. By the time crisis emerged, this fear was in the background. But I have suggested that the fear of an Iraqi threat was also based on previous Iraqi behavior in the region, and on threatening statements by the Iraqi leadership that were unrelated to Israel. In any case, this perception of an Iraqi threat was there in the background.

How does one reconcile this threatening perception of Iraq with the conventional wisdom that the United States continued to "appease" Iraq up until the Iraqi invasion of Kuwait? I have suggested that this accusation does not match Iraqi and Arab perceptions of U.S. behavior in the spring and summer of 1990; Arabs, including Kuwaitis and Egyptians, believed that the United States was not appeasing Iraq, but targeting it on behalf of Israeli interests. Here too, perceptions and expectations both in the United States and in the Middle East are highly colored by the Arab-Israeli conflict.

I have also argued that the Palestinian-Israeli crisis of October 1990 explains the sudden escalation of U.S. deployment. This conclusion rests on another implicit assumption: The Arab-Israeli conflict accentuates the tension between the domestic and the international realms of U.S. foreign policy, which often translates into tension between Congress and the White House on matters related to the Middle East. The United States has had a tough time reconciling its commitment to Israel with its interests in the Arab world. The basis of this difficulty is not the commitment to Israel, but the continuation of the Arab-Israeli conflict. Only a settlement of this conflict will improve United States policy choices and reduce the tension between the domestic and international realms of U.S. policy in the Middle East.

My explanation of the October decisions pertained primarily to the question of timing; what could we have expected had the Palestinian-Israeli conflict not threatened the cohesion of the U.S.-led alliance? Would war have been avoidable? My argument, based on my implicit assumptions, has been that the United States had to prevail eventually, and that prevailing meant that Iraq would be humiliated either diplomatically or militarily; whether war would have been avoidable or not depended therefore on what Iraq decided to do. War remained a sure "win" for Mr. Bush.

This last conclusion assumed that the relative costs of the war to the United States were always acceptable. I have argued that this assessment of potential costs was never much in doubt. One may wonder, then, how in the U.S. public debates there were many serious people who worried about the costs. This discrepancy is partly explained by the tactical dilemma of the Bush administration: On the one hand it needed to portray Saddam Hussein as a monster who, if not stopped, could become the Hitler of the Middle East; on the other hand, it wanted to assure Americans that Hussein could be defeated quickly, and without much cost. In the end, there were bound to be Americans who believed one assertion over the other.

Notes

1. James R. Kurth, "A Widening Gyre: The Logic of American Weapons Procurement," *Public Policy* 19(3) (1971): 373–404.

2. For a good summary of theories of U.S. imperialism, see Thomas Weiskopf, "Capitalism, Socialism, and the Sources of Imperialism," in *Testing Theories of Economic Imperialism*, ed. Steven Rosen and James Kurth (Lexington, MA: D. C. Heath, 1974): 57–136.

3. For a nice historical account of the importance of oil, see Daniel Yergin, *The Prize: The Epic Quest for Oil, Money, and Power* (New York: Simon & Schuster, 1991).

4. "A Collective Effort to Reverse Iraqi Aggression," 22 and 30 August 1990, *Current Policy* 1296 (Washington, DC: U.S. Department of State, Bureau of Public Affairs, 1990).

5. Senate Committee on Armed Services, *Crisis in the Persian Gulf: U.S. Policy Options and Implications* (11 September 1990): 8–22.

6. See Shibley Telhami, *Power and Leadership in International Bargaining: The Path to the Camp David Accords* (New York: Columbia University Press, 1990): 72–75.

7. For an account of the possible implications of an Iraqi takeover of Saudi oil resources, see Stephen Van Evra, "The United States and the Third World: When to Intervene," in *Eagle in a New World: American Strategy in the Post-Cold War Era*, ed. Kenneth A. Oye, Robert J. Lieber, and Donald Rothchild (New York: Harper Collins, 1992): 128.

8. As Edward N. Luttwak pointed out, "It soon became clear that the supposed beneficiaries of the American effort to secure their oil supplies, Germany, Japan, and the rest of them, were (correctly) persuaded that the price of oil would continue to depend on the substitution cost . . . and not on who controlled the oil of the Persian Gulf. Hence they flatly refused to contribute seriously to the effort" (Edward N. Luttwak, "Saddam and the Agencies of Disorder," *Times Literary Supplement*, 18 January 1991: 3–4).

9. Japanese concern about Congressional criticism apparently led the Japanese government to warn its businesses not to actively seek Kuwaiti contracts. See Sam Jameson, "Japan Warns Its Firms to Go Easy on Kuwait Bids," *Los Angeles Times* (31 August 1990).

10. See, for example, his syndicated column "How the Crisis is Rupturing the Right," *Tribune Media Services* (25 August 1990).

11. See, for example, Joe Stork, "Israel as Strategic Asset," in *Reagan and the Middle East*, ed. Nassir Aruri, Fouad Mougrabi, and Joe Stork (Belmont, MA: Association of Arab-American University Graduates, 1983).

12. See, for example, Eric M. Uslander, "One Nation, Many Voices: Interest Groups in Foreign Policy Making," in *Interest Group Politics*, ed. Allan J. Cigler and Burdett A. Loomis (Washington, DC: Congressional Quarterly Press, 1986); and Hedrick Smith, *The Power Game: How Washington Works* (New York: Ballantine Books, 1988).

13. See, for example, Shibley Telhami, "Middle East Politics in the Post-Cold War Era," in *Beyond the Cold War: Conflict and Cooperation in*

the Third World, ed. George W. Breslauer, Harry Kreisler, and Benjamin Ward (Berkeley: Institute of International Studies, 1991): 293–314; and Jon Krosnick and Shibley Telhami, "Public Attitudes and American Policy Toward Israel" (unpublished paper, 1992, available from author, Department of Government, Cornell University, Ithaca, NY 14853).

14. For example, in a hearing on 4 April 1990, Representative Lantos, referring to Saddam Hussein, declared, "I am old enough to remember when another maniac in power in Germany spoke of eliminating hundreds of thousands or millions of children and women by poison gas. . . . I really wonder if there is anybody in this room over the age of 10 who has the slightest doubt that Saddam Hussein has no moral scruples whatsoever in unleashing chemical warfare" (Hearing before the Subcommittee on Europe and the Middle East of the Committee on Foreign Affairs, House of Representatives, 4 April 1990:41).

15. For example, on 4 May 1990 Safire criticized the Bush administration for doing business with "the nation that gasses its Kurds, develops missiles to develop binary poison gas warheads, and hangs a newsman who dared investigate a mysterious explosion" (*New York Times*, 4 May 1990: A35). Charles Krauthammer wrote on 27 July 1990 in the *Washington Post*: "Hitler analogies are not to be used lightly. . . . The time has come, however, to bestow the compliment on a tyrant who is truly a nightmare out of the 1930s: Saddam Hussein, president (soon for life) of Iraq" (A-27). It should be noted, however, that these columnists, although generally pro-Israel, have always taken hawkish foreign policy decisions and have generally supported military interventions in cases where Israel was not involved (Panama, Grenada, and Bosnia).

16. See, for example, commentaries by Rosenthal in the *New York Times* on 9 August 1990; and by Safire on 24 August 1990.

17. See Patrick Buchanan's column, "How the Gulf Crisis is Rupturing the Right," which appeared in several newspapers on 25 August 1990, and is reprinted in Micha L. Sifry and Christopher Cerf, *The Gulf War Reader* (New York: Random House, 1991): 213–15.

18. Van Evera, "The United States and the Third World," 129, points out that "Israel might be unable to defend itself against a single Arab regime that controlled both the oil wealth of the Persian Gulf and the human power of the eastern frontline states."

19. On 3 December 1990, for example, when it appeared that the United States was open to a diplomatic solution to the Gulf crisis, several ministers in the Israeli government warned of "the deep worry that they and most Israelis share that the United States might find a peaceful solution to the Persian Gulf Crisis that would leave Iraq's military power intact." (Joel Brinkley, "Top Israelis Warn of Deep Worry Over Diplomatic Accord in Gulf," *The New York Times*, 4 December 1990:A-13). Two days later, Israeli Foreign Minister David Levey was reported by *Haaretz*, to have told

the U.S. Ambassador William Brown that, "if the United States failed to confront Iraq militarily, Israel might attack Iraq" (Sabra Chatrand, "Israel Warns Against a Gulf Retreat," *The New York Times*, 6 December 1990: A-18).

Aware of Israeli interests, Arab allies of the United States, including the Saudis, who wanted to see Iraq stopped, were fearful that Iraq might be weakened too much to be able deter Israel (see Caryle Murphy, "Many Saudis Want Iraq Left Able to Deter Iran, Israel," *Washington Post*, 12 November 1990:1).

20. Israeli Foreign Minister Moshe Arens contrasted Bush administration policy with the policies of the Reagan administration this way: "The Reagan administration also objected to settlements, but did not make such a big issue out of it and did not highlight differences of opinion, as the incumbent Administration does" (FBIS-NES-90-091, 10 May 1990:27).

21. See William Safire, "Humiliating Israel," *New York Times* (2 March 1992): A-15; and A. M. Rosenthal, "Mideast: Forgotten Realities," *New York Times* (25 February 1992): A-21. In Israel, characterizing the Bush administration as being anti-Israel was common even earlier. Israel's radio, *Qol Yisra'el* (Voice of Israel) quoted Israeli government minister Rehav'am Ze'evi as having said "Bush is hostile to Israel, his policy smacks of anti-Semitism" (FBIS-NES-91-184, 23 September 1991:46).

22. Kenneth Waltz, the most prominent proponent of theoretical realism (see his *Theory of International Politics*, Reading, MA: Addison-Wesley, 1979), opposed military intervention in the Gulf. See Kenneth Waltz, "A Necessary War?" in *Confrontation in The Gulf*, ed. Harry Kreisler (Berkeley, CA: Institute of International Studies, Univ. of California, Berkeley, 1992): 59–65. Other proponents of realism also questioned the wisdom of U.S. intervention. See Robert W. Tucker, "Imperial Temptation: The New World Order and America's Purpose," *Council on Foreign Relations* (New York, 1992).

23. See Ted Galen Carpenter, "Bush Jumped the Gun in the Gulf," *New York Times* (18 August 1992).

24. Van Evera, "The United States and the Third World," 127–31.

25. As an example of the literature on the role of the military in foreign policy, see Paul Baran and Paul Sweezy, *Monopoly Capital* (New York: Monthly Review Press, 1966); and Michael Reich and David Finkelhor, "The Military Industrial Complex: No Way Out," in *Up against the American Myth*, ed. Tom Christoffel, David Finkelhor, and Dan Gilbarg (New York: Holt, Rinehart and Winston, 1970).

26. For an account of General Powell's reluctance to use force, see Bob Woodward, *The Commanders* (New York: Simon & Schuster, 1991). General H. Norman Schwarzkopf, commander of Desert Storm speculated that the "contingent of hawks in Washington" were mostly civilian: "These were guys who had seen John Wayne in *The Green Berets*, they'd seen *Rambo*,

they'd seen *Patton*, and it was very easy for them to pound their desks and say, 'By God, we've got to go in there and kick ass.' Of course, none of them was going to get shot at" (Quoted in *Newsweek*, 28 September 1992: 52).

27. Marcy Darbovsky, L. A. Kaufman, and Billy Robinson, "Warring Stories: Reading and Contesting the New Order," *Socialist Review* 21(1) (1991); excerpted in *The Gulf War Reader*, ed. Micah L. Sifry and Christopher Cerf (New York: Random House, 1991): 480–86.

28. In noting the presidential risks entailed in going to war, John Mueller pointed out that during the Korean and Vietnam wars, as casualties climbed from 100 to 1,000, support for the war dropped by 15 percentage points; as casualties rose from 1,000 to 10,000, support decreased by another 15 percent. Quoted by James Bennet, "How They Missed That Story," *Washington Monthly* 22, no. 11 (December 1990): 8–16.

29. For example, Elizabeth Drew suggested "that Bush was proving something to himself and the world—showing what a tough guy he is" (Drew, "Letter from Washington," *New Yorker*, 4 February 1991). For psychological approaches to U.S. behavior, see *The Political Psychology of the Gulf War: Leaders, Publics, and the Process of Conflict*, ed. Stanley Renshon (Pittsburgh: Univ. of Pittsburgh Press, 1993).

30. I do not here challenge the possibility that personal characteristics can account for some decisions in foreign policy, although, in this case, I find it difficult to discern what the behavioral implications of a "wimp factor" are. Ultimately, my argument is that whether or not Mr. Bush was a "wimp," his behavior would have been the same because of other overriding factors. For an interesting account linking Bush's personal characteristics to the Gulf War, see Jean Edward Smith, *George Bush's War* (New York: Henry Holt and Company, 1992).

31. Kurth, "A Widening Gyre," 373–404.

32. For example, Representative Tom Lantos, in criticizing the administration policy with Iraq, said "our government contributed richly to that Alice in Wonderland quality by treating Iraq as a very favored entity with all kinds of credits and grants and loans and what have you and leaning on our one dependable tiny beleaguered democratic ally with increasing ferocity" (Hearing of the Subcommittee on Europe and the Middle East of the Committee on Foreign Affairs, U.S. House of Representatives, 17 July 1990).

33. That the Amman speech was important is indicated by the audience (the presidents of Yemen and Egypt, and the King of Jordan), but also by substantial reference to it made by the Iraqi president in the Baghdad Arab summit conference in May; Hussein indicated that his analysis in Amman should be a basis for the discussions at the Baghdad Summit: "We will make the analysis we presented in Amman a basis for a brotherly and thorough discussion" (FBIS-NES-90-103, 29 May 1990).

34. Speech to the Arab Cooperation Council (FBIS-NES-90-039, 27 February 1990:4, 5).

35. Speech by Saddam Hussein to the Arab Summit Conference in Baghdad (FBIS-NES-90-103, 29 May 1990:5).

36. Telhami, "Middle East Politics"; Krosnick and Telhami, "Public Attitudes."

37. In my visit to Syria, Iraq, Jordan, Egypt, and the West Bank in May and June 1990, while on the staff of the chairman of the Subcommittee on Europe and the Middle East of the U.S. House of Representatives, this perception was conveyed in every place I visited.

38. FBIS-NES-90-124 (27 June 1990): 22.

39. FBIS-NES-90-118 (19 June 1990): 2.

40. FBIS-NES-90-095 (16 May 1990): 4.

41. Speech to the Arab Cooperation Council (FBIS-NES-90-039, 27 February 1990:2, 3).

42. In a report prepared following a visit to the Middle East after the Arab Summit conference in Baghdad at the end of May, I concluded that anti-Americanism at the popular level was approaching the anti-British sentiment of the 1950s; Iraq had become the most influential Arab state; and the personal popularity of Saddam Hussein had increased dramatically, despite his shortcomings. Driving Arab sentiment were the following factors: a perception that the Arab-Israeli peace process was dead, the tilt to the right in Israeli politics, a U.S. veto of a UN Security Council resolution on protecting Palestinians, a U.S. congressional resolution declaring Jerusalem the united capital of Israel, and Soviet Jewish immigration to Israel. The prevailing sentiment was concisely summarized by Ashraf Ghorbal, a former Egyptian ambassador to the United States: "Arabs are sick of their governments pathetically begging the United States to plead with Israel to please let them have peace" (interview, Cairo, June 1990). By the end of June 1990, following the suspension of the U.S.-PLO dialogue, even Kuwaiti newspapers were calling on the Arabs "to adopt serious and objective stands against the United States, which persists in a position hostile to the Arab causes" (FBIS-NES-90-122, 25 June 1990:22). Egyptian president Husni Mubarak also warned that "the biased U.S. positions will certainly return the region to dependence on the military option" (FBIS-NES-90-108, 5 June 1990:10).

43. In his speech to the Arab Summit conference in Baghdad, Saddam Hussein spent much time reminding his Arab colleagues of what the "Arab masses" wanted, concluding that "it is not possible to divorce popular matters from official and material ones" (FBIS-NES-90-103, 29 May 1990:3). Alluding to the power of Arab public opinion, Hussein declared in his Amman speech in February, 1990: "We are not thus out to antagonize or to incite public opinion against the United States. . . . However, America must respect the Arabs and their rights" (FBIS-NES-90-039, 27 February

1990). It is clear that by June 1990 there was a perception of internal vulnerability in Arab states that were friendly with the United States. Yassir Arafat said that he believed that even the Saudi government was facing some serious internal challenges (interview, Baghdad, Iraq, June 1990).

44. Despite his conclusion that the United States emerged as the undisputed global power, Hussein also noted that "All strong men have their Achilles' heel." His conclusion was that the Arab ability to stand up to a powerful United States depended on the extent of Arab unity: "All of us are strong as long as we are united, and all of us are weak as long as we are divided" (Speech to the Arab Cooperation Council, FBIS-NES-90-039, 27 February 1990).

45. It may not have been a coincidence, for example, that the planner of the Palestinian operation on the shores of Tel-Aviv in May 1990, Abu Abbas, was stationed in Baghdad and received Iraqi support. Although Yassir Arafat did not authorize this operation (interview, Baghdad, June 1990), the consequence of this operation was the end of the U.S.-PLO dialogue, which led to the aggravation of the anti-U.S. sentiment in the Middle East.

46. In an interview with Egyptian writer and former presidential adviser, Muhammad Hassanin Heikal, he told me he was phoned by Iraqi foreign minister Tariq Aziz during Aziz's visit to Cairo immediately following the Iraqi invasion. According to Heikal, Aziz had one thing on his mind: surprise about the Soviet reaction. Soviet envoy, Yevgeni Primakov, also reported that Saddam Hussein was surprised by the Soviet reaction (quoted by *Paris Europe Number One*, 28 April 1991, as reported in FBIS-SOV-91-083:11).

47. In his account of the crisis, General H. Norman Schwarzkopf, commander of Desert Storm, wrote that "Not until mid-September did we see a clear indication that Iraq was abandoning the idea of invading Saudi Arabia and assuming a defensive posture" (quoted by *Newsweek*, 28 September 1992:58).

48. For example, the president said on 8 August that the mission of U.S. troops was "wholly defensive" (George Bush, "The Arabian Peninsula: U.S. Principles," 8 August 1990). More specifically, Secretary of Defense Richard Cheney stated that the military mission was to deter attack and prepare to defend (United States Senate, Committee on Armed Services, *Crisis in the Persian Gulf Region: U.S. Policy Options and Implications*, 11 September 1990). These objectives changed in November when the United States began to pursue a military strategy of compellence, with the president declaring on 8 November that additional troops were needed for "adequate offensive military option."

49. Ronald Reagan, *An American Life* (New York: Simon & Schuster, 1990), 466. Using similar language, and noting that "Nobody wanted another Vietnam," General Schwarzkopf quoted General Powell as having

told him in October that "If we go to war, we will not do it halfway. The United States military will give you whatever you need to do it right" (quoted in *Newsweek*, 28 September 1992:59).

50. Viewed from this perspective, it is not surprising that members of the administration provided a variety of justifications for U.S. intervention: defeating aggression, oil, new world order, commitment to friends, and jobs. Moreover, given the international task, effective implementation of controversial policies demanded that bureaucratic hesitation, disagreements, or projections of uncertainty not be tolerated.

51. For an account of Arab calculations during the Gulf War, see Shibley Telhami, "Arab Public Opinion and the Gulf War," in *The Political Psychology of the Gulf War*, ed. Stanley Renshon (Pittsburgh: Univ. of Pittsburgh Press, forthcoming).

52. General Schwarzkopf indicated that military contingencies assuming that Iraq was an aggressor state were developed in the summer of 1989; "I thought of the many Arabs who had said I shouldn't worry about Iraq, and the few who'd said I should. I decided worrying was the prudent course." A war game based on this contingency, Internal Look, was played in July 1990 (*Newsweek*, 28 September 1992:54–55).

Red flags in Congress and the State Department went up primarily after the February speech by Saddam Hussein to the Arab Cooperation Council in Amman, Jordan. Although the administration had been accused of continuing to appease Iraq during the Spring of 1990, this was not the prevailing perception in the region, not only by Iraq, but also by Egypt and Kuwait. For examples of the Arab perceptions of U.S. policy toward Iraq, see note 44.

53. Woodward noted that the option of reducing Iraq's military potential was considered very early in the crisis. *The Commanders* (New York: Simon & Schuster, 1991): 290–96.

54. On 12 August 1990 the Iraqi president presented a proposal that linked the withdrawal from Kuwait to "the immediate and unconditional withdrawal of Israel from the occupied Arab Territories" (see FBIS-NES-90-156:48–49).

55. For a discussion of the evolution of Arab public opinion during the Gulf Crisis, see Shibley Telhami, "Arab Public Opinion and the Gulf War," in *The Political Psychology of the Gulf War*, ed. Stanley Renshon (Pittsburgh: Univ. of Pittsburgh Press, forthcoming).

56. A *Christian Science Monitor* reporter wrote that this Palestinian-Israeli confrontation "was an acid test of whether the Gulf crisis was about to become "Israelized." He quoted a Saudi close to the royal family as having said (in reference to UNSC Resolution 672) "If the United States had vetoed the resolution, even I would have burned my bridges with America" ("Saudis Uneasy Over Implications of War with Iraq," *The Christian Science Monitor*, 30 October 1990:1).

57. Paul Lewis, "U.N to Weigh Iraqi War Crimes Inquiry: The U.S. Wants to Shift Attention away from Israel" (*The New York Times*, 21 October 1990): 12.

58. Quoted in *Newsweek* (28 September 1992): 58–59.

59. On 18 October, for example, the Arab League urged the United States "to change its policy in order to favor the national rights of the Palestinians and Arabs and to halt aid to Israel" (*The New York Times*, 19 October 1990:13). The Arab League's resolution also called for sanctions against Israel. On the same day, the United States reportedly "expressed fears that any new punitive Security Council action against Iraq so soon after last Friday's vote condemning Israel might encourage Arabia and other third world countries to press the Council to take similar measures against Israel as well" (Paul Lewis, "Top 5 in UN Council Near Accord Over Claims Against Iraq," *The New York Times*, 19 October 1990:1).

60. Jackson Diehl, "Crisis Seen Hindering Israeli-Arab Peace Steps," *The New York Times* (30 October 1990): 16.

61. *New York Times* (30 October 1990).

62. Interview with Prince Sultan Bin Abd-al Aziz, *Riyad SPA* (22 October 1990) in FBIS-NES-90-206:22–23.

63. Rowland Evans and Robert Novak, "Coalitionitis in the Gulf," *New York Post* (22 October 1990): 17.

64. Colin Powell reportedly told General Schwarzkopf on 22 October: "I'm not sure we can bring more troops to the Gulf without a clear mandate from Congress and the American public" (*Newsweek*, 28 September 1992:59).

65. *Newsweek*, 28 September 1992:59.

66. *Washington Post* (4 December 1990): A-1 and A-34, quote on A-34.

67. Woodward points out that military deployment scheduled dictated decisions in October about future deployments. *The Commanders* (New York: Simon & Schuster, 1991): 298–99.

68. Even if the administration felt that it did not need legal authorization from Congress, there was a feeling that domestic support was required: One "principle" of intervention articulated by the Reagan-Bush administration was that the "actions we take will have the support of the American people and Congress. (We felt that the Vietnam War had turned into such a tragedy because military action had been undertaken without sufficient assurances that the American people were behind it)" (Ronald Reagan, *An American Life*, New York: Simon & Schuster, 1990: 466).

69. See reports of Soviet calculations in FBIS-SOV-90-229: 18–19.

70. Woodward, *The Commanders*, 303–7.

71. See testimony to Senate Armed Services Committee (3 December 1990).

72. *New York Times* (4 December 1990).

73. In one reflective discussion with a member of the staff of General

Colin Powell during the crisis, we both noted, to our relief, how the two of us agreed on certain interpretations of events, although because of an emerging outside conventional wisdom, each of us had begun to doubt what we both knew.

74. This conclusion is similar to the conclusion of Leslie H. Gelb and Richard K. Betts about the U.S. decisions to deploy in Vietnam: Conventional and unanimous interpretations of the "national interest" were that communism must be stopped in Vietnam, whether or not this position was objectively reasonable; as a consequence, "the commitment in principle always determined the scale of the commitment" (*The Irony of Vietnam*, Washington, DC: Brookings Institution, 1979:353).

75. Van Evera, "The United States and the Third World."

8
The New World Order and the Gulf War

Rhetoric, Policy, and Politics in the United States

Enid Hill

New world order became the catch phrase of U.S. policy in the Gulf during the crisis and war. It seems to have entered the vocabulary of U.S. foreign policy makers, however, largely by accident. As the story goes, in early August 1990, shortly after Iraq occupied Kuwait, National Security Adviser Brent Scowcroft, while discussing with White House press aides how to explain U.S. confrontation of Iraq, is reported to have said, "Tell them we can't just let Iraq get away with this—there is a new world order developing." Shortly thereafter a CNN correspondent came by. "We told her it's a 'new world order,'" one of the group said later. "She liked it, and 30 minutes later it was on CNN. . . . The philosophy came later."[1]

The "philosophy" that unfolded was heavy in rhetoric and light in substance. The new world order swung between something newly emerged (an international system without the cold war and the dangers of bipolar confrontation) and a condition that the United States as sole surviving superpower sought to establish. The latter interpretation implied a new era of peace where a benign internationalism would be imbued with liberalist values and institutions in rising democracies. What "internationalism" in actuality signified for U.S. policy in a world of unchallenged military superiority was made manifest in the Gulf War and its aftermath.

In the weeks and months following the creation of the idea of a new world order, the phrase appeared prominently in the rhetoric of President George Bush and Secretary of State James Baker when they sought to explain and justify the large-scale military involvement in the Gulf. In various public statements the implications of a new world order for U.S. foreign policy during the Gulf crisis were suggested. These statements, in turn, were given focus in the commentaries and critiques of media pundits and others. But, as usual, it is in the actions of states where the concrete meaning of policy is manifested.

Following the war, the interests of the United States and intentions for a new world order became intertwined with the forward planning of the U.S. military and with domestic politics in the 1992 presidential election campaign.

Bush-Baker Rhetoric

One month into the Gulf crisis, the creation of a new world order was specified as an objective in the Gulf, albeit in fifth place. Speaking to Congress in September 1990, the president said: "We stand today at a unique and extraordinary moment. The crisis in the Persian Gulf . . . offers a rare opportunity to move toward a historic period of cooperation. Out of these troubled times, *our fifth objective—a new world order*—can emerge; a new era . . . in which nations of the world . . . can prosper and live in harmony" (emphasis added).[2] This new world "struggling to be born" would be "quite different" from the one we had known, he said. It would be a world of peace, "where the rule of law supplants the rule of the jungle, a world in which nations recognize the shared responsibility for freedom and justice, a world where the strong respect the rights of the weak." The occupation of Kuwait by Saddam Hussein was the first assault against this new world.[3]

Secretary of State Baker said substantially the same thing during a news conference in Brussels while attending a NATO meeting: "We believe Iraq's unprovoked invasion and continued occupation of Kuwait is a political test of how the post–cold war world will work." He elaborated: It would be a test of "the institutions of collective security" or rather of Western security (NATO and the Western European Union), of how well they could be adapted to confront today's dangers and tomorrow's threats."[4] When the fighting ceased the following spring, the president then claimed that the "first test" of the new world order had been passed.[5]

Inherent in the idea of the creation of a new world order was the principle of countering aggression. The aggressor in this case was Saddam Hussein, a new Hitler, who was "trying to wipe a country off the face of the earth."[6] His aggression challenged "the better world that we all have hoped to build in the wake of the cold war."[7]

The fact remained, however, that Saddam Hussein was not just any aggressor nor Kuwait just any state. Important economic interests were at stake. U.S. audiences could be counted on to understand the importance of oil. "We cannot permit a resource so vital to be dominated by one so ruthless," Bush told Congress at the beginning of the crisis. Not only did Iraq control 10 percent of the world's proven oil reserves, with the addition of the fields in Kuwait it would control double that amount. Moreover, "an Iraq permitted to swallow Kuwait would have the economic and military power, as well as the arrogance, to intimidate and coerce its neighbors." The neighbors he was speaking of were those states that "control the lion's share of the world's remaining oil reserves."[8]

In March 1991, Bush again addressed Congress and spoke of "the world after war." Challenges unfortunately still remained: "Our commitment to peace in the Middle East does not end with the liberation of Kuwait." Echoing statements suggested by Baker a month earlier, Bush spoke of setting up "shared security arrangements" in the region and of the need "to control the proliferation of weapons of mass destruction." There were now "new opportunities for peace and stability in the Middle East." In spite of previously rejecting any linkage of the Gulf conflict with the Palestinian question, "a new momentum for peace in the Arab-Israeli conflict" was identified: "We must do all that we can to close the gap between Israel and the Arab states and between Israelis and Palestinians." In spite of having just rejected diplomacy as a viable alternative in the Gulf, for the Arab-Israeli conflict "there can be no substitute for diplomacy. A comprehensive peace must be grounded in UN Security Council Resolutions 242 and 338 and the principle of territory for peace. This principle must be elaborated to provide for Israel's security and recognition at the same time for legitimate Palestinian political rights. . . . The time has come to put an end to Arab-Israeli conflict."[9]

By March 1991, however, the Bush-Baker scenario for the world after the Gulf War clearly needed more substance. Groping for bearings in unknown territory, historical reference points suggested themselves. "Out of the horrors of war," said Bush, "two times before in this century . . . hope emerged for enduring peace." But both times it was proven to have been "a distant dream, beyond the grasp of man." Now there were changed conditions. What had been previously impossible could now take place. The UN was "freed from the Cold War stalemate" and was thus "poised to fulfil the historic vision of its founders." Winston Churchill's vision for the postwar world could be fulfilled: a world where "the principles of justice and fair play protect the weak against the strong" was now possible.[10] So much for rhetoric. To articulate and implement policy was another matter.

At the beginning of the crisis Bush had remarked that U.S. interest and involvement in the Gulf "is not transitory." He could not have spoken more aptly. U.S. interest in the area had indeed predated Saddam Hussein's adventure in Kuwait and "will survive it." There would be, Bush said, "a lasting role for the United States in assisting the nations of the Persian Gulf."[11] The new world order was thus not so new after all. It was to be a continuation of past interests and involvements.

In a statement to the House Foreign Affairs Committee in February 1991, Baker commented at length about "our ideas on post-crisis challenges and arrangements as we begin the process of examining what our policy should and will be in the aftermath of the crisis."[12] Although declining to "lay out a detailed blueprint" for the Gulf or the region as a whole, Baker indicated that it was clear to him what would bring "greater security for all" and "enduring peace." "What was needed for this vital region," he said, "are new and different security arrangements." The states of the Gulf and regional organizations such as the Gulf Cooperation Council (GCC) will be expected to "take the lead in building a reinforcing network of new and strengthened security ties." There was also a role for the international community, including the UN. Its role, said Baker, will be "to encourage such arrangements and to stand behind them." As for the United States, "we have deployed small naval forces in the Persian Gulf . . . ever since 1949." There have also been "strong bilateral ties" with Saudi Arabia and other states of the region that have included joint military exercises and provision of military equipment.

The particulars of the security arrangements would need to be worked out: whether to have local troops under the UN or the GCC, and how the international community could reinforce deterrence in the Gulf "through other political arrangements such as resolutions or security commitments." Having postulated the need for regional security using local capabilities with international additions, Secretary Baker specified "arms limitation" as a second challenge. He proposed "to change the destructive pattern of military competition and proliferation in this region and to reduce arms flow." A third challenge concerned economic reconstruction and recovery.[13]

Fourth on the list of the secretary of state was the need "to resume the search for a just peace and real reconciliation for Israel, the Arab states, and Palestinians. . . . Let's not fool ourselves, though. The course of this crisis has stirred emotions among Israelis and Palestinians that will not yield easily to conciliation. Yet, in the aftermath of this war, as in earlier years, there may be real opportunities for peace if the parties are willing. . . . We will be consulting and working very closely with our friends and all parties who have a constructive role to play in settling this conflict."[14] At face value there was nothing especially new here. Curiously, this last "challenge" did become part of U.S. policy in the months that followed.

In this statement to the House committee, Baker put the new world order in the context of being coincident to the new relationship of cooperation between the United States and the Soviet Union. In the new order, freedom and democracy would flourish "secure from the fears of the cold war." Free from such fears, Baker could see "more clearly than we could have ever imagined a year or even six months ago" a world "shaped by the United States of America and by its international allies." It is to be a world that is "a fitting place for free peoples to live [in]."[15]

In fact, it is the world once envisioned as coming into being after World War II. Although mention was made of burying the "spectre of Vietnam" in the desert sands,[16] this episode of U.S. foreign policy was not the main reference point for Bush and Baker. Nor could the containment of communism be a relevant policy for countering Saddam Hussein. Rather, the two world wars and their intended aftermaths of "collective security" provided Baker with more suitable analogies. Churchill is quoted in order to discount the viability of a policy of appeasement for dictators. The disaster avoided in the Gulf was not Vietnam but Munich! When he addressed the nation on 8 August 1990, immediately after the decision to deploy U.S. air and ground forces to Saudi Arabia, Bush likened the crisis to "the struggle for freedom in Europe." At that time "we and our allies remained stalwart." Now, "keeping the peace in the Middle East will require no less." As was the case with Hitler, there is again "an aggressive dictator threatening his neighbors."[17]

The order envisaged to come after the Gulf War was akin to the vision that had animated the founders of the UN in 1945. It had been aborted when the Soviet Union challenged the other wartime allies in their project of orchestrating postwar international relations. Liberated from cold war shackles, a revitalized UN would now finally be able to implement an international order of Wilsonian idealism, a world safe for democracy and for free peoples. No mention was made of that other Wilsonian principle, self-determination.

However well crafted were the statements that explained and justified U.S. actions in the Gulf, there were those in the United States, also intimately connected with the formulation of foreign policy, who were critical. First and foremost, of course, was the U.S. Senate, the constitutional partner of the president in making foreign policy. Although the principal spokesmen of policy endeavored to explain the aims and objectives of U.S. engagement in the Gulf region, members of Congress expressed both support and concern.

"War-Powers" and the Senate

In the wake of the Vietnam War and the civil disobedience and suspicion of executive deception and abuse of power that accompanied it, the War Powers Act was passed in 1973. It was a direct reaction to President Richard Nixon's unilateral decision to bomb Cambodia. By this law, the president of the United States was required "in every possible instance to consult Congress" before U.S. forces were committed to hostilities. Thus, when he committed troops to Saudi Arabia in August 1990 by presidential order, Bush "presented Congress with a dilemma." His action was tantamount to committing the nation to war without consulting Congress. By doing so, a "constitutional issue" was raised, said the official commentary of the *Congressional Quarterly*. Congress "repeatedly" raised the issue of presidential violation of the War Powers Act, but it did so "indecisively."[18] More than a year and a half later, the Bush administration continued to be unhumbled before Congress and the War Powers Act. When an emboldened Hussein defied UN inspectors in July 1992, Secretary of Defense Richard Cheney appeared on television, saying, "We always have the option, *if the President makes the decision*, to once again use military force to enforce those U.S. resolutions. We did it before. We can do it again" (emphasis added).[19]

The so-called War Power debate in the Senate, however, did underscore the fact that Bush's commitment of troops to the Gulf was a straightforward disregard of a duly enacted law. Moreover, to all intents and purposes this action was also unconstitutional. The framers of the U.S. Constitution had, "with studied care, . . . *vested the question of war in the legislature*," wrote James Madison, because "the history of all governments demonstrates that the executive is

the branch of power most interested in war, and most prone to it."
By deliberate intent, the Constitution had been framed to deny to
the U.S. president "the English King's power to make war on his
own."[20] Yet this was exactly what the president of the United States
had done. Notwithstanding the Constitution and the War Powers
Act, George Bush had unilaterally set the country on a trajectory toward war.

During the first few days following the Iraqi invasion, Bush
"pressed Saudi Arabia to ask for American troops." The Saudis responded on 8 August. The initial number of troops planned for deployment at that time was 250,000. The press was told 50,000. On
31 October, this number doubled but was not announced until after
the congressional election in November. Bush still insisted that the
mission of the United States in the Gulf was defensive. On 29 December, he gave the order to go to war at 3 A.M. on 17 January "if
Iraq had not withdrawn from Kuwait. Never at any moment in that
process did the President doubt his power to take the country into
war. Just before Christmas he told ambassadors of the 28 coalition
countries that *if he decided to go to war, he would do so whether
Congress and the people agreed or not"* (emphasis added).[21]

This action set a precedent for U.S. foreign policy. Whereas other
presidents had committed troops for brief actions, none had embarked on "such a massive offensive war" by presidential fiat. By
usurping the war powers of Congress, Bush accrued "more personal
power to make war than the leader of any other significant democracy."[22] In the light of such undeniable disregard for law and the war
powers of the Constitution, the performance of Congress was certainly lackluster.

When the Senate did eventually debate the war powers issue, its
mood was mainly supportive of the president's actions. Those who
voiced opposition expressed discomfort rather than outrage. Indeed,
the country generally seemed unconcerned about the fine points of
presidential law-breaking. *The Congressional Record* recorded dissent, but that dissent had no tangible effect. The resolution supporting the commitment of U.S. military forces in the Gulf passed overwhelmingly by a vote of ninety-six to three, demonstrating strong,
bipartisan support for the Bush policy in Congress, the intention of
the debate.

Reservations expressed by some Democratic senators are revealing, however. Senator Herbert Kohl, Democrat from Wisconsin, was
"less than pleased" when asked to assent after the fact to the presi-

dential movement of troops abroad. "The president may not like the War Powers [Act] but it is the law of the land, and one of the issues at stake in the Persian Gulf is respect for the rule of law." Kohl was also concerned about the conduct of U.S. foreign policy generally in the Middle East. "Over the past few years we have bounced from one policy extreme to another: We have shifted goals, altered alliances, modified the means we are willing to use. It is really time for us to figure out what our policy in the region is going to be. . . . Our nation has a need to develop a comprehensive and consistent policy in the Middle East."[23]

Senator Robert Kerrey, Democrat from Nebraska, approved of "the emphasis that the president [placed] on the role of the United Nations" and viewed maintenance of "the international consensus in support of our presence in the region" to be "a critical element" for the success of U.S. policy. But he warned;

> If there is one lesson . . . to be learned from this crisis, it is the fact that . . . the United States . . . has to realize that unilateral action will threaten seriously our own long-term security. . . . Only by promoting a truly international security system based on the rule of international law and the United Nations can our Nation hope to promote both our own and wider global security.
>
> The fact that the president has been sensitive to the need for responding to this crisis under the United Nations auspices and framework, has been a very important consideration in my support for his policy, . . . and is thereby making an important contribution in the long overdue requirement for strengthening multilateral responses to present and future crises.[24]

Senator Joseph Biden, Democrat from Delaware, found the policy debate "long overdue" because sending U.S. Armed Forces to the Gulf indicated the presence of a new U.S. doctrine: "Ten years ago, . . . President Carter articulated a doctrine that now bears his name. He said: 'An attempt by any outside force to gain control of the Persian Gulf region will be regarded as an assault on the vital interests of the United States.'" It was understood then that "an alien hand—at the time, a Soviet hand—grabbing control of this essential resource" could not be countenanced by the United States. Now President Bush had produced a corollary: "We will not permit an unfriendly Arab nation to control Gulf oil." The senator noted that this was "a dramatic shift in American foreign policy . . . a new

American doctrine to justify massive U.S. intervention in the Middle East."[25]

Senator Biden's main concern, however, was to ensure the preservation of the constitutional role of Congress to declare war. "Congress must have a role to play in authorizing the current deployment of troops," he said, as well as "any further action" in the Middle East. "Simply put," the Congress has "an obligation to approve sending U.S. forces into combat, if that unfortunate situation were to occur." He also counseled, "some guidelines for U.S. policy" should be set down "in order to clarify our objectives in the Gulf, and to provide signposts for future actions."[26]

Senator Ernest F. Hollings, Democrat from South Carolina, also was not happy with the situation. "In a time of crisis, such as we now face" he had serious doubts about "our evolving policy in the Persian Gulf." Although he supported the initial deployment to defend Saudi Arabia, he said, "we have now moved beyond that limited purpose." He did not believe "that preservation of Kuwait's territorial integrity and the emir's regime [was] of vital interest to the United States justifying the expenditure of American blood." Moreover, "such a war would have catastrophic consequences for future U.S. relations vis-à-vis the Persian Gulf and the nations of the Arab masses." Saddam Hussein "is not primarily our problem. He is the Arab world's problem."[27]

The president had already decided otherwise. On 8 August he told the United States that political leaders of the Middle East, Europe, and the Americas "all agree that Iraq cannot be allowed to benefit from its invasion of Kuwait." All agreed "that this is not a U.S. problem or a European problem or a Middle East problem: It is a world problem."[28] Nevertheless, the words and actions of the president *did* make it essentially a U.S. problem. Or rather, he made Saddam Hussein a U.S. problem; he did not take responsibility for what would happen to the people of Iraq.

Rationalizing the military buildup as the only viable response to an evil aggressor, a new Hitler, initially found support in the establishment press. The tone noticeably changed, however, when the large increase in the deployment of U.S. forces was announced in mid-November, which some were quick to interpret as indicating the administration's intention to go to war. As for the rhetoric about a new world order, it was obvious that the term needed to be spelled out in policy terms, that it was not a self-defining policy. What it portended for future policy remained wide open to speculation, and thus to criticism by the media pundits, academics, and anyone else who presumed to be an expert on foreign policy, like former presidential advisers Henry Kissinger and Zbigniew Brzezinski.

"A Slogan in Search of Substantive Meaning"

Before the Gulf crisis, there had been a need to rethink U.S. foreign policy. With the collapse of eastern Europe and the weakening of the Soviet Union, the erstwhile cornerstone of foreign policy that had served the United States for forty years—containment—had suddenly become outdated and irrelevant. Commentators had begun to notice the vacuum of policy and urged a basic reappraisal of foreign policy in the light of new international realities. At the same time, issues of U.S. involvement in the Gulf, first as crisis, then as war, and of its relationship to the new world order, conflated not into questions of what U.S. policy *should be* but rather *what it actually was.*

The enduring, historically conditioned divides of U.S. foreign policy—internationalism versus isolationism and idealism versus realism—were reflected in the commentaries on the Gulf War and the new world order. Also reflected were dimensions of conservative and liberal opinions. Not infrequently, when it is the Middle East that is discussed, the stereotypes of political opinion in other contexts do not carry over consistently. The benchmarks of conservative and liberal positions become confused.

Owen Harries, editor of the *National Interest* (a prominent mouthpiece for conservative, nationalistic trends in Washington), reassessed his initial support for the Bush handling of the Gulf crisis. "The policy now seems to me to be deeply flawed," he wrote. The thrust of his critique directly concerned what U.S. actions in the Gulf portended for a new world order. Had the president been serious about establishing a new way of doings things, he should not have set in motion the "immediate, unqualified, and unilateral commitment of American power" to achieve Iraqi withdrawal from Kuwait. Harries's point was not that the commitment of troops and war matériel was wrong, however. It was premature; thus it lost Bush the leverage to "get other countries to play their part." By ensuring that the United States would play the predominant role, he also made it inevitable that the United States would bear the major part of the burden. "If the president had really wanted to establish that the old way of doing things was yielding to a 'new world order' as he insisted he did, he should have made it clear at the outset that the days of leaving it to the United States to bear the burden of responsibility and leadership—to 'do the hard work of freedom'—were over."[29]

In short, the president was too eager to follow "the unhealthy American habit" of cold war days, not consulting anyone, taking control, "and then complaining bitterly that others were not backing it up and sharing the burden." But that was not the most serious result of U.S. insistence on dominance, according to Harries. "The country has become much more attached to its role of superpower and leader of the free world than it cares to admit."[30]

There was also "disproportion" in Bush's Gulf policy. Harries considers the number of bombs dropped to be out of all proportion "to the original provocation and its perpetrator." He finds it ironic in the extreme that such vast amounts of firepower were used in the "first year of the new world order." Most seriously, far from being "a decisive precedent for the new world order," the sheer size of the arsenal assembled and used to counter Iraqi adventurism in Kuwait "ensures that it cannot be a convincing precedent." Walter Lippmann's admonition about the importance of keeping "ends and means in balance" was called forth.[31]

The conservative stance reasserted its fundamental isolationist tendencies. In conclusion, Harries reminded us of how, historically, the Middle East had been treacherous for political careers. "From Napoleon to Anthony Eden, it is difficult to recall a modern Western statesman who, in the end, enhanced his reputation by taking initiatives in the Middle East."[32] The message was clear: since involvement in Middle Eastern affairs is a risky business, it is better to stay out.

Isolationism has deep roots in the United States. William R. Hawkins, a contributor to the *National Interest* wrote of those conservatives who, for forty years, "favored the vigorous projection of U.S. power abroad" but who, with the end of the cold war, questioned that position. "For some conservatives, it seems, containment of the Soviet Union . . . was the only goal that could justify a sustained American commitment abroad."[33]

There were those who, during the Gulf War, had been concerned about the effects on U.S. society of an overextended foreign policy. This position was expressed by a senior editor of the *National Review* in dissent from that journal's official position. "With the end of the cold war, conservatives ought to be redoubling their efforts to achieve the domestic goal of restoring a limited republic, not sacrificing this purpose to global empire."[34]

Conservative thought in the United States also has an interventionist-militarist dimension that was exhibited by the Bush government in the Gulf crisis. A brief description of its meaning for the new world order also appeared in the *National Interest*. James Kurth, professor of political science at Swarthmore College, found the "likely military and economic pillars of the new world order" to be very similar to "the world order set up in 1945." Specifically, he noted, "An American international security order could again be based on American high-tech weaponry—in this case smart bombs, precision missiles, and stealth aircraft—and the strategy of conventional deterrence."[35]

Veteran statesman of Middle Eastern affairs Henry Kissinger wrote of the new world order in the *Washington Post* several months after the war in the Gulf. He compared President Bush's definition of the new order—"emerging from the ashes of the Cold War"—to the principles proclaimed by Woodrow Wilson in 1914. But Wilson and Bush were not alone. Kissinger noted that "with few exceptions, all U.S. leaders since Wilson have shared the propensity to disclaim national interest as their motivation."[36] It is the usual lament of the political realist. But if Kissinger really thought that the president disavowed U.S. national interests, he did not listen very carefully. It was Bush's interpretation of the national interest that was at issue.

Kissinger was writing to recommend that what is needed is "a definition of national interest that commands consensus at home while accommodating the interests of other societies." There are now problems in both areas and Americans need to be reoriented to the new realities. For example, "the widespread perception that the Gulf War certified America as the last remaining superpower" is erroneous. The Gulf War did not signify "a new dawn for American predominance." It was, rather, "a glorious sunset of the cold war world." The belief that the United States is "the only remaining superpower" is an illusion. In the new order of things in the world, "power will be the nexus of political, military and economic assets"; thus the United States will be one power among others that are emerging in Asia and Europe. "The new order will be more like the European state system of the eighteenth and nineteenth centuries than the rigid patterns of the cold war." There will be six major states: the United

States, Europe, China, Japan, "whatever emerges in the Soviet Union, and probably India." There will, of course, be a lot of lesser states.

The United States must make major adjustments in its foreign policy, Kissinger believes, since the other major players will bring "somewhat different values and very different historical experiences" to the international arena. These experiences "bear little resemblance to how America has viewed the problem of world order." Collective security is not viable except in "the most overwhelming challenges to international order." Because the major players of the new world have such a "dramatically different background," there will be insufficient basis for collective security to work. The new preeminent states will not perceive threats identically, nor will they be prepared to run the same risks. New perceptions and policies to accord with the new era, Kissinger speculates, will require a redefinition of national security that includes a new concept of national interest. Such a concept should be "more discriminating in its purpose, less cataclysmic in its strategy and, above all, more regional in its design" than that of the cold war. "Any other approach will court progressive irrelevance."[37]

Where in all this is the Middle East, Dr. Kissinger? If economic assets are part of the nexus of power, the sources of oil should not be discounted. And in whose "regional security" zone are the oil-rich areas of the Gulf? Other writers spoke more directly about U.S. interests in the Middle East.

Zbigniew Brzezinski, national security advisor to President Carter, dubbed the post-cold war era as "the third grand transformation of the organizing structure and motivating spirit of global politics" of the century. Under existing conditions, he wrote, "a truly new world order based on consensus, rule of law, and peaceful adjudication of disputes" was still far away. Although such an order "may eventually become a reality," the phrase is presently "a slogan in search of substantive meaning."[38]

The present global situation is full of security challenges: "Naked ambition, lust for power, national uprisings and underdevelopment, are combining to create . . . destabilization and conflict, aggravated by the proliferation of weapons of mass destruction."[39] Brzezinski recommended "pragmatic nationalism" to deal with these "complex and dynamic circumstances" in this "third transformation of global politics." He identified "four large structural dilemmas" of the post-cold war world. One of these dilemmas is the Middle East.[40] "How will the Middle East be pacified? Can the United States, now so deeply absorbed in the Middle East's complex problems, afford not to promote energetically a framework of security and accommodation; or are the region's problems so intractable that the wiser course dictates a policy of cautious diplomacy?"[41]

The Gulf War was a direct consequence of the end of the cold war, Brzezinski postulated, a situation that allowed the United States complete "freedom of action" in the region. However, as a result of the war, the United States has been plunged "into a deep, probably protracted, political and military absorption in the Middle East's various crises." He questioned in particular whether the "preconditions for movement toward a solution of the Arab-Israeli conflict" have been created. Brezezinski saw this issue as "ultimately that of American political will to sustain and push forward the needed peace process"—not exactly a new revelation.[42]

In conclusion, Brzezinski issued a warning. The present "special status" of the United States in security matters "is threatened by its own domestic shortcomings" and its need of "domestic renewal." Retrenchment to domestic concerns is relevant to U.S. foreign policy and its interests abroad. "This will require a more subtle American contribution to sustaining global security than was the case during the Cold War. More emphasis will have to be placed on cooperation with genuine partners, including shared decision-making . . . [and on] widening and increasingly self-reliant regional cooperation."[43]

The assessments described all presume in one way or another that the United States will continue to be the preeminent enforcer of global security, albeit with "regional cooperation," in the new world order. The Gulf area, indeed the whole Middle East, is such a region. The future may produce a countervailing power, but at present there is no viable counterpart to U.S. military power. Thus, as Noam Chomsky wrote in January 1991, "The U.S. is completely free to use force arbitrarily, anywhere it likes. . . . Statesmen and strategic analysts [are] aware of this. . . . They talk about it. It's obvious."[44] The interesting question is not, however, how the United States can but *why it does* choose to use force when acting as guarantor of the new world order.

Chomsky's argument is that, in the world system of the new world order, "there is one very powerful military force" (the United States) and a "lieutenant" (Great Britain) with a "reasonably powerful military force." However, "neither of them is dominant economically" and both are "very weak politically." This means that they "try to shift the confrontation to the arena in which they are strong," that is, "they move the thing over into an arena in which [they are] likely to win" and, in the process, show that "force is the way you rule the world. That's the new world order."[45]

Diplomacy is not an option, according to Chomsky, as both the United States and Britain are "politically weak" because of "the policies they followed, particularly in the Third World." These policies are "extremely unpopular" creating such strong antagonism that it "even [turned] into overwhelming support for Saddam Hussein, a hated tyrant." Furthermore, Chomsky observed, "We look at ourselves as 'noble cause' and benign. They look at us as what Winston Churchill really was and a million other things like it. So diplomacy is not the strong card [and is why] the U.S. and England are politically weak."[46]

As for economics, the world is now tripolar: "Germany-led Europe, Japan and its periphery, and the United States." The U.S. economy, although still the world's largest, is declining and its decline has been worsened due to Reagan-Bush policies.[47] It is no longer a source of capital as "Germany-led Europe" and Japan are. But the Gulf oil producers possess capital, and therein lies the key to why Britain and the United States are so concerned with being the protectors of this region's security. That is why the "test" of the United States as military enforcer of the new world order occurred in the Gulf, rather than in any one of the half dozen other conflicts presently also disturbing world order.

That the Gulf is important to the United States because of its oil is not disputed. However, neither the United States nor Britain was desperate for the Gulf's oil at the time of the crisis. "What they really needed was the profits" from oil production which "tend to flow back to the American and British economies [by way of] treasury securities, U.S. financial institutions, . . . imports of American manufactured goods, construction companies, arms, etc."[48]

The Gulf region is clearly an exceptional case for the U.S. policy of enforcement of order in the post-cold war world. Moreover, the coincidence of interests between the United States and those states with present liquidity (Japan, the Gulf states, and "Germany-led Europe") has, in this case, turned the United States into a mercenary, for it also collected monies from them for the Gulf War. Although the United States is paramount militarily, someone must pay the bills for costly military adventures. Thus, future enforcement of the new world order using U.S. force will require a coincidence of interests.

A coincidence of interests continues in the Gulf, for nothing has basically changed with regard to the centrality of the Gulf oil to the developed, industrialized states as well as to the Gulf states. While the rest of the world is left to its own devices—to tear itself to pieces if it chooses in the name of ethnic purity or any other excess of national identity—the Gulf can count on continuing involvement. And as the region continues to rumble with the inconclusive results of the war, scenarios for new and future action in the Gulf area continue to animate the U.S. policymakers.

After the War: A New U.S. Policy for the New World Order?

During the Gulf crisis and war, the new world order appeared quite suddenly to have become the new foreign policy of the United States. Created in rhetoric and made palpable with military force, it was pressed into service provisionally to provide a foreign policy that could be sold to the U.S. public in place of the now irrelevant "containment." It was clear, however, that to be useful as policy in the future it needed more definition.

A year after the Gulf War—fought in the name of a new world order—*New York Times* editorial writer Thomas Friedman noted with nostalgia the "beauty of containment." Containment had a straightforward logic and served as a "seemingly easy guide for policymakers." It directed them to "what was important," "what was a threat to American interests," and "where they should put their resources." Its salience was that it defined U.S. foreign policy as "one central problem from which all others emanate and which could be used to galvanize the public."[49]

Containment of the Soviet Union and its surrogates had served the United States for more than forty years as its major pillar of foreign policy. It originated in an anonymous article published in July 1947 in *Foreign Affairs.* The author was soon named and acknowledged thereafter as George F. Kennan, who became head of policy planning in the State Department. The editors of *Foreign Affairs* today dream of the appearance of another "X," that is, "someone who can come along and write the single article laying down the architecture that will shape our foreign policy for the next 40 years."[50]

With the "driving force [of] the Soviet threat" gone, "we are cut loose from a lot of our certainties," said Les Aspin (Democrat from Wisconsin), chairman of the House Armed Services Committee. "We must ask ourselves first-principles questions which haven't been asked in 40 to 50 years."[51] It is agreed that the U.S. role in the world must be redefined. What is needed is "an affirmative purpose that will command domestic political support" not least for "the spending it would require to implement," said Harvard's Michael Sandel.[52]

The Gulf War did define the U.S. role in the world; it did provide an "affirmative purpose" if only briefly—for it was a short war. Both its role and its purpose were pursued, as discussed, in the name of a new world order ostensibly being protected or to be created. The end of fighting in Iraq, however, proved to be singularly inconclusive, and the situation that followed far from orderly. Indications of what U.S. foreign policy in the post–Gulf War world might mean began to emerge in various parts of the government. Opinions were far from uniform. Pronouncements, speeches, actions, and ditherings flowed from Bush and those around him as they reacted to the unsettled conditions in Iraq. The Pentagon created a plan for military preparedness. Disclosures appeared incidentally during investigations by congressional committees of what U.S. policy toward Iraq had been prior to the Gulf War and how it had been carried out. Rational policy formulation was not helped by the fact that 1992 was a presidential election year.

The survival of Saddam Hussein was definitely an embarrassment to George Bush and made his status as hero of the Gulf War politically problematic. His popularity evaporated like the morning mist as the public increasingly tuned out foreign affairs. People generally couldn't care less about a new world order except insofar as they believed it directly affected them. They were more engrossed in the problems of the domestic economy—widely believed to be a shambles. Standing on a record of foreign affairs became increasingly difficult during the 1992 presidential election year; however, foreign affairs and the need to articulate U.S. policy did not disappear.

At the same time, Saddam Hussein's defiance in the face of UN sanctions, restrictions, and inspections increased. Opposition groups in Iraq were in the news again. What would the United States do to restore order in other places of turmoil such as Bosnia? Comparisons were made of U.S. inaction in Bosnia and the great zeal for protecting order in Iraq. But that was not all. Reminders of another debacle of U.S. foreign policy in the preceding Reagan administration—"Irangate"—popped in and out of the news during the preparations to prosecute former Secretary of Defense Caspar Weinberger, implicated in the Iran-Contra affair. That affair concerned the indirect sale of U.S. weaponry to Iran and the use of the proceeds to supply arms to the Contras in Nicaragua. "Irangate" refers to the cover-up of involvement in this affair by members of the Reagan administration.

Meanwhile, a new cover-up—"Iraqgate"—was in the making. Disclosures formed a pattern of administration irresponsibility, if not malfeasance, in pursuing a policy of aid to Iraq before the war. The search for new skeletons in old closets occupied the press and several congressional committees during the spring and summer of 1992, although the disclosures seemed to have little effect on the general political consciousness or on the candidates. Bush dismissed it all as "pure politics." The larger question of an *overall* approach to foreign relations found articulation as neoisolationism in the country and among presidential candidates. Within the executive branch, planning for a new policy of unipolar militarism was uncovered.

"America First" or "America Only" in the New World Order?

During the primary campaigns in New Hampshire, a "reporter, not even an American, had the gall to stand up . . . and ask the candidate a question" about America's future role in the world. "My friend," answered the notoriously isolationist Pat Buchanan, "this campaign is not about the outside world. It is about the U.S.A."[53]

Selling "America First" was not original with Buchanan or his campaign. It had been the slogan of U.S. isolationists of the 1930s and 1940s, those who tried to prevent U.S. entry into World War II.[54] Not far beneath the surface of U.S. political culture is antipathy to foreign involvements. As the presidential election drew near in 1992, even George Bush, who liked to take credit both for victory in the Gulf War and the defeat of communism, seemed "embarrassed about his interest in the world."[55]

The other extreme was presented by Pentagon policy planners. In February 1992, documents emerged that set forth detailed plans for budgetary planning for the rest of the century. In these documents the Gulf War was characterized as "a defining event in U.S. global leadership" and its aftermath as a "new international environment."[56] The Pentagon clearly sought to justify the continuation of large military expenditures at least to the end of the century, to ensure that America retained its position as the "one and only unrivalled superpower. . . . We will retain the pre-eminent responsibility . . . for addressing those wrongs which threaten not only our interests, but those of our allies or friends, or which could seriously unsettle international relations."[57] The Pentagon did not intend that the United

States would be "the world's 'policeman' . . . righting every wrong," a role the documents explicitly rejected. Rather, "American interests" were to determine U.S. involvement in international affairs, and military reactions would be "selective."[58]

The "first objective" was "to prevent the reemergence of a new rival" and "to prevent any hostile power from dominating a region whose resources could, under consolidated control, be sufficient to generate global power." In order to do this, the United States must "establish and protect a new order that holds the promise of convincing potential competitors that they need not aspire to a greater role or pursue a more aggressive posture to protect their legitimate interests." It must "account sufficiently for the interests of the advanced industrial nations to discourage them from challenging our leadership or seeking to overturn the established political and economic order. . . . [And] we must maintain the mechanisms of deterring potential competitors from even aspiring to a larger global role."[59]

In the Middle East "our overall objective is to remain the predominant outside power in the region and preserve U.S. and Western access to the region's oil." Therefore, "It remains fundamentally important to prevent a hegemon or alignment of powers from dominating the region. This pertains especially to the Arabian peninsula. Therefore we must continue to play a strong role through enhanced deterrence and improved security."[60]

Also included in these Pentagon documents were scenarios for seven "hypothetical" future conflicts intended as guides for budgeting by the various armed services for the years 1994 to 1999. These "alarming scenarios" were characterized by Patrick Tyler of the *New York Times* as being designed for use by the Pentagon "to prevent further reductions in forces or cancellations of new weapon systems from defense contractors."[61] Although characterized as "illustrative and not predictive," the Pentagon planners nevertheless indicated which regions and what kind of disruptions the Pentagon would respond to with military force.

Prominence was given to a "hypothetical" invasion of Kuwait and Saudi Arabia by Iraq.[62] It was predicated on the possibility that sanctions would peter out and Iraq could rebuild its military forces and weaponry. Presumably learning from mistakes the last time around, Iraqi forces could "promptly take control of the oil fields and major export terminals in Kuwait and northeastern Saudi Arabia." The key difference in the 1990 invasion was that "the United

States would not have six months to mobilize and deploy a large army to the Arabian desert. . . . *The United States would respond with an immediate request to the governments of Kuwait and Saudi Arabia to come to their defense* with nearly five Army divisions, a Marine expeditionary force, 15 fighter squadrons and four heavy bomber squadrons and three aircraft carrier battle group" (emphasis added).[63] This would be, however, only the initial deployment. The strategy would be to "deter, defend, and delay" until reinforcements arrived.

There were other differences: No mention was made of any allies or coalition partners and no mention of any role for the UN. Note also in the last quotation that there is no pretense about asking the countries involved to request U.S. forces.

Just to make sure that there would be no substantial cuts in the U.S. military arsenal, another hypothetical scenario postulated the occurrence of an invasion of South Korea at the same time. As one expert remarked during congressional hearings, "If during the cold war we did not have to worry about fighting Iraq and North Korea simultaneously, why do we have to worry about it now?"[64]

Thus, while cutbacks of U.S. troops in Europe were planned along with a reduction in "the most expensive new weapons systems," the conflict scenarios envisaged that "the United States would need to keep aircraft carriers and their escort warships dispersed around the world to deal with potential trouble from the Baltic Sea to the South China Sea."[65] The intentions of the military planners could not be indicated more clearly. The U.S. military is to be relied upon to maintain world order and will be deployed to wherever in the world U.S. interests are considered to be threatened. The level of expenditure for the U.S. military arsenal (the Defense Department's "menu of weapons and forces") indicated that by 1995, "military budgets [would] have to grow by tens of billions of dollars a year."[66]

On being confronted with the Pentagon's draft proposal, members of Congress were "skeptical." An unsigned editorial in the *New York Times* commented, "For America to go it alone would be obtuse, expensive and dangerous. The administration better say so soon."[67] It did. White House and State Department officials strongly criticized the draft report and its assertion that the mission of the United States in the new era would be to prevent friend and foe alike "from competing with the United States for superpower status." One official was quoted as calling it a "dumb report . . . that in no way or shape represented U.S. policy." A senator called it "myopic, shallow and disappointing" and "counterproductive to the very goal of world leadership that it cherishes." Alarms went off in many capitals, and the State Department disavowed the document.[68]

In an op-ed piece in the *New York Times*, Secretary of Defense Richard Cheney challenged the contention appearing earlier under Patrick Tyler's byline, that the Pentagon documents were "a rejection of collective internationalism." Cheney denied "the absurd charge" that "we advocate a 'go it alone' defense strategy." Rather, he recommended "retaining our ability to influence the events that will most affect our security and freedom in the years ahead. This means recognizing the critical importance of America's world role and preserving the ability to fulfill it effectively." The difference would seem more semantic than substantive, a question of repeatedly mentioning "our allies" but still emphasizing the United States as a "global leader." Cheney particularly wanted to set the record straight about "our allies in Europe and Asia." To "forsake this leadership position and abandon our friends and allies at a time of global change" would be "a grave mistake." They are important to global military actions for peacekeeping, and they will be pressed "to take on a greater share of responsibility" in maintaining "international security."[69]

Nevertheless, the Pentagon documents had been clear about the nature of "our leadership" in relation to "our allies": "We will retain the pre-eminent responsibility for addressing selectively those wrongs which threaten not only our interests, but those of our allies or friends." And the United States "must sufficiently account for the interests of the advanced industrial nations to discourage them from challenging our leadership or seeking to overturn the established political and economic order."[70] Tyler had called this the "benevolent domination by one power."[71]

Although the White House and the State Department declined comment on the Pentagon documents, presidential contestants and members of Congress expressed opinions. Republican presidential challenger Pat Buchanan called the Pentagon plan "a formula for endless U.S. intervention in [other peoples'] quarrels and wars." The Democrats were, generally, for greater reductions in military spending and collectivism in international security. Senator Joe Biden criticized the report as "an inappropriate Pentagon instinct to erect a 'pax Americana'" supported by U.S. military power. An "advance in civilization" would be rather "a collective power through the United Nations." A campaign manager for Democratic presidential candidate Bill Clinton characterized the documents as "an excuse for big budgets instead of downsizing." Paul Tsongas, another Democratic presidential candidate in the primaries, called for "participation in a new internationalism truly based on the principle of collective security."[72]

The director of foreign policy studies at the Brookings Institution, John Steibruner, pointed out that the chauvinism of the policy advocated by the Pentagon was likely to produce exactly the effect that it sought to prevent. Taking the position that "no collection of nations can aspire to regional domination" would in itself set such nations "on a path of global rivalry with the American superpower."[73] In the words of Secretary of Defense Cheney, such an open bid by the United States for domination of a new world order, however benevolent, produced "reverberations around the world among our allies."[74] Pentagon spokesmen emphasized that this was not the final version; it was only a draft.

A revised document surfaced in mid-April. Gone was the controversial assertion that the major concern of U.S. security policy would be "to thwart the emergence of a new rival to American military supremacy." Rather, the highest defense priority was to maintain the post–World War II "system of alliances" upon which "sustained cooperation among major democratic powers" had been built. Instead of emphasizing that military planners should insure that the United States act unilaterally in future crises, the revised version "recasts American military preeminence as a catalyst—not an alternative—to collective action."[75]

Although the most provocative assertions of the February draft document had disappeared, many of the draft's "most sensitive passages remain implicit in the new document." The "sovereign right" of the United States "to defend vital interests unilaterally" was retained, and the military planners were still "directed to base budget requests on a set of seven classified scenarios depicting potential roads to war." There was no reason to believe that the scenarios, now more securely classified, had substantively changed. Other "sensitive assessments" of areas of impending crisis had also disappeared from the April version of the report. They would "still hold," Pentagon planners told the press, "But [we] preferred not to write [them] down."[76]

As though in contradiction to specifying scenarios of future U.S. military conflict, Chairman of the Joint Chiefs of Staff General Colin Powell reportedly wrote in a document accompanying the Pentagon draft report that "the real threat we now face is the threat of the unknown, the uncertain."[77] That is, one cannot predict what kind of hostile force will challenge the interests of the United States in the future. The underlying premise of Powell and the revised Pentagon report—one could call it the "Pentagon Doctrine"—was clearly that the use, or threat, of military force by the United States would be the future policy to maintain "world order."

Mr. Bush's Doctrine and Its Corollary

Foreign policy can be defined not only by what a country's leaders do but also by what they fail to do. The nonaction of the United States in the conflict in Yugoslavia is instructive as it further defines the policy ostensively designed to promote a new world order after the Gulf War. Ethnic conflicts in Yugoslavia were not viewed as a threat to world order; therefore, U.S. military involvement, or what one member of the press called the "Bush Doctrine," was not relevant. Bush's "doctrine," which surfaced as Croatians, then Bosnians, pressed the United States to intervene in their conflict, was "I don't want to send young men into a war where I can't see that they're going to prevail and prevail rapidly."[78]

To stop the bloodshed in Yugoslavia is obviously no simple matter, nor does it represent "the direct threat to U.S. interests that Iraq's invasion of Kuwait did."[79] Although direct U.S. military intervention in the Yugoslavian conflict may well be ill advised, the reaction of Bush, and the underlying premise of the Pentagon report—its "all or nothing" approach, its preference for the quick military fix—illustrated the gaping void in present U.S. foreign policy. What happened to diplomacy as an instrument for solving threats to world order? And where is the reasoned discourse of leadership in the world's self-appointed paramount state?

Lack of action in Bosnia seems to have made a mockery of the new world order "based on America's power, sense of justice and vision" or of a "unipolar world disciplined and shaped by American power" as the basis for the future. Writing in the *Washington Post*, Jim Hoagland asked, "How can Sarajevo happen in a unipolar world where America is all-powerful and wiser than others? . . . Bosnia shows that we do not live in a unipolar world." It also shows that the United States has devalued further "the coercive power of American diplomacy,"[80] and in doing so U.S. policy makers were indeed not very wise. The unwillingness, or inability, to use diplomacy was starkly demonstrated during the weeks preceding the war with Iraq when diplomacy was steadfastly rejected as an option. Ultimatums were stridently issued. "No negotiations" was repeated many times.

This "all or nothing" approach, "crush them in a week or don't get involved,"[81] invites a corollary to the "Bush Doctrine" of quickly in with military force and quickly out. Political issues will only be considered threats to world order within the scope of what the United States decides to solve, if there can be a clearly defined and easily executable military objective. Not only was diplomacy lost somewhere—perhaps in the oil-rich desert sands— but so was the conception of leadership based on diplomacy's adroit use.

Presidential Politics 1992 (I): The Continuing Problem of Order in the Gulf

In March 1991, Bush received a standing ovation from Congress at the conclusion of the Gulf War. This high point of his popularity was destined to decline. A year later, Saddam Hussein, the "Hitler" against whom the war had been fought, remained in power. As Bush's popularity ratings fell, Hussein became increasingly defiant. Meanwhile, revelations of how the Iraqi regime had acquired its military hardware and built defense industries, as well as the nature of these acquisitions, emerged from UN inspections and investigations in the U.S. Congress. Startling disclosures of hitherto classified documents concerning U.S. involvement in Iraq's military industries were revealed. These documents seemed to show that the Bush administration knowingly allowed Hussein to build up threatening military capabilities, including chemical and nuclear components.

To the politically dangerous revelations of congressional committees was added the embarrassment that Saddam Hussein continued to be the strongman of Baghdad. There were also pressures to assist opposition groups within Iraq. The Bush administration responded with "covert action" planning. In January 1992, plans to back an internal revolt to topple Saddam were reported in the *New York Times* and elaborated in two subsequent articles by Patrick Tyler.[82] Congress had been notified "last fall," he claimed, that increased covert actions in Iraq were undertaken by the administration and that these "intended to foment a coup against Saddam Hussein that could be supported by U.S. military forces if necessary."[83] The Saudis were said to be "pressing the Bush administration to organize a large covert action campaign in Iraq" with the aim of arming Kurdish rebels, Shia fighters, and Sunni opposition forces in order to "hasten Mr. Hussein's downfall while leaving the formation of a successor government clearly in Iraqi hands." President Bush was reported to be particularly eager that Saddam should fall "before November's election." In a statement to mark the first anniversary of the Gulf War, Bush praised "thousands of brave Iraqis who [were] resisting Saddam's rule."[84]

Tyler claimed to have been told by administration officials that the Central Intelligence Agency (CIA) was actively "working with dissidents in the Iraqi power structure." The goal of this "covert action" was "to divide the Iraqi military by building a network of opposition forces that could challenge Mr. Hussein's control of the countryside and ultimately challenge his stronghold in Baghdad." Saudi Arabia and Kuwait were said to be cooperating "both in financing . . . and in providing logistical support for whatever military or paramilitary operations might then evolve." New overtures to Kurdish clan leaders were reported as were claims of cooperation in these endeavors by Turkey and Syria.[85]

Some canny op-ed writers thought Tyler and the press were being "used" to create a "war of nerves," a dangerous and ill-advised game, because such tactics could well lead to real rebellions of Kurds and Shia.[86] Although Bush and his administration appeared to be encouraging civil rebellion in Iraq among Kurds and Shia to undermine Hussein's power, they were patently unenthusiastic about such groups ruling in Baghdad and were not ready to commit U.S. ground forces to help Kurd or Shia rebellions following the war in 1991. General Powell was reported to have warned that the success of U.S. military intervention in support of "an indigenous challenge to Mr. Hussein's authority" could only be assured if ground forces were committed.

Kurd or Shia opposition groups were clearly problematic from the U.S. point of view. Whether or not they would be indeed helpful in toppling Hussein, they were not viewed as likely candidates for a viable alternative government. And there were other considerations. If the Iraqi Kurds were encouraged too much, the Kurds in Turkey and Iran could be emboldened to join in fomenting rebellions in their own states and to seek an independent Kurdist state. As for the Shia, their natural links to Iran were feared by some to contain the seed of an Islamic fundamentalist movement, which could lead to another Islamic state. Given such views of the hazardous nature of "indigenous" rebellions, the administration's statements of encouragement could hardly be other than ambiguous. The kind of opposition that U.S. officials *did* take seriously, and which they were vocal in encouraging, was rebellion within the military. This too was admittedly problematic because ultimately "they had to start asking themselves what they should do if it happened and Iraqi units pleaded for U.S. help, including military intervention." However, "having finally asked the right question, they apparently have not figured out an answer."[87]

General Powell gave an answer, reported Tyler. The United States "could support a coup by Iraqi military units if the Iraqi commanders asked for air support and other help in advance" although a large number of combat troops "would have to be sent back to the region to insure success."[88] There was no getting around it; the top military strategist insisted on ground troops if there was to be military intervention in support of any opposition movement. This policy was not what Bush wanted to hear during an election year when the electorate was turned off by foreign policy.

Meanwhile, the Iraqi regime became increasingly obstructionist and prevented UN inspectors from identifying and destroying nuclear and chemical warfare installations.[89] Reports out of Iraq noted that attacks on the Shia in the southern marshlands had been stepped up since March.[90] The Bush administration dithered over how to react, or whether it should react at all. Inaction won, for the moment. Some administration officials said that military force would be necessary "to eradicate Iraq's remaining capacity to make weapons of mass destruction." The more politically minded let it be known that a new U.S.-led attack was unlikely "because of the political debate it would stir" in a presidential election year and it would be seen as "a crass attempt to garner votes."[91] Nevertheless, by August the political damage of inaction was obviously calculated to be greater than some kind of reaction.

An "air exclusion zone" south of the thirty-second parallel "to protect Shiite Muslims in southern Iraq" from attacks by Hussein was declared, and flights to enforce it (from the USS *Independence*) began on 27 August.[92] The temptation to label it "political" was great. "It shows the lengths to which George Bush will go to win reelection, and how far his foreign friends will lean to help him," wrote Leslie Gelb in the *New York Times*. A "new element" was said to allow the flights, the introduction of "fixed wing aircraft" into the south. But helicopters had been used for eighteen months "to slaughter the Shiites," wrote Gelb. A "deeper reason" was attributed to administration officials. They sought "to face the highly nationalistic Iraqi military with a choice between preserving the unity of the country and retaining Saddam."[93] Preventing continued genocide in the southern marshlands was not, it seems, the driving force behind the new involvement.

Nor in truth was the sudden revelation, reported by "Bush aides," that "Iraqi Shiites are more 'Iraqi' than 'Iranian' so that the allies can safely aid the Shiites without actually splitting this territory from Iraq," wrote Gelb. Rather, the crucial element that catalyzed the new policy occurred in presidential election politics: "Bill Clinton pulled way ahead in the polls and Mr. Bush began searching . . . for a magic campaign bullet." This columnist was not, however, opposed to the Bush administration "getting tough" with Saddam. He found it a demonstration "that crass political motives sometimes lead to good foreign policy."[94]

While the Bush administration wavered throughout the spring and summer of 1992 on whether, and how, to become directly engaged with the issues of Hussein and the opposition groups inside Iraq. Congress and the press were investigating how Iraq's ability to threaten world order and U.S. interests had come about in the first place. Why had the "Iraqi dictator" been allowed to grow into such a "menace"? "The answer to that question . . . is shocking," wrote Anthony Lewis in a *New York Times* editorial, "Who Fed This Caesar?"[95]

Presidential Politics 1992 (II): Investigations of Bush's Prewar Iraq Policy

The continuance of Saddam Hussein in power after the Gulf War was not the only indicator of a failed Bush policy or the only embarrassment deriving from U.S. relations with Iraq in an election year. It became increasingly clear from the many classified documents made public through congressional investigations that the war was testimony to a glaring failure of the Bush administration's prewar policy and how it had conducted its relations with Iraq. Bush cried politics, "pure gut politics," as the disclosures multiplied in the spring and summer of 1992, but most investigations had started before the election campaigns.

Congress began exercising its powers of oversight over the executive branch on matters related to the Gulf War and U.S. policy toward Iraq shortly after the war's end. From early 1992, revelations from congressional investigations and hearings multiplied. They included matters related to the conduct of the war and disclosures that the U.S. prewar relationship with Iraq had greatly helped Hussein build his military strength. There were other disclosures about the Patriot missiles being less successful than had been claimed.[96] Reports from the UN Special Commission in Iraq to supervise the destruction of Iraq's weapons indicated much less success in destroying Iraq's Scud launchers than had been claimed.[97] A bipartisan congressional report of the House Armed Services Committee, released 23 April, claimed there had been as much as a four-to-one advantage, that at the time the allied forces numbered roughly 700,000 the Iraqis had as few as 180,000.[98]

Combined with election year politics were "genuine concerns about the policy failure before the invasion." The wisdom of the Bush-Baker policy was questioned, that is, whether "Mr. Bush [could] have avoided the war if he had moved to restrain rather than reward the Iraqi leader earlier." There were also assertions that the administration policy of "supporting Iraq before the war was not only misguided, but criminal."[99]

"Almost every Monday" during February and March 1992, Democratic Representative Henry Gonzales of Texas, "the feisty chairman of the House Banking Committee," read "more classified documents into the *Congressional Record* than anyone since the Vietnam War" and, in the process, constructed a picture of corruption and coverup. These documents portrayed a complex web of relationships and dealings of questionable legality on the part of Iraqis, U.S. government officials, and private U.S. companies. The authority for these dealings was the Bush administration's policy of pursuing "improved economic and political ties with Iraq"[100] generally and as mandated in National Security Directive 26 signed by Bush on 2 October 1989.[101]

Why was the chairman of the House Banking Committee interested in Bush's Iraqi policy? Congressman Gonzales entered the arena of U.S. prewar relations with Iraq through the investigation of the "Bank Lavoro scandal." Bank Lavoro was the Atlanta branch of the Italian Banca Nazionale del Lavoro (BNL). Centrally featured in some disclosed classified documents was a scandal involving "a massive fraud to pump billions of dollars in illegal loans and credits out of BNL-Atlanta, far above the amounts reported to the Federal Reserve." The scandal first surfaced when bank documents were seized in August 1989 in a raid by the Federal Bureau of Investigation (FBI) and Federal Reserve officials of the Atlanta branch of the

BNL.[102] The case had been prepared and the Atlanta prosecutor was ready to bring an indictment in January 1990. The record set forth in the congressional disclosures indicated the possibility of interference from the Justice Department as well as telephone calls from staff inside the White House. Indictments had been postponed for a full year.[103]

The Commodity Credit Corporation (CCC) of the Department of Agriculture, which had granted credits to Iraq, was also involved. Officials in the Agriculture Department were alleged to have known in October 1989 that "their $1 billion a year CCC program was riddled with corruption."[104] On 13 October 1989, a meeting of lawyers and other officials of the CCC took place. The minutes of this meeting reportedly stated that "although additional research needs to be done, it appears more and more likely that C.C.C. guaranteed funds and/or commodities may have been diverted from Iraq to third parties in exchange for military hardware."[105]

There was also evidence of loans having been provided "to various U.S. firms for the illegal export to Iraq of missile-related technology."[106] At the 13 October meeting, "top legal officials of the Agriculture Department" were also aware, it was claimed, that "payments required by Iraq of exporters wishing to participate in the Iraqi market may have been diverted into acquiring sensitive nuclear technologies."[107]

Congressman Gonzales accused administration officials of "conflicts of interest" and "failure to pursue diligently the circumstances of loan guarantees to Iraq by both the Export Import Bank and the Commodity Credit Corporation." There was also the matter of "making false and misleading statements to Congress."[108]

Evidence of influence and pressure exerted by government officials was uncovered. Officials in the departments of State, Commerce, and Agriculture and in the White House were involved. This course was taken purportedly in the interests of maintaining Iraqi friendship and thereby exerting influence over Hussein. Bush was quoted as explaining that "the United States originally tried to help Iraq because of its war with Iran." After the Iran-Iraq war ended in 1988, the administration sought "to bring Iraq into the 'family of nations.'" Bush also "repeatedly" said that aid "provided to Iraq to counterbalance Iran [was] a way to stabilize the Middle East."[109]

At issue was not just a policy gone awry due to poor judgment or lack of foresight. Bush and other officials were accused of hiding behind "a cloak of national security" to avoid disclosure that they had aided the unreliable regime of Saddam Hussein "long after it was prudent to do so."[110] But this, too, begs the question of what was really behind all the subterfuge in the prewar years. The "cloak of national security" hid interventions by high officials to circumvent established standards and procedures, as well as manipulation of government processes, in order to expedite loans to Iraq after they were well aware of many alleged abuses that later came to light in Congress.

In mid-July 1992 Congressman Gonzales was still producing documents and reading them on the House floor, whether they were classified or not. One disclosure was a "secret CIA document" dated 6 November 1989 that reflected "a seeming lack of concern about the unfolding bank scandal," considering it a "minor irritant" in the U.S.-Iraq relationship, and speculated that any strain in relations would "probably be short-lived," particularly if Baghdad believed that "additional credits [would] be forthcoming." The report also described Iraq's "complex procurement networks of holding companies in Western Europe to acquire technology for its chemical, biological, nuclear, and ballistic missile development programs."[111]

Another "secret report" of the CIA, known as a "national intelligence estimate," issued in early November 1989, warned that failure to approve a pending $1 billion agricultural loan guarantee program to Iraq "would create further tensions in American-Iraqi relations." For the most part, the report "followed the conventional wisdom of the Bush administration that President Saddam Hussein of Iraq was a leader who could be worked with." But it included a lengthy discussion of Iraq's ambitious weapons programs and procurement network and "also noted" the possibility of "illegal transactions involving the U.S. government loan program through the Atlanta branch of the BNL." The latter warning was, however, "reportedly in a single paragraph buried deep in the 25-page report."[112]

Many documents were declassified in response to investigations by other congressional committees. New material provided to a House Foreign Affairs subcommittee, headed by Sam Gejdenson (Democrat from Connecticut), included State Department memos, cablegrams, letters, and interviews with senior administration officials that revealed fierce internal battles over the transfer of high-technology equipment and U.S.-backed agricultural loans to Iraq. Other controversies involved human rights violations and support of terrorism. Most documents declassified for Mr. Gejdenson's committee, however, were dated prior to the election of President Bush. They were revealing, nonetheless. A 1988 document apparently warned that Iraq had emerged from the war with Iran as "a great military and political power" and was "aiming higher."[113]

By early July, more declassified documents indicated that "Iraq was diverting technology to its nuclear-weapons program as early as 1985." This was "much earlier than previously known." These documents included Department of Defense memos that "sought restrictions on exports of U.S. technology with nuclear uses to Iraq." Gejdenson claimed that an analysis of U.S. exports to Iraq showed that "between 1985 and 1990" there were "192 instances in which technology with potential nuclear applications was licensed for sale." Bush cried politics and denied that he or the State Department knew anything about it.[114]

The House Committee on Energy and Commerce, John D. Dingell (Democrat from Michigan) chairman, investigated the circumstances behind warnings in 1989 issued by the CIA's "top authority on the spread of bomb manufacturing gear," particularly items that had dual civilian and military uses and about Iraq's "major effort to build an atomic bomb as rapidly as possible." All of Dingell's findings were "ignored." The committee held closed hearings on the subject in April 1991 and evaluated secret intelligence data. Congressman Dingell reportedly called the unheeded warning "a major Governmental failure in which an opportunity for timely action was missed." Evidence coming out of Iraq since the war was reporting that "Baghdad came perilously close to getting the bomb."[115]

By the summer of 1992, revelations emanating from several congressional committees on U.S.-Iraqi relations and the formulation and execution of policy vis-à-vis Iraq pointed to "a pattern of obstruction of justice and lying to Congress."[116] There was, it appeared, a complex web of obfuscation and denials, a "cover-up" by administration spokesmen about activities of doubtful legality and policies of questionable prudence, whereby Iraq was allowed to defraud a U.S.-registered bank and the U.S. government in order to develop its military capabilities. Predictably, it began to be called "Iraqgate."

"Iraqgate": The "Little Details" of Coverup

For several months the House Judiciary Committee investigated whether there were violations of U.S. laws by administration officials. Headed by Representative Jack Brooks (Democrat from Texas), the committee initially investigated allegations that officials in the Bush administration had used influence to delay the indictment of several Iraqis and officials in the Atlanta branch of the Banca Nazionale del Lavoro, which made illegal loans of U.S. $5 billion to Iraq. The committee also uncovered the possibility that the Commerce Department had "tampered with documents submitted to Congress."[117] Since August 1991, "at the request of one congressman," the Justice Department had pursued a criminal investigation into this alleged alteration in late 1990 of Commerce Department records, subpoenaed by Congress, on U.S. exports to Iraq.[118] And there was an allegation of "perverting the use of Agriculture's farm export guarantees" by the State Department. These "little details of bureaucratic deception . . . form a mosaic of cover-up," wrote William Safire in the *New York Times* in June 1992.[119]

Included in the "little details" were telephone calls from the White House counsel's office to the prosecutor in Atlanta in November 1989, which "reminded her of the 'embarrassment level'" should there be an indictment of Saddam Hussein's family.[120] Other documents indicated that a federal prosecutor was sent to Atlanta shortly before the indictment in January 1990 with a "different theory" about who was largely responsible for the loan frauds (the Italian bank not the Iraqi officials who were about to be indicted by the Atlanta prosecutor). The case was postponed for a year, until after the war, when the original charges were made.

The Judiciary Committee was to consider "whether to request the appointment of an independent counsel" to investigate "the administration's policy of helping Saddam Hussein" before the Gulf War. Mr. Brooks sent a request on 12 June 1990 to President Bush to "direct top administration officials to testify before [his] House committee" and submitted a list of names. The administration claimed that "the Democrats [were] exploiting the investigation for election-year purposes." Mr. Brooks pointed out that the investigation "began more than two years ago" and would have ended a long time ago if the administration had been forthcoming with documents. "Should noncompliance result," the *New York Times* quoted him as having written in his request, "the case for an independent counsel— with full subpoena and prosecutorial powers—would be bolstered for that reason alone."[121] Although the president "resisted sending high level officials to testify," it seemed that he "wisely" notified departments "to respond to Judiciary's request for documents" and lower level civil servants began appearing before Congress.[122]

All but one of the twenty-one Democrats on the House Judiciary Committee voted to request the attorney general to begin the process of appointing an independent counsel "to investigate serious allegations of possible violations of federal criminal statutes by high-ranking officials." The list included names of persons in the White House. Bush denounced the congressional request for an independent prosecutor as "purely political."

As a *New York Times* editorial suggested, "to call the congressional request 'political' is to obscure the point of the independent counsel law." This law intends that the party out of power can "press the executive branch whenever high executive officials have a conflict of interest that threatens their impartiality." Such requests may well be politically inspired. But what matters is not that. It is whether the congressional request "is based on reasonable suspicion of crime that the Justice Department is too embarrassed to pursue." When the Iran-Contra scandal broke in 1986, "even [Attorney General] Edwin Meese recognized . . . that the Reagan Justice Department could not be seen as an impartial investigator of criminality."[123]

Attorney General William Barr was not Ed Meese. Barr rejected the Judiciary Committee's call for "a prosecutor not beholden to the Bush administration." In doing so, wrote Safire, "he [took] personal charge of the cover-up." It is "an unprecedented refusal to recognize a 'political conflict of interest' as called for in the law." The political purpose of the refusal was clear: "contain Iraqgate until after the election."[124]

"Has the attorney general committed an impeachable offense?" the columnist inquired and answered "yes." Meanwhile more detailed documents continued to flow. Safire mentioned another memo, this time an internal State Department memo, dated 16 October 1989, addressed to Secretary Baker from subordinates. It concerned the importance of giving U.S. $1 billion in U.S. grain credits to Iraq: "Our ability to influence Iraqi policies . . . will be heavily influenced by the outcome of the Commodity Credit Corp. negotiations." At that time, the BNL scandal had broken and administration officials were aware of the involvement of Iraqis in various other alleged illegalities. Notes mentioned phone calls to the U.S. attorney in Atlanta and a suggestion to "wall off" the agricultural credits for Iraq from the BNL investigation. Meanwhile, Congressman Gonzales "was preparing to answer the attorney general's defiance with a bill of impeachment."[125]

Conclusion

The Bush administration's foreign policy seemed to move from one extreme to another. Before the war, the United States was determined to be conciliatory toward Iraq, to "bring it within the family of nations," to "moderate Saddam Hussein's behavior." The policy of conciliation, of bending the law (perhaps breaking it) to allow Saddam to have what he wanted, was continued "even after it had ceased to be prudent to do so." At the other extreme was absolute hostility and refusal to negotiate or compromise. Saddam was portrayed as a "Hitler," the apotheosis of evil. He was issued ultimatums with which the administration obviously did not expect him to comply.

Schizophrenic tendencies in U.S. policy are not limited to pre- or postwar Iraq. Although recent manifestations of policy in the Gulf often seem to lack rationality, coherence, or even common sense, they are symptomatic of U.S. policy toward the Middle East generally. The usual concerns and calculations of strategic advantage and national interest would appear to be far removed from the minds of those who formulate U.S. policy for the Middle East.

What is going on? Leslie Gelb called the prewar policy toward Saddam's Iraq a "blunder," something Republicans would claim a "soft-headed Democrat" might be expected to do.[126] One could conclude that U.S. policy in the Middle East suffers from a lack of political understanding of the issues at stake in particular parts of the area, compounded by the arrogance of power and lapses of principle.

There is certainly a new world order in the making, given the metamorphosis of the Soviet Union and the dissolution of socialist power, of pending European unity, of dramatic economic development in China as well as an expansion and ferocity of ethnic conflict not known for decades. How this new world will relate to the Middle East is unclear. Given the declared interest of the United States in the Gulf region, however, U.S. foreign policy will assuredly continue to affect the area, one can only hope with more salutary effects than hitherto.

Notes

IHT   *International Herald Tribune*
NYT   *New York Times*
WPW   *Washington Post Weekly*

1. Thomas Friedman, "Bush's Roles on World Stage: Triumphs, but Troubles, Too," *NYT*, 16 June 1992.

2. "Towards a New World Order," address by President Bush before a joint session of Congress, 11 September 1990, *U.S. Dept. of State Dispatch*, 17 September 1990, 91. The other four objectives were Iraqi withdrawal from Kuwait "completely, immediately, and without condition"; the restoration of the legitimate government of Kuwait; assurance of "the security and stability of the Persian Gulf"; and protection of U.S. citizens abroad.

3. Ibid., 92.

4. "News Conference Following North Atlantic Council Session," opening statement by Secretary Baker and excerpts from news conference, Brussels, Belgium, 10 September 1991, *Dispatch*, 17 September 1990, 95.

5. "Defeating Aggression in Kuwait," radio address to U.S. Troops by President Bush, 2 March 1991, *Dispatch*, 11 March 1991, 164.

6. Bush address, 11 September 1990, 92.

7. "U.S. Increases Troop Commitment in Operation Desert Shield," opening remarks by President Bush at a news conference at the White House, 8 November 1990, *Dispatch*, 12 November 1990, 258.

8. Bush address, 11 September 1990, 92.

9. "The World after the Persian Gulf War," address by President Bush before a joint session of Congress, 6 March 1991, *Dispatch*, 11 March 1991, 161.

10. Ibid.

11. Bush address, 11 September 1990, 93.

12. "Opportunities to Build a New World Order," Statement by Secretary Baker to the House Foreign Affairs Committee, 6 February 1991, *Dispatch*, 11 February 1991, 81.

13. Ibid., 82–83.

14. Ibid., 83–84.

15. Ibid., 84.

16. Bush address, 2 March 1991, 164.

17. President Bush, "Address to the Nation," 8 August 1990, in *Historic Documents of 1990* (Washington: *Congressional Quarterly*, 1991), 539.

18. "War Powers Debate, 2 October 1990," *Historic Documents of 1990*, 663–64.

19. Andrew Rosenthal, "Bush Is Still Unsatisfied with Iraq's Compliance," *NYT*, 27 July 1992.

20. Quoted in Anthony Lewis, "'On His Word Alone,'" *NYT*, 12 January 1992.

21. Ibid.

22. Ibid.

23. "War Powers Debate," 667, 668.

24. Ibid., 670.

25. Ibid., 671.

26. Ibid., 672–74 passim.

27. Ibid., 676.

28. Bush address, 8 August 1990, 539.

29. Owen Harries, "Drift and Mastery, Bush Style," *The National Interest* 23 (Spring 1991): 5.

30. Ibid.

31. Ibid., 6–7.

32. Ibid., 7.

33. William R. Hawkins, "Isolationism, Properly Understood," *The National Interest* 24 (Summer 1991): 61.

34. Joseph Sobran, quoted ibid.

35. James Kurth, "Things to Come: The Shape of the New World Order," *The National Interest* 24 (Summer 1991): 4.

36. Henry Kissinger, "What Kind of New World Order?" *The Washington Post*, 3 December 1991.

37. The "truly international" issues, Kissinger predicts, will be subjects such as population, environment and nuclear proliferation, "never previously . . . the topic of global arrangements." The issue is whether "societies of such different cultural origins will be able to define even the genuinely global issues in a compatible manner?"

38. Zbigniew Brzezinski, "Selective Global Commitment," *Foreign Affairs* 70, 4 (1991): 1.

39. Ibid., 6, quoting Jacques Delors, president of the EC Commission.

40. The other three are how Europe will define itself, how the Soviet Union will be transformed, and how the Pacific region will organize itself.

41. Ibid., 6–7.

42. Ibid., 17, 18.

43. Ibid., 20.

44. Noam Chomsky, "The New World Order," Bates College lecture, 30 January 1991, Open Magazine Pamphlet Series, 24.

45. Ibid.

46. Ibid., 23.

47. Ibid.

48. Ibid., 21–22.

49. Thomas Friedman, "Rethinking Foreign Affairs: Are They Still a U.S. Affair?" *NYT*, 7 February 1992.

50. Ibid.

51. Ibid., quoting Les Aspin, Democrat from Wisconsin, chairman of the House Armed Services Committee.

52. Ibid., quoting Michael Sandel, Harvard political theorist.

53. A.M. Rosenthal, "Running from the World," *NYT*, 18 February 1992.

54. These isolationists of the 1930s and 1940s had a considerable following. It was only when directly attacked by the Japanese at Pearl Harbor

that the United States formally entered the conflict with a declaration of war.

55. Rosenthal, *NYT*, 18 February 1992.

56. "Excerpts from Pentagon's Plan: 'Prevent the Re-Emergence of a New Rival,'" *NYT*, 8 March 1992.

57. "America Only," editorial, *NYT*, 10 March 1992.

58. Patrick Tyler, "U.S. Strategy Plan Calls for Insuring No Rivals Develop: A One-Superpower World," *NYT*, 8 March 1992.

59. "Pentagon's Plan," *NYT*, 8 March 1992.

60. Ibid.

61. Patrick Tyler, "Pentagon Imagines New Enemies to Fight in Post-Cold-War Era: Plans for Hypothetical Conflicts and Big Budgets," *NYT*, 17 February 1992.

62. Other scenarios postulate conflicts with North Korea (invading South Korea) and Russia (invading the Baltics); coups in Panama (threatening the canal) and in the Philippines (threatening substantial numbers of American lives); and the emergence of "a new, anti-democratic and expansionist superpower" that would "threaten U.S. interests" from within the former Soviet Union "or from some combination of powerful nations." The seventh scenario postulates the Gulf invasion happening simultaneously with an invasion of South Korea. Ibid.; "Pentagon's Plan," *NYT*, 8 March 1992.

63. Ibid.

64. Patrick Tyler, "War in 1990s: New Doubts. Pentagon Plans Evoke Skepticism in Congress," *NYT*, 18 February 1992.

65. Tyler, *NYT*, 17 February 1992.

66. Estimate of the Congressional Budget Office, quoted in *NYT*, 18 February 1992.

67. "America Only" editorial, *NYT*, 10 March 1992.

68. Patrick Tyler, "Senior U.S. Officials Assail Lone-Superpower Policy," *NYT*, 11 March 1992.

69. Richard Cheney, "Active Leadership? You Better Believe It," *NYT*, 15 March 1992.

70. "Pentagon's Plan," *NYT*, 8 March 1992.

71. Tyler, *NYT*, 8 March 1992.

72. Patrick Tyler, "Lone Superpower Plan: Ammunition for Critics," *NYT*, 10 March 1992.

73. Ibid.

74. Barton Gellman, "On Second Thought, We Don't Want to Rule the World," *WPW*, 1–7 June 1992. The words quoted are from a speech by Secretary Cheney in New York on 22 May 1992.

75. Ibid.

76. Ibid.

77. Tyler, *NYT*, 18 February 1992.

78. Jim Hoagland, "Yugoslavia: Again, Bush Should Have Charted a Middle Course," *IHT*, 18 June 1992, quoting a statement made by Bush during a television interview on 7 January 1992.

79. Ibid.

80. Ibid.

81. The language is Hoagland's.

82. Patrick Tyler, "Saudis Press U.S. for Help in Ouster of Iraq's Leader: A Plan to Back Uprisings," *NYT*, 19 January; "Gates in Mideast Is Said to Discuss Ouster of Hussein: Next Turn of the Screw," *NYT*, 7 February; "Congress Notified of Iraq Coup Plan: Bush Told Lawmakers in Fall about Covert Operations," *NYT*, 9 February 1992.

83. Tyler, *NYT*, 9 February 1992.

84. Tyler, *NYT*, 19 January 1992.

85. Ibid.

86. William Safire, "Waging a War of Nerves," *NYT*, 20 January 1992; Leslie Gelb, "Ousting Saddam or Trapping Bush: Covert Games U.S. Aides Play," *NYT*, 24 January 1992.

87. Gelb, *NYT*, 24 January 1992.

88. Tyler, 9 February 1992.

89. Michael Wines, "U.S. Sees Increasing Need for a Strike on Iraq," *NYT*, 15 March 1992.

90. Chris Hedges, "Deep in the Marshes of Iraq, Flames of Rebellion Flicker," *NYT*, 15 March 1992.

91. Wines, *NYT*, 15 March 1992.

92. John H. Cushman, Jr., "U.S. Planes Unchallenged as Flight Ban Starts in Iraq," *IHT*, 28 August 1992.

93. Leslie H. Gelb, "Now Bush Gets Tough on Saddam," *IHT*, 24 August 1992.

94. Ibid.

95. Anthony Lewis, "Who Fed This Caesar?" *NYT*, 15 March 1992.

96. Coincident with a study commissioned by Congress was a day-long hearing by the House Government Operations Subcommittee on National Security, 7 April 1992, on the Patriot, discussed in George Lardner, Jr., "Did the Patriot Missile Obey the Hippocratic Oath? A New Study Says it Did Little Harm to Scuds," *WPW*, 20–26 April 1992.

97. No mobile Scud launchers had been destroyed and only twelve of our twenty-eight fixed site launchers, reported a member of the commission. Mark Crispin Miller, "Desert Scam: Not One Mobile Scud Launcher Was Destroyed," *IHT*, 25 June 1992.

98. John Lancaster, "Cutting the Iraqi Army Down to Size," *WPW*, 4–10 May 1992.

99. Elaine Sciolino with Michael Wines, "Bush's Greatest Glory Fades as Questions on Iraq Persist," *NYT*, 27 June 1992.

100. George Lardner, Jr., "The U.S.-Iraqi Courtship: A Chairman on the Hill Is Uncovering the Administration's Prewar Dance with Baghdad," *WPW*, 30 March–5 April 1992.

101. Inter alia, see Elaine Sciolino, "CIA Advice to Bush on Iraqi Loan Program Minimized Bank Scandal," *IHT*, 20 July 1992.

102. Lardner, *WPW*, 30 March–5 April 1992.

103. William Safire, "Iraq: The System Punishes Scam Plus Cover-Up," *IHT*, 26 June 1992.

104. Lardner, *WPW*, 30 March–5 April 1992.

105. Quoted in Dean Baquet, "Documents Charge Iraqis Made Swap: U.S. Food for Arms: Bank Fraud and Bribery," *NYT*, 27 April 1992. Under the Commodity Credit Corporation, "the Government co-signs bank loans for poor countries that want to buy millions of dollars worth of grain, corn and other farm products. The Government agrees that if the country defaults, it will repay the bank up to 98 percent of the loan amount, as well as a portion of the interest."

106. Lardner, *WPW*, 30 March–5 April 1992.

107. Baquet, *NYT*, 27 April 1992.

108. Martin Tolchin, "Bush Is Asked to Direct Aides to Testify on Iraq Aid," *NYT*, 13 June 1992.

109. Baquet, *NYT*, 27 April 1992.

110. Lardner, *WPW*, 30 March–5 April 1992.

111. Elaine Sciolino, "CIA Advice to Bush on Iraqi Loan Program Minimized Bank Scandal," *IHT*, 20 July 1992.

112. Ibid.

113. Elaine Sciolino, "U.S.Documents Raise Questions Over Iraq Policy," *NYT*, 7 June 1991.

114. Douglas Frantz and Murray Waas, "How Much Did Bush Know? Pentagon Warnings on Iraqi Nuclear Goals Date to 1985," *IHT*, 3 July 1992.

115. William J. Broad, "Warning on Iraq and Bomb Bid Silenced in '89," *NYT*, 20 April 1992.

116. William Safire, "Iraqgate: Act Now to Avoid a Whitewash," *IHT*, 10 July 1992.

117. Tolchin, *NYT*, 13 June 1992.

118. R. Jeffrey Smith, "Trying to Pry Lid Off Pro-Iraq Policy," *IHT*, 14 July 1992.

119. Safire, *IHT*, 26 June 1992.

120. Safire, *IHT*, 10 July 1992.

121. Tolchin, *NYT*, 13 June 1992. Pursuant to the Ethics in Government Act, a majority of the Judiciary Committee's twenty-one Democrats must request the appointment of an independent counsel. The attorney general is required to conduct a "threshold inquiry" and report back to Congress in thirty days. If he finds "reasonable grounds for further inves-

tigation," the attorney general must apply to a special three-judge panel of the Court of Appeals for appointment of an independent counsel. Such counsel, formerly called "special prosecutor," was appointed in the Watergate and Iran-Contra cases.

122. Safire, *IHT*, 26 June 1992.

123. "A Special Prosecutor on Iraq," *NYT*, 18 July 1992.

124. William Safire, "Justice Stoops to Politics in an Iraqgate Cover-Up," *IHT*, 1 September 1992.

125. William Safire, "An Impeachable Offense? Evidence in a 1989 Memo," *IHT*, 11 September 1992.

126. Leslie H. Gelb, "Bush's Iraq Policy was No 'Mistake,'" *IHT*, 10 July 1992.

9
The Making of the New World Order

The Role of the Media

Malcolm Hayward

To understand Arab-American cultural relations as they evolved during the Gulf crisis and how they related to President George Bush's conception of a new world order, one must account for three factors. First, there are what Edward Said (1983) termed our interpretative situations. A series of events, such as the Gulf War, or the vision of a new political domain, such as Bush's new world order, are interpreted according to the belief patterns of a particular culture. If one needed only to define how these patterns develop, an analysis might be relatively straightforward; however, a second factor influences the understanding of events and ideas, that being the narratives used by participants to relate those events. We rarely see events first hand; they are related to us and encased in a story shaped by the presenter. Similarly, political ideas are embedded in story lines informed by three elements: the exigencies of the situation, the need to persuade an audience, and the politician's conception of how the events fit within the larger context of policy. A third factor for understanding Arab-U.S. cultural relations is the mode of presentation and its effect on the audience; different presentational modes (television, a speech, or a newspaper story) significantly shape the public's views of events and ideas. The Gulf crisis and Bush's new world order can be seen, thus, in rhetorical terms with attention given to the audience, narrative, and mode of presentation.

In all three areas, the media had a crucial role. It did not achieve its potential, however, because it failed to offer critiques of the messages it delivered and their mode of presentation. The media stands at the center of Americans interpretations of the Arab world. During the Gulf crisis, the media drew upon academic scholarship and political narratives to shape the image that Americans had of the

Middle East. Moreover, the forms in which the actual images of the Middle East and the participants in the Gulf crisis were presented impacted significantly upon Americans' understanding of the issues. This in turn affected how President Bush presented his image of the new world order, a concept having implications well beyond the local realm of the Gulf.

The Interpretative Situation

There are numerous principles that Americans feel should govern a state and its culture. The fact that these principles are often subverted does not deny their importance as constructs by which Americans measure other cultures. First, rationality and logic are held in high esteem; Americans prefer leaders who seem self-possessed and allow emotional responses only within narrowly defined ranges, such as patriotism and righteous indignation. As Catherine Lutz noted, "American cultural belief does not deny that men may become emotional," but it only allows "certain types of emotion," such as anger (Lutz 1988:73).

A second principle is that actions must be sanctioned not only by their logical consequences, but also by the doctrine of fair play, particularly to those who may be at risk, need protection, or lack power, such as children and women. An aspect of this principle is that in order to ensure fairness, the rules of fair play must be codified and made available to all. Once a rule is established and written down, all members of society should adhere to it; according to the American mind, all members of society should abide by these rules to settle grievances and disputes or to access the benefits allowed by the rules. Fairness is related to another concept, that of consent. In general, Americans feel that a society should operate by the common consent of the governed. Democracy, then, is seen as an outgrowth of the freedom of individual choice; a government is fair if it allows equal participation of the people it governs. Consensual democracy is seen as a more highly evolved form of governance than other political systems, often distinguished as unevolved, or rooted in tradition.

Finally, the evolved society finds proof of its worth in its technological innovations and superiority. Technology is seen as the appropriate outgrowth of both a logical approach to solving problems and the freedom of individuals to pursue individual goals in a society working on democratic principles (Stewart 1972:66–67). Although there are other principles to which Americans are deeply committed, at least in name, these four—rationality, codified fairness, government by consent, and dependence on technology—form a backdrop for interpreting the Gulf crisis and understanding the place of the Arab world within the construct of Bush's new world order.

To see how the Gulf crisis was understood in the United States in terms of these principles, one should look at the analysis proposed by Edward Said (1978) in *Orientalism*. Said defines the intersection of three groups that are responsible for Western views of Arab people and culture: orientalists, the media (in this case, primarily the news media), and politicians. None of the three act in isolation, but interact with one another. As Said points out in *Covering Islam*, "the canonical, orthodox coverage of Islam that we find in the academy, in the government, and in the media is all interrelated and has been more diffused, has seemed *more* persuasive and influential, in the West than any other 'coverage' or interpretation" (Said 1981:161).

These three groups, moreover, pursue agendas faithful to goals that they define as being in the "best interests" of their constituencies, based on their interpretative situations. Another way to phrase this issue is in terms of "ideologies," as defined by Terry Eagleton in *Ideology: An Introduction*. Eagleton describes six overlapping but distinct ways in which ideology may be defined: as social or cultural processes, class beliefs, the promotion of class interests generally, the advocacy of class interests by a dominant power, such advocacy using distortion, and distortion arising from social processes generally (Eagleton 1991:28–30). Here we are concerned with his fourth meaning of ideology, which "attends to the *promotion* and *legitimation* of the interests" of a social group in a dominant position (Eagleton 1991:29). To some extent, we are also concerned with his fifth definition, "in which ideology signifies ideas and beliefs which help to legitimate the interests of a ruling group or class specifically by distortion and dissimulation" (Eagleton 1991:30), whether or not such distortions or dissimulations are purposeful or arise from a fundamental misunderstanding or misconstrual of the issues and events.

Interpretative Situations: The Academic Perspective

The rhetoric of the crisis found all three groups—scholars, media, and politicians—characteristically shaping their pronouncements to agree with their underlying suppositions about the East. There was, moreover, a dynamic interchange among the three. In *Covering Islam*, Said shows that orientalists, often unknowingly, set their interpretations of Islam "in a profoundly and in some ways an offensively political context" (Said 1981:xvii). Politicians and the media then used these marginalized and politically biased studies to "take over the dissemination of racist caricatures of the Islamic peoples" (Said 1981:141). Failure to examine their biased interpretations resulted in the group's failure to understand, intellectually and politically, the dynamics of Arab culture.

Interpretations of the Gulf War were heavily influenced by academic commentary. On 10 August 1991, the *Wall Street Journal* published an essay by historian David Pryce-Jones, author of *The Closed Circle*. In it, Pryce-Jones attempted to place Arabs within a cultural context Westerners could understand. He wrote: "To Westerners, this [aggression of Saddam's] makes him out to be a little Hitler, defying his neighbors and even the world community in a way that appears irrational, if not mad. An effort of imagination and some knowledge of history are required to understand that he is not in the least deranged but behaving in accordance with ancient customs in the Middle East. Arabs do things differently from us, and always have" (A-10).

What Pryce-Jones proposes to do here is symptomatic of many orientalists. Trying to establish a cultural perspective outside of the U.S. vision of the world (Saddam's action only "appears irrational"), he invites another perspective, equally Eurocentric and equally culture-bound. The problem is not Saddam's irrationality; the problem is that all Arabs are "different." Having assumed that U.S. culture and values are the norm, Pryce-Jones uses the "otherness" of the Arabs as the basis for dismissing their views and culture. If Saddam seems deranged, it is only because he is following irrational ancient customs. If that message is not clear from the above passage, it certainly is from what follows:

> Throughout the Arab Middle East there is no check of any kind on absolute power; no government by consent, no representative parliament or loyal opposition, no free speech. Treaties, frontiers, sovereignty are Western concepts easily brushed aside in the absence of institutions to realize them. What might look like Arab nation-states are therefore much closer to tribes held together by military-type rulers according to custom and sanctioned by honor. Everywhere the strong feel it only normal to

oppress the weak. That is why the Middle East is so violent and backward.

Given such a perspective, Pryce-Jones offers a political solution to the Middle East drawn from Kipling's nineteenth-century view of the "White Man's Burden": "At this point in history there is no question of conquest or imperialism. This is a clash of quite a different kind, between past and present, between tribal custom and government by consent. Before Arabs can take their place in the modern world as they deserve, rulers of the stamp of Saddam have to be exposed as the savage and outmoded tyrants that they are."

Pryce-Jones thus tries to convince his readers that eastern and western cultural differences are analogous to the old, savage, tribal society (the East) and the new, consensual, evolved democratic society (the West). From this perspective, there is no question in his mind as to which society "ought" to prevail. Despite the extremity of Pryce-Jones's view, the themes he touches on in this early analysis of the crisis are precisely those adopted by George Bush in his attempts to manipulate public opinion in the United States and provide a rationale for his view of the "American century" to come. Clearly, Pryce-Jones' interpretation of the events valorizes Western values such as democracy, the institutionalization of boundaries and frontiers, and the codification of societal relations, as opposed to a strong central leader, a certain fluidity in conceptions of land ownership, and a reliance upon custom and honor as a legitimate basis for contractual obligations between groups. If one agrees with Pryce-Jones's interpretation, Arab customs become irrational and destructive.

This image of Arab irrationality was embraced by news reporters throughout the period. On 10 February 1991, for example, Patrick Tyler reported in the Sunday *New York Times*: "As he holds out in his bunker, Mr. Hussein has not left the briefings to his generals, as Mr. Bush has done. The Iraqi leader uses no pointer, no charts; he briefs with rhetoric, distortion and his own social mythology about the subjugation of the have-nots by the haves—all of it designed to inflame Arab and other third-world sensibilities about the return of the colonial powers to visit destruction on Arab lands and Islamic shrines" (E-5). This is, in fact, the same argument that David Pryce-Jones made, although the terms are not quite as obvious. Tyler contrasts the pointers and charts of President Bush's generals—objects associated with reason and logic—with Saddam's "rhetoric, distortion, and social mythology," including the mythology that Arabs were subjugated by capitalist interests. Just as Pryce-Jones argued that U.S. interests are not imperialist, so too for Tyler, the "return of colonial powers" became part of the mythology.

Criticism is not directed at Saddam alone. How are we to understand the phrase "to inflame Arab sensibilities" other than as an indictment of emotionalism, of incipient madness, within the Arab world? Arabs are, in this view, susceptible to being "inflame[d]." Said describes the negative images of Arabs in his essay "Orientalism Now" in *The World, the Text, and the Critic* (Said 1983:285–87). For example, one dogma of orientalists, cited by Said, is a belief in "the absolute and systematic difference between the West, which is rational, developed, humane, superior, and the Orient, which is aberrant, undeveloped, inferior" (Said 1983:300).

This attitude is also apparent in Patrick Tyler's seemingly more objective viewpoint. For example, in his 3 June 1991, *New York Times* article, "U.S. Officials Believe Iraq Will Take Years to Rebuild," there are repeated references to "Western technology," the need for "foreign equipment and expertise," the loss of "foreign health workers," and "spare parts and chemical additives produced outside the country" (A-1, A-8), implying Iraq's dependency on the West and ignoring Western dependency on the resources of the Arab world. Technology, seen as a proof of Western superiority, is used here as a standard to denigrate the Arab culture. As a consequence of this assumed dependency on Western technology, the Orient becomes, as Said says in *Orientalism*, "at bottom something either to be feared . . . or to be controlled (by pacification, research and development, outright occupation whenever possible)" (Said 1978:301).

Similarly, the 28 January 1991, issue of *Time* prints an analysis by Lance Morrow on "Saddam and the Arabs." In it, Saddam's strength and position with his people is, predictably, an emotional bond: "Saddam also represents the yearnings of the Arab people: a defiant assertion of dignity, unity and honor. He has given fierce expression to the emotions of many Arabs on matters that mean the most to them. . . . So powerful are these emotions that millions of ordinary Arabs, from factory workers to university professors, are willing to tolerate Saddam's otherwise evil performance" (64). It is difficult to know what Morrow means by "ordinary Arabs"; presumably they are ones who are swayed by powerful emotions only, as compared to those who are swayed by all emotions. Or perhaps he means that only the extraordinary Arab will oppose evil. This assertion corresponds to a view presented by Edward Mortimer in a review of Samir al-Khalil's *Republic of Fear*: "it is also true that coercion is a method of government that Iraqis have been conditioned to regard as normal, and the ability of the regime to use it may actually be evidence of its legitimacy, rather than the reverse" (Mortimer 1990: 12). At any rate, we are presented with the conclusion that "millions of ordinary Arabs" can "tolerate evil" since, in this view, conditioning has taught them that coercion is normal, as though Arabs, like animals, can be conditioned to behavior Westerners would not accept.

Other characterizations of Arabs emerge from Morrow's article. Arabs live in the past: "In a universe of sometimes incapacitating grievance, a practical Arab future opening onto a larger world, onto a new century, may be more difficult to imagine than a romantic past. The past has a powerful, seductive glory. It seamlessly encloses itself within fundamentalist Islamic virtue" (Morrow 1991:64). Together with this capacity for being seduced, Arabs have "a sense of violation, of second-class status" from "centuries of foreign domination." So too, Arabs have, for Morrow, "an obscure, almost magic sense of inevitability," and they "cling to their spiritual distinctiveness" (Morrow 1991:65). All of these generalizations depict an Arab mind unable to deal with the assumed real world of the West, an Arab mind that is injured, superstitious, weak, and which clings to false values.

This image of the Arab world throughout the Gulf crisis was predicated upon the Americans' image of themselves as rational, fair, democratic, and modern human beings. Orientalists and, following their lead, the media used this projected image to conceptualize Arab culture (particularly the Iraqis) in terms that Americans would, from their own background and standards, read as pejorative. There was little attempt made to understand Arab culture—or more precisely, the range of cultures existing in the areas most affected by the war— either on its own terms or in ways which would suggest a critique of the relativity of U.S. values.

Narrative Structure

Political documents and decisions are phrased for public consumption. Although political statements do not directly reflect the thinking behind a political decision, some insight may be gained of the ways in which politicians interpret U.S. understanding of the Arab world and the reasoning behind actions taken in that world.

In Bush's remarks on opening the air campaign against Iraq on 16 January 1991, political self-interest in the war is scarcely concealed. In his speech, Bush mentioned the danger to the "fragile economies of the Third World, emerging democracies of Eastern Europe, to the entire world, including to our own economy." The president's justification for war is also instructive. "While the world waited [for sanctions to work], Saddam Hussein systematically raped, pillaged and plundered a tiny nation no threat to his own. He subjected the people of Kuwait to unspeakable atrocities, and among those maimed and murdered [were] innocent children" (Bush 1991:A-14). Bush included several strong and significant themes in this part of his message. First, he describes the attack in sexual terms, and then he associates this sexual violation of a country with the violation of children. In Bush's fantasy of sexual violence, the word "systematically" takes on a more ominous connotation. Not only is Saddam Hussein portrayed as embodying the stereotypical quality of sexual excess; he is described as directing this against children. Such remarks would have an emotional impact on Americans who are strongly committed to protecting children from sexuality.

Bush's political vision is re-articulated in this same speech in which he justifies bombing Iraq. He refers to his 11 September 1990 address to the U.S. Congress: "This is an historic moment. We have in this past year made great progress in ending the long era of conflict and cold war. We have before us the opportunity to forge for ourselves and for future generations a new world order, a world where the rule of law, not the law of the jungle, governs the conduct of nations" (Bush 1991:A-14). This apotheosis of U.S. idealism, in which Bush suggests a new world order based upon American values, is marked by a concomitant denigration of the Arab world. In justifying the bombing, Bush combined a number of themes referred to earlier. In opposition to a United States whose Western values include reason, protection of the weak, and straight-dealing, Bush presents an image of the insane Arab, enslaved to his emotions; the menacing Arab, threatening women with rape and children with worse horrors; the guileful Arab, hiding a systematic plan for evil beneath a placid exterior. This political message is consistent with those iterated by both the experts and the media.

These images fuel a narrative that is very familiar to Americans: a story evoked in countless westerns and police shows of an evil man in search of power, an innocent and helpless victim, and a protector who appears on the horizon to save the victim. A typical western defines the bully searching for power as the large landowner wanting to increase his holdings by driving the peaceful farmer from his small plot, the equivalent of Bush's characterization of Kuwait as a peaceable "tiny nation no threat to his [Saddam Hussein's] own." The established forces of law are insufficient to oust the bully; the sheriff is weak or a tool of the landowner. Only the intervention of an outsider, the hero, will save the farmer, and incidentally the region, by killing the evil landowner and reestablishing the rule of law. Police shows follow the same format, except in these the issue is usually not territory but power, power that is often expressed in violent sexual terms. In one common plot, the gang leader exploits women, not hesitating to rape and murder his victims. Because the city streets operate by the "law of the jungle," the normal course of arrest and prosecution seldom works (the equivalent of waiting for sanctions). Thus, the police detective or private eye must take the law "into his own hands," but always with the purpose of restoring the legitimacy of that "rule of law." Violence is thus legitimized because the goal is moral and just. The criminal is usually not brought to court but is gunned down publicly in the streets (as happens frequently in a western), or hunted and killed in his bunker or hideout.

In his narrative of the Gulf War, Bush conflated two very common American plot structures in which the bully is called to account for his crimes and a new order is reasserted. Scripting the Gulf crisis in this manner validated the president's actions, for it follows familiar lines. The characters—Saddam and his "henchmen," as Bush termed them—and the plot—"crimes and tortures committed against the innocent people of Kuwait"—once identified to the audience, provide their own justification for war. The pursuit of a criminal and the attempt to re-establish justice need no further rationale, for the familiar story line is accepted without question.

Media Presentations of the Gulf Crisis

Throughout the crisis, television was crucial in determining public perceptions, conveying the strongest and most immediate images. At different stages during the war, three iconic representations of Saddam Hussein were displayed repeatedly on U.S. television and played a prominent role. The first, shortly after the invasion of Kuwait and the detention of "human shields," shows Saddam standing with children held, according to U.S. television, as "human shields." The image shows the children, Saddam, other officials, and some adults gathered in a large room. The second image, shot in November, is a clip of Saddam visiting his troops in Kuwait. As he strides forward, one of the soldiers reaches for Saddam's hand and bends as if to kiss it. The third, after the bombing has begun, shows Saddam in his bunker conferring with his troops. The first and third images were sometimes portrayed as still shots, but the second was always seen as a videotext with motion.

The three images convey their own messages to U.S. viewers. Even while the voice of the newscaster may pretend to deliver objective commentary, the imagery presented on the video screen is anything but objective. In fact, the images are designed to provide acceptable answers to U.S. viewers' questions about the war. In August and September 1990, the issue was phrased as what danger does Iraq (or Saddam or the Arab world generally) hold for Americans? The first image, that of Saddam and the children (or at times other Iraqi leaders and the children and their parents) evoked powerful reactions. In fact, in its 7 January 1991 issue, in which George Bush was chosen as "man of the year," *Time* presented a television picture of Saddam and a five-year-old British hostage as the lead picture in a section called "Images." It shows the boy standing in a short-sleeved shirt beside a seated and smiling Saddam; beneath the picture are quoted lines from the Koran, Sura 49: 9, and beneath that an identification of the picture with the content that Saddam "had his own ideas about justice and fairness." This first image might be read thus: our children (our future) are held hostage to an Arab world which may pretend benevolence but which is actually menacing. The fear was that Saddam would, through the control of oil, control U.S. destiny; Americans read their future in the fate of the hostages or human shields. To emphasize this message, the facing picture showed a tearful Florida guardsman hugging his sons as he said goodbye. Thus, the danger from Saddam Hussein was graphically phrased as a danger to American children, although this was only one of the political messages the president tried to impress upon the American people.

As fall progressed and war became more likely, the images changed. Questions were frequently raised concerning Saddam's effectiveness. Why did the Iraqis follow him? The picture showing an Iraqi soldier reaching to clasp Saddam's hand had a very negative element of emotionalism. This spoke to the distrust that Americans had of emotions. They liked to believe that their rulers acted with consideration and reason, and that the military's approach was businesslike and logical. The video-image reinforced the notion that Iraqis (and probably all Arabs) were strongly emotional and followed their leaders only because of an emotional bond. In contrast, General Norman Schwarzkopf was shown in a briefing room, delivering his message in a straightforward manner. Because Americans felt that those led by emotions were erratic and weak, the video-image challenged the effectiveness of Saddam's army and his ability to control it. It is ironic that the reaction of many Americans to the war was strongly emotional and that Bush reinforced this by using emotional language and images to maintain support for U.S. military actions during the crisis.

The image of Saddam in his bunker was projected frequently following the bombing offensive against Iraq. The questions in the minds of Americans were, "Is the bombing successful?" and "What effect has it had on the Iraqis?" Now Saddam has become the cowardly Arab holding out—or perhaps hiding out. The image reinforced the message, relayed most often by the military, of the Iraqis "hunkered down," laying low, waiting out the bombing. The media eagerly seized any evidence of the Iraqis' willingness to give up, from the planes flown to Iran, to soldiers surrendering or deserting. These messages were meant to depict the Arab fighting forces as weak and vacillating as compared to the open, forthright bravery of the U.S. troops.

The video-images had a special impact because of their immediacy. As a number of commentators on the effect of the media during the Gulf crisis pointed out, television in this war had a greater impact than in previous wars. Even in the Vietnam War, videos from the field were delayed and edited, creating a distance between the viewers and the events. The live broadcasts of CNN, however, invoked a sense of drama and immediacy for the audience, which carried over into videos replayed for days afterwards. Viewers thus engaged were less prone to question the legitimacy of such texts or their veracity. Their immediacy validated their authenticity even though such texts should have been questioned on the same basis as any texts chosen to document an event: Are they truly representative? What messages are they delivering? Are they honest in regard to the event described and the participants in that event?

The Making of the New World Order

It is clear that such images, their mode of presentation, and the interpretative situations that lay behind them, had implications for Bush's concept of a new world order. First, it is important to remember that the conception of this order evolved within several specific contexts: the Gulf War as a response to a crisis, and the rapidly changing U.S.-Soviet relations due to the imminent breakup of the Soviet state. Thus the new world order had some of the shapelessness of an emerging paradigm whose shadowy outlines were designed to fit both events as well as Bush's view of the U.S. foreign policy role in the 1990s. It is, in other words, both a contingent vision and an attempt to articulate a broader perspective. Yet even this broader perspective had to respond to, be consistent with, and encompass the events of the Gulf War in order to serve as a rationale for Bush's actions within the Gulf. This dual role for the new world order explained, in part, the lack of definition and specificity of its agenda, not only in terms of the Gulf, but also for other areas of potential conflict—Eastern Europe, for example, or the Far East—in which the United States's role as a mediator had not been clearly defined or had been complicated by past actions, such as Vietnam.

President Bush's conception of the new world order was first generated through meetings with Mikhail Gorbachev in the context of nuclear arms control and the rapid thaw in relations between the two superpowers. The Iraqi invasion gave Bush the opportunity to use this concept as justification for what was portrayed as a united world front standing against Iraq. That Bush would follow this tactic emerged from his summit meeting with Mikhail Gorbachev on 9 September 1990. The text of their joint statement, as reported in the *New York Times* said, "We are united in the belief that Iraq's aggression must not be tolerated. No peaceful international order is possible if larger states can devour their smaller neighbors" (A-6). Bush again referred to this "peaceful international order" in his 11 September address to Congress:

As you know, I have just returned from a very productive meeting with Soviet President Gorbachev. And I am pleased that we are working together to build a new relationship. In Helsinki, our joint statement affirmed to the world our shared resolve to counter Iraq's threat to peace. . . .

A new partnership of nations has begun.

And we stand today at a unique and extraordinary moment. The crisis in the Persian Gulf, as grave as it is, also offers a rare opportunity to move toward an historic period of cooperation. Out of these troubled times, our fifth objective [the other four refer to Iraq's withdrawal, the restoration of Kuwait's government, the stability of the Gulf, and protection of American citizens abroad]—a new world order—can emerge: a new era, freer from the threat of terror, stronger in the pursuit of justice, and more secure in the quest for peace. An era in which the nations of the world, east and west, north and south, can prosper and live in harmony.

A hundred generations have searched for this elusive path to peace, while a thousand wars raged across the span of human endeavor. And today that new world is struggling to be born. A world quite different from the one we've known. A world where the rule of law supplants the rule of the jungle. A world in which nations recognize the shared responsibility for freedom and justice. A world where the strong respect the rights of the weak. (Bush 1990:A-20)

Within this new world order, the American role was for Bush, quite clearly, as the world leader. He portrayed the invasion of Iraq as a test of his vision:

America and the world must defend common vital interests.
And we will.
America and the world must support the rule of law.
And we will.
America and the world must stand up to aggression.
And we will.
And one thing more: In the pursuit of these goals,
America will not be intimidated. (Bush 1990:A-20)

Finally, after detailing his plans for Iraq and Kuwait, and appealing for a passage of his budget, Bush returned at the end of his address to this theme: "Once again, Americans have stepped forward to share a tearful goodbye with their families before leaving for a strange and distant shore. At this very moment they serve together with Arabs, Europeans, Asians and Africans in defense of principle and the dream of a new world order. And that's why they sweat and toil in the sand and the heat and the sun" (Bush 1990:A-20).

It is useful to analyze this text both in terms what is stated and what is not stated. What is readily apparent is the emphasis on law and justice: adherence to rule is highly esteemed. Peace and freedom are, for Bush, only possible within the context of a highly codified and rigid set of world laws. Law enforcement takes precedence within such a system; he assumes that rights will be at risk without a police force to ensure them.

What is not readily apparent, but equally present in the stated text, is the cultural bias implied and inherent in the terms used and the assumptions underlying these. It is impossible for an American to hear a phrase such as "rule of the jungle" (later used by Bush in his 17 January 1991 speech on the bombing as the "law of the jungle") without making a connection to Africa or Asia. In this way, world rule or world law becomes the province of the first world, the "civilized" world. So too, the "threat of terror" is associated with the Arab world generally, and not particularly with Iraq. Even suitably friendly allies participate in the generation of Bush's vision of the Other, if they chance to be Arabs. For example, in the conclusion to the speech, Saudi Arabia becomes a "strange and distant shore" where Americans are forced to "sweat and toil in the sand and the heat and the sun." The country is pictured as alien to *normal* human beings. Its strangeness and foreignness is not just because it is a new place for those sent there. Rather, it is a place outside of civilization, where even nature is inhospitable to human endeavor, the civilizing force at work toward the "defense of principle and the dream of a new world order."

The term "new world order" contains a curious double entendre that should remind us of Bush's vision of the U.S. role in the future. On the surface, it seems that he refers to a world order which is new, a *new* world order. Even here, there are two senses in which the phrase might be taken. Perhaps the world order is new because the old ordering forces have given way: before there was the rule of the jungle, now there is the rule of law. A new order has replaced an old order. If read this way, the argument is legitimated by the idea of progress, and the new order is set against an image of an un-evolved world order based on Darwinian struggles, as each nation was free to display naked aggression, unchecked but for the strength of others. The old order in this case may be read as the stabilization that results from the strategic limits of a country's or ruler's powers. The other sense in which this phrase might be taken is that the world order is new because prior to this, no world order existed: Before there was chaos or anarchy, now there is the chance for harmony—or at least there might have been before Saddam Hussein. In either case, however, the emphasis is on a "world order" that encompasses the United States and all other individual states in the world.

Both readings, however, miss the force of Bush's image and vision. An alternative reading of the phrase would define it as an order brought about by or through the United States, the new world, that is a *New World* Order, as one might say the New World Symphony. This new world order is to be defined by American standards and values. Though such a reading of the phrase may not have been intended, it is in fact a more accurate assessment of the phrase, as seen in Bush's repetitions, "America and the world." This is a case of the ideological strategy that Eagleton calls "universalization." By use of this device, according to Eagleton, "Values and interests which are in fact specific to a certain place and time are projected as the values and interests of all humanity. The assumption is that if this were not so, the sectoral, self-interested nature of the ideology would loom too embarrassingly large, and so would impede its general acceptance" (Eagleton 1991:56). By the phrase "America and the world," Bush seeks to identify U.S. interests as identical to world interests.

This vision is described as a new world that is "struggling to be born. A world quite different from the world we've known." In other words, Bush is reaching here for an image, not just of a new order for the world, but for a new world that would encompass or include certain ordering principles. These principles emerged during the Gulf crisis as the backdrop to the political and media renderings of the war from the U.S. interpretative background, namely rationality, codification, government by consent, and a dependence on technology. Within the construct of the new world order, however, these four principles become locked in a particular dynamic interrelationship, the pivotal point of which is "economic interest."

Economic self-interest forms the cornerstone for Bush's conception of the new order. After his rhetoric concerning matters of principle, Bush turns, in his 11 September address, to the heart of the matter: "Vital economic interests are at risk as well. Iraq itself controls some 10 percent of the world's proven oil reserves. Iraq plus Kuwait controls twice that. An Iraq permitted to swallow Kuwait would have the economic and military power, as well as the arrogance, to intimidate and coerce its neighbors, neighbors who control the lion's share of the world's remaining oil reserves. We cannot permit a resource so vital to be dominated by one so ruthless. And we won't" (Bush 1990:A-20). Here, Bush has transferred the oil assets, of not only Iraq and Kuwait, but of the entire region, from those countries to the world. Although the phrase "world's . . . oil reserves" could mean oil reserves in the world, the possessive here suggests that these are reserves that belong to the world. In the new order, then, economic assets that a powerful country, such as the United States, consider to be vital to its growth are liable to appropriation, since they are seen as not properly the possession of the particular country in which they are located but as commodities that belong to the world market.

This is particularly the case for commodities that might support the growth of a country's technology because an "advanced" country requires technology for its economic growth. The ability to exploit such commodities depends upon a controlled and codified market place based upon a reasonable economic system—capitalism. Finally, because one strong individual (such as Saddam Hussein) might disrupt the free interplay of market forces under capitalism, which assumes a dispersal of power to stimulate competition and guarantee access to commodities and to the market, government by consent becomes a key element in the political structure of the new world state.

What Bush omits from his depiction of the new world order is any concern for the root problems that plagued the old regime: the economic exploitation of nations, an inequitable distribution of resources among the people of the world, an unwillingness to accept cultural differences, and the racial and ethnic bias that permits one group to feel justified in dictating its principles to another group. Until these concerns are addressed, no true harmony will exist in the world. The new world order, if it comes in Bush's terms, will remain as he has formulated it: a series of repressive laws enforced by the powerful in order to retain their position of economic and political privilege within the world.

Implications for the Future

The interpretative situation from which Americans viewed the Gulf crisis, the narrative in which the crisis was presented, and the media images presented of the crisis are complementary and cumulative.

They result in ways of thinking about the Arab world bound by academic tradition as well as popular stereotyping of Arab peoples. Unless these patterns are re-evaluated and rethought, it seems unlikely that U.S. understanding of the Arab world will change significantly in the 1990s. A change will only be effected by political action and education to force those in positions of power to transmit those understandings—academics, politicians, media representatives—to alter their own understandings and presentations of the inhabitants of the Middle East. If a new world order is not to become by default a new U.S. order, concerted, aggressive action must force such re-examination and re-interpretation.

The media has an important role to play in this regard. As we have seen, the media was at the center of U.S. understanding of the Gulf crisis. The media interpreted the academic reading of the Arab world—or, as I have shown earlier, perpetuated the misunderstandings of orientalists. They also promulgated the political narratives developed during the period. Yet the media scarcely questioned these narratives. Finally, the media images themselves shaped U.S. feelings, not only about Iraq and the war, but about Arabs in general. In order to fulfill its duties to the U.S. public and the world public, the media must engage in more forceful critical commentary concerning both the content of its messages and the mode of their display.

References

Bush, George. "Transcript of President's Address to Joint Session of Congress." *New York Times* (12 September 1990): A-20.

———. "Transcript of the Contents by Bush on the Air Strikes Against the Iraqis." *New York Times* (17 January 1991): A-14.

"Images." *Time* (7 January 1991): 40–53.

Eagleton, Terry. *Ideology: An Introduction.* London: Verso, 1991.

Lutz, Catherine A. *Unnatural Emotions.* Chicago: Univ. of Chicago Press, 1988.

Morrow, Lance. "The Devil in the Hero." *Time* (28 January 1991): 64–66.

Mortimer, Edward. "The Thief of Baghdad" (Review). *New York Review of Books* (27 September 1990): 7–15.

Pryce-Jones, David. "And If the West Shames Him, He Will Fall." *Wall Street Journal* (10 August 1991): A-10.

Said, Edward. *Orientalism.* New York: Pantheon, 1978.

———. *Covering Islam.* New York: Pantheon, 1981.

————. *The World, the Text, and the Critic.* Cambridge: Harvard Univ. Press, 1983.

Stewart, Edward M. *American Cultural Patterns: A Cross-Cultural Perspective.* Yarmouth, ME: Intercultural Press, 1972.

"Text of Joint Statement: Aggression 'Will Not Pay'." *New York Times* (10 September 1991): A-6.

Tyler, Patrick. "Battle Plans are Deadly Simple; The Strategic Weapon is Politics." *New York Times* (10 February 1991): E-1, E-5.

————. "U.S. Officials Believe Iraq Will Take Years to Rebuild." *New York Times* (3 June 1991): A-1, A-8.

10
Defeating the Vietnam Syndrome

The Military, the Media, and the Gulf War

Andrew T. Parasiliti

> *Such was the lingering impact of the Vietnam War that the Persian Gulf conflict at times appeared as much a struggle with its ghosts as with Saddam Hussein's Iraq."*
>
> George C. Herring, "America and Vietnam."[1]

On 16 January 1991, the day the air war against Iraq began, President George Bush promised the American people that "this will not be another Vietnam." During the Gulf War, the Bush administration formulated its policies toward the media based on the assumption that critical reporting undermines U.S. foreign policy. The U.S. Department of Defense devised a media containment policy to avoid the perceived negative effects of "another Vietnam." The media's response to this policy was schizophrenic and ambiguous, reflecting in part its own battles with the ghosts of Vietnam.

Some leading news organizations and reporters challenged the Pentagon's restrictions. In general, however, media coverage of the Gulf War, especially network television, accepted the containment policies. The result was a public relations landslide for the Bush administration and a relatively uncritical view of U.S. participation in the Gulf War presented to the American people. The media's Gulf War performance has forced it to reconsider its role in covering U.S. military operations.

The Media and Vietnam

Military-media relations are by nature ambiguous, especially during war. The press' desire for independent coverage inevitably clashes with the requirements of military security. Historically, the U.S. military imposed some degree of censorship on the press during war. In these cases, the media acquiesced to rules restricting the dissemination of information that could jeopardize U.S. military operations or security. Generally, the military did not restrict and indeed facilitated media access to troops in the battlefield. Military censors reviewed journalists' stories for any potential breaches of security.[2]

Such was the case in Vietnam. Many U.S. policymakers and military officers believed, however, that critical reporting by the media was responsible for turning U.S. public opinion against the Vietnam War. The conflict in southeast Asia left a legacy of tension in military-media relations. Lieutenant General Bernard E. Trainor observed that "it is clear that today's officer corps carries as part of its cultural baggage a loathing for the press."[3]

According to this view of an oppositional media, the press had the power to de-legitimize government policies. Simon Serfaty terms this general phenomenon "medialism," defined as "an important and powerful international communications network capable of circumventing the control of any government and supported by its own working ideology . . . medialism represents a force that political leaders ignore at their own peril."[4]

The view that critical reporting by the media somehow undermined U.S. policy in Vietnam is not supported by empirical analysis. Michael Mandelbaum points out that television coverage of the Vietnam War generally portrayed Americans in successful combat operations. The argument that the media focused excessive attention on scenes of dying and wounded Americans is exaggerated.[5] Daniel Hallin's careful study of media content during the Vietnam War indicated that critical coverage did not occur until the war had become unpopular within official government circles, for example, following the 1968 Tet Offensive when public figures such as U.S. Senator J. William Fulbright challenged the policy. The real causes of decline in U.S. support for the Vietnam War were the lack of clearly defined political objectives and increasing casualties, not critical media coverage.[6]

Hallin instead argues that the media reflects what he terms an establishment orientation. Reporting is guided by two principles: first, a commitment to objective journalism, or the belief that the press transmits information to the public in a relatively passive manner, and second, a tendency to rely mainly on official sources—government representatives and associated analysts—for information. Only when debate over a policy occurs within official policy circles does the media expand its coverage to present other views.[7]

The press underwent self-evaluation after the Vietnam War in response to criticism of its alleged oppositional role. This process led to an even more entrenched establishment orientation. According to Hallin, the press became

> integrated into the process of government . . . journalists gave up the right to speak with a political voice of their own, and in turn they were granted a regular right of access to the inner councils of government. . . . These standards involved not merely renouncing the right to make partisan criticisms of political authority, but also granting to political authorities certain positive rights of access to the news and accepting for the most part the language, agenda, and perspectives of the political establishment.[8]

Any ambiguity in the media's relationship with the government began to fade between the Vietnam and the Gulf wars. By the time of Operation Desert Storm, the media's ability to provide independent analysis had been substantially reduced. The media containment policies of the U.S. military ensured that press coverage of this conflict would not be undermined by the perceived influence of an oppositional media.

Prelude: Grenada and Panama

The Gulf War media containment policy originated in the U.S. invasions of Grenada and Panama. Department of Defense (DoD) media controls proved effective in restricting the ability of the press to provide independent coverage of these two military operations.

U.S. Chairman of the Joint Chiefs of Staff, General Colin Powell, cited the Grenada operation as an influential precedent for the military's media policy during the Gulf War.[9] The invasion represented a turning point in military-media relations. The press was literally left behind as U.S. troops attacked Grenada on 25 October 1983. Journalists who chartered boats to the island nation were intercepted and detained by U.S. Navy vessels. The DoD did not lift media restrictions until 30 October. The success of the military operation in Grenada and the restricted media coverage may have indicated a shift among U.S. policymakers from the "Vietnam Syndrome" to the

"Grenada Syndrome"—"the fear of repeating the Vietnam experience showed sign of giving way to a desire to relive it in an idealized form."[10]

A February 1984 investigation of military-media relations during the Grenada operation by Major General Winant Sidle recommended that combat correspondent pools be established to facilitate media access to military operations. Media representatives on Sidle's panel initially opposed the idea of pools, but they eventually considered them a necessary compromise in order to assure future access to military operations. The panel's report recommended that pools be "terminated as soon as possible and full coverage be allowed."[11]

The U.S. invasion of Panama in 1989 provided the next test for the media-military relationship. The Department of Defense, following a Sidle Panel recommendation, had established the DoD National Media Pool in 1985 to "enable reporters to cover the earliest possible action of a U.S. military operation . . . while still protecting the element of surprise."[12] U.S. Secretary of Defense Richard Cheney, however, interpreted pools as a means of restricting, not facilitating, media coverage of U.S. military operations. After the media pool arrived in Panama, they were detained by U.S. military personnel until the fighting was over.

A subsequent Department of Defense investigation of the military's media policy by a former official, Fred Hoffman, highlighted the problems with the Panama operation. The report argued that excessive military concern with either secrecy or reporters' safety is not an excuse for limiting pool reporting. The Assistant Secretary of Defense for Public Affairs was asked to "weigh in aggressively" with his superiors to facilitate press access. The Hoffman report suggested that military surveillance of media personnel be reduced in the future.[13]

Containing the Media: Pools, Escorts, and Censors

Secretary of Defense Richard Cheney termed the administration's media policy during the Gulf War "a model of how the department ought to function."[14] According to one administration official, the policy was "much shrewder than Iraq's . . . this sophistication was no accident, but the result of an agonizing reassessment by the military in the wake of Vietnam."[15] Pools, military escorts, and censors permitted the Bush administration greater opportunity to control the flow of public information about the war. Television audiences viewing apparently routine non-combat reports from the Gulf became accustomed to the omnipresent by-line "reviewed by military censors." *Washington Post* Assistant Managing Editor Bob Woodward, who had access to DoD officials during the formation of this policy, wrote, "the public and the world were going to see an incredibly limited and antiseptic version of the war. The media were going to be kept away. Even the videos from the gun cameras in the bombers showing the attacks were going to be distortions when they were made public."[16]

On 13 August 1990, the Department of Defense established the Joint Information Bureau (JIB) in Dhahran, Saudi Arabia. The JIB coordinated all media activities under the supervision of DoD authorities. Captain Ron Wildermuth, chief public affairs aide to General H. Norman Schwarzkopf, U.S. Central Command (CENTCOM) commander and commander in chief of UN coalition forces in the Gulf, outlined media policy on 14 August in a ten-page document entitled "Annex Foxtrot." Captain Wildermuth wrote that "news media representatives will be escorted at all times. Repeat, at all times." Moreover, all interviews of military personnel would be coordinated through DoD or military public affairs personnel or pool escorts.[17]

The DoD justified media pools as necessary because of the large number of reporters in Saudi Arabia and the perceived difficulty of their operating independently in the desert theater of operations.[18] The pool system also allowed the military to influence news stories by controlling reporters' access to field locations. Television coverage of Operation Desert Shield generally focused on the rather innocuous issues of high-tech weaponry, Christmas in the desert, troop preparation and morale (which was usually favorable, given the constant presence of military public affairs officers during interviews of enlisted men), and "covering the war" (stories about the journalists themselves).[19]

Participation in the combat correspondent pools became a contentious issue.[20] The Department of Defense limited pool membership to 126 of the over 1,000 journalists in Saudi Arabia. DoD officials made their selections based upon fitness tests and politicking among the news organizations in Saudi Arabia. CENTCOM gave preference to "media that principally serve the U.S. public and that have had a long-term presence covering Department of Defense military operations."[21]

To facilitate favorable media coverage during Operation Desert

Shield, the Pentagon established the "Hometown News Program." Journalists from predominantly small newspapers in the United States were allowed to spend up to four nights in the field with military units from their area of the country. The Pentagon paid the full cost of this program. Air Force Lieutenant Colonel Michael Fox, the officer in charge of the program, explained why these journalists were granted access denied to many reporters already in Saudi Arabia: "There was just a safer feeling. If they knew that they're getting a free ride and they can't afford the $2,000 ticket, there's probably going to be a tendency to say "We'll do good stuff here.'"[22]

The final version of the DoD "Guidelines for News Media," released on 14 January 1991, stated that

> media pools will be established to provide initial opportunity to join CENTCOM media pools, providing they agree to pool their products. News media who are not members of the official CENTCOM media pools will not be permitted into forward areas. Reporters are strongly discouraged from attempting to link up on their own with combat units. U.S. commanders will maintain extremely tight security throughout the operational area and will exclude from the area of operation all unauthorized individuals.[23]

Publicly, Assistant Secretary for Public Affairs Pete Williams claimed that media pools were necessary to ensure press access to combat operations given the difficult logistical situation created by the presence of so many reporters. Military personnel strictly enforced the pool rules to preempt any unilateral reporting once hostilities began. Williams, in a teleconference briefing with the Joint Information Bureaus in Dhahran and Riyadh on 12 January 1991 explained the DoD policy toward unilaterals. "If reporters show up at units and refuse to leave . . . we will treat them like any other nonmilitary person who shows up at a unit . . . if that means they'll be detained, or some very large burly guys escort them back, that may happen. But the point is we can't be flexible on this at the beginning or we've lost all control over the pools. . . . We might want to consider pulling a person's credentials if they do that several times or even once."[24] Edward Cody of the *Washington Post* said that although most military men were inclined to be cooperative, "they had been told by their commander [Gen. Schwarzkopf] that cooperation was to be limited."[25]

The battle between UN coalition and Iraqi forces at the Saudi

Arabian border town of Khafji illustrated the effect of the media pool restrictions on press coverage. The U.S. military did not take pool reporters to Khafji until eighteen hours after the battle began. After arriving, military personnel restricted press pool reporters to rear areas away from the battle. Pool reporters, working with information provided by their military escorts, erroneously reported that coalition forces had retaken the town while, in fact, the battle was still in progress. Guy Gugliotta of the *Washington Post*, frustrated at the "virtual non-existence of usable pool reports," attempted to operate independently. A U.S. military public affairs officer threatened to turn Gugliotta and his companions over to Saudi authorities if they did not leave. Colonel William Mulvey, chief of the Dhahran JIB, gave the Saudis a memo containing the names of eight reporters who attempted to operate unilaterally at Khafji. Mulvey encouraged the Saudis "to pull a few visas to make a point."[26]

U.S. Marines confiscated at gunpoint a French television crew's film of the fighting at Khafji for operating outside of the media pools. On 6 February, an NBC reporter verbally abused Robert Fisk, a reporter for the London *Independent*, when Fisk tried to approach a U.S. Marine unit for more information.[27]

U.S. military personnel strictly enforced the media pool restrictions. On 3 February 1991, an Alabama National Guard unit blindfolded and held *Time* photographer Wesley Boxce for 30 hours after accusing him of spying for the Iraqis. On 5 February, the U.S. First Cavalry detained Fred Bayles of the Associated Press for six hours for operating outside the pool system. The *London Times* reported on 8 February that U.S. Marines held a wire service photographer for six hours and threatened to shoot him if he left his car. Chris Hedges of the *New York Times* was detained after asking to speak with a public affairs officer at a U.S. military hospital and later had his press credentials revoked for interviewing a Saudi shopkeeper without an escort.[28] Retired army Colonel David H. Hackworth, *Newsweek's* Gulf War correspondent and a Vietnam war veteran, wrote that "I had more guns pointed at me by Americans or Saudis who were into controlling the press than in all my years of combat."[29]

Censorship and delay of nonsecurity threatening material became routine during the Gulf War. The DoD argued that security could be jeopardized because of the instantaneous communication made possible through satellite technology and computers.[30] The "Guidelines for News Media" stated that "material will be examined solely for its conformance to the attached ground rules, not for its potential to express criticism or cause embarrassment." According to the Society of Professional Journalists, however, the policy of "security review at the source" turned military public affairs officers (PAO) "into editors and producers and constitutes an unnecessary prior restraint on the news."[31]

Following the Gulf War, Assistant Secretary Williams wrote that "at no point in the security review procedure were Department of Defense personnel authorized to make any changes to any media story" and that he was personally unaware of any such incidents.[32] A July 1991 DoD report on the Persian Gulf conflict acknowledged, however, that some PAO's "overzealously" performed their security review responsibilities.[33] The Department of Defense's final report to Congress on the Gulf War also noted the slow processing of pool reports.[34]

James LeMoyne of the *New York Times* reported that "three Pentagon officials in the Gulf region said they spent significant time analyzing reporters' stories in order to make recommendations on how to sway coverage in the Pentagon's favor." LeMoyne's scheduled interview with General Schwarzkopf was cancelled after he was critical of President Bush in one of his articles. Military officials warned reporters not to appear "anti-military."[35]

On 16 January 1991, Carol Morello of the *Philadelphia Inquirer* was aboard a U.S. aircraft carrier in the Gulf when the air war began. She and her colleagues were ushered into a room in order not to bear witness to the "initial euphoria" of the pilots. Military censors changed the word "fighter-pilot" to "fighter" in an article by Malcolm Browne of the *New York Times*. Censors also changed the word "giddy" to "proud" when describing the mood of Air Force pilots following attacks against Iraq in one of Frank Bruni's articles for the *Detroit Free Press*.[36]

Media personnel found their access to U.S. troops limited by the presence of military public affairs officers who arranged and supervised interviews and field visits. After Stephanie Glass of the *San Antonio Light* asked a PAO if the airmen she was interviewing could finish their own sentences, he told her that if she was going to be a "smart ass" she would be "put back on the bus." Albert Hunt of *The Wall Street Journal* said that PAOs interrupted interviews on several occasions. The Ad Hoc Media Group, representing seventeen of the leading American news organizations, reported that in general newspeople had to deal "repeatedly with escorts who stepped in front of a camera to stop an interview, stared menacingly at G.I.s making unfavorable comments, locked up reporters to prevent them from witnessing spontaneous excitement at the start of the war and jaw-boned about the content of stories."[37]

Another notable addition to the range of military censorship during the Gulf War was the restriction on casualty information and photographs. Although the DoD's "Guidelines for News Media" only forbade pictures of "recognizable" casualties, in practice casualty pictures were strictly limited. In fact, the Pentagon banned media access to Dover Air Force Base, where the bodies of U.S. soldiers killed in action were sent.

The Briefings

The pool restrictions and enhanced censorship controls allowed the Bush administration to exploit official sources as the main conduit of public information. The media, even without such restrictions, rely on official sources as a matter of routine practice. Regularly televised briefings allowed military officials to speak directly to the American people without the press being able to verify the information presented due to DoD pool restrictions and censorship.

The briefings became a central part of an overall White House marketing strategy. The Bush administration modeled its media policy after a 1980s-style U.S. political campaign. At daily press briefings, White House Press Secretary Marlin Fitzwater tested a proposed "message of the day" about the war before the cameras were turned on. If the response to the message was favorable, the message would be faxed to political and business leaders around the country urging that the message be disseminated to the public.[38]

The major news networks routinely covered the military briefings, which were usually shown in their entirety on the Cable News Network (CNN). President Bush and his senior advisers closely monitored these sessions; the president reportedly watched at least part of virtually every briefing. The regular appearance of Schwarzkopf and Powell at the forums gave these traditionally rough-and-tumble information-gathering sessions for reporters an enhanced stature in the eyes of the public. Lieutenant General Thomas Kelly, a regular briefer, usually had his staff seek out potential questions from reporters in advance of the briefings in order to rehearse answers before going on the air. The briefings included videos of high-tech weaponry in apparently successful military operations.

The briefers perceived the sessions as a means of controlling, not enhancing, the flow of information about the war. On 17 January 1991, an airforce officer briefing journalists said "I don't like the press, your presence here can't possibly do me any good, and it can hurt me and my people." On 7 February General Schwarzkopf told reporters that "we will continue to be deliberately conservative in what we tell you and the American people" in order not to allow a "credibility gap to generate."[39]

"Warspeak" concealed the true nature of war from the American people. Military euphemisms, which originated in the terminology of the DoD systems analysts of the 1960s, replaced clear language about military engagements. War dead were now simply "KIA" (killed in action); civilian casualties became "collateral damage;" bridges and civilian targets bombed by coalition aircraft were "serviced."[40]

Aircraft and tanks, however, could be killed. Even though General Schwarzkopf testily told reporters on 30 January 1991 that "body count means nothing, absolutely nothing" in reference to human casualties of war, seven days earlier General Powell used "body count" to refer to the number of Iraqi aircraft destroyed by coalition bombing. In fact, DoD officials reportedly encouraged journalists to use "body count" to refer to the destruction of Iraqi military hardware.[41]

The briefings also allowed military officials to dictate the relative importance of issues on the media agenda. For example, General Schwarzkopf began his briefing on the morning of the first notification of U.S. casualties in the war with "rather sensational" graphics of U.S. precision-guided "smart bombs" annihilating their targets. He followed this with a more restrained announcement of "twelve KIA." That evening network news coverage gave roughly equal time to the bombs and marine casualties.[42]

Military briefers obscured the definition of a "successful" bombing mission. On 18 January, Lieutenant General Kelly claimed that coalition aircraft performed with "80 percent effectiveness." But after being questioned about the 80 percent success rate at a briefing three days later, Kelly defined success as meaning that "the sorties are launched, they go to their targets, they successfully drop their ordnance."[43] Whether the bombs hit their targets is left out of this definition of a successful mission.

Despite the sensational videos of U.S. precision-guided weapons employed at military briefings, the celebrated "smart bombs" in fact constituted only 7 percent of the bomb-tonnage dropped on Iraq.

Secretary Cheney said that DoD did not release footage of errant bombings because it was "pretty dull, boring stuff."[44]

Lieutenant General Kelly described the briefings as the "most significant part of the whole operation." He explained:

> for the first time ever the administration—the Department of Defense—was talking directly to the American people, using the vehicle of a press briefing, whereas in Vietnam everything was filtered through the press. I think that it was a major advantage for the government. The press, wittingly or unwittingly, between Riyadh and Washington, was giving us an hour-and-a-half a day to tell our story to the American people . . . the American people were getting their information from the government—not from the press. . . . I think the lesson for the future is, that we should endeavor to do that more.[45]

The Media Rallies Round the Flag

Media coverage of Operation Desert Shield and Operation Desert Storm reflected clear support for the Bush administration's policies. DoD containment policies reinforced the media's post-Vietnam drift toward a more pronounced establishment orientation. *Newsday* reporter Sydney Schanberg, noted that the media's own scars from Vietnam, including accusations of a lack of patriotism and renewed fears of offending the political establishment, may have influenced the pro-war orientation of the press.[46]

An analysis of newspaper editorials following Bush's decision to send troops to Saudi Arabia revealed generally strong support for the president's policies, including a warning on 27 August by the *Los Angeles Times* that it would be "bad policy" for Congress and the president to quarrel over Middle East policy. Interestingly, on 11 August the *Times* criticized increased military deployments to the region. During the two weeks following President Bush's 8 August decision to send troops to defend Saudi Arabia, however, 76 percent of all references to the president in the major print media were favorable. As U.S. support for the president's policies solidified and congressional opposition was practically nonexistent, twenty-four of the nation's twenty-five leading newspapers expressed editorial approval of Operation Desert Storm (the *Rocky Mountain News* was the lone exception).[47]

The Bush administration defined the terms of debate, and the press usually followed its lead. Both the government and media increasingly focused on the ruthlessness of the Iraqi regime and whether Iraq would withdraw unconditionally from Kuwait, rather than the implications of war in the Middle East. Eye-catching information boxes and graphics at times replaced investigative journalism and analysis in the print media. David Ignatius of the *Washington Post* said that "we spent so many months focusing on whether Saddam would pull out, the overriding question we didn't ask was what kind of world would we face after a war? . . . Could we have been clearer before the fact, telling readers what war is like?"[48]

Television coverage of Desert Shield also reflected the Bush administration's agenda in marketing the war to the American people. NBC News held a live mock confrontation between George Bush and Saddam Hussein on 9 August 1990 that concluded with Hussein threatening to hang U.S. hostages held in Iraq.[49] On 17 August 1990, ABC anchorpersons Ted Koppel and Barbara Walters lectured Iraq's ambassador to the United States, Mohammed al-Mashat, for his faulty comparison of Iraq's invasion of Kuwait to the United States's invasions of Panama and Grenada. Koppel said that "*We* did not go in and seize Panama. *We* did not go in and seize Grenada." A survey of guests on ABC's *Nightline* and PBS's *MacNeil-Lehrer News Hour* in August 1990 showed that almost half were current or former government officials (47 to 48 percent) and that no guest argued against the U.S. military intervention.[50] Television news networks used video news releases provided by Hill and Knowlton, a Washington public relations firm hired by the Kuwaiti government, without attribution, in their broadcasts.[51]

The administration compared Saddam Hussein's Iraq to Adolf Hitler's Germany as part of its campaign to justify the war to the American people. On 8 August 1990, President Bush described Iraq's invasion of Kuwait as occurring in "blitzkrieg fashion." On 15 October, the president referred to Saddam Hussein as "Hitler revisited."[52] The media accepted and accentuated this characterization of Saddam Hussein. A *New Republic* cover photo of the Iraqi president included a doctored mustache so that Hussein more closely resembled Hitler. Syndicated columnists, such as Charles Krauthammer and William Safire, used the analogy in expressing their support for the war.[53]

Consensual reporting by the major news networks may have increased support for the Bush administration's war policy.[54] The major networks employed patriotic images in its programming. NBC's coverage, entitled "America at War," had, as its symbol, a fighter bomber imposed over a U.S. flag. In response to fears of having their products associated with the war, CBS executives assured advertisers that their commercials would be preceded by "specially produced" segments with "upbeat images or messages about the war."[55] A CNN reporter described American warplanes taking off to bomb Iraq at the start of the air war as a "sweet beautiful sight." On 17 January 1991, Charles Osgood of CBS called the bombing of Iraq "a marvel."[56]

The media imitated the Bush administration's tendency to portray attacks on Iraq as personally directed at Saddam Hussein. Ann Compton of ABC mentioned that the United States made "more attacks on Saddam Hussein's head" in a remark characteristic of this approach. Reporters usually cited Saddam Hussein as the person who launched the Scud missile attacks on Israel and Saudi Arabia.[57] This personalization of the conflict reinforced the administration policy of vilifying Saddam Hussein while correspondingly dehumanizing the human toll of the war on Iraq.

Following the Pentagon's lead, network analysts and reporters referred to Iraqi civilian casualties as propaganda or collateral damage. This terminology proved effective as a euphemism to minimize the U.S. public's sensitivity to Iraqi civilian casualties. Fifty-five percent of a group polled during the war were "fairly or very concerned" about "collateral damage," while 82 percent expressed the same sentiments about the "number of civilian casualties and other unintended damage."[58] Referring to possible civilian casualties of coalition bombing, Tom Brokaw of NBC said that "we must point out again and again that it is Saddam Hussein who put these innocents in harm's way." On 27 January 1991, Dennis Murphy of NBC said, when describing footage of Iraqi civilian casualties, that "until we get some Western reporters in there to vouch for it, I think we'll have to call it propaganda." When the U.S. military announced that it had bombed hydroelectric dams and other civilian structures, media analysts never referred to this as a violation of the Geneva Protocols on the conduct of war. Ted Koppel described 23 January 1991, when 2,000 sorties were reportedly flown against Iraq, by saying "aside from the Scud missile that landed in Tel Aviv, it's been a quiet night in the Middle East."[59] On 16 February 1991, an article in the *Washington Post* by television critic Tom Shales described as Arnett's Syndrome (a reference to CNN's Peter Arnett, who covered the air war from Baghdad) a "seemingly inexhaustible concern for the welfare of the Iraqis."

"Expert" network television analysts may have a "substantial impact on public opinion" because of "high perceived credibility."[60] During the Gulf War, the experts generally supported Operation Desert Storm and at times reinforced negative stereotypes of Arab society. One analyst compared Western and Arab minds by saying that "we go in a straight line. They zig-zag." On 16 January 1991, NBC analyst Edward Peck, former head of the U.S. interests section in Baghdad, described the Middle East in the following way: "Where we in the West tend to think of the New Testament heritage, where you turn the other cheek and you let bygones be bygones and forgive and forget, the people of the Middle East are the people of the Old Testament, if you will—if the Muslims will let me say that— where there's much more of an eye for an eye and . . . you carry on the vendetta and the struggle long after people in the West would be prepared to say all right, it's over."[61]

The media also hyped the potential for terrorist reprisals against Americans by Arabs or even Arab-Americans. Dan Rather, CBS News anchorperson, asked Federal Bureau of Investigation Chief William Sessions on 16 January 1991, "if you're an American mother who happens to be of Jewish heritage . . . do you send your children to school? . . . What should our attitude toward Americans of Arab descent be?" Correspondingly, acts of discrimination against Arab-Americans, which increased during the Gulf War, received little media attention.[62]

The media reinforced the military's emphasis on U.S. high-tech weaponry employed in apparently successful operations. On 17 January 1991, Arthur Kent of NBC termed Iraq's Scud missile "an evil weapon, but an accurate weapon." Peter Jennings of ABC called the Scud a "horrifying killer" while admiring the "brilliance of laser-guided bombs" employed by U.S. forces. The lack of independent combat footage probably contributed to this infatuation with the weaponry of war.[63]

The Press Reconsiders Its Role

After the Gulf War, Peter Jennings of ABC described the media-military relationship as a "pact with the devil." The media realized relatively late in the game that the DoD policies had accentuated the dangerous precedents set during the Grenada and Panama conflicts. Although many journalists in the field offered admirable reporting under difficult conditions, for the most part they spent "too much energy interviewing each other on the failure of the system—'Vietnam was never like this,' everyone kept saying—and not enough time figuring out how to turn it to our advantage."[64]

Those reporters who challenged the pool system occasionally achieved impressive results. Forrest Sawyer of ABC broke from the pool system, hooked up with Saudi and Egyptian forces, and ended up being the only Western reporter to fly on a bombing mission and bring back pictures from the front. Probably the most memorable television scoop of the war was achieved by Bob McKeown of CBS, who left the pool system and brought the first televised pictures of a liberated Kuwait City to U.S. audiences. This historic event may not have been recorded without McKeown's shirking of the pool system.[65]

In January 1991, some press organizations, including *The Nation* and *Agence France-Presse*, legally challenged the DoD press controls on the grounds that they violated First Amendment rights guaranteed under the U.S. Constitution. During the war, Pentagon spokespersons were not allowed to appear on radio or television with any of the plaintiffs in the lawsuit. On 16 April 1991, U.S. District Court Judge Leonard B. Sand dismissed the case, ruling that the issue was "too abstract and conjectural" to be ruled on, especially since the war had ended.[66]

Although not participating in the lawsuit, fifteen leading U.S. news organizations and television networks sent a letter to Secretary of Defense Richard Cheney on 29 April 1991, protesting media restrictions during the Gulf War. The letter claimed that the "flow of information to the public was blocked, impeded, or diminished" and that the media restrictions "meant we could not tell the public the full story of those who fought the nation's battle." Finally, the letter declared that "we are intent on not experiencing again the Desert Storm kind of pool system."[67]

In May 1992, DoD officials and representatives of twenty major news organizations agreed on revised principles for future war coverage. The agreement stated that while "pools are not to serve as the standard means of covering U.S. military operations," they "may sometimes provide the only feasible means of early access to a military operation." Military public affairs officers were called on "to act as liaisons" but "not interfere with the reporting process."[68]

The Gulf War was indeed a "critical moment" for the media, and especially for television journalism, a time when journalistic standards require re-evaluations in the context of an event of magnitude.[69] The use of satellite technology for instantaneous reporting, although originally feared as a potential security threat by the military, actually contributed to the media's substandard performance. Because of pool restrictions, censorship, and its reliance on official sources, the media, especially television, lost valuable time to analyze and sort out its information.

The U.S. public didn't seem to mind, giving apparent credence to those supporting the Pentagon controls. Over 80 percent of Americans polled in one survey rated the press coverage of the war as "good or excellent." Eighty-three percent thought that military restrictions on news reporting was a good thing. General Schwarzkopf received a 62 percent "very favorable" rating, the second highest ever for an American public figure.[70]

The public's favorable view of war coverage, in fact, underscores the serious problems in military-media relations. The public watched and approved of television coverage of the war, but knew less about the politics of the Middle East. Another survey of Americans who followed events in the Gulf on television revealed that 74 percent of those polled believed that the United States had threatened sanctions before Iraq invaded Kuwait. Only 13 percent knew that U.S. officials had declared neutrality on "Arab-Arab disputes" as late as July 1990 and that the United States did not have a defense treaty with Kuwait at the time of Iraq's invasion. Only 31 percent of those polled knew of Israeli occupation of Arab territory and only 3 percent of the Syrian occupation of Lebanese territory. In contrast, 81 percent knew the name of the Patriot missile used to intercept Iraqi Scuds.[71]

Conclusions

Following the Gulf War, George Bush said, "by God, we've kicked the Vietnam Syndrome once and for all."[72] In defeating Iraq, U.S. political and military leaders also declared victory over the legacy of defeat and frustration that characterized the United States' involvement in Vietnam. The DoD's media containment policies reflected the government's obsession with the myths and legacies of Vietnam in regard to the role of the press during war.

The press, struggling with its own Vietnam Syndrome, tried to have it both ways during the Gulf War—challenging the DoD controls while championing the war. The results proved that such a response to the Pentagon's containment policies could only result in diminishing the press's ability to report the news in a truly independent manner.

The military-media relationship is by its nature ambiguous and contentious, and must remain so in a democracy. The Gulf War was a setback for the healthy tension that should characterize a balanced military-media relationship. This is unfortunate, because there can only be Pyrrhic victories when one side "wins" in the course of this struggle.

Notes

1. George C. Herring, "America and Vietnam: The Unending War," *Foreign Affairs 70* (Winter 1991-92): 104.

2. For an historical overview of military-media relations prior to Grenada, see Jack A. Gottschalk, "Consistent with Security . . . A History of American Military Press Censorship," *Communications and the Law 5* (Summer 1983): 35-52.

3. Lt. Gen. Bernard E. Trainor, "The Military and the Media: A Troubled Embrace," in *The Media and the Gulf War*, ed. Hedrick Smith (Washington, DC: Seven Locks Press, 1992): 69.

4. Simon Serfaty, ed., *The Media and Foreign Policy* (New York: St. Martin's Press, 1991): 2. The literature supporting the oppositional media hypothesis is cogently summarized in Daniel C. Hallin, "The Media, the War in Vietnam, and Political Support: A Critique of the Thesis of an Oppositional Media," *The Journal of Politics 46* (February 1984): 2-24.

5. Michael Mandelbaum, "Vietnam: The Television War," *Daedalus 111* (Fall 1982): 160-62.

6. See William M. Hammond, *Public Affairs: The Military and the Media, 1962-1968* (Washington, DC: U.S. Government Printing Office, 1982): 388; and John E. Mueller, *War, Presidents, and Public Opinion* (New York: John Wiley and Sons, 1973): 53, 60-61, 266.

7. Hallin, "The Media, the War in Vietnam, and Political Support."

8. Daniel C. Hallin, *The Uncensored War: The Media and Vietnam* (Berkeley: University of California Press, 1989): 8.

9. Jason DeParle, "Long Series of Military Decisions Led to Gulf War News Censorship," *New York Times*, 5 May 1991, 1. The U.S. military may also have been influenced by press restrictions employed by the British government during the Falklands/Malvinas War. See Jacqueline E. Sharkey, *Under Fire: U.S. Military Restrictions on the Media from Grenada to the Persian Gulf* (Washington, DC: The Center for Public Integrity, 1991): 61-66.

10. Hallin, *The Uncensored War*, vii.

11. *Final Report of the Chairman of the Joint Chiefs of Staff (CJCS) Media-Military Relations Panel (Sidle Panel)*, prepared by Major General Winant Sidle, (Washington, DC: Office of the Assistant Secretary of Defense-Public Affairs, 23 August 1984): 8.

12. U.S. Department of Defense, *Conduct of the Persian Gulf Conflict: An Interim Report to Congress* (July 1991): 19-1.

13. Fred S. Hoffman, "Review of the Panama Pool Deployment: December 1989," (Washington, DC: Assistant Secretary of Defense for Public Affairs, March 1990). In Committee on Governmental Affairs, U.S. Senate, *Pentagon Rules on Media Access to the Persian Gulf War*, Senate Hearing 102-178, (Washington, DC: U.S. Government Printing Office, 1991): 780–800.

14. Jason DeParle, "Keeping the News in Step: Are the Pentagon's Gulf War Rules Here to Stay?" *New York Times* (6 May 1991): 9.

15. James P. Pinkerton, "General Schwarzkopf's New Paradigm: Domestic Lessons of Desert Storm," *Policy Review* (Summer 1991): 22–23. Mr. Pinkerton served as deputy assistant to the president for policy planning in the Bush administration.

16. Bob Woodward, *The Commanders* (New York: Simon & Schuster, 1991): 375.

17. "Approved Annex F (Foxtrot) TO OPORD Desert Shield Public Affairs, U.S. Central Command (CENTCOM), 14 August 1990. Declassified by R.E. Wildermuth, Capt., U.S.N., 22 May 1990." In *Pentagon Rules on Media Access to the Persian Gulf War*, 279–88.

18. See U.S. Department of Defense, *Conduct of the Persian Gulf War: Final Report to Congress*, April 1992, S-1, for a list of the complications that provided the rationale for the Pentagon's media policy.

19. Michael Massing, "Is the Most Popular Evening Newscast the Best?" *Columbia Journalism Review* (March/April 1991): 31.

20. See Frank A. Aukofer, "The Press Collaborators," *Nieman Reports* (Summer 1991): 24–26.

21. "CENTCOM (Central Command) Pool Membership and Operating Procedures," 30 January 1991.

22. DeParle, "Long Series of Military Decisions . . . ," 1. The Pentagon also gave preferential treatment to Quantum Diversified, a Minneapolis firm, to shoot an apparently pro-military video on the National Guard. See Sharkey, *Under Fire*, 113–15.

23. U.S. Department of Defense, "Guidelines for News Media" (14 January 1991).

24. "Groundrules and Guidelines: Teleconference briefing by Pete Williams, Assistant Secretary, Public Affairs, with Joint Information Bureaus in Dhahran and Riyadh, Saudi Arabia, 12 January 1991." In *Pentagon Rules on Media Access to the Persian Gulf War*, 409.

25. The Ad Hoc Media Group, "Problems of News Coverage in the Persian Gulf (Letter and Report)," 25 June 1991.

26. Ibid.

27. Robert Fisk, "Free to Report What We're Told," in *The Gulf War Reader: History, Documents, and Opinions,* ed. Micah L. Sifry and Christopher Cerf (New York: Times Books/Random House, 1991): 378.

28. Events cited in Nicole Volpe and James Ridgeway, "How to Win: 32 Examples of the Press on a Leash," *Voice,* 26 March 1991, 17-18, and the Ad Hoc Media Group (Letter and Report).

29. "Newsweek's Troops in the Persian Gulf," *Newsweek* (11 March 1991): 4.

30. See "Groundrules and Guidelines: Teleconference Briefing by Pete Williams," 391, for a discussion of the influence of technology on the policy of security review at the source.

31. "Letter responding to revised groundrules and guidelines from The Society of Professional Journalists, 10 January 1991." *In Pentagon Rules on Media Access to the Gulf War,* 612-13.

32. "Response from Pete Williams, Assistant Secretary of Defense for Public Affairs, 24 May 1991." In *Pentagon Rules on Media Access to the Gulf War,* 145.

33. U.S. Department of Defense, *Conduct of the Persian Gulf Conflict: An Interim Report to Congress* (July 1991): 19-4.

34. U.S. Department of Defense, *Conduct of the Persian Gulf War: Final Report to Congress* (April 1992): S-1.

35. James LeMoyne, "Pentagon's Strategy for the Press: Good News or No News," *New York Times* (17 February 1991): E-4.

36. Malcolm W. Browne, "The Military vs. The Press," *New York Times Magazine* (3 March 1991): 27-30.

37. The Ad Hoc Media Group (Letter and Report).

38. See DeParle, "Long Series of Military Decisions . . . ," and "The President's Spin Patrol," *Newsweek* (11 February 1991): 31. Also see Brian Schriner, "The War of Images: The Media and the Gulf War," *Journal of South Asian and Middle Eastern Studies* 15 (Winter 1991): 9-14, for a discussion of the White House strategy of manipulating media coverage of the war.

39. See Volpe and Ridgeway, "How to Win," 17-18, and Article 19, *Stop Press: The Gulf War and Censorship* no. 2 (London: The International Centre on Censorship, May 1991): 8-13, for two useful chronologies of press restrictions and censorship during the Gulf War.

40. See Sharkey, *Under Fire,* 28, and Douglas Kellner, *The Persian Gulf TV War* (Boulder, CO: Westview Press, 1992): 238-42. Also see Harry G. Summers, Jr., *On Strategy: A Critical Analysis of the Vietnam War* (Novato, CA: Presidio Press, 1982): 35-36, for a discussion of military euphemisms employed during the Vietnam War.

41. Cited in Sharkey, *Under Fire*, 160–61.

42. See "The President's Spin Patrol," 31.

43. Cited in Sharkey, *Under Fire*, 149–52.

44. In DeParle, "Keeping the News in Step: Are the Pentagon's Gulf War Rules Here to Stay?" *New York Times* (6 May 1991): 9.

45. In Sharkey, *Under Fire*, 129.

46. Sydney H. Schanberg, "Censoring for Political Security," *Washington Journalism Review* 13 (March 1991): 25.

47. See James Bennett, "How They Missed That Story," *Washington Monthly* (December 1990): 10–16, and Arthur E. Rowse, "The Guns of August," *Columbia Journalism Review* (March–April 1991): 26–27, for two useful analyses of major print media coverage of the events leading to the Gulf War.

48. In Thomas J. Colin, "As Television Glanced Off the Story, Newspapers Surrounded It," *Washington Journalism Review* 13 (March 1991): 33.

49. See Jim Naureckas, "Media on the March: Journalism in the Gulf," *Extra!* 3:8 (November-December 1990): 3–8, for examples of media bias and control leading up to the Gulf War.

50. Examples cited in Ibid., and Rowse, "The Guns of August."

51. See Sharkey, *Under Fire*, 116–17, for a discussion of the role of public relations firms on media coverage of the war.

52. Dan Balz, "President Warns Iraq of War Crimes Trials," *Washington Post* (16 October 1990): A-19.

53. LaMay et al. found 1,170 examples of the Hitler-Hussein comparison in the media. See Craig LaMay et al., *The Media At War* (New York: Gannett Foundation Media Center, 1991): 42.

54. A study of the effect of television news on the U.S. public's attitude toward major foreign policy issues observed that "when collective opinion does move, the news that is broadcast on network television accounts for a large part of the magnitude and the direction of change." In Donald L. Jordan and Benjamin I. Page, "Shaping Foreign Policy Options: The Role of T.V. News," *Journal of Conflict Resolution* 36(June 1992): 237. This study analyzed the effect of television news coverage on public opinion regarding thirty-two foreign policy issues from the 1970s and early 1980s.

55. See Daniel Hallin, "TV's Clean Little War," *The Bulletin of Atomic Scientists* (May 1991): 17–19, for a discussion of the use of patriotic imagery, and Volpe and Ridgeway, "How to Win," 18, for the citation on CBS advertising policy.

56. Cited in Jim Naureckas, "Gulf War Coverage: The Worst Censorship Was at Home," in *Extra! The Gulf War Special Issue* (May 1991), 3, 5.

57. Ibid., 3.

58. Times-Mirror Center for the People and the Press, "The People, the

Press, and the War in the Gulf Part II" (Washington, DC, 25 March 1991).

59. Events cited in *Extra! The Gulf War Special Issue*, 6–8; Larry Cohler, "Molding the Media is the Message," *Washington Jewish Week* (21 February 1991): 7; and James Ledbetter, "Deadlines in the Sand," *Voice* (5 February 1991).

60. Benjamin I. Page, Robert Y. Shapiro, and Glenn R. Dempsey, "What Moves Public Opinion," *American Political Science Review* 81 (March 1987): 35.

61. Cited in *Extra! The Gulf War Special Issue*, 4, 9.

62. Cited in *Extra! The Gulf War Special Issue*, 8.

63. Ibid., 5.

64. David Lamb, "Pentagon Hardball," *Washington Journalism Review* (April 1991): 35.

65. U.S. military personnel in Saudi Arabia had orders to "stop CBS" when they learned that McKeown had made a break for Kuwait City. See Volpe and Ridgeway, "How to Win," 18. Also see "Clippings from the Media War," *Newsweek* (11 March 1991): 52.

66. "Opinion. United States District Court Judge Leonard B. Sand. United States District Court. Southern District of New York, April 16, 1991." In *Pentagon Rules on Media Access to the Persian Gulf War*, 1440.

67. Letter to Secretary of Defense Dick Cheney concerning need to improve future combat coverage and improved understanding between the military and the media, from: *Time, The Chicago Tribune, The New York Times*, CBS News, *The Wall Street Journal*, NBC News, *The Washington Post*, Knight-Ridder, Inc., *Newsweek*, Cox Newspapers, Hearst Newspapers, ABC News, Cable News Network, *The Los Angeles Times*, Associated Press, 25 June 1991 [29 April 1991]. In *Pentagon Rules on Media Access to the Persian Gulf*, 728–29.

68. Howard Kurtz and Barton Gellman, "Guidelines Set for News Coverage of Wars," *Washington Post* (22 May 1992): A-23. News organizations endorsing the principles included *The Washington Post, New York Times, Los Angeles Times*, ABC, CBS, NBC, CNN, the American Society of Newspaper Editors, American Newspaper Publishers Association, and the Radio and Television Directors Association.

69. Barbie Zelizer, "CNN, the Gulf War, and Journalistic Practice," *Journal of Communication* 42 (Winter 1992): 66–81.

70. "The People, the Press, and the War in the Gulf, Part II."

71. Center for Studies in Communication, "The Gulf War: A Study of the Media, Public Opinion, and Public Knowledge," February 1991.

72. Cited in Ann Devroy and Guy Gugliotta, "Cease-fire Talks Delayed by Technical Details," *Washington Post* (2 March 1991): A-13.

Part III
The Gulf War and the
Middle East Order

11

Iraq and the New World Order

Marion Farouk-Sluglett and Peter Sluglett

It is both difficult and distressing to write about Iraq in the aftermath of the Gulf War. The invasion of Kuwait some two years after the end of a futile and destructive war with Iran was not a popular move in Iraq. Few Iraqis believed that Saddam Hussein's action was taken to rectify an old wrong, but as U.S. determination and Saddam Hussein's intransigence combined to make a showdown inevitable, many Iraqis hoped that one positive outcome might emerge: Saddam Hussein would not survive the confrontation, and more than two decades of nightmare would end.

But in the fall of 1993, two and a half years after the end of the ground war and the savage suppression of the Kurdish and Arab uprisings (during which anywhere from a quarter to three-quarters of a million people were killed), Saddam Hussein was still in power. Quite apart from those killed in the war and its aftermath, thousands have since died of exposure, malnutrition, and the lack of proper sanitation and drinking water. A medical team from Harvard visited Iraq in October and November 1991 and reported a serious increase in mortality rates among children under five. The economy was kept alive by the regime's printing of unlimited quantities of paper money. The UN drafted proposals that would permit Iraq, under strict international supervision, to sell some oil to buy essential imports. These proposals were rejected by the Iraqi government on the grounds that the terms constituted an infringement of its national sovereignty. The Arab-Israeli "peace process," the presidential campaign in the United States, and the short attention span of the media and of world, especially U.S., public opinion, all gave Saddam Hussein and his circle breathing space, providing yet another opportunity to regroup and rearm themselves against the Iraqi people.

Although public utilities were restored in Baghdad and Basra, the situation in most of the country remains grim. Substantial numbers of middle class Iraqis—including those considered to have formed the social base of the regime—have either left the country or are desperately trying to do so. The devastation confronting most Iraqis every day is far greater than anything that could have resulted from the most rigorous and thorough application of sanctions, but Saddam Hussein is still in power and there is no obvious prospect of unseating him. Survival seems to be the only priority of the leadership, regardless of the cost to the country and its people.

That this state of affairs could have come to pass seems almost incomprehensible. This chapter examines the sequence of events and looks at some of the ways in which the Iraqi opposition would like to see the situation develop in the future. Although the generally rentier nature of the economy is clearly crucial in any overall assessment of what has happened,[1] what may be called "Iraq-specific" political requirements and historical conjunctures have shaped and changed the regime itself over time. A brief look at contemporary Iraqi history shows how the Ba'ath consolidated power and how Ba'ath rule gradually turned into the absolute dictatorship of a narrow group of Takritis around Saddam Hussein. It also reveals the way in which the Iran-Iraq War and the militarization that accompanied it changed the nature of the regime and the aspirations of its leader.

The Creation of Modern Iraq

Briefly, the modern state of Iraq was created in 1920 as part of the peace settlement after World War I.[2] The victorious allies divided the Arab provinces of the former Ottoman Empire among themselves. Great Britain, which had occupied the provinces of Basra and Baghdad for most of the war and Mosul by the end of the war, was appointed mandatory power under the new system of international trusteeship established by the League of Nations.

Although parts of the country had been united under a single government at various times in the past, the entity that emerged in 1920 had no previous independent existence as a nation state. Britain imported a king, Faisal, the son of Sharif Hussein of Mecca, and endowed Iraq with a constitution and a bicameral legislature. The mandate, a form of indirect rule where Arab ministers and officials were closely supervised by British advisers whose advice had to be taken, ended in 1932 when Iraq was admitted to the League of Nations as an independent state. By this time, Britain had secured

Iraq's present northern boundary, had ensured that the concession for oil exploration and exploitation was given to the Iraq Petroleum Company (a conglomerate of British, Dutch, French, and American oil interests), and had created a social base for the monarchy by appointing tribal leaders who had full possession of what had previously been the customary land holdings of "their" tribes. In addition, Britain retained military bases in Iraq and generally continued to exercise strong political and economic influence.

In 1941, a group of Iraqi officers led a short-lived campaign against Britain that resulted in a second British occupation until the end of World War II. Between 1945 and 1958, the country was governed by a succession of twenty-four cabinets, most of which contained the same handful of individuals, often headed by the veteran pro-British politician Nuri al-Sa'id. Genuine opposition parties were banned for most of this period, which meant that there was little scope for the development of a democratic tradition. Many Iraqis believed that the country's most urgent need was national independence, which would be followed by economic development and social reform, both of which were blocked or denied by the monarchy and its British sponsors. At the same time, the state was seen as the "natural" vehicle to carry out these reforms and implement the development so badly needed. This kind of thinking—usually but not always associated with "socialism"—had wide acceptance in the Middle East during the postwar period and was by no means unique to Iraq.

During and after World War II, members of the rising middle class were expanding their investments in manufacturing, commerce, and real estate. This accelerated in the 1950s when oil became a major force in the economy. Although oil revenues were modest in comparison to those of later decades, they were sufficient to finance the expansion of the bureaucracy, the educational system, and other services. The increase in government expenditure served as a direct stimulus to the economy

Private capital continued to be concentrated in the hands of a few families who controlled more than half of all private corporate commercial and industrial wealth. Far below them in status and wealth were medium to small property owners, religious dignitaries and local notables, wholesale and retail merchants, manufacturers, owners of workshops and repair shops, and petty traders, as well as the newly emerging intelligentsia of professionals—lawyers, army officers, and civil servants. This latter group, together with large sections of the urban poor, were acutely aware of the shortcomings of the political system and formed the core of the independence movement in the 1940s and 1950s. A working class also emerged, particularly in the mostly foreign-owned large enterprises such as the railways, the Basra port, and the Iraq Petroleum Company. Because of its close links with the independence movement, organized labor developed into an effective political force in the years preceding the revolution.[3]

Ethnic and Sectarian Divisions: Historical and Present Realities

The major social and economic changes taking place during the period between 1920 and 1958 should not obscure the fact that Iraqi society contained (and continues to contain) elements that had never previously been combined in an independent and separate polity. Then as now, the population (some 18 million in 1990) was divided into a variety of overlapping categories—ethnic, religious, occupational, regional origin, and tribal background. Apart from the Christian (3.6 percent), Sabean, and Yazidi (1.4 percent) communities some 95 percent of Iraqis are Muslims. About a quarter of the Muslims are Kurds (mostly Sunni Muslims) while the remaining Muslims are Arabs. The Arab Muslims are divided into Sunnis and Twelver Shi'is, the latter forming the largest single religious community in the country. Of course, neither the communities nor the sects ever constituted single monolithic entities.[4]

As far as it is possible to make any calculations (because only generalized *religious* affiliation—"Christian" or "Muslim"—is recorded in an Iraqi census), some 72 percent are Arabs, about 22 percent Kurds, and the remainder are Turcomans, Armenians, and others. Most Kurds (apart from the Yazidis), and all but a tiny minority of Arabs (who are Christians), are Muslims. To that extent, Iraq's heterogeneity should not be exaggerated unduly, as some 70 percent of the population is both Muslim and Arab, and recent manifestations of Sunni-Shi'i sectarianism are more the result of discriminatory government policies (including large-scale expulsions of Shi'is in the late 1970s and 1980s) than reflections of "primordial hostility" between the two sects.[5]

The Kurds' status and political aspirations are primarily defined by considerations of language and ethnicity. Since the formation of the state of Iraq, Kurdish politics generally have focused on the quest either for a "Grand Kurdistan" embracing the Kurdish population of Iran, Iraq, and Turkey or, more realistically, some kind of autonomous status for the Kurdish area within the state of Iraq, either federated or in some other close relationship with Baghdad. Although most Kurds are Sunni Muslims, this is not significant in the sense that the fact that they are members of the same sect does not bind them to the Sunni Arabs, although it is equally incorrect to conclude from recent events that there is any "innate antipathy" between Kurds and Arabs.[6]

Between two-thirds and three-quarters of the Arab population (some 14 million) are Shi'is; thus there are nine to ten million Shi'i Arabs, and four to five million Sunni Arabs. Apart from Baghdad, which has mixed Sunni and Shi'i quarters as well as quarters with particularly strong Shi'i or Sunni representation,[7] it is generally true that Sunni and Shi'i Arabs inhabit distinct parts of the country. Historically, the Sunni Arabs constituted the majority of the urban population and were politically dominant, both under the monarchy and under the republic; this was partly because the Ottoman Empire was a Sunni institution and employed only Sunnis in its administration. In addition, when modern state education appeared in Iraq at the end of the nineteenth century, few Shi'is attended the new state schools.

Consequently, when the state of Iraq was created in 1920, there were few qualified Shi'is able or willing to take part either in the government or the administration. This situation continued at the level of cabinet participation throughout the mo]narchy (although there were Shi'i ministers and even Shi'i prime ministers)[8] and with key power positions under the republic.[9] Shi'i tribal leaders were among the richest landowners and Shi'i businessmen among the richest merchants by the time of the revolution in 1958, and the rapid rise in educational provision produced increasing numbers of qualified Shi'is. Thus, by the mid-1950s, the Shi'i-Sunni division was less significant and, in addition, the quest for national independence in the 1930s, 1940s, and 1950s had a generally unifying effect, a tendency that continued for some years in spite of the deep political divisions that emerged after the revolution. In addition, the secular atmosphere and the general sense of optimism in Iraq and the Middle East in the 1950s and early 1960s prompted the hope that the significance attached to such sectarian divisions would gradually disappear.[10]

The situation in the early 1990s seems a far cry from those days. A simplistic image of Iraqi society emerged, influenced by the Middle Eastern "experts" of the U.S. defense establishment: "the Arab

Sunnis" supported the "Sunni" regime of Saddam Hussein, and the "somewhat less Arab" Shi'is (a sort of Iranian fifth column) bitterly opposed it, with the Kurds in another category altogether. It is certainly the case that the combination of the general revival of Islamic sentiment, the Iranian Revolution and the Iran-Iraq War have all contributed to the reemergence and reassertion of sectarian feeling. Far more crucial in the reinforcement of sectarianism, localism, and other forms of communal solidarity, however, has been the sense of the individual's powerlessness in the face of an arbitrary and repressive political system. This has generally had the effect of forcing men and women to have recourse to pre-state networks of sect, locality, or family. In Iraqi terms, having recourse to such networks means strengthening loyalties to a particular Shi'i or Sunni (or Kurdish or Christian) tribe, region or family. Thus, at least part of the explanation for the degree of "Islamic revival" that has taken place is that the reassertion of the other loyalties encompasses and includes the promotion of ways of life and value systems deeply embedded in Arab-Islamic consciousness.

Here the Ba'ath government has acted as one of the main causes of the reproduction of heterogeneity rather than contributing to its demise. Support for the present regime rests with the Takriti clans and longstanding individual associates of Saddam Hussein, and cannot be represented a priori as Sunni support for a Sunni government. On the other hand, it is possible that broad sections of the Sunni population who might otherwise not have supported Saddam Hussein may have done so out of fear of the advent of a Shi'i fundamentalist regime. At the same time, many secular-minded Shi'is outside the holy cities of Karbala' and Najaf probably shared such fears and sided with the regime for similar reasons.

The Role of Political Parties before the Revolution

For a variety of reasons, no liberal democratic party could muster mass support or build an effective machinery under the mandate and monarchy (1920-1958). The parties that existed tended to be loose organizations centered around prominent personalities.[11] After the mid-1920s, most of the leading Iraqi participants in the Arab revolt made their peace with the mandatory power and became dependent on Great Britain for the maintenance of the status quo and their own positions within it. As long as they remained in control, it seemed impossible for an effective pluralistic democratic system to emerge, and no genuine opposition party could gain power through the ballot box.

It is a peculiarity of Iraqi politics that the independence movement functioned almost exclusively underground, and that it was most strongly influenced by the Communist Party (founded in 1932), which organized most of the massive demonstrations and strikes of the 1940s and early 1950s. After Gamel Abdel Nasser's rise to power in Egypt in 1952, the pan-Arab nationalists and the Ba'athists also gained influence, especially among the Sunni population. Before Nasser, partly because of Iraq's ethnic and communal heterogeneity, pan-Arabism made little headway; locally, Iraqi nationalism had more appeal. Even in the late 1950s, there was no Nasserist party as such, and the Ba'ath, founded in Syria and brought to Iraq by Syrian schoolteachers in the early 1950s, had only 289 members in 1955,[12] the year when Saddam Hussein joined. After the nationalization of the Suez Canal in 1956, however, Arab nationalism emerged as a political force to be reckoned with; Nasser became the emblem of the successful defiance of imperialism and his pictures appeared everywhere in Iraq.

The Iraqi Republic[13]

On 14 July 1958, a group of military officers seized power, overthrew the monarchy, and abolished the old political order. Under the self-styled Free Officers led by Brigadier 'Abd al-Karim Qasim, cabinets consisted of a combination of military and civilian members. The feebleness of the parliamentary tradition and the limited commitment to parliamentary democracy became obvious when the Free Officers began to put out feelers to the more moderate civilian parties to whom they might hand over the reins of government after a period of reconciliation. Although these politicians were well-known and respected, none had a properly functioning political party at his disposal; they had never held office and had no experience of how to run a government.

In addition, there seemed to be an unspoken agreement among these politicians and the Free Officers that it was important to block communist participation in government. Probably overestimating the number who would vote for the Communist Party, the Qasim regime preferred to stall the democratic process. An ironic consequence of this was that the main pressure to hold elections came from the communists themselves, who organized massive demonstrations (in 1959 and 1960) in favor of free elections and the legalization of the Communist Party. Because no elections were held, the amount of influence the communists actually possessed remains a matter of conjecture.

In the aftermath of the revolution, in the autumn of 1958, the main focus of political contention centered around the question of whether Iraq should join the United Arab Republic of Egypt and Syria, which had been formed the previous February. The nationalists and Ba'athists wanted to join, partly out of conviction and partly as a means of controlling the communists, because Nasser had made political parties illegal. The communists opposed it, again partly out of conviction and partly because they understood its implications for their own political future. For his part, Qasim had no desire to defer to Nasser and thus, quite fortuitously, found himself on the same side as the communists, whose political views he did not share. In an attempt to distance himself from them, Qasim clamped down on the leftists and dismissed from the army and other key positions individuals suspected of having communist sympathies. In doing so, he undermined his own political base (because he had irretrievably alienated himself from the pan-Arabists in the early 1960s) and fell easy prey to a coup engineered by nationalist and Ba'athist officers in February 1963.

At the time, the atrocities of February 1963 marked the most savage repression perpetrated against its population by any government in the Middle East. Qasim was killed and a Ba'athist-Arab nationalist junta seized power under the leadership of 'Abd al-Salam 'Arif, which proceeded to establish a reign of terror against its communist adversaries. The most notorious of those involved in this bloodshed, particularly 'Ali Salih al-Sa'adi, were the Ba'athists. Nine months later, the Ba'athists fell out with the Nasserists and with 'Arif; the Ba'athist leadership was sent into exile in Spain, and the intensity of political persecution diminished. 'Arif's presidency was mainly occupied with fighting a fruitless and expensive war in Kurdistan and keeping himself in power. After his death in a helicopter accident in 1966, his brother, 'Abd al-Rahman 'Arif, became president, but was ousted by another Ba'ath military coup in July 1968.

The Principal Political Groups in Post-Revolutionary Iraq

The main groupings that continued to play a significant role in Iraqi politics after 1958 were the communists, the Kurds, and the pan-Arab nationalists, both Nasserist and Ba'athist. The communists, with their roots in the shantytowns, the emerging labor movement, and the professional middle class, continued to be a significant political force in the years immediately after the revolution, but their position was ambivalent. They supported 'Abd al-Karim Qasim partly because of his welfare state measures and his attempts to negotiate with the Iraq Petroleum Company (apart from his housing and welfare programs, Law 80 of 1961 was the first legislation enacted to restrict the activities of foreign oil companies in any Arab country).[14] They also supported Qasim because the communist leadership was reluctant to support the idea of a military takeover by the party. This issue was to remain highly contentious within party circles for many years, although any possibility of a takeover had passed by 1961, as most of the party's supporters in the army had by then been dismissed.

The second political force, the Kurdish national movement, was divided into numerous factions, the most important of which was the Kurdish Democratic Party led by Mulla Mustafa Barzani. Since the formation of the state, most Kurdish politicians and parties have sought some form of regional or local autonomy within Iraq. There had, however, been a history of armed confrontation between Kurdish organizations and the authorities in Baghdad, either because Baghdad refused to countenance such aspirations, or because such undertakings fell far short of the Kurds' minimum demands.

The party that achieved the greatest long-term success in post-revolutionary Iraq was the Ba'ath, which is still in power. The basic tenets of Ba'athism, "One Arab Nation with an Eternal Mission," expressed in the slogan "Unity, Freedom, and Socialism," were first developed in Syria by Michel 'Aflaq and Salah al-Din al-Bitar in the 1940s and early 1950s. *Unity* refers to the unity of the Arab nation, *freedom* is freedom from imperialism and Zionism, and *socialism* expresses a general aspiration toward state-directed economic development supported by a mixed economy. Hence, Ba'athism was a variety of pan-Arab nationalism based on the general premise that there is a single Arab nation that was divided artificially, first by the Ottomans, and subsequently by European and U.S. imperialism, and Zionism.

Once the Arabs are liberated and united, it is believed, social and political conflicts within particular states (or "regions of the Arab nation") will subside.

Ba'athism first came to Iraq in 1951 but was slow to take root, partly because pan-Arab nationalism had never attracted a particularly widespread following in Iraq before the rise of Nasser, and partly because the political scene was dominated by the communists. Nevertheless, the small Iraqi Ba'ath Party joined a national front with the communists and other parties in 1957 and welcomed the revolution of 1958. Although the Ba'athists never attracted mass support, they eventually seized power and held onto it by a combination of a skillful organization, ruthlessness, and an alliance with key military officers.

The Second Ba'ath Coup

On 17 July 1968, a group of Ba'ath officers led by Ahmad Hasan al-Bakr (prime minister in 1963–1964) organized another Ba'ath coup and took over the government two weeks later. Both al-Bakr, who became president, and his relative, deputy and successor, Saddam Hussein, came from Takrit, a small town about 100 miles north of Baghdad. The highest organ in the new regime was the Revolutionary Command Council (RCC) of the Ba'ath party; the RCC (and in later years, the president) appointed the cabinet. The cabinet had no real power and rubber stamped the decisions made by the party and its president. The Ba'ath had only a small following in 1968 and was primarily remembered for the reign of terror that it introduced in 1963.

Realizing that it had to trim its approach to appeal to a left-leaning constituency, the Ba'ath tried to convince its main rivals, the Communist Party and the Kurdistan Democratic Party, if not of its good faith at least of its progressive credentials. Hence, it advocated and legislated a series of wide-ranging social and economic reforms, pursued apparently anti-imperialist foreign policies, and launched strident attacks on Zionism and imperialism. In this general spirit, fortified by a fifteen-year treaty with the Soviet Union in 1972, the government moved to nationalize the Iraq Petroleum Company in that same year.[15] Largely because of their espousal of such policies, the Ba'athists convinced their main rivals, the communists, to join them in a National Progressive Front.

For various reasons, the Kurds did not join the National Progressive Front although Saddam Hussein and the Ba'ath realized the importance of distracting the Kurdish leadership's attention while the Ba'ath consolidated its authority. In the early 1970s, there were lengthy negotiations on Kurdish autonomy between the Ba'ath and Mulla Mustafa Barzani, which, if successful, would have created a federal structure for the Kurdish area. But because the regime refused to take a census and, in particular, refused to consider Kirkuk as part of the Kurdish area,[16] a major conflict between the armed forces and the Kurds erupted in the spring of 1974.

The Kurds were supported by the shah of Iran, who had taken the Ba'ath's radical and leftist rhetoric seriously and was also worried about Soviet influence in the region. The Ba'ath capitalized on the Shah's support for the Kurds, and presented itself as the victim of an imperialist conspiracy masterminded by the West and its agents. In the end, the Ba'ath leadership's eagerness to resolve the Kurdish problem once and for all (as it probably believed) induced Saddam Hussein to conclude an agreement with the shah in Algiers in March 1975. As a result, Iran immediately withdrew its heavy artillery and closed the border to the Kurds; the Kurdish resistance collapsed and Barzani went into exile. Relations between Iraq and Iran now became extremely cordial and remained so until the Iranian revolution of 1979.

Political and Economic Developments

By the time of Saddam Hussein's takeover of the presidency of Iraq in 1979, the dividing lines between the Ba'ath party leadership and the state had almost disappeared, and the state and its institutions were transformed into an instrument of the party leaders. This was largely facilitated by the massive rise in oil prices that followed the Arab-Israeli War of October 1973; between 1972 and 1974, oil revenues increased tenfold, from U.S. $575 million to U.S. $5,700 million. Huge sums were spent on welfare and infrastructural projects, and the higher wages and salaries, together with the new employment opportunities generated by an expanding economy, substantially improved living standards. As nationalization had given the Ba'ath leadership absolute control over the oil revenues (with little pressure to make it accountable as to how the monies were spent), increases in receipts from oil gradually accelerated the independence of the government from the rest of society.[17]

Having "solved" the Kurdish question, the Ba'ath was no longer in need of communist support and once again turned against them.

In July 1978 a blanket decree was enacted making any non-Ba'athist political activity illegal, and membership in any other political party punishable by death for all members and former members of the armed forces (which, in the context of universal conscription, applied to all adult males). Over the next few years, tens of thousands of individuals of various political persuasions were imprisoned, murdered, or forced into exile.

Between 1975 and 1979, Iraq gradually returned to the Western orbit on a global level and toward the moderate Arab states on a regional level. Within the Ba'ath party, real power moved away from the party organization and the RCC and became concentrated almost exclusively in the hands of Saddam Hussein and a few particularly trusted subordinates. The party was transformed into an instrument of the leader and gradually assumed the characteristics of a national rally, in which adulation of the party and its leaders replaced whatever political or ideological discourse may once have existed.

The combination of the independence given him by the new oil money and the successful elimination or subordination of most of the opposition after his takeover in July 1979 gave Saddam Hussein a major boost of confidence. He promoted a spectacular personality cult, with massive portraits and statues of the benevolent leader visible everywhere; towns, suburbs, public buildings, and streets were renamed in his honor. The oil wealth also permitted him to equip several parallel security services, generally commanded by men from Takrit, with the most up-to-date means of surveillance and riot control imported from the East and West. Together with a greatly expanded communications system, these security services made the state machinery more efficient than ever before. During the 1980s, security was further refined, with the construction of huge underground complexes, mostly designed and built by British firms, to serve as emergency headquarters in the event of attacks upon the regime. These were put to use with considerable effect when Iraq was attacked by the coalition forces early in 1991. In this way, the regime became more distanced from the population and more apparently invulnerable.

The Growth of Opposition to the Regime

While surveillance was directed against all opposition, the Ba'ath was concerned about potential Shi'i opposition even before the Iranian revolution.[18] The existence of a Shi'i political movement in Iraq dated back to the late 1950s, when a number of religious leaders in Najaf, led by Ayatullah Muhammad Baqir al-Sadr, formed a political organization, the Association of Najafi *'ulama*. Its aim was to raise the consciousness of the Muslim community as a whole and to arrest the spread of communism and atheism. By the late 1960s, the *'ulamas'* main concern was no longer communism but the Ba'ath party, and the Najafi *'ulama* formed themselves into a political group called al-Da'wa al-Islamiyya (The Islamic Call). The foundation of al-Da'wa was partly a reaction against the secularism of the Ba'athist state, but more particularly against the state's new-found determination to interfere directly in the affairs of the Shi'i clerical hierarchy, a highly sensitive area from which all previous Iraqi governments (including the Ottomans) had tended to keep their distance.

The Ba'ath responded to al-Da'wa's activities in familiar fashion; in 1974, five *'ulama* were executed without trial; in February 1977, numerous arrests were made in the holy cities during the Muharram ceremonies, after which eight members of the clergy were executed and fifteen were sentenced to life imprisonment. In 1979, encouraged by the Iranian Revolution, al-Da'wa engaged the government in open conflict, attacking Ba'ath party offices and police posts, and openly declared its support for the new government in Iran. The Ba'ath responded by intensifying its campaign against al-Da'wa, making membership of the party punishable by death. In April 1980, Ayatullah Muhammad Baqr al-Sadr and his sister Bint Huda were executed. A few months after this, Iraq invaded Iran; this shifted Shi'i opposition to the regime to a different plane, in the sense that support for al-Da'wa could be interpreted as an attack on Iraq and Arabism and thus tantamount to treason.

It is difficult to gauge how strong the appeal of al-Da'wa was. Although the majority of Iraqi conscripts (like the majority of Iraqis) were Shi'is, there was no mass desertion or any other manifestation of widespread feelings of common cause between Iraqi and Iranian Shi'is during the Iran-Iraq War. This was primarily because the majority of Iraqi Shi'is considered themselves Iraqi Arabs first and Shi'is second, rather than the reverse, and had little instinctive sympathy with their Iranian counterparts simply on the ground that they were also Shi'is. On the other hand, the Shi'i community became the principal target of the government's domestic repression throughout the war. In particular, the massive deportations of members of the community to Iran after April 1980 on the grounds that they were "really" of Iranian origin (and the sequestration of their properties and assets that followed) heightened sectarian loyalties.[19] Hence, although such repression effectively preempted the revival of al-Da'wa, it made many Shi'is more profoundly aware of their Shi'ism, without, of course, somehow turning them into Iranians.

The Iranian Revolution and the Iran-Iraq War

The Iranian Revolution of 1978-1979 had momentous significance for Iraq. In particular, the fall of the shah meant the de facto abrogation of the Algiers agreement and put the Kurdish question back on the agenda. In addition, the establishment of a populist Shi'i government in Iran was a matter of grave concern for the regime in Iraq where, as elsewhere in the Arab world, populist Islam was beginning to fill the void created by the evident ideological bankruptcy of Arab nationalism and Arab socialism. Misjudging the situation on several levels, Saddam Hussein resurrected the old disagreements over the boundary between the two countries in the Shatt al-'Arab and the status of the southwest Iranian province of Khuzistan-Arabistan. He took the frequent cross-border incidents as a pretext for going to war with Iran on 22 September 1980. In his calculations, a quick defeat of the new Islamic republican regime in Iran would make him into the undisputed master of the Gulf and make Iraq into a major regional power.

Although Iraq met with initial success, Iranian forces were more resilient than expected. The war dragged on for more than eight years instead of producing the speedy victory that the Iraqi regime had anticipated. For several years, the confrontation developed into a stalemate where both contenders were bogged down in entrenched positions with no end in sight. In time, the burden of having to support Iraq financially strained the economies of Kuwait and Saudi Arabia, while Kurdish forces under Barzani's son Mas'ud gradually regrouped and managed to gain control over much of the Kurdish area. Eventually, worried about the repercussions of an Iraqi collapse on the region, Iraq's Arab neighbors committed themselves unequivocally to its support. In this way, Saddam Hussein achieved his objective of regionalizing the war and drawing Saudi Arabia, Kuwait, and their Western allies more seriously into it. By the spring of 1987, the United States was firmly aligned on the Iraqi side, a decisive factor in Iran's eventual loss of the war.[20]

Although greatly weakened, Iran could still inflict serious damage on Iraq and occupy Iraqi territory. In the spring of 1988, Iran launched an offensive in northern Iraq with the assistance of the two most prominent Kurdish organizations, the Patriotic Union of Kurdistan and the Kurdistan Democratic Party, capturing the Iraqi city of Halabja on 15 March. The next day, the Iraqi air force bombed Halabja with poisonous gas, causing some 5,000 civilian deaths. By this time, Iranian resistance was clearly crumbling, and a series of military reverses resulted in the Ayatullah Ruhollah Khomeini announcing in mid-July that his government would accept UN terms for a cease-fire without conditions.

Although the effects of the war were devastating, Iraq emerged as a substantial military power. Between 1979 and 1980, the Iraqi army numbered some 190,000 men; by the late 1980s, it had more than quintupled to around one million, and there were comparable increases in military hardware.[21] In addition, there was now a major armaments industry whose products included a surface-to-surface missile based on the Soviet Scud. A new Ministry of Industry and Military Industrialization was created to oversee these activities, headed, until the fall of 1991, by Hussein Kamil Majid, Saddam Hussein's son-in-law.[22] By 1990, the scale of military production prompted serious international concern as it became widely known that Iraq was manufacturing chemical weapons and sophisticated missiles, and was not far from acquiring the means to produce nuclear weapons. The essential components of the weaponry were provided by firms in Western Europe and the United States. Although the increased significance of the military was an implicit threat to Saddam Hussein, because there was always the possibility that a serious rival or challenger could appear from within its ranks, the overall effect of the military buildup served ultimately to consolidate his power.

During and after the Iran-Iraq War, Saddam Hussein made use of his "victory" over Iran to make explicit claims to the leadership of the Arab world, which he and the "noble people of Iraq" had so assiduously defended for eight years. His real power base resided almost entirely in his extended family, people incorporated into it by marriage, or considered part of it by long association with him. Thus his son, 'Udayy, was married to the daughter of the Vice-President, 'Izzat al-Duri; Hussein Kamil Majid, Minister for Industry and Military Industrialization between July 1988 and November 1991, himself a distant cousin of Saddam Hussein, was married to Hussein's daughter Raghad, and his brother, Saddam Kamil, a colonel in the missile brigade, to another daughter, Rima'. Until his untimely (and somewhat unseasonable) death in a helicopter accident in a sandstorm near Basra in April 1989, 'Adnan Khairullah Tulfah, a maternal cousin of Saddam Hussein and the brother of his wife Sajida, was Minister of Defense; 'Adnan's wife was the daughter of the former president, Ahmad Hasan al-Bakr, and 'Adnan and Sajida's father, Khairullah Tulfah, a former primary school teacher, was for some years mayor of Baghdad, during which time he became a wealthy businessman. Qusayy, Saddam Hussein's youngest son, was married to the daughter of General Mahir 'Abd al-Rashid, but apparently separated from her when her father fell out of favor in the autumn of 1988. 'Ali Hasan al-Majid, the minister of the interior responsible for putting down the rising in the spring of 1991 and now (November 1993) minister of defense, was also a cousin of Saddam Hussein. The president's two closest colleagues outside his family circle, Tariq 'Aziz, a Christian from Mosul, and Taha Yasin Ramadhan, from the Jazira (northwestern Iraq), were closely associated with him well before the Ba'ath takeover in 1968.

Infitah

The Ba'ath's increased development expenditures since the oil price rise of 1973 not only stimulated the economy but also made the state into the principal generator of opportunities for private business.[23] Local firms profited enormously, by acting either as contractors or as middlemen for foreign firms, a particularly lucrative activity. Nevertheless, although Ba'ath rule provided a multiplicity of opportunities for individuals to make money, the might of the state remained dominant in the economy, and oil still accounted for over 90 percent of foreign exchange.[24]

In the early years of the war, the regime encouraged private capital to diversify from its preoccupation with quick money from real estate, contracting, commerce, and services into light and medium manufacturing. The extension of private enterprise into agriculture reduced food imports, promoted a better quality and more regular supply of food items, and broadened support for the regime among the entrepreneurial middle classes. As the war progressed, Saddam Hussein made a series of declarations and policy statements known collectively as the administrative revolution (*thawra idariyya*). Their intent was to reduce state interference and, correspondingly, limit the powers of the bureaucracy. This implied a reduction in the influence of members of the Ba'ath party who controlled the key positions within the administrative and bureaucratic structures. By this time, both the party and its ideology had become largely redundant as "political" forces and, in Samir al-Khalil's vivid descriptions, the "Republic of Fear" was firmly in place.[25]

The much vaunted economic initiatives, heralding a return to or an advance toward greater liberalization, were accompanied by declarations of intent to move toward greater political liberty, and vague assurances were given that opposing political parties would be licensed at some time in the future. Needless to say, no political liberalization actually occurred. In addition, the various economic measures had no significant long-term effect on the crisis in which Iraq was floundering in 1989 and 1990, largely because the kind of administrative reform that Saddam Hussein thought would set Iraq on the road to reconstruction could not be achieved without a thorough transformation of the political system and the establishment of the rule of law. He thus found himself trapped by the incompatibility between his desire to maintain and expand his personal dictatorship and the basic requirements of a market economy.

The Background to the Invasion of Kuwait

Although Iraq's economic situation after the war was precarious, it could not be described as desperate given the country's very substantial oil reserves; prudent housekeeping, tight control of imports, and checks on government spending would have brought about its gradual economic recovery, provided that there was no further disastrous collapse in the price of oil. Such policies were not adopted, however; while the rebuilding of the cities, the infrastructure, and industry were important targets, U.S. $5 billion per year was allocated to rearmament over the period between 1988 and 1992, and only half this sum, $2.5 billion, to reconstruction—the latter included such projects as "victory" monuments and a new presidential palace.

At the same time, the various efforts to restructure the economy led to high inflation and steep rises in the cost of living. As might have been expected, private capital responded to the privatization measures by speculative or quick, rather than sustained, investment, which meant that the rich got richer and the middle and lower classes got poorer. Also, the "cuts" imposed on the bureaucracy since 1987 led to high unemployment, which meant that rapid military demobilization was politically impossible. In addition, after eight years of war and suffering, there were widespread hopes that peace would bring greater prosperity and security.

Saddam Hussein saw himself as a triumphant leader who had brought his country to a great victory and was now entitled to take his rightful place in the counsels of the Arab world. As well as believing that his defense of the Arab nation entitled him to a major leadership role within it, events taking place elsewhere in the world—the vast upheavals in the Soviet Union and eastern Europe—strongly influenced his actions.

Two important points should be made here. In the first place, in spite of the fact that Iraq has one of the most, if not the most, vicious and tyrannical regimes in the Middle East, Saddam Hussein always managed to attract a following both within Iraq and in the rest of the Arab world. Some of this was opportunistic, in the sense that it was bought, but where it was not bought directly, Saddam Hussein's strident anti-imperialist and, until 1984,[26] anti-Zionist, rhetoric found an echo on the streets and in the refugee camps, especially in Jordan, the West Bank, and Gaza. There was also the sense both in the Arab world and in Western business circles that, however wicked and ruthless Saddam Hussein might be, he "got things done," somewhat in the spirit of a certain Italian dictator who "at least" made the trains run on time.

In addition, although he would have lost the war with Iran had it not been for the arms and support that the West supplied, the folk memory in the region was sufficiently selective (or short-term) for it to be widely believed that, unlike most other Arab rulers, he was not afraid of standing up to the West. In this respect, Saddam Hussein always had his finger on the pulse of certain sentiments in the Arab world and knew how to exploit them.

Second, in the context of Soviet policies in the Middle East, it had long been clear, well before Gorbachev's assumption of power in 1985, that the Soviet Union was too concerned about its relations with the West to throw its weight wholeheartedly behind any Arab policy or maneuver that might crucially threaten Israel. As no Arab state or combination of Arab states had seriously entertained such ideas since 1973, however, this consideration gradually became less important, because Soviet support continued to be vital in a variety of other ways. It was not until 1987, for example, that the United

States and the West felt it prudent to make the high technology weaponry available to Iraq that enabled it to defeat Iran in 1988 and invade Kuwait in 1990. Most of Iraq's basic weaponry came from the Soviet Union, and as long as the old men remained in power in Moscow, Iraq could always count on a certain measure of Soviet support if it fell out of favor with the West. Thus between 1985 and 1989, Iraq spent nearly U.S. $12 billion on arms, of which nearly U.S. $7 billion went to the Soviet Union; France, Iraq's second major supplier, received just over U.S. $2 billion over the same period.

However welcome it was elsewhere, the new atmosphere of *glasnost* and *perestroika* was highly unsettling to Saddam Hussein. A familiar world was in complete disarray and none of the former certainties seemed to count. Hence, when the report of the U.S.-based Human Rights Watch on Iraq was questioned in Congress in February 1990,[27] Saddam Hussein understood this and other portents as indications that the West was going to turn against him, and that the close relationship forged with the West was coming to an end.

With his extraordinary ability to swim abreast of the changing political currents in the region, including his theatrical espousal of Islam in the 1980s when that seemed to serve his purpose, Saddam Hussein made use of the widespread and by no means unjustified unease felt among the broad left in the Arab world that the defection of the Soviet Union might well lead to unchallenged Western, particularly U.S., dominance in the region. He thus launched a virulent campaign against the United States, presenting himself as the only steadfast Arab leader capable of defending the Arab nation against the West and its allies in the region.

These sentiments were summarized in a major speech to members of the Arab Cooperation Council assembled in Amman on 24 February 1990. He laid out the possible consequences for the Arab world of the decline of the Soviet Union as a world power and the affirmation of U.S. superiority that this implied; the Gulf would become an American lake, and the United States would use its military and naval power to control the price of oil. To preempt the permanent establishment of U.S. hegemony, the Arabs should agree on a definite plan of action to build themselves into a regional power capable of determining the agenda on a more equal basis.

Over the next few months, this discourse became more strident. Several incidents enabled Saddam Hussein to present himself as "embattled," the victim of conspiracies forged by Zionism, imperialism, and the agents of imperialism in the region. The trial and execution of the thirty-two-year-old British journalist Farzad Bazoft followed shortly after the Human Rights Watch report became public. In April, a scandal erupted over the so-called Iraqi supergun and later over the discovery of essential parts for nuclear weapons in the baggage of Iraqi travelers passing through Heathrow Airport in London. These incidents were represented as evidence of machinations against Iraq and the Arab nation, and the virulently anti-U.S. campaign that followed echoed around the Arab world.

Iraq's neighbors were also accused of betraying Iraq or the interests of the Arab nation. Early in 1990, Iraqi officials lobbied the Gulf rulers to lower their oil production and push the price up from U.S. $18 to U.S. $20 per barrel. At the same time, Saddam Hussein was determined to provide Iraq with access to a deep water anchorage on the Gulf, probably to accommodate the new fleet of frigates and corvettes that he had ordered from Italy. Iraq was confined to the port of Umm Qasr and the shallow narrows at the head of the Gulf; Saddam Hussein was casting his eyes on the Kuwaiti islands of Bubyan and Warba, which could provide a useful alternative anchorage. In the spring of 1990, he raised the stakes by demanding access to the islands and resuscitating Iraq's claim to that part of the Rumaila oilfield that ran from Iraq into northern Kuwait. He also castigated Kuwait for allegedly having the temerity to demand repayment of some of Iraq's debts, and for having been instrumental in keeping oil prices low. In July 1990, part of the Iraqi army was sent to the border, and on 2 August, when Kuwait refused to give in to Saddam Hussein's demands, Iraq invaded and subsequently annexed Kuwait.

Western Reaction and the "War Aims" of the Coalition

When the crisis began the attitude of the U.S. administration was incoherent and constantly shifting, although it soon became clear that it was determined to remove Saddam Hussein from Kuwait. As the military build-up increased in the late autumn of 1990 and Saddam Hussein remained intransigent, the crisis developed its own momentum. Two clear-cut and consistent, if undeclared, objectives emerged. First, it was vital that the Gulf area, which contains some 62 percent of the world's oil reserves, should not fall under the control of interests hostile to the United States. Second, Iraq's military capacity should somehow be cut down to size.

Although this may have been the hidden agenda, the stated ends were quite different. Initially, the declared aim was the expulsion of Iraq from Kuwait and the restoration of the rule of the Sabah family. As the autumn wore on and the hostage crisis intensified, and accounts of Iraqi atrocities in Kuwait seeped through to the media, the focus shifted to Iraq's appalling human rights record. During the aerial bombardment and the land war, the notion increasingly gained ground that the removal of Saddam Hussein would not be unwelcome, and indeed that things might change dramatically if he were to be overthrown.

It is a measure of the extent to which Saddam Hussein had become the prisoner of his own rhetoric and the degree to which he misjudged the situation—as he had misjudged the strength of Iran in the past—that he did not realize that such excesses as the annexation of an oil state would not be tolerated by the major consumers of oil. He also failed to realize that his neighbors would not condone such an infringement of the territorial sovereignty of another Arab state.

The Aftermath of the Gulf War

According to one observer,[28] the invasion of Kuwait and the war (that is, the period between 2 August 1990 and 27 February 1991) resulted in at least 100,000 deaths among the military and civilian populations of Iraq and Kuwait, and some 300,000 wounded. Hundreds of thousands of people were displaced (in the sense of being forced to leave their homes and places of work); over U.S. $170 billion in property and infrastructural damage occurred in Iraq, perhaps U.S. $60 billion worth in Kuwait, excluding the environmental effects of the firing of the Kuwaiti oil wells. Two hundred thousand Palestinians and 150,000 Egyptians were forced to leave Kuwait, as well as 600,000 Asians from India, Pakistan, Sri Lanka, and Bangladesh. A further 350,000 Egyptians left Iraq when Egypt joined the coalition.

A few days after the war ended, popular insurrections broke out in southern Iraq and Kurdistan; by 4 March 1991, Kurdish forces had taken Sulaimaniyya and by 24 March, they were in control of most of Kurdistan, including the towns of Arbil and Kirkuk. Although the so-called rebels gained control of large areas between the end of February and the beginning of March, units of the Republican Guard responded with exceptional brutality and were able to gain the upper hand quickly in southern Iraq, especially in Basra, Najaf, and Karbala'. The terms of the cease-fire did not include an embargo on the Iraqis' use of helicopters; in fact, just before Iraqi troops recaptured Samawa on 26 March, the United States explicitly announced that it would *not* shoot down Iraqi helicopters. In the southern cities, the insurgents captured and killed local Ba'athist officials, members of the security services, and their families, venting their hatred for the regime upon them. When the Republican Guard regained control of the southern cities, they carried out indiscriminate mass executions. Tanks were painted with the slogan "No Shi'is [will survive] after today" and there was widespread destruction of Shi'i shrines and other mosques in the holy cities.

In the last week in March, Iraqi helicopters and troops launched raids on Kirkuk and other Kurdish cities. Kirkuk was recaptured after a massive bombardment on 28 March and Sulaimaniyya on 3 April. A mass exodus of Kurds to the Iraqi-Turkish and Iraqi-Iranian borders began; by the end of April, there were about 2.5 million refugees, both Kurds and southerners. The Kurds fled largely because they feared a repetition of the bombing of Halabja in March 1988 with chemical weapons, which had killed more than 5,000 people. The number of casualties in these uprisings is difficult to estimate and, in addition, tens of thousands died of exhaustion and exposure on the borders of Iran and Turkey. The problem remained acute throughout the spring and summer of 1991 and, although some Kurds returned to Kirkuk, Dohuk, and Zakho, hundreds of thousands did not.

The U.S. and British troops that went to northern Iraq in April and May to encourage the Kurds to return and to protect them when they did so left during the course of the summer and were replaced by a small UN force. Partly in response to the scale of the disaster in Kurdistan and partly in keeping with the opportunism that they had frequently displayed in the past, the Patriotic Union of Kurdistan and Kurdistan Democratic Party leaders spent several months in Baghdad, apparently negotiating Kurdish autonomy with Saddam Hussein. The Iraqi population—Kurds, Shi'is, and Sunnis—remained at the mercy of the "pariah president" whom British Prime Minister John Major urged them to overthrow on 28 February 1991.

These and similar calls to action were followed by claims that such calls had never actually been made. On 2 April 1991, for instance, a U.S. State Department spokesperson declared that the

United States "never, ever stated, as either a military or a political goal of the coalition, or the international community, the removal of Saddam Hussein." Maybe not. But very broad hints were dropped in January and February of 1991—until, that is, the implications of Saddam Hussein's possible overthrow were analyzed by the so-called Middle Eastern experts in Washington. Iraq would become "Lebanonized"; the Kurds would join forces with other Kurds in Turkey and Iran; the Iranians would help the clerics in southern Iraq to create an Islamic Republic of Iraq; the Saudis would be extremely concerned if militant Shi'is took over in the south; many of the regimes in the region would be at risk—whatever that meant—if some sort of quasi-democratic replacement for Saddam Hussein emerged. Most of these assumptions were inaccurate. Nevertheless, an emasculated Saddam Hussein seemed, at least for the time being, the favored option and probably the easiest scenario to control.

An Uncertain Future

Although events in Iraq have clearly been overshadowed by the Arab-Israeli "peace process," it is clear that U.S. and Western policy in the region have been found severely deficient by Arabs of a variety of political persuasions. Suspicion of the West's intentions deepened, particularly among the small but influential oppositional groups in the Gulf states and Saudi Arabia, who had expected to see a more fundamental transformation of regional politics than actually occurred. Was "all this" simply to ensure Western hegemony in the region, to ensure Western access to oil, or is the United States also committed to advocating the implementation of the rule of law in Iraq and other Arab countries? The grave inadequacy of the U.S. policy in the latter respect lent credibility to the opinion in the Arab world that the United States is not serious about encouraging political reform there, in marked contrast to its sustained pressure in previous years on the states of Eastern Europe. Even those Arabs who supported the coalition feel let down by the West's continued commitment to "stability" while failing to encourage the most elementary forms of democracy in the Arab world.

At the same time, it is clear that there are considerable obstacles in implementing such a process.[29] For a number of reasons, it seems that there is every likelihood that Saddam Hussein can survive at least in the short or medium term. The uprisings in south Iraq and in Kurdistan were brutally crushed, and it is likely that most organized opposition within Iraq itself—outside the Kurdish areas—was destroyed. The initial preparedness of the Kurdish leadership to negotiate with Saddam Hussein was also symptomatic of the general assumption that he was there to stay for the foreseeable future.

In the regime, as noted before, power is vested primarily in Saddam Hussein, his sons and sons-in-law, and some 700 Takritis, who are either in senior positions in the armed forces or in charge of the various security services. Most of these people are not only implicated in some way in the regime's various crimes and excesses but also have strong material reasons for ensuring that Saddam Hussein stays in power. The logistics of any assassination or coup attempt are daunting, given the high security surrounding Saddam Hussein and the regime's control of the cities. It is difficult to see how the regime's power to dominate domestically could be challenged, and there is, therefore, little likelihood of it being removed by some form of popular insurrection.

A number of persistent misconceptions about Iraqi politics continue to muddy the analytical waters. One is the notion, broadly stated, that a fundamentalist Shi'i regime might come to power in close association with Iran. In the first place, none of the major Shi'i groups has proposed the establishment of an Islamic state—much less an Islamic state tied to Iran—and second, Shi'i opposition to Saddam Hussein is sectarian rather than religious. The greater visibility of the Shi'i opposition somewhat distorts the true state of affairs; no automatic dividing line separates the Shi'i opponents and Sunni supporters of the regime, as opposition and support could come from either community. As mentioned before, Iraqi history cannot be understood in terms of Sunni-Shi'i antagonism. If any generalization can be made, the dividing line is between the Takriti power-holders and the majority of the disenchanted and disenfranchised population, both Sunni and Shi'i. Hence, the claim put forward by some commentators that particular measures—like the continuation of sanctions or increasing the pressure on the regime—would somehow rally the "Sunni population" behind Saddam Hussein is speculative rather than axiomatic.

Again, Shi'i opposition is sectarian rather than religious in the sense that the Shi'is have felt discriminated against under all Iraqi governments and they feel particularly threatened since the mass expulsions of the 1980s. In brief, the Shi'i opposition believes that if there is to be stability in Iraq, the "Shi'i problem" must be properly addressed and adequate mechanisms found to bring what is seen as Sunni hegemony to an end. The Shi'is form between 70 and 80 percent of the Arab population; as the war between Iran and Iraq demonstrated convincingly, the Iraqi Shi'is feel themselves Arab and Iraqi first and Shi'i second. Second, the bulk of Iraqi Shi'is are not particularly religious. al-Da'wa was unable to establish widespread ideological roots, and there has been no Shariati to mobilize a popular following among the middle and lower middle classes. In addition, there is a history of tension between the higher clergy and the religious establishments of Najaf and Karbala' on the one side and the Qum on the other. Finally, although those most heavily involved in the excesses of the present regime would certainly be held accountable if it fell, the notion that "the Shi'is" will rise up and massacre "the Sunnis" can only be described as fanciful.

Hence, in contrast with the protest movement in Iran under the shah in the 1970s, the Iraqi Shi'i opposition seeks the enfranchisement of the whole population under a functioning democratic system rather than the installation of an "Islamic Republic of Iraq." The pronouncements of some spokesmen of the Shi'i opposition abroad are an accurate reflection of the feelings of Shi'is in Iraq, many of whom have long felt excluded as Shi'is from positions of political influence and authority. They believe that this imbalance can only be properly redressed under a more genuinely democratic state which enfranchises both communities. On the other hand, it is also the case that, inevitably, the longer the present dictatorship continues, the greater the likelihood of support for a more radical religious opposition. The same is true, *mutatis mutandis*, for the Kurds; they also want some form of local self-government or federal state structure, and realize that there is little prospect for the materialization of any kind of Grand Kurdistan embracing Iranian and Turkish Kurdistan.

It is widely felt in the Middle East that the West is once again pursuing its own short-term interests in a manner that will not ultimately serve it well. Now that the Soviet Union has changed tracks and communism no longer poses a threat to the status quo in the region, the United States and the West should make a fundamental reassessment of their policies in the Middle East and put their weight wholeheartedly behind the democratic forces in the region. Supporting such forces would not only create a more stable situation in the long run, but would also convince the people of the region that the U.S. policy has not once again been formed almost exclusively on serving its own immediate interests and those of its regional allies. In sum, this is the only new world order worth considering.[30]

Notes

1. See Marion Farouk-Sluglett, "Iraq: Rente Petrolière et Concentration du Pouvoir," *Maghreb-Machrek* 131 (January 1991): 3–12.

2. For a detailed discussion of the origins and early years of the modern state, see Peter Sluglett, *Britain in Iraq 1914–1932* (London: Ithaca Press, 1976).

3. These developments are discussed in Hanna Batatu, *The Old Social Classes and the Revolutionary Movements of Iraq; A Study of Iraq's Old Landed Classes and its Communists, Ba'thists and Free Officers* (Princeton, NJ: Princeton University Press, 1978): especially 53-361, 465-82, and *passim*; for several interesting critiques and appreciations of Batatu's book, see Robert Fernea and Wm. Roger Louis, eds., *The Iraqi Revolution of 1958: The Old Social Classes Revisited* (London: I. B. Tauris, 1991).

4. For a useful discussion of this issue see Dale Eickelman, "Ethnicity and Cultural Identity," *The Middle East: An Anthropological Approach* (Englewood Cliffs, NJ: Prentice Hall, 1989): 207-27.

5. For a sense of the changing nature of Sunni-Shi'i relations, compare our two articles, "Some Reflections on the Present State of Sunni-Shi'i Relations in Iraq," *Bulletin of the British Society for Middle Eastern Studies* 5 (1978): 79-87; and, "Sunnis and Shi'is Revisited: Sectarianism and Ethnicity in Authoritarian Iraq," in *The Modern Middle East in Historical Perspective: Essays in Honour of Albert Hourani*, ed. John P. Spagnolo (London: Ithaca Press, 1992): 279-94. For a more optimistic interpretation see Amatzia Baram, "The Ruling Political Elite in Ba'thi Iraq: The Changing Features of a Collective Profile," *International Journal of Middle East Studies* 21 (1989): 447-93.

6. For a more detailed discussion of the Kurdish issue, and of recent developments, see our article, "The Kurds," in *The Times Guide to the Middle East*, eds., Peter Sluglett and Marion Farouk-Sluglett (London: Harper Collins, 1991): 51-67.

7. For a relatively recent study of the city, see Bassim al-Ansari, *'al-Thawra, Quartier de Bagdad,' Thèse du 3e Cycle*, EHESS (Paris: Universite Paris VII, 1979).

8. Salih Jabr was prime minister from March 1947 to January 1948; Muhammad al-Sadr from January 1948 to June 1948; Fadhil Jamali from September 1953 to April 1954, and 'Abd al-Wahhab Mirjan from December 1957 to March 1958. Batatu, *Old Social Classes*, 182.

9. It can safely be asserted that under the present regime which has been in office since July 1968, no Shi'i has held a significant power posi-

tion; Hasan al-'Amiri, Na'im Haddad, and Sa'dun Hammadi, who held relatively high offices in the late 1970s and 1980s have all disappeared from view. (Hammadi also appeared regularly as a government spokesman in 1990 and 1991.)

10. See Farouk-Sluglett and Sluglett, "Some Reflections" and "Sunnis and Shi'is Revisited."

11. The situation in Syria provides an interesting contrast. In 1954, in what were probably the last generally free elections in the Arab world, the Communists, Ba'thists and smaller parties gained only 29 out of the 142 seats in the Chamber. Hizb al-Sha'b, with thirty seats, al-Hizb al-Watani, with nineteen seats, and the Independents, with sixty-four seats, attracted the great majority of the votes. See Patrick Seale, *The Struggle for Syria: A Study of Post-War Arab Politics 1945-1958*, 2d ed. (London: I. B. Tauris 1986): 181-83.

12. Batatu, *Old Social Classes*, 743.

13. This period forms the central concern of our *Iraq since 1958: From Revolution to Dictatorship*, 2d extended ed. (New York: St. Martin's Press, 1990).

14. The best account of the fortunes of Iraqi oil affairs until the mid-1970s is in E. Penrose and E. F. Penrose, *Iraq: International Relations and National Development* (Boulder, CO: Westview Press, 1978). See also Farouk-Sluglett and Sluglett, *Iraq Since 1958*, 215-54, and Nirou Eftekhari, "Le pétrole dans l'économie et la société Iraqiennes," *Peuples Méditerranéens* 40 (1987): 43-73.

15. Michael E. Brown, "The nationalization of the Iraq Petroleum Company," *International Journal of Middle East Studies* 10 (1979): 107-24.

16. Still a major bone of contention between the two sides.

17. Farouk-Sluglett, "Iraq."

18. See Farouk-Sluglett and Sluglett, *Iraq Since 1958*, 190-200; Hanna Batatu, "Iraq's Underground Shi'a Movements; Characteristics, Causes and Prospects," *Middle East Journal* 35 (Autumn 1981): 578-94; Chibli Mallat, "Religious Militancy in Contemporary Iraq; Muhammad Baqer as-Sadr and the Sunni-Shia Paradigm," *Third World Quarterly* 10 (1988): 699-729; and P. Martin, "Les chi'ites d'Iraq; Une Majorité Dominée à la Recherche de Son Destin," *Peuples Méditerranéens* 40 (1987): 127-69.

19. Dilip Hiro, *Iran under the Ayatollahs* (London: Routledge & Kegan Paul, 1985): 167. According to Amnesty International (Report of an Amnesty International Mission to the Government of Iraq, 22-28 January 1983, London, 1983) the Iraqi Revolutionary Command Council announced in July 1980 that "any Iranian family which is proved to be disloyal to the [Iraqi] revolution and the homeland is subject to deportation even if it holds the Iraqi nationality certificate." At least 100,000 Shi'is, possibly more, were deported in this way.

20. As well as giving substantial military assistance, the United States also signed a five-year economic and technical agreement with Iraq on 26

August 1987. This was accompanied by U.S. $1 billion in food aid. The net effect of these deals was to make Iraq the third largest export market for the United States in the Arab world. See Ofra Bengio, "Iraq" in *Middle East Contemporary Survey, 1987* (Tel Aviv, 1990).

21. Kamran Mofid, *The Economic Consequences of the Gulf War* (London: Routledge, 1990): 87–88.

22. Hussein Kamil Majid had been commander of the Republican Guard at the time of Saddam Hussein's major purge of the Revolutionary Command Council in July 1979. For details of arms manufacture, see Economist Intelligence Unit, *Iraq: Country Report* 1988 no. 4; and ibid., 1989 no. 2.

23. The early stages of this process have been described and analyzed in 'Isam al-Khafaji, *al-Dawla w'al-Tatawwur al-Ra'smali f'il-'Iraq, 1968–1978* (The State and Capitalist Development in Iraq) (Cairo: Dar al-Mustaqbal al-'Arabi, 1983). See also R. Springborg, "Infitah, Agrarian Transformation and Elite Consolidation in Contemporary Iraq," *Middle East Journal* 40 (1986): 33–52.

24. The extent of the country's continuing dependence on oil is discussed by Eftekhari, "Le pétrole dans l'économie," and by Farouk-Sluglett, "Iraq: rente pétrolière."

25. Samir al-Khalil, *The Republic of Fear: Saddam's Iraq*, 2d ed. (London: Hutchinson Radius, 1990).

26. A few days after Iraq's resumption of diplomatic relations with the United States, Foreign Minister Tariq 'Aziz, declared on U.S. television, "Iraq does not consider itself to be a direct party to the [Arab-Israeli] conflict because Israel is not occupying any part of Iraqi soil." *al-Nahar*, Beirut, 2 December 1984.

27. This report was subsequently published: See David A. Korn, "Middle East Watch," *Human Rights in Iraq* (New Haven: Yale University Press, 1990).

28. Joost Hilterman, *Middle East Report* (July 1991).

29. The following paragraphs are based on conversations with members of the Iraqi opposition in London in the summer of 1991.

30. These conclusions were generally agreed upon in the course of a workshop held at Princeton in May 1991. See John Waterbury, ed., *Towards New Orders in the Middle East: The Role of United States Policy* (Princeton, NJ: Princeton University, Center for International Studies, 1991).

12
Iran and the New World Order

Scheherazade Daneshkhu

During the summer of 1991, the Iranian embassy in London launched a series of lectures on Iran. Two of the British guest speakers were academics; both were asked to speak about the new world order and the case of Iran. Like other countries, Iran was striving to understand what was meant by the new world order and its undefined consequences for Iran and the region. Iran's interest was governed by two major considerations: the Islamic republic's own turbulent relations with the United States and the composition of a new security structure in the Persian Gulf in the aftermath of the U.S.-led war against Saddam Hussein in January 1991.

Soviet support for the United States, although probably the most notable aspect of the war, was more a consequence of the collapse of Soviet power and a redefined foreign policy than the successful implementation of George Bush's vision of a new world order. This vision was reiterated in his State of the Union address on 29 January 1991 when he defined it as an attempt to achieve the universal aspirations of mankind: peace, security, freedom, and the rule of law.[1]

Although change is inevitable in the conduct of international relations because of the increasing disintegration of the Soviet Union, what replaces it is still an open question. Will it mean a Pax Americana, or will the United States retreat to isolationism now that it is no longer threatened by external forces? Could it lead to more smaller power blocs, for example, Europe, or could it mean an increased role for the United Nations? Or will it mean chaos?

There is little to suggest, during either the conduct of the war or its aftermath, that the United States implemented a new world order policy toward Iran or the Gulf. The indecisive resolution to the Gulf War suggests a caution that would have been uncharacteristic of the Reagan presidency, but the decision to let Saddam Hussein remain in preference to his overthrow by the Kurds or Shi'a reveals that the United States is still intent on manipulating events to its advantage.

The emphasis on order rather than democracy in the new world order rhetoric is disheartening. Once committed to democracy at least in rhetoric, President Bush's pragmatism in letting it fly out the window to make more plausible his defense of Kuwait and Saudi Arabia does not inspire confidence that the new order will be a positive development for the rest of the world. The deterrence of aggression can also be viewed subjectively. Although there is no doubt that Saddam Hussein's invasion of Kuwait was a flagrant act of aggression, many Palestinians would argue that they are subjected daily to Israeli aggression on the West Bank and in Gaza; the West counters aggression only when it is in its interests to do so.

Recent U.S. policy toward Iran was predicated on the release of Western hostages, with little mention of human rights or democracy in that country. Moreover, President Bush's view that in a rapidly changing world U.S. leadership is indispensable does not sound like the views of an isolationist.[2] There is little reason to believe that the United States will cease to continue a foreign policy based on its own interests, although there may be some confusion about what constitutes those interests.

At least there is one certainty in the new world order—the collapse of the Soviet empire. Some fear that the lack of superpower competition will mean that weak states will have no one to turn to, but the Soviet Union certainly had little reason to claim it could counterbalance the United States to promote a fairer or better system. The communists in Iraq would be the first to point out that the Soviet Union supported Saddam Hussein in his suppression of the Iraqi Communist Party.

Yet, despite the dangers of a Pax Americana, the disintegration of an autocratic system in the Soviet Union that to date has involved little violence can only be regarded as a positive development and stands as an example to other autocratic governments in the developing world. Iran welcomed the collapse of communism primarily as an ideological victory that involved the demise of a materialist doctrine opposed to Islam. Iran supported Mikhail Gorbachev's rise to power because this led to increased recognition of the demands of its neighboring Muslim states to the south, states that Iran had once ruled.

Hashemi Rafsanjani's government did not, however, make as much of the dismantling of communism as it could have. This is in part because of a new orientation in foreign policy. Iran's reaction to the new world order and the Gulf War was as much a function of internal events as of external developments. Internally, the domestic factors to be considered included an increasing polarization of political views within the ruling hierarchy, a redefinition of the meaning of Islam as an ideological doctrine, and concern over the state of the economy.

From 1986, there were signs of a new, less ideological trend emerging in Iran, spearheaded by Rafsanjani, who was then speaker of the *majlis* (parliament). This pragmatic faction sought a face-saving end to the Iran-Iraq War and wished to normalize relations with other states. It wanted to encourage trade and relax the strict social conditions prevailing at home. By contrast, the hardliners remained committed to continuing the war, exporting revolution, and maintaining a state of permanent revolution. When Ayatollah Ruhollah Khomeini died in June 1989, the hardliners lost their most valuable asset.

Despite the increased tension between the two factions, a new foreign policy was implemented and Iran now is represented in more countries than at any time since the revolution. Iran changed its image from that of a hot-headed revolutionary state intent on intervening in the internal affairs of others to a respectable and responsible member of the international community, whose voice should be listened to. In recent years, Iranian officials defined the export of revolution to mean building Iran into a model Islamic country for others to emulate. This did not mean the abandonment of terrorism as a political weapon at home or abroad. Political executions continue within the country and outside; the 1991 murder of Shapour Bakhtiar, the shah's last prime minister, served as a reminder that the Iranian government, split as it may be, can still be as ruthless as it used to be.

A clear statement of the abandonment of an isolationist foreign policy was made by President Rafsanjani on 2 July 1988: "One of the wrong things we did in the revolutionary atmosphere was to constantly make enemies. We pushed those who could be neutral into hostility and did not do anything to attract those who could become friends. It is part of the new plan that in foreign policy we should behave in a way not to needlessly leave ground to the enemy."[3]

The shift in foreign policy hoped to attract foreign investment to reactivate the country's economy. President Rafsanjani termed the second decade of the Islamic republic as the decade of reconstruction, as opposed to the first decade of revolution. Rafsanjani also hoped to entice the private sector to invest in industry and production rather than property speculation and trade. Another aim was to persuade the Iranian exiles (approximately 1 million), many of whom were Iran's former elite industrialists and managers, to return, repatriate their wealth, and help run the factories. For these developments to take root, Rafsanjani needed to project the image of a more stable country with which Westerners and the private sector could do business.

The U.S.-led coalition against Iraq helped Iran move several steps closer to achieving these ends. The impact of the war was multifaceted and gave impetus to the country when it was in a stalemate. First, Iraq handed Iran victory in order to secure, at the very least, Iranian neutrality in the Gulf War, even though Iran had effectively lost the Iran-Iraq War. This was a personal victory for President Rafsanjani who was criticized by his hardline rivals for negotiating with Iraq. Second, it allowed Iran to feel vindicated as the aggrieved party in the 1980 Iran-Iraq War and indeed, Western opinion became more favorable toward Iran; this was aided by Iran's neutrality during the hostilities. Third, the Gulf War altered the strategic balance of power in the region. The Gulf Cooperation Council (GCC) was revealed as the paper tiger it always was and the Arab Gulf states moved closer to Iran as a way of counterbalancing Iraq's aggression. With the elimination of its main regional rival, Iran renewed its assertion that, as the largest country in the region, it should have the largest say, particularly in matters of security.

Finally, in order to play the role of the main regional power both militarily and economically, Iran had to reassess its relations with the United States. Cordial relations are a long way off, but both countries see it is in their best interests to improve relations. There seems to be a slow thaw; the United States relaxed some of its trade sanctions while Iran agreed to release the remaining Western hostages in Lebanon.

Iraqi-Iranian Relations

The Gulf War changed the balance of power between Iran and Iraq in Iran's favor. This was an unexpected and unearned reversal of fortune for Iran, which had been the effective loser in the Iran-Iraq War.

Iran informed the UN of its acceptance of Security Council Resolution 598 on 18 July 1988 after a series of battlefield defeats. A fortnight earlier, an Iranian civilian airliner was shot down by a U.S. naval vessel's missile resulting in the death of 290 civilians, the overwhelming majority of them Iranian. The United States later acknowledged that the ship's crew had mistakenly thought the aircraft was hostile, but the occasion was seized by Rafsanjani, then commander in chief, as an indication that the United States might enter the war on Iraq's side. Unlike Saddam Hussein, the pragmatic Rafsanjani knew that Iran would be the sure loser in a war against the United States: "World arrogance had decided to prevent our rapid victory. . . . An example of this was the strange obduracy of Americans in the Persian Gulf with the downing of the passenger plane; the allegation that it was a mistake is not acceptable in any way. In our opinion this was to be considered a warning rather than anything else."[4]

Iraq celebrated Iran's acceptance as a victory and subsequently dragged its heels over the implementation of the resolution in the hope of influencing the terms of any peace agreement in its favor. Iraq insisted on direct talks with Iran instead of those conducted through the UN. Iraq still occupied some 2,500 square kilometers of Iranian land that it refused to give up until Iran ceded total sovereignty over the Shatt al-Arab boundary waterway, which had been the ostensible *causus belli*. According to the 1975 Treaty of Algiers, Iran and Iraq agreed that sovereignty would be divided down the *thalweg*, or median line. The treaty was torn up by Saddam Hussein on the eve of Iraq's invasion of Iran in September 1980.

Relations between the two countries remained cool despite a series of UN-sponsored talks from the autumn onward. As if to drive home the point that Iran was at Iraq's mercy, Farzad Bazoft, an exiled Iranian who worked for the British newspaper, *The Observer*, was charged with spying and was hanged. The Iranian response to this was muted, mainly because Bazoft was seen to be as much an enemy of Iran as was Iraq. But the execution led to a sharp deterioration in relations between Great Britain and Iraq. Days later, British officials arrested five people for trying to smuggle U.S.-made electronic triggers to Iraq for their suspected nuclear use.

By April 1990, Saddam Hussein accused the United States and Britain of supplying Israel with political and diplomatic cover to attack Iraq. He said that he had advanced chemical weapons capable of destroying half of Israel. This and other statements caused an outcry in the West and, in a battle between Israel and the West against the Arab world (albeit one spearheaded by Iraq), Iran would at least publicly support Iraq. Thus, the secretary general of the

Iranian Foreign Ministry, Hossain Mussavian, said in May 1990 that Tehran would stand by Baghdad if war broke out between Iraq and Israel.[5]

Saddam Hussein sought to exploit the Iranian dilemma. His shift away from the enemy on the eastern flank to the West and Israel altered the framework in which Iranian-Iraqi negotiations were conducted and helped account for the first breakthrough since the 1988 cease-fire. In May 1990, Saddam Hussein initiated a direct correspondence with Hashemi Rafsanjani, much to the surprise of the Iranians, in a process that culminated in Iran and Iraq holding direct talks at the UN on 3 July. The Kuwaiti news agency reported in June that Iraq had ordered its media to refrain from attacks on Iran's leadership and to use correct forms of address.[6]

The events leading to the Kuwaiti invasion wrong-footed Iran as much as it did other nations. On the eve of the invasion, Iran said that the buildup of Iraqi forces signaled an attempt to pressure Kuwait and other Organization of Petroleum Exporting Countries (OPEC) members who had exceeded their quota during the OPEC meeting held in Geneva in late July. Both Iran and Iraq supported higher prices.

During the Iran-Iraq War the Gulf Arab states supported Iraq. Iran embarked on a policy of renewing relations with its smaller Gulf neighbors in an effort to portray itself as a nonbelligerent that need not be feared by the sheikhdoms to support its self-appointed position as guardian of the Persian Gulf. This followed President Rafsanjani's revised foreign policy goals of normalizing Iran's relations with the rest of the world and ensuring that, in its own region, Iran remain the dominant power. It involved portraying Iraq, not Iran, as the unstable force in the region. This would also serve to vindicate Iran as the victim of Iraqi aggression in the 1980 war if the UN found Iraq responsible for its outbreak.

The Iraqi invasion of Kuwait provided Iran with the ideal opportunity to demonstrate to the West the dangers of Saddam Hussein and to drive home the point to the Gulf Arab states that they were wrong to have supported Iraq in the Iran-Iraq War. Iran called for an Iraqi withdrawal from Kuwait, but opposed outside intervention in helping to achieve this. Iran's foreign ministry issued the following statement after the invasion:

> The Islamic Republic of Iran rejects any form of resort to
> force as a solution to regional problems. It considers Iraq's mil-

itary action against Kuwait contrary to stability and security in the sensitive Persian Gulf region and condemns it. Although the recent developments are the consequences of past [Kuwaiti] collaboration with the aggressor, which Iran has repeatedly pointed out to the regional countries, Iran considers respect for sovereignty and territorial integrity and noninterference in their internal affairs an absolute principle of intergovernmental relations.[7]

At a stroke, Iran tried to deny its past involvement in supporting opposition groups in a number of the Arab Gulf states—notably Bahrain, Saudi Arabia, and Iraq—during the early 1980s and to present itself instead as a rational actor committed to maintaining the status quo. It was particularly important for Iran to re-emphasize that it would not tolerate any change in the geographical boundaries of the region because it was Saddam Hussein's desire to redraw the Shatt al-Arab boundary that had ostensibly caused the Iran-Iraq War. For this reason too, Iran emphasized the integrity of Iraq's territory after the war. Iran's foreign policy had changed but Iran was now implicitly denying the policies it had pursued under Ayatollah Khomeini.

When Saddam Hussein announced that he accepted the Treaty of Algiers on 15 August 1990 (the treaty he had torn up before invading Iran in 1980), he clearly hoped for Iranian support over Kuwait. In his letter to President Rafsanjani he wrote of the need for "a serious interaction with all the believers to confront the evil doers who seek to inflict evil on Muslims and the Arab nation."[8] Iran was not taken in by the use of Islamic rhetoric by Saddam and warned the public not to be fooled by it.

Reports of Iranian help to Iraq surfaced at the time,[9] but apart from smugglers seeking a good profit and food and medicine that Iran announced it would give to Iraq in accordance with the UN's provisions for humanitarian aid, there was little evidence that the Iranian government was aiding Iraq. It certainly was not in Iran's interests to do so. An Iraq that could hold on to Kuwait would become a maritime Gulf power in direct challenge to Iran, and victory would likely spur Saddam Hussein to challenge Iran at a later date for the Shatt al-Arab. Moreover, there was no love lost by Iranian officials for Saddam Hussein, who they believed gave the West the green light to invade Iran in an attempt to weaken the new Islamic government to a point where it could be overthrown.

Iran celebrated its victory and used the invasion of Kuwait to illustrate that it had been the victim of a similar aggression ten years earlier. President Rafsanjani said, "Now everybody says it was clear who was the aggressor and who was the victim. A nation was defending its own rights for ten years, all alone by itself, and yet it was accused of being adventurist and fundamentalist and so forth."[10]

Nevertheless, Iran was now in a delicate position. It had outstanding business with Iraq: a peace settlement to be formulated, tens of thousands of prisoners to be repatriated, the dredging of the Shatt al-Arab to be completed, and the withdrawal of all Iraqi troops. On the other hand, it was opposed to the stationing of Western troops in the region and although it wished to see the demise of Saddam Hussein, it despaired that this had to be at the hands of the West and to the net advantage of the United States and Israel.

Iranian officials spoke repeatedly of two separate files—the "peace" file with Iraq and the "Kuwait" file, and indeed it attempted to exploit its position of being on speaking terms with the Iraqis as a vantage point to launch a regional peace initiative to make the presence of U.S. military forces unnecessary. Thus, Iran proposed a five-point Islamic peace plan outlined by the speaker of parliament, Mehdi Karrubi, in January 1991. A week or so later, President Rafsanjani offered his services as mediator but was tartly turned down by the United States. The degree to which Iran welcomed the weakening of Iraq became clear when Rafsanjani gave tacit approval for a U.S. strike at Iraq during the first month of the Kuwaiti invasion: "We warn that once the calamity is over, when Iraq sees the light of wisdom—whether she pulls herself out voluntarily or is forced to pull out of Kuwait—then these [foreign] forces have no cause to remain in the region."[11]

The "peace" file caused Iran and Iraq to resume diplomatic relations on 10 September. An additional bonus of these improved relations was the Iraqi clampdown on Iranian opposition groups that had used Iraq as a base to carry out dissident operations. Radio stations of Iranian opposition groups using Iraqi facilities to broadcast to Iran were closed down.[12]

Cordial relations were maintained throughout the autumn and winter while Iran continued to call for an Iraqi withdrawal from Kuwait. Its schizophrenic position on the increasing inevitability of a coalition war against Saddam Hussein, in which Iran's main Arab ally, Syria, would be involved, resulted in contradictory statements. On 18 December, in answer to students' questions, Rafsanjani said,

"We are very strongly opposed to the Iraqis being crushed by the Americans. . . . Our solution is that Iraq should withdraw unconditionally from Kuwait. She should not raise any conditions. On the contrary, she should be answerable for the evil actions she has committed. . . . We hope, we beseech God, we pray the war will not happen. But if it does take place, they [the Iraqis] themselves are responsible for it."[13]

As mentioned earlier, despite Iran's public stance against a war, it welcomed a strike against Saddam Hussein. Inaction on the part of the United States aroused far greater concern about its intentions in the region than its use of force. Like other countries, Iran had no illusions about U.S. motives to protect Israel and safeguard its oil supplies above any principle of nonaggression. When the war broke out, President Rafsanjani was pressured by his domestic opponents to help Iraq, its Muslim neighbor, in the fight against the twin Satans—the United States and Israel. Hojatoleslam Sadeq Khalkhali, the notorious hanging judge and a member of parliament, called for a military pact between Iran and Iraq to fight Israel while former interior minister,[14] Hojatoleslam Ali Akbar Mohtashemi, appealed to the *majlis*: "The great leader [Khameni] described confrontation with America in the Persian Gulf as jihad for the sake of God and being slain as martyrdom for the sake of God. Is that defending Saddam? Or is it in defense of our Islamic homeland, the Muslims, and the Islamic tradition?"[15]

Ayatollah Sayed Ali Khameni, the spiritiual leader, supported Rafsanjani's position of neutrality:

These gentlemen who have brought the country of Iraq under the boot of aggressive invaders—what have they got to say to the Iraqi nation? What right did you have to involve the Iraqi nation in an unwanted war to satisfy your ambitions? Are you the guardians of the people of Iraq that you should occupy Kuwait and then turn Iraq and its oppressed nation into targets for the abject enemy? This issue cannot be defended in any way and anyone who defends it and justifies their stance is deceiving himself.[16]

Rafsanjani laid out Iran's strategic concerns clearly in a Friday prayer sermon describing Iranian participation in the war as suicide:

Now I raise an important question for some gentlemen who advocate our entry into the war to help Iraq. What will happen

to us if Iraq were to be seated on the southern coast of the
Persian Gulf? . . . Does it mean that we must go to war to
help Iraq to remain in Kuwait? After all, that is what Saddam
wants. Then our border with Iraq will extend close to the
Strait of Hormuz. Then tomorrow the Persian Gulf will become the Arabian Gulf and the like. Is that not suicide in your
view?[17]

While condemning the coalition forces, Rafsanjani and Khamenei
cleverly blamed their presence in the region and their resort to force
as Saddam Hussein's fault. By so doing, they justified the sacrifice of
ideology to pragmatism. Fears of a secret Iranian-Iraqi alliance re-
surfaced with the extraordinary flight by over 100 Iraqi fighter and
other planes to Iran. The reason for the flight of the Iraqi air force is
still unclear; even if there had been collusion, Saddam Hussein mis-
calculated. To date, Iran has not returned the planes, maintaining in
any case that it only has around twenty planes. It is highly unlikely
that they will be returned unless Iran is substantially pressured to
do so.

Given the lack of Iranian support for Iraq and its continued sanctuary for the main Shi'a opposition group, the Supreme Assembly
for the Islamic Republic of Iraq (Sairi), it was not surprising that
the tension showed. From February 1991 onward, a distinct chill
crept into Iraqi-Iranian relations. Iraq pointedly snubbed Iran's peace
dialogue while Iran accused it of making a series of miscalculations
that would lead to disaster. Iranian radio also broadcast news of an-
tigovernment disturbances in Iraq and days after the war ended,
Ayatollah Ali Meshkini, chairman of the Assembly of Experts (the
body that appoints a spiritual leader), called for the first time on the
Iraqi people to overthrow their leader. "You gentlemen of the Iraqi
nation! Brothers! Are you going to sit there and let Saddam rule
over you? Saddam's weakest day is today. That honorable gentle-
man from Sairi [Hojatoleslam Mohammad Baqr Hakim] has put
forward a good suggestion. He has said that Saddam should go and
the nation choose a leader for itself. Oh you Iraqi nation. His remarks are good. For God's sake take some action."[18]

The Shi'a uprisings in the aftermath of the war led to a speedy
breakdown in the restrained politeness that had prevailed. For Iran,
the combination of the achievement of its 1980 war aims, Iraq's capitulation to the coalition forces, and an expectation of Saddam Hussein's imminent overthrow proved too much. A new radio station

hostile to the Iraqi government, the Voice of the Islamic Republic in Iraq, broadcast from Iran in March, and Iran's own news agencies covered extensively the disturbances in the Shi'a south. Iraq accused Iran of sending agents to help foment the troubles, and although Iran denied this, it stretched credibility to imagine that Iran had no hand in assisting the rebels.

The failure of the rebellion and the uneasy peace that prevailed since the end of the war caused tense relations to persist. These were exacerbated further in April 1992 when Iran mounted an air raid inside Iraq against the Mosahedin-E Khalq opposition group, and cross-border accusations continued throughout the year. Iranian leaders would like Saddam Hussein to go, and although their first preference for a replacement government would be a Shi'a Islamic republic led by Seyyed Hakim, they realize that this will not occur and therefore they have not pushed as hard as they might for such an Islamic republic. Instead, the Iranian government championed the cause of the Shi'a population, resenting as hypocritical the world's focus and sympathy for the problems of the Kurds at the expense of the Shi'a.

While Saddam Hussein remains in power, Iraq represents a potential danger to Iran, although by the same token, it is unlikely that the United States will ever let Saddam Hussein accumulate sufficient power to threaten any country in the region. If a Shi'a republic is impossible, Iran would instead hope for a government with which they could do business, be it Ba'athist or not. Iranian leaders would not welcome any increase in power for the Kurds, fearing that Iran's own Kurdish minority might become unruly and demanding.

Iran Vindicated?

The overall effect of the war benefitted Iran, mainly by shifting the balance of power to Iran and allowing its leaders to play for Western sympathy for its own losses sustained in the Iran-Iraq War. Thus, the Iran government said that if Kuwait was to be compensated for war damages, Iran should be as well. A team of inspectors from the UN visited Iran in June 1991 to assess the damage resulting from the Iran-Iraq War. (Iran asked that all paragraphs of UN Security Council Resolution 598 be implemented; it called on an impartial body to determine responsibility for the war.) This process has been put on the agenda again because of the Gulf War.

Iran also benefitted from the fact that Saddam Hussein replaced

Ayatollah Khomeini as the West's most hated villain. Tales of Saddam Hussein's atrocities toward his own people, which were the staple diet of the Western press after the invasion of Kuwait, shifted critical attention away from Iran and made the Iranian regime look better in comparison. Moreover, Iran won respect for its handling of the refugee crisis in contrast to the obstacles strewn in the path of refugees by Turkey. It was the refugee situation that led Iran to accept its first consignment of U.S. aid.

Relations with Persian Gulf States

The coalition war against Iraq made a shift in the balance of power in the region inevitable. The existing security structure—the GCC, which included Saudi Arabia, Kuwait, the United Arab Emirates, Oman, Qatar, and Bahrain—was created in 1981 with the express intention of leaving out Iran and Iraq, which were mistrusted by their neighbors. The GCC was dominated by Saudi Arabia, which was resented by some members of the pact. During the Iran-Iraq War, the littoral states had little choice but to support Iraq against what was perceived as a greater threat from Iran. But even during the war, Iran's relations with the six Gulf Arab states were not uniform. The best relations were with Oman and the United Arab Emirates: The latter had strong trading links with Iran while Oman hoped to boost its international image by acting as a mediator between Iran and Iraq. Bahrain and Qatar were neutral but wary of Iran, while there was open hostility with Saudi Arabia and Kuwait, both branded by Iran as stooges and lackeys of the West. They in turn regarded Iran with fear and suspicion as threatening their governments through the sponsorship of pro-Shi'ite liberation movements. Iran held Kuwait responsible for bringing foreign forces to the Persian Gulf when it asked for protection for its oil tankers, first from the Soviet Union and then from the United States. Iran saw the presence of U.S. forces at its doorstep as a direct threat to its own security and retaliated against Kuwait by mining its harbors.

Iran's acceptance of UN Security Council Resolution 598 was welcomed by the GCC, and Iran, now on the defensive, sought to gain as many friends as it could in the hope of pressuring Iraq to implement the resolution. Relations with Kuwait improved rapidly. By the autumn of 1989, the two countries agreed to restore diplomatic relations, and Iran's foreign minister, Ali Akbar Velayati, visited Kuwait in July 1990. By the summer of 1992, Iran agreed to return to Kuwait six Kuwaiti Airways Corporation aircraft that were moved to Iran during the 1991 Gulf War despite the absence of an arrangement regarding parking fees.

The cooling of Iran's Islamic fervor and its talk about good neighborliness and relations based on mutual respect allayed some of the fears of the Gulf states. On 2 June 1988, Velayati delivered a speech to the UN that crystallized Iran's policy toward the Persian Gulf: "The Islamic Republic of Iran has repeatedly stated that it will not permit the Persian Gulf to become a playground for the superpowers and that it is to the advantage of peace and security that this area should be free from all kinds of rivalry and the presence of foreign forces. The security of the Persian Gulf is the responsibility of the littoral states alone. The Islamic Republic, which has the longest coastline, desires peace and stability in this waterway more than any other country."[19]

The general secretary of the GCC, Abdullah Bishara, opposed Iran's isolation and stated that the GCC countries were determined not to be provoked into a conflict with Iran: "We preferred the old approach of coexistence with the Iranians."[20] In December 1990, the GCC announced talks with Iran about its possible inclusion in a new security structure, an approach welcomed by Iran and in part a result of Velayati's active diplomacy; he visited all the GCC countries, apart from Saudi Arabia, that did not have diplomatic relations with Iran. In June 1992, Bishara reiterated the GCC's desire that relations develop with Iran and said that foreign ministers at the forty-third meeting of the GCC had laid a framework for cooperation with Iran.

The Iraqi invasion of Kuwait demonstrated the Iranian government's ability to withstand its domestic critics and maintain the new orientation of its foreign policy—support of Kuwait. While hardliners such as Hojatoleslam Mohtashemi called for attacks on foreign ships and "the palaces of kings and sheikhs in the region," the Iranian foreign ministry welcomed members of the ousted al-Sabah family to Tehran.[21] President Rafsanjani used the opportunity to point out to his Arab neighbors how mistaken they had been in supporting Iraq during the Iran-Iraq War: "Our southern neighbors are now regretting the fact they gave so much money and assistance to them [the Iraqis]. They say: Why did we utter so much nonsense and adopt such oppressive measures toward this noble neighbor of ours [Iran] and help that aggressive neighbor [Iraq]."[22]

Iran knew that it could only play a major role in the Persian Gulf if relations with Saudi Arabia, aborted after the 1987 *haj* riots, were restored. Ayatollah Khomeini vowed after the Mecca riots that, even if it were possible to forgive Saddam Hussein, it would never be possible to forgive Saudi Arabia. Nevertheless, discussions about the number of pilgrims Saudi Arabia would allow to the *haj* proved a good opportunity for both sides to maintain a dialogue.

By September 1989, Velayati said he would welcome efforts by the GCC to mediate between Tehran and Riyadh, an offer taken up most energetically by Oman. There was a setback with the execution by Saudi Arabia of sixteen Kuwaiti Shi'as, some of Iranian origin, for their role in a bomb attack in Mecca in July 1989, but the two countries resumed negotiations on the haj quota within months. In August 1990, the Jeddah-based Islamic Development Bank approved U.S. $6.5 million in project financing for small industries in Iran.

The 1990 Iraqi invasion of Kuwait and Saudi fears for its own security hastened negotiations with Iran. Days after the invasion, Prince Nayif Bin Abdul Aziz, the Saudi interior minister, outlined his country's predicament:

> The Kingdom did not stand against Iran at all. . . . But we were in a position with no alternative—we had to stand by an Arab state [Iraq] defending itself and protecting us from evil. But circumstances change. Nobody imagined that the Iraqi people and the Iraqi army would agree to divert its force, after having triumphed in the war with Iran, to invade and occupy a small Arab and Muslim state which is a neighbor of Iraq. . . . What are we going to do? Either we are occupied by Iran or Iraq—at least the latter is an Arab and Muslim."[23]

In part, Saudi Arabia needed a rapprochement with Tehran to balance its politically embarrassing situation of having hundreds of thousands of U.S. troops stationed on its land. King Fahd made conciliatory noises by claiming that Kuwaiti and Saudi financial assistance to Iraq had not been aimed at an invasion of Iran but at Iraq's defense. He said that he had personally tried to dissuade Saddam from invading Iran and referred to past events between Iran and Saudi Arabia as "aberrations."[24]

By the end of March 1991, the two countries finally announced the restoration of diplomatic relations, much to the dismay of Iranian hardliners who had criticized the policy of talking to Riyadh. "Have we forgotten that the Imam [Khomeini] used to say graciously that if we forgive Saddam we cannot forgive Fahd and his house? What has happened for the crimes of the principal enemies of Islam and the Muslims, the world-devouring America and the treacherous House of Saud, to be forgotten, and for some to favor forming relations with Fahd's mercenary regime?" fulminated Mohtashemi in the majlis.[25] But Rafsanjani defended his policy by saying that it was Khomeini's desire that Iranian pilgrims carry out the haj. For this, it was necessary to restore diplomatic relations with Saudi Arabia.

The terms of the restoration of relations were in Iran's favor. Whereas Riyadh had previously insisted that no more than 45,000 Iranian pilgrims could attend the haj in the face of Iranian demands for at least 150,000, it agreed to compromise on 110,000. The inclusion of Iran in a strategic security relationship was also mooted. Velayati said that as part of the deal "the two leading countries in the Persian Gulf, Iran and Saudi Arabia, have decided to maintain close, strategic and comprehensive cooperation on ensuring regional security."[26]

The *haj* passed uneventfully in June, and later in the month Saudi Arabia released a number of Shi'a prisoners in an amnesty. In 1992, about 120,000 pilgrims performed the haj uneventfully, and President Khameni's edict to the pilgrims that "any act which weakens the religion or causes discord among Muslims is harmful and the faithful must avoid them" helped slowly improve Saudi-Iranian relations. In July 1992, deputy Iranian foreign affairs minister, Mohammad Ali Besharati, announced that King Fahd and President Rafsanjani planned a summit meeting soon, although this had not materialized by June 1993.

It was perhaps unsurprising that Iran wanted to show that it still maintained cordial relations with Saudi Arabia when much of its good work at regaining the trust of its regional neighbors was severely harmed by the 1992 Abu Musa affair. Abu Musa and the islands of the Greater and Lesser Tunbs had been invaded by the shah on the eve of the British withdrawal from the region in 1971. The shah concluded an agreement with Sharjah that allowed for joint sovereignty of the strategically important island of Abu Musa and the stationing of Iranian troops there. Ras al-Khaima, which comprised one of the sovereign states of the UAE and to which the islands belonged, was unable to prevent the occupation of the Greater and Lesser Tunbs by the Shah who claimed sovereignty over them.

The 1992 dispute began in April and intensified in September when

Iran refused entry to a ship carrying passengers from the United Arab Emirates (UAE). Iranian officials demanded that non-Sharjan residents should produce Iranian permits and that all foreigners intending to land on Abu Musa should advise the Iranian authorities in advance. Iran claimed that it had already warned the UAE of these measures. Iran denied that it demanded visas of emirate citizens, but a report on Syrian radio after Syrian's foreign minister, Faruq al-Shara'a, visited Iran to mediate on the dispute attributed a statement to Iranian deputy foreign minister, Mohammad Besharati, that emirate citizens would be allowed to return to Abu Musa without a visa.

The incident caused an outcry and dominated the Arab regional press. At its Qatar meeting on 9 September, the GCC issued a "strong condemnation of the measures taken by Iran on Abu Musa, which are a violation of the sovereignty and territorial integrity" of the UAE. The statement rejected "completely" Iran's occupation of the Tunbs islands. The GCC said it "totally supported all the measures taken by the UAE to affirm its sovereignty over the island." Syria, which had been allied to Iran during the Iran-Iraq War, also came out in support of its fellow Arabs.

Iran underestimated the degree to which its actions might alarm the UAE and its Persian Gulf neighbors. The government took a defensive line, with President Rafsanjani claiming that security measures on the island had to be increased following an incident in which armed strangers landed there. He said one of these, a Dutchman, was arrested. At other times, Tehran appeared to distance itself by blaming overzealous officials on the islands, while President Khameni blamed the argument on the West for trying to create divisions between Iran and its neighbors. While the Arab states played up the incident, Iran downplayed it. The Foreign Ministry issued a statement referring to the "misunderstanding" that had arisen between Iran and the UAE. The Foreign Ministry official responsible for Gulf affairs, Mostafa Fumani-Ha'eri, while conceding that some non-Sharjah Arabs on the island might have been "disturbed" as a result of the measures, denied that Iran's policy towards the island had changed.

There are reasons to believe that Iran underestimated the degree to which its actions would be regarded as provocative. First, its policy toward the Arab states of the Persian Gulf tried to improve relations rather than alienate them. Second, Iran was concerned about its own security and had embarked upon a program of rearmament, including the purchase of submarines from the former Soviet Union. Tehran regarded the three islands in the Persian Gulf, particularly Abu Musa, which is almost equidistant between the shores of Iran and the UAE, as strategically important. It based its surface-to-air missiles in the Iran-Iraq War there. At a time when the littoral states had signed bilateral defense pacts with the United States (with the exception of Saudi Arabia and the UAE) and Kuwait and the United States were preparing for joint maneuvers in the Persian Gulf, Iran decided to take extra defensive measures of its own. It was also threatened by the continued presence of 25,000 troops in the region. Third, Iran appeared to go out of its way to resolve the dispute. It agreed to the Syrian initiative even though Syria could not be regarded as an honest broker, having already declared its support for the UAE. Fumani-Ha'eri traveled to Abu Dhabi to hold direct talks with his UAE counterpart, Saif Said, after Iran backed down from an earlier position that it only wanted to talk to Sharjah about the problem. The talks failed, partly because the UAE used this opportunity to include the Tunbs islands, which was unacceptable to the Iranians. For its part, the UAE's reaction was also understandable and the feeling among the states of the GCC was balanced between wanting to continue to improve relations with Iran and fearing that failure to check an "aggressive" Iranian move now might mean greater trouble in the future.

The Gulf War created the conditions that would enable Iran to accelerate its policy of improved relations with its Arab neighbors. This would enable it to make friends of former enemies and thus become less isolated than it had been during the Khomeini years and establish its dominance of the Persian Gulf through diplomatic means. The Iraqi invasion of Kuwait turned Iraq overnight from an ally defending the Arab homeland to an enemy. It was therefore in the interests of the littoral states to re-establish at least a working relationship with Iran to avert an Iraqi-Iranian collaboration.

Persian Gulf Security and Iran-U.S. Relations

Iran profited from the Gulf War and hopes to emerge as the main power in the Gulf region. This objective is not without a foundation: Iran's coastline stretches the entire length of the Gulf and, with sixty million inhabitants, it has by far the largest population in the region. With the embargo on Iraqi oil, it is also the second largest oil producer in the region after Saudi Arabia. Iran was the dominant Gulf power under the shah. The U.S. twin pillars policy of promoting Iran and Saudi Arabia to maintain American interests in the region translated into a pillar and a half, because Saudi Arabia could not compete in terms of the size of its armed forces or manpower.

It is understandable that the Gulf Arab states might not welcome such a dominant non-Arab power on their Eastern shores. Iran's seizure of the islands of Abu Musa and Greater and Lesser Tunbs in the Gulf from the UAE and the shah's claims to Bahrain nearly provoked an international crisis. Iran's support for Iraq's Kurdish rebels ensured the Iraqi government's capitulation to Iranian demands for the 1974 Treaty of Algiers in exchange for a promise from Tehran to stop funding the rebels. The Gulf littoral states feared that an Iran unchecked might mean an Iran with unlimited power to dictate policy in the Gulf. Their fears are not without foundation. On the one hand, the Iranian government denies that it wished to dominate the region. On the other hand, however, Iran describes itself as the largest country in the region with the greatest degree of interests in Persian Gulf affairs, entailing that it should have the greatest say in those affairs.

There are, therefore, alternate views of security in the Persian Gulf; the Arabs, Iran, and the United States each have their own agenda, while powers farther afield, such as Egypt and Pakistan, also have an interest in the matter. The Iranian government asserts that security in the region must rest with the littoral states, which should cooperate to ensure stability and security. The GCC countries agree that this is the ideal security arrangement, but they do not trust Iran or one another as the guardian of their interests. The UAE called for Iran's inclusion in a Persian Gulf security system and the GCC wanted Iran to have a participatory role in future regional security arrangements. But by calling for international guarantees, it is clear that Kuwait and Saudi Arabia do not believe that a regional arrangement will be enough to maintain order.

Kuwait shares this view. In July 1991, Kuwaiti Defense Minister Sheikh Ali al-Sabah al-Salim said that Kuwait wanted "to guarantee politically and militarily that neither Iraq nor any other country will attack Kuwait. Therefore, there must be security arrangements with foreign countries, excluding the presence of foreign forces."[27] In September 1991, Kuwait signed a bilateral, ten-year defense pact with the United States. This, along with internal quarrels, derailed the

Damascus Declaration of March 1991, which envisaged a security structure comprised of the GCC states, Egypt, and Syria (the 6 + 2 arrangement).

The Kuwait-U.S. treaty and the Damascus Declaration were greeted with dismay by Iran. Iran's First Deputy Foreign Minster, Mohammad Ali Besharati, criticized Egypt and Syria for seeking to play a role in the security of the region. He commented that Egypt, "because of its worsening economic conditions, is not the right country to pay attention to Persian Gulf security." This provoked an angry response from Egypt and threatened to disrupt the painfully slow process of restoring relations between the two countries.[28]

Iran opposes any outside, particularly U.S., presence in the region and wishes to avert a reversion to the gendarme policy that prevailed under the shah. It wants to be at the center of any regional security arrangement:

The method of domineering powers in the Persian Gulf has been that of creating a power in the form of a gendarme of the region who would administer the region's affairs in the way desired by colonial powers. . . . "Iraq lacks the necessary resources to play such a role," said Mr. Rafsanjani at the end of an international conference on the Persian Gulf in Tehran in 1989. "We are not ready in any way to be the guardian and protector of others in the Persian Gulf and yet we will not allow anyone to wear the mantle of guardianship and gendarme of the Persian Gulf. . . . The way we suggest is that of cooperation between the region's countries on the basis of recognized Islamic, humanitarian and international criteria."[29]

In part, the rhetoric is aimed at deflecting criticism that the Islamic Republic's foreign policy sounds extremely similar to the shah's Persian nationalism. There is, however, a strong dose of nationalism contained in Rafsanjani's foreign policy, with an increasing emphasis on Iran's interests rather than those of Islam. Any suggestion to rename the Persian Gulf the Islamic Gulf was firmly rebutted in Tehran.

Despite its opposition to U.S. involvement in the region, there is little that Rafsanjani's government can do. The government warned the United States not to intervene in the area after the Iraqi invasion of Kuwait but however strong the propaganda, the resources at Iran's disposal to prevent the United States from intervening in the area are limited. And, despite the warnings, Iran stayed neutral in the Gulf War and used its influence to ensure the release of Western hostages from Lebanon. An aggressive U.S. foreign policy might backfire by giving added ammunition to the hardliners in Iran who criticize Rafsanjani and, perhaps, carry out terrorist operations. For now, the hardliners are on the defensive and President Bush has watered down the U.S. strategic imperatives in the region by making a concerted effort for an Arab-Israeli peace conference.

U.S.-Iranian relations are slowly improving. Iran has consulted with the International Monetary Fund and is undertaking its fiscal reform in accordance with its guidelines. It has also talked to the World Bank. U.S. companies have increased their trade with Iran: In 1991 the Ford Motor Company awarded a U.S. $15 million contract to rebuild oil shipping facilities in southern Iran.[30] In September, Iran released David Rabhan, a U.S. citizen who was a pilot for former president Jimmy Carter, after eleven years in prison. Despite these changes, however, the United States extended its declaration of a national emergency with respect to Iran for another year, until November 1991; this declaration restricted trade between the two countries. The United States relaxed the declaration a few months later by allowing some U.S. oil companies to buy Iranian oil on the condition that Iran deposit its payment in the security account at the Hague for the compensation of the U.S. claims resulting from the 1979 revolution.

The United States had made it clear that it would only consider a normalization of relations with Iran once all the Western hostages are released from Lebanon, a process that has already taken place. It was Iran's studied neutrality during the Gulf War that won it a degree of trust from the United States and prompted talks between the two countries.[31] In March 1991, President Bush publicly expressed a desire for improved U.S.-Iranian relations and hoped that Iran would become better integrated with the other countries of the region. "We want better relations with Iran. . . . I don't think they should be treated forever as enemies by all the countries out in the GCC or others."[32] Clearly, the United States saw a role for Iran in security arrangements in the region but the Clinton administration has been far warier of Iran than Bush and has accused it of being a terrorist nation and an "international outlaw." While U.S. and Iranian interests remain fundamentally opposed, it is debatable how great a say Iran will have in security matters.

Conclusion

The coalition war against Iraq was a boon to Iran and precipitated its move to integrate itself with other countries of the region. This is a stabilizing development although future GCC-Iranian relations will likely come up against the brick wall of bilateral security arrangements between the GCC states and the United States.

Iran will express disapproval in strong rhetorical terms, but because it, too, needs to improve relations with the United States and since the decisive military victory against Iraq is likely to prove an effective cautionary legacy to those daring to challenge U.S. interests, there may be less substantive Iranian opposition than might be expected.

Pride plays an important part in a government's behavior. Iran had been under siege since the creation of the Islamic republic, much of it deserved but some undeserved. Now that it can play a constructive role in the region's affairs, it would be short-sighted of the United States to fail to recognize that Iran seeks to restore its national pride by playing an important role in the formation of a postwar security structure. From the U.S. perspective, it would be short-sighted of Washington to thwart such a development, as long as this does not clash with vital U.S. interests.

The tension between U.S. and Iranian interests hinges on the price of oil and on political issues such as the Palestinian question. Yet, an Iran that no longer seeks to overthrow Washington's friends in the region increasingly becomes an Iran that the United States can do business with. Although far from an ideal government from the U.S. perspective, Iran is at least no longer the destabilizing force it once was. And, if its government is able to appear cohesive, and is no longer conducting a contradictory foreign policy, the United States will be able to cooperate with Iran.

No one will argue that the formation of a postwar security structure will be easy. Despite the success in countering Saddam's aggression in Kuwait, there is little indication that tensions in the region will disappear. Egypt and Iran clashed verbally and a dispute between Qatar and Bahrain arose after complaints by Qatar that its vessels had been harassed by Bahraini gunboats. Qatar and Saudi Arabia also renewed their border dispute.

Although most security structures are designed to ensure cooperation among regional states against an outside attack, the greatest threat to the security of the Gulf countries is likely to come from inside the Gulf region. With the demise of the Soviet Union, some of the states in the region will defer to the protection of an outside power, the United States and perhaps France or Great Britain, as a protection against its putative allies in the defense structure. For this reason, an all-inclusive security structure is virtually meaningless.

What would be the common interest binding Iran, Iraq, the GCC states, Syria, and Egypt? It cannot be said that these states share a common opinion vis-à-vis Washington. Instead, those countries that are already allies of the United States will likely develop closer ties with Washington and hope to achieve a workable relationship with other states in the region. The strategic relationship with the United States may be of assistance to the governments of these states in the short term, but in the long term the risk of domestic opposition to increased U.S. involvement is greater.

The Iranian government, which demonstrated its pragmatism in the coalition war against Iraq, will likely continue to seek its own security through the continuation of a policy designed to deter threats, be they external or internal. What finally emerges may not resemble anything as ordered as a security structure, but will likely be an arrangement that conforms with U.S. strategic interests. It will have little to do with democracy, human rights, justice, or the like. Attempts to impose this pax Americana too energetically or to prevent the larger states in the region (Iran, Iraq, and possibly Saudi Arabia) from having roughly equal political weight (a situation that proved the most stabilizing in the past) may, however, prove explosive in the future.

Notes

1. Quoted in *Survival* 33 (March/April 1991): 183.
2. *Ibid.*
3. Hashemi Rafsanjani, 2 July 1988, BBC Summary of World Broadcasts/Middle East 0794 (5 July 1988).
4. *BBC Summary of World Broadcasts/Middle East* 0207 (20 July 1988).
5. Radio Monte Carlo, Paris on 12 May, in *BBC Summary of World Broadcasts/Middle East* (15 May 1990).
6. Kuna, Kuwait, on 29 June, in *BBC Summary of World Broadcasts/Middle East* (30 June 1990).

7. Voice of Islamic Republic on 2 August, in *BBC Summary of World Broadcasts/Middle East* (4 August 1990).

8. Republic of Iraq Radio, Baghdad, on 15th August, in *BBC Summary of World Broadcasts* (16 August, 1990).

9. See for example, Youssef M. Ibrahim in the *International Herald Tribune* (3 August 1990).

10. Voice of Islamic Republic of Iran, Tehran, on 24 August, in *BBC Summary of World Broadcasts/Middle East* (27 August 1990).

11. Voice of the Islamic Republic of Iran, Tehran, on 24 August, in *BBC Summary of World Broadcasts/Middle East* (27 August 1990).

12. BBC Monitoring in *BBC Summary of World Broadcasts/Middle East* (18 October 1990) reported that four radio stations using Iraqi facilities to broadcast in opposition to Iran were no longer being heard. These were the Free Voice of Iran, Radio Iran (first program), the Voice of the Mojahedin-Khalq, and the Voice of the Ahwaz Revolution.

13. Voice of the Islamic Republic of Iran, Tehran, on 18 December, in *BBC Summary of World Broadcasts/Middle East* (20 December 1990).

14. *Middle East Mirror* (11 September 1990).

15. Voice of the Islamic Republic of Iran, Tehran, on 24 January, in *BBC Summary of World Broadcasts/Middle East* (25 January 1991).

16. Voice of the Islamic Republic of Iran, Tehran, on 24 January, in *BBC Summary of World Broadcasts/Middle East* (26 January 1991).

17. Voice of the Islamic Republic of Iran, Tehran, on 25 January, in *BBC Summary of World Broadcasts/Middle East 0980* (28 January 1991).

18. Voice of the Islamic Republic of Iran, Tehran, on 1 March, in *BBC Summary of World Broadcasts/Middle East* (4 March 1991).

19. Velayati address to the UN on 2 June 1988, in *BBC Summary of World Broadcasts/Middle East* (7 June 1988).

20. Kuna, dateline Washington, on 25 February, in *BBC Summary of World Broadcasts/Middle East* (27 February 1988).

21. Agence France Presse, datelined Tehran, quoted in the monthly *Bayan* published by Ali Akbar Mohtashemi on 29 September, in *BBC Summary of World Broadcasts/Middle East* (1 October 1990).

22. Voice of the Islamic Republic of Iran, Tehran, on 21 September, in *BBC Summary of World Broadcasts/Middle East* (24 September 1990).

23. Kingdom of Saudi Arabia Radio, Riyadh, on 19 August, in *BBC Summary of World Broadcasts/Middle East* (21 August 1990).

24. King Fahd in *Middle East Mirror* (31 January 1991).

25. Voice of the Islamic Republic of Iran, Tehran, on 24 January, in *BBC Summary of World Broadcasts/Middle East* (25 January 1991).

26. Voice of the Islamic Republic of Iran, Tehran, on 27 April, in *BBC Summary of World Broadcasts/Middle East* (29 April 1991).

27. Quoted in *Middle East Economic Survey* (1 July 1991).

28. Quoted in *Middle East Mirror* (25 June 1991).

29. Voice of the Islamic Republic of Iran, Tehran, on 22 November, in *BBC Summary of World Broadcasts/Middle East 0620* (24 November 1989).

30. *Middle East Economic Digest* (31 August 1991).

31. Reuters report quoting *IRNA* in *The Independent* (11 August 1991).

32. Quoted in *Middle East Economic Digest* (22 March 1991).

13

The Gulf War, the Palestinians, and the New World Order

Cheryl A. Rubenberg

In the aftermath of the Gulf War, no actors were in a weaker or more vulnerable position than the Palestinians. They lost the financial support of their major Arab state backers and the political support of a significant number of other states, their bargaining power was markedly diminished, the Intifada had come to a virtual halt, their leadership was in crisis, and a new exodus of Palestinians had begun—this time from Kuwait—adding another painful chapter to the Palestinian tragedy. In addition, the transformation of the international system into a unipolar structure with a hegemonic United States purposefully promoting its design for a new world order in the Middle East was not beneficial for Palestinian interests. The United States has consistently rejected fundamental Palestinian rights, refusing to acknowledge the Palestinian right to self-determination, to an independent state, or to leaders of its own choosing—that is, the Palestine Liberation Organization (PLO).[1]

U.S. diplomacy in the post-war period evidenced no change in any aspect of this traditional stance. Moreover, in the aftermath of the Gulf crisis, the regional balance of power was more strongly in Israel's favor than at any time in the history of the Arab-Palestinian-Israeli conflict, and Israel had less incentive to make concessions in a settlement with the Palestinians than before.[2]

The new world order, the collapse of communism—economically and politically—in the Soviet Union and Eastern Europe, and the consequent dissolution of the bipolar world into the global political-military domination of the United States, fundamentally and negatively altered the Palestinian situation. Although the Soviet Union had never been a strong supporter of the Palestinians or the PLO,[3] its position on an international conference, its relationship with Syria and Iraq, and its general counterpoint to the United States in the region provided Palestinians with some hope that the U.S.-Israeli behemoth might be contained and Palestinian interests realized. In the context of *perestroika* and *glasnost*, however, the Soviet Union was enormously eager for trade, aid, investment, and loans from the United States; thus, Moscow readily acquiesced to U.S. interests in the Middle East. Indeed, as the *New York Times* noted, the Soviet Union was quite willing "to squeeze the Syrians and Palestinians on Washington's behalf and to restore relations with Israel."[4]

The United States' foremost interest in the Middle East involves ensuring continued access to oil, adequate production of oil, and the stabilization of prices at U.S. $18 to U.S. $22 a barrel.[5] Middle Eastern markets for U.S. goods, services, and investment opportunities are also significant. Finally, regional stability and the prevention of nationalist (or radical Islamic fundamentalist) movements have been consistent and enduring interests. Until the recent thaw in U.S.-Soviet relations (and the subsequent disintegration of the Soviet Union), an important U.S. goal was containing the spread of Soviet influence. In the new world order, however, the Soviets were no longer considered a threat and the "Russians" became a "junior-partner" in the U.S. grand design.[6]

Following from the definition of its national interest, U.S. policy has opposed, axiomatically, all manifestations of Arab nationalism in the region, including Palestinian nationalism. The United States has also opposed regimes that were not "pro-American" or were aligned with the Soviet Union, for example, Syria. Similarly, the United States was antagonistic to Iraq when that country was a Soviet ally and was defined as a "radical Arab nationalist" state. In the context of the Iran-Iraq War and the extreme U.S. animosity to the Iranian fundamentalist and nationalist revolution, however, the United States attempted to woo Iraq from its alignment with the Soviets through the sales of arms and other goods. But in that war's aftermath, militarily powerful, oil-rich, revenue-hungry, and independent-minded Iraq again became a concern to U.S. policymakers. When a Kuwaiti-Iraqi dispute over the production and pricing of oil led to Baghdad's invasion of its neighbor, the United States quickly seized the opportunity to "cut Iraq down to size" (and to establish a permanent U.S. military presence in the Gulf in order to "secure" the region for U.S. domination). In the context of the new world order, the Soviet Union provided essential support to the U.S.-led coalition against Iraq and, at the same time, decreased its support for Syria.

The United States has considered Israel its main "surrogate power" or "strategic asset" in the achievement of its national interests in the

Middle East. Indeed, Israel's importance has been such that the United States has supported all of Israel's self-defined national interests. In practice, U.S. backing of Israel's interests has been significantly strengthened as a consequence of the powerful impact exercised on U.S. domestic politics by Israel's U.S. friends.[7]

Israel's first and foremost national interest—the preeminent objective of both the Labor and Likud parties—has been the creation, expansion, security, and development of *Eretz Israel* (the land of Israel) usually defined to include the West Bank, the Gaza Strip, and East Jerusalem as well as Israel in its pre-June 1967 borders. This, in turn, explains Israel's hostile attitude toward Palestinians and the PLO; Israel cannot acknowledge the Palestinians as a people or Palestinian nationalism when it intends to transform all of Palestine into a Jewish state. Soviet policy toward Israel and on Palestinian rights changed significantly as Moscow sought to win favor in Washington. What measure of support the Palestinians had enjoyed evaporated, and Israel's interests were accommodated.

In order to expand and develop *Eretz Israel*, the Jewish state needs immigrants, and Soviet Jews have long been considered a valuable pool. Washington pressured Moscow on behalf of Israel in the context of the new world order, which resulted in Moscow permitting 71,200 Jews to leave the Soviet Union in 1989, 187,000 in 1990, and 113,000 between 1 January and 31 July 1991.[8] This massive emigration could bring as many as one million Soviet Jews to Israel in the next five years and will inextricably alter the nature of the Palestine-Israel conflict. Palestinian land and water resources are being used to settle Soviet Jews in the West Bank, East Jerusalem, and the Gaza Strip as well as in Israel proper. By June 1991, Israeli confiscation of Palestinian land was estimated at 70 percent of the West Bank and 50 percent of the Gaza Strip. Construction of settlements and infrastructure in these areas accelerated in 1990 and 1991 with expenditures in that fiscal year (ended 1 April 1991) at U.S. $500 million.[9] One Israeli analyst noted that the settlements "represent an ideological imperative shared by an overwhelming majority of [Israel's] people . . . [that had] begun in earnest in the early 1970s by the then-Labor government."[10] Another commentator remarked that settlement construction in the occupied territories "in the last year [1991] thus constitutes a real revolution."[11] Israel's intention to transform Arab East Jerusalem into a Jewish enclave was evidenced in its plan to settle 195,000 Jews there by the end of 1991, a situation that would marginalize the Palestinian population of approximately 150,000 and effectively remove the issue of East Jerusalem from the "peace" agenda.[12]

Further, the immigration of Soviet Jews is deeply affecting Palestinian economic life. As part of its effort to transform the West Bank and Gaza into a Jewish state, Israel has pursued deliberate policies to keep the economies of these areas underdeveloped and tied to its own economy in structural relations of dependence and subordination that have included severe restrictions on economic development and the consequent employment of 40 percent of the West Bank's and 50 to 60 percent of Gaza's labor force inside Israel.[13] New immigrants from the Soviet Union are replacing Palestinians from the territories who work in Israel, contributing significantly to the misery of the Palestinians—a process that was greatly accelerated after the Gulf War. Finally, the massive influx of Soviet Jews is altering the "demographic factor" in the Israel-Palestine conflict decidedly in Israel's favor.[14] Israelis who support trading parts of the territories for peace have long used the argument that higher Palestinian birth rates would give Arabs a majority in the Jewish State if Israel held on to the West Bank and Gaza. But with the Soviet Jewish immigration, this argument has become moot and the position of the doves weakened.

The myriad problems facing Palestinians as a result of the massive immigration of Soviet Jews is a consequence not only of Moscow succumbing to U.S. pressure on behalf of Israel, but also of the United States bowing to Israeli pressure to limit its own immigration quotas for Soviet Jews so that they have to go to Israel.[15] Israeli analyst Boaz Evron commented aptly on this phenomena: "We all know that Israeli and Zionist Organization emissaries have left no stone unturned in persuading the nations of the world to bar entrance to Jewish refugees, in order to force them to come to Israel, the one country which most of them would not otherwise choose as their destination. After all, it is clear to all of us that if the choice was theirs, 97 percent of them would 'drop out'."[16] In the new world order then, human rights have no more precedence than in the old. Also noteworthy is the important role played by the United States in the May 1991 immigration of 16,000 Ethiopian Jews to Israel.[17] Some of these immigrants, too, are being housed in the Occupied Territories and are taking Palestinian jobs.

In addition to acceding to Israel's wishes on the issue of Soviet Jews, *glasnost* heralded a general improvement in Israeli-Soviet relations including an exchange of consuls, agreements for exchanging trade and expertise in a range of areas, numerous visits by Israeli ministers to Moscow, and many influential voices in the Soviet Union pushing for the restoration of full diplomatic relations between the two countries.[18] Moreover, as one analyst noted, the growing independence of the republics under *glasnost* caused them to make their own foreign contacts and

> Israel has skillfully exploited the opportunity this has opened up, capitalizing on the presence of Jewish communities in all the Soviet republics to open up business deals, give religious and cultural support to Jews and sow good will generally. It has given practical help to victims of the Armenian earthquake and the Chernobyl disaster. The policy is paying off, with the republics now independent, or hoping to become so, declaring that they want to have missions in Israel.[19]

Indeed, by 1992 Israel had technical agreements, agricultural and diplomatic missions, and offers of expertise including "defense" assistance with all six former Soviet republics. In the view of some analysts, Israel has positioned itself as a "strategic asset" against the new "threat" (that is, pan-Islamism) to the United States posed by Central Asia.[20]

Also notable in the evolving relations between Moscow and Tel Aviv was the memorial service held by the Soviet Union on 5 October 1991 to commemorate the Nazi atrocities at Babi Yar.[21] Support for Holocaust ideology is a major component of Israel's foreign policy objectives.[22] And, on 18 October 1991, the Soviet Union restored full diplomatic relations with Israel.[23]

The transformation of the international system also significantly affected the question of how to resolve the Arab-Palestinian-Israeli conflict. There had long been an international consensus, disputed only by the United States and Israel, on the proper means and substance of an Arab-Palestinian-Israeli peace settlement. That consensus was expressed in the UN General Assembly Resolution 38/58 passed on 13 December 1983 calling for an "international conference" under the auspices of the Security Council with the United States, the Soviet Union, Israel, the PLO, Syria, Lebanon, Jordan, and Egypt participating on an equal footing in conformity with certain principles including (1) the right of self-determination and the right to an independent state of the Palestinians; (2) the right of the PLO to represent the Palestinians; (3) the inadmissibility of the acquisition of territory by force; (4) the exchange of land for peace; and (5) the right of all states in the region to exist within secure and internationally recognized borders.[24] Soviet and European support for this version of an international conference were significant counterweights to the U.S.-Israeli position. In the new world order, however, Moscow acceded to the United States' perspective on a peace settlement contributing to Arab state capitulation and, as a consequence, none of the principles on Palestinian rights were included.

When, in the aftermath of the Gulf conflict, the United States resumed discussion of an international conference, Syria initially insisted that the UN play a major role in any conference, that UN resolutions (242, 338, and others) be the basis of a settlement, that the conference be an ongoing affair, that the United States and the Soviet Union be co-sponsors, and that they be able to intervene to help the parties overcome obstacles. Israel rejected these demands, insisting that the conference be simply a one-day ceremonial opening to direct talks between Israel and its Arab neighbors. Israel also made it clear that the Jewish state would not exchange territory for peace—negating Resolutions 242 and 338 (the territories for peace formula)—and demanded a veto over the composition of a Palestinian delegation.[25] It specified that such a delegation could only participate as part of a Jordanian delegation and could contain no Palestinians from East Jerusalem, living in the diaspora, or affiliated with the PLO.

The United States, working strictly on formalities and procedural matters, proposed a "compromise" plan in which the Israelis and Syrians would agree that the UN be represented by an "observer" who would have no functional role in the talks, and that the conference would only be reconvened provided both sides were agreeable, and then only to hear reports of progress but not interfere in the talks. This meant in effect that (1) the conference would be chaired by the United States, not the UN, along with a weakened Soviet Union; (2) the UN and the Europeans would have only token observer roles; (3) the conference would be largely symbolic without any binding power and with follow-up meetings indeterminate; (4) relevant UN resolutions would serve merely as a "basis for talks" rather than being binding; (5) the conference would set the stage for separate, bilateral talks between Israel and individual Arab states; and (6) the Palestinians would likely achieve none of their fundamental objectives.[26] Despite its favorable features for Israel, the Jewish state rejected the U.S. compromise plan, but in mid-July 1991 Syria accepted the U.S. proposal.[27]

By acceding to the U.S. framework for a Middle East peace conference, Syria tacitly acquiesced to the Israeli demand that the PLO "disappear" by agreeing that it not have a seat at the conference and that only non-PLO Palestinians from the West Bank and Gaza participate.[28] Syria's acceptance of the U.S. proposal, a substantive Israeli victory, also meant that Syria (as well as Jordan and Lebanon) could reach separate peace agreements with Israel without any consideration of Palestinian concerns.[29] In addition, it set the stage for Saudi Arabia, Kuwait, and the other Gulf states to agree to direct negotiations with Israel, by which they declared in effect their readiness to recognize Israel, despite Israel's absolute rejection of basic Palestinian rights.[30]

After Syria agreed to participate in the U.S. "compromise" conference, Israel was also pressured to accept. Thus, in early August Israel gave a conditional "yes" to attend;[31] however, Israel stipulated that it have a veto over the composition of the Palestinian delegation and that its sovereignty over the West Bank, East Jerusalem, and Gaza remain absolute. Israel then reinforced its position through public declarations and the rapid construction of new settlements.[32]

Syria's capitulation to the United States on an international conference was only part of the change in Syrian-Soviet relations. In the context of the new world order, the Soviet Union gradually but significantly diminished its support for Syria. Thus, when the crisis in the Persian Gulf took shape, the Syrians aligned themselves with the Western coalition and sent troops in support of the U.S.-led drive against Iraq. The reasons for these actions by Syria's leaders included their desire to weaken their traditional foe Iraq, to gain financial aid from Saudi Arabia, and, more important, to curry favor with Washington and move into the U.S. sphere. It was only one step from there to Syrian support for the U.S.-Israeli position on the nature and substance of a peace conference, the need for direct negotiations with Israel, and the abandonment of the Palestinians.

The "peace" conference opened in Madrid, Spain, in October 1991; but the real position of the Israeli government was confirmed in June 1992 by former Israeli Prime Minister Yitzhak Shamir, who commented on the negotiations with the Palestinians: "I would have conducted the autonomy negotiations for 10 years, and in the meantime we would have reached half a million souls in Judea and Samaria."[33] By October 1992, six sessions of the peace conference had been held; Shamir had been replaced by the Labor Party and a new prime minister, Yitzhak Rabin; and the Palestinians were no closer to achieving their fundamental objectives than they had ever been.

Another effect of the transformations in the international system and their regional consequences involved Palestinian decision making in the Gulf War. The Palestinians were frustrated over many factors: The Soviet Union no longer counterbalanced the United States in the Middle East; the Arab world was divided and support for the Palestinian cause had waned in many capitals; Israel's occupation over the territories was more brutal than ever; and Israel had rejected all Palestinian peace initiatives, in particular the PLO's November 1988 unilateral declaration of Israel's right to exist and its renunciation of terrorism.

Palestinian despair over these events led them into a highly detrimental alignment with Iraq that alienated them from nearly all the Arab regimes. The PLO did not support Iraq's occupation and annexation of Kuwait; however, it did stand with Iraq in opposition to the U.S.-led coalition arrayed against Saddam Hussein.[34] As one Palestinian analyst described: "The PLO took the position that while Iraq had violated a basic tenet of the Arab political order—the inviolability of state sovereignty—Saudi Arabia and its Gulf allies in the Gulf Cooperation Council (GCC) also challenged the institutionalized rules of conflict resolution within the 'Arab family' by acquiescing in U.S. military intervention."[35] In standing with Iraq, the PLO responded to the sentiments of its constituency in the Occupied Territories, where support for Saddam Hussein, who seemed the only Arab leader willing to challenge Israel, ran high. During the early stages of the conflict, PLO Chairman Yasser Arafat attempted to mediate a settlement between Kuwait and Iraq, but his efforts, ridiculed by the United States, further antagonized Arab leaders.

One consequence of the Arab states' displeasure with the PLO was the suspension of all financial support for the organization, which from Saudi Arabia and Kuwait alone exceeded U.S. $100 million per year.[36] In addition, Palestinians in the West Bank and Gaza suffered enormous losses due to the termination of remittances from migrant workers in Saudi Arabia and the Gulf. Approximately half of the Palestinians who had worked in Kuwait fled the country after 2 August 1990, and those who remained could not get money out of the country. This resulted in the loss of some U.S. $100 million dollars in annual contributions to the Occupied Territories.[37] In the wake of the Gulf War, Saudi Arabia quietly replaced its Palestinian workers with Egyptians at an undisclosed but presumably significant loss for the West Bank and Gaza.[38] Subsequently, Qatar and other Gulf states began to restrict the entry of Palestinian workers.

Moreover, in the war's aftermath, Kuwait engaged in brutal repression against Palestinians living in that country, turning them into scapegoats for the policies of the PLO. Palestinians were indiscriminately imprisoned, tortured, deported, and killed. Government harassment involved forced unemployment, withdrawal of social services, confiscation of property, and denial of access to public education for Palestinian children. Those who fled at the beginning of the Iraqi occupation—some 200,000 persons constituting over half of the community—were not permitted to return. The employment contracts of all public sector Palestinian employees, a prerequisite for residence rights, were terminated.[39] Traditionally, Kuwait has made it very difficult for Palestinians to obtain permanent residency and almost impossible to obtain citizenship, despite the fact that Palestinian engineers, physicians, educators, laborers, and others virtually built modern Kuwait. In June 1991, the *New York Times* reported that "in conversations with government officials, Kuwaiti citizens and the Palestinians themselves, nobody disputes that the goal is to drive them out."[40] By August 1992, Kuwait had expelled all but 20,000 of the 450,000 Palestinians who had resided in that country prior to the Gulf War.[41] After mobilizing the entire UN in defense of Kuwait, it was remarkable that in the new world order extreme Kuwaiti human rights violations against Palestinians were not a subject of concern for the United States.

Palestinian interests also suffered a significant setback as a consequence of a new intensity and openness in relations between Arab states and the United States. To a considerable extent, this was due to the Soviet Union's withdrawal as an independent player from the region, making the United States "the only game in town," but it was also related to traditional state and personal interests of a number of Arab leaders. Long-standing U.S. allies such as Kuwait, Saudi Arabia, Egypt, and Jordan were, in the aftermath of the Gulf War, so eager for closer ties with the United States that U.S. leverage increased considerably and these states offered extraordinary concessions to Israel to please their patron. Toward the end of July 1991, *New York Times* columnist Leslie Gelb noted that "Mr. Shamir can make a powerful case that he has squeezed almost every gettable concession from the Arabs . . . and almost everything from the Bush administration save love."[42]

Of the traditional allies, Saudi Arabia and Kuwait in particular wished to demonstrate their gratefulness to the United States for coming to their defense against Iraq. Thus, at no small political risk domestically, in July 1991, Saudi Arabia announced its willingness to suspend the Arab boycott of Israel if Israel would stop building settlements in the Occupied Territories.[43] Notably, the Saudis did not make their offer contingent on Israel's dismantling the existing settlements or adhering to UN Resolution 242, nor did they call for the establishment of a Palestinian state, or even for the inclusion of the PLO in the peace process. Moreover, although Saudi King Fahd publicly pleaded with U.S. Secretary of State James Baker to help ease the plight of Palestinians, the Saudi government worked behind the scenes to delegitimize the PLO. *New York Times* columnist Thomas Friedman aptly commented on the Saudi position: "Everyone in the region knows the Saudis much prefer the Israelis over Yasser Arafat or Jordan's King Hussein for controlling the progressive, potentially radical Palestinians in the West Bank and Gaza Strip."[44]

In addition, Saudi Arabia (together with Kuwait and the other Persian Gulf states) agreed to send the secretary general of the Gulf Cooperation Council (GCC) to the compromise U.S.-designed international conference. Each of the six GCC states also agreed to send a national delegation to side talks with Israel on single topics such as arms control, water rights, and economic cooperation.[45]

By August 1992, Kuwait, in the words of one analyst, had undergone an "earthquake" in its relations with Palestine and Israel. Kuwaiti officials openly discussed the establishment of diplomatic relations with Israel. The Arab boycott was, in practice, terminated with businesses "brazenly selling coke, Ford automobiles, and Marks and Spencer swimsuits" as well as other products "creating a crack in the old Middle East economic order that forced Western businesses to choose between trade with the Jewish State or trade with the Arabs." And, moreover, there was a significant transformation in the tone of rhetoric with the Palestinians now demonized and the former hostility to Israel (for example, references to the Zionist entity) dropped.[46]

Egypt, whose peace treaty with Israel in 1979 set the norm for separate agreements between Arab states and Israel and for the negation of Palestinian rights, stepped up its criticism and isolation of the Palestinians in the aftermath of the Gulf War. In August 1991, Egyptian Foreign Minister Amr Moussa declared that Arafat was no longer welcome in Egypt, saying, "We are all upset with what happened, with all those who supported the occupation of Kuwait. We think they did a very big injustice to the Arab system and the Arab image and morale. They have made a grave mistake."[47] Egypt was the first Arab state to call for an end to the Arab economic boycott of Israel and was instrumental in persuading Saudi Arabia to take a similar stand.[48] As a close American ally, Egypt typically seeks to align its position on Middle Eastern issues with the United States; moreover, the Egyptians were well aware of the quid pro quo expected of them for the U.S. decision during the war to "forgive" Egyptian debt. Also, significant in terms of Egyptian-PLO relations was the 15 May 1991 election by the Arab League of an Egyptian, Esmat Abdel-Meguid, as its secretary general, thus restoring Cairo's role as the center of Arab diplomacy.[49] Arab League headquarters had been returned to Cairo on 1 January when Egypt organized the Arab coalition against Iraq.

Syria, as noted earlier, although not a traditional ally, nevertheless aligned itself with the United States during the Gulf crisis and its aftermath and, at the expense of the Palestinians, agreed to participate in the U.S.-designed international conference. Syria was also responsible for the loss of the Palestinians' last area of independent operation in Lebanon. In early October 1990, Syria led the Lebanese army in disarming the various militias that had exercised control over sections of Lebanon since the mid-1970s. In doing so, it had tacit approval from the United States, obtained by sending troops in support of the U.S.-organized coalition against Iraq. Then, in July 1991, with Lebanon stabilized under a pro-Syrian government, the Lebanese army moved into Sidon and the surrounding Palestinian refugee camps and "disarmed" the 5,000 to 6,000 guerrillas in a quick and humiliating defeat for the PLO.[50] The Lebanese army's takeover of traditional Palestinian strongholds marked the end of two decades (interrupted by Israel's 1982 invasion) of autonomous Palestinian activity in Lebanon and added geographic restriction to the organization's political isolation in the aftermath of the Gulf War.[51] Shortly after its military move against the PLO, Lebanon announced that it was prepared to engage in direct negotiations with Israel.[52]

In early June 1991, King Hussein called for face-to-face negotiations between Jordanian and Israeli heads of state. Jordanian officials, including the king, had been meeting with Israelis for years but this was the first time the monarch had been so direct in public.[53] On 21 July, Jordan (joining Syria, Lebanon, Egypt, and Saudi Arabia) accepted the U.S. invitation to attend the U.S.-sponsored "peace" conference and, in so doing, consented to become custodian for the Palestinians. At the same time, Jordan joined Saudi Arabia and Egypt in calling for an end to the Arab boycott of Israel.[54] In September 1991, as the international conference took shape, excluding the PLO and omitting any requirement for Israel to withdraw from the Occupied Territories, King Hussein declared, "We are on the threshold of reconciling with our enemy, Israel."[55]

In the aftermath of the war against Iraq, the liberation of Palestine, once the cornerstone of Arab nationalism, clearly disappeared from the Arab states' agenda. No longer were the Arab regimes committed to the PLO as the legitimate representative of the Palestinians (as a 1974 Arab League resolution mandated), nor were they willing to demand an independent state for the Palestinians in the West Bank and Gaza in exchange for normal relations with Israel. Anti-imperialism, the other hallmark of pan-Arabism, was also vanquished from the Arab scene as the Arab governing elites rushed to embrace the United States. Indeed, even the idea of Arab nationalism or pan-Arabism seemed moot by the summer of 1991.

Certainly, a strong case could be made that Arab nationalism died long ago—perhaps as early as 1967—or possibly that it never existed.[56] For many years, there had been an enormous dichotomy between Arab state rhetoric and practice on the question of Palestine. Jordan colluded with the Zionists even before the creation of Israel as a means of absorbing the West Bank. Jordan further raised questions about the sincerity of its commitment to Palestinian interests on several occasions including the Black September fiasco in 1970 when King Hussein drove the PLO from Jordan and massacred thousands of Palestinians, the king's reluctant acceptance of the 1974 Arab League legitimation of the PLO, and his 1986 unilateral abrogation of a 1985 Jordanian-Palestinian accord. Syria also pursued a two-faced policy, on the one hand championing the Palestinian cause, while on the other actively harming Palestinian interests. For example, Palestinian guerrilla activities were prohibited on Syrian soil after 1967; Syria brutally suppressed Palestinians in 1976 during its volte face in Lebanon; it sponsored Lebanese militia attacks on Palestinians in 1983, 1985, and thereafter; and President Hafez Assad continuously tried to undermine the leadership of Yasser Arafat. Moreover, it should be noted that in 1982 when Israel unleashed a massive war against Palestinians in Lebanon, no Arab state offered support.[57]

Still, there was a difference in 1991 that was expressed in the boldness and brazenness with which the Arab regimes flaunted Palestinian rights and interests. In the past Arab leaders were constrained by the strength of mass sentiment regarding the Palestinians to at least give lip-service to the Palestinian cause. But with the advent of the new world order—in particular the promise of U.S. force to maintain the status quo should disgruntled masses make their voices heard—no major Arab state seemed either willing or able to demand rights for the Palestinians. Too, the Arab masses appeared less interested in the Palestinian issue by 1991, although it is difficult to gauge public opinion in closed societies especially given the strength of the Arab states' security apparatus. Nevertheless, it was difficult to imagine that the Zionist affront to Arab honor had been removed to the extent that the behavior of the states suggested.

The Palestinians also found that their support in Europe had weakened after the Gulf crisis. In the aftermath of the war the Europeans retreated significantly from their long-standing position (articulated in the 1980 Venice Declaration) that the PLO was the sole legitimate representative of the Palestinians.[58] The twelve member states of the European Community (EC) exerted considerable pressure on the PLO to acquiesce in a non-PLO Palestinian delegation to an international conference and influenced Syria to accept the U.S. proposals for such a gathering. In June 1991, the EC went further than it had gone before in offering Israel a privileged, long-term economic and trade relationship.[59] And in mid-July, in the framework of the Group of Seven (the industrial nations of Britain, Canada, France, Germany, Italy, Japan, and the United States) the Europeans asked the Arab states to end their economic boycott of Israel and were instrumental in shaping the Egyptian and Saudi positions on this matter.[60]

Some analysts argued that in the aftermath of the Gulf War, the credibility of the United States as the leader of the new world order would mandate that it act consistently and in a principled manner to find a just resolution to the Palestinian issue. Those who took this position misunderstood the nature and purpose of U.S. foreign policy. U.S. antipathy to basic Palestinian interests has been strong and consistent, a position that is congruent with its long-standing "national interests" in the Middle East as traditionally defined by the ruling elite. Likewise, the United States has been consistent in the means utilized to secure those interests, which have included opposition to nationalist movements, firm support for Israel's interests, and a strong preference for "stability" or the status quo.[61] In addition, the United States stood alone as the hegemonic power in a unipolar world and therefore had greater leverage over regional political issues and could impose its geopolitical will with far greater ease than previously. Thus the Arab states fell in line with U.S. wishes, and the Palestinians were left without any significant support.

Even the form of the U.S. "peace" effort suggested that it would work against the Palestinians. The U.S. two-track strategy of separating Israeli-Arab state and Israeli-Palestinian negotiations seriously weakened the Palestinian position. Unlike the comprehensive settlement that UN Resolution 38/58 envisioned, the U.S. plan pursued separate, bilateral agreements, and the United States was far more committed to a just solution of the Israeli-Arab state conflict than to the Israeli-Palestinian one. Moreover, the United States demonstrated its attitude toward the Palestinians in countless instances including its 1990 veto of a UN Security Council resolution on sending observers to the Occupied Territories; the termination that same year of a low-level dialogue with the PLO reluctantly began by the United States in 1988; and the pressure U.S. Secretary of State Baker exerted on West Bank and Gazan Palestinians in the spring and summer of 1991 to find a group of non-PLO Palestinians to join a Jordanian delegation to negotiate with Israel on some form of "autonomy" for the Palestinians.[62] The United States was primarily interested in ending the Arab state economic boycott of Israel and terminating the Palestinian Intifada in order to get the various parties to the negotiating table.[63] Washington admitted openly that it had "no plan" to resolve the differences between Israel and the Palestinians when a conference was convened.[64] The Bush administration's position remained consistent with long-standing U.S. opposition to any recognition of the PLO as the legitimate representative of the Palestinians, or recognition of the Palestinian right to self-determination and to an independent state in the West Bank and Gaza.[65]

The Bush administration also maintained the nature, structure, and closeness of the traditional U.S.-Israeli relationship. Although the media made much of the seemingly strained relations between Washington and Tel Aviv, the problem was more personal than political. President Bush was not fond of Israeli Prime Minister Yitzhak Shamir, who openly defied "official" U.S. policy, and the Bush administration was relatively candid about its wish to see a Labor Party victory in the June 1992 elections in Israel. But that the so-called "rift" between the two countries was not serious was evident in numerous circumstances.

For example, some analysts considered the Bush administration's September 1991 decision to defer Israel's request for U.S. $10 billion in loan guarantees for Soviet Jewish housing a sign that there were deep differences between the United States and Israel, and that the administration was going to pressure Israel to withdraw from the territories and return them to Arab control. But as the *New York Times* noted "nobody in Washington is challenging Israel's need for the loan guarantees" and "the Bush administration's whole approach to peacemaking is almost entirely based on terms dictated by Prime Minister Yitzhak Shamir."[66] In fact, the delay in approval of the loan guarantees was designed with two purposes in mind: (1) to influence domestic Israeli politics to bring about a Labor victory, and (2) to ensure that the Arabs came to the conference table by making the United States appear as an impartial mediator. Indeed, no one in the U.S. government considered forcing Israel to return to the Palestinians the 70 percent of West Bank land and the 50 percent of Gaza land that it had confiscated, to turn over to Palestinians the more than 200 settlement locales illegally constructed by Israel, or to ask the 225,000 Jewish settlers to leave the West Bank, Gaza, and East Jerusalem. Nor did the United States demand that Israel relinquish the 75 percent of West Bank water that it had diverted to Israel.[67] In reality, the United States was only interested in supporting Israel's old "autonomy" concept for the Palestinians.[68] The issue of the loan guarantees was resolved in Israel's favor on 11 August 1992 when President Bush announced, with Prime Minister Rabin at his side at the president's home in Kennebunkport, Maine, that the United States was now prepared to provide the U.S. $10 billion in loan guarantees.[69]

It is also notable that throughout the "difficult" years of the Bush-Shamir relationship, Israel remained an important "strategic asset" to U.S. Middle East objectives, even in an era in which the Arab states were virtually flocking to the U.S. fold! For example, in early June 1991 the United States began stockpiling U.S. $100 million worth of U.S. military equipment in Israeli bunkers "for use in any regional conflict."[70] In principle, the stockpiled weapons were to be used by U.S. military forces, but in practice they could also be of great use to the Israeli military. The Pentagon's announcement of its intention to stockpile weapons in Israel came just one day after Secretary of Defense Richard Cheney said that the United States would give Israel twenty-five more F-15 fighter planes including fifteen promised in 1990 and would provide U.S. $210 million in additional funds that supply three-quarters of the money for an on-going U.S.-Israeli anti-ballistic missile project, the Arrow.[71] It is remarkable that in the new world order, the United States strengthened its military relationship with Israel, provided it additional weapons, and made no effort to require the Jewish state to dismantle its massive stock of chemical, biological, and nuclear weapons—all despite much talk about regional "arms control."

Indeed, in light of U.S. insistence that Iraq be permitted no atomic or nuclear capability of any sort, the deafening silence in Washington as to Israel's nuclear doctrine of targeting the Soviet Union as well as the Arab states, its nuclear "blackmail" of the United States, and its possession of " 'hundreds' of tactical and strategic nuclear weapons, including more than 100 nuclear artillery shells, nuclear land mines in the Golan Heights, and hundreds of low yield neutron war heads capable of destroying large numbers of enemy troops" was shocking.[72] As analyst Seymour Hersh noted, however, "America's policy toward the Israeli arsenal was not just one of benign neglect; it was a conscious policy of ignoring reality."[73]

On 10–11 August 1992 when President Bush entertained Prime Minister Rabin at his home and announced the United States' willingness to grant the loan guarantees, the *New York Times* reflected the president's relief that the Labor Party was at the helm in Israel and that the diplomatically skillful Mr. Rabin was in charge. The *Times* added that the visit "was intended to signal an end to the tensions in the American-Israeli relationship."[74] The president made much of Israel's importance as a surrogate for the United States in describing the meeting with Rabin: "Our time together can best be described as a consultation between close friends and strategic partners," and he referred several times to Israel's "strategic importance" to the United States. Further, Bush "signaled that he was ready to move forward with military cooperation between the two countries, and reaffirmed Washington's longstanding policy of assuring that Israel had a 'qualitative military edge' over [the combined strength of] its Arab neighbors."[75] That nothing had changed for the Palestinians was made clear by Prime Minister Rabin in early September 1992 when he condemned the Palestinian negotiating strategy of seeking to end the occupation and move toward self-government, stating: "I hope the Palestinians keep in mind we are in control of the territories.

We will not budge one inch."[76] That the Palestinians would get nothing more than "administrative" autonomy over some minor aspects of their lives excluding control over land, water, immigration, security, or other crucial matters, could not have been made clearer. The "change" from Likud to Labor was merely cosmetic.

The continued strength of the U.S.-Israeli relationship was also reflected in the amount of economic assistance that flowed to Israel during the Bush administration. In 1991, total U.S. aid to Israel was U.S. $5.147 billion including U.S. $3 billion under the foreign aid program, U.S. $70 million in additional interest by receiving aid at the beginning of the year instead of quarterly like all other aid recipients, U.S. $700 million in U.S. weapons, U.S. $650 million in emergency assistance related to the Gulf War, U.S. $485 million worth of oil to be pre-positioned in Israel, U.S. $200 million in U.S. military equipment, and U.S. $42 million to develop the Arrow missile.[77]

The intimacy of the U.S.-Israeli relationship was further evidenced in the number and position of high officials in the Bush administration with strong pro-Israeli sentiments. In late October 1991 the composition of the U.S. delegation to the Madrid conference was made public. The U.S. group consisted of the top Middle Eastern advisors, who had surrounded the administration since its inception, including Dennis B. Ross, director of the State Department's Policy Planning Staff; Aaron David Miller, State Department Policy Planning staff member; Daniel C. Kurtzer, deputy assistant secretary of state, Policy Planning Staff; William J. Burns, principal deputy director of State Department Policy Planning Staff; and Richard N. Haass, special assistant to the president for national security affairs. Publicly, only one of these men was identified as having pro-Israeli sentiment—Kurtzer, "an Orthodox Jew."[78] Three of the others came to the Bush administration from the Washington Institute for Near East Policy, a pro-Israeli think tank founded in 1985 by Martin Indyk, a former deputy director of research for the American Israel Public Affairs Committee (AIPAC, the registered U.S. pro-Israel lobby).

In September 1988, the Washington Institute published a 113-page report entitled *Building for Peace: An American Strategy for the Middle East.* One of its authors had this to say about the report: "Both the process of the development of the report and the report itself produced a consensus on the direction for the future of U.S. policy, and that can clearly be seen in the Baker Approach."[79] Dennis Ross was a senior fellow at the institute and a major participant in writing the report. Richard Haass participated in the preparation of the report, although he was a lecturer at Harvard University's John F. Kennedy School of Government at the time. Aaron David Miller was a State Department Middle Eastern specialist and was technically prohibited from engaging in an activity such as the preparation of *Building for Peace*; nevertheless, he did participate and was known to have strong pro-Israeli ties.[80] Little was known about William Burns in this regard. Noteworthy also was that while each of these individuals was profiled in some detail in the *New York Times*, nothing of their connection to the Washington Institute for Near East Policy, their participation in the preparation of *Building for Peace*, or their other pro-Israeli affiliations were mentioned.[81]

Indeed, not only could the Palestinians hope for little from the United States in the aftermath of the Gulf War in terms of the fulfillment of their basic objectives, but Israel was more intransigent than ever on the Palestine issue. In part, this was related to the defeat of Iraq, a situation aptly summarized by Republic of Yemen UN Ambassador Abdalla Saleh Al-Ashtal:

> With the destruction of Iraq, which was the only important military force in the Arab world, Israel can continue to ignore UN resolutions with impunity. Indeed, there will be such an imbalance in military power, notwithstanding the forces of Egypt and Syria, that Israel will be even more intransigent than before. . . . The increased imbalance in the area makes a solution [to the Israeli-Palestinian conflict] even more difficult. The Israelis simply will not allow it, and the Arab countries friendly with the United States do not have the leverage to bring it about.[82]

Israel's massive settlement drive in the Occupied Territories exemplified its real intentions regarding the Palestinians. Israeli analyst Amiram Goldbloom wrote in this regard that the new settlements set up during Secretary Baker's visits to the Middle East had enormous political significance in that "they are intended to prove to the Palestinians, and . . . to the Arab world, that the Israeli government thumbs its nose at the U.S. efforts to advance peace in the region. . . . The government is now mobilized to torpedo any chance for peace."[83] Goldbloom also noted that while the Israeli government continually justifies its settlement of the West Bank, East Jerusalem, and Gaza by saying that it is unacceptable that any area should be "Judenrein," in fact the real objective is to make all of *Eretz Israel* "Arabenrein."[84] Another Israeli analyst noted in the same vein that the intention of the Israeli government "is clearly visible on the ground—to push the Palestinians into a corner from which there is no exit, thus compelling them, sooner or later, to pick up and leave."[85] Subsequent to the Israeli elections in June 1992, much was made of the Rabin government's more "liberal" policy on settlements even though it was the Labor Party that began the settlement and colonization of the West Bank, East Jerusalem, and the Gaza Strip in 1967 and continued it through 1977 when Likud came to power. Moreover, Rabin never promised to cease settlement construction; instead, he made a highly ambiguous distinction between "security" and "political" settlements, and said only that additional political settlements would not be built. In key areas such as the Jordan Valley and "greater Jerusalem," the prime minister made it clear that there would be no settlement freeze, and in the words of one analyst, " 'security' settlements designed as physical obstacles separating the Palestinians from Jordanian territory, or as guarantees of Israel's continued hold on Jerusalem, will be supported as lavishly by Rabin as they were by Yitzhak Shamir and Ariel Sharon."[86] Moreover, Rabin permitted construction of 5,000 of the 10,000 homes in the Occupied Territories that the Shamir government had planned.[87]

The Israeli government's objective of driving out the Palestinians was clearly evident during the Gulf War when its cabinet included the Moledet (Homeland) Party, which advocated expulsion of all the Palestinians from *Eretz Israel*. Rehavam Ze'evi founded the party on the eve of the 1988 Knesset elections to take over from Meir Kahane's Kach Party, which was disqualified from running.[88] As a consequence of the elevation of retired General Ze'evi (with his openly racist ideology) to a prestigious government ministry and to the special inner cabinet that dealt with security and foreign affairs, the movement for expulsion of Palestinians gained new legitimacy in Israel. That the Labor Party and its "leftist" coalition partner, Meretz, did not deviate from this tradition was evident in their unanimous decision in December 1992 to expel en masse 413 Palestinians for allegedly having ties to the Islamic fundamentalist organization, Hamas, but against whom Israel had no evidence of any illegal activity. Further, the arrest on 30 January 1991 of Sari Nusseibeh, an internationally respected moderate and professor of philosophy at Birzeit University, on unsubstantiated charges of "subversive activities of collecting security information for Iraqi intelligence" pointed to the vulnerability of all Palestinians. Nusseibeh was held without formal charges or trial under a three-month administrative detention order.

Of further significance in Israel's stance toward the Palestinians was the hostile position taken by several members of the Israeli "left" or "peace" camp, most notably Yossi Sarid, who declared that because the Palestinians were "cheering" for the Iraqis, he was washing his hands of their cause.[89] Commenting on the effects of these phenomena, Israeli journalist Danny Rubenstein wrote: "The financial blow [the cut off of funds from the Arab states] was dwarfed by the political damage dealt to the image of the PLO and the Palestinians. All the support they had acquired during the three years of the Intifada disappeared into thin air."[90] Thus, with the distinction between the "left" and the "right" increasingly blurred in Israeli politics, and the United States designing its "whole approach to peacemaking almost entirely . . . on terms dictated by Prime Minister Yitzhak Shamir," the outlook for Palestinians was not hopeful.

Many analysts saw the election of Yitzhak Rabin in June 1992 as a signal that the Palestinian situation would markedly improve. The preceding discussion outlines several reasons why this is unlikely to occur. In addition, it should be noted that Rabin was prime minister from May 1974 through 1977 during which time he presided over a vigorous expansion of settlements throughout the Occupied Territories, which he repeatedly maintained were permanent and would never be surrendered. For example he told a settlers' meeting in Gush Etzion (south of Bethlehem) that "the bloc will be an integral part of Israel in any political settlement and that it will have territorial continuity with Israel."[91]

Rabin was defense minister under Prime Minister Shamir and the architect of the brutal suppression of the Intifada including the iron fist policy of "force, might, and beatings." On 7 July 1992, the *New York Times* reported that he stated he was still prepared to use an "iron fist" against the Palestinians. He has been consistent throughout his political career in categorically opposing an independent Palestinian state and has indicated no change in that position. Rabin sports a more "moderate" face than Shamir and his Likud colleagues, but on the issue of political independence for the Palestinians he does not differ. In his first speech as prime minister, Rabin offered Palestinians rapid movement toward "autonomy with all its advantages and limitations" as a five year interim arrangement before final status negotiations.[92] As noted previously, however, autonomy provides no control over land, water, security, immigration, or foreign affairs and gives the Israeli army the right to enter the territories when "necessary" while "security" settlements will continue to be built. Moreover, although Rabin made several symbolic gestures, such as releasing several hundred political prisoners (but only those who were within a few days of completion of their terms), he maintained the detentions of thousands of others and also authorized the army to pursue its death-squad "find and kill" policy against Palestinian activists.[93] In the judgment of this writer, the transformation from Likud to Labor meant no substantial change for Palestinians.

The disintegration of the Intifada in the aftermath of the Gulf War—its transformation from a mass-based popular movement with extremely widespread participation to a more narrowly based movement of committed activists—also weakened the Palestinian position. The reasons for the decline of the uprising were many, but prominent among them was the devastating psychological impact of the forty-five-day curfew imposed during the Gulf crisis coupled with the abrupt shift from euphoria over Saddam Hussein's proclamations about liberating Palestine to despair when he was crushingly defeated, and the concomitant isolation of the Palestinians. The extended curfew was only one of the many brutal tactics employed against the Palestinians that cumulatively weakened the Intifada.[94] Israel's "iron fist" policy (designed by Yitzhak Rabin) resulted in the following from 9 December 1987 through 31 May 1992: 1,057 deaths; 122,802 injuries requiring hospitalization; 66 expulsions; 15,240 administrative detentions; 89,635 acres of land confiscated; 2,184 house demolitions or sealings; 143,000 tree uprootings; and 11,523 curfews including areas with 10,000 or more persons under twenty-four-hour or longer curfews. In addition there were almost continuous curfews over the entire West Bank and Gaza during the 16 January to 28 February 1991 period.[95]

In addition, the Intifada was hurt as a consequence of the desperate economic situation in the territories resulting from the cut-off of subsidies from Arab states; the serious decline in remittances from Palestinian workers in the Gulf, many of whom lost their jobs and businesses, and themselves became refugees; the refusal of Israel to permit Palestinians to return to work in Israel; and the lack of an indigenous economy in the West Bank and Gaza—all of which contributed to a general malaise on political issues because attention was focused on bare survival.[96] For the first time in the history of the Palestine conflict, Palestinians were hungry and there did not appear to be a quick or satisfactory solution to the severity of the economic deprivations.[97] Moreover, there was a disintegration of the general social order: an upsurge in crime by Palestinians against Palestinians; indiscriminate killings unrelated to collaboration; and brutal inter-party conflict as, for example, that between Hamas and Fateh in Nablus in early June 1991 and in Gaza in May, June, and July 1992.[98] So deep and widespread was the sense of despair and hopelessness that people were virtually immobilized and incapable of participating in organized resistance.[99] And, without a strong, organized, active Palestinian movement in the Occupied Territories that could make itself felt in Israeli society, Israel had no incentive to deal fairly with the Palestinians.

Moveover, when the Intifada did reignite in December 1992 and the months following, it was met with the most brutal policies ever used in Israel—mass expulsions, mass house demolitions, and indiscriminate killings. The intensity of the repression, occurring at a time when the United States was doing nothing to stop Serbian genocide in Bosnia, led many to conclude that Israel had an essentially "free hand" (from its U.S. patron) to kill and expel as many Palestinians as it might choose.

Finally, the Palestinian cause was hurt in the aftermath of the Gulf War as a consequence of the weakened position of its leadership, the Palestine Liberation Organization. Much of this has been discussed above in terms of the PLO's alienation from the Arab states as a consequence of its support for Iraq during the war. But in addition, there were increasing demands from inside the Occupied Territories for a larger role for the Intifada leadership in Palestinian decision making. And, Hamas, the fundamentalist Islamic movement, was stronger and posed an increasing challenge to the organization, partly because of Palestinian dissatisfaction with the PLO but considerably abetted by funding from the Gulf at a time when funding for PLO institutions had seriously diminished and general economic hardship prevailed throughout the West Bank and Gaza. There were also problems within the Fateh leadership: Israel's assassination of Abu Jihad (Khalil al-Wazir) on 16 April 1988 and Abu Nidal's more recent (1990) assassination of Abu Iyad (Salah Khalaf) deepened a number of visible and hidden rifts in Yasser Arafat's faction.[100] Arafat's own brush with death in an April 1992 plane crash (and his subsequent brain surgery) only served to exacerbate these problems, which included issues of succession, potential power struggles, and power sharing or collective versus unilateral authority.[101] There were also disputes over the proper Palestinian position in the "peace process" and the extent to which the PLO should accommodate the United States.[102] There is, however, little doubt that the overwhelming majority of Palestinians continued to consider the PLO their sole legitimate representative.

In sum, there seemed little reason to hope that in the new world order Palestinians could expect a just settlement of their long-standing conflict with Israel. Palestinians no longer possessed any independent military capability, and their political influence was seriously weakened. Their Arab "brothers" no longer even feigned support, and Israel was more committed than ever to retaining hegemony over the land and resources of East Jerusalem, the West Bank, and the Gaza Strip. As such, the prospects for an independent state in the West Bank and Gaza seemed more remote than at any previous time. The United States, as the unchallenged leader of the new world order, was in a position to impose its political agenda in the Middle East without countervailing pressure, but that agenda did not include the satisfaction of fundamental Palestinian objectives. Human rights, justice, political freedom, and self-determination for the weak were in as short supply in the new world order as in the old.

Acknowledgments

Special thanks to Dario Mareno, Ibrahim Abu-Lughod, and Naseer Aruri for their reading and critique of this piece.

Notes

1. For two detailed articles on U.S. policy toward the Palestinians see Cheryl A. Rubenberg, "U.S. Policy Toward the Palestinians: A Twenty Year Assessment," *Arab Studies Quarterly* 10 (Winter 1988): 1–43, and Cheryl A. Rubenberg, "The U.S.-PLO Dialogue: Continuity or Change in American Policy," *Arab Studies Quarterly* 11 (Fall 1989): 1–58.

2. For an analysis see Thomas L. Friedman, "Syria's Tactical Leap Into the Peace Process," *New York Times* (21 July 1991).

3. See, for example, Galia Golan, *The Soviet Union and the Palestine Liberation Organization* (New York: Praeger, 1980) and Galia Golan, "The Soviet Union and the PLO Since the War in Lebanon," *The Middle East Journal* 40 (Spring 1986): 285–305.

4. Thomas L. Friedman, "Peace Talks But No Dove," *New York Times* (20 October 1991).

5. See, for example, the analysis by Louis Uchitelle, "Gulf Victory May Raise U.S. Influence in OPEC: Oil Prices of $18 to $22 a Barrel are Considered a Suitable Level," *New York Times* (5 March 1991).

6. For a detailed analysis of U.S. national interests see Rubenberg, "U.S. Policy Toward the Palestinians."

7. Cheryl A. Rubenberg, "Introduction," *Consistency of U.S. Foreign*

Policy: The Gulf War and the Iran-Contra Affair, ed. Abbas Alnasrawi and Cheryl A. Rubenberg, (Belmont, MA: Association of Arab American University Graduates, 1989): 1-19. Also see Cheryl A. Rubenberg, *Israel and the American National Interest: A Critical Examination* (Urbana: Univ. of Illinois Press): especially 329-76 on Israel's role in domestic affairs. Also, see Edward Tivnan, *The Lobby: Jewish Political Power and American Foreign Policy* (New York: Simon & Schuster, 1987).

8. The figures on Soviet emigration are given by Michael M. Phillips, "Jewish Leaders Fear a Cutoff In Emigration," *Miami Herald* (21 August 1991): 15-A. The issue can be looked at in a slightly different way. The Israeli journal, *New Outlook* (Tel Aviv 34[1], December 1990-January 1991: 25) states that 200,000 people immigrated to Israel in 1990 including 185,000 from the Soviet Union. And, "this was the largest annual immigration figure since 1951." In addition to Soviet Jews immigrating to Israel, in 1991 a large number of Ethiopian Jews arrived.

9. Amiram Goldbloom, "Are Settlements An Obstacle to Peace?" *New Outlook* (Tel Aviv) 34(4) (June-July-August, 1991): 7-9.

10. Alon Ben-Meir, "Israeli Settlements: A National Imperative," *Miami Herald* (9 June 1991).

11. Goldbloom, "Are Settlements An Obstacle to Peace?," 7.

12. See the analysis and statistics provided by Hanan Ashrawi, "Israel's Real Intentions," *The Palestinians After the Gulf War: The Critical Questions* (Washington, DC: Center for Policy Analysis on Palestine, 1991): 19-25. On 3 October 1991 the Israeli weekly *Kol Ha'ir* (Hebrew) revealed details of a secret master plan of the Israeli Housing Ministry for the construction of 4,000 homes for Jews in the heart of Arab East Jerusalem (*Miami Herald*, 5 October 1991). Population figures for Jerusalem are always somewhat variable. One source notes that there are 500,000 inhabitants in Jerusalem of which 71.7 percent are Jews; 25.4 percent are Muslims; and 2.9 percent Christian. See John N. Tleel (World Council of Churches), "Ecumenical Life in Jerusalem," *Al-Fajr* (Jerusalem-Palestinian Weekly-English) (20 September 1992): 9.

13. Cheryl A. Rubenberg, "Twenty Years of Israeli Economic Policies in the West Bank and Gaza: Prologue to the Intifada," *Journal of Arab Affairs* 8 (Spring 1989).

14. For analyses and statistics on demographic issues see Meron Benvenisti with Ziad Abu-Zayed and Danny Rubenstein, *The West Bank Handbook: A Political Lexicon* (Jerusalem: West Bank Data Base Project, 1986) and Meron Benvenisti, *1987 Report: Demographic, Economic, Legal, Social, and Political Developments in the West Bank* (Jerusalem: West Bank Data Base Project, 1987). For an interesting article on the broader demographic issue and the Palestinians see Bernard Sabella, "The Demography of Conflict: A Palestinian Predicament," *New Outlook* (Tel Aviv) 34(3) (April-May 1991): 9-11.

15. See, for example, the analysis by Karen Elliott House, *The Wall Street Journal* (25 September 1991).

16. Boaz Evron, "Captives of [Israeli] Immigration," *Yediot Ahronot* (Hebrew) (4 April 1991), transl. Israel Shahak, "From the Hebrew Press: Monthly Translations and Commentaries from Israel," *American Educational Trust* 3(6) (Washington, DC, June 1991).

17. Jane Perlez, "Reversal on Ethiopia: Plight of Jews and the Prospects for Chaos Aroused U.S. Interest in a Mediation Role," *New York Times* (31 May 1991) and Clifford Kraus, "Israelis Begin Airlift of Ethiopia's Jews," *New York Times* (25 May 1991).

18. Julia Slater, "The Middle East and the New Soviet Union," *Middle East International* 409 (27 September 1991): 17–19.

19. Slater, "The Middle East and the New Soviet Union," 18.

20. See the lengthy and excellent analysis by Jane Hunter, "Making Islam the Enemy," *Israeli Foreign Affairs* 8 (25 March 1992): 1–3.

21. William E. Schmidt, "Today at Babi Yar the Spirits Will Rest," *New York Times* (5 October 1991).

22. See, for example, Marc H. Ellis, *Beyond Innocence and Redemption: Confronting the Holocaust and Israeli Power* (New York: Harper & Row, 1990).

23. Serge Schmemann, "New Soviet Era Opens with Israel's Embassy," *New York Times* (25 October 1991).

24. See the analysis and documentation in Rubenberg, "U.S. Policy Toward the Palestinians."

25. In August 1992 the newly elected Israeli prime minister, Yitzhak Rabin, declared that Israel now would recognize Resolution 242 but that it would only give up "some kilometers" of the Golan Heights and would "never come down from the Heights" (Clyde Haberman, "Israel Tells Arabs It Accepts UN's Land-for-Peace Plan," *New York Times*, 26 August 1992). Also, Israel declared that it would never withdraw from Jerusalem and that it would "not budge one inch" from the West Bank and Gaza (Clyde Haberman, "Rabin Strongly Criticizes Palestinian Negotiators," *New York Times*, 3 September 1991).

26. See the analysis by Haim Baram, "A Jubilant Shamir Gets What He Wanted," *Middle East International* 405 (26 July 1991): 3.

27. Thomas L. Friedman, "Israel Rejects Baker's Plan for Talks," *New York Times* (16 May 1991): A-6.

28. Thomas L. Friedman, "Syria Accepts Bush's Compromise on ME Peace Conference," *New York Times* (15 July 1991); Thomas L. Friedman, "Syria's Move Toward Peace Talks: Is It Primarily to Improve U.S. Ties?," *New York Times* (17 July 1991); and Thomas L. Friedman, "Syria Approves Bush's Plan for a Mid East Conference: Baker Seeks Israeli Assent," *New York Times* (19 July 1991).

29. For statement and analysis see Thomas R. Mattair, "The Bush

Administration and the Arab-Israeli Conflict," *American-Arab Affairs* 36 (Spring 1991): 62–63 and 52–72 *passim.*

30. *Ibid.*, 63.

31. Serge Schmemann, "Israelis Give U.S. Conditional 'Yes' on Mideast Talks," *New York Times* (2 August 1991).

32. Thomas L. Friedman, "Shamir is Unyielding on Makeup of Palestinian Delegation," *New York Times* (25 July 1991).

33. Former Israeli Prime Minister Yitzhak Shamir in interview with Israeli daily *Ma'ariv* (Hebrew) (26 June 1992), reprinted in *The Washington Report on Middle East Affairs* 11 (August–September 1992): 34.

34. Muhammad Hallaj, "The Palestinians and the Gulf War," *American-Arab Affairs* 35 (Winter 1990–1991): 117–25.

35. Naseer Aruri, "The Palestinians After the Gulf War: What Options," *The Palestinians After the Gulf War: The Critical Questions* (Washington DC: The Center for Policy Analyses on Palestine, 1991): 6.

36. Yahya Sadowski, "Power, Poverty, and Petrodollars: Arab Economies After the Gulf War," *Middle East Report* 170 (May–June 1991): 10.

37. Sadowski, "Power, Poverty and Petrodollars," 10. Also see Ann M. Lesch, "Palestinians in Kuwait," *Journal of Palestine Studies* 20 (Summer 1991): 42–54 and Nadim Jaber, "Writing on the Wall for Kuwait's Palestinians," *Middle East International* 403 (28 June 1991): 3–4.

38. Thomas L. Friedman, "There's A New Era. Then There's the Middle East," *New York Times* (28 July 1991): E-1, E-4.

39. Lesch, "Palestinians in Kuwait," 42–54; John H. Cushman, "Under Harassment, Many Palestinians in Kuwait See No Choice but to Leave," *New York Times* (9 June 1991); Jaber, "Writing on the Wall for Kuwait's Palestinians;" and Youssef M. Ibrahim, "For Refugees in Jordan, Misery Without End," *New York Times* (3 October 1991).

40. Cushman, "Under Harassment."

41. Carol Rosenberg, "Kuwait Softens Stance on Israel," *Miami Herald* (13 August 1992).

42. Leslie H. Gelb, "Victory for Mr. Shamir," *New York Times* (24 July 1991).

43. See Thomas L. Friedman, "With a Condition, Saudis Offer End to Israel Boycott: Lebanese also Back Baker," *New York Times* (21 July 1991): 1, 6.

44. Thomas L. Friedman, "There's a New Era."

45. Thomas L. Friedman, "With a Condition." For a good analysis also see Mattair, "The Bush Administration," 63.

46. Carol Rosenberg, "Kuwait Softens Stance on Israel."

47. Carol Berger, "Egyptians Step Up Criticism of PLO Leader," *Christian Science Monitor* (22 August 1991): 5.

48. Thomas L. Friedman, "Egypt Offers Plan on Israel Boycott," *New York Times* (20 July 1991).

49. Alan Cowell, "Egyptian is Named Arab League Chief," *New York Times* (16 May 1991).

50. Jim Muir, "The Syrian-Lebanese Treaty: Grounds for Concern or Hope?," *Middle East International* 401 (31 May 1991): 3–4; Jim Muir, "The Palestinians Lose their Lebanese Foothold," *Middle East International* 404 (12 July 1991): 3–4; Barbara M. Gregory, "U.S. Relations With Lebanon: A Troubled Course," *American-Arab Affairs* 35 (Winter 1990–1991): 62–93; Augustus Richard Norton, "Lebanon After Ta'if: Is the Civil War Over?," *The Middle East Journal* 45 (Summer 1991): 457–73.

51. See the analysis by Lamis Andoni, "PLO Isolated and Uncertain," *Middle East International* 404 (12 July 1991): 4–5.

52. Thomas L. Friedman, "With a Condition."

53. Joel Brinkley, "Israel Accepts Jordan King's Call to Meet," *New York Times* (3 June 1991).

54. Thomas L. Friedman, "Jordanians Agree to Join Talks on Mideast Peace," *New York Times* (22 July 1991): 1, 4.

55. Youssef M. Ibrahim, "Jordan Cautions on Peace Session," *New York Times* (19 September 1991).

56. See, for example, the analysis by Abbas Alnasrawi, *Arab Nationalism, Oil, and the Political Economy of Dependency* (New York: Greenwood Press, 1991) or earlier, Malcolm Kerr, *The Arab Cold War: Gamal 'Abd al-Nasir and His Rivals, 1950-1969*, 3d ed. (New York: Oxford Univ. Press, 1971).

57. For an analysis see Cheryl A. Rubenberg, "Conflict and Contradiction in the Relations between the Arab States and the Palestine National Movement," in *Palestine: Continuing Dispossession*, ed. Glenn E. Perry (Belmont, MA: Association of Arab-American University Graduates, 1986): 121–43.

58. John Palmer, "The European Community," *Middle East International* 406 (16 August 1991): 17–18.

59. Palmer, "The European Community," 18.

60. Cherif J. Cordahi, "G7 Back Baker," *Middle East International* 405 (26 July 1991): 7 and "G7 Summit Declaration" (Document), *Middle East International* 405 (26 July 1991): 22.

61. Rubenberg, "U.S. Policy Toward the Palestinians," and "The U.S.-PLO Dialogue."

62. Serge Schmemann, "Baker Makes Case to 3 Palestinians for October Talks," *New York Times* (3 August 1991) and Henry Kamm, "Palestinians Call Issues Unresolved," *New York Times* (3 August 1991).

63. See the analysis by Thomas L. Friedman, "Bush Makes Aid to Israel Subject to Conditions," *New York Times* (6 October 1991): E-3.

64. Thomas L. Friedman, "U.S. Hopes Sessions on Mideast Create a New Atmosphere: Won't Push Its Own Plan," *New York Times* (27 October 1991).

65. Rubenberg, "U.S. Policy Toward the Palestinians," and "The U.S.-PLO Dialogue."

66. The first quote is from Friedman, "Bush Makes Aid to Israel Subject to Conditions," and the second is from Thomas L. Friedman, "A Window on Deep Israel-U.S. Tensions," *New York Times* (19 September 1991): A-9.

67. The statistics may be found in Thomas L. Friedman, "Peace Talks But No Dove," *New York Times* (20 October 1991) and in more detail in *Report on Israeli Settlement in the Occupied Territories* 1 (May 1991): 1, 6.

68. Israel was clear that it would permit Palestinians administration over such things as "garbage collection, local police authority, traffic, and education," but absolutely no control over land, water, security, immigration, or ultimate authority. See Thomas L. Friedman, "Peace Talks But No Dove."

69. Andrew Rosenthal, "With Rabin Beside Him, Bush Lauds Israelis," *New York Times* (12 August 1992).

70. See the data and analyses by Joel Brinkley, "U.S. Begins Storing Military Supplies in Israeli Bunkers," *New York Times* (1 June 1991) and Donald Neff, "An Empty Gesture," *Middle East International* 402 (14 June 1991): 6.

71. Brinkley, "U.S. Begins Storing Military Supplies"; and Neff, "An Empty Gesture."

72. Joel Brinkley, "Book on Israel's Atomic Arms Goes Beyond US Estimates," *New York Times* (20 October 1991) reporting on a new book by Seymour M. Hersh, *The Samson Option*. Also noteworthy in regard to Israel's nuclear weapons is the special issue of the Israeli journal *New Outlook* (Tel Aviv) 34(5) (September–October 1991) entitled "The Middle East: Approaching The Nuclear Edge?"

73. Brinkley, "Book on Israel's Atomic Arms."

74. Andrew Rosenthal, "With Rabin Beside Him, Bush Lauds Israelis."

75. Ibid.

76. Clyde Haberman, "Rabin Strongly Criticizes Palestinian Negotiators," *New York Times* (3 September 1992).

77. Since 1949 Israel has received more than U.S. $46 billion in U.S. assistance. For additional analysis see *Report on Israeli Settlement in the Occupied Territories*, a Bimonthly Publication of the Foundation for Middle East Peace, Washington DC, beginning in January 1991 with vol. 1(1). Also see *Breaking the Siege* (The Newsletter of the Middle East Justice Network) 3(2), June–July 1991.

78. Thomas L. Friedman, "U.S. Hopes Sessions on Mideast Create a New Atmosphere," *New York Times* (27 October 1991).

79. Alfonso Chardy, "U.S. Policy Parallels Group's Ideas," *Miami Herald* (19 June 1989).

80. Chardy, "U.S. Policy Parallels Group's Ideas"; Steve Niva, "The Bush Team," *Middle East Report* 158 (May–June 1989): 31; *Middle East Report* 158 (May–June 1989): 4–5; Rubenberg, "The U.S.-PLO Dialogue," 34–36.

81. Friedman, "U.S. Hopes Sessions on Mideast."

82. "The Gulf Crisis, The UN, And The New World Order: An Interview With Ambassador Abdalla Saleh Al-Ashtal," *Journal of Palestine Studies* 20 (Spring 1991): 38.

83. Goldbloom, "Are Settlements an Obstacle to Peace?," 9.

84. *Ibid.*, 8.

85. Danny Rubinstein, "Burying Peace," *New Outlook* 34(4) (June-July-August, 1991): 6.

86. Peretz Kidron, "Partial Settlement Freeze," *Middle East International* 431 (7 August 1992): 7.

87. "PLO Urges Caution on Loan Deal," *Miami Herald* (12 August 1992); and Peretz Kidron, "Rabin and Baker Work Towards a Deal," *Middle East International* 430 (24 July 1992): 3–4.

88. Yoav Peled, "An Extremist Goes Mainstream," *Los Angeles Times* (13 February 1991), reprinted in *Israeli-Palestinian Digest* (An Information Service of the Jewish Committee for Israeli-Palestinian Peace, Washington, DC) no. 9 (Spring 1991): 7.

89. Yossi Sarid, "They Know Where to Find Me," *New Outlook* 33(9) (September-October-November, 1990): 10–12.

90. Danny Rubinstein, "A Faith Betrayed," *Tikkun* 6 (May–June 1991): 20.

91. Statement from Geoffrey Aronson, *Israel, Palestinians, and the Intifada*, 35, repeated here from Nancy Murray, "Rabin and the Labor Party: Is the Past Prologue?" *Breaking the Siege* (The Newsletter of the Middle East Justice Network) 4 (August/September 1992): 4.

92. *Ibid.*, 4, 5.

93. Kidron, "Partial Settlement Freeze," 7. For an analysis of these Israeli death squads see *Targeting to Kill: Israel's Undercover Units*, Palestine Human Rights Information Center, Jerusalem, (published in cooperation with The Center for Policy Analysis on Palestine, Washington, DC) May 1992.

94. For analyses of the Israeli policies toward the Palestinians during the Intifada and their effects see Ze'ev Schiff and Ehud Ya'ari, *Intifada: The Palestinian Uprising—Israel's Third Front* (New York: Simon & Schuster, 1990); Don Peretz, *Intifada: The Palestinian Uprising* (Boulder, CO: Westview Press, 1990); Jamal R. Nassar and Roger Heacock, eds., *Intifada: Palestine at the Crossroads* (New York: Praeger, 1990); David McDowall, *Palestine and Israel: The Uprising and Beyond* (Berkeley: Univ.

of California Press, 1989); M. Cherif Bassiouni and Louise Cainkar, eds., *The Palestinian Intifada—December 8, 1987–December 8, 1988: A Record of Israeli Repression* (Chicago: DataBase Project on Palestinian Human Rights, 1989).

95. "Human Rights Update: May 31, 1992" (Chicago: Palestine Human Rights Information Center, 1992).

96. For an analysis of the economic problems of the West Bank and Gaza, including a discussion of the dependence on the transfer of funds from external sources rather than from income generated locally, see Cheryl A. Rubenberg, "Twenty Years of Israeli Economic Policies in the West Bank and Gaza: Prologue to the Intifada," *Journal of Arab Affairs* (Special Issue on the Intifada) 8 (Spring 1989): 28–73.

97. See, for example, Oded Lifshitz, "Gaza is Hungry," *New Outlook*, (Tel Aviv) 34(4) (June-July-August 1991): 37–39.

98. Daoud Kuttab, "Worries About the Intifada," *Middle East International* 402 (14 June 1991): 12–13. See also Carol Rosenberg, "In Isolation, Gaza Palestinians Put Hopes on Peace Process," *Miami Herald* (6 October 1991); Daoud Kuttab, "Gaza Besieged," *Middle East International* 427 (12 June 1992): 7; and Tahir Shriteh, "Hamas versus Fateh," *Middle East International* 430 (24 July 1992): 11.

99. For discussions about the decline in the Intifada see, for example, Kuttab, "Worries About the Intifada," 12–13 and Penny Johnson, "Letter from the Curfew Zone," *Middle East Report* 170 (May-June, 1991): 38–39. Also, this writer spent ten days in Brueij Camp in the Gaza Strip in August 1991 and observed first hand the despair, social disintegration, and the stalled Intifada.

100. See the analysis by Lamis Andoni, "Succession Debate Stifled," *Middle East International* 427 (12 June 1992): 6–7.

101. See the analysis by Lamis Andoni, "PLO: Leaving the Door Ajar," *Middle East International* 399 (3 May 1991): 14; and Andoni, "Succession Debate Stifled."

102. Chris Hedges, "PLO Drops Abu Abbas From Top Policy Council," *New York Times* (29 September 1991); Thomas L. Friedman, "U.S. Maneuvering Gingerly After PLO's Nod on Talks," *New York Times* (29 September 1991); Carol Rosenberg, "Arafat Urges New U.S.-PLO Dialogue," *Miami Herald* (29 September 1991), and "Palestine Council OKs Conditioned Peace Talks," *Miami Herald* (28 September 1991).

14
Israel and the New World Order

<hr>

Meir Porat

The disintegration of the Soviet Union and the ensuing economic, social, and political crises that preoccupied its political successors created the perception that the United States came out of the cold war as a victorious and powerful state. This perception was reinforced by the role it played during the Gulf crisis and the conduct and conclusion of the Gulf War.

In an address to a joint session of the U.S. Congress on 11 September 1990, George Bush declared that out of the troubled times: "a *new world order* can emerge: a new era, freer from the threat of terror, stronger in the pursuit of Justice, and more secure in the quest for peace. An era in which the nations of the world, east and west, north and south, can prosper and live in harmony."[1]

After the conclusion of the Gulf War, President Bush delivered a similar message. On 6 March 1991, he stated to a joint session of Congress that

> Now, we can see a new world coming into view. A world in
> which there is the very real prospect of a new world order. In
> the words of Winston Churchill, a "world order" in which "the
> principles of justice and fair play . . . protect the weak
> against the strong. . . ." A world where the United Nations
> freed from cold war stalemate, is poised to fulfill the historic
> vision of its founders. A world in which freedom and respect
> for human rights find a home among all nations. The Gulf War
> put this new world to its first test, and my fellow Americans,
> we passed the test.[2]

Most of the cliches contained in the two addresses were repeated in the past, but never translated into actions or results. The phrase "new world order" caught the attention of many, however, and provided a fertile ground for interpretations, elaborations, and commentaries. In fact, these words assumed the status of a concept and the significance of a theoretical discovery. Whether the assumption of this status or significance is justified may be open to debate.

Contrary to President Bush's declarations, the Gulf War demonstrated that military power is still the most effective means to resolve international conflicts. Iraq used its military power to resolve its outstanding disputes with Kuwait in the context of the old world order. But when the United States used its military power to resolve a dispute with Iraq, President Bush considered it a manifestation of a *new* world order. It is difficult to comprehend what distinguishes the *old* from the *new world order*. Bush's reference that the "Gulf War put this new world to its first test" and that the Americans passed the test makes sense only in the context that for the first time the United States succeeded in obtaining the unanimous support of the permanent members of the UN Security Council in providing international legitimacy to what was mainly a U.S. action to further its own national interests and foreign policy objectives.

The two main pillars of U.S. post-World War II foreign policy were global hegemony and allied containment. The dissipation of the cold war in 1989 was not accompanied by a corresponding change in the foreign policy and objectives of the United States. But this should not come as a surprise as the "cold war ended essentially through the unilateral acts of the Soviet Union," and therefore the United States was not compelled to change or modify its foreign policy objectives. Moreover, it appears that in the Gulf War U.S. post-World War II policies did not change but were given "a new lease on life."[3] So although President Bush spoke about the establishment of a new world order, this is merely a new name representing old policies and objectives. This is the reason why Shaykh Abbasi Madani, the leader of the Algerian Islamic Front "expressed fears that the West would exploit the crisis for its own purposes."[4] These purposes were consistent with the efforts of the United States to sustain its global hegemony and allied containment.

The purpose of this chapter is to examine whether a new world order was created in the Middle East and, if so, to uncover the nature and scope of the interrelation between Israel and the so-called new world order. The role played by Israel on the international scene was always influenced by global, regional, and domestic considerations. For the purposes of this paper, only the regional and domestic concerns will be addressed. To be sure, in reality all these considerations are intertwined and inseparable, but analytical expediency requires that each of the two groups of considerations be examined separately to demonstrate that there is nothing new about the new world order in the Middle East.

Regional Considerations

The establishment of the state of Israel in 1948 and its subsequent development played a major role in Middle Eastern politics. Usually this role was a passive one; however, regardless of whether Israel pursued any particular policy, its mere existence was sufficient to stimulate antagonism and active hostility from most countries in the region. The only two exceptions to this were Iran and Egypt. Until the fall of the shah of Iran in 1979, Israel maintained a close relationship with Iran, including diplomatic, military, and economic activities and cooperation. In the same year, Israel signed a treaty with Egypt ensuing from the Camp David Accords that established a stable peace between the two states. But this peace did not translate into any significant interrelationship except for the Israeli purchase of some U.S. $150 million per year of Egyptian oil.

Since its establishment in 1948, Israel held the position that no one state or any combination of states in the region should be able to pose a military threat. Since 1967, the United States helped Israel to become a regional military superpower. Consistent with this position were continuous Israeli efforts to foster division among its neighboring states and prevent them from forming a united front against Israel. Also, Israel pursued a policy of deterrence that required a military capability sufficient to meet any conceivable military threat from its neighbors. An important component of this deterrence policy was the ability to launch when necessary preemptive and punitive attacks, or wage war, inside the territory of its adversaries.

The Gulf War demonstrated that preemptive, or even punitive, military action by Israel, or anyone else for that matter, could no longer be relied upon as an effective deterrent. In this war, the Iraqis did not march into the Kingdom of Jordan to establish an anti-Israeli "Eastern front" as expected by Israeli strategists, but rather chose to threaten with the use of missiles. Eventually, the Iraqis acted on their own threats and used Scud missiles, which exposed the Israeli urban centers to a new kind of warfare and demonstrated the unpreparedness of the Israeli state for missile warfare.[5]

The Gulf War also demonstrated that the strength of the military forces of Israel, including the rumored possession of nuclear capabilities, did not deter the Iraqis from launching unprovoked Scud missile attacks against Israel. This is not surprising, because even the overwhelming power of the U.S. military machine, together with military contingents from other countries, did not deter Iraq from conducting a losing war and launching missiles against Saudi Arabia and Israel. In any event, Iraq seemed prepared to sacrifice more than Israel was willing or able to sacrifice in terms of either people or matériel.

It was also apparent that Israel could no longer rely on preemptive military action as an effective deterrent against an adversary such as Iraq. It is questionable whether Israel could mount any effective military action without crossing Syrian or Jordanian territory and without alerting the Iraqis. It is also quite clear that even if the Israelis could overcome these two obstacles and take preemptive military action, the United States could prevent such action. The United States actually did so in October 1973 and again in January 1991. The alternative was to prevent any potential danger from getting out of control, which in turn would force the Israelis to escalate a developing crisis.

Another unchanged aspect of the regional politics of the Middle East was Saddam Hussein. The consensus was that as long as he maintained his position as the undisputed ruler of Iraq, Middle Eastern stability would remain elusive. Actually, it is safe to assume that "anything short of the removal of Saddam Hussein, or severe international constraints upon his activities, will leave the Iraqi leader as an influential actor in the Middle East. He will still enjoy the sympathy of millions of disaffected and frustrated Arabs and possess a powerful military capability that he can use at some other point in time."[6] The Israelis also subscribed to this view.[7] In conclusion, the Iraqis still pose a great danger to Middle Eastern stability, and this danger was not removed by the Gulf War.

As far as other aspects of Middle Eastern politics and issues are concerned, the Gulf War had no impact. If the issues were not linked directly to Iraq, the Gulf War did not influence them. For instance, the general danger inherent in a Syrian-Iraqi rivalry for leadership in the Arab world, coupled with the fact that Syria had also managed to assemble an impressive arsenal of modern military hardware and was historically hostile toward Israel, made Syria a dangerous adversary prior to and after the Gulf War. Syrian policies, menacing from Israel's point of view, were exacerbated by Syria's domination of Lebanese affairs and influence on the policies of the Kingdom of Jordan.

The water crisis in the Middle East is another area of great importance. In the joint invitation issued to participants invited to the Madrid Peace Conference, George Bush and Mikhail Gorbachev listed water "as one of the important region-wide issues on which the third-stage multilateral negotiations should focus."[8] The relevance of this issue was recently underscored: The Palestinian and Israeli delegations at the sixth round of talks in Washington in September 1992 agreed in principle to the creation of a subcommittee to discuss water issues. The availability of and control over free flowing fresh water resources affects the Arab-Israeli relationship as much as it affects the relations among Turkey, Syria, and Iraq and relations between Egypt and Ethiopia.

In October 1991, Lieutenant General Mohammed Tantawi, Egypt's new defense minister, predicted that "the struggle for water" would lead to future conflicts in the Middle East "because any attempt to control water resources will be considered a direct threat to the national security of the beneficiary states."[9] Turkey, where the source of the Tigris and Euphrates is situated, is in the process of harnessing its water resources to generate relatively inexpensive electrical power. This may result in a complete stoppage or a substantial reduction of water flowing to Syria and Iraq. Syria can do the same with regard to any water flowing to Iraq through its territory. Similarly, Ethiopia controls the source of the Nile River, which is, in effect, the only major source of fresh water in Egypt.

During the 1960s, Syria attempted to divert water from the source of the Jordan River to reduce the volume of water flowing into Israel. These attempts "led to recurrent and increasingly serious armed clashes between Israel and Syrian forces." Syria refused to recognize Israel as a party interested in the question of Jordan River water, and "evidence is mounting that there has been no fundamental change in the Syrian policy of nonrecognition."[10] This problem will continue as long as peace is not attained between Israel and Syria and the dispute over the Golan Heights is not settled.

The growing shortage of water supplies threatens the precarious stability that prevails presently in the Middle East. But there is no evidence to indicate that the water crisis assumed any new dimensions as a result of the Gulf War except perhaps insofar as the relative military power of Turkey vis-à-vis Iraq increased. From the Israeli perspective, the water issue is far from being satisfactorily resolved and therefore may develop into a major conflict.

Another regional phenomenon affecting Israel is the military arms race, which accelerated as a result of the Gulf crisis.[11] For unknown reasons the United States decided to supply Saudi Arabia with massive additional armaments. In addition to the large amounts of military matériel left by the United States in Saudi Arabia after the Gulf War, the kingdom decided to acquire more sophisticated weaponry. On 11 September 1992, President Bush announced the sale of seventy-two F-15 fighter planes to the Saudis bearing a U.S. $9 billion price tag.

Because Israel refuses to accept any change to the prevailing regional military balance, which is tilted to its advantage, the U.S. action resulted in a renewed escalation in the arms race. U.S. willingness to supply Israel and Arab countries with billions of dollars worth of military hardware led to the unavoidable conclusion that "the only justification for the additional arms deals is the need of the United States to provide work for its huge arms producing industries." This policy "may eventually be the cause of an unprecedented conflagration whose link with the Gulf Crisis would be that it indirectly enabled such an outbreak."[12]

The regional arms race was further complicated by the development and acquisition of nuclear weapons and technology. In 1981, the Israeli air force launched a devastating attack on the Iraqi nuclear facility located at Osiraq. This retarded Iraq's nuclear program, but did not destroy it. At the time of the outbreak of the Gulf War, it was rumored that Iraqi scientists were one to two years away from developing a nuclear bomb. Similarly, it was rumored that Israel already had nuclear weapons.

The possession of nuclear weapons may, however, be of negligible importance in the Middle East. In the case of Israel, the United States would never allow it to use such weapons. Israel would also be unable to use nuclear weapons against enemy targets located within 100 km of its borders because at such distances the fallout from nuclear explosions could cause untold devastation and deaths in Israel. Third, Israeli nuclear capacity encouraged its Arab neighbors to acquire a similar capacity. Finally, the Gulf War provided sufficient evidence that knowledge of Israel's nuclear capacity did not deter Iraq from launching missiles against Israel and thus neutralized the element of deterrence supposedly inherent in the possession of such weapons.

These considerations may be the real reason behind Israel's proposal for a nuclear weapons-free zone in the Middle East. But this proposal is unlikely to be accepted by the Arab countries as long as no one can agree on an inspection formula. The Israelis insist on mutual inspection by the parties and they refuse to give the role of inspector to any international agency or intermediary. The Arab countries demand compliance with the Nonproliferation Treaty and expect that the International Atomic Energy Agency will restrain the Israeli nuclear program.[13] It is uncertain whether the Israeli proposal will result in some kind of agreement. Nor is it certain that the nuclear issue will be dealt with as an integral part of a comprehensive Middle Eastern peace settlement. It is clear, however, that the Israeli proposal was not a result of the Gulf War, nor was it linked to it in any other manner.

In June 1990, approximately seven weeks before the Iraqi invasion of Kuwait, Prime Minister Shamir stated in a speech to the Knesset that Israel was "also calling for an international agreement on the disarmament of nonconventional arms that will eliminate these horrible destructive weapons from the world."[14] Thus it can be safely concluded that the idea, if not the real intention, for a nuclear weapons-free zone originated before the outbreak of the Gulf War and even before the Gulf crisis.

On another front, Iraq's ambitious policies and actions provided impetus to Arab nationalism, Islamic fundamentalism, and the rising expectations among the masses of the so-called developing and underdeveloped countries. This impetus posed a threat to U.S. hegemony. Contrary to belief in the United States, however, the Iraqi domestic momentum required to topple the Iraqi president did not materialize, and Saddam Hussein not only survived the war but managed to enhance his political stature in the eyes of millions of Arabs and non-Arab Muslims throughout the world. After all, he not only challenged the United States and other Western powers, but managed to withstand and survive a military onslaught, the magnitude of which is unparalleled in Middle Eastern history.[15]

These developments are reflected in the changing mood of the Arab and non-Arab Muslim countries where the Gulf War stimulated a nationalist and fundamentalist excitement. It is apparent that

> great anger is accumulating among wide segments of the population in Egypt and other Arab states. This anger is directed against the Arab governments that ostensibly aided Western imperialism—the "historic enemy of the Arabs and of Islam"—to return to the Middle East "through the back door" and through Saudi Arabia in order to regain control of oil resources, to humiliate the Arab nation and to destroy Saddam

Hussein, the modern Saladin, fighting heroically against "the new Crusaders"—the Western, Christian allies, and Jewish Israel.[16]

This testimony is significant because it is delivered by an Israeli.[17] If true, it is natural to expect that Arab nationalism and Muslim fundamentalism will continue to play an important role in future U.S. political and strategic configurations.

Recognizing these developments, the Israeli leadership will closely monitor U.S. foreign policy for any change in its objectives. As long as the United States maintains its traditional policies so will Israel. It is important that Israel's foreign policies are consistent, and overlap to some extent, with those of the United States.

The Palestinian issue was also not affected by the Gulf War in spite of Iraqi and Palestinian efforts to link the two. The reality was that the "Gulf Crisis cannot ultimately end until the Arab-Israeli crisis has also been resolved," nor can the Arab-Israeli crisis be resolved without the resolution of the Palestinian issue. So, although there is "an unprecedented interest in the West in resolving the Arab-Israeli conflict, the chasm among the principal players in reality is as deep as ever."[18]

It is noteworthy that although the United States and Israel professed a desire to resolve the Palestinian and Arab-Israeli crises, such a resolution could be detrimental to the fundamental objectives of the foreign policies of both states. A peaceful and stable Middle East may lead to the development of an anti-Western Arab or Islamic united front. Such unity would increase the political, economic, and bargaining powers of the Arab Middle East to the detriment of the United States as well as Israel. On the other hand, a solution to the Arab-Israeli conflict could extract the unifying and transcending Palestinian issue from Arab political concerns leaving them disconnected to pursue their individual national objectives. The Arab-Israeli conflict cemented the Arab states; a comprehensive peace could well fragment this unified stance against Israel and the United States.

For now, it is clear that Israel failed totally in fulfilling its desire to integrate constructively into the regional economy and political system. The Gulf War did not change this reality; therefore, it is difficult to substantiate the claim that the disappearance of the Soviet Union on one hand, and the Gulf War on the other, created a new world order in the Middle East.

Domestic Considerations

The complex issues that dominated Israeli domestic politics were further complicated by the consequences of the Gulf War. Some of these issues require special consideration.

Politics

The Israeli political spectrum is dominated, quantitatively, by "doves" on the left and "hawks" on the right. In the middle is a plethora of small political parties and movements among which a coalition of small religious parties is the most important. This results from Israel's multiparty political system in which the two largest blocks (Likud and Labor) cannot muster the support of more than 30 to 40 percent of the seats in the 120-seat Knesset (the Israeli parliament).

The religious parties traditionally held the political balance of power and still do. Thus, even if the Gulf War affected the policies and principles of the so-called "peace camp" or the right-wing nationalist camp, the religious parties had a neutralizing effect on the political system regardless of external and regional events.

The Gulf crisis and war caused some confusion within the Israeli peace camp, exacerbated "when Palestinian leaders and rank-and-file in the territories went out of their skins to proclaim their ecstatic support for Saddam Hussein." Whether this confusion was real or imagined, a spokesman for the peace camp rejected the notion that the Gulf War was linked to its agenda. He admitted that the war "brought home to a growing number of Israelis how horrible war is," and that the missile attacks proved that the "40-60 km of strategic depth provided by the territories [was] meaningless in terms of today's warfare."[19] But many Israelis presented the same views some time before the Gulf crisis.

The hawks, on the other hand, argued that pro-Saddam Palestinian demonstrations and fervor were further proof that they could not be trusted. It should be noted, however, that this argument was made by the Israeli political right many times in the past. It is extremely difficult to determine which are the causes and effects when it comes to the ongoing saga between Israel and the Palestinians. What is clear, however, is that the Gulf War did not change the nature of Israeli-Palestinian relations, and they are still characterized by mutual distrust.

In addition to distrust, the Israelis cannot produce a consensus about the Palestinian issue. This inability will persist as long as the present electoral system prevails because the Israeli political system lends itself to the establishment of coalition governments that are permanently on the verge of collapse and depend on the fragile and unreliable support of capricious and marginal political parties of the extreme right or left. As a consequence, the latter play a political role far greater than is warranted by the number of voters supporting them.

In recent years, growing numbers of Israelis joined the ranks of those pressing for radical political and electoral reforms including the election of prime ministers in direct popular elections. In April 1991, in the single largest mass protest since the 1982 invasion of Lebanon, nearly 200,000 people marched to demand political and electoral change in Israel. A long-time opponent of the idea of a direct vote for the premiership, former Prime Minister Yitzhak Shamir, finally opened a free vote in the Knesset on this question, which led to the March 1992 decision. From 1996 onward, the Israeli voters will be able to elect their premier through a direct vote.

The efforts in this direction may receive some impetus from the rising tide of Arab nationalism and Muslim fundamentalism in the Middle East because any effective defense against them requires that Israel develop a more decisive government as well as a more responsive electoral system. Without an effective political system, the Israeli government will realize sooner or later that, besides a Palestinian issue, it must also deal with a restive Arab population that is part of its citizenry.

The Israeli Arabs

Israeli Arabs cannot remain immune to the general political and religious change sweeping through the Middle East. These Arabs formally enjoyed full Israeli citizenship rights, but in practice they were not allowed to integrate into Israeli society. Although economically they may be better off than many Arabs in other Middle Eastern countries, they were not allowed to reach a level of economic parity with the average Israeli Jewish citizen. The same is true of their political status as manifested in the total exclusion of Israeli Arabs from many state departments, agencies, and corporations.

The first signs of restiveness among the Israeli Arabs developed in response to the Intifada, the Palestinian uprising that began in 1988 in the West Bank. As long as the Intifada lasts among West Bank and Gaza Palestinians, the Israeli Arabs will be restive. This is quite natural because Israeli Arabs and the Palestinians in the Occupied Territories are related by blood, language, and culture. In many cases the two groups shaped the 1948 and 1967 wars between Israel and its neighboring Arab countries.

To counterbalance the natural growth rate of Israeli Arabs, which is higher than that of Israeli Jews, the Israeli government encouraged Jewish immigration by whatever means available. The end of the cold war witnessed a thaw in the attitudes of the Soviet Union and Israel toward each other. This was marked by the permission given to Soviet Jews to immigrate to Israel without too many obstacles. Since 1989 hundreds of thousands of Soviet Jews took advantage of the opportunity, and the tide of immigration continued unabated. Even the advent of the Gulf crisis and war did not effect this immigration. The only element that could slow down this immigration would be Israel's inability to absorb such large numbers of newcomers in a relatively short period of time. This recent wave of Jewish immigration from the Soviet Union provided some breathing time, but is not a long-term demographic solution. The situation is made more difficult by a declining birthrate among the Jewish population of Israel as well as Jewish emigration from Israel.

The entrenchment of the definition of Israel as a Jewish state in the basic laws of the country, as well as the unlikely prospects of integrating Muslim and Christian Arabs into an Israeli society and political system defined mostly in terms of Jewish religious identity, precluded any possibility of reversing a growing schism between Israeli Arabs and Jews. Any such potential reversal is made even more remote by the lingering and persistent inability to resolve the Palestinian issue. But this problem predates the Gulf crisis by many years.

The Palestinians in the Occupied Territories

The fact that Israeli Jews and Palestinians perceive each other as wolves was reinforced by the events of the Gulf War. First, what "added the additional layer of hatred and mistrust is not so much the dancing on rooftops (which can be understood even if not sympathized with), but the persistent support for Saddam Hussein."[20] Israelis failed, or refused, to put these events in a proper context.

The sight of Palestinians dancing on rooftops while Iraqi Scud missiles landed on Israeli territory, as unpleasant to Israeli Jews as it may have been, was definitely not worse than ultraorthodox Jews in Israel dancing in the streets and on rooftops claiming that finally retribution was meted out to nonbelieving Jews. According to them, these claims were supported by the fact that no missiles landed in orthodox neighborhoods. The point of this observation is that no Israeli labeled these orthodox Jews as wolves nor did these orthodox Jews suffer any repercussion for their actions. A similar act by the Palestinians, however, was deemed proof of their disloyalty and untrustworthiness and elicited more hostile and derogatory remarks from Israelis.[21]

As indicated earlier, Saddam Hussein was a symbol and voice of Arab nationalism and perhaps even heroism. The Palestinians expressed support for him in the context of their own national aspirations and frustrations, and not because of his personal attributes and characteristics. Israelis were not the only people frustrated by the conflict. Palestinian discouragement was a response to the lack of solutions to their demands. The 1988 declaration of an independent Palestinian state and the Palestinian Liberation Organization's (PLO) renunciation of terrorism were only the more important of several unsuccessful steps taken by Palestinians toward peace, steps that were largely ignored by Israel and the United States. The lack of momentum for their demands naturally generated frustration; therefore, it is easy to see how they would be excited by the romantic specter of an Arab leader standing up against all odds to a Western superpower and refusing to back off. This is the reason that the United States was alarmed by Saddam Hussein and why it intervened in the Gulf crisis.

The crux of the problem was that Palestinian and Israeli national aspirations always collided because they were directed toward the same territory. The hostility between the two was only a by-product and not the cause of conflicting national aspirations. Unless these conflicting aspirations can be satisfied, there is no chance of finding a permanent solution to the Israeli-Palestinian or Arab-Israeli conflicts.

It was argued that the Palestinian issue is only "a symptom of the Arab-Israeli conflict rather then its 'root cause',"[22] and therefore it is necessary to resolve the two in one single package. It is unlikely that Israel will be successful in dealing with a group of Arab countries divided among themselves when it cannot resolve the Palestinian issue over which it has more control. The attempt to resolve both conflicts simultaneously will in effect delay any possibility of resolving the Palestinian issue. It should be noted, however, that as long as the Arab-Israeli conflict is controlled, the United States can present its involvement in the Middle East as a legitimate action to protect the only democracy in the region.[23] Without such a conflict, the United States would need to develop a new way of legitimizing its involvement in the Middle East.

One way to prolong the conflict is to delay the resolution of the Palestinian issue. The question is how long Israel will be able and willing to sustain a status quo that strains Israeli society and its political system. Israel could be more flexible with the Palestinians if they wanted to satisfy only U.S. objectives. In fact, the Israelis have their own reasons to delay any final settlement of the Palestinian conflict. First, Israelis know that any such settlement must involve a withdrawal from all or substantial parts of the Occupied Territories. Any voluntary withdrawal from the West Bank or the Gaza Strip could be tantamount to political suicide for the leader of the country during such a withdrawal. At the same time, it is doubtful whether the Palestinians, with or without the support of Arab countries, will have the capacity to force Israel to withdraw. Therefore, the only possible way to get Israel to relinquish its occupation of the West Bank and the Gaza Strip is through U.S. pressure. As indicated, this is not likely to happen in the near future.

Second, the *aliyah*, or Jewish immigration, strengthened Israel in many areas including militarily. To settle immigrants, Israel needs all the land that it can control including the West Bank and the Gaza Strip. As it happens, "the convergence, however inadvertent, between Washington and Israel in capping the Jewish refugee quotas to the United States and in diverting this human flood of Soviet Jewish refugees towards the shores of the Eastern Mediterranean . . . have generated a well founded fear that this vast new *aliyah* will bring in its wake what earlier *aliyah* have brought and constitute a prelude to an even greater Israeli hegemony in the region."[24] But even if Israel's goal is not necessarily to increase its hegemony, some of its leaders definitely cherish the idea of a "greater Israel."

The third reason is that, demographically, most of the Israeli population is concentrated within the Haifa-Tel Aviv-Jerusalem triangle. This area is already congested and cannot absorb many additional people. The only tracts of land large enough and available for development are in the southern part of Israel, which is a barren desert with insufficient water and infrastructure, and is too remote from the Israeli main cities. Consequently, the only practical places for expansion are inside the Occupied Territories, but populating this area carries other strategic considerations. Despite the freeze on Jewish settlement building in the Occupied Territories demanded by the

United States as a condition of granting the U.S. $10 billion in loan guarantees to Israel, the current Labor government exempted the so-called "security settlements" from this. The building of Jewish settlements will continue around Jerusalem, the Golan Heights, and the Jordan River valley.

Another reason dictating against a release of, or withdrawal from, the West Bank and the Gaza Strip is that almost 100,000 Israelis are already settled in these territories. No Israeli politician seems willing to risk repeating the 1982 forceful removal of Jewish settlers from the Sinai by the Israeli Army. Therefore, the difficulties involved in removing them are bound to make the Palestinian issue linger for as long as Israel can afford to delay it. These settlers live in newly developed towns and settlements that are intertwined with Palestinian cities, towns, and villages in a very intricate web that is going to be difficult, if not impossible, to untangle. Whether Palestinians will consider any future peace plan that leaves such a substantial and growing Israeli minority in their midst remains to be seen. Under the current Israeli proposals for autonomy of the Occupied Territories, Jewish settlers would be exempt from Palestinian jurisdiction, but because Israelis and Palestinians cannot agree on the form of autonomy this is hardly the problem. The Israelis would probably do whatever they can to avoid reaching this stage by making postponements and indefinite delays.

It is clear, however, that despite the benchmark talks in Madrid in 1991 the Palestinian issue is almost exactly where it was prior to the Gulf crisis and war. All sides to the Palestinian-Israeli dispute propose ideas of how a settlement can be reached, but since the Camp David Agreement of 1979 there is absolutely no noticeable progress, and the Israelis still take autonomy to mean municipal rule while the Palestinians envision statehood. The Israeli masses are still frustrated with living in a permanent state of siege as is amply manifested in their daily economic, political, social, and cultural life. At the same time, the Palestinian masses are frustrated with the lack of progress in their struggle to satisfy political and national aspirations. Given the present state of affairs, however, neither the Gulf War nor peace conferences made any difference.

Defense Policy

It was stated that the devastation inflicted upon the Iraqi army by the U.S.-led coalition "confirms Israel as the undisputed superpower of the Middle East."[25] This is, of course, a truism; Lebanon, Syria, the Kingdom of Jordan, and Egypt did not require such an announcement. They did not have any doubts about Israel's military capabilities.

On the other hand, the Gulf War demonstrated again that the United States is willing and able to intervene militarily in the Middle East to further its interests and support its regional allies. This, however, was also known to Israel's Arab neighbors. Thus, in effect, the Gulf War did not change any of the military considerations or premises that prevailed before its outbreak.

Another important feature of the Gulf War was Israeli self-restraint. Traditionally, when a serious military threat developed, Israel pursued a policy of preemptive military action such as that taken in the 1967 Six Day War. Whenever Israel was attacked, it pursued a policy of retaliatory military action. This time, Iraqi threats against Israel before the Gulf War and the launching of Scud missiles against Israeli urban centers failed to provoke an Israeli military response.

A few analysts and commentators believed that the United States was "pleading" with the Israelis "not to interfere with the fighting over Iraq in any way that could undermine the coalition with the Arab states that has made possible the presence of U.S. troops in the region."[26] Although this contention deserves some credence, it is highly questionable whether the United States had to plead its case before Israel. It is more likely that the United States "was insisting that Jerusalem exercise complete restraint,"[27] emphasis being on the word *insisting*.

Israel calculated that by "accommodating" U.S. "pleas" for self-restraint, Israel would be more successful in obtaining additional massive economic and military aid after the war. Although these calculations were based on the Israeli experience of the 1973 Yom Kippur War,[28] it was not certain that the United States would actually provide such massive aid without linking it to Israeli concessions with regard to the Arab-Israeli and Palestinian-Israeli conflicts.

Second, although the psychological impact of Scud missiles landing on Tel Aviv and Haifa should not be disregarded, the actual physical damage inflicted upon Israel in terms of destruction and war-related economic losses was significantly less than the damage that Israel would have incurred by direct and active participation in the war.

Third, no Israeli preemptive or retaliatory military action could have had any meaningful effect on an adversary such as Iraq under

Saddam Hussein. Even the massive and general devastation inflicted upon Iraq by the U.S.-dominated coalition did not seem to affect the Iraqi leadership.

Finally, the Israeli policy of self-restraint should not be considered a manifestation of or a response to a new world order. A very strong case can be made in support of the view that this policy was consistent with Israeli self interests and objectives. First, this policy facilitated U.S. efforts to create and lead an anti-Iraqi political and military coalition, which intended to deal a devastating blow to one of Israel's most powerful adversaries. U.S. and Israeli consultation and cooperation during the Gulf War, which included among other things the tracking of mobile Iraqi SCUD missiles, serves as an example.[29] It is worth noticing that this type of concerted activity was not unusual but fell within the bounds of the 1984 "memorandum of understanding" governing U.S.-Israeli strategic concerns.

The Economy

The influx of hundreds of thousands of new immigrants and the huge amounts of money associated with the absorption and integration of these people into the general matrix of Israeli society stretched Israel's economic capacity to the limit. Without U.S. aid, Israel could not sustain its economy even before the war. Israel's requirement for additional massive injections of economic aid must be satisfied before it can develop an economy that produces money and not an economy that collects or raises money.[30]

The precarious state of the Israeli economy was exacerbated by the Gulf War, which demonstrated that Israel was unprepared for an unconventional war, or to conduct a defensive war. Consequently, it will require vast amounts of money to cure these deficiencies as quickly as possible. Thus, from an economic perspective, the Gulf War escalated military expenditures in many Middle Eastern countries, not only Israel, in direct contradiction with the declared principles of a so-called new world order.

Conclusion

The preceding review of some of the more important issues permeating Middle Eastern affairs in general, and Israeli policies and attitudes in particular, demonstrates that the new world order in the

Middle Eastern region is not different from the *old* world order. The same complex cluster of elements that influenced the Middle East before the Gulf War continues to hold the region in its firm grip. Although certain conditions may change with the passage of time, the essential composition of the Arab-Israeli and Israeli-Palestinian conflicts remains intact.

Because rising Arab nationalism and Muslim fundamentalism will affect the present and future political stability of the Middle East, it is possible that the climate in the region is not yet ripe for lasting peace settlements. The proliferation of literature and articles originating in Israel that advance the thesis that a real and lasting resolution of all conflicts in the Middle Eastern region will be possible only if and when the Arab countries adopt democratic political systems may simply be a tactic intended to divert everyone's attention from the lack of progress toward a negotiated resolution of the Arab-Israeli and Israeli-Palestinian conflicts.[31]

If the idea of democratization as a prerequisite for enduring political stability takes root in the minds of decision makers in Western democracies, it will address two issues of concern to Israel. First, because Israel has the only Western style democratic system in the Middle East, it will help to link future political prospects with those of the Western democracies.

More important, however, is the calculation that if democratization is to be a prerequisite for enduring settlements in the region, Israel could continue to hold the Occupied Territories and adhere to its policy of no compromise for as long as its Arab neighbors fail to adopt effective democratic political systems. From the present vantage point, this may take a very long time, if it happens at all. In any event, as far as substance is concerned, there seems to be no evidence to support the contention that the disintegration of the Soviet Union and the consequences of the Gulf War created a new political climate or a new world order in the Middle East.

Notes

1. George Bush, "Address to Joint Sessions of Congress, Washington, DC, 11 September 1990" (excerpts), *Journal of Palestine Studies* (Documents and Sources) 20(2) (Winter, 1991): 195.

2. George Bush, "Address to Joint Session of Congress on the Middle East, Washington, DC, 6 March 1991" (excerpts), *Journal of Palestine Studies* (Documents and Sources) 20(4) (Summer 1991): 181.

3. Bruce Cummings, "Trilateralism and the New World Order," *World Policy Journal* 8(2) (Spring 1991): 215, 212.

4. Walid Khalidi, "The Gulf Crisis: Origins and Consequences," *Journal of Palestine Studies* 20(2) (Winter 1991): 15.

5. Gadi Yatziv, "The Doctrine of Security is Falling Apart," in *War in the Gulf*, ed. Nathan Shaham and Tsvi Raanan (Tel Aviv: Sifriat Poalim, 1991) (in Hebrew): 65.

6. Hermann Frederick Eilts, "The Persian Gulf Crisis," *Middle East Journal* 45(1) (Winter, 1991): 16.

7. President Chaim Herzog's Independence Day Address (Jerusalem, 17 April 1991), *Middle East Focus* 13(3) (Fall 1991): 18.

8. George E. Gruen, *The Water Crisis: The Next Middle East Conflict?* (Los Angeles: The Medi-Press, 1991): 1.

9. Interview with the Egyptian daily, *Al-Ahram*, quoted by Tony Walker from Cairo, "Turkey Postpones Regional Water Supplies Conference," *Financial Times* (London) (8 October 1991), as cited in Gruen, *The Water Crisis*, 2.

10. Gruen, *The Water Crisis*, 3.

11. Interview with Mattityahu Peled, "The Gulf Crisis: An Israeli View," *Journal of Palestine Studies* 20(2) (Winter 1991): 111.

12. *Ibid.*

13. Peter W. Rodman, "Middle East Diplomacy After the Gulf War," *Foreign Affairs* (Spring 1991): 15.

14. Prime Minister Itzhak Shamir, "Speech to the Knesset Presenting His New Government, 11 June 1990" (excerpts), *Journal of Palestine Studies* (Documents and Source Materials) 20(1) (Autumn 1990): 170.

15. Uri Avneri, "Nasos Shirt," in *War in the Gulf*, ed. Nathan Shaham and Tsvi Raana (Tel Aviv: Sifriat Poalim, 1991) (in Hebrew): 80.

16. Moshe Maoz, "Moslem Fury Gathering Strength," *The Jerusalem Post International Edition* (week ending 16 March 1991): 25.

17. Professor Moshe Maoz is a Middle Eastern expert at the Hebrew University in Jerusalem.

18. Robin Right, "Unexplored Realities of the Persian Gulf," *Middle East Journal* 45(1) (Winter 1991): 27, 28.

19. Yossi Goell, "Ideology Springs Eternal," *Jerusalem Post International Edition* (week ending 16 March 1991).

20. Susan Rolef, "Adding to the Layer of Mistrust," *The Jerusalem Post International Edition* (week ending 23 February 1991): 8.

21. *Ibid.*

22. Editorial, *The Jerusalem Post International Edition* (week ending 23 February 1991): 24.

23. Rodman, "Middle East Diplomacy," 106.

24. Khalidi, "The Gulf Crisis," 20.

25. Donald Neff, "The U.S., Iraq, Israel, and Iran: Backdrop to War," *Journal of Palestine Studies* 20(4) (Summer 1991): 23.

26. Yossef Goell, "A Convincing Indirect Deterrent," *The Jerusalem Post International Edition* (week ending 23 February 1991): 8; Ze'ev Schiff, "Israel After the War," *Foreign Affairs* 70(2) (Spring 1991): 21.

27. Schiff, "Israel After the War," 27.

28. *Ibid.*

29. David A. Welch, "The Politics and Psychology of Restraint: Israeli Decision-making in the Gulf War," *International Journal* 68(2) (Spring 1992): 335–39, 349.

30. Shimon Peres, "Peres is Strategic Depth," in *War in the Gulf*, ed. Nathan Shaham and Tsvi Raana (Tel Aviv: Sifriat Poalim, 1991) (in Hebrew): 27.

31. See for example, Gad Yacobi, "Towards a 'New Order'," in *War in the Gulf*, ed. Nathan Shaham and Tsvi Raana (Tel Aviv: Sifriat Poalim, 1991) (in Hebrew): 58; N. B. Argaman, "Why Democracy Still Eludes the Arab World," *Jerusalem Post International Edition* (week ending 9 March 1991): 12; Paul Eidelberg, "The Idol of Self-Determination," *Jerusalem Post International Edition* (week ending 16 March 1991): 26.

15
Jordan and the Gulf War

Kamel S. Abu Jaber

The 1990 Gulf crisis and its aftermath will continue to severely challenge the Arab order, not only because of the defeat of Iraq, but also because of the psychological, political, military, and economic scars it inflicted. The multiplying effect of the war will be a destabilizing factor for the Middle Eastern region for some time. By leaving the Arab world so weakened in the presence of other regional powers such as Israel, Turkey, and Iran, the war created a power vacuum that will invite more instability. In addition, the war deepened and entrenched divisions in Arab ranks. The Arabs are no longer divided just along political (progressive centrist and reactionary) and economic (rich and poor) lines, but now are also totally dependent on outside powers for their military and political security.

In spite of the half-hearted efforts by Arab leaders to close ranks again and recreate the prewar fig leaf atmosphere of the Arab sister nations relating in a brotherly fashion, the cleavages created by the war will take time to bridge. Many observers, both Arabs and non-Arabs, believe the cleavages can never be bridged because certain Arabs "hired" foreign armies to destroy Iraq. The ruthless destruction was only matched by the later continued and deliberate espousal of the causes of various minorities within the country. The sudden and for the first time "strengthened" United Nations provided legitimacy to Western actions in collusion with Israel for the destruction of the last Arab power. And although few in the Arab world, including Jordan, condoned the annexation of Kuwait and, in fact, called for the restoration of Kuwait to its preinvasion status, the destruction of Iraq and continued visible Western presence was viewed as a punishment totally out of proportion to the original deed.

For whose benefit was the Arab world so totally reduced and exposed? Jordan never wanted nor could it condone the annexation of Kuwait. In fact, from the beginning it made its position on Iraq very clear: Iraq must evacuate the country and restore the original regime.

Yet while saying this, Jordan, ever cognizant of the real and present danger of Israel, wanted the restoration of the original situation to be brought about peacefully, and a solution worked out within the Arab system. Whatever reservations it may have had vis-à-vis Iraqi action or power were diminished when weighed against the imminent danger of Israel. Iraqi power, if it could be made to behave within the Arab system, was an absolute necessity to counterbalance the ever growing power of the Israeli Likud Party.

Further, Jordan's view of the crisis evolved against the background of a totally frustrated and thwarted Arab world that, since the advent of modern times, found itself not only challenged, but ridiculed, abused, and rendered helpless at every turn. Also in the background was the vision of the Arab world badly defeated in 1967 and the West's covert and overt glee over the event. With the help of the Zionist propaganda machine and the West the Arab world was turned into an "ugly pariah," an outlaw, and a terrorist on the international scene. So badly did the situation evolve that it became palatable for the West to resort to its moral double standard in treating Arab and Israeli actions. Jordan's position also evolved in the wake of the unresolved internal as well as external challenges and crises facing the Arab world: the faltering economies, the uneven development, the questions of political legitimacy and social justice, in addition to problems and crises in Palestine, Lebanon, Southern Sudan, and the Western Sahara. That is why Jordan, then and now, insisted on not isolating the Iraqi invasion of Kuwait from its milieu and historical background.

Jordan found itself in the midst of a crisis not of its own doing; its position was further complicated by conflicting commitments to the two opposing belligerent sides, neither willing to heed its advice. Among the immediate side effects of the crisis were the tens of thousands of refugees that poured into the country, adding further pressures to Jordan's limited resources and exasperating its already deep economic crisis. Although Jordan had experienced massive waves of forced refugees in 1948 and 1967, this refugee movement was truly a tragic one, not only of a more permanent Palestinian dimension but of a transitory multinational one as well. The number of Palestinian "returnees," the name given to Palestinian refugees forced out of Kuwait, the Gulf countries, and Saudi Arabia, was estimated at three to four hundred thousand.

The new status quo that emerged in the region, shattering its already fragile stability and its future course, emphasized the need for new and innovative thinking concerning how to deal with the new circumstances. Can the so-called Arab solidarity—the Arab system and the Arab League—be restored to any semblance of a working order? As weak and perhaps ineffective as they were before the conflict began, they did at least provide two services to the Arabs: first as an umbrella under which the Arab leaders met at the summit and second as a fig leaf of solidarity presented to the world. Skeptical as it may be, Jordan always viewed these two vehicles as important channels for the Arabs to communicate with each other and even infrequently decide on something. Now even these have disappeared, and earnest efforts are underway to revive them.[1]

Jordan's Position

Caught between powerful conflicting poles—its traditional pro-Western policies, its friendship and strong ties with the Gulf regimes and Saudi Arabia, and its equally strong relations with Iraq—Jordan decided to stand in the middle. Doing so, it hoped to influence the course of events in such a way as to avoid military conflict. Underestimating and perhaps unaware of the undercurrents of Western (principally British-U.S. and Israeli) long-term strategy, Jordan found itself in the unusual situation of being isolated with Iraq. In effect, the economic blockade applied to Jordan as well, making it a secondary target; its very survival hung in the balance for the entire duration of the crisis, from 2 August 1990 to March 1991.

From the beginning, Jordan realized the gravity of its position, which was complicated by pressures from within the country. From the time of the parliamentary elections of November 1989 and the restoration of parliamentary life in Jordan, popular pro-Iraqi sentiment was so strong it could not be ignored, even if the regime had wished to do so. On the mass street level, the view of Iraq in Jordan, in spite of the way Iraq dealt with its internal opposition, was of a rising, technologically advancing, nationalistic Arab state that offered to redress the military imbalance tipped in Israel's favor vis-à-vis the Arab world.

Jordan's population (approximately half Jordanian and half Palestinian) saw the rising Iraqi military power as the only hope of either liberating all of Palestine for the radical elements or, at least, forcing the Israelis to negotiate a viable, palatable, peaceful settlement for the moderate elements. In Jordan's democratic atmosphere, this strong sentiment was expressed in mass rallies, speeches, radio and television programs, parliamentary debates, conferences symposia, and magazine and newspaper articles; it could not be ignored by the regime.

Strengthening this sentiment and giving it more substance were numerous factors, chief among them Israeli intransigence and that country's total disregard for UN resolutions, international law, or the Geneva Conventions, which called for the protection of civilian populations under occupation. The latter could be seen in the ruthless treatment of the Palestinians in the course of their Intifada. Frustration deepened as the days and weeks of the Intifada turned into months and years, with the entire Western world not only turning a blind eye on the atrocities committed against the Palestinians, but finding excuses for why the Israeli soldiers committed such atrocities.

In the background, also, was the apparent Iraqi victory against Iran in its long war with that country. Many felt that this was the first time in many centuries that Arab soldiers had won a battle, and soon comparisons were made between Saddam Hussein and the legendary liberator of Jerusalem, Salah al-Din al-Ayubi. The powerful symbolism and imagery moved the masses to intensely support Iraq.

Also motivating the mass sentiment and, to a large extent, the officialdom of Jordan, was the failure of the United States as the sole influential international actor on the Middle Eastern scene to move Israel to the negotiating table.[2] Since 1967, U.S. support for Israel increased and developed into a political, military, technological, and economic alliance. The once symbiotic relationship developed into an organic one to the point where it became difficult, if not impossible, to distinguish who was influencing whom. The resultant despair at not having even a modicum of fair treatment turned not only to xenophobic anti-U.S. and anti-Western feeling, but also to stronger support for Iraq.

The United States and the West were further blamed for Egypt's withdrawal from the Arab-Israeli conflict and the signing of its peace treaty with Israel, leaving the Arab world exposed before the expanding Israeli military and political power. The allotment of blame as to who and what induced Egypt to abandon the cause of Palestine was laid at the doorstep of the United States, the argument being that the West, especially the United States, could not be trusted. This did nothing to help its traditional friends, such as Jordan, nor even those who revolved in its orbit such as Egypt: Iraq offered the only hope.

Linked to these motivating regional and international factors for

Jordan's behavior were other, uniquely Jordanian factors. In the years since the Iran-Iraq War, coordination and personal friendships developed between Jordanian and Iraqi leaders. The public could not miss the frequent, sometimes weekly visits exchanged at the top leadership level, nor could they miss the outpouring of mass media support in the newspapers and on the official radio and television stations. Jordan television devoted much of its newscasting to Iraqi news and other special events in addition to the transmission of weekly programs broadcast directly from Baghdad.

On the economic level, two developments should be noted, especially because they were important in influencing Jordanian behavior. The first concerned U.S. pressure on Jordan: the continued refusal to sell arms to Jordan following the signing of the Camp David Accords and the peace treaty between Egypt and Israel.[3] U.S. pressure on Jordan to follow the Egyptian pattern moved from the political to the economic level with U.S. aid decreasing in the 1980s to the point of being negligible. Further, the United States induced its Arab allies in the Gulf (with the exception of Saudi Arabia and Oman and to some extent the United Arab Emirates) to withhold aid from Jordan. These developments diminished the influence of these traditional donor countries on Jordan and also increased Jordan's dependency on Iraq. In fact, it was a matter of pride for Jordan to associate with a progressive, nationalistic Iraq and receive aid from it rather than from the United States and its associates in the region.

The Jordanian economy eventually became strongly intertwined with Iraq's. Iraq not only provided Jordan with oil at concessionary prices, but freely allowed Jordanian goods into the country. Busy with its war with Iran in the 1980s, Iraq needed much of the agricultural produce and many Jordanian manufactured products. By the time the crisis erupted in August 1990, nearly 40 percent of Jordan's economy depended on Iraq.[4] Iraq was a neighbor and a sister Arab Islamic country that was working toward the twin goal of Arab unity and the liberation of Palestine. Geographical contiguity and the facilitated transportation system added to the growing relationship. Many Jordanians felt that to support Iraq was a natural, nationalistic duty.

There were additional reasons for Jordan's initial position as well as its later refusal to support the condemnation of Iraq's invasion of Kuwait. U.S.-Western and Arab pressure on Jordan to condemn the invasion and annexation did not bear fruit primarily because Jordan did not wish to provide Arab cover for Western military action and intrusion into the area. It was also prompted by Jordan's desire to maintain a link between Iraq and the rest of the world even though it did not condone Iraq's action. Arab condemnation, Jordan felt, would take the whole matter out of Arab hands and provide a legitimate cover for whatever was contemplated for the area. Foreign intrusion would further weaken the entire Arab world and leave Israel in a position of military hegemony.[5] Jordan also feared for Iraq's military power, not only in its strategic depth against Israel, but as a check against possible Iranian or even Turkish designs. As events unfolded, Jordan's assessment was accurate of the consequences of a diminished Iraq not only internally but vis-à-vis Israel, Iran, and Turkey.

Jordan reasoned that an Iraqi defeat would create a regional power vacuum with untold consequences. Jordan was a central buffer state surrounded by powerful neighbors: Israel, Syria, Iraq, Turkey, and Iran. Any disturbance of this status quo, however much tension it might produce at times, could shatter the geopolitical and geostrategic balance beyond repair, perhaps at the expense of the very survival of the country.

Throughout the crisis and its aftermath, Jordan viewed with trepidation and much suspicion the personalization of the conflict against Saddam Hussein and the way in which the Western powers prevented any meaningful dialogue with Iraq. Not only was Western-Iraqi dialogue somehow excluded, but so was Arab-Iraqi dialogue. The entire Western world spoke of international law, principles of the UN, and the necessity of upholding certain moral values. The United Nations suddenly acquired teeth, and for a few weeks its secretary general became an important and serious political broker. Why were any of these lofty ideas not adhered to in the case of Israel?

Thus, Jordan's vision and its consequent stand emanated from highly complex factors, none of which were apparent to the sometimes overly simplistic explanations in the Western mass media. On the Iraqi-Kuwaiti level too, Jordan felt that, in the words of King Hussein, the crisis "did not come out of the blue."[6] Jordan's choice, considering its domestic, regional, and international situation, was not between good and evil, but between the lesser of two evils. In fact, Jordan was surprised at Western reaction to its stand: "My objective and that of Jordan was to avoid war and to reverse the occupation of Kuwait peacefully," said Hussein. Later he added, "Let me be very clear: we were against Iraq's action in Kuwait and we were against Iraqi intransigence in not taking any of the opportunities to move out of Kuwait and to resolve this question peacefully."[7]

In fact, Jordan could not take any other stand than to oppose the occupation of Kuwait as a matter of principle; it cultivated good relations with Kuwait and was a member of both the Arab League and the UN.[8] Ever cognizant of the conspiracies against its survival, Jordan could not but be against the forceful annexation of one state by another. Further, for Jordan to condone the annexation of Kuwait, either morally or legally, would deprive it of one of its most important arguments against the Israeli annexation of Arab lands in the West Bank, including Jerusalem, the Gaza Strip, the Golan Heights, and South Lebanon. Unlike the West, Jordan cannot back up and sustain a double standard. To do this would deprive it of strong arguments aimed at its very survival by the Israeli Likud government in their deliberately misleading call that "Jordan is Palestine."

Understandably, Jordan attempted to convince Iraq to withdraw peacefully from Kuwait, thus preventing the Arab and Western coalition from destroying it. Obviously, Iraq had other visions as to how it would deal with the crisis and was bent on following its own course. In answering a question addressed by this author to Crown Prince al-Hassan bin Talal in the second week of August as to whether Jordan was counseling Iraq to withdraw from Kuwait or suffer terrible consequences, he replied that Jordan was doing its best toward that end but that the Iraqis would not listen. Answering a similar question in July 1991, King Hussein replied, "I was frank and honest, right from the word go. If I didn't succeed it is to my sadness and regret."[9] Iraq played into the hands of its enemies, providing them with an excuse to strike at it under an Arab-Islamic cover, and its military effort was largely funded by Arab money.

Jordan's attempts to diffuse the situation and contain it within the Arab fold must be viewed against this background. During the two decades prior to the eruption of the Gulf crisis, especially since the mid-1970s, Jordan was forced, ironically, by its traditional allies (the West and conservative Arab regimes), into an isolated position in the hope of forcing it to succumb and sign a Camp David-type treaty with Israel. The pressure not only failed to coerce Jordan, but instead pushed it closer toward Iraq, a position that would not have been anathema under normal circumstances. When Iraq predictably acted violently against its version of Kuwait's behavior, Jordan found itself in a precarious predicament. Since its establishment, Jordan, because of its paucity of natural resources, its refugee burdens, and its security needs, as well as its central geostrategic position as a buffer, always needed a powerful economic and military ally. To put it bluntly, Jordan's position is determined to a very large extent by its geography and demography.

But for the traditional centrism and moderation of its leaders, especially its king, the country could have had a more volatile, radical, and militant complexion. Its moderation and following of a cautious, rational course had been the greatest "hidden strength" of the country and were instrumental in giving Jordan its uniquely liberal socioeconomic and political experiment, and allowing it to face and survive the successive crises it faced over the decades.

Throughout the Gulf crisis, Jordan insisted that it had not abandoned either its traditional moderation or its friends. As the militarily and economically weakest link in the chain of states of the Middle East, it could not then, nor can it now, ignore its powerful neighbors. By personalizing the conflict between Saddam Hussein and George Bush, Jordan felt that both Iraq and the United States had painted themselves into a corner from which neither could escape easily. Jordan's choice between the two sides was an impossible one made more difficult by the accusations of the Western mass media that it had abandoned its traditional friends, a charge that Jordan continues to deny.[10] Internally the country was liberalizing and broadening the base of the regime. The November 1989 elections brought in a parliament that included many fundamentalists, leftists, various radicals, nationalists, and many independents.[11] Their vocal support of Iraq against Western aggression could not be ignored even if the regime wished to do so. In the words of Ann Lesch "the Jordanian public and government were predisposed to support Iraq, given their yearning for a strong Arab leader who would stand up to the West, defend them from Israeli attack, and compel the oil-rich regimes to use their wealth to support Arab causes."[12] It was also true that the king had "given the impression" of sympathizing with Iraq. Days after the Iraqi invasion, the king told NBC News that Saddam Hussein was "a person to be trusted . . . an Arab patriot in the eyes of many."[13]

Later, however, it appeared that the king was not happy with what he called "Iraq's intransigence in not taking any of the opportunities to resolve the question peacefully." It was also revealed that he sent President Hussein "a very tough letter . . . in September [1990] but that the latter did not heed the advice."[14] And, in discussing his support of Iraq, the king said, "this is the second time that this happened in my life. In 1967 I was sitting on the beach in Aqaba when I heard the news that the late-Egyptian President Jamal Abdul Nasser had put his troops in Sinai and closed the Gulf of Aqaba. . . . We are still suffering until now."[15] In the same interview, he added that he had not spoken with Saddam Hussein even by telephone since the first few days after the occupation of Kuwait.[16]

Obviously then, Jordan's position was grossly misunderstood. Whether the misunderstanding was deliberate on the part of the West, especially through its mass media apparatus, remains to be seen. True to its traditional moderate and conciliatory tone, Jordan, risking its very survival, stuck to its cause, hoping that, in the words of King Hussein, the truth about Jordan and its people would soon be revealed and others would realize their mistakes.[17]

Beyond the Crisis

One year later, commemorating the first anniversary of the attack on Iraq, Secretary of Defense Richard Cheney stated that the use of force against Iraq for a second time could not be ruled out unless that country fully complied with UN Security Council resolutions.[18] Saddam Hussein was still in power, Kuwait was rebuilding itself, and Shamir was as coy as ever vis-à-vis any meaningful negotiations with the Palestinians.

Although it is obvious that the use of force against Iraq accomplished much for Israel and the West, it pushed the Arab world further back from entering the modern world and communicating with it. Iraq unleashed powerful forces and fearful passions when it invaded Kuwait. It challenged the borders marked by the colonial powers after World War I and brought into question the political legitimacy of the regimes that were then established. The Gulf War prompted many questions: Are the borders laid down by colonial interests and the regimes untouchable? Is Arab unity feasible, and how can it be accomplished? Who owns Arab wealth (oil), especially when it is contemplated that the colonial powers made sure that wealth remained in the hands of the minority with poverty the lot of the majority, making it easy to control both? Are the more populous states on whose shoulders rests the burden of maintaining Arab national security entitled to a share in this wealth? Should not the smaller but wealthier states carry part of the burden albeit only financially? Why is not at least part of the Arab surplus money, invested and sometimes squandered in the West, invested in the Arab world? Is it because the Arabs remain divided into the poor and the rich, the have and the have-nots? Whose oil is it? These questions unleashed by the Gulf crisis challenge not only the West but the Arab body politic as well.

Although leadership in most Arab countries acted one way, popular sentiment still searches for reasonable answers. To be sure, the crisis made for very strange bedfellows. "Progressive" and so-called "reactionary" regimes cohabited easily, the old rhetoric relegated to the dustbin of history. New alignments and new fragmentations emerged, and with them the search for ways of coping with the new circumstances. Who is friend and who is foe? It is as if the entire Arab world, already disoriented and in search of itself, was placed in a giant mixer.

How does a small, problem-ridden country cope with the new circumstances? Every time Jordan hoped that a new plateau of stability was approaching, another problem shattered the situation. The old friends, whether in the Arab world, in the region, or in the West, are still not happy with Jordan. In the West, they feign astonishment and even dismay at Jordan's behavior, choosing deliberately to misunderstand that a small, weak country such as Jordan must play games to survive. Jordan could not have acted in any other way. Too many powerful forces from within would have torn its fabric asunder. What would have happened, for instance, had Jordan condemned Iraq and invited foreign troops into its territory? Would Iraq have remained aloof, or would it have crossed through Jordan on the way to liberate Jerusalem, an idea that is very appealing not only within Jordan but elsewhere in the Arab world?

Under the circumstances, Jordan's behavior, questioned by many within Jordan who thought it should have militarily involved itself on the side of Iraq, was designed to assure the country's survival and prevent the further spread of the conflict. Although the West continuously preached the benefits of the spread of democracy in various parts of the world, it hypocritically criticized Jordan for responding to its own internal popular pressure in support of Iraq.

The crisis created new wounds and deepened old ones in the Arab body. Yet, it brought new realizations to the fore. For one thing, it starkly revealed how limited Arab independence and Arab scope of action are. The Arab world, whether for or against Iraq, was easily manipulated by outside forces and the entire Arab world had no real friends or allies either regionally or internationally, especially in the West. The Western powers are still willing to resort to classic military action and although Western military forces were physically removed from the region following independence, the forces were simply moved to ships and bases close by or to their home countries in the West, always ready to return quickly.

With the wounds came possibilities. If Jordan could rehabilitate its relationship with the United States, its traditional ally, it could weather the crisis and look toward a better future. One of the most important lessons for Jordan, which may help in honing its sense of survival, is that Arab and Islamic solidarity slogans are no more than the desert mirages of Arabia. When the chips were down, every Arab state, regardless of brotherly declamations to the contrary, acted purely from self interests.

Power, Jordan realized, resides with the powerful and, in the words of Adnan Abu Odeh, political advisor to King Hussein, "the entire world seems to have accepted American leadership, even the Europeans who hold contrary private opinions have surrendered." The implication is that Jordan should follow suit. Jordan would be happier to live in a world of pan-America if a peaceful settlement of the Palestinian situation could be accomplished. Toward that end, it continues to push for a greater U.S. role in the region. At the same time, it views any further isolation and possible destruction of Iraq as dangerous to the stability of the whole region vis-à-vis Israel, Turkey, and Iran.

For a small country, the situation cannot be black or white. Such a reduction is not just hypocritical but unnatural as well. It is this vision that caused Jordan to follow the course it did and now impels it to pursue reconciliation. No sooner had the military operations against Iraq ended than King Hussein declared in one of his speeches to the Arab nation that it should turn a new page based on "re-conciliation."[19]

In a land where myth and reality have been interlocked since time immemorial, Jordan's style and conduct is only part of the scene. This is an area of shifting ideas and conflicts. While the people involved declare their versions of the truth in absolute, eternal terms clear to themselves alone, the Jordanian leadership learned that only foggy shades of grey exist. Today, on the intellectual as well as the official levels in the Arab world, there is an earnest search to "purify the Arab atmosphere." Jordan is keen to restore the Arab "order," or disorder as the case may be, that existed in the area prior to the crisis. The Amman-based Arab Thought Forum held a symposium in Cairo in September 1991 on precisely this theme.

When the dust settles, questions will continue to arise in Jordanian minds. How was Kuwait, ever so careful, cool, and calculating in its relations with others, made to behave the way it did, ignoring Iraq's pleas, threats, and the presence of over one hundred thousand Iraqi troops on its borders? Was it the presence of U.S. flags over its ships or was it given assurances to ignore Iraq's angry protests over the Rumailah oil field, the construction on the Iraqi border territory, and the deliberate depression of oil prices on the world market?

Iraq's behavior, to be sure, was more predictable considering the nature of its leadership and its ambitious pan-Arab Ba'athist ideology, as well as its euphoric sense of triumph after the war with Iran. Yet, how was Iraq lured to send its armies unprotected into the desert at Hafr al-Batin? Ambassador April Glaspie's testimony, despite its later elaborations, does not give satisfactory answers, and the Bush administration remained silent.

How did the entire international scene become so suddenly receptive to what took place under the aegis of a UN that hitherto was paid scant attention by the very actors who now suddenly proclaimed their adherence to its principles? This occurred, coincidentally, with the collapse of the Soviet communist system and the ensuing Soviet Jewish immigration to Israel.

Who induced whom and who paid the price? Were both Kuwait and Iraq the victims of a pre-arranged, well-thought-out, well-executed and -planned Desert Shield: an operation designed to place majority control over the flow, price, and distribution of oil in the hands of the British-U.S. partnership at the international level, leaving Israel in a position of regional military and political hegemony? When were the plans made? Were its antecedents the various doctrines issued by most U.S. presidents since Franklin D. Roosevelt to protect the oil of Arabia as a "vital interest of the United States" as well as the U.S. Rapid Deployment Force constructed in the early 1980s? Was the whole affair from start to finish a historical accident, the "daughter of its moment" as the Arabs say, or was it a well-laid-out plan awaiting the right movement to come to fruition?

Scholars will continue to search for answers to these and many other questions in the decades to come, especially as the Arab world becomes weaker. The structural internal weakness will be due to the inability of its component parts, either individually or collectively, to cope with internal or external problems in a rational manner. For

the present, Jordan, like every other small country, must bow its
head before the Desert Storm. From the beginning, Jordan guessed
that should the crisis get out of Arab hands, the entire Arab world
would be reduced and marginalized, jeopardizing its very survival as
a reasonable political presence. The crisis quickly metamorphosed
from a crisis of borders to that of survival—*Azamat Hudud ila
azamat Wujud.*

Addendum, from His Majesty King Hussein's Speech to the Nation, 5 November 1992.[20]

> We can rightfully ask ourselves about the measure of our
> achievements in the face of the national setbacks and upheav-
> als that have beset our nation and world in these turbulent
> times. We thank God that we have achieved a great deal. We
> have established in this land the foundations of a modern dem-
> ocratic state. This was due to God's bounty in the first place,
> and also to the positive response of this noble people, who, re-
> gardless of their origins and habitats, have been aware of the
> message, cognizant of their roles, and conscious of the chal-
> lenges they have had to meet. It has likewise been due to a un-
> ified vision shared by the leadership and the people over a
> whole century. We should strive for a further strengthening of
> these foundations and for a further release of energy. We
> should build up a new life in this democratic climate, so that
> Jordan could remain a land of the free and the proud who
> bow their heads only to God; a land of responsibility whose
> people recognize balance in all things, especially between rights
> and obligations; a land of credibility that is capable of forgoing
> ahead in times of deepest darkness and profoundest challenge;
> a land of integrity enjoyed by everyone of its own citizens as
> well as by the free who seek its protection and by the true who
> seek to join their people's quest to preserve the nation's right to
> life and to lead it out of its disarray, weakness, despair and loss
> and forge a unified, free, dignified and immortal nation.
>
>   We have passed through a difficult time, but you have been
> capable of rising to the level of your responsibilities. I have
> been with you as you strove to prevent the collapse of the na-
> tional edifice. I have been with you and among you as with
> your blood you drove away the darkness of the night. Because

of your courage, I consider myself all the more proud, all the more strong and all the more capable of providing support. I have known you to be the bravest of people in the defence of right and freedom. I have lived among you as you clasped to your hearts brethren of yours when they were rocked by tragedy of shaken by misfortune. I shouldered your cares in my youth and early manhood. And here I am now observing the generations which are moving to build a democratic Jordan, a Jordan true to its nation's ideals. I have observed how they derived their vision and mode of action from the message of the revolt, from the constitution and the chapter—without any recklessness, fanaticism, upheaval or overbearing behavior. And we recall a time when we were waging our battles alone—weaving the flag of a union between the two banks, Arabizing the army command, establishing universities and house of learning, setting up national institutions of which we are truly proud, and rallying "La crème de la crème" among our religious and legal minds to establish our pioneering civil law based on Muslim Sharia. We also recall a time when we held fast against intellectual disarray, conspiracy, and lack of responsibility when we stood up to those who infringed the rights of the Arab citizen, denigrated the reverence of the great message, played fast and loose, aborted opportunities for freedom and growth, and willfully tampered with a nation's unity. We remember how we fought the nation's wars even when we had been kept in the dark about the date of battle, how we shed our blood on the plains of Karama, how we told the nation on that rosy morning that we had the upper hand, that the road to Jerusalem lay in our sacrifice, our river, our unity and our determined steadfastness, and that we would never surrender one iota of our nation's rights—from the Arab sea to the last outpost to the distant sea.

These, then, are the traits of our common journey of Jordan's immortal March, rooted in the nation's spirit, its martyrs and its all-engulfing challenges. I am proud that throughout my entire life it has also been my own journey. Let us together launch an appeal to our beloved nation—one that would renew itself across distance, direction and time—to stand up to the ambitious and to the renegades; to protect its capitals from those who would advocate tyranny or who would tie the destiny of nations to individuals; and to open wide the gates of freedom, democracy, pluralism and respect for human rights. Our own model is open to the whole nation. Let them come to our universities, our institutions, our schools, and our newspapers. Let them support this proud national voice, for the sake of the entire nation, and not for our sake. Let there be established in Amman a center for the study of freedom, democracy and human rights in the Arab world. For the light of righteousness must wipe out the dark of wrongfulness. And *bani hashem* must be the vanguard, for their grandfather Hashem was the first to forge a pact among them and protect the caravans of quarish. And their grandfather Abdul Muttaleb was the first to provide Mecca with fresh water and to paint Al-Ka'ba in Gold. Their history is a record of sacrifice for their nation. Never did they seek personal gain or the glory of palaces. Whenever they set out, it was to support their divine faith—true to their pious spirit and heedful of the honor bestowed upon them by God's holy book: "And Allah only wishes to remove all abomination from you, ye members of the family, to make you pure and spotless." I say this because some are prone to forgetfulness. The blood of our martyrs is sacred. Our ancestors' vision is constantly before us, and our struggle is permanently engraved on the strong arms of our people. Along with our nation, we have remonstrated against those who have done wrong, have guided those who have erred back to the fold, and have helped those in need. We have refused to support wrongful occupation or liberation that infringes on sovereignty. We have warned against the designs and conspiracies of the foreigners, and have always sought God's favors. My conscience has been truly vindicated in that I have held fast to the pledge I made to you forty years ago when I said: "I have pledged to shun all repose in working for your prosperity and building our dear homeland, in which we live and in which we shall die." From that moment, I have consecrated myself to the people of this blessed land; to the concept that the Hashemite Jordanian state is the vanguard of a new Arab era imbued with the scent of freedom, justice and democracy; and to the view that the Jordanian people perceive the dream to be at hand while others see it as distant prospect. I have fully believed that the Jordanians represented the legitimacy of the great revolt through the blood of their martyrs shed over an area from Bab al-wad to Karama, from the Yarmouk to

Tafila, and through their concern for the poor, for orphans and for prisoners of war. I am certain that they will be amply rewarded for their noble endeavors.

Fellow Citizens,
Beloved Brethren,

No sooner had one journey ended than another began. The history of this land has been one of tireless activity, since the time the Martyr King Sharif Abdullah Ibn Al-Hussein laid down the cornerstone of the illustrious salt school, presented the flag to the first battalion of our Arab legion and recited the *fatiha* in honor of the first martyr. Of the army the martyr king had said, "This is an army which does not shame its commanders, does not disappoint its generals, does not let down its people, does not hold back, does not shirk the task of protecting its rights and those of the its country. The army is only an army. It is the country's sword, its shield, its pride, its voice, its whip, the bane of its enemies and the apple of its king's eye." It has been so since the time the king—God rest his soul— declared the enlightened message of Jordan, where no one is stronger than the oppressed until their rights are restored, or weaker than the oppressors until their rights are taken away from them, where its people stand united while others are plagued by disarray; where they advance while others hold back; where they keep up the struggle to ensure that none in the land remains poor, afraid or downtrodden.

Notes

1. Immediately after the end of hostilities against Iraq, almost every Arab leader, as well as the newspapers, began speaking of "closing the Arab ranks" again or of "purifying the Arab atmosphere."

2. See, for example, Ann M. Lesch, "Contrasting Reaction to the Persian Gulf Crisis: Egypt, Syria, Jordan and the Palestinians," *Middle East Journal* (50)1 (Winter, 1991): 31–33, 44.

3. Stanley Reed, "Jordan and the Gulf Crisis," *Foreign Affairs* 69 (Winter 1990–1991): 23.

4. *Ibid.*, 24.

5. This view was expressed by Adnan Abu Odeh, special political advisor to King Hussein, in his lecture, "The Gulf Crisis," World Affairs Council, Amman (12 January 1991).

6. Lesch, "Contrasting Reaction," 44.

7. Interview with King Hussein, "The Great Survivor," *Time* (22 July 1991): 14.

8. Abu Odeh, "The Gulf Crisis."

9. *Time*, "The Great Survivor," 14.

10. *Ibid.* In this interview the king stated that Jordan would soon issue a white paper explaining its position.

11. For the results of the 1989 elections and the composition of the Parliament, see my study with Shireen Hunter "The 1989 Jordanian Parliamentary Elections," *Orient* 1 (March 1990).

12. *Lesch*, "Contrasting Reaction," 44.

13. Reed, "Jordan and the Gulf Crisis," 21.

14. *Time*, "The Great Survivor," 14.

15. See *Jordan Times* (16 July 1991): 1.

16. See *al-Dustur* (17 July 1991): 15.

17. *Ibid.*

18. *CNN Television News* (2 August 1991).

19. *Al-Duster* (2 March 1991): 7.

20. This chapter was completed before Abu Jaber was appointed Minister of Foreign Affairs in October 1991. To update the chapter, the editors excerpted a section from a speech to the nation given on 5 November 1992 by His Majesty King Hussein I.

16
Syria, the Kuwait War, and the New World Order

Eberhard Kienle

Damascus and the End of the Cold War

As the second cold war subsided and official declarations on its death were ritually repeated by politicians in the East and West, international cooperation and the peaceful resolution of conflicts appeared to be the hallmarks of the coming age. After leaving Afghanistan, the Soviet army began its withdrawal from the Eastern European countries, the two German states were united, and various regional conflicts, in which the two superpowers had opposed each other by proxy, were diffused. The two Yemens merged before the two Germanys, and tension eased in Central America and South Africa. After subtle signs that the Arab-Israeli conflict could not escape this trend, the Madrid conference ushered in the most spectacular changes outside of Europe and North America.

In Europe, the "Soviet bloc" collapsed as most of its member states emulated the political and economic systems of the liberal democracies in the West.[1] The Soviet Union began to democratize and introduce some elements of market economy, thus initiating a process that President Hafiz al-Asad of Syria once defined as a belated version of his "corrective movement" (*al-Haraka al-tashihiyya*) of 1970. Long before the regime changed in Moscow, the economic decline and moral erosion of what once was seen as communism helped to remodel the world in the image and interest of the much celebrated "West," which stands not so much for a geographical entity, but for a specific version of capitalism with its salient economic, social, political, and cultural features (bearing in mind, of course, the rather unsophisticated character of these categories). Almost ipso facto this process seemed to entail less openly conflictual relations between states.

On the surface, there was the chance for what President George Bush called an "era in which the nations of the world, East and

West, North and South, could prosper and live in harmony."[2] The harmony that epitomized the new world order as conceived by Bush was obviously disrupted by the Iraqi invasion of Kuwait in August 1990. But another, less publicized, aspect of the new world order was in danger as well. The danger came from the emergence of nuisance powers able to challenge or disrupt the new world order. The West had just contributed to the large-scale erosion of the East, and its leaders were increasingly unable to oppose Western policies and interests. At last, opposition to shaping and reshaping the world in accordance with rules laid down in the West seemed to be minimal. This view did not take into account Saddam Husayn, who, by invading Kuwait, asserted his claim to pursue interests out of tune with the new harmony. Thus Iraqi action challenged not only the expectation that conflicts between states would be settled more peacefully, but the growing sense of comfortable hegemony prevailing in the West as well. The liberation of Kuwait reasserted the West's claim to ultimate rule-making and enforcement, but only because, due to developments elsewhere, this new world order was already in gestation.

The lessons of the Gulf War for the new world order were twofold: Conflicts should be resolved by peaceful means, and Western claims and interests should be defended. As for the future prospect of peaceful conflict resolutions, the *reconquista* of Kuwait should serve as an example to deter future Saddam Husayns from settling disputes with their neighbors by force, but because it was a military enterprise, it may have nipped in the bud this version of a new world order. At any rate, its value as a deterrent did not seem to apply to major military powers should they try to impose their aims by force (an action many Arabs felt occurred during the recent crisis). Indeed, the need to settle disputes peacefully was not even considered in areas as near as Damascus, where during the military buildup in the Gulf the regime decided to launch its final offensive against General Michel 'Awn in Lebanon.

It appears more rewarding to look at the impact of the war on the new world order from the second point of view—Western claims and interests. With regard to Syria, the question is to determine how the war prompted that country's regime to reformulate its policies toward the Western winners of the cold war. On the surface at least, it appears that such a shift occurred when Syria agreed to military action against Iraq and even participated in the coalition.

One can argue that, unlike its counterpart in Baghdad, the Asad regime understood the implications of the end of the cold war. This understanding, together with a number of other (partly connected) considerations, led the regime to seek closer relations with the West prior to the Kuwait crisis. At that time, however, there were limits to such a rapprochement because the Western powers continued to suspect Damascus of sponsoring or protecting international terrorists. In the United States, moreover, the less conciliatory aspects of Syrian policy in the Arab-Israeli conflict continued to be seen as more pertinent than its accommodating features. In this conjuncture the Kuwait crisis came as a godsend and enabled Damascus to demonstrate its willingness to play the new game. Hence the crisis merely provided an opportunity, but not the cause, for Syria to openly support the new world order. Syria seized this opportunity, but did not make unnecessary concessions and, in the process, sought to reshape to its advantage the regional order in the Middle East.

Siding with Kuwait and Saudi America

The Syrian regime was the first in the Arab world to condemn the Iraqi invasion of Kuwait on 2 August 1990 and to ask for the immediate withdrawal of Iraqi forces.[3] A few days later, Damascus clearly condemned Baghdad's decision to annex the emirate. At the same time, President Asad was the driving force behind the Arab emergency summit, which began its deliberations in Cairo on 9 August, a day after the annexation. Not surprisingly, from the beginning of the crisis his regime supported all relevant UN resolutions, including Resolution 678, which authorized the use of force against Iraq. At the Cairo summit, Syria, Egypt, and Morocco committed troops to the defense of Saudi Arabia. Soon, a small Syrian contingent arrived and on 10 September Damascus announced the dispatch of an armored division. Although Syrian officials repeatedly insisted that their troops would not move into Iraq, they did not rule out the possibility that beyond the defense of Saudi Arabia they might participate in the liberation of Kuwait.[4] Either for logistical reasons or because Damascus sought firm financial commitments on the part of Riyadh, the bulk of Syrian forces—an armored division of some 15,000 troops—did not arrive in Saudi Arabia until early November. They took up positions on the Iraqi border and successfully engaged Iraqi troops that crossed into Saudi Arabia during the war; after Iraq's rout in the ground war, they moved into Kuwait alongside other allied troops.

In addition, the Syrian regime vigorously enforced the embargo and declined an Iraqi request, presented in person by the oil minister, to reopen the trans-Syrian oil pipeline. Finally, Syria allowed Kurdish and other Iraqi opposition movements to operate from Damascus and to convene a major congress in Beirut that led to the approval of a charter calling for the overthrow of the Husayn regime and for a pluralistic, democratic Iraq.

During the crisis, many Syrians disagreed with the government line. There were unconfirmed rumors of riots in some towns in the east of the country, and leading intellectuals and lawyers published communiqués opposing the use of military forces against Iraq. For many Syrians, it was unacceptable to participate in a war against another Arab country, particularly against Iraq, whose president appeared to be the one Arab leader standing up to Israeli intransigence. Not that Syrians ignored the tyrannical nature of his regime, but as many of them put it, he was, at least, an Arab tyrant. Worse, in this war Syrians fought alongside Americans who had been castigated over the years as imperialists and allies of Zionism.

But as usual, such misgivings did not affect the resolve of the Syrian regime. On the contrary, President Asad clearly savored the visits by U.S. envoys to Damascus, among them Secretary of State James Baker. These contacts were crowned by the talks between President Asad and President Bush in Geneva on 23 November 1991, which brought a great degree of diplomatic rehabilitation to a regime condemned and ostracized as one of the masterminds behind international terrorism. During the crisis, contacts were also intensified with other Arab countries, especially Egypt and Saudi Arabia, as well as with Iran, from which Damascus emerged as one of the centerpieces of a new regional and Arab order. Such a "new Arab order" was explicitly referred to in the Damascus Declaration of 6 March 1991 in which Syria and Egypt agreed to contribute to the defense of Saudi Arabia and the other member states of the Gulf Cooperation Council (GCC) in exchange for economic cooperation—a euphemism for financial support.[5] The mere fact that this declaration was made in Damascus and not in Cairo points to the success of Syrian diplomacy during the crisis; that it largely remained *lettre morte* does not disprove this assertion.

Syria's New Strength

Thanks to its choices during the crisis, the Syrian regime found its post-crisis position strengthened in various ways. Through rapprochement with the West and the Gulf states, the crisis enabled Damascus to remove the remaining obstacles to its domination of Lebanon. Participation in the anti-Iraq coalition allowed Damascus to evict General 'Awn from his last positions and bring an end to the de facto partition of the country. This led to the full implementation of the Ta'if agreement of October 1989[6] and the Syro-Lebanese Treaty of Friendship, Cooperation, and Coordination of May 1991,[7] which formalized Syrian overlordship over the country. By the same token, the pacification of Lebanon and its transformation into a client state consolidated and even improved Syria's strategic position vis-à-vis Israel as well as other Arab states.

Thus, the short-term occupation of Kuwait by Iraq resulted in the long-term domination of Lebanon by Syria. Ironically, although its action was intended to strengthen Iraq, it led to its demise as the major Arab power and resulted in the rise of Syria, its chief competitor for regional influence and hegemony for over two decades.[8] Not only did this further weaken parts of the Syrian opposition, which received support from Iraq, but it enabled Damascus to act more freely on the regional scene. Syria could now pursue its policies toward Israel and the Palestinians in a more flexible manner and without interference from Baghdad. The latter's permanent attempts to outbid Syria in this matter would hardly have helped in convening the Madrid conference. Now, however, Baghdad could not exert any such pressure to thwart Syrian concessions. To some extent, however, Syria may use its new strength to avoid such compromises. Damascus, for the time being, succeeded in establishing itself as an unavoidable interlocutor for external powers ranging from the United States to the USSR (now Russia) whose consent and assent is needed for the settlement of the Arab-Israeli conflict.[9]

In purely financial terms, the dispatch of troops to Saudi Arabia earned the Syrian regime some U.S. $1 billion during the crisis alone.[10] Compared to an estimated budgetary expenditure of approximately U.S. $5.52 billion in the exercise of 1990,[11] this was a considerable amount of additional cash. Moreover, during the crisis, the Syrian treasury benefitted from the temporary rise of oil prices, which over the second half of 1990 reached an average of roughly U.S. $26 per barrel, compared to about US $18 per barrel before the crisis. Oil revenue increased substantially thanks to the increase in exports from some 130,000 barrels per day in 1989 to about 210,000 barrels per day in 1990; almost half of this was high quality light crude.[12] Taking into account the income from refined products,

Syrian oil revenue (before deductions for oil companies) rose from about U.S. $1.25 billion to U.S. $2.4 billion. Finally, the European Community released grants and loans worth U.S. $190 million that were frozen in 1986 after a British court concluded that Syria was involved in the aborted attack against an Israeli passenger plane. Payments under the fourth European Community financial protocol were frozen by the European parliament in early 1992 because of continued human rights violations in Syria, but several member states of the European Community continued bilateral aid.[13] Over the same period, Syria suffered the loss of up to U.S. $130 million per annum in remittances from nationals working in Kuwait and elsewhere in the Gulf, but the victims were individuals and families, not the regime.

The additional income resultant from renting out troops and selling more oil during the crisis, in all likelihood, would not continue after the defeat of Iraq. Used as capital to yield profits at a later stage, however, the monies accrued during the crisis would strengthen the regime's position. One way to achieve this aim was to invest the funds in military aircraft, tanks, and other weaponry systems. Such use had been rumored since the end of the war, but it is difficult to check. Czechoslovakian tanks, as well as Korean and Chinese missiles, were ordered or actually bought.[14] The response from the former USSR, once Syria's chief supplier, to rumors of recent purchasing plans remained ambiguous; some sources even affirmed that it was negative.[15] Additional military investment would enable Damascus to fulfill its commitments under the Damascus Declaration and, provided its services were in demand, to benefit from further financial fallout. Secondly, it would strengthen Syria vis-à-vis Israel and hence enable it to protect its territory and economy as well as its new position in Lebanon. By the same token, it would enhance its bargaining position in the yet unconcluded "peace process" and possibly amortize military expenditure through additional material gains exceeding the amount initially invested.

Although some financial pay-offs from the crisis ceased, others continued and some may reappear. With its new image as a conservative power in the region, Syria remains eligible for European and other overseas aid. The same applies to Arab aid, even though the patterns of its disbursement are more erratic. If the Damascus Declaration ever results in a more institutionalized defense arrangement, the services provided by Syrian troops would again be charged to Gulf customers.

In addition, the reconstruction of Lebanon is occurring after the country's pacification. As illustrated by various contracts for the re-building of downtown Beirut, these efforts afford the Syrian regime and those individuals closely associated with it new opportunities to siphon off part of the funds flowing into this new protectorate. The flows of cash and capital will continue to provide resources for Leb-anon, even though they are bound to remain limited because of the continued conflict with Israel and the nature of the Pax Siriana.

Its enhanced position could make Syria more reluctant to abide by the rules of a new world order that was shaped without its con-tribution. Memories of the regime's past involvement in terrorist ac-tivities, alleged and real, seem to confirm such fears, as much as the lingering idea that Israel wants peace and the Arabs do not.

Apart from the questionable truth of these conceptions, however, it must be noted that, historically, Syrian interests converged with Western interests. The initial intervention in the Lebanese civil war in 1976 attested to that as much as policies vis-à-vis the Palestine Liberation Organization, not the least of which was the expulsion of Arafat and his troops from Tripoli in Lebanon in 1985. First as Minister of Defense and then as President, Hafiz al-Asad also stopped *fida'yun* infiltrations into Israel from Syria. Furthermore, he accepted UN Security Council Resolutions 242 and 338, which imply the recognition of Israel's right to exist as a state, and con-tinued to recognize their validity at a time when the Likud govern-ment in Jerusalem denied all substance of the resolutions.

Nor did Syria's position toward Israel become more inflexible after the end of the Gulf War. On the contrary, Damascus repeatedly welcomed aspects of U.S. peace plans. During a visit by the Soviet Foreign Minister Alexander Bessmertnykh in the spring of 1991, Syrian officials and media referred to a "peace conference" without insisting that this be an "international peace conference" under UN auspices. In his letter to President Bush dated 14 July 1991, Presi-dent Asad largely accepted the U.S. proposals for a regional peace conference, which indeed came close to direct negotiations with Is-rael.[16] Soon after, Damascus accepted an invitation to the Madrid conference in autumn 1991 and Foreign Minister Faruq al-Shara"s address at the opening session did not prevent the Syrian delegation from adopting a constructive attitude once the Likud was voted out of office. Far from calling for a Palestinian state, Damascus ulti-mately accepted a transitory period of some three to five years, after which the Occupied Territories should accede to their final status.

Except for the demand that this final status be defined from the outset, the proposal resembled the Shamir and Baker plan.[17] Damascus certainly purchased or attempted to purchase arms from the Soviet Union, China, and elsewhere, but so did Israel from the United States.[18]

Hence, there was no reason to believe that Syria opposed an equitable settlement of the outstanding differences with Israel even though, like all political actors, it sought to defend its interests as thoroughly as possible. Due to its relatively improved position, Syria could challenge Israeli interests in well-defined instances, but always within the general acceptance of the rules governing the new world order.

Continuing Weakness

Asad's cautious policy in the aftermath of the war seems to be derived, as always, from a realistic assessment of the resources available to his regime. Although reinforced by the outcome of the war, the regime's strength remains limited and in some respects precarious and vulnerable.

First, it is worth noting that the recent war did not make Syria as strong as Iraq had been prior to the Iran-Iraq War. Syria thus cannot reasonably aspire to the role played by Iraq in its golden age. The resources available to the Syrian regime are more limited than those that were available to the rulers in Baghdad and that would, under more fortunate circumstances, be available to them now. Unlike Iraq, Syria is not a major oil producing country, although its production and revenue have increased considerably over the last two years. Syria's entire production of just over 400,000 barrels per day in 1990 (to some 550,000 barrels per day in 1992)[19] amounted to roughly 10 percent of Iraq's export capacity by the end of 1989.[20] While Syrian revenue from the combined export of crude oil and refined products reached about U.S. $2.4 billion in 1990 (including temporary price rises, cf. supra), Iraqi revenue in 1989, calculated on a price of U.S. $18 per barrel, amounted to US $26.28 billion for crude oil alone, thus corresponding to its income from oil in 1980, before the war against Iran. With an oil revenue exceeding U.S. $5 billion per annum since 1974, the Iraqi regime could launch important investment and military programs at a time when Syria still had to spend foreign currency to import crude oil as well as refined products. In the absence of any major income from other industries, Syria was at an obvious disadvantage in accumulating capital.

This difference was reflected not only in the developmental effort but also in the military expenditure and strength of the two countries. Though clearly unsustainable in the face of more than U.S. $70 billion of foreign debt, Iraqi defense expenditures in 1988 amounted to an estimated U.S. $12.87 billion while, in the same year, Syria's were budgeted at a maximum of U.S. $1.6 billion.[21] Qualitative implications for Syria were a smaller armed force and the absence of any significant military industry or locally developed weaponry systems, be they missiles or nuclear devices.

Generally weaker than Iraq had been, Syria now must accept the precarious nature of its new strength. The Damascus Declaration may not be implemented, as the oil states prefer military cooperation with the United States, France, and Great Britain. Moreover, if accrued, any additional revenue from troops stationed in the Gulf or in protection money from Lebanon could be termed as rent. It would not be premised on any significant degree of productive activity and thus threatens to reinforce, or at least consolidate, parasitic rentier tendencies.[22] Such economies based on "circulation" (as is already largely the case in Syria) would obviously be highly dependent and vulnerable.[23]

Although financial transfers may continue to keep the regime afloat temporarily, the Kuwait crisis quite obviously did not lead to any improvement in the country's economic structure.[24] Despite the limited recovery of some manufacturing industries in 1989 and 1990, the industrial infrastructure remained in precarious shape. Nor were the main agricultural development schemes, for instance, in the Euphrates Valley, successful.[25] Earnings from agriculture were certainly more than satisfactory since 1990, largely because of factors beyond the regime's control such as the climate and world market prices for cotton. The only recent long-term improvement was the increase in oil production and thus in oil revenue. This, however, is neither linked to the war nor sufficient to propel Syria into the league of major producers such as the Gulf monarchies.

Some of the chief economic indicators have improved since 1988. Syria's gross domestic product, after a negative growth period in 1987, improved, although in a rather erratic pattern. Also in 1989, the current account balance returned to the black, even jumping to

U.S. $717 from U.S. $-164 in 1988. At the same time, the decline of foreign exchange reserves was apparently arrested; possibly it was even reversed so that slow recovery could occur from the critical lows. In 1985 and 1986, the reserves at times did not cover a month of imports. The country's foreign debt, entirely owed by the state, appears to be rather dramatic now that World Bank statistics include data supplied by Eastern European countries. Some confusion exists as to whether the recent figure of US $16.4 billion for 1990 includes at least part of Syria's debt to the former USSR, but even then it compares unfavorably with a gross national product of some U.S. $24.4 billion in 1990 and U.S. $20.6 billion in 1992. The country will have to repay an average of US $1 billion per year until 1998 with the debt service in 1990 reaching 33 percent of its total exports of goods and services.[26]

In a sense, the economic situation is particularly critical because Syria can no longer count on the relative leniency that its Soviet and East European creditors showed in the past. With the end of the cold war, Syria lost its strategic importance for Moscow. In the Gorbachev era, even the former Soviet government had increasingly diversified its interests; in the Middle East, this ranged from the reflagging of Kuwaiti ships during the Iran-Iraq War to better relations with other conservative states such as Jordan and Saudi Arabia. The same applied to relations with Egypt and, more recently, Israel. Under these conditions, Moscow is in a better position to insist on the repayment of its debt and to link itself to future arms supplies. For these, however, Syria continues to rely on Moscow, be it only for spare parts to repair its largely Soviet-made equipment. Soviet reminders and representations in the late 1980s, including the refusal to help Syria attain strategic parity with Israel, illustrated how seriously the matter was taken in Moscow.[27]

Whatever the improvements in terms of growth, current accounts, and foreign exchange reserves, one cannot forget the more somber developments in Syria's economy. These constraints limit the regime's political choices and leeway after the war. Already, prior to the Kuwait crisis, the economic performance was certainly insufficient for the political ambitions of a regime that sought to establish itself as the major Arab power next to Egypt. As the regime identified shortage of capital as one of the major ills of the Syrian economy, it was only logical to devise policies to attract foreign investment and incite technological transfers.[28] The choice was indeed a necessity, considering the huge amounts needed to repay the foreign debt, a continuously high birth rate, and the numerous parasitic internal "security" and secret police forces with all their material privileges.

In terms of quality and quantity, the West seemed the obvious place to seek the needed financial and technological resources. Neither the major oil economies, threatened by Iraq, nor the crumbling Soviet Union were viable alternative sources. Iraq, with a debt of at least U.S. $70 billion, was even less of an alternative. Consequently, in the Kuwait crisis, it was out of the question to challenge the West which alone was and is able to cater to these needs. Combined with the long-standing Syro-Iraqi conflict over regional influence and hegemony,[29] and a realistic assessment of the global political warming, sheer economic necessity determined Syrian decisions in August 1990.

Syria, too, had been accused of numerous evils and figured prominently on the famous U.S. list of sponsors of international terrorism. The appearance of a villain (Iraq) even worse than itself was a welcome opportunity to join the just against the unjust. Hence the political basis was laid for the necessary transfer of economic resources. Shortly after Desert Storm had calmed, the People's Assembly passed a new investment law, which was signed by President Asad in May 1991. With its implicit bias in favor of external (foreign as well as expatriate Syrian) as opposed to domestic capital, Law No. 10 authorized investors to import equipment and materials tax and duty free, to open foreign currency accounts in Syrian banks, which are exempt from currency regulations, to repatriate imported capital five years after the start of the respective project, and to immediately transfer profits abroad. Moreover, the companies and their shares and profits were largely exempt from tax for up to seven years.[30] These were significant changes compared to the previous rules which restricted the investment of non-Arab foreign capital to a few narrowly defined areas.[31]

If successful, opening the country to Western capital will certainly increase its dependency on the West. Its regional power will take the form of a loan with strings attached. But the rulers in Damascus find this a more comfortable perspective than languishing in dearth and insignificance.

Whether the attempts to attract capital are successful is as yet unknown. Official Syrian figures portray the policy as effective, but on closer inspection one realizes that they include numerous projects that would have been set up even without the new law, as well as rather obscure enterprises in which the import of private cars stands for investment.[32]

Future Policies

Syria's choices during the Kuwait crisis not only illustrated its readiness to accept the new world order, but also helped it to join this order more successfully. The defeat of Iraq enabled Syria to show greater flexibility in the conflict with Israel and to participate in the peace talks; the alliance with the West also reduced pressure from there, indirectly enhanced Syria's position vis-à-vis Israel, and improved its chances for capital transfers.

In any sizeable quantity, however, such transfers were premised on more than just siding with the West against Iraq and laying the legal basis for foreign investment. They implied further measures to inspire confidence. Foremost among these were guarantees against external military threat and hence credible and convincing moves towards a formal arrangement with Israel. This seemed to be the lesson of the Egyptian experience in the 1970s, although the latter could not be reduced to bilateral détente alone.[33]

It is, of course, not certain whether the Syrian regime seeks to open up its economy to external capital to the same degree as did Egypt. Any increase in the share of the private sector in the economy threatens to reduce the power and position of the regime, which rests on the control of the public sector and the military and "security" apparatus. Indeed, the members of the present regime have not really attempted to play an important economic role outside of the state; they have extracted enormous numbers of commissions and bribes from their clients and protégés[34] but, with few exceptions, they failed to transform them into any significant capital.[35] External investors, especially expatriate Syrians, would probably demand various guarantees, for example, against military destruction. Syrians who detain large amounts of capital outside of the country, by the very fact of their nationality, remain more vulnerable to blackmail, sequestration, and nationalization. They would hardly transfer funds without substantial and concrete concessions from the regime, which could include control over certain military units.[36]

It may be safer for the Syrian regime to promote the reconstruction of Lebanon and to siphon off part of the capital transferred there. Notwithstanding the obstacles already mentioned, there is probably a greater readiness among the Lebanese to invest in Lebanon than there is among Syrians to invest in Syria. Despite Syrian overlordship, political pressures are likely to be more mediated and indirect than in Syria proper, and the private sector's legal framework provides quite different business opportunities than those available even with the latest laws in Syria. If ever the reemergence of a strong private sector on Lebanese soil should imperil the position of the Syrian regime, these dangers could be warded off more easily due to the continuous formal distinction between the two countries. This distinction at present enables the Asad regime to dominate Lebanon and, at the same time, minimizes Lebanese claims to enfranchisement.

One of the major issues of debate among the ruling circles of Syria will certainly be the ways in which the strengthening of private capital, be it domestic or external, can be reconciled with the privileges and survival of the regime. But as the rulers do not intend to cut back on their ambitions, they will make every possible effort to tap external resources and integrate themselves into the new world order. Their choices in the Kuwait crisis facilitated this policy, but were its result rather than its cause.

Notes

1. For an eloquent exposition of this convergence of systems through the collapse of one of these systems, see F. Halliday, "The Ends of Cold War," in *New Left Review* 180 (March–April 1990): 5–24. If such a convergence of systems is the outcome of the end of the cold war this need not, as Halliday suggests, imply that the cold war was a conflict between systems. Cf. M. Kaldor, "After the Cold War," in *New Left Review* 180 (March–April 1990): 25–40.

2. George Bush, "Address to Congress, 11 September 1990," in *The New York Times* (12 September 1990).

3. For a detailed chronology of events see *The Middle East Journal* 1–3 (1991).

4. For example, interview with the commander of Syrian forces in Saudi Arabia, 'Ali Habib, with *al-Khalij* (7 October 1990); also in *Washington Post* (12 November 1990); *Tishrin* (15–17 November 1990 and 12–14 January 1991).

5. For details, see *Middle East International* (22 March 1991): 9, 10.

6. For details, *The Middle East Journal* 44(1) (1990): 122, 123; *BBC Summary of World Broadcasts* (24 October 1989).

7. *BBC Summary of World Broadcasts* (23 May 1991); *Middle East International* (31 May 1991): 3, 4.

8. E. Kienle, *Ba'th v. Ba'th, The Conflict between Syria and Iraq 1968-1989* (London: I. B. Tauris, 1990).

9. See also L. Rokach, "I passi verso l'unificazione fra Iraq e Siria: un disegno politico che tende alla 'restaurazione'," in *Politica Internazionale* (Luglio 1979): 35-43.

10. The *New York Times* (6 December 1990) alleges Saudi financial support for Syria amounting to U.S. $1 billion. Other less realistic estimates go beyond this amount.

11. The Economist Intelligence Unit, *Syria: Country Report* 1 (1990): 14; Office Arabe de presse et de documentation, *Rapport économique syrien 1989-90* (1990): B-120. Figures based on official exchange note.

12. The Economist Intelligence Unit, *Syria: Country Report* 1 (1990): 17-20; 3 (1990): 15, 26. For production figures see *ibid.* and *Middle East Economic Digest* (5 April 1991): 20, (12 April 1991): 4, 5. For more recent figures of oil production, *Syria: Country Report* (1992 quarterly).

13. *Middle East Economic Digest* (22 March 1991): 22; The Economist Intelligence Unit, *Syria: Country Report* 1 and 2 (1992).

14. *The Washington Post* (31 January 1992).

15. *Middle East Economic Digest* (15 February 1991): 20; *Middle East Economic Digest* (19 April 1991) referring to *Al-sharq al-awsat*. A plan to purchase Czechoslovakian tanks worth U.S. $200 million may, in part, replace such deals with the USSR, but it should be pointed out that Syria's military debt vis-à-vis this country is estimated at U.S. $1 billion (see *Middle East Economic Digest*, 17 May 1991: 22). Soviet hesitations to accede to Syrian demands surfaced in 1989 (see *Middle East Economic Digest*, 8 December 1989: 35).

16. For the visit by Foreign Minister Bessmertnykh see *Le Monde* (11 May 1991); *Tishrin* and other Syrian newspapers (8 and 9 May 1991); for Asad's acceptance of the proposals put forth by Bush, see *al-Ba'th* (15 July 1991); *BBC Summary of World Broadcasts* (16 July 1991).

17. *Le Monde* (14 April 1991, and 11 May 1991).

18. Wide publicity was given to Israeli reports claiming that Saudi Arabian payments worth U.S. $2 billion for Syrian military support were to be used for the acquisition of new weapons systems from the USSR. See *The Guardian* (20 March 1991) referring to *Ha'aretz*. On the other hand, U.S. Secretary of Defense Cheney assured Israel one day after President Bush called for arms reduction in the Middle East that the United States will provide an additional ten F-15 aircraft and make a significant contribution to the cost of Israel's Arrow missile program. See also *The Guardian* (31 May 1991); other examples could be added.

19. The Economist Intelligence Unit, *Syria: Country Report* 3 (1990): 15, and 1-4 (1992).

20. *Middle East Economic Digest* (3 November 1989): 19.

21. International Institute for Strategic Studies, *The Military Balance 1989-1990* (London, 1989): 101, 114. Syrian defense expenditures then seemed to rise sharply to U.S. $2.49 billion in 1989, but returned to U.S. $1.13 billion in 1991. See also International Institute for Strategic Studies, The Military Balance 1992-1993 (London, 1992). Figures are based on official exchange notes.

22. In spite of its growing oil production, Syria still remains largely an "induced rentier state" benefiting from the rent accruing to other states that control "rentable resources" (see H. Beblawi, "The Rentier State in the Arab World," in *The Rentier State*, ed. H. Beblawi and G. Luciani, London: Croom Helm, 1988: 49-62.

23. In the sense of the concept of an "economie de circulation" close to that of the rentier state, introduced by M. Chatelus and Y. Schemeil, "Towards a New Political Economy of State Industrialization in the Arab World," *International Journal of Middle East Studies* 16 (1984): 251-65.

24. For Syria's economic situation on the eve of the Kuwait war, see V. Perthes, *Staat und Gesellschaft in Syrien 1970-1989* (Hamburg/Berlin, 1990); V. Perthes, "The Syrian Economy in the 1980s," *The Middle East Journal* 46 (Winter 1992): 37-58. Economic developments before and after the Kuwait war are covered by E. Kienle, "Entre jama'a et classe: Le pouvoir politique en Syrie contemporaine," *Revue du Monde Musulman et de la Méditerranée* 59-60 (1991): 211-39; V. Perthes, "The Syrian Private Industrial and Commercial Sectors and the State," *International Journal of Middle East Studies* 24 (1992): 207-30. For figures see also the quarterly country reports by the Economist Intelligence Unit.

25. J. Hannoyer, "Grand projets hydrauliques en Syrie," *Maghreb-Machrek* 109 (1985): 24-42; V. Perthes, *Staat und Gesellschaft in Syrien 1970-1989*; M. Seurat, "Etat et industrialisation dans l'Orient arabe," *Industrialisation et changement sociaux dans l'Orient arabe*, ed. CERMOC (Beirut: CERMOC, 1982), 27-67.

26. GDP growth picked up from -4.5 percent in 1986 to +1.56 percent in 1987, +11.3 percent in 1988, and an estimated +1.5 percent in 1989 and +9 percent in 1990, as calculated by Economist Intelligence Unit, London, *Syria: Country Report* 2 (1991) and 2-3 (1992). The current account balance was at U.S. $-860m in 1985, -164m in 1988, and an estimated +700m in 1989; there are, however, serious doubts as to the validity of the 1989 figure: The World Bank, *World Tables*, (1989-1990 edition): 546; Economist Intelligence Unit/Business International, *Syria: Country Report* 1 (1990), 3 (1990), and 2-3 (1992). Foreign exchange reserves, excluding gold, improved slowly but insufficiently from U.S. $83 million in 1985 to U.S. $223 million in 1987, declined to U.S. $191 million in 1988 and rose to an estimated

U.S. $280 million in 1989. International Monetary Fund, *International Financial Statistics* (June 1991): 510; Economist Intelligence Unit, *Syria: Country Report* 3 (1990); 2-3 (1992). Until recently, total external debt was supposed to have grown from U.S. $3.54 billion in 1985 to U.S. $4.70 billion in 1987, U.S. $4.89 billion in 1988 and an estimated U.S. $5.0 billion in 1989. Revised World Bank figures released in 1992 put the country's external debt at a minimum of U.S. $16.4 billion compared to U.S. $10.8 billion for 1985. The World Bank, *World Tables* (1989-1990 edition): 546; Economist Intelligence Unit, *Syria: Country Report* 3 (1990) and 2-3 (1992). As to the debt to the USSR, which amounts to U.S. $12 to $15 billion, see, for example, *Syria: Country Report* 2 (1990) and 2-3 (1992).

27. See, for example, *Middle East Economic Digest* (8 December 1989): 34; *Middle East Economic Digest* (19 April 1991); E. Karsh, *Soviet Policy Towards Syria Since 1970* (London: Macmillan, 1991): 176.

28. For example, interview of Minister of the Economy Dr. Muhammad al-'Imadi with *al-Hayat*, 27 July 1991.

29. E. Kienle, *Ba'th v. Ba'th*.

30. *Middle East Economic Digest* (17 May 1991): 22. For full text see Mu'assasat al-Nuri, ed. *Qanun istithmar al-amwal fi al-Jumhuriyya al-'arabiyya al-suriyya* (Damascus, 1991); translated text in: Damascus Chamber of Commerce, *Law No. 10 of Encouraging Investment* (Damascus, 1991).

31. I. Bashur. "Al-atar al-qanuni fi al-istithmar fi al-Jumhuriyya al-'arabiyya al-suriyya," in *al-Iqtisad* 4 (Damascus, 1986): 3-26 and 5 (1986): 14-32; V. Perthes, *Staat und Gesellschaft*, 102; V. Perthes, "Syrian Economy."

32. *al-Hayat* (9 August 1992); *The International Herald Tribune* (18 August 1992) quoting official Syrian sources, which put investment under Law No. 10 at U.S. $1.6 billion roughly one year after its promulgation.

33. J. Waterbury, *The Egypt of Nasser and Sadat: The Political Economy of Two Regimes* (Princeton, NJ: Princeton University Press, 1983): 144-57, 201.

34. Y. Sadowski, "Ba'thist Ethics and the Spirit of State Capitalism: Patronage and the Party in Syria," in *Ideology and Power in the Middle East: Studies in Honour of George Lenczowski*, ed. P.J. Chelkowski and R.J. Pranger (London, 1988): 160, 184.

35. E. Kienle, "Entre jama'a et classe," 211-39.

36. *Ibid.*

17
Imagining Egypt in the New Age

Civil Society and the Leftist Critique

Raymond William Baker

I took to the streets on January 16, only twenty-four hours after having attended a conference at the Cairo Book Fair where I warned against the murder of a quarter of a million Arabs. Isn't that what actually happened?

Yusuf Chahine

When Egyptian university students erupted in protest by the thousands, their opposition to the Egyptian role in the U.S.-led coalition's war against Iraq did not go unrecorded. Egypt's great film director, Yusuf Chahine, obsessed with images of the coming slaughter and angered by official compliance with the U.S. strategy, met them—his camera ready—on the campus and in the street. Later, Chahine wove dramatic footage of the student demonstrators at Cairo University into his arresting documentary, *Cairo Illuminated by Her People.* This brief film assessed the consequences of the Gulf War for Egyptians and for the Arab world from an independent, leftist perspective.

Chahine's powerful articulation of the leftist alternative to official policy, still banned from public showings in Cairo, pressed on the limits of debate in civil society.[1] All of Chahine's best works, feature films such as *Cairo Station, The Earth,* or *Alexandria, Again and Again?,* commented obliquely but perceptively on the dilemmas of Egyptian society. Faced with the crisis in the Gulf, Chahine turned for the first time to the medium of the documentary to speak his truth—the truth of the independent Egyptian Left—about Egypt's role in the Gulf tragedy.

The government celebrated the outcome of the Gulf War, announcing that Egypt's strengthened partnership with the United

States would bring prosperity and an enhanced regional role in the U.S. new world order. Chahine's controversial documentary, *Cairo Illuminated by Her People*, read the Egyptian postwar future differently. Although accepting the linkage between domestic and foreign policy, he questioned official promises that Egypt would benefit significantly from participation in the international coalition. Chahine did so by examining the damaging ways in which the Gulf crisis would affect the lives of ordinary young people. The film's sober vision emphasized the continuing weight of domestic problems such as massive unemployment, crushing food prices, and the particularly devastating housing shortage; he gave no credit to government claims that relief would flow from Egypt's enhanced ties to the United States as a result of its docile adherence to the U.S.-led coalition.

Chahine's worried vision of Egypt's future concentrated on the obstacles that frustrate and disfigure young lives. Yet, the director described the film's subject as "Cairo as I love it and as I see it." And rightly so: His unvarnished documentary expressed the unfounded optimism of those who know and care for Egypt. Chahine's camera embraced and caressed his damaged but beloved subject, capturing the magic of Cairo illuminated and unblemished by night and the incredible warmth and goodwill of her people by day, only as someone who cherished both could. Chahine's Egypt has great problems, but even greater and unexpected possibilities. For Chahine, that unfounded promise originated from the restless and dissatisfied populace and not from the limited and bankrupt regime that misled it.

Critics close to official circles were angered by the film's suggestion that the best representatives of a renewed Egypt stood against government policy in the Gulf. Chahine's most controversial scene used actual footage of university students demonstrating against the Gulf War in the face of official bans. His empathic camera probed not only the politics of the student opposition but also the hopeful mystery of how these fervent young people mustered the spirit and courage to respond to tragedies larger than the burdensome day-to-day problems that limited their lives and prospects.

Articles in the national press attacked Chahine for injecting opposition politics into his art. Chahine responded in a series of public forums, defending his right to free expression. Skillfully, he turned each occasion designed to discredit him into an even more explicit critique of official policy and a lesson in democratic expression. "I stated my political opinion openly," said Chahine, "because I believed that at that time we were pursuing a dangerous course that should be avoided." Chahine thought that there was "a conspiracy against the Arabs, and I did not think that we should participate in the destruction of an Arab power." Chahine argued that anyone concerned with Egypt's social problems as he was could not avoid politics and foreign policy because "politics controls society and what controls politics is foreign policy." With no hint of apology, the director remarked that "I am a free man; I expressed my opinion freely and I will not change it." Chahine ridiculed the "stupid" charge that his film supported Saddam Hussein: "There are dictators less harsh than Saddam Hussein and I have no tolerance for them. So how could I support Saddam Hussein, the bloody dictator? I stated my opinion against the war only."

Chahine grounded his opposition to the war in moral outrage over the slaughter of Iraqi innocents. The Iraqi president, in Chahine's view, made a terrible mistake. But he asked "of what are a quarter of a million Iraqi citizens guilty?" Chahine heaped scorn on U.S. talk about smart weapons or clean bombs that killed human beings by the tens of thousands: "They died in ten days. It was a horrible thing." Impatient with the position of the West that Iraqis should bear responsibility for their fate, having installed and maintained Saddam Hussein, Chahine retorted that "in fact, all the rulers in the West contributed in bringing Saddam Hussein to power. Who among them did not give him weapons and armaments?"

Chahine made no claims to special political expertise. But as an artist he did claim the role of "a professor" who is "responsible for educating my students." To those who sought to limit his freedoms, he responded: "What do they want from me as an artist? To be a photographer? To say what they are dictating?"[2]

For Egyptians, Chahine's uncompromising vision as director and social critic opened the gap between official promises and more probable outcomes. Chahine spoke for civil society in insisting that all Egyptians, whatever their political stance, ask: "What precisely did the Americans have in mind for the Gulf and the Arab world when they announced the beginning of a new world order? What role exactly had they reserved for Egypt in their global vision, and with what consequences for the Arab future?" He raised all the key issues: the link between Egypt's foreign policy and resolution of its dire social and economic problems, democracy, and decision making; the destruction of Iraq and the Arab future; U.S. global hegemony; and the Arab system. And Chahine was not alone. In equally revealing ways, other actors in Egyptian civil society explored the same critical terrain. The Gulf War energized political life as groups and individuals across the political spectrum debated the wisdom of the Mubarak decision to bind Egypt's future to the U.S. vision of a new world order.

The Gulf War and the New World Order

If, as Yusuf Chahine asserts, foreign policy shapes politics, then U.S. foreign policy counts most in giving form to the arena of global politics in the post-Cold War era. U.S. President George Bush announced a new era of law and collective action to maintain peace on a global level. The slogan of a new world order captured a sense among the U.S. public of important changes that would come with the end of the Cold War. It also spoke to vaguely expressed concerns: What did the decline of the Soviet Union mean for the United States' place in the world? How would the rise of global economic powers such as Japanese and the Germans affect the U.S. position? With a peace dividend in hand, could U.S. citizens at last turn to their own pressing domestic problems?

Conceptually, the notion of a new world order harbored at least three analytically distinguishable models, all of which responded to the changed character of global power relations. The first conception envisioned a new world system structured by an enhanced role for the UN and international law. The second looked to the several poles of the industrialized centers of Europe, Japan, and the United States, while the third recognized only the single pole of U.S. power. President Bush relied on this ambiguity in his efforts to rally support for his Gulf policy. On the one hand, he articulated a broad vision of a search for a resolution of the Gulf crisis that combined respect for the UN and international law and appreciation for the enlarged international role of the European, Japanese, and Arab allies. On the other hand, the record showed that as early as October the president had in fact decided unilaterally for the war option. From the outset his thinking emphasized the unique global power of the United States and relegated international law and coalition diplomacy to a distinctly minor role.

The conflict with Iraq received wide recognition as the first major international crisis of the post-Cold War era. In the U.S. domestic debate over the Gulf crisis, it was perceived that the stakes were particularly high, as the conduct and outcome of the crisis would help shape the character of post-Cold War international politics. The controversy centered on the issue of sanctions versus war, and each option carried a quite different conception of what form the new world order should take and what the U.S. role should be in it. Those who felt that the new world order should allow a greater scope for the UN and collective diplomacy favored the sanctions option, while those who followed the president in leaning toward the U.S. hegemonic model argued for war.

The most effective critics of official policy, such as Stanley Hoffman of Harvard, attacked the unilateral impulse that lay not too far beneath the U.S. appeals to international law and coalition politics. Hoffman sketched a complex appraisal of the new power conditions of a world order no longer structured by the bipolarity of the superpower age. For all the pre-crisis talk of U.S. decline, stimulated by the weakened performance of the U.S. economy, the United States alone possessed a combination of political, economic, military, and demographic weight. Other major powers such as Europe and Japan based their claim to a large world role on only one or two of these factors. At the same time, the problems of the U.S. economy and the unsettling economic challenges from Japan and Europe introduced uncertainty into any calculation of the U.S. capacity to use its cumulative power position in a coherent and constructive way. Before the Gulf crisis, Hoffman expressed a profound uneasiness over the capacity of the United States, given its economic weakness, to direct a world system whose engine was the global economy: "The world is like a bus whose driver—the global economy—is not in full control of the engine and is himself out of control; in which children—the people—are tempted to step on either the brake or the gas pedal; and adults—the states—are worried passengers."[3] At the height of the crisis, Hoffman argued that the United States might best exercise global leadership, not unilaterally as the war option ultimately would require, but through a steering group operating in the UN that would rely on diplomatic and economic pressures. Hoffman joined those critics of official policy who called for punitive sanctions to contain and discipline Iraq followed by a grand multilateral diplomatic initiative that would address the underlying political and economic issues of regional security, peace, and development. Global commitments tempered along these lines might also reserve for the United States the resources it would need to resolve its own pressing economic and social problems.

Instead, President Bush conducted diplomacy and war in the Gulf with a view to the dominant world position of the United States, based on military power, and with only calculated references to the UN, international law, and coalition politics. The president opted for war in early October, probably making that outcome irreversible by ordering the massive military buildup in November. Discussion at the highest levels recognized that a sanctions-only option could succeed; indeed, General Colin Powell, chairman of the Joint Chiefs of Staff, stated this position. The president, however, decided against it. The most plausible reconstruction of Bush's thinking comes from Bob Woodward, who gave this account to C-Span of the discussion among the commanders:

> What Powell said to the president and said to [Brent] Skowcroft, the national security adviser, Cheney, his boss, the secretary of defense, Jim Baker, the secretary of state is—and this is in October, midway through the period leading up to the war from the invasion of Kuwait—he said: "Look, there are two alternatives here—war or continuing the economic sanctions, and both will achieve the objectives. **Economic sanctions may take a year or two, but it will work**" [Emphasis added]. Bush rejected that and said, "No, we're going to develop the offensive capability and option," and eventually decided to go to war. So he [Powell] wasn't opposed to war. He said there is an alternative that in his judgment would succeed. The president felt the alternative would not succeed or that the political consequences would be so great internationally and domestically that he would not proceed on the sanctions-only option.[4]

The president took the lead in defining the stakes of the crisis in extreme terms as a threat not only to the Gulf states but to "the American way of life." Shortly after the invasion, he declared that "our jobs, our way of life, our own freedom and the freedom of friendly countries around the world will suffer if the control of the world's great oil reserves falls into the hands of Saddam Hussein."[5] With this presidential definition of the crisis, Bush signaled that there could be no question of handing over responsibility for resolving the crisis to the UN, to international law, or even to the European allies.[6]

When Secretary of State James Baker first outlined the administration's course for Congress, he offered a breathtaking vision of the U.S. world role:

Our strategy is to lead a global alliance, political alliance if you will, to isolate Iraq politically, economically, and militarily. . . . We remain the one nation that has the necessary political, military, and economic instruments at our disposal to catalyze a successful response by the international community. Geographically, of course, we stand apart from much of the world, separated as we are by the Atlantic and the Pacific. But politically, economically, and strategically there are no oceans. And in a world without oceans a policy of isolationism is no policy at all. **Only American engagement can shape the peaceful world that our people so deeply desire** [Emphasis added].[7]

The Bush doctrine in action relied on a commitment to unfettered and unchallengeable U.S. military power. Pressure by the only superpower member of the UN would assure its compliance. The allies in turn would be relegated to the status of regional guardians of stability and protectors of the sea lanes. "This is the comfortable and familiar role," noted British political analyst Martin Walker, "played for a generation by Israel in the Middle East, and to a degree by Britain in the Atlantic."[8] The president continued to speak throughout the crisis as often as possible of the UN Security Council vote authorizing the use of force and of the participation of a broad coalition of European and Arab states in the international force. But when the coalition mobilized and the strike came, U.S. military power dominated the scene. "It is difficult to think of any other nation, at any other time in history, that could within six weeks have deployed 150,000 army personnel some 3,000 miles from their bases, with tanks and guns and warplanes to match, and without denuding any of its other outposts around the world."[9]

This display of unrivaled U.S. power and the political will to use it was aimed at an audience larger than the peoples and governments of the Gulf and the Middle East. Paradoxically, the rapid decline of the Soviet Union threatened to diminish U.S. global standing. Talk of the U.S. decline, prompted essentially by flawed economic performance, accelerated as the sudden disappearance of the Soviet Union from the superpower club led to an even greater stress on economic prowess. The collapse of the Communist threat that had cemented the Western alliance removed a central argument for allowing the United States to take the lead. The U.S. management of the

Gulf crisis engineered an end to this thinking. The *Economist* reported the change in stark terms:

> Now, quite suddenly, it is again clear that economic power does not always outrank military power, and that the value of military clout did not vanish with the ending of the Cold War. To be a great power, economic strength is necessary but not sufficient, as Japan and Germany have amply demonstrated in recent months. America has proved—and the world has noticed—that it can project its military might abroad to secure its (and other people's) economic and other interests.[10]

The strike against Iraq thus provided general notice of U.S. global supremacy while also chastening any other would-be Third World challengers. The world saw that, with low U.S. casualties in a high-tech conflict, neither destruction on a massive scale nor huge Iraqi casualty figures stimulated an anti-war movement of proportions serious enough to affect presidential decisions. In the new world order heralded by President Bush, neither the Soviet Union nor an aroused U.S. domestic public could curb U.S. willingness to use its overwhelming military power. Overall, as Martin Walker summed up, the Gulf crisis perfectly suited U.S. global purpose as defined by George Bush:

> Iraq is not the Gothic hordes. It is, instead, the perfect fall guy, offering the United States the perfect crisis. Saddam Hussein is the perfect villain (though the Bush administration may yet pay a heavy price for giving Saddam Hussein such an obvious opportunity to appeal to the poor and nonwhite majority of the human race). The rich but impotent Gulf states are the perfect protectorates. The Soviet Union, grateful at this beleaguered moment to be treated as a strategic equal by Bush, is the perfect associate. And Moscow's complacence has made the UN Security Council into the perfect vehicle to legitimate American power with the mantle of the international community.[11]

Viewed in this way, Iraq appeared less as a threat than an ideal demonstration case for the efficacy of U.S. power in Third World interventions. The U.S. public could be counted on to accept the military strikes provided the human losses were either screened from view or the victims sufficiently dehumanized. In the Gulf conflict, censorship and smart bombs achieved the masking objective with startling success, while skillful reliance on the prevailing Western stereotypes of Arab societies desensitized the public to the human tragedies of the war.

Politics in Arab and other Third World states was routinely discussed in terms of anti-U.S. mobs and authoritarian rulers with little sense of principled political actors with whom ordinary Americans might identify. The "lessons" of the Gulf War were meant to impress the irrational and dangerous crowds in the streets on the one hand, and the brutal governments that alone could discipline them on the other. Experience with Iraq reflected both sides of the coin. Despite the Hussein regime's deplorable human rights record, the United States showed little restraint in helping Saddam Hussein to build his power base, especially during the Iran-Iraq War. In fact, the brutality of the regime proved to be an asset. During the conflict with Iran, the Iraqi regime avoided nothing, certainly not the terrible loss of young Iraqi and Iranian lives or the slaughter of dissident Kurds to secure the objective shared with the United States of preventing Iranian domination of the Gulf through the export of the Islamic revolution. The United States showed little displeasure as the two strongest powers in the Gulf maimed and murdered a multitude of their young men. Then, when the Iraqis showed signs of emerging not only victorious but capable of rebuilding their power with expanded oil revenues, the United States, without a hint of embarrassment, discovered the reprehensible character of the Iraqi ruler. The regime's vile record of abusing its power could then justify the deadly U.S. strikes in which poor Iraqi conscripts (and uncounted civilians) died once again by the thousands. If the U.S. public gave these victims any thought at all, they saw only the ugly face of Saddam Hussein.

In the official U.S. calculus, only the authoritarian state system and its ability to maintain order, and not civil society and the values it espoused, counted at all. Ironically, domestic critics of the official Gulf policy reinforced this assessment. Dismayed by the unsubtle displays of mass opinion in political systems with only limited political participation at best, and disappointed in the perceived unwillingness of Arab intellectuals to challenge state power directly, they fell into bleak and exaggerated characterizations of the absence of democracy in the Arab world as the fundamental political reality and the cause of all its ills. This tendency inadvertently reinforced the view that the wounds of the Arab world were primarily self-inflicted; that is, the dilemmas of Arab politics were caused more by outmoded traditions that failed to provide for basic freedoms and human rights guarantees than by contemporary political forces such as Western economic, political, and military interventions or the assertions of Israeli power. The perceived absence of any role for civil society suggested that the only notable political actors in the Arab arena were the mob or the authoritarian ruler. Ironically, this view provided little guidance or encouragement for those in the West—often including these critics themselves—searching for alternatives to the present U.S. resort to military interventions as the preferred course in resolving conflicts with the Third World. Although the Mubarak regime took a clear position in support of the Bush strategy, that position did not go uncontested in Egypt.

Official Egypt Reacts: The Government Position

In the official view, Egypt had backed the winner in the Gulf contest by paying attention to issues of both principle and power. President Mubarak denounced Saddam Hussein's deceptive personal pledge that no strike would occur against Kuwait while negotiations were under way. Unimpressed by the Iraqi claim that the attack came only after the breakdown of talks, Mubarak asserted that the crisis in the Gulf derived ultimately from the unacceptable aggression of one Arab state against another. Pointing to a deep current of support within Egypt for the coalition effort and apparently feeling personally insulted by Saddam Hussein, the president contrasted his own liberalized rule in Egypt to the dictatorial impositions of the Iraqi ruler. Moreover, the president explained that Saddam wanted "to usurp Egyptian leadership [of the Arab world]" as the return of the Arab League (under an Egyptian general secretary) to Cairo and then the Cairo Summit at the height of the crisis proved.[12] Finally, President Mubarak pointed to the immediate economic dividends from the partnership with the United States in the form of important debt relief and a new appreciation of Egypt's foreign aid needs on the part of international agencies. At the same time, the president expressed the hope that Egyptians and all Arabs would reap the benefits of a re-energized U.S. commitment to a resolution of the Palestinian question already in evidence by the fall of 1991.

Debate in Egyptian civil society questioned all of these propositions. In particular, the U.S. propensity to rely on military force drew harsh criticism and warnings directed at U.S. policy and the Egyptian regime's support for it. The relative openness of Egyptian society allowed these opinions to surface with greater clarity than elsewhere. It is important for domestic critics of U.S. policy to note that there are active if not ruling political forces in the Arab world that should be recognized and supported for the possibilities of co-operation they offer to curb unrestrained state power. Despite its circumscribed role, a great deal can be learned, and not all of it de-pressing, from the response of civil society in Egypt to the Gulf cri-sis. Egyptian civil society does not yet speak with its full voice. The political liberalization begun in the 1970s has not yet altered the fundamental realities of power concentration in a regime grounded in and sustained by military and security apparatuses. Foreign pol-icy formulation, even on issues that sharply divide the population, remain the preserve of the powerful Egyptian presidency.

Yet, the liberalization of the last two decades has significantly en-hanced the prospects of civil society. Although unable to affect policy outcomes directly, civil society increasingly assured presentation of broad policy alternatives; it could also reflect more accurately the po-litical costs and advantages of different policy choices.

The Mubarak regime, unlike its predecessor, does distinguish be-tween criticisms of policy and direct power challenges. Although two of the most powerful political forces in the country—Nasserism and Islamism—did not yet have full legal representation when the coalition attacked Iraq, the multiparty system nevertheless functioned in circumscribed ways to focus political opposition to regime poli-cies.[13] Professional organizations and university forums provided re-spected platforms for alternative views. Most important, the media offered some openings for the expression of alternative perspectives.

This public arena in Egypt saw the imposition of important restric-tions, and serious limitations marred the quality of the debate in civil institutions and the media.[14] The realities of power and compliant constitutional provisions ensured that Egypt's participation in the military strike against Iraq was solely a presidential decision. Neither parliament nor the recognized political parties participated in any meaningful way in the decision to join the international coalition against Iraq. Moreover, any inclination to challenge the presidential prerogative encountered not only official resistance and intimidation but a variety of inhibitions specific to the Gulf events. Mass senti-ment on the underlying issues was initially unclear, as ordinary Egyptians reacted with considerable confusion to the events in the Gulf. Both the conspicuous and arrogant consumption of the Ku-waitis as well as the brutality of the Iraqi regime made an impression on Egyptian society. Intellectuals, to whom the public might have looked for clarification, often mirrored rather than clarified these contradictory assessments. The mainstream Islamist trend associated with the Muslim Brotherhood, in recent years the most self-assured in its criticisms of state policy, suffered the consequences of a divided response. As a transnational current, the Islamists found themselves caught between radical pressures from the Sudanese and North African movements and the conservative stances of the Saudis and the Kuwaitis. Instead of taking the lead in formulating an alternative to the government stance, the Islamists in Egypt found themselves preoccupied with important divisions within their own camp. Finally, important civil institutions concerned with foreign policy such as think tanks and university forums assumed a low profile, the result, in some cases, of recent brushes with harsh official measures.

Although it would be unwise to downplay these restrictions on the internal Egyptian debate, it would be just as unhelpful to ignore the partial clarifications provided by civil society despite these obstacles. The restrictions and limitations do not tell the whole story. The Egyptian political arena split over the Gulf crisis. The parties of the right, notably the Wafd and al-Ahrar, lined up with the government, while the Islamists and the Left, in a tacit and unforeseen rapprochement, led the forces opposing the Gulf policy. Divisions occurred within all political blocks as a result of the confusions and uncertainties of the Gulf crisis. In many ways the Islamist current, pulled in all directions because of its transnational affiliations, had the most difficulty in achieving a unified position.

In these confusing circumstances, the broad Left current assumed greater importance than one might have expected in articulating the opposition stance on Egypt's role in the Gulf.[15] Throughout the crisis, the Egyptian Left suffered from the legal restrictions and periodic repression that denied it a presence in political life commensurate with the support it enjoyed in society. The primary political institution of the Left remained the National Progressive Unionist Party (NPUP), with its frustrating amalgam of leftist currents. The Nasserists, the leftist orientation with the largest potential mass support, continued but were handicapped by the denial of any legal status to either of the two parties that vied for the Nasserist mantle. In the major universities, the Left enjoyed a strong presence, particularly evidenced by the student demonstrations against the war and in the efforts of the well-received Students' Committee for the Defense of Democracy.[16] The professional organizations also witnessed an active Left component, although it was the media where the Left had its most important base. *Al-Ahaly*, the paper of the NPUP, was joined by *al-Yassar* as the forum of a broad and often unaffiliated progressive public opinion. In the mainstream, the distinguished journal *Rose al-Yusuf* consistently brought a leftist orientation to its largest public audience. Drawing on these considerable resources (and leaving aside the subterranean leftist forces such as the various illegal communist groupings), the Egyptian Left, operating in civil society, succeeded in engaging the official position with a coherent alternative.

The Left Alternative

The Left contested every aspect of the official reading of the crisis and its consequences: Egypt was a satellite and not a partner of the United States; the Iraqi regime made a grave mistake in invading Kuwait, but the response should have been an Arab or UN resolution and not a Western military intervention. Whatever the flaws of Saddam's regime, the strike against Iraq destroyed an important Arab power, weakening the Arab system and strengthening the Israeli-U.S. hold on the area. The complete U.S. domination of the Gulf would only worsen the uneven distribution of Arab resources, with Egypt deriving scant economic benefit from its participation in the coalition. And in the wake of the war, prospects for a just settlement to the Palestinian question would fade even further under the smoke screen of an endless and unproductive "peace process."

The Left's position opened with a critique of presidential leadership, attacking President Mubarak's monopoly on decision making and his failure to provide the public with the full facts of the situation confronting the nation.[17] Although some critics ceded that President Mubarak had managed to maneuver with considerable skill in an extremely difficult situation, all agreed that real national leadership would have seized the initiative and shaped circumstances for Egypt's benefit.[18] They reminded the public of Mubarak's initial opposition to an Arab summit on the grounds that it would be divisive and destructive, only to then reconsider and convene the Cairo Summit. They reported that the president had initially spoken at the summit of a call for simultaneous Iraqi and U.S. withdrawal, but that crucial phrase was removed from the final communiqué. They noted that the president initially argued that Egypt's role would be purely defensive, but he reversed himself dramatically as Egypt assumed the prominent Arab position in the final assault on Iraq.[19]

The Left ascribed the president's radical and confusing shifts in position to U.S. pressure.

The official language of partnership and friendship, according to the Left, masked more than it revealed when applied to the Egyptian-U.S. relationship. Egypt, in fact, had become a U.S. outpost, a regional surrogate whose interests were subordinated in all essentials to those of the United States. Moreover, the U.S. regional system had a profoundly reactionary character. Egypt, once in the vanguard of progressive Arab states and more recently linked economically in 1989 to Iraq, Jordan, and North Yemen in the Arab Cooperation Council (ACC), now found itself allied with the tribal regimes of the Gulf.[20] The Left seized the opportunity afforded by the Gulf crisis to attack the backward and corrupt Gulf states, focusing attention on such issues as skewed income distribution and the mistreatment of women.[21]

One important U.S. aim in binding Egypt into this system was to secure its neutralization, making total Israeli ascendency in the area possible. Unimpressed with the argument that the crisis revealed that Israel was not as important to the area, the Left contended that the Israelis performed a variety of intelligence and other back-room services for the coalition that guaranteed its continued favored position. Strains might surface between Washington and Tel Aviv, but the underlying relationship would hold. Whatever the complexities of the Gulf situation, one fact remained for the Left: Egypt had cooperated fully in the destruction of an Arab power and the deaths of as many as a quarter of a million conscripts and citizens in one of the great centers of the Arab world. At the same time, Egyptian links to the Gulf states provided a cover of legitimacy for their continuing monopolization and corrupt waste of precious Arab resources. The United States, hiding behind calls for legitimacy and stability, blocked all movement toward democracy or reform.

In the end, the Left judged that Egyptians received much less than was expected for these considerable services to U.S. power. The first casualty of the about face was, of course, the ACC, which aimed to link Egypt, Iraq, North Yemen, and Jordan in a loose economic union.[22] At the same time, the supposed gains from the strengthened Gulf connection went to the Americans first and then the Europeans rather than to the Egyptians or the Syrians. Neither the expanded Egyptian security role in the Gulf nor the expected Egyptian share in Gulf reconstruction materialized. In both instances the United States dominated, leaving Egypt little more than crumbs. At the same time, the domestic liberalizations that supposedly went with the U.S. external link were as much a facade as a reality; as Hussein Abdul Razik put it in *al-Yassar*, "there is no rational Egyptian who can believe that there is democracy in Egypt."[23] The Left saw these outcomes as clear evidence that the so-called new world order was, to use Mohammed Sid-Ahmed's characterization, "nothing more than a consecration of U.S. global hegemony following the disappearance of the Soviet pole." Because the U.S. strategy aimed to make "the destiny of the world subject to the will of one country, [it] is more blatantly imperialistic than any similar project in the past."[24]

Elaborations: Voices of Civil Society

Using the resources of civil society, the broad Left current cooperated with other political and social forces, notably the Islamists, to bring this critical assessment of the Gulf crisis before Egyptian and Arab publics. This effort greatly enhanced debate and reflection in civil society on the meaning of the Gulf War for Egypt. Into this enlarged arena stepped respected national figures emerging from the Left, but transcending the narrow confines of any particular political orientation by speaking directly to and for the entire nation. Coming from the universities and research centers, the press, professional associations, and previous government service, they provided new information and integrating interpretations that gave force and depth to the Left's critique of official policy. The impact of the new postwar circumstances on complicated domestic problems such as the national debt and privatization were given special attention. Regional questions such as the Egyptian security role in the Gulf, the peace process, and the future of the Arab system also received probing treatment. At the same time, distinguished commentators examined the hopes raised by talk of an expanded role for the UN, international law, and international human rights organizations and added their assessments to the worldwide discussion of these prospects. Thanks to these courageous interventions, critical issues—important for Egypt, the region, and the world—received consideration in the public spaces of civil society, often in the face of active state discouragement.

For Egypt

Ordinary Egyptians, many of whom had friends or relatives in the Gulf, felt that the crisis dealt Egypt a severe blow on a variety of levels. Analysts on the Left could find little consistency or coherence in the policy of the Mubarak regime toward Iraq. In the late 1980s, the Egyptian regime consolidated relations with Baghdad that resulted from Egyptian assistance during the Iran-Iraq War. In 1989 the regime announced Egyptian adherence to the ACC. Although giving rhetorical support to this limited Arab union, the Left had clear misgivings. Reservations focused on the council's impact on the Palestinian question, the autocratic character of the decision to form the council, and the exclusion of such key Arab actors as Sudan and Syria. At this stage, the Left criticized the regime for embracing the Iraqis too hastily with little regard for the potential costs.[25]

During the Gulf crisis, the Left found itself ironically attacking the opposite excess; the Egyptian government, as the Left saw it, moved from a thoughtless embrace of Hussein's regime to the mindless annihilation of the Iraqis. The Left understood that the majority of Egyptians blamed Iraq for the crisis by its invasion of Kuwait. Ahmed Abdullah, an independent political analyst who had played a leadership role in student politics in the 1970s, explained that the Egyptians lost a great deal from the crisis, ranging from their dashed hopes for leadership of a stable Arab world to the more immediate deprivation of employment opportunities in the Gulf. Abdullah concluded that "it seems logical for Egyptians to ally with the rest of the 'frightened' in the Gulf in their support of the U.S. campaign and their opposition to the Iraqi regime." Yet, although Abdullah recognized the Iraqi "mistake" and the necessity to check Iraqi power, he dissented firmly from the drive to destroy Iraq, criticizing the headlines of official papers "that expressed eager anticipation for the onset of military operations." The deep feeling of competition with Iraq for leadership of the Arab world was "different from seeing a brother killed by someone because he misbehaved." Warning that "any axis standing on the corpse of Iraq must be weak," Abdullah concluded that "the correct stance from the Arab and Egyptian perspective was to rectify the mistake of the Iraqi brother without resorting to a paid killer."[26]

The Egyptian regime, the Left argued, fell too easily into demonizing Saddam Hussein. Following the U.S. lead, the official press characterized the conflict as originating in Saddam Hussein's excessive ambition and flawed character. Galal Amin, a distinguished university economist, spoke for progressive opinion in Egypt when he opined that "it is very improbable that what occurred is simply an expression of the strange ambitions of the one ruler."[27] The so-phisticated Left, while eschewing the old Marxist dogmatisms, never-theless insisted that forces larger than personal ambitions and flawed characters moved important historical events like the Gulf War. Such forces had a class character in both their international and purely Egyptian dimensions. According to Amin, anecdotes about the "end of the Left" and the "bankruptcy of leftist thought" in no way dimin-ished the importance of class analysis for major political and social events.[28]

Sober voices of civil society warned that the U.S.-inspired eco-nomic restructuring undertaken by the government had a political rather than economic logic. The U.S. ideological commitment to the market economy meant a reflexive hostility to the public sector and to such socialist measures as food subsidies that protected the most vulnerable segments of the population.[29] The International Monetary Fund (IMF) pushed to reduce subsidies, fire public sector employees, and decrease funding for social services like education and health. The regime used the preoccupation with the Gulf to accommodate these demands in order to receive "millions of dollars in cash aid," but at the price of "tight budgetary constraints."[30] The bitter pill was presented as more palatable because of the financial gains, notably debt relief, that rewarded Egypt's role in the Gulf.

The Left challenged these claims, drawing special attention to the mishandling of the national debt and exaggerated official claims for the impact of debt relief secured in the wake of the crisis. For fifteen years, the Left had warned that the mushrooming national debt con-stituted a threat to Egyptian national independence as serious as the European financial claims against Egypt in the nineteenth century that led to the eventual occupation of the country. Galal Amin ex-plained that the full scale of the debt had been hidden by the gov-ernment, under a barrage of deliberately misleading characterizations, such as "the debts are not as huge as some thought they are, that the debt services are still at a reasonable level, that Egypt is paying its debts on time, that this or that international agency testified to the good health of the Egyptian economy, and that what the state gets are grants that are not paid back or easy loans that do not burden the Egyptian economy."

The real extent of the debt crisis surfaced, although indirectly, when the government hailed debt relief as a major Egyptian gain from participation in the U.S.-led coalition. The official press re-ported that the United States forgave U.S. $7.8 billion and the Gulf

Arabs an additional U.S. $14.4 billion. President Mubarak stressed the importance of this reprieve, giving thanks to the Lord and telling Egyptians that he had been unable to sleep worrying about the mounting interest payments on the national debt.

Taking this personal presidential revelation as a point of departure, Galal Amin took up the question of the debt in *al-Yassar* of February 1991. Amin reminded readers that the government had made assurances for fifteen years that the debt was not beyond Egypt's capacities, and asked why the president should have trouble sleeping over an issue of so little importance. Amin calculated the total external debt, including late interest charges, at a staggering U.S. $55.7 billion. Taking this base figure, the debt relief granted in response to the crisis represented an approximate 25 percent reduction. While recognizing the obvious gain for Egypt, Amin nevertheless argued that the remaining massive debt still far exceeded Egypt's capacity for repayment. The impossible strain on the economy was indicated by Egypt's failure from 1986 to 1989 to meet interest payments, with these huge sums then added to the principal each year. "If our economic conditions do not see a tangible change," wrote Amin, "we will remain unable to repay our debts even if we are exempted from one billion dollars annually." From these harsh facts, Amin concluded that ordinary Egyptians would sense no improvement in their condition from the much heralded debt relief and that the national independence would remain threatened for the foreseeable future by this intolerable financial burden.[31]

The perilous condition of the Egyptian economy, and the shift of its burden to the poor, was not the only issue in the region with a class dimension. Saddam Hussein's characterization of the conflict in the Gulf as a struggle of the rich against the poor had a transparently manipulative character. The Egyptian Left cautioned, however, that it would be a mistake to conclude that the slogans of redistribution and economic justice had no resonance in the Arab world. Clearly, the issue was more complex than Saddam's clumsy rhetoric claimed.

As Galal Amin pointed out, Iraq, with its oil, was hardly a poor state, nor had it displayed any great interest in distributing its oil wealth to less fortunate Arab peoples. The class dimension of the conflict was enacted in less dramatic, but no less important, arenas, and it ignored state boundaries. The Left noticed that on entering Kuwait, the United States rescued the emirs and princes, yet left poor Palestinians, Yemenis, Egyptians, and Asians to their fate. The

Iraqi poor, in the guise of conscripts, died by the thousands. And the Egyptian balance sheet showed the same class results. When *al-Ahram* published the list of Egyptians who died in the war, Galal Amin was not alone in noticing that none came from Cairo or a regional capital. Egypt's martyrs, noted Amin, had their origins in the remote villages rather than the prosperous suburbs of the capital. "Their names," wrote Amin, "are purely and authentically Egyptian: Khamis Allam Hamed, Abdul Azim, and Subhy, while their sisters are Om Hashem and al Sayyidda, Samia, and Badria. . . . These are the people who cultivate the land in peacetime and die in wartime." For Amin, the truth of the Marxist notion that workers have no country was underlined:

> Following the cease-fire, some reporters took pictures of large numbers of Iraqis walking in the desert to return to Iraq. They were in a desperate state, hungry and tired and many of them had lost their shoes. The same reporters took pictures of other large numbers of people walking in the reverse direction. Kuwaitis and Egyptians going South, after being released. The two groups met on the way, the Iraqis going to the North and the Egyptians and the Kuwaitis moving south. And pictures showed them greeting each other. Why not? None of these groups carried any animosity toward the other at any moment. They had absolutely no interest in this war.[32]

Egypt's policy in the Gulf linked the country with the least progressive elements in the Arab world, at the cost of the poor and disenfranchised. In this outcome, the regime saw strategic advantages in the U.S. new world order. Opposition voices from civil society contested those claims as well.

For the Region

The Egyptian regime anticipated an important security role in a new partnership with Saudi Arabia and Syria in the post-war Gulf region. In addition, Egypt looked forward to economic gains from the reconstruction of Kuwait. These gains, it was thought, would more than offset the potential gains of the new links that had been forged with Iraq during the Iran-Iraq War, culminating with the economic ties promised by the ACC. On both accounts the regime suffered harsh disappointments. From the outset, the Left warned that Egypt's and Syria's only leverage with the United States was their capacity to provide an Arab face for the interventionist forces that would mobilize support for the UN and promote favorable world public opinion. Once used in this way, the Left argued that Egypt and Syria would be summarily denied any substantial strategic or financial gains.

The blow came on 19 September 1991, when the United States and Kuwait signed a ten-year military cooperation agreement. The new arrangement provided for U.S. stockpiling of military supplies, authorized visits by U.S. war planes and ships, and regular joint military training and exercises.[33] Meanwhile, Egypt having withdrawn its troops from the Gulf, claimed that while general principles for an Egyptian role in the Gulf had been agreed to, the details required further negotiations. Egypt, it seemed, had been pushed aside.

The high point of Egyptian hopes came with the Damascus Declaration of March 1991. Issued in the wake of the war, the agreement provided for 35,000 troops from Egypt and another 30,000 from Syria to provide an Arab security guarantee for the Gulf. In exchange, the Gulf states pledged generous economic support in the form of a Gulf fund totaling U.S. $15 billion on which the Egyptians and Syrians could draw. The deal unraveled almost immediately. Within three weeks, the Gulf Arabs, with the tacit support of the United States, reneged on the arrangement. The fund was reduced in size and was opened to non-Arab states.[34] The Kuwaitis further angered the Egyptians by downplaying the Egyptian role in the fighting and indicating an even stronger interest in a U.S. rather than an Arab security shield. In response, Egypt withdrew the bulk of its forces, while the Kuwaitis struck their deal with the United States.

Cairo's disillusionment also extended to its role in the Kuwaiti reconstruction. Egyptian hopes for a large role in the Gulf were expressed most clearly by Housing and Construction Minister al Kafrawi, who made the case that "we have the experience of having rebuilt our country after the wars of 1956, 1967, and 1973, and we reconstructed the [Suez] Canal region in thirty months and returned 1.5 million people to their homes."[35] The Kuwaitis responded that a cold calculus of efficiency, not sentiment, would dictate the contract awards. The United States got the lion's share while the Egyptians got only an estimated U.S. $20 million of the billions awarded.

The Left understood these outcomes as the indirect consequence of the U.S. military response to the crisis. The U.S.-led attack demolished not only Iraq, but also the prospects of a revived and strengthened Arab regional system. Muhammad Sayyid Said, a senior political analyst of the al-Ahram Center for Political and Strategic Studies, described the impact of the Gulf crisis as "an earthquake hitting the whole area." Said explained that the crisis erupted at a time when the United States was laying the groundwork for a Pax Americana. Furthermore, Said reasoned that the massive scale of technologically advanced military power used in the war was aimed at more than Iraq. He argued that the terrible destruction of Iraq was "a lesson for the entire Third World, warning it not to challenge the American system."[36]

The massive reconstruction effort in Kuwait and the new security system for the Gulf, both marked by U.S. dominance, attested to the extreme weakness of the Arab regional system, now completely penetrated and dominated by U.S. power. In backing the U.S. military strike, the regime destroyed Egypt's only prospect to use the Gulf crisis for the reconstruction of an Arab regional system in which Egypt could play a leadership role on behalf of general Arab interests. The U.S. military strike destroyed not only Iraqi power, but diplomatic and political prospects for Egypt as well.

To make this case, the Left had to establish that there was a workable alternative to the complicated role that Egypt played in the United States' use of massive military power. Muhammad Sayyid Said, among others, recognized the practical constraints on Egyptian policy. In the face of Iraqi power, a purely Arab resolution to the crisis was probably unavailable. But Said believed that Egypt had the opportunity to weigh in on behalf of the various diplomatic initiatives, all of which would have used the UN forum instead of relying solely on U.S. military power.

> The system could have contributed through pressuring for the crystallization of a new power of Western Europe and the USSR. The failure to do so gave the U.S. a monopoly position in directing the crisis beyond its abilities and international position. This encouraged the U.S. to implement a vehement and contradictory stance in conducting the war against Iraq, leading to the material and moral destruction of this beloved Arab state to "the pre-industrial era," to use the expression of the general secretary of the UN.[37]

Instead of backing the diplomatic alternative, Egypt simply followed the U.S. line that negotiations could begin only after withdrawal, thereby effectively cancelling that option. As Abdullah argued, "never in human history had negotiations taken place following the with-

drawal of the forces."[38] Egypt failed to effect any workable negotiations, to find an Arab solution, or to support a broader diplomatic
effort that would not have led so obviously to the imposition of a
U.S. solution. After the Cairo summit, Egypt simply fell in line behind the Americans.[39] As a result, Egypt failed to support effectively
important diplomatic opportunities by the Jordanians, the Yemenis,
the French, and the Russians. "The word 'negotiations' appeared
very rarely in the Egyptian official press," noted Ahmed Abdullah.
When the Islamist political opposition, led by Adel Hussein and Ibrahim Shukry, attempted to mediate, they were condemned and de-
famed in the government press. Not only did the regime fail to use
its modest room to maneuver, it blocked the efforts of others and
thereby helped assure serious damage to the regional Arab system.

According to the Left, the U.S. resolution also adversely affected
the Arab system by fostering the uncoupling of the Gulf states from
the Arab world. The issues of Gulf security and reconstruction are
important here. The real thinking of the Gulf states, once the rhetoric of an Arab common front was no longer required, emerged
most clearly from the details of the Gulf Fund dispute that led to the
Egyptian withdrawal. The fund, created for the purpose of development assistance to the Arab world, saw its capital drop from U.S.
$15 billion to U.S. $10 billion over a three-year period beginning in
1991. Important from the Egyptian perspective was the decision to
open the fund to non-Arab powers, notably the Iranians, and "to
include the IMF and the World Bank in orienting the fund's work
and supervising it, so that the new financing becomes a support for
the economic programs supervised by both the Bank and the IMF."[40]
In addition, the Gulf states built a privatization strategy into the
fund's working relations by making grants to private sector projects
directly rather than to governments.

These new arrangements, despite their ostensibly economic rationale, had clear political implications. The Gulf states could use the
fund effectively to settle accounts with Arab regime that did not
fully support their cause in the crisis; at the same time, the private
contracting system enabled the Gulf regimes to build a network of
clients within individual Arab states who had benefited directly from
the Gulf connection. These circles could then be counted on to function as interest groups on behalf of the Gulf states. At the same time
and with obvious relevance to the uncoupling strategy, the Gulf states
altered their demographic composition by reducing the number of
visiting Arab workers, thus further diluting their ties to the Arab
world.

Putting these various elements together, the Egyptian Left concluded that the Gulf states had opted decisively for reliance on U.S. military power and close alliance of their economics and societies to the West, while securing "the silence of the other Arab States whether by selective or distinctive financial support [through the fund], by local pressure groups, or even through pressures from the international financial institutions."[41] Furthermore, the Left warned, the separation of the Gulf States was not the worst consequence of the blow to the Arab system.

Muhammad Hassanein Haikal, editor of *al-Ahram* during the Nasser years, explained the harsh implication of the extreme weakness of the Arab system for the Palestinian issue: "I see no real possibilities for a settlement. In any settlement there is an exchange. Obviously, the Arabs are ready to talk, but they have nothing to offer; whereas, the Israelis have everything, but they are not ready to offer anything."[42] Haikal argued that the talk of movement on the peace process was really a cover for imposing Israeli conditions rather than the beginning of real negotiation. "What is the form of this settlement that is now being discussed?" Haikal asked. He pointed out that discussion focused not on the shape of the settlement, but simply on the abstract idea of getting a process started. "This is what they ask the Arabs to participate in," continued Haikal; "it is like asking them to catch a plane before it takes off without telling them where this plane is heading." Haikal found the argument that the process would generate its own dynamics unacceptable because the Arabs had so little leverage, and the Israelis had set such harsh conditions, for example, dictating the composition of the Palestinian delegation and precluding a Palestinian state as an outcome. Muhammad Sayyid Said concluded that "contrary to all previous stages in Arab history since the end of WWII, it would be incorrect for us to call for a quick move to end the Palestinian problem at the current stage and before the rehabilitation of the Arab world." The only outcome possible at the present time, according to Said, would be "the 'solution' proposed by the fanatic right wing in Israel, the U.S., and the West. . . to achieve peace and normalize relations without having to give back the 1967 Occupied Territories and without granting self-determination to the Palestinians and their right to have an independent country."[43]

The absence of a genuine settlement resulted from the U.S. concept that the United States could "impose its will and monopolize politics in the Middle East, regardless of international legitimacy," Said commented. The new U.S. assertiveness might create strains with Israel, but these would be over marginal questions, although their importance would undoubtedly be magnified to better position the United States as a mediator. Nonetheless, the U.S. bias toward Israel is unlikely to change as a result of the Gulf conflict because "it stems from the heart of the ruling institutions of the United States."[44]

When the Israelis advanced their post-Gulf slogan of "peace for peace" instead of the principle of "land for peace" embodied in UN Resolution 242, the Left saw this hardened position as a direct result of the improved Israeli position in the wake of the Gulf War. The destruction of a major Arab power and the further weakening of the Arab system emboldened the Israelis. Their new language, as Haikal understood it, meant "that the Arab states must sign the agreement with Israel or they have before them the example of Iraq." Haikal concluded that although he could understand the U.S. incentives for desiring to "pacify conditions in the ME," they had to realize that "this must take place in a more just way."[45]

For the World

In the wake of the disaster following the Iraqi invasion of Kuwait, the late Philip Galab, one of the most highly respected of Egypt's leftist journalists, announced a momentous discovery "that could change all the diplomatic and political formulas that have prevailed for centuries." Galab reported with mock seriousness that "the U.S. together with Great Britain and Israel have discovered something called international law, the violation of which should be punished either under the banner of the UN or without it."[46] Galab underscored the irony of the U.S. appeal to values that it had, in the case of Palestine, consistently violated.

In a quite different style, Muhammad Hassanein Haikal discussed the power dimension of the U.S. claim that the end of the Cold War had brought a new and better international order: "I don't think there is a new world order. We had a British system that went on for the 18th and 19th centuries and until the mid-20th century. Then we saw a new system with the second world war, it is an American system." Haikal understood the Gulf crisis as essentially a reassertion of this U.S. system against challenges from the Japanese and the Europeans. "What happened during the crisis," Haikal explained, "is that the Americans were not happy with some of the changes in the international balance of power and therefore they reemphasized their domination." Haikal, in fact, saw little immediate prospect in a displacement of U.S. dominance, although in time it might confront an effectively unified Europe or Asia capable of containing its power.[47]

In this widely endorsed view, what was really behind the Gulf War was competition among the United States, Europe, and Japan that was becoming tougher all the time. Referring to U.S. fears of a unified Europe, Amin remarked that because "the U.S. possesses the greatest force in the world, it would be very strange if the U.S. did not use this force to improve its relative position in the international economy and strengthen its negotiating position with Western Europe and Japan."[48]

The U.S. postwar initiatives to control the arms flow to the Middle East reflected these same underlying realities. Amin Huwaidy, a former interior minister from the Nasser years and a specialist on military affairs, analyzed the ways in which the Bush initiative would buttress U.S. ability to shape regional political outcomes. Huwaidy wrote that in the contemporary unipolar world, the United States would determine the standards of international legitimacy, changing those standards to suit its purposes. For example, the Bush arms regulation initiative, approved by the London Conference on Arms Exports, banned the building of missiles and nonconventional weapons while limiting exports of conventional weapons into the Middle Eastern region. The initiative made these determinations based on the notion that any state does have a legitimate need to defend itself. Yet, Huwaidy asked pointedly, "Who determines these threats and who would determine the size and the quality of the necessary weapons to counter them?" Huwaidy pointed out that the United States clearly intended to assume that responsibility within the purview of the new world order. He judged that the U.S. control over the arms transfer process would be critical because the balance of force in the area would dictate the balance of interests. Huwaidy concluded with two pointed questions: "How can we achieve stability if the U.S. is controlling the weapons market and is biased toward Israel? How will we deal in the international arms trade if the rules for interaction became more political than commercial?"[49]

Alongside these realist assessments by the broad leftist current, however, came an emphasis on the Arab interest in cultivating some alternative to this unconstrained U.S. dominance. Muhammad Sayyid Said reasoned that the Arabs had essentially two strategies available to them. The first, a "revolutionary" option, reasoned that the Gulf crisis revealed the Arab system to be so corrupt and dependent on the West that the only solution "is to destroy the entire Arab system and comprehensively combat the West and achieve Arab unity even if this necessitates the usage of military force and even if it ends in complete chaos in the whole area."[50] Said rejected this argument, arguing that such an outcome would effectively undermine any remaining sense of political morality in the Arab world. In Said's view, the only Arab unity worthy of the name must be attained with democracy and respect for human rights. He attacked the Iraqi regime for using the call to unity as a cover for regional ambitions while it brutalized its own people. "What is the value of a unity which is led by those who dare to kill and slaughter thousands of their own people?" asked Said.

Raising an even more sensitive issue for the Left, Said questioned the wisdom and morality of an abstract anti-foreign impulse. "Undoubtedly, we do admit that any patriot should reject the military presence in the Gulf if it comes by force and against the will of the nation, or even if it is not against their will if the arguments for it are not persuasive," wrote Said. Yet, he pushed harder and asked, "Shall we reject foreign intervention because it is foreign on the basis that anything foreign is evil and anything Arab is good? These arguments would have meant that we would have given Kuwait forever to Iraq, because there was no Arab force able to evacuate Kuwait, and we all know this fact well." From this perspective, Said returned to the question of the role of international law and the UN as an alternative to reliance on U.S. power, arguing that "the preferred position is not to reject a foreign presence entirely, but to call for a role for the UN, so that Arabs, through that organization, can deter Iraq."[51]

On the international as well as domestic plane, figures at the very core of the Egyptian Left, like Mahmud Amin al-Alim and Rifa'at al-Said, emphasized democracy in addition to the traditional demand for social justice as critical to an Arab revival. Such prominent leftists argued that during and immediately after the crisis, the cause of democracy was highlighted alongside the social cause. Later events in Algeria, where Islamist forces flourished in a quasi-democratic environment, would dampen the enthusiasm of the Left for acceleration of Egypt's democratic experiment.[52] But, in al-Said's words, the immediate response to the Gulf War was a rethinking of the democracy issue as meaning that "democracy in the Arab arena is no longer concerned simply with having more than one party or with human rights, but it is an essential element for the Arab nation."

More concretely, al-Said argued, "If democracy existed in Iraq, it wouldn't have decided to invade Kuwait. . . . If Saudi Arabia had democracy, it wouldn't have decided to invite the Americans in. . . . If it existed in Kuwait, the system wouldn't have fallen apart the way it did. . . . And Egypt wouldn't have been able under a democratic system to undertake the emergency measures to provide an umbrella for the Americans."[53]

Sayyid Yassine pointed out that although this democratic current emerged well before the Gulf War, it was accelerated by it. Yassine provided one pointed example of the attempt to make democracy a more integral part of the Arab system. In 1984, the Center for Unity Studies sponsored a conference on the crisis of democracy in the Arab world. No Arab government would agree to host it, so the meeting was held in Cyprus. Yassine reported that over a hundred Arab intellectuals attended and follow-up practical work was done in the human rights field by the Arab Organization for Human Rights, which now has branches throughout the Arab world and was recognized by the UN.

The new interest, especially among younger Arab intellectuals, in questions of international law and human rights rather than rigid ideologies, reflected an openness that characterized the post-Cold War age. Yassine commented that a new world was emerging based on a new, post-Marxist revisionist critique of modernity in its ratio-nalist aspect. Neither capitalism nor socialism fulfilled their promise. "So, the door is open before multiple ideas and innovations," con-cluded Yassine. "Post-modernist philosophy opens the door before human history without having a final or ready-made solution," he noted, "and this is the essence of the cultural dialogue that occurs today in the world."[54]

In the Gulf conflict and debate, Yassine saw this underlying cul-tural contest reflected indirectly. An old world—represented by a brutal Iraqi invasion and a savage U.S. counterattack—that sought to reimpose the old certainties confronted the new possibilities rep-resented by the calls for reliance on international law and a revived UN. For the moment, military force carried the day. An Iraqi dicta-tor opened the door for the forcible reentry of the West into the Arab arena, forecasting parallel interventions and disruptions on a global scale. In the United States and in the Western world gener-ally, a "new racism and ethnocentrism reasserted itself to contest the post-modern claim that respects the particularity of every human culture." Yassine argued that this policy debate was the surface reflex of a more profound cultural contest that represented "a very important struggle because it will produce political and economic policies: the cultural role will become more important than the political because it will determine the other."[55] For the moment, force and the old world have had their way. But in civil society in Egypt and around the world, the struggle continues.

Civil Society and the Common Good

Egyptian intellectuals of national stature, respected throughout the Arab world and in the West, raised the issue of civil society's role in decision making as the events in the Gulf made politics once again important to all Egyptians. In doing so, they attempted to rally Egyptian intellectuals to act more effectively as independent critics of government policy.

In a spirit of self-criticism during and immediately after the crisis, the shortcomings in the discharge of this responsibility received great emphasis. Galal Amin reminded his readers that "the researcher for the truth in Egypt is always one who tries to solve puzzles or decode a secret language." Amin complained that "half the truth is purposefully hidden from you, while half of what is said is similarly distorted to mislead people." One may find the truth in the end, Amin concluded, "but for the most part only after it's already too late.[56]

Amin argued that too many Arab intellectuals simply abandoned the quest for reasons that, while perfectly understandable, should be somehow resisted. "We live in a very tough world. There is a lack of vision, a deterioration of the progressive forces, the absence of a clear intellectual alternative, in addition to inflation that humiliates man. And the problem is not that of Arab intellectuals only, but the intellectuals of the whole world." With mordant wit, he sketched portraits of the various responses to the crisis, linking each "dependent" response to the "requirements" of one of the five Arab regimes that played key parts in the crisis (Kuwait, Iraq, Saudi Arabia, Jordan, and Egypt). Sarcastically, Amin noted that the ruler of each state required quite different qualifications and talents of the intellectuals who would serve it. Those who would back Saddam Hussein, he explained, must display "a high level of progressiveness, or at least be able to use progressive terminology. It also requires a good understanding of the benefits of Arab nationalism and socialism as well as the role of the hero in history, regardless of whether there is any chance of achieving Arab unity or socialism. What is important is to talk and to receive the different awards of Saddam Hussein and his different gifts such as a Mercedes car."[57]

In sharp contrast, Shaikh Gaber al Ahmed of Kuwait would need intellectuals who could evoke Islam, but in moderate dosage and without the least hint of any socialist or Arab nationalist shading. The Saudi demands were in some ways more difficult to fulfill, Amin added. King Fahd's intellectuals should be completely fluent in Koranic terminology, "particularly knowledgeable about the words related to the punishment on the day of atonement and the different forms that are taken by the devil in daily life, while able to skirt any mention of foreign and domestic policy, Israel, or the situation of the mass of Muslims in Saudi Arabia itself." The intellectual who won the favors of Jordanian King Hussein, in contrast, must have the skills of an acrobat, and be able to preserve the complex balances the regime seeks to maintain. For the Jordanian advocate, "there is nothing wrong with Arab nationalism, socialism, and even Israel, provided all this talk is academic in nature and remote from current affairs and any critique of a specific Arab government." With just a touch of flattery for his Egyptian readers, Amin allowed that "the dependency of the Egyptian intellectual was better than other types because it did not sanctify the ruler as was the case in Iraq, or abstain from any real discussion of the subject as in Kuwait, or mouth the sad stupidities that were uttered in support of the Saudi regime." Amin explained the contrast: "Hypocrisy Egyptian-style is full of light spirit and good cheer, lacking for the other regimes. Both the hypocrite and the subject of hypocrisy are not taken seriously in Egypt and both of them know that what they are saying is not true. They function rather like the singer at weddings who celebrates the beauty of the bride while everyone knows that she is very ugly."[58]

Assessment of the obstacles facing Egyptian intellectuals and explanations of their flawed performances received considerable and often quite blunt treatment. Sayyid Yassine, director of the al-Ahram Center for Political and Strategic Studies, registered candidly the difficult circumstances under which Arab intellectuals everywhere labored, namely repression and temptations to corruption. "The traditional critical role of the Arab intellectual," wrote Yassine, "is rendered more difficult due to the political repression that limits the intellectual freedom of the thinker and through financial temptations from the part of certain systems." Yassine described the "trap" facing the government critic "who is either repressed and silenced or emigrates or struggles in a tyrannical context where human rights are violated and he is subjected to financial temptations, skillfully exploited by the Arab systems permitting the purchase of many pens."[59]

During the Gulf crisis, these political obstacles were heightened by the profound splits that had already divided informed opinion into secularists versus Islamists, reformists versus revolutionaries. At the same time, although with different force in the various Arab societies, a powerful distorting pressure arose from below in the form of mass opinion opposing any foreign intervention in Arab affairs. Yassine noted that where the popular trend supporting Iraq acquired great strength, some intellectuals feared to analyze the crisis in ways that would challenge mass sentiment. Yassine put the matter pointedly: "Is the role of the intellectual to follow the popular feelings whatever their rationality is, or is it to offer opinions from a critical perspective even if it opposed the popular orientations?"[60]

When such characterizations are echoed in a Western context, as they often are by Arab émigrés to the West, they only reenforce prevailing stereotypes of Arab politics and Arab intellectuals and thereby enhance the Western inclination to ignore actual Arab public opinion. In local contexts, they function quite differently. Those who offer them to Arab readers have risked remaining in an Arab political arena; such assessments then have the character of action arousing appeals to revive and strengthen the best traditions of public inquiry.

To this end, even the most trenchant local critics back away from despair that would depress rather than stimulate the revival and strengthening of civil society. Sayyid Yassine remarked that "fairness dictates that we register the positions of the Arab intellectuals who were not dependent on the authority but expressed their views against the authority, especially some of the Egyptian, Moroccan, and Tunisian intellectuals, most notably those from the opposition parties."[61] Galal Amin dropped his satirical tone to account for the fact that among Egyptians there was "a larger number of intellectuals who did not sell themselves as opposed to those who did." He conceded that "I really believe that some intellectuals were supporting Saddam Hussein out of personal convictions but I think they are wrong." Amin noted, however, that even on the Arab scene, it was the corrupt intellectual who received greatest attention for two reasons: "The one who doesn't sell himself to the media isn't dealt with by the media, and the bad smell is the one that attracts attention."[62]

Expressing the concerns behind his sarcasm and his hopes for the future, Amin remarked:

> The situation of the Arab intellectual is very unfortunate today and sorrowful. But that situation is not worse than that of the politician or the army officer. And anyway, this sorrow is not new. It is old and the wound has been reopened anew by the calamity of Kuwait. The disaster of the Gulf led to even infecting the wound. It is the last straw for our generation of politicians and intellectuals that was growing old even before the disaster of Kuwait, a generation that was weakened in the sixties with the war of 1967 and whose morals were destroyed in the seventies with the treasons of Sadat and whose energies were exhausted with the inflations and the humiliations inflicted by the United States. Our hope is for a new generation that does not forget anything, does not forgive anything, and understands everything.[63]

Taking advantage of the interest sparked by the Gulf War, Yassine offered not only the distant vision of a generation of truly independent social critics, but also a practical scenario, workable within existing political realities, of immediate steps Egyptian intellectuals could take to strengthen their positions vis-à-vis the state and the masses. To this end, Yassine prudently clarified that the target was not the state. He argued that "our struggle is not against the regime; from our nationalist perspective, we don't want to weaken the state as a state because this would benefit foreign forces." But Yassine added that "we want a strong state but not an authoritarian state; we want a modern state capable of fulfilling the basic needs of the people."[64]

Yassine rounded out his analysis with a call to Arab intellectuals—indeed, to intellectuals everywhere—to rethink global problems in the light of the changed circumstances illuminated by the Gulf War and, most important, to develop a new language that directly and effectively addresses broad publics and strengthens civil society and the humane values on which it rests. Yassine argued that the role of the intellectual was not marginal because the intellectual "tries in the midst of all these difficult circumstances of economic temptations and political repression, to undertake the role of independent critic." Yassine urged that intellectuals in the Arab world and beyond rethink global problems in ways free from the old rigidities of the past and open to an uncertain future; he urged them to fulfill their responsibilities by risking involvements "in practical tasks that contribute to the revival of civil society" in their states and in the world.[65]

Acknowledgments

I am grateful for the help I received in researching and writing this article from Nevine Mounir Tewfih, Manar Shorbagy, and Kamel Ahmed Attia, my friends and colleagues at the American University in Cairo. Paul Schemm and Norman Spaulding, my research assistants at Williams, helped in editing the manuscript.

Notes

1. In contemporary political terms, civil society is usually taken to mean all those institutions, associations, and groupings of citizens situated between the formal structures of the state and the private or familial sphere of action. In Egypt, however, civil society connotes something more specifically political, namely, the broad realm of political action that seeks to limit or check arbitrary executive power.

2. Chahine's film and his public comments were reported widely in the Egyptian press. The most complete statement of his views, from which these quotations are drawn, comes from an interview with Dr. Abdul Mon'eim Sa'ad, "The Knight of the Cinema Opens Fire on Everyone: A Heated Dialogue with Yusuf Chahine Who Has Become an International Figure" *The Cinema and People* (13 September 1991): 16-19. Important critical statements by other artists and writers also appeared in the opposition press. Representative is "Intellectuals, Writers, and Artists Express their Shock at the American Aggression and their Disapproval of Egyptian Media Coverage," *al-Ahaly* (23 January 1991).

3. Cited on p. 793 of Martin Walker, "The U.S. and the Persian Gulf Crisis," *World Policy Journal* (Fall 1990): 791-99.

4. Woodward made these comments in a C-Span interview for the "Booknotes" program.

5. On other occasions, President Bush reached for higher moral ground: "Some people never get the word. The war is not about oil. The fight is about naked aggressions that will not stand" (Julius Jacobson, "The Gulf Crisis: Villains and Victims," *New Politics*, Winter 1991: 5-19).

6. The official attitude has been, "the American way of life is thought to be at stake" (Edward Said, "Arabesque," *New Statesman & Society*, 24 August 1990).

7. Cited on p. 791 of Walker, "The U.S. and the Persian Gulf Crisis."

8. *Ibid.*, 798.

9. *Ibid.*, 794.

10. "On Top of the World?" *The Economist* (9 March 1991) 15–16.

11. Walker, "The U.S. and the Persian Gulf Crisis," 795.

12. *al Ahram* (28 September 1990).

13. A Nasserist party was recognized by the regime only in the postwar period.

14. But, as Ahmed Abdullah points out, "until now there has not been any large scale persecution for the supporters of Iraq in Egypt (with the exception of ending general Tal'at Musallam's contract with the Ahram Center for Political and Strategic Studies because of his apparent support for Iraq)." Ahmed Abdullah, *Trilogies, The Second Gulf War: A Perspective from the Point of View of the Generation that Will Pay the Price!* (Cairo: Dar Al'Arabiya lil Tiba'a wa al Nashr wa al Tawzi, 1991): 21.

15. For a brief discussion of the dissension within the National Progressive Unionist Party (NPUP), see "The Leaders of the NPUP Reject the Party's Position on the Gulf Crisis," *al-Akbar* (10 September 1990). The article focuses on the resignation of Amr Muhieddine from the party and its central committee, while also reporting on the reaction to the party position on the Gulf of three other party leaders.

16. See *al-Sha'ab* (5 March 1991), for a report of a meeting with the representative of the Students' Committee for the Defense of Democracy with the Minister of Education.

17. See Hussain Abdul Razik, "Our Position: Change, Is It Made by the Individual Ruler or by the Popular Forces," *al-Yassar* (June 1991). Abdul Razik charged that the president monopolized information and facts and hid them from the political forces, disregarding the first principle of democracy, which is the right to know. Abdul Razik went on to criticize the unilateral character of key decisions, unsuccessfully masked by the "the talk of institutions, the ministerial council, the prime minister, the ruling council and the people's assembly." Abdul Razik concluded that "the real decision maker in Egypt is the president."

18. Muhammad Hassanein Haikal, editor of *al Ahram* during the Nasser era, made this point: "Egypt's stance in the Gulf was in spite of some criticisms supported by most Egyptians. But leadership is another story. Egypt adapted to the prevalent conditions internally, in the area, and in the balance of international power. By doing so, it did its best in a very contradictory position. Leadership, however, is something else" (Muhammad Hassanein Haikal, interview by Muhammad Salmawy, in the *Ahram Weekly* from *al Sha'ab* 4 June 1991).

19. "Our Position: Loopholes in the Arab Umbrella," *al-Yassar* (August 1990).

20. Formed in 1989, the ACC aimed for economic integration and the construction of common markets to reduce trade barriers.

21. The attitude toward women became an emblem of all the reactionary characteristics of Gulf society. See, for example, "The Saudi Woman, a Strange, Strange, Strange World," *al-Yassar* (August 1991). This unsigned article reports that in Saudi Arabia,

> women are the major worry for religious people, callers, scholars, and legislators. Their speeches, whether in the mosques, TV, radio, or tapes and publications that are spread everywhere in the cities, are about women. For example, there is this caller whose tapes were distributed during the crisis devoting himself and calling on his listeners to devote themselves to fighting enemies and tyrants. The listener would imagine that it is a call for volunteering [for combat against Iraq]. But quickly it becomes clear that the enemies are those who urge girls to seek their liberation. According to the speech there is a conspiracy woven by the enemies of Islam and the enemies of women to spread corruption, calling upon women to be educated, the spread of TV programs where girls appear as old as thirteen, the calls for employing women as teachers, teaching girls five English classes per week, the charity associations for women which are regarded as women's clubs, the existence of gardens where male and female children interact, the work of women in some governmental circles, the publishing of pictures of women volunteers with their faces uncovered, the call to train women to carry weapons and defend themselves, and the call for allowing women to drive cars. So, for this caller, the phenomenon are the work of the spies of the Jews, the Christians, and the enemies who are conspiring to corrupt Saudi society.

22. It is true that the Left had responded cautiously to the ACC idea. But, on balance, the Left welcomed this effort to foster Arab union. See the cautious treatment of the ACC in the editorial of *al-Ahaly* (22 February 1989). In the same issue Muhammad Sid Ahmed spells out some of the reasons for the restraint, notably that "this new gathering is a step towards building an alternative Arab system, in which the struggle against Israel is no major concern."

23. Hussain Abdul Razik, "Our Position: Change."

24. Muhammed Sid Ahmed, "New Strains in U.S.-Israeli Relations," *al Ahram Weekly* (19 September 1991).

25. For instructive examples of leftist thinking on the ACC, see Abdul Azim Anis, "Questions About Arab Regional Blocs," *al-Ahaly* (1 March 1989), and "The ACC is Not a Pure Economic Gathering," in *al-Ahaly* (22 February 1989) where Muhammad Sid Ahmed argues that "it is no secret that a partner of the new ACC (Egypt) has a peace treaty with Israel; hence, this new grouping is a step towards building an alternative Arab system in which struggle against Israel is not the major concern." Also important are Muhammad al Maraghy, "And the Layman Asks About His

Benefits," *al-Ahaly* (22 February 1989), and "On the Project of the Arab Economic Grouping," *al-Ahaly* (8 February 1989).

26. Ahmed Abdullah, *Trilogies.*

27. Galal Amin, "In Defense of the Conspiracy Theory," *The Arabs and the Calamity of Kuwait* (Cairo: Madbouli Press, 1991): 69.

28. Galal Amin, "On the Sorrows of Samia, Badriyya, Awatif, and Hannia," *ibid.*, 100.

29. On privatization as an indiscriminate and economically irrational dismantling of the public sector, see Galal Amin, "Six Remarks on the Selling of the Public Sector, *al-Ahaly* (20 April 1990).

30. *The Middle East* (April 1991).

31. Galal Amin, "The Truth Concerning Debt 'Relief'," *Al-Yassar* (February 1991): 105.

32. Galal Amin, "On The Sorrows of Samia."

33. *International Herald Tribune* (20 September 1991).

34. *The Middle East* (July 1991).

35. *The Middle East* (April 1991).

36. Muhammad Hassanein Haikal, interview by Muhammad Salmawy in the *Ahram Weekly*, from *al Sha'ab* (4 June 1991).

37. Muhammad al Sayyed Said, "Rehabilitating the Arab System: A Chance for Success. . . . But," *al Ahram* (31 May 1991).

38. Ahmed Abdullah, *Trilogies*, 14–16.

39. *Ibid.*, 18–19.

40. Magdy Sobhi, "The Political Economy in the Postwar Era," *International Politics* (Cairo: July 1991).

41. *Ibid.*

42. Muhammad Hassanein Haikal, interview by Muhammad Salmawy in the *Ahram Weekly*, from *Al Sha'ab* (4 June 1991).

43. Muhammad al-Sayyed Said, "The Future of the Palestinian Question Following the Gulf Crisis," *al Ahram* (26 April 1991).

44. *Ibid.*

45. Muhammad Hassanein Haikal: "We're going on a trip of losing ourselves. . . . What the Arabs are offered today is to sign the agreement with Israel or they will be subject to what happened to Iraq" (interview by Mustafa Bakry, *Masr al-Fatah* (26 August 1991).

46. Philip Galab, "The Greatest Discovery: International Law," *The Other Opinion on the Disaster in the Gulf* (Cairo: Madbouli Press, 1991): 17–18.

47. Muhammad Hassanein Haikal, interview.

48. Galal Amin, "In Defense of the Conspiracy Theory," 71–72.

49. Amin Huwaidy, "Meditation: The Power Concept Following the Desert Storm," *al-Ahaly* (25 September 1991).

50. Muhammad Sayyed Said, "The Iraqi Aggression: The Political and Moral Crisis," *al Ahram* (17 August 1990).

51. *Ibid.*

52. In January 1992, Muhammad Sid Ahmed expressed these leftist misgivings about moving too rapidly in the democratic direction directly to Egyptian President Husny Mubarak in a public exchange. Shireen T. Hunter, *The Christian Science Monitor* (12 June 1992), comments critically on this premature inclination in the region "to use the Algerian experience as an excuse for putting the brakes on democratization."

53. The views of Mahmud Amin al-Alim and Rifa'at al-Said were given in a conference of prominent leftists reported in *al-Ahaly* (15 May 1991).

54. Sayyid Yassine, interviewed by Zeinab Montasser, "The Press in the Arab World is 'Imprisoned'," *Rose al-Yusuf* (9 September 1991): 34–37.

55. *Ibid.*

56. Galal Amin, "The Truth Concerning Debt 'Relief'," *al-Yassar* (February 1991)

57. Galal Amin, "The Arab Intellectual and the Crisis of the Gulf," *The Arabs and the Calamity of Kuwait* (Cairo: Madbouli Press, 1991): 59.

58. *Ibid.*, 50–57.

59. Sayyid Yassine, "The Arab Intellectuals Confronting The Gulf Crisis," *al Ahram* (8 March 1991).

60. *Ibid.*

61. *Ibid.*

62. Galal Amin, "The Arab Intellectual."

63. *Ibid.*

64. *Ibid.*

65. Ibid.

18

Turkey, the Gulf Crisis, and the New World Order

Tozun Bahcheli

Following Iraq's invasion of Kuwait on 2 August 1990, Turkey played an important role in the U.S.-led coalition. It did so by shutting the twin pipeline that transported half of Iraq's oil exports from Kirkuk to the port of Yumurtalik on Turkey's Mediterranean coast. The subsequent Saudi cut-off of the Iraqi pipeline that stretched to Yanbu on the Red Sea and the prevention of Iraqi oil exports through the Gulf by the navies of the coalition members thus denied Baghdad the ability to export petroleum.

Although Turkish troops did not engage the Iraqi military, Turkey nonetheless served the coalition in two important ways. First, it massed an estimated 100,000 troops along its 240-kilometer border with Iraq, thus forcing the Iraqis to commit an equivalent force. This deployment caused Iraq concern as it feared that the coalition forces would initiate a second front in the north. Second, the Turks allowed the United States to use bases (principally the Incirlik air base in southeastern Turkey) to bomb targets in northern Iraq during the Gulf War.

In view of the traditional reticence of Turkey to be involved in disputes between states in the region, many observers were surprised by the Turkish government's unequivocal commitment to the U.S.-led coalition against Iraq. In Turkey, the government was vigorously criticized by the opposition parties and most newspapers for its risky commitments that could embroil Turkey in a war with Iraq. A majority of Turkish people also opposed their government's Gulf policy. Ultimately, though, given the outcome of Operation Desert Storm, Turkish President Turgut Ozal could boast that Turkey had emerged from the war on the winning side.

Ozal's role

The architect of Turkey's Gulf policy was President Ozal, who acted in tandem with the Bush administration from the beginning of the crisis to help defeat Iraq. Ozal's determination and stewardship of Turkey's Gulf policy was remarkable in many respects. Since the introduction of multiparty democracy in Turkey in 1950, the role of Turkish presidents was essentially ceremonial; real executive power was exercised by the prime minister and his cabinet. Before being elected to the presidency by the unicameral Turkish parliament, Ozal had served as prime minister for five years. During the election of 1987, his Motherland Party received 32 percent of the national vote but was able to capture a majority of seats in parliament. In the local election held in March 1989, Ozal's party received only 22 percent of the vote. Eight months later, when his standing in the polls fell to a new low, Ozal used his party's parliamentary majority to get elected to the presidency. Also, Ozal handpicked Yildirim Akbulut, a lackluster and compliant politician, to succeed him as party leader and prime minister. In this way Ozal succeeded in appropriating many of the powers of the prime minister's office. The opposition parties bitterly criticized Ozal's maneuver to get elected to the seven-year presidency and his administration of the country from the presidential palace.

None of this controversy diminished Ozal's determination to control the government and to take charge personally of Turkey's response to the Gulf crisis. During the first week of the crisis, when Turkey was pressured to shut off the oil pipelines, the announcement that the pipelines were being closed was made by Ozal without Foreign Minister Ali Bozer's prior knowledge.[1] Bozer's feathers were further ruffled when Ozal omitted him from the substantive talks with President George Bush and his aides in Washington in late September 1990. Bozer subsequently resigned on 18 October 1990. Barely a week later, Defense Minister Safa Giray, a senior member of the cabinet, also resigned, although his departure reportedly "came less as a result of disputes over departmental policy than as part of the continuing battle between the liberals and religious conservatives within the party."[2]

There were fears of more damaging political fallout when Turkey's chief of its armed forces, Necip Torumtay, resigned. It was widely reported that in addition to his displeasure with Ozal over a personal snub,[3] Torumtay's resignation was related to the military chiefs' anxiety over the possibility that Ozal's Gulf policy might involve the Turkish military in a war with Iraq. The military brass had good reason to be concerned, particularly with the missiles and unconventional weaponry in the Iraqi arsenal; in contrast, the Turkish military was outfitted with Korean War-vintage arms. Still, Ozal promptly appointed a new military chief; he brushed aside his critics at home, and stayed the course. During the months leading to and after the outbreak of the war, he was regularly interviewed on U.S. and European television, and he used those opportunities to underline Turkey's support for the international coalition against Iraq. This did not just enhance his international profile but, to some extent, helped publicize the linchpin role that Turkey played in the strategy to force Iraq to give up Kuwait.

However much the style of the Turkish president and the risks of his Gulf policy bothered some Turks, it could not be said that Ozal acted in a political vacuum. The rationale for his actions was widely shared by some foreign policy bureaucrats, military leaders, and even some of the politicians who criticized his brazen handling of the crisis.

The Gulf crisis came about at a time when many of Turkey's policymakers were lamenting the diminution of the strategic utility of their country to the Western alliance because the confrontation between the superpowers was substantially diminishing. For the previous forty years, Turkey's strategic value to the West had been based on the perceived threat of the Soviet Union. As the cold war ended, Turkish policymakers were just beginning to absorb the implications of the epochal changes in the international environment and to reflect on how best to protect Turkey's influence in a rapidly changing world.

Against this background, Ozal saw the crisis as an opportunity for Turkey to garner both short- and long-term diplomatic and military advantages. "More importantly, the very nature of Turkey's short-term relationships with the United States and the European Community was suddenly opened up to longer-term evaluation."[4] Ozal hoped to improve Turkey's case for membership in the European Community and to strengthen the perception of Turkey as an asset in the Middle East for both the Americans and Europeans.

Because of its implementation of UN sanctions against Iraq, Turkey's economic losses were substantial. According to one estimate, Turkey "lost up to $7 billion in revenue from exports, pipeline fees, tourism, and contracts."[5] Although the Turks were disappointed with the level of support which they received, the effect of the crisis on their economy was not as severe as initially feared. The United States provided U.S. $82 million in emergency funds for a start, and made a commitment to increase the annual military assistance from U.S. $515 million in 1990 to U.S. $700 million in 1992. In addition, the Bush administration doubled Turkey's textile quota. The Japanese also assisted with U.S. $300 million, and an equal sum was pledged by the Kuwaiti government in exile. Additional aid was provided by the European Community, while the Saudis offered U.S. $1 billion in oil. Nonetheless, in spite of this compensation, the aid received covered only an estimated third of Turkey's losses.[6]

Turkey's Stake in the Crisis and Relations with Iraq

Turkey's alacrity in joining others to confront Iraq appeared to some as extraordinary. After all, quite apart from the general proclivity of the Turks to stay out of their neighbors' affairs, Turkey's relations with Iraq were not marred by deep-seated animosities. Moreover, in recent years, Turkey had emerged as one of Iraq's main trading partners. What then were the motivations guiding Turkey's Gulf policy?

To begin, the Turks saw Iraq's invasion of Kuwait, as did the vast majority of states, as a blatant case of aggression by one country against another sovereign state. In taking an unequivocal position on Kuwait, Turkey demonstrated its commitment to the protection of the existing state system in the Middle East. If Iraq were allowed to have its way, what future claims would other states face on legitimacy and borders?

Beyond these considerations, Turkey was agitated by the potential shift in the balance of power posed by Iraq's action. If Iraq incorporated oil-rich Kuwait, it would become a stronger power and be in a much better position to dominate other states in the region. President Saddam Hussein's track record worried the Turks. Turkey remained neutral during the course of the Iran-Iraq War, and made some attempts to help negotiate an end to it, but along with other governments, Ankara was convinced that Saddam Hussein's precipitation of the war was motivated by a desire to dominate the region.

It suited Turkey's purposes that neither Iraq nor Iran won the eight-year war. The Islamic Republic of Iran had aggravated Turkey because of its periodic intervention in domestic Turkish politics on the side of the Islamist groups. On several occasions, Ayatollah Khomeini and other senior members of the Iranian government had offended the mainstream Turkish leaders by criticizing the secularism of the Turkish state.

Although Turkey's relations with Iraq in the 1980s indicated considerable pragmatic cooperation, and there were fewer irritants, new stresses had appeared. Turkish leaders worried about the enhancement of Iraq's weapons capabilities, as did the rest of Iraq's neighbors. As one writer stated, "Turkey has been alarmed at the stockpiling, use and increasing threat of use of nonconventional weapons by Iraq."[7] In particular, Iraq's development of long-range missiles capable of hitting targets in Turkey made the Turks uneasy. This did not mean that the Turks expected the Iraqis to make war on their country. There were no territorial disputes between the two countries, and none of their disagreements had made war a credible contingency. Nevertheless, Iraq and Syria (which Turkey also suspected of aspirations of regional hegemony) were threats to Turkey. Turkish leaders were concerned that an assertive Iraq, growing stronger by the year, might confront Turkey more aggressively in the future.

Of the bilateral issues that appeared on the diplomatic agenda of Turkey and Iraq, the most important was water. Since Turkey had embarked on the mammoth Southeast Anatolia Project (known in Turkey by its acronym GAP) during the 1980s, relations between Turkey and Iraq (as well with the other affected riparian state, Syria) had soured. The GAP project, which cost Turkey an estimated U.S. $21 billion, involved the construction of twenty-two dams on the Euphrates and Tigris rivers (both originating in eastern Turkey) that will bring water to the semi-arid southeastern part of the country and increase Turkey's electricity generation by 50 percent. The Euphrates flows from Turkey into Syria and then to Iraq, whereas the Tigris flows directly from Turkey into Iraq. When the project is complete, it will irrigate at least 1.88 million acres and will eventually double the nation's agricultural output.

While Turkish spokesmen trumpeted the great promise of GAP, the Syrians and Iraqis, beginning in the 1980s, increasingly voiced their concerns regarding the sharp reduction in the amounts of water they would receive, and the adverse economic implications for their countries as Turkey moved ahead with the project. On 13 January 1990, Iraq and Syria realized their vulnerability when Turkey diverted the waters of the Euphrates for an entire month to fill the giant Atatürk Dam, the centerpiece of the project. Although Turkey warned

Baghdad and Damascus of its plans, both the Iraqi and Syrian governments protested the damage done to their economies. "Indeed, the dramatic drop in the flow of the river caused a great outcry in the entire Arab world. By the time the normal flow was restored, the water issue was cited as a possible future cause of war."[8] Syria and Iraq lobbied effectively to deny the project credits from the Islamic Development Bank, and the Iraqi government was instrumental in the Arab League's censure of Turkey for its diversion of the Euphrates.

In an interview granted to a Turkish journalist in early May 1990, Iraqi Vice President Taha Yasin Ramadan identified water as the most troublesome issue between his country and Turkey and stated that the future of Iraqi-Turkish relations was predicated on the mutually agreed upon sharing of the Euphrates waters.[9] Clearly, Turkey's GAP project was a reminder to Iraq of its reliance on Turkey's good will.

According to a scholar well-versed in Iraqi-Turkish relations, Baghdad felt growing unease and irritation over its increased dependence on Turkey during the 1980s when Iraq was engaged in its exhausting war with Iran.[10] When Iran forced Iraq to close its Gulf ports in the early stages of the Iran-Iraq War, Turkey became an important transshipment route for Iraq. "Turkey's location made it the obvious and cheapest route for Iraqi imports from Europe. Moreover, the land link between Turkey and Europe meant that imports could travel by road as well as by sea."[11]

The war with Iran also forced Baghdad to rely more heavily on Turkey for exporting its petroleum. When Syria shut off Iraq's oil pipeline in April 1982 to punish the Baghdad regime for engaging in war with Iran, the Iraqi government responded by expanding the capacity of the Iraqi-Turkish pipeline (which opened in 1977), and constructed a second line which began operations in 1987. Both Iraq and Turkey benefitted economically from this interdependence, but as the subsequent closure of the pipelines following Iraq's invasion of Kuwait illustrated, Turkey gained strategic leverage over Iraq that it did not previously have.

It is true that Iraqi and Turkish governments share a common interest on the Kurdish issue, and have periodically collaborated to contain the threat of Kurdish nationalist groups. It is estimated that twelve million Kurds live in Turkey,[12] concentrated in the southeastern and eastern areas of the country bordering Syria, Iraq, and Iran: They comprise between 15 and 20 percent of the total population. By comparison, the Kurds' share of Iraq's total population may be as high as 20 to 25 percent.[13] Both states view Kurdish national aspirations as a threat to their territorial integrity and have been frustrated by their inability to deal with the issue effectively.

In Turkey, the most pressing challenge has been posed by the Kurdistan Workers Party (PKK), a Marxist-oriented Kurdish organization dedicated to creating a Kurdish state on Turkey's southeastern border. The insurgency that the PKK initiated in 1984 has claimed the lives of more than 4,500 people. The Turkish government was hampered in dealing with the PKK's hit-and-run operations, particularly because Kurdish fighters often operated from neighboring Syria as well as from Iraq.

When the Baghdad regime was preoccupied with its war against Iran, Iraqi Kurds were able to exercise control in much of Iraqi Kurdistan, save for the major cities and other strategically important areas. Ankara complained that Kurdish guerrilla fighters operating on Iraqi soil were waging hit-and-run attacks on Turkey, and the government pressed Baghdad to give Turkey rights of pursuit. Given its own interest in averting separate Kurdish national entities on its own soil or next door, Iraq complied. An agreement was reached in 1984 to enable Turkish personnel to pursue PKK fighters across the border with Iraq.

Even the potential convergence of Turkish-Iraqi interest on the Kurdish issue did not prevent the two countries from getting upset with one another. When Iraq launched its infamous attack on the Kurds by using chemical weapons after its cease-fire with Iran in August 1988, tens of thousands of Iraqi Kurds sought refuge across the border in Turkey. Turkey felt obliged to grant many of them sanctuary, which angered the Baghdad regime. "The Iraqis felt that Turkey had trifled with its security in an attempt to curry favor with the United States and the EC, and to garner votes for Turgut Ozal among Turkish Kurds. Having 'infuriated' their neighbors by this policy, the Turks then experienced a 'cooling' in bilateral relations."[14]

During the two years between the end of Iraq's war with Iran and its invasion of Kuwait, other issues ruffled Turkish-Iraqi relations. In 1989, when the "hot pursuit" accord expired, the Iraqis refused to extend it unless the water issue was resolved to their satisfaction. The Turks in turn upset the Iraqi government by impounding and returning to Britain parts of the Iraqi "supergun." They also turned down Iraq's request that Turkey increase the amount of the Euphrates water it would release from 550 square meters per second to 750 square meters per second.[15] Both governments also quibbled over Iraq's failure to pay for the credits that Turkey extended to its neighbor for its purchase of Turkish goods. By 1990, Iraq owed Turkey U.S. $2 billion. It took a series of tough negotiations to reach agreement on rescheduling the U.S. $1.4 billion that Iraq was unable to repay in 1989. In early May 1990, Turkish Prime Minister Akbulut visited Baghdad to help smooth the strained bilateral relations, but his talks with the Iraqi leadership failed to reduce the growing mistrust between the two neighbors; some Turkish newspapers complained of the cool treatment that Iraqi leaders had given to the Turkish premier.[16]

The New Order after the Gulf War and Turkey's Role

When the Gulf War ended, Turks were relieved that their country was spared any direct involvement or damage. Ozal boasted that "siding with the winner was always advantageous."[17] Ozal was certainly vindicated by the results of the Gulf crisis. Without committing any troops to combat or suffering any retaliation from Iraq, Turkey increased its stock among the Western capitals and even among its neighbors. If Ozal's detractors at home had their way, Turkey would have emerged from the crisis on the sidelines, scrambling to be heard.

The defeat of Iraq benefited Turkey in that Iraq, its powerful and potentially troublesome neighbor, will deal with the Turks from a position of weakness for some time. Hussein reportedly gave some assistance to the PKK to spite Ankara,[18] but the urgency of its domestic needs and continued external vulnerabilities should keep the Iraqi regime preoccupied. Besides, the Iraqis need the Turks to export their oil. In regard to the water issue, the Turks will use their newly achieved clout and press ahead with the completion of the GAP project without having to worry as much about Iraq's (or Syria's) hindrance. During a visit to Turkey in March 1991, Iraq's Tariq Aziz declared his country's readiness to let bygones be bygones.[19]

In spite of their economic losses in the Gulf crisis, the Turks capitalized on their role by gaining substantial amounts of modern hardware, which their armed forces badly needed. According to one report, Turkey received U.S. $8 billion worth of arms "available as a result of disarmament on the Central European stage. These included 1,000 tanks, 700 armored personnel carriers, and a range of missiles."[20]

Notwithstanding its enhanced military capabilities, Turkey was most unlikely to become directly involved in the new security arrangements in the Gulf area.[21] There was a period during the early months of the crisis when it appeared possible that Turkish troops would join a deterrent Gulf force (alongside those of conservative Arab states like Saudi Arabia and Egypt) once Iraq was forced out of Kuwait. Apparently there was disappointment in Ankara that Turkey had not been invited to the meeting of member states of the Gulf Cooperation Council, Syria, and Egypt to discuss Gulf security in March 1991. Syrian and Egyptian leaders were even more disillusioned that the "Declaration of Damascus" (6 March 1991) was unfulfilled, and that Gulf states preferred U.S. military commitments. It was unrealistic, then, to expect a direct Turkish role in Gulf security.

In any case, Ankara became increasingly preoccupied with the volatile new politics in the neighboring Balkans and the Caucasus where Turkish involvement was solicited by some of the parties engaged in conflict. Many Turks have expressed an affinity for Bosnian Muslim Slavs and have displayed a strong interest in their tragic predicament. Over two million Bosnians have settled in Turkey over the past several decades, and this helped buttress Turkish interest in Bosnia. The besieged government of Bosnia-Herzegovina repeatedly sought Ankara's help to stem the advance of the militarily superior Serbian nationalist forces.

Turkey's leaders resisted any recourse that would result in the unilateral deployment of the Turkish military. Ankara joined others in providing substantial humanitarian assistance and was in the forefront of the diplomatic efforts to secure Western military intervention in the new Balkan state.

Turkey's assistance has also been solicited by Albania and Macedonia, both of which feared Serbian and, to a lesser extent, Greek designs. If the Serbian forces extended their military campaign from Bosnia and Croatia into the formerly autonomous province of Kosovo, where the Albanians constituted 90 percent of the population, Albania would be unable to resist direct involvement. Such an escalation would put additional pressures on Turkey to extend its level of involvement from economic and diplomatic to military. Turkish leaders do not relish such a scenario, but at the same time, pressure from the Balkan Muslim peoples to help, and the desire to be a participant in the restructuring of the Balkans, will make Turkish involvement unavoidable.

The ongoing conflict between Armenia and Azerbaijan over Nagorno-Karabagh threatened to draw Turkey into the troubled affairs of yet another region on its borders. Of the newly independent Turkic states that were part of the former Soviet Union, Azerbaijan was the nearest and had forged the closest relations with Turkey. Turkish leaders strenuously avoided any direct involvement in the fighting between Armenian and Azeri forces and joined Russia, Iran, and the United States in encouraging a pacific settlement of their disputes. Ankara was well aware that an overt alliance with Azerbaijan against Armenia could cause serious damage to its international standing and influence.

Although conflicts beyond its immediate borders invited interest and involvement, Turkey was also increasingly challenged by a Kurdish nationalist insurgency at home. From the Turkish point of view, one of the unwelcome (and unexpected) consequences of the Gulf War was the new international attention claimed by the Kurds of Iraq. Turkey's refusal to accept large numbers of desperate Kurdish refugees in the aftermath of their failed rebellion against the Hussein regime was widely criticized in some European capitals and drew attention to the Turkish Kurds as well. Turkish leaders believed that the acceptance of hundreds of thousands of Kurds on Turkish soil would exacerbate their own Kurdish problem. To deal with the refugee problem, Ozal proposed creating safe havens for the Kurds in northern Iraq. The idea was subsequently accepted and acted upon by the British and U.S. governments.

Clearly, the Turks are intensely interested in the fortunes of the Kurdish national movement in Iraq because of its effects on Turkish Kurds. In an important policy shift, Ankara opened a dialogue with Iraqi Kurdish groups; Jelal Talabani, leader of the Patriotic Union of Kurdistan (PUK) and Masoud Barzani, head of the Kurdish Democratic Party (KDP) regularly visited Ankara for discussions with Turkish officials. These leaders consider Turkey's good will and cooperation indispensable for maintaining Kurdish autonomy in northern Iraq in the allies' security zone above the thirty-sixth parallel. It is primarily through Turkey that the Kurds of Iraq receive substantial supplies of food and medicine, as well as some fuel.

For their part, Turkish leaders enlisted the help of Iraqi Kurdish leaders in pushing the PKK fighters from northern Iraq where they had launched attacks across the border in Turkey. Ankara expressed its opposition to the declaration of a federated Kurdish state in northern Iraq during October 1992, however, and stated its opposition to the partition of Iraqi territory. Clearly, the Turks were concerned that a Kurdish state across its borders in northern Iraq would encourage Kurdish nationalists in Turkey who aspired to autonomy or independence in the southeast.

In a remarkable reversal of policy, Turkish authorities removed the decades-old ban on speaking and publishing in Kurdish. It is widely expected that Turkish Kurds will soon enjoy other cultural rights, and that the Kurdish language will be part of their educational institutions and the media. There is, however, no indication that these measures will stem the tide of Kurdish separatism.

Indeed, there is a growing sense of gloom among many Turks that the Kurdish issue will increasingly burden the Turkish state, and that a long, drawn-out struggle between the Turkish authorities and Kurdish nationalist groups is inevitable. Fighting between Turkish forces and the Kurdish PKK during the first eight months of 1992 alone claimed nearly 1,500 lives. Turkey also faces the prospect of problematic relations with Europe for the harsh measures it applied against some Kurdish communities in the southeast, as it sought to win a military victory against the PKK.

Ironically, the desire to contain Kurdish nationalism probably prompted many Turkish officials to begin normalizing relations with the Baghdad regime.[22] For Turkey, the economic benefits of renewed trade with Iraq, as well as the resumption of Iraqi oil exports through the Kirkuk-Yumurtalik pipeline, would be considerable. It is not conceivable, however, that Turkey will resume normal relations with the Hussein regime as long as the UN sanctions against Iraq continue.

As a result of the close collaboration between the United States and Turkey during the Gulf crisis, Turkish President Ozal hoped that in the new world order proclaimed by President Bush, Ankara and Washington would usher in a broadened strategic relationship, with Turkey assuming a more prominent regional status in Washington's global calculations.

These heady expectations failed to materialize. Many Turks criticized the Western powers' nonintervention policy toward Bosnia. Moreover, various political groups on the left as well as the right suspected ulterior motives in the U.S. policy of protection for the Kurds of northern Iraq. These groups believed that Washington wanted Iraq and Turkey to be partitioned. Most Turkish government officials do not share this view as it applies to Turkey, but are wary about further collaboration with the United States against Iraq. Thus, in July 1992, Ankara refused to allow the U.S.-led anti-Iraq coalition access to airbases for prospective raids against Baghdad.

Furthermore, Turkish support for Operation Provide Comfort has weakened considerably.

Clearly, Ankara and Washington do not see eye to eye on some issues, but it is still true that there is a considerable convergence of interests between the two countries. Turkey remains a stable, pro-Western state in an unstable region. The United States is promoting Turkey, with its secularism and parliamentary democracy, as a role model for the newly independent Turkic states in Central Asia. Moreover, the United States and Europe expect Turkey to play a pivotal and stabilizing role in the precarious Balkans and the Caucasus. For their part, the Turkish leaders still assign the highest priority to maintaining close ties with the West, even as the prospect of Turkish entry into the European Community becomes more uncertain. While many Turks believe that their country has incurred more costs than derived benefits for its role during the Gulf crisis, the Demirel government, which assumed office after the Gulf War, is essentially following the same path as his predecessor. This is a vindication of Ozal's political vision.

Notes

1. Philip Robins, *Turkey and the Middle East* (New York: Council on Foreign Relations Press, 1991): 70.

2. The Economist Intelligence Unit, *Turkey: Country Report* 4 (1990): 10.

3. Robins, *Turkey and the Middle East*, 72.

4. *Ibid.*, 68.

5. Reuters report in the *Middle East Times* (28 January–4 February 1992).

6. *New York Times* (13 March 1991).

7. Robins, *Turkey and the Middle East*, 63.

8. *Ibid.*, 90.

9. *Milliyet* (4 May 1990).

10. Robins, *Turkey and the Middle East*, 58-64.

11. *Ibid.*, 60.

12. Sami Kohen, "Turkey Cautiously Moving Toward 'Normalizing' Relations with Iraq," *The Washington Report on Middle East Affairs* (July 1991): 16.

13. See Mohammed M. Malek, "Kurdistan in the Middle East Conflict," *New Left Review* 175 (May–June 1989): 80.

14. Robins, *Turkey and the Middle East*, 63-64.

15. *Günes* (7 May 1990).

16. *Turkiye* (7 May 1990); *Sabah* (6 May 1990).

17. *New York Times* (13 March 1991).

18. *Ibid.* (20 October 1991).

19. Kohen, "Turkey Cautiously Moving."

20. Robins, *Turkey and the Middle East*, 71.

21. Nonetheless, one writer wrote, "The war has already underscored the 'return' of Turkey to the Middle East in a militarily significant way. Turkey will gain from the crisis to the extent that the weakening of Iraq does not entail a corresponding military threat from either Iran or Syria, or from Kurdish insurgents infiltrating the Turkish border" (see Shahram Chubin, "Post-war Gulf Security," *Survival* 33 [March–April 1991]: 145.

22. Robert Olson, "Turkey and Iraq: Toward Normalization?," *Middle East International* (7 August 1992): 19.

Part IV
Political Trends and
Cultural Patterns

19
The Middle East in the New World Order

Political Trends

Louis J. Cantori

Political trends in the Middle East in the aftermath of the Gulf War can be viewed from the three levels of analysis perspectives of the international system, the regional or subordinate system, and the domestic system. The recent dramatic global changes in the international system profoundly impacted the Middle Eastern regional system and significantly affected its politics.

The Changing International System

The end of the cold war in 1989 prepared the way for a U.S.-dominant unipolar international system in the 1990s. The political dissolution of the USSR reinforced that outcome. Concomitant with this, U.S. foreign policy needed to readjust from one attuned to the global activities and ambitions of the Soviet Union to one with new definitions of security and political interests.[1]

The international system's long-term future is likely to be one of regionally based multipolarity, such as Germany in Europe, China and Japan in East Asia, and Russia in Eurasia. Such great powers' interests are likely to compete in third regions, for example, Russia and the United States in the Middle East and China and Japan in Southeast Asia. Thus the current unipolarity of the international system represents a likely transitional phase from bipolarity to a possible regionally based multipolarity.

The Middle Eastern Subordinate System

Not surprisingly, a transitional unipolarity in the international system has impacted on the Middle Eastern international subordinate system, suggesting a similar state of transition there as well. The Middle Eastern regional system was unique in its relation to the international system for the historical intensity of superpower involvement and for the less-dependent nature of that involvement. The high level of local conflicts, such as the Palestinian question, Lebanon and the Gulf, combined with geopolitical and energy resource factors, always incurred intense superpower involvement. Seldom, however, were the superpowers able to determine Middle Eastern foreign policy (for example, the relative policy independence of Syria vis-à-vis the USSR and Israel vis-à-vis the United States). Such an intrusive system imposed by external great powers on regional actors might be characteristic of most regional systems world-wide, but the Middle East previously had eluded this oppressive type of relationship.[2] The end of superpower bipolarity in the international system resulted in the potential for greater superpower influence. In the absence of a regional actor to play one power off against the other, the single superpower has become more important.

Trends in the Intrusive System

The unipolar character of this intrusive system could have a stabilizing affect if U.S. policy remains active in the region, and if that policy is perceived as pursuing an equitable solution to the Palestinian problem or other mutually identifiable problems. In other words, the U.S. effort to parlay the military success of the allied coalition of the Gulf War into a diplomatic one is a contingent issue. If U.S. policy fails to be equitable, then U.S. paramountcy will decline, and the system will likely return to the more parochial interests of the region's states even while the United States remains regionally engaged in security and economic assistance, especially to Israel and Egypt. Unipolar intrusion is thus a conditional status.

More specifically, U.S. foreign policy in the Middle East previously centered on denying the region to the USSR, guaranteeing access to its oil, preserving the security of Israel, and accessing the crossroads of sea and air lanes that intersect the area. With the decline of the Russian threat to the area, the most salient issue now is oil, although the security of Israel remains an important concern. During the cold war Israel was viewed as not only a responsibility but a strategic asset. After the cold war, this was no longer the case, as illustrated in the Gulf War. Although Israel came under missile attack, it was important that it remain a noncombatant so as not to sabotage the coalition of Arab states aligned with the United States. The lines of sea and air communication were an important assurance as part of close U.S.-Egyptian ties. The emphasis on oil in U.S. policy resulted in the protection of the Gulf region with military security rather than the development of significant political diplomatic terms for the area. Nonetheless, the stability of the Middle East is of primary importance, and post-Gulf War U.S. policy did identify some goals: a security regime in that subregion, arms control, the Palestinian question, and economic development.[3]

The Palestinian problem seems to be the Gordian knot that should be cut to achieve regional stability, assurance of the security of Israel, a solution to arms proliferation, and possible economic redistribution in the region. Hence a peace settlement should be a priority in contemporary U.S. policy.

Middle East and Gulf Interdependencies

There was always a tendency on the part of U.S. policy to separate the politics of the Gulf from those of the Middle East as a whole. Illustrative of this has been the Gulf-centric nature of U.S. policy. It is the oil of the Gulf and the security of friendly states that have been the focal point of U.S. policy.[4]

Although the United States assumed that the Gulf acted independently of the Middle East, there are, in fact, five factors that deny this premise. The first (often overlooked) concerns the regional foreign policy ambitions of Gulf and non-Gulf Arab states and the emergence of a regional multipolar, potentially Egyptian, hegemonic system. In the case of the Gulf states, the continuing afterglow of the Gulf War should not obscure the fact that Saudi and other Gulf leadership depend for their legitimacy on supporting the Palestinian movement as an Arab cause and regaining Jerusalem as an Islamic cause. Toward this end, money flows outward in large amounts from Saudi Arabia to Islamic groups throughout the Arab and Islamic world. More important is the Egyptian assumption of its natural hegemonic leadership role in the Arab world including the Gulf.[5] In the latter case, its credible military role in Desert Storm held the promise of a regional collective security role in the Gulf, which thus far has been denied in favor of the United States. The broader point is that presently there is a dynamic at work in the Middle East revolving around the emergence of a multi-polar regional international system in which Egypt, Syria, and Saudi Arabia are current actors, but in which Iran and eventually Iraq will be significant players.

A second regional factor is that the Gulf states are dependent upon accepted principles of political legitimacy, which they share with the region as a whole. Two interconnected sub-issues tie in with political legitimacy. One of these is the unresolved nature of the Palestinian issue. Prior to August 1990, the Gulf states dealt with this issue largely through rhetoric and large-scale financial support of the Palestinian Liberation Organization (PLO). A second issue is that hundreds of thousands of Palestinians were welcomed for their advanced skills as employees in private and public sectors in the Gulf. When the PLO embraced Saddam Hussein, these lines were severed with an as yet unknown potential for instability. The Palestinians were subsequently expelled from the Gulf along with highly skilled Jordanian workers. In the short run, opposition sentiment in the Gulf states has accepted these actions, but they could contribute to the weakening of legitimacy in the long run.

In addition to the political aspects of the legitimacy issue and its potential for Gulf state instability, there has been a third related factor of economic transfers to the nonpetroleum-producing countries in the form of remittances by Jordanians and Palestinians. The sudden severing of these transfers in the aftermath of the Gulf War is having a devastating effect on the economies of Jordan and the Occupied Territories, increasing the prospects for instability there as well.

The broader regional perspective affects the Gulf in a fourth way: U.S. power projections and the need to maintain good relations with key Middle Eastern states in order to gain air and sea passageways in case of a major buildup. Egypt is probably the single most important Middle Eastern country in this regard. Its large size and geopolitical locations in northeastern geographical Africa and the eastern Mediterranean make it a strategic air passageway, and its control of the Suez Canal assures its importance in terms of a sea passageway.

A fifth factor relates to military forward presence and prepositioning. In reference to the former, the politics of the Middle East tends to preclude this option. The memory of colonialism and the strength of nationalism preclude all except the most nominal forward presence, such as the pre-Gulf War sea plane headquarters of the U.S. Navy in Bahrain. In the ebullience of the immediate post-Gulf War

Middle East there was talk of such a forward presence, but this receded even while rumors persisted of a covert U.S. troop presence in the eastern province of Saudi Arabia. In the past, overt pre-positioning as a presumably less provocative policy than forward presence proved impossible in the Middle East. One example is the much discussed Ras Bannas military base in Southern Egypt in the 1980s. The only overt pre-positioning possible until now was in Israel, but the use of such material in a regional conflict would have a political liability resembling that of possible Israeli participation in Desert Storm. Covert pre-positioning in Turkey and, to a more limited degree, Egypt is politically more feasible. The recently concluded bilateral agreements with Kuwait, Bahrain, and Oman and similar agreements with other Gulf states are noteworthy for their public character and carry potential destabilizing baggage.[6]

Related to the foregoing is the substitution for a kind of forward presence and peaceful engagement by periodic deployments and joint maneuvers. Egypt again is instructive in this regard. In general, periodic deployments of U.S. forces in Egypt occurred that were technically outside of Egyptian authority, as battalion-sized units assigned as UN truce supervisory units in the Sinai. In addition, the joint maneuvers of Operation Bright Star were carried out in near secrecy with the help of the internal Egyptian press, out of respect for Egyptian domestic political sensibilities. Gulf leadership, although not bothered by the issue of a free press as was Egypt, may still feel politically vulnerable.[7] Kuwait has permitted large-scale joint maneuvers, such as those that occurred in the summer of 1992.

U.S. Foreign Policy, U.S. Security Assistance, and Arms Control

U.S. foreign policy in the Middle East has expressed itself through diplomacy and security measures. The Gulf War dramatically illustrated the latter, while the continuing peace process illustrates the former. Access to Gulf oil and the relation of this access to oil pricing gives this sub-area of the Middle East its importance in U.S. international security policy.[8] Forward presence and military prepositioning were indicative of this security policy.

Security assistance in terms of military assistance and sales are also related to international security policy. In fact, one is tempted to characterize security assistance as the "magic wand" of U.S. international security policy. It is supposed to substitute for the decline in the U.S. defense budget as a way of increasing regional military capability and gaining goodwill. Clearly implied is that security assistance will increase military capabilities on a nearly cost free basis and lessen the need for U.S. force commitments. From this point of view security assistance is nowhere in more dramatic evidence than in the Middle East where, since the end of Desert Storm, billions of dollars of sales were authorized and approved.

There are two dimensions to such security assistance that might be commented on. The first is the tension between the advocacy of the alleged benefits of security assistance to U.S. policy and the advocacy of arms control. One policy objective appears to contradict the other.[9]

A second dimension of security assistance is the lack of evidence to support its alleged benefit of increasing military capability. For political reasons, security assistance in the Middle East had a major impact in Israel and Egypt. The resulting enormous military capability of Israel benefitted U.S. policy because Israel became militarily self-reliant. The potential benefit of Israel's military capability as a military ally was nullified by Israel's political liabilities, as recently seen in its mandated nonperformance in Desert Storm.

Egypt illustrated a second feature of military capabilities via security assistance. It alone among the Arab countries possessed the population and power to benefit from such assistance and was unique among Arab non-Gulf states in being politically eligible for such assistance. Security assistance to the Gulf states was politically important in terms of presumed goodwill toward the United States and of marginal military importance because of small populations and low power capabilities. Again, this was illustrated by the relative military unimportance of the Gulf Cooporation Council (GCC) forces in Desert Storm. Egypt thus was the single state that truly benefited and will likely continue to benefit from security assistance. But the full benefit of this to U.S. policy was denied by Egypt's apparent exclusion from the regional security regime in the Gulf.

A Regional Security Regime for the Gulf

Attention to an indigenous and mutual regional collective security appears to be a missing link between the U.S. national security interests and security assistance as a means of increasing military capability. The present policy of large amounts of security assistance and U.S. force commitments suggests a degree of redundancy. The former seems to deny the necessity for the latter. This failure to address the possibilities of regional security arrangements rather than U.S. force guarantees further illustrates that the United States is not supporting regional self-reliance.

At an Arab summit meeting in Syria in March 1991, a "Damascus Declaration" was issued that called for Syria and Egypt to assume security responsibilities in the Gulf.[10] Since that date, however, this indigenous Arab approach was quietly dropped in favor of a prominent U.S. role in Gulf security, which in turn was supplemented by a Saudi decision to double its force levels and become more self-reliant.[11] The reason for the apparent abandonment of a Syrian and Egyptian role in the Gulf probably reflects a long-standing Saudi Arabian fear of Egyptian hegemony. It is better to have a U.S. commitment that might in practice be slipped back "over the horizon" than an Egyptian commitment with its attendant political ascendancy and attendant threatening republican nonmonarchical principles.[12]

Subordinate System Relations

There are broad changes at work within the regional system. The most general change is that Islamism was added to its basic Arabism. Islam, the more universalizing phenomenon, reduced the alienation of two of its peripheral states, Turkey and Iran. In the case of Turkey, increasing domestic religious sentiment made the country receptive to Islamic cultural influences and caused Turkish policy to increasingly think of itself as a broker between the Middle East and the West. This was reinforced by a Turkish realization that its opportunity for European Community membership was probably waning. This sentiment also acted as a constraint on Turkish policy in the recent Gulf War.[13]

The case of Iran was more profound. Whether in Lebanon in the front ranks against Israel or in the Gulf where Islamic solidarity was used to ameliorate Arab Gulf state fears even while its Shiism acted in the opposite direction, Iran had now joined the core grouping of Middle East states.[14] In the core, the international Islamic Conference Organization (consisting of all Islamic states in the world) facilitated Egypt's reentry into the Arab state system, and Saudi subventions to Islamic organizations in other countries abound. Most important, the Israeli occupation of the holy places of Jerusalem animated Islamic sentiment in all Middle Eastern states and groups on the Palestinian question.

The Gulf War, and the special Arab coalition developed to pursue it, continues to have diplomatic bounce even though the bounce may be declining in energy, and old alignments may be reemerging as new ones arise. Among the old alignments are Saudi reservations about Egyptian and Syrian ambitions, which have subsequently denied those states an important security force role in the Gulf. In addition, Egypt and Saudi Arabia joined Syria in reestablishing diplomatic ties with Iran. Iran as an important Gulf War benefactor is catered to in order to constrain its potential for Gulf hegemony. Lebanon reemerged and was stabilized by its restoration as a Syrian sphere of influence; this resulted in the resolution of the conflict in Lebanon, with the exception of the Israeli occupation of the southern part of the country.[15]

A major paradox is that even while the leadership of the PLO and Intifada were in disarray, the Palestinian problem was energized by the U.S. diplomatic initiative that attempted to expand upon the singularity of a military victory in expelling Iraq from Kuwait in the Gulf War. But Iraq still retains a significant conventional fighting force and Saddam Hussein remains in power. There is a potential U.S. domestic political question of exactly what the war achieved.[16] Therefore, the "linkage" question of the Palestinians that was denied by the United States during the war is being addressed: to stabilize the region for security reasons, to enlarge for U.S. domestic political reasons the claims of success in the Gulf War, and to assuage the United States' wartime Arab allies. Thus, the new alignments, especially of Syrian, Egyptian, and intra-Arab cooperation, are sustained by the problematic peace initiative.

In light of the foregoing, Iraq's defeat failed to revise regional international relationships and therefore could not impose its will on the Gulf and Palestinian questions. With two exceptions, the U.S.-led allied victory returned Middle Eastern relationships to their pre-Gulf War position. The exceptions are Israel and Iran; they are the winners in the Gulf War in that their common adversary, Iraq, has been vanquished at little cost to themselves. But while they may be beneficiaries, the inertia of Israel's settlement policy remains a destabilizing factor, however, and Iran's Gulf policy is enigmatic. Equally destabilizing could be the ascendancy of more radical regimes in key Arab countries and their possible acquisition of the missile guidance systems and "smart" weapons technology that are present in the international arms market.[17]

Regional Issues

The Pre-Gulf War Background

The pre-August 1990 period held both diplomatic hope and some accomplishment toward resolving the three major conflicts of the Gulf region. Therefore, significant disappointment was felt on the eve of the war. Among the three major conflicts, the Palestinian question was the most complex (the others being Lebanon and the Iran-Iraq War). The 1982 Israeli invasion of Lebanon weakened but did not eliminate the PLO. As settlement of the Occupied Territories increased in the late 1980s, the Palestinian "internals" (those inside the Occupied Territories) took control of their fate and in December 1987 launched the Intifada. Their initiative coincided with the efforts of Egypt to play the Palestinian hand to gain reentry into the Arab state system (after its exclusion in the wake of the 1979 peace treaty with Israel).[18] The intersection of these two developments resulted in the November 1988 declaration by the PLO "externals" (those outside the Occupied Territories) of their acceptance of UN Resolutions 242 and 338. This signified the PLO's recognition of Israel and its willingness to sit down with Israel and negotiate land for peace. Israel was reluctant to abandon its policy of annexing the Occupied Territories and, in spite of diligent U.S. efforts to pursue a peace process, by the spring of 1990, the effort proved fruitless. This was followed by Israeli repression during which over 800 Palestinians were killed, a hardline Israeli government was elected, and U.S. talks with the PLO broke off on 20 June, as a result of an abortive Palestinian beach front raid in Israel. All of these events caused the spirits of Palestinians both inside and outside of Israel to be at a low ebb by the summer of 1990.[19] Saddam Hussein's rhetoric of justice for the Palestinians and the reality of his missile attacks upon Israel therefore received understandable but ill-considered support from "internals" and "externals" alike.

The Lebanese conflict began with the civil war of 1975 and ended when Syria intervened in 1976, only to be reopened by the Israeli invasion of June 1982. The pathology of the militia wars and Western hostage-taking ensued. Numerous attempts to cease hostilities failed until a meeting of the still surviving members of the 1972 parliament was convened in Taif, Saudi Arabia in October 1989. The members agreed to constitutional reforms that reduced the Christian role in government and reformed the system. Even with Syrian, UN, and U.S. support, this reform had to await the downfall of General Michael 'Awn, a Marionite military commander who had been embattled in Beirut since March 1989. His military defeat by Syrian forces did not occur until October 1990, well into the Gulf crisis.[20]

Similar to the foregoing cases, but more dramatic, the situation in the Gulf brought relief at the end of the Iran-Iraq War in 1988 but a new crisis that began in July 1990. Without doing much more than taking passing note of an event that resulted in more than 1,000,000 dead on both sides, it is important to observe that the 1980 to 1988 war devastated the Iraqi economy and brought Iraq's long-standing grievances with Kuwait into focus. These grievances consisted of the Kuwaiti extraction of Iraqi oil, Kuwaiti insistence on the immediate repayment of war-time loans used to defend Kuwait against Iran, and Iraq's historical territorial claims on Kuwait.

In summation, by August 1990 the Palestinian question was deflated and the moderate internal leadership discouraged while HAMAS, an organization of Muslim militants in Gaza, gained in popularity. Lebanon arrived at a conflict resolving formula in the Taif agreement, but hundreds were still dying in the effort by General 'Awn to hold out, and Iraq was on a course set for war. In short, regional tensions were ready to erupt by the time Iraq invaded Kuwait.

The Iraqi Invasion and the Allied Coalition

Frantic efforts to avert the war were pursued in the days before 2 August by the Jordanians, the Saudis, and the Egyptians. The latter became incensed in the process because it was clear that Iraq was determined to achieve its objectives by the threat or actual use of force, and possibly to rival Egypt for regional leadership. These efforts at an Arab solution to the crisis thus came to nothing. Contributing to this was a shared Saudi and Egyptian sense that Iraq had betrayed them in its assurance that it would not go to war. This may also have been aggravated by the diplomatic abrasiveness of Kuwait.[21] The conflict thus became irreconcilable, inviting the intrusion of the United States as the Western state most vitally concerned about the invasion in terms of the threat posed to Saudi Arabia and the security of 65 percent of the world's oil reserves in the Gulf. It was the directness of the threat to Saudi Arabia and the GCC states that energized Saudi Arabia. Egypt, on the other hand, was motivated by its rivalry with Iraq for regional hegemony and a sense of betrayal by Iraq in the pre-invasion diplomacy.[22] U.S. diplomacy therefore had fertile ground on which to construct a successful Arab and international coalition.

Trends in the Structure of International Relations

The structure of Middle Eastern international relations has progressed through three discernible phases in the past three decades. In the 1960s, these relations centered on the content and leadership of Arab nationalism and socialism, aptly termed the "Arab cold war."[23] The 1970s saw this ideological rivalry replaced by a concrete need to recover the territory lost to the Israelis in the 1967 war. Thus Egypt and Syria planned the 1972 war with this objective in mind. The Sinai I and II agreements subsequently sought and achieved this. The crowning event was the 1979 Egyptian-Israeli peace treaty. Although Egypt succeeded in regaining Sinai, this success was countermanded when the country was ostracized by the Arab state system, the members of which protested the failure to arrive at a settlement for the Palestinians.

The marginalization of Egypt coincided with the territorial expansionism of Israel in its invasion of Lebanon, its settlement policy in the Occupied Territories, and the Iran-Iraq War of 1980 to 1988. At the end of the decade, Egypt reentered the Arab state system to provide a counterweight to Iran in the Gulf.[24] Israel still retained territory in southern Lebanon and its settlements not only continued to increase, but tens of thousands of Soviet Jews began to arrive. These conflicts in Lebanon and the Gulf diffused the Arab state system in that to a significant extent they were either surrogate conflicts or, in the case of the Gulf, geographically distinct conflicts. Egypt backed the Syrian presence in Lebanon as did most Arab states, but neither Egypt, because of its treaty with Israel, nor the other Arab states directly intervened in Lebanon. As a result, regional subordinate international relations were significantly intruded upon by the United States and the Soviet Union. Thus, this diffusion of interests and involvements of the members of the Arab state system in the 1980s coincided with the greater intensity of intrusive powers, that is, the

U.S. intervention in Lebanon and the Soviet support of Syria and Iraq.

The Iraqi invasion of Kuwait created a crystallization of diplomatic positions that ended the earlier diffusion of such relationships. The intrusive power penetration was now of a unipolar variety—the United States. Its leadership created an international alliance (legitimated by UN resolutions), the Arab members of which consisted of Egypt, Syria, Saudi Arabia, and Morocco. While the Arab League supported the alliance, nearly half of the Arab League members invoked pan-Arabism to condemn both the invasion and the U.S.-led reaction to it. The shared characteristics of these rejectionist states were that they were undergoing domestic upheavals due to revenue shortfalls resulting from oil price declines, economic austerity programs dictated by International Monetary Fund (IMF) insistence upon reforms, Islamic revivalism, and tentative steps toward democratic participation.[25] These states emerged as a potential revisionist faction seeking a greater expression of Arabism and possible Islamism and promoting a redistribution of regional wealth and justice for the Palestinians. As Iran pursues its regional foreign policy of justice for the Palestinians, it may have a leadership role in the emergence of this Middle Eastern revisionist alliance. Central to this emerging status quo versus revisionist polarization in the Middle East is the Palestinian question. If the United States is successful in obtaining peace on this issue, the emergence of the two blocs may not occur. If the effort fails, however, Syria may join Iran in a revisionist stance and contribute to the future destabilization of the Middle East.

The Domestic Politics of the Post-Gulf War Middle East

The Gulf War exacerbated an emerging problem of domestic instability caused by an economic downturn in certain key Middle Eastern states. The underlying reasons for the downturn concerned economic problems resulting from the oil glut of the late 1980s and were aggravated by the coincidence of IMF insistence upon reforms in Morocco, Algeria, Tunisia, and Jordan. These reforms were intended to cause movement toward a market economy. Political disturbances had occurred prior to the war, but Saddam Hussein's pan-Arab, anti-imperialist rhetoric found a resonance among economically desperate populations. As a defensive reaction to the basic unrest, a "democratic bargain" was struck by these regimes to allow greater political participation.[26] This bargain generally succeeded in that all the leaderships were able to retain power. The policy consequence, however, was that Jordan supported Iraq, Morocco withdrew its military commitment to the allied alliance, and Algeria, Tunisia, and Yemen opposed the allied counterinvasion.[27] The regionwide Islamic revival was also in vehement opposition to U.S. involvement and, at the same time, tended to be equivocal in its support of Saddam Hussein because of his pronounced secularism.

The post-1990 configuration of Middle Eastern relations and domestic politics was thus shaped by events that occurred before the August 1990 invasion. The Arab members of the allied coalition, principally Saudi Arabia, Egypt, and Syria, were not faced with pressing domestic issues at the time of the invasion, although in varying degrees all three were coping with the economic fallout from declining oil prices. Saudi Arabia had its own vast resources to turn to. Egypt's hard currency earnings from its own oil earnings, Suez Canal dues, tourist income, worker remittances, and foreign economic assistance buffered its economy. Syria, although marginally worse off, would receive (with Egypt) monetary payments from Saudi Arabia and Kuwait for committing to the alliance.[28] None of the three states were imperiled by the significant domestic unrest that characterized the opponents to U.S. policy.

The Palestinian reaction to the invasion of Kuwait was set by Arafat's statement of support for Saddam Hussein. The underlying reasons were complex. The bases for this support were four-fold. First, by August 1990, the PLO's November 1988 endorsement of a two-state solution to the crisis and the implied acceptance of the state of Israel seemed to die as the U.S. peace initiative was turned down by the Israelis. Second, this suggested that, at least momentarily, the sacrifices of the Intifada were not bearing diplomatic fruit in spite of the heavy human toll. Third, the moderate secular West Bank leadership thought that Saddam Hussein's appeal to Arab nationalism and justice for the Palestinians was, perhaps, an antidote to the pressure exerted by the more radical Muslim group HAMAS.[29] Fourth, from Arafat's point of view, the PLO was under attack by Syria, and Iraq was an alternative Arab state that might narrow the Arab military gap vis-à-vis Israel. The Scud missile attacks on Israel seemed to justify this expectation. The fact that the PLO endorsed the illegal military occupation of another people was appreciated by some within the movement as perhaps hypocritical while others saw it merely as appropriate action for Iraq to regain territory to which it had historical claims.[30]

The states that sought an Arab solution to the crisis were neither economically nor politically stable. Jordan was an acute illustration of this. Its economy had been in decline in the 1980s, and its efforts to meet the credit requirements of the IMF resulted in a startling revolt by the very Bedouins who were the backbone of the regime. This revolt shocked the regime into parliamentary elections that resulted in one-third of the representatives coming from the Muslim Brotherhood.[31] Jordan had a more direct connection to the crisis as it had benefitted economically during the Iran-Iraq War by using the port of Aqaba to ship Iraqi war matériel to Baghdad. The invasion thus found Jordan caught between its domestic complexities, including its large Palestinian population, and its economic ties to Iraq. Simply to survive, King Husayn had to bob and weave and, in the process, incurred the enmity of the members of the allied alliance. He survived and demonstrated his diplomatic agility in playing an important interlocutor role in the post-Gulf War, U.S.-initiated peace process.

The Moroccan monarchy, similarly and over a longer period of time, felt the aftershock of mandated monetary fund reforms. In June 1981 in Casablanca, and in other major cities in January 1984, hundreds of demonstrators were killed by the security forces. For years, Morocco had a parliamentary system that presented a democratic facade while the reality was one of repression and manipulation of individuals, parties, and elections. With the relative absence of a democratic parliamentary safety valve and a rising Islamic tendency, the demonstration of 300,000 in the capital of Rabat in February 1991 defeated the token Moroccan military commitment to the allied coalition in the Gulf War.

The stories of Algeria and Tunisia were no less dramatic. In Algeria, the most recent pattern of economically motivated disturbances began in April 1985. Islamic militant clashes followed in October of that year. Student demonstrations in several cities occurred in November 1986. The greatest and most intense rioting, resulting in hundreds of fatalities, took place in January 1988 in several cities, followed by further disturbances in October. The regime responded with a vigorous democratic reform program that resulted in local and provincial elections in June 1990 in which the Islamists won control of thirty-two of the forty-eight provinces compared to only fourteen for the National Liberation Front (FLN), the government party. Similarly, free elections initially were promised for June 1991, but in May, widespread rioting broke out in protest against allegations of government plans to rig the elections. As was the case in Jordan and

Morocco, the mobilized disgruntled masses responded positively to Saddam Hussein's challenge to the political status quo, and the government, in turn, denounced the presence of Western forces in Saudi Arabia.

Much the same pattern of events occurred in Tunisia as well. In December 1983, riots began in the south of the country regarding the monetary fund's mandated removal of government price subsidies on flour and spread in early January 1984 to Tunis and other cities, with nearly 200 persons killed. In November 1987, the aged President Habib Bourquiba was replaced in a popular coup by Zine el-Abidine Ben Ali, who promised more democratic elections. The elections of April 1989 were significantly democratic, but the Islamic al-Nahda (Renaissance) Party was not allowed to compete in the parliamentary elections. Running as independents, the party received almost 15 percent of the votes cast and up to one-third in three major cities, including Tunis. By utilizing a party-list electoral system, the government's Constitutional Democratic Rally won all 141 parliamentary seats. The government, having succeeded electorally, began to repress the al-Nahda Party. In the fall of 1990, hundreds were arrested and in May 1991, an Islamic conspiracy was announced. In the midst of this internal tumult, Tunisia found it expedient to do the popular thing and positively responded to Saddam Hussein's challenge to the status quo while publicly opposing the military role of the West.[32]

The Republic of Yemen's opposition to the Western presence differed somewhat. It, too, was poor, but perhaps more important was the nationalist euphoria that accompanied the unification of the People's Democratic Republic of (South) Yemen and the (North) Yemen Arab Republic in May 1990.[33] Neither the South nor the North had any fondness for Saudi Arabia (this dated back to the latter's support of the Yemeni monarchy in the 1962 revolution). Undoubtedly, a reinforcing factor to this was the anti-imperialist position of the Yemen Socialist Party and the emergence of an Islamic tendency.

Conclusion

In conclusion, there are a number of points that can be made about the pronounced character of the intrusive system and the U.S. leadership role in the region, the redefinition and characteristics of the subordinate system of regional relations, and future political trends.

Unipolarity and the Intrusive System

Unipolarity in the international system combined with a lack of independent political power or alliance relationships in the subordinate system has resulted in short-term domination by the United States as a single superpower. The U.S. became a unipolar intrusive power first in the Gulf and subsequently in the entire region. The mounting intensity of this intrusive role (and the primacy of oil as a concern in the subarea of the Gulf) has caused the United States to direct its policy to stabilizing the entire region, hence the consistency of the pursuit of the peace process from one U.S. administration to another.

Redefining the Middle Eastern Subordinate System

Whereas in the pre-1980 era, Turkey and Iran could be placed with Israel in an alienated Middle Eastern subordinate system periphery, this is no longer the case. Arabism has remained important, but the Islamic revival has resulted in greater participation by Turkey and Iran in the Middle Eastern subordinate system, such as Turkish cooperation in the Gulf War and Iranian policy through Hizbollah in Lebanon.

Related to the foregoing, Israel in the alienated periphery is no longer a strategic asset to the United States in the aftermath of the cold war. The United States has sought political stability in the region while Israel, until the Rabin Labor government came to power, had sought destabilizing objectives of territorial annexation; thus Israel was a provocation and a security burden. Whether the de-acceleration of the settlement process in the context of an ongoing peace process will alter this characterization remains to be seen.

It is striking that in the aftermath of the Gulf War North Africa appears to be more involved with Middle Eastern international relations and issues. The regional issues of economic redistribution and the Islamic revival are being internalized in each North African state and are creating the political instability that the appeal of Saddam Hussein's leadership illuminated.

The Middle Eastern subordinate system now is better defined and more consolidated. The U.S. leadership role expanded the invasion of one Arab country by another into a regionwide crisis. The maldistribution of national wealth in the region emerged as a regional issue and formed part of a new, incipient pan-Arabism. This re-emergent cultural factor was reinforced and expanded by Islamism, causing Turkey and Iran to become involved in the affairs of the region in a new and vigorous way.

Although a new balance of power system has yet to emerge in the Middle East, one thing is clear. The unipolarity of the international system has a similar transition structure in the Middle East in the form of U.S.-supported Egyptian hegemony. The reality, however, of military force strengths equal to or greater than Egypt in Syria and Iraq suggests the potential for multipolarity.

In the medium long term the oil wealth of Iraq and Iran will give these states the ability to challenge the status quo in the Gulf and to support movements and states elsewhere in the region. This could become the basis for alliance relations that could challenge U.S. unipolarity and its client states of Egypt and Israel.

Political Trends

Arms limitation in the region is nearly impossible as long as Israel remains committed to an Israeli settler population in the Occupied Territories and the Palestinian issue is unresolved. Israel's nuclear capability promotes the poor man's alternative of chemical and biological weapons of mass destruction while improved "off the shelf" ballistic guidance and warhead technologies constantly advance.

A stable Gulf security regime remains elusive due to Saudi Arabian antipathy toward an Arab force presence and to domestic religious sentiment that is hostile to the foreign presence of the United States.

The U.S. role as the guarantor of Gulf stability maintains a high profile, with the attendant risks of domestic GCC instability and international incidents, for example, Iraqi radar lock-ons, retaliations, and so on.[34] This is part of a generally high political Gulf profile especially when the United States is involved in military force reductions.

It is true, however, that as far as the level of conflict in the region is concerned, the Lebanese domestic issue is being resolved, the Gulf is temporarily secure, and the Palestinian issue is being addressed in the U.S.-initiated peace effort.

The two major beneficiaries of the war were Iran and Israel. Iraq was eliminated as a serious security threat to both, and they are now free to continue their military buildup. Iran can now increase its influence in the Gulf and its ties with the West and Japan. Depending on the outcome of the most recent peace process, Israel may be able to consolidate its hold upon South Lebanon, the Golan Heights,

Jerusalem, and the Occupied Territories and in general press a hard position in the peace process. Even under a new more moderate Labor government, it will not be able to disengage without a difficult to achieve comprehensive settlement.

The Arab/Islamist opposition grouping to the war, however, suggests that the "have-not" economic sentiment could create a radical bloc with Iran as this country has already rejected the peace process. Syria, with its continued ties to Iran, could become a "swing" radical leader if it is disappointed in the present peace process.

Domestic political factors of economic impoverishment and Islamism are creating "democratic bargaining" strategies of elite survival in a number of Arab states. This domestic phenomenon lies behind the significant opposition to the U.S. role in the Gulf and leadership neutrality in the present peace efforts. Should these efforts fail, it will further radicalize domestic politics and contribute to the instability of the region.

For reasons amply documented in the foregoing, the United States emerged in post-Gulf War Middle East as preeminent and should retain this prominence. Russia, however, although temporarily in eclipse, has long-term Middle Eastern geopolitical interests that are likely to reemerge. Key among these is the region as a market for weapons sales and the complexities of Middle Eastern Islamism for the stability of the Central Asian republics.

The post-Gulf War political trends in the region are, therefore, best understood as transitory ones in which the unipolarity of the international system is mirrored in the status of Egypt and Israel as U.S. client states. Islamism, however, has begun to be linked to the injustices of economic inequality and of the Palestinian situation. The potential is one of regime instability and the emergence of conflictual multipolarity in an "expanded" regional system that now includes Iran, Turkey, and North Africa.

Acknowledgments

An earlier version of this chapter was presented to an international colloquium, "Conflicts and Boundaries: Ethnicity, Regional Structures, and International Influence in the Middle East," Deutsche Forschungsgemeinshaft, Free University, Berlin, 13–14 December 1991. I am grateful to Dr. Friedemann Buettner, of the Free University and Dr. Eberhardt Kienle of the University of London and other German colleagues for their critical comments.

Notes

1. For the post-cold war period as one of Third World conflicts, see Richard Norton, "The Security Legacy of the 1980s in the Third World," in *Third World Security in the Post-Cold War Era*, ed. Thomas Weiss and Meryl A. Kessler (Boulder, CO: Lynne Rienner Publishers, 1991): 19–33.

2. See Louis J. Cantori and Steven Spiegel, *The International Politics of Regions* (Englewood Cliffs, NJ: Prentice-Hall, 1970) for the concept of intrusive systems and L. Carl Brown, *International Politics and the Middle East: Old Rules, Dangerous Game* (Princeton, NJ: Princeton University Press, 1984) for the same idea applied historically.

3. George Bush, Speech to Congress on the End of the Gulf War, 6 March 1991. Reprinted in *American Arab Affairs* 35 (Winter 1990–1991): 166–71.

4. See, for example, Joint Chiefs of Staff, 1991 *Joint Military Net Estimate* (Washington, DC: U.S. Department of Defense, March 1991): 4/3.

5. Salah Bassiouny, the former Egyptian ambassador to the USSR, has stated the Egyptian case even more forcibly by saying that if Iraq had not been built up by the Gulf states and foreign powers and if Egypt's leadership role on the Palestinian issue had not been undermined by Western support for Israel, then Egypt might have led an Arab force to deter Iraq's invasion of Kuwait. In any case, Egypt seeks regional peace by being the leader of its balance of power ("The Dilemma of Egyptian Foreign Policy," *Middle East Papers*, "Special Dossier: The Gulf Crisis," Cairo: National Center for Middle East Studies, November 1990: 6, 8).

6. For an account of the pattern of what might be termed the "sticking together" of a pattern of U.S.-Gulf state security agreements, see Steven Simon, "U.S. Strategy in the Persian Gulf," *Survival* 34 (Autumn 1992): 81–87.

7. For example, even in Kuwait, the nineteen members of the Islamic grouping of the thirty-one of fifty seats opposition representatives in Kuwait's parliamentary elections have reported reservations regarding the closeness of U.S. ties (*New York Times*, 7 October 1992:12). A petition signed by 107 Muslim clerics submitted to King Fahd of Saudi Arabia said that inviting "atheist" troops to defend Saudi Arabia as in August 1990 should be avoided in the future (*New York Times*, 8 October 1992:6).

8. Joint Chiefs of Staff, *1991 Joint Military Net Estimate* (Washington, DC: U.S. Government Printing Office): 11–21.

9. Joshua Sinai, "Arms Sales to Middle East: Security or 'Pattern of

Destructive Competition"?" *Armed Forces Journal* (August 1991): 40–44. See also the special issue of *Middle East Report* 177, "Arms Race or Arms Control," 22 (4) (July–August 1992).

10. From *Mideast Mirror* (6 March 1991), reprinted in *Journal of Palestine Studies* 20 (Summer 1991): 161.

11. *The Washington Post* (20 October 1991). For Saudi Arabian foreign policy reflecting its long-term consistency, see David Long, "Saudi Arabia in the 1990s: Plus ça change," in *The Gulf, Energy and Security*, ed. Charles Doran and Stephen Buck (Boulder, CO: Lynne Rienner Publishers, 1991), 85–105.

12. Regarding the Egyptian withdrawal of forces, see Fawaz A. Gerges, "Regional Security After the Gulf Crisis: The American Role," *The Gulf, Energy and Security*, ed. Charles Doran and Stephen Buck (Boulder, CO: Lynne Rienner Publishers, 1991): 63–64. For the Gulf Cooperation Council perspectives, see Charles Tripp, "The Gulf States and Iraq," *Survival* 34 (Autumn 1992): 44–47, and John Duke Anthony, "Betwixt War and Peace: The 12th GCC Heads of State Summit," *Middle East Insight* 8(6) (1992): 54–61.

13. For this point see Sabri Sayari, "Turkey: The Changing European Security Environment and the Gulf Crisis," *Middle East Journal* 46 (Winter 1992): 13–14.

14. See Shahram Chubin, "Iran and Regional Security in the Gulf," *Survival* (1992): 62–80 and Rouhallah Ramazani, "Iran's Foreign Policy: Both North and South," *Middle East Journal* 46 (Summer 1992): 393–412.

15. Augustus Richard Norton, "Lebanon After Taif: Is the Civil War Over?" *Middle East Journal* 45 (Summer 1991): 457–73.

16. For example, see the cover story, "Was It Worth It?" *Time* 138 (5 August 1991) and also Mark Crispin Miller, "Operation Desert Sham," *New York Times* (24 June 1992): 21.

17. The explosive character of this technology and its transfer in the Middle East and the Third World is noted by Janne E. Nolan to be a matter more of diplomacy rather than indigenous technical development due to the increasingly packaged nature of this "off the shelf" technology. See Janne E. Nolan, *Trappings of Power: Ballistic Missiles in the Third World* (Washington, DC: Brookings Institution, 1991) and her contribution to Supplement, Report to the Chairmen, Senate and House Committees on Armed Services, *Perspectives on Worldwide Threats and Implications for U.S. Forces* (Washington, DC: U.S. General Accounting Office, April 1992): 69.

18. See Louis J. Cantori, "Egypt Reenters the Arab State System," in *The Middle East from the Iran-Contra Affair to the Intifada*, ed. Robert O. Freedman (Syracuse, NY: Syracuse University Press, 1991): 341–66.

19. Ann Lesch, "Notes for a Brief on the Palestinian Question in the Context of the Non-International Regional Middle Eastern's Order" (Con-

ference Group on the Middle East, American Political Science Association, Washington, DC, 31 August 1991): 1.

20. See Norton, "Lebanon After Taif."

21. This intransigence was the Iraqi point of view, conveyed to the author in Baghdad by the deputy foreign minister, 25 July 1990. Joseph Kostiner, an Israeli specialist on the Gulf, has made a similar point regarding Kuwait's unjustified sense of security, which is quoted in Judith Miller and Laurie Mylroie, *Saddam Hussein and the Crisis in the Gulf* (New York: Times Books, 1990): 215.

22. Muhammad Muslih, "Strategies Behind Arab Reactions to the Gulf Crisis." (American Political Science Association, Washington, DC, 31 August 1991): 3-4. Revised version incorporated into Muhammad Muslih and Augustus Richard Norton, *Political Tides in the Arab World* (New York: Foreign Policy Associations Headline Series, Summer 1991).

23. Malcolm Kerr, *The Arab Cold War*, 3d ed. (New York: Oxford University Press, 1971).

24. See Paul Noble, "The Arab System: Pressures, Constraints and Opportunities," in *The Foreign Policies of Arab States*, 2d ed., ed. Bahgat Korany and Ali E. Hillal Dessouki (Boulder, CO: Westview Press, 1991): 49-102.

25. See Muslih, "Strategies Behind Arab Reactions," 10-20 for a discussion of the noncoalition dissenting group.

26. The phrase is used by Daniel Brumberg in reference to Algeria in Louis J. Cantori et al., "Democratization in the Middle East," *American-Arab Affairs* 36 (Spring 1991).

27. Cantori et al., "Democratization in the Middle East," and especially Mark Tessler, "Anger and Governance in the Arab World: Lessons from the Maghrib and Lessons for the West" (American Political Science Association, 31 August 1991, Washington, DC, to appear in a special issue of *Jerusalem Journal of International Relations*).

28. For a political economic analysis of Syrian politics, see Fred Lawson, "From Neo-Baath to Ba'th Nouveau: Hafiz al-Asad's Second Decade," *Journal of South Asian and Middle Eastern Studies* 14 (Winter 1990): 1-21.

29. Related to the author in Jerusalem by a prominent West Bank leader on 10 August 1990.

30. On this general point see Lesch, "Notes for a Brief on the Palestinian Question" and Emile Sahliyeh, "The Gulf Crisis: Implications for the Palestinian-Israeli Conflict" (Washington, DC: American Political Science Association, 31 August 1991): 9-10.

31. Laurie Brand, "Democratization in Jordan" in "Democratization in the Middle East," ed. Cantori et al., *American Arab Affairs* 36 (Spring 1991): 21-23.

32. For references to the North African states, see Tessler, "Anger and Governance in the Arab World"; Clement Henry Moore, "Democratic

Passions and Economic Interests," in "Democratization in the Middle East," ed. Cantori et al., *American-Arab Affairs* 36 (Spring 1991): 7-10; Daniel Brumberg, "The Prospects for a 'Democratic Bargain' in Contemporary Algeria," in "Democratization in the Middle East," ed. Cantori et al., *American-Arab Affairs* 36 (Spring 1991): 23-26; Michael Hudson, "After the Gulf War: Prospects for Democratization in the Arab World," *Middle East Journal* 45 (Summer 1991): 414-18 for Algeria, 418-20 for Jordan.

33. Charles Dunbar, "The Unification of Yemen: Process, Politics and Prospects," *Middle East Journal* 46 (Summer 1992): 456-76.

34. On this point see Louis J. Cantori, "The Middle East: Political Trends and Their Implications for U.S. Force Structure," in *Perspectives on Worldwide Threats and Implications for U.S. Forces* (Washington, DC: U.S. General Accounting Office, April 1992): 64-65.

20
Islam, Democracy, and the Arab Future

Contested Islam in the Gulf Crisis

Raymond William Baker

There is no God but God,
George Bush is the Enemy of God
Islamist Student Slogan at Cairo University

On 6 August 1990, after reviewing U.S. satellite intelligence of the Iraqi military buildup on the Saudi border, King Fahd, "Guardian of Islam's Holy Places," formally invited the United States to deploy troops in Saudi Arabia. Islamic scholars from Saudi Arabia, Kuwait, and other Muslim countries supporting the decision explained the Saudi policy by analogy with the Prophet Muhammad's reliance on an unbeliever for assistance in a time of dire threat. A consensus of Arab states had already judged Iraq's invasion and subsequent annexation of Kuwait to be unlawful. But Fahd's decision to bring the United States full force into the Gulf sharply divided Arab governments and peoples, making the Gulf crisis the most significant political question for Arabs in the 1990s.

On the state level, Fahd's decision not unexpectedly prompted the threatened oil-rich Gulf states to join Iraq's traditional strategic rivals, Syria and Egypt, in backing the U.S. intervention, while poorer Arab states tended to side with Iraq or to declare their neutrality. The surprise came when ordinary Muslims by the hundreds of thousands sided with Iraq. They did so under Islamist banners, not always in accord with the policy of their governments.

Whatever its other consequences, the Gulf crisis energized Islamic forces in the entire region.[1] At the same time, the spectacle of Arab pitted against Arab and Muslim against Muslim raised the most basic questions about the health of the Arab-Muslim order in the Middle East. Intellectuals judged that the "sickness" of the Arab order resulted from a lack of democratic regimes. Some considered the relevant examples to be the authoritarian and corrupt Gulf monarchies whose insensitive greed generated the underlying conditions of inequality that produced the crisis, while others focused on the brutal dictatorship of Saddam Hussein, whose flagrant aggression made war inevitable. Thus, the invasion of a vulnerable but extraordinarily wealthy Gulf sheikhdom by one of the region's best armed tyrannies ironically succeeded in placing the issue of Islam and the political order—more specifically Islam and democracy—on the agenda for debate throughout the Arab world.

By examining the role Islam played in the various responses of the Arab world to the Iraqi invasion and Western intervention, this chapter illustrates that, contrary to the reductionist interpretation given by the West, Islam functioned in complicated and nuanced ways that could not be fairly generalized as either predictably irrational or undemocratic. This examination first sketches the different understandings and uses of Islam produced in the various geographic, political, and social conditions throughout the Arab world, and then explains how the standard Western interpretation of Islam obscures these complexities. In particular, Western readings for the most part overlooked self-consciously rational and democratic interpretations of the Gulf crisis expressed in Islamic terms, such as the one offered by the centrist and independent Islamists in Egypt.

The Islamist Tableau from Yemen to Morocco

The Islamist character of the framework within which questions about the meaning of the war were raised represented a break with the past. Previous Middle Eastern wars in 1956, 1967, and 1973 saw nothing like the spontaneous rallying around Islamist symbols. Furthermore, Iraq, in its conflict with Saudi Arabia, seemed an improbable object of Muslim sympathies. The Iraqi Ba'athist regime had a strictly secularist national program with only transparently manipulative gestures in the Islamist direction.[2] During the war with Iran, Saddam Hussein announced his claim of descent from the Prophet Mohammed and other similar religious themes to counter the appeal of the Iranian revolution, while at the same time continuing the vigorous repression of even the hint of an Iraqi Islamist movement.[3]

In contrast to this shifting pattern, the Saudis had consistently presented their state as a model of Islamic rule, at the same time generously supporting Islamist movements and causes beyond their borders. In early September, the Saudis sponsored a meeting in Mecca of the World Muslim League, an offshoot of the Organization of the Islamic Conference based in Jeddah. The conference concluded with a statement by the assembled Muslim dignitaries reaffirming the Saudi decision to resort to non-Muslim forces as conforming to Muslim law, provided the non-Muslims departed as soon as the precipitating danger subsided.[4] Despite such efforts, Muslims in impressive numbers turned their backs to the Saudis and the Kuwaitis (with their dependence on the United States) in favor of Iraq and what they saw as resistance to foreign intervention aimed at asserting Western hegemony over the Arab Muslim world.[5]

From Yemen to Morocco, support for the Iraqi cause was strongest among the poorer segments of the population. Islam, whether on the streets or in elected parliaments, provided the most powerful vocabulary to express this mass opposition to U.S. intervention in the Gulf. Publics in Jordan and the West Bank rallied immediately to the Iraqi side and were soon followed by large-scale, pro-Iraq demonstrators in Yemen, Lebanon, Algeria, Libya, Tunisia, and the Sudan.[6]

In Jordan, once considered among the most pro-American of Arab states, a wave of anti-U.S. sentiment seized the population. The Muslim Brotherhood, holding almost half the seats in parliament, threw its important political resources behind the massive wave despite the Brotherhood's opposition to the invasion of Kuwait and their reservations about Saddam Hussein's anti-Islamist stands. When thousands assembled in Amman's Roman amphitheater or marched on the U.S. and Kuwaiti embassies, Islamist chants filled the air. Friday prayers became occasions for officially sanctioned but clearly spontaneous efforts to rally sustained mass support for Iraq. Activists based in mosques joined the efforts of unions and charitable organizations to break the embargo against the Iraqis by shipping food.[7]

On the West Bank, Palestinians, sympathetic to the Islamic Resistance Movement (HAMAS) financed largely from Kuwaiti sources, initially took a strong pro-Kuwaiti line. But public opinion, including Palestinians who identified with HAMAS, became wildly pro-Iraqi.[8] Pressured from below, the HAMAS joined the more militant of the nationalist groups like the Popular Front for the Liberation of Palestine (PFLP) and the Popular Liberation Front (PLF) in urging active resistance to U.S. troops in the Gulf. The HAMAS activists expressed widespread fears that the United States would establish a permanent military presence in Saudi Arabia and the Gulf, in effect occupying the lands most sacred to Islam.

The Islamist-dominated military junta in the Sudan announced strong support for Iraq, with Hassan al-Turabi leading the National Islamic Front (NIF) in a particularly militant stand against the West. The official position of Yemen attempted to preserve some semblance of balance in its reaction by initially criticizing the Iraqi invasion while also expressing sympathy for the Iraqi claims against Kuwait and calling for negotiation. But on the mass level, pro-Iraqi sentiments overwhelmed all else, not surprising given the strong influence of Sudanese-style militant Islamism in Yemen.[9]

Meanwhile, North Africa, regardless of the old divisions between so-called moderate and radical states, was angered at the Western intervention. All governments of the area, whatever their initial reactions to the crisis, had no choice but to respond to the wave of outrage at the U.S.-led intervention in the Gulf. President Mu'ammar Qadaffy, who had no love for the royalist Gulf regimes, seized the initiative and personally led Libyan mass demonstrations through the streets of Tripoli against the Western presence in the Gulf.

Other North African regimes responded to the mass wave with less enthusiasm and as thousands took to the streets under Islamist banners, the worried governments tried to contain the powerful political emotions unleashed. Under the leadership of Shaikh Abbas Madani, Algeria's largest opposition party, the Islamic Salvation Front (FIS), demanded that the government take the lead in organizing volunteer squads to fight in Iraq. Madani traveled to Baghdad where he declared that "any aggression against Iraq will be confronted by Muslims everywhere."[10] Alarmed, the Algerian regime responded by enlisting its reservists, increasing security around Western embassies and, in a particularly revealing gesture, around government buildings as well. Al-Nahda (Renaissance), the major Islamist party in Tunisia, assumed a more restrained stance, although its exiled leader, Rashid al-Ghannushi, also journeyed to Baghdad in a show of support. The Tunisian government limited its response to suspending regular television programming and replacing it with calming news reports and solemn music. King Hassan of Morocco faced stern demands from the Islamist opposition to bring home the 1,500 troops he had committed to the coalition in the Gulf; he responded by closing schools and banning all street rallies. Whatever their earlier difference in attitudes toward Iraq, all the governments of the Maghreb were eventually forced to issue official statements at least vaguely sympathetic to Baghdad.

Even the Arab countries that joined the coalition such as Morocco, Syria, and Egypt witnessed demonstrations of pro-Iraqi sentiment, again usually under Islamic banners. King Hassan of Morocco threatened martial law to contain the demonstrators, while not even the repressive Syrian regime could completely silence voices raised to protest the official policy.[11] To dampen opposition in Egypt's cities, the Egyptian government delayed the opening of the national universities. But once the students were allowed to return, anti-war rallies of up to 30,000 students became an almost daily occurrence on Egyptian campuses throughout the country. The regime's subsequent crackdown left at least one dead and many injured. Although student activists represented a broad spectrum of political opinion, slogans and pamphlets of Islamist inspiration dominated, indicating that important leadership came from the Islamist societies that regularly won the student union elections at all the national universities since the mid-1970s.

No observer could fail to notice the dominant Islamic dimension of the political reactions to the Gulf crisis. Yet its precise meaning when acted out on such a broad stage remained open to question.[12] Faced with diverse and confusing indicators that political life in the Arab world bears the powerful stamp of religion, how are we to make sense of Islam, politics, and the Arab world?

Muslim "Rage" and the New World Order

Many Western observers in government, the media, and the universities relied on a durable but ultimately misleading answer to these complex issues: They judged the origins and motives of this latest Islamist wave as a predictable expression of a profound cultural antipathy between Islam and the West. And given the deep historical roots of Muslim antagonism, they doubted that policy and politics in any form could do much to mollify it.[13] According to this influential view, anger at the West originated in bitter Muslim resentment at Western civilization because it had eclipsed Islamism.[14] The United States was an object of Muslim hatred as the triumphant representative of an aggressive, modern civilization whose virtues (Western liberalism and democracy) and successes (the material prosperity generated by market economies) unintentionally exposed Islam's own inability to respond creatively to historical change. Because of its Islamic foundations, the Arab world was judged immune, for the most part, to the interest in democracy stimulated worldwide by the collapse of communism. Moreover, despite the surface appearance of immediate political and policy causes, the animosity toward the West arose from these deep historical causes that predated and will endure long after the disappearance of concrete issues such as U.S. military interventionism or support for Israel. Therefore, U.S. policymakers should pursue U.S. interests in the area calmly and decisively, paying mind only to the Islamic sensibilities of allied Muslim governments, with as little attention as U.S. security interests will allow to the disturbed reactions of hostile governments and mass oppositions.

The U.S. public encountered the Muslim "rage" and the profound "uneasiness" of Muslim societies expressed in the complex prose of academic specialists, summarized in the urgent prescriptions of policy analysts, and taken for granted as the common sense of harried journalists covering fast-breaking news.[15] It should be noted that this understanding of Islam and politics played directly into the Bush strategic vision and the reliance on military means to enforce it.

George Bush's new world order and the Middle East's special place in it assumed that the United States is entitled, by virtue of its exemplary history of political and market freedoms, to a preeminent global role with unchallenged control of global resources. In the wake of the U.S. triumph in the Cold War, the most serious challenges to U.S. primacy came from the industrialized centers in Europe and Japan. The Gulf War, whatever its local causes, provided an occasion for the assertion of U.S. military power to contain the economic threats from the Europeans and the Japanese. The display of U.S. military power to defend unfettered access to Gulf oil drove home the point that the United States alone was the ultimate protector of the well-being of all industrialized centers. With the decline of the Soviet Union and the chastening of the competing Japanese and European industrial centers, a variety of so-called terrorist Third World nations and movements emerged as the only remaining dangers to the U.S. global position. The necessary curtailment or elimination of these dangerous and irrational individuals, movements, and states required military action.[16] Support for democratization had only a circumscribed role in U.S. regional policy, limited to cosmetic improvements in the systems of closely allied states. The drive behind support for Kuwait today, as for Iraq in the past, is regional stability, not democracy. Threats were defined in terms of the capacity to disturb the balance that served U.S. interests. On the regional level, the Gulf War defined Iraq as a terrorist state only to the degree that the growth of Iraqi power threatened U.S. hegemony in the Gulf. For an Arab state such as Egypt, alliance with the United States required commitment to the neutralization of Iraq in the region and the containment of the fundamentalists at home.

In the context of this strategic vision and the broad understanding of Islam on which its proponents could draw, two alternative but ultimately related definitions of Islam were generated in media and policy discussions of the Gulf crisis. The first, seeking to make sense of Islamist opposition, saw Islam as an essentially anti-modern, anti-Western belief system, easily swayed toward terrorist purposes. This dominant definition reflected the primary strategic concern that sees Islam as a destabilizing force that challenged the U.S. position. This conception impels the use of force to contain or destroy the Islamic threat when it is directed against U.S. interests or, less frequently, to exploit it when directed against a perceived enemy.

A second, ancillary definition treated Islam as a benign cultural sensibility. This subordinate conception served the strategic purpose of accommodation with Muslim regimes, notably that of the Saudis, that backed the United States and played a role critical to the success of its Gulf policy. This view argued for tolerance of cultural differences on issues such as consumption of alcohol, the status of women, and antipathy to democracy, provided that such allowances did not hamper the underlying purposes of the strategic cooperation.

Despite their contrasting policy implications, both definitions of Islam share certain characteristics. Each casts Islam as a unified and unchanging cultural complex, whether judged positively or negatively, whose essential character was set more than a millennium ago. In this way, each casts Islam as a force standing outside and in most ways against history and politics as Westerners understand them. Thus, Western analysts could simultaneously hail the triumph of democracy as the benchmark of our age, while still judging the Arab world to be congenitally hostile to the liberal ideal.[17] To comprehend an Islam viewed in this way requires a grasp of an unchanging core of precepts and psychological dispositions—outside of history and resistant to change—that, despite surface variations, remain essentially the same.

Media coverage of the Gulf War relied overwhelmingly on this understanding of Islam that left it suspended in a historical and political vacuum. Islamist opposition was, for the most part, reported as "irrational" and "dangerous" manifestations of political extremism, or was ignored altogether. The Islamic dimensions of the political life of allied states such as Egypt or Saudi Arabia were treated generally as a public relations challenge to which Westerners should be sensitized. Security analysts, psychology experts, and public relations specialists—often innocent of any direct experience of Arab political life, not to mention history, culture, languages or religions of the area—helped to give an appearance of depth to these ahistorical and apolitical conceptions.

Given the early presidential commitment to the war option and the power of the U.S. president to shape the national agenda on foreign policy issues, media reliance on retired generals and former national security advisers as their major resources to explore the war option in exquisite detail had a certain logic. The operative questions of debate set in these terms pertained to differences of opinion over the existing balance of military resources, the likely costs of the fighting, the most suitable timing for a strike, and the reliability of coalition partners. Islam figured in, if at all, only as part of the vaguely acknowledged political context for the coming conflict.[18]

Although the national security experts defined the poles as balanced in the so-called debate of the Gulf crisis, they did not completely monopolize the public arena. The president's insistent focus on the aberrant personality of Saddam Hussein guaranteed a place for psychological profiles of leadership. The psychological experts narrowed discussion to the question of the rationality of key actors and the sources of their appeal: Is Saddam Hussein crazy, as the president repeatedly alleged, or a calculating and shrewd, if brutal, dictator? Could we negotiate with Saddam Hussein and the crowds who rallied to him? Are punitive sanctions really an option against an irrational leader of angry crowds of Muslims whose boundless anti-Western rage targets the West as a whole and not particular policies or actions? When the "talking head" is a clinical psychologist with little or no training in the history and politics of the Muslim world, complex political questions dissolved into personalities and historical conflicts into failed opportunities for rational dialogue.[19]

An even more drastic psychological reductionism characterized the approach of the public relations experts who were charged with smoothing the rough edges of the unavoidable contacts with the United States' Muslim allies. In a manipulative version of cultural relativism, the Defense Department addressed the problem of Muslim sensibilities by distributing material to the troops in Saudi Arabia, telling them that they "must appreciate the religious, cultural and political sensitivities surrounding our presence." In practice, this meant assuming the worst about the Saudi hosts and other Arab allies in admonishing the U.S. troops to avoid discussing with Arabs such subjects as "the Jewish lobby," "U.S. strategic cooperation with Israel," "women's rights," "censorship," and "moral standards." In addition, the Pentagon advised against wearing "crucifixes or Stars of David."[20] These guidelines were, of course, perfectly consonant with the larger commitment to overlook the human rights shortcomings of a regime such as Syria and the disinterest of the Kuwaiti rulers in anything like democratic reform. The only principle underlying the cooperation with the Arabs would be stability in the Gulf, by which the Bush administration meant conditions that allowed unimpeded Western access to the oil reserves of the Gulf at acceptable market rates.

Although they implicitly claim general applicability, the definitions and prescriptions of the strategic, psychological, and public relations experts provided little help in making sense of Islam in contexts other than that of the dominant U.S. strategic vision and for purposes other than those of furthering U.S. interests. In particular, these perspectives on Islam obscured the debate and the varied political contexts in which it occurred around the issue of Islam and the prospects for democracy in the Arab world.

Muslims: Interpreting Islam

The task of clarifying the partisan struggles over the Gulf crisis in specific Arab countries without any special reference to U.S. strategic aims was only obstructed by the ahistorical and apolitical conceptions that were at the heart of the dominant Western reading of Islam. Knowledge of actual political struggles over the interpretation of Islam, as opposed to the much grander cultural clashes between Islam and the West, would entail local rather than general knowledge. The understanding gained would be explanatory on the historical rather than theoretical plane and would be entangled in the purposes of the actors rather than our own.

Much less will be lost than might be feared by this lowering of sights. After all, rare are the states and even rarer the individuals who respond to the world around them in terms of the grand cultural motives regularly attributed to Islamist activists. Deep historical experiences do leave their trace on us. Yet, the meanings of these markings remain open-ended and ambiguous. No simple formulas, somehow above the maddening complexities of particular histories and politics, can capture them. The transparency such formulas promise should be caution enough: How many of us would dare speak with certainty of the motives and the aspirations of those with whom we share our most intimate lives, let alone distant strangers who inhabit different political worlds? When the subjects of our studies regain their histories and their politics, ambiguities about Islam collapse into human struggles, into human lives lived on the changing and indeterminate political surface. The issues, policies, and actions that surround the efforts of Muslim political actors to fix the meaning of Islam do matter and their importance does vary with time and place.

A sense of the actual politics of interpreting Islam emerges more clearly when we approach our subjects with the open-ended questions we have heard them ask of their own experience: How can Islam as a spiritual and political force in our lives help us grasp the meaning of the Gulf War? Who should express these meanings of Islam and how? The importance of these local questions emerges with special force when the crisis in the Gulf unexpectedly and urgently placed democracy on the political agenda of the Arab world.

How Does Islam Help Us Grasp the Meaning of the Gulf War?

Millions of ordinary Arabs, from the Gulf to North Africa, gave urgency to this question as they took to the streets, chanting Islamist slogans. But the universal appeal to Islam provided perhaps the only common thread in the Arab response. Regardless of whose side they took, people everywhere invoked Islam as their inspiration and guide. Jordanians and Palestinians spoke of Islamic commitments as they signed up to fight alongside their Iraqi brethren. Egyptians did the same as they volunteered to help save Kuwait and defend Saudi Arabia and the Holy Places. The Muslim Brotherhood of Kuwait rallied to the royalist Kuwaiti regime, invoking Islamic values in support of the coalition, while the Muslim Brotherhood in Jordan appealed to those same values to support the liberalizing Jordanian king in his defiant criticism of the international intervention.[21] Impatient Algerian Islamist radicals turned more and more to the streets, while Islamist moderates in Egypt cautioned that electoral victories would prove more lasting. Islam found a place on both sides of the battle lines and the political street, but only as the object of intense political contest.

Confronted with Islamic justifications for contradictory actions and positions, Muslim intellectuals and activists entered into the struggle over how to interpret Islam's purposes in the terrible events unfolding in the Gulf. Islamist self-understandings, far from unified, competed with rival interpretations of the role Islam should play. The West, of course, had its own well-known view.

Western policymakers, journalists, and analysts had surprisingly little trouble in accounting for the contradictions in Islam's role. As we saw, the available definitions of Islam easily accommodated the "irrational and violent" reactions of the oppositions and the "benign if not particularly sensible" religious sensitivities of the Muslim allies. In both cases, analysts recognized a unitary and unchanging Islam that was demonstrating its essential irrelevance to the modern world, either by fueling anti-Western outbursts or by needlessly complicating the serious business of coalition-building. Strategic questions about how and when to deploy superior Western power, either to rescue allies or destroy enemies, made any further interest in the politics of the Islamist reaction to the Western role or its implications for democratic development a distinctly minor matter.

Arab public opinion, especially in those areas such as the Maghreb, Lebanon, and Egypt, where a measure of press freedom exists, treated the question of Islam in a manner strikingly different from the West. Islam was almost universally recognized as a powerful political resource that had, in the last decades of the twentieth century, become the most important ideological force in the area, eclipsing its nationalist and socialist rivals in its hold on the masses. All factions, it was assumed, would maneuver to gain access to this incomparable political resource. Thus, Arab analysts tended to treat the question of Islam as an important arena of political struggles. More than one commentator warned that the process of engaging Islam in this way risked damaging the faith.[22]

A second broad explanation of Islam's political role, favored by the left, emerged from this internal Arab debate. Arab leftists, face to face with a powerful rival, encountered political Islam as an immediate historical phenomenon. The left appreciated the tactical flexibility of Islamist groups, although they naturally viewed the politics surrounding Islam as an exercise in opportunism. The left drew a sharp distinction between political Islam, manipulated by a variety of unscrupulous political groupings, and the genuine Islamic faith of the Arab peoples. What real content could Islam have as a political ideology, the left asked, if it could accommodate itself so easily to both camps in the military contest? Why should the masses trust the language of political Islam when it could mount arguments both to defend and condemn the Iraqi invasion or the Saudi decision to invite Western intervention?

Clearly, there is no single Islamist position or response to the theoretical question of Islam's relevance to political life in general or to specific policy issues such as the Gulf War. Each of the factions in the multifaceted Islamist current had its own "nuanced" and "interested" view. The character of the course chosen resulted less from the "dogmatic givens" of the faith than from the tactics and strategies adopted in a given time and place to achieve the ends that groups set for themselves.

The relationship of a given group to the political authority and the character of the general rules of the political game that prevailed in that system usually constituted the key elements of the local circumstances that shaped Islamist political action. But these important generalizations, based on observed empirical regularities, were the only ones possible. The definition of Islam's role is always contested and shaped in highly charged, contemporary political environments; to grasp it, attention must be paid to prevailing patterns of power and the strategies adopted by Islamist groupings to achieve their concrete political purposes within these constraints.

In Jordan, for example, the Muslim Brotherhood rallied to the king's pro-Iraqi tilt out of fear that the kingdom itself was in jeopardy, or that a weakened King Hussein might be replaced by his brother Prince Hassan, whose stronger Arab nationalist orientation the Brotherhood feared. In contrast to this defensive logic of the Jordanians, Turabi's National Islamic Front in the Sudan seized the opportunity presented by Sudanese anger at the West to push the Islamist-inclined junta and accelerate Islamization, including "the extension of Islamic law to the southern parts of the country."[23] In each case, the definition of the Islamist political project responded to limits and opportunities as they appeared to specific Islamist actors.

In Egypt, the contest over Islam's meaning to the events in the Gulf was enacted in a sophisticated civil society. Its openness made it easier to track these formative political circumstances. For the last decade, a broad and diverse Islamist current thrived in the liberalized Egyptian political arena. Naturally, given Egypt's pivotal role as a major Arab player, all factions in the rich spectrum of Islamist opinion registered their views on the Gulf crisis. But they did so in a fluid and changing political context that precluded reading any generic Islamist response from some fixed dogmatic text as Western analysts frequently attempted to do. There were surprises on the Gulf issue in the Egyptian context that were in no way predictable: the tactical rapprochement between the Islamists and the left arrayed against the regime and the parties of the right, important splits in the Islamist Alliance of the Brotherhood and the Labor Party, and a wrenching debate over the implications of events in Algeria for the place of democracy in Islamist thinking and action.

The Islamists could play such an active role in the Egyptian debate because President Husny Mubarak had continued the democratization set in motion by his predecessor, Anwar Sadat. From the outset, the Mubarak regime registered a more refined appreciation of the differences between criticism and direct challenges to state power.[24] During the 1980s and early 1990s, the broad Islamist current benefited from these developments and won an ever larger presence in public life.

The early record of the Muslim Brotherhood in Egypt showed that it could play according to democratic rules. As early as 1941, its members decided to enter elections whenever the opportunity arose. Hasan al-Banna, the movement's founder, used the threat to run for office as a lever to press the government into social reforms advocated by the Brotherhood. In 1945, al-Banna and five other prominent movement figures did run for parliament, although none won office in the government-rigged election. After 1952, Nasserist authoritarianism interrupted these experiments in democratic political participation, and they could not be resumed until the Sadat liberalization of the 1970s.

In the 1970s, Sadat returned the Muslim Brotherhood to public life as a counterweight to the Nasserists and the left. The Brotherhood opted for a strategy of working within the Sadat system, even cooperating with the regime to contain the more radical Islamist elements.[25] The Mubarak era then opened the way for a return to electoral politics, although in circumscribed form because the official party—the National Democratic Party (NDP)—continued to dominate the political field. Before the Gulf crisis, the regime recognized eight opposition parties including the three major ones, Wafd, the National Progressive Unionist Party (NPUP), and the Islamist-inclined Labor Party. The remainder included smaller groupings such as the Liberal Party. Two major political forces, however, the Nasserists and the Muslim Brothers, were still denied official representation. The Nasserists gained legal recognition only in the post-war period.

The Muslim Brotherhood remained a political force by affiliating with existing parties. In the 1984 parliamentary election, they allied with the Wafd to win twelve seats. Then in 1987, the Brotherhood formed a coalition with the Labor Party that was later joined by the Liberal party to form the Muslim Alliance.[26] This Alliance increased the Brotherhood's parliamentary strength to thirty-two seats.[27]

Today the Islamists play a prominent role in Egyptian politics, economics, and cultural life. They enter elections, run companies and financial institutions, publish books and newspapers, and open schools. They also play a key role in the respected institutions of civil society including faculty clubs and student unions, syndicates such as those of the engineers and the doctors, and a wide variety of volunteer philanthropic organizations.

Responding to this growing Islamist sentiment, the ruling NDP published an electoral platform assuring Egypt's Islamic identity and affirming adherence to the implementation of Islamic law as the main source of legislation. The NDP commitment to "rebuild society according to Islamic teachings" yielded such measures as the enhanced role of religious studies in the public school curriculum, more media time devoted to Islamic programs, and the publication of an official Islamic weekly, *al-Lewa al-Islami*.

During the Gulf crisis, the regime extended government-controlled platforms to sympathetic Islamist figures such as the mufti, Shaikh Muhammad Sayyid Tantawy, and officially favored Islamist notables such as the popular Shaikh Metwally Sha'rawy. Their statements were aimed at consolidating mass support for the official position. The Mufti issued a religious ruling declaring that "the invasion of Kuwait [was] illegitimate from a religious point of view."[28] The most effective defense of government policy, however, came from Shaikh Sha'rawy. On the central issue of foreign intervention near the holy places, Sha'rawy cited two examples of the Prophet's reliance on nonbelievers for assistance and even weapons when the community of Muslims faced dangers it could not meet unaided. In Sha'rawy's view, Muslims should have resolved the conflict themselves without resort to outsiders, but their inability to do so in the face of the Iraqi aggression legitimated Egypt's policy. Sha'rawy argued that the holy places were holy because of religious law, and if the law as the Prophet understood it found nothing illegitimate in resorting to unbelievers, then clearly there was no cause for concern. "If their interests coincide with ours," asked Sha'rawy, "where is the harm?" Sha'rawy acknowledged that the Iraqis also invoked Islam to justify their course. In rejecting the justice of that appeal, Sha'rawy complained that one symptom of the moral decline of the contemporary age was precisely this fact that "everyone who makes untruthful claims refers to Islam today, but we must be aware of this."[29]

The major parties of the right, the Wafd and al-Ahrar, sided with the regime and official Islam. Wafdist leader Fuad Serrag Eddine's denunciation of Iraq exceeded even government rhetoric with the charge that the Iraqi "aggression affirms what Israel says about the Arab's aggressive intentions." The official Wafdist statement demanded "the unconditional and immediate withdrawal of all Iraqi forces from Kuwait."[30]

What could not easily be foreseen in the Egyptian reaction to the war was the tactical agreement of the left and the Islamist current. Despite years of competition and hostility, these two important political forces drew together to oppose the Western presence in the Gulf. The Egyptian Communist Party denounced all foreign intervention and condemned the regime for its active participation in the coalition effort. The leftist NPUP adopted a similar position and emphasized the necessity of an Arab resolution of the conflict. The NPUP statement also called for "the creation of a democratic Arab institutional order to guarantee that Arab wealth would be used for Arab development and not for exercising control over other Arabs." The Labor Party and the Muslim Brotherhood, in separate statements, adopted virtually the same stance. Naturally, nuanced differences defined their respective positions: The left emphasized the economic issue and the Islamists stressed the Western intrusion on the Holy Places of Islam. But the two groups strongly opposed reliance on the West and preferred an Arab and Islamic alternative resolution to the crisis.

The debate in Egypt over the meaning of Islam for the crisis in the Gulf provided a particularly illuminating case of the extremely fluid politics of interpreting Islam. Although traces of the struggles were clearer in Egypt, the general point that emerged from the Egyptian case held throughout the Arab world. No prior certainties about Islam's meaning for the political life of Arabs could be sustained in the face of often highly volatile contests to fix its meaning for particular events and causes. Throughout the Arab world, those meanings emerged painfully and unpredictably during the course of complex contests over power, ideas, and values in no preordained mix.

In this, as in other matters, the political lives of Arabs displayed no more rigidity or predetermination than our own. Like us, they were open to local contingencies as well as global pressures; they were shaped and misshaped by acts of collective human creativity that do not lend themselves to sure prior prediction; they are understood best according to the logic of actual political struggles.

Who should Express the Meaning of Islam for Political Life and How?

For those who accept the contrary view that Islam plays its role in the political life of Arabs as the repository of fixed meanings and automatic emotions, the question of who speaks for Islam has only slight importance. Cultural forces, and not mere political actors pressing for their particular agendas, emerge when cultures clash— Islam versus the West. In this case, a core political conflict was obscured in the Arab world. The shift from cultural imperatives to human political subjects enmeshed in tactical and strategic struggles raises the issues of intentionality and knowledgeability. For what kind of world, enlivened by what kind of values, do Islamist actors struggle? How do they understand the forces that press on them to actualize or thwart their goals? In broadest terms, the battle lines are drawn between the officially recognized Muslim scholars or *'ulama* and independent Muslim intellectuals and scholars who contest the right of the scholars to pronounce on the truth of Islam.

Established political authorities have had a relatively easy time in exerting their power over the networks of religious scholars. Schools, universities, and mosques can be managed by controlling the appointments of shaikhs and apportioning budgets, including salaries. Independent intellectuals who manage to persuade others that they have the right to interpret Islam by virtue of their learning, Islamist institutional base, or personal charisma, are another matter.

In Egypt a broad spectrum of official and independent Islamist opinion made its way into the debate in civil society over the Gulf policy. The turning point in Egyptian policy came with the Cairo Summit of 10 August, hastily called by President Mubarak, ostensibly to reach an Arab solution to the crisis. The representatives of twelve Arab states agreed to send troops to help defend Saudi Arabia in case of an Iraqi attack; this outcome meant the endorsement by the majority of the assembled Arab states of the intervention by the U.S.-led international coalition.

Islamists in Egypt, whatever their position on the spectrum of Islamist opinion, reacted strongly to Egypt's pivotal role in legitimating the Western presence in the Gulf. Their response revealed a great deal about their particular visions of Islam's meaning for the crisis, signaling as well their complex relationships to the government and to each other. The Mufti anchored one end of the Islamist spectrum securely in the government camp and obtained, as we have seen, supporting statements from prominent pro-government Islamist figures such as Shaikh Sha'rawy. Other prominent independent Muslim intellectuals, such as Ahmed Baghat and Khaled Muhammad Khaled, also found an easy outlet in the mainstream press for their convictions in favor of official policy.[31] Islamist elements identified with the liberal right relied on *al-Nur*, the Islamist newspaper of the al-Ahrar Party, to express support for the government.[32]

With the suspension during the crisis of the Saudi-financed Muslim Brotherhood publications, the Brotherhood, on the other hand, used its important platforms in the professional syndicates and statements in both the government and opposition press to explain its more ambivalent reaction to crisis. Torn between condemnation of the invasion and wariness of the Western role, the Brotherhood necessarily equivocated, distancing itself from both the official stance and the extreme pro-Iraqi views. Brotherhood antipathy to the presence of Western troops in the Gulf provided the basis for cooperation with the Egyptian left and allowed them to use the leftist publications. Islamist figures identified with the Islamic left issued statements in leftist papers such as *al-Yassar* and *al-Ahaly*, emphasizing their shared objections to the Western presence and downplaying their reservations about the Iraqi invasion.[33]

The equivocation of the Brotherhood created the opportunity during the crisis for the emergence of a new political party with an Islamist orientation more radical than the Muslim Brotherhood. The Labor party leadership of Ibrahim Shukry and Adel Hussein anchored the oppositional end of the Islamist spectrum. Throughout the crisis, *al-Sha'ab* gave voice to the most virulent opposition, Islamist and otherwise, to Egypt's participation in the U.S.-led international coalition arrayed against Iraq.

The lack of subtlety of the extreme positions and the intense passions that often moved the regime's most ardent defenders and harshest critics inevitably preempted attention within Egypt and abroad. Attention to the full range of institutionally based positions expressed in Islamist terms provided an important corrective to this distorted perception of the character of public debate. Civil society in Egypt does sustain a center, and the moderates, including the Islamist moderates, do play a more important political role than the focus on the extremes of the government and its most vocal (or violent) opponents would suggest.

As a spokesman for the moderates, Fahmy Huwaidy, a prominent Islamist of the center, coordinated preparation of a "Statement to the Nation."[34] Huwaidy and the distinguished panel of independent Islamists, "preoccupied with the issues of Islam but not members of any organization, group or agency working under the name of Islam" intervened in the national debate to provide Egyptians with "another Islamic view." In his introduction to the statement, Huwaidy explained the dismay of the moderates that Iraq's calculated appeal to Islamic jihad had evoked a positive response from some Islamic forces throughout the Arab world, thereby "putting themselves in the same camp as the criminal." The moderates objected that "those who fiercely rejected the foreign intervention should be aware that we face two crimes: the first is the invasion and the second is the foreign intervention, and that the latter was a mere result of the former."

The writers of the "Statement to the Nation" argued that if the crime of the occupation of Kuwait and the overthrow of its regime by force was a great evil that should be vigorously confronted, the resistance should consist of an Arab and Islamic nature. Aware of the practical absence of such an alternative, the writers reasoned that "if the Arabs and Muslims cannot carry out this task, then we insist that it must be carried out internationally under the umbrella of the UN, and not under the flag of any specific Eastern or Western Country." The importance of the statement for Arab affairs emerged clearly with the characterization of "Arab leaders [who] stood paralyzed and amazed, content with merely issuing statements and exchanging accusations in a way that indicates a deep rooted incapability and decline in the Arab lands" at a time when "Arabs faced the advent of a new century in which the challenges will be the most dangerous ever faced by the Arab nation, threatening even its survival in view of a New World Order that implies Western hegemony." The signatories concluded with a diagnosis of the causes of Arab decline that focused bluntly and provocatively on the absence of democratic freedoms, protection of human rights, and political participation to remedy the situation "in most countries where the individual ruler is surrounded by an idolatrous sanctity that destroys any sense of dignity and respect and intensifies all values of tyranny and bigotry."

Two important assumptions were made by the powerful statement of Egypt's moderate Islamists. First, they assume that the perils facing Egyptians are part of a general crisis facing Arabs and other Muslims. They recognize the immediate cause of the crisis to be the criminal act of a dictatorial Arab regime that the Arab Muslim system was unable to contain. Yet, on a more fundamental level they also signal that the Arab weakness and disunity revealed by the crisis is particularly dangerous because of the larger threat of the assertion of unconstrained Western hegemony in the so-called new world order. Second, the moderates argue that the remedy for the ills of the Arab and Muslim world is democratization, which is understood to entail respect for human rights and political participation that will lead to the rapid "eradication of social, economic and political injustice." Each of these components of the democratic vision are described as "fundamental to our Muslim and Arab culture." Throughout the crisis, the moderates responded to those in the Arab world who sought to turn discussion from these necessities of internal, democratic reform by defining the Gulf issue simply as an Arab-Western confrontation.

Islam, Democracy, and the Arab Future

Ironically, the aggression ordered by the Iraqi dictator that precipitated the Gulf crisis also placed the issue of the relationship of democracy and Islam on the Arab agenda. The Egyptian moderate Islamists who had been lonely pioneers in the rethinking of the democracy issue from an Islamist perspective now found themselves at the very center of an area-wide debate. The importance of this debate over democracy in Islamist circles as part of the Gulf crisis belied the traditional Western assumption of Islam's inherent and automatic antipathy to the democratic idea. The partisan contests, in which democratization figures as an issue for Islamists, speak against any of the facile assumptions, expressed more recently, about what democratization would mean for the relationship of the world of Islam and the West. Advocates of democracy, such as the Algerian Islamists, often were the most bitter opponents of the U.S. policy in the Gulf. In Egypt, the most biting critics attacked the regime's close cooperation with the United States. Their attacks coincided with those of militants elsewhere in the Arab world. They were able to draw on these transnational linkages and publicize their views precisely because of the regime's commitment to a limited democratization. Discussions of the compatibility of Islam and democracy occurred as part and parcel of political struggles over the strategies that would best advance the Islamist project in particular circumstances. Recent experience, especially in Algeria and Egypt, illustrated that for all the ambiguities that accompany open-ended political struggles everywhere, it is clear that dogmatic givens of the faith will not automatically determine the outcome against the democratic possibility, as is so often assumed in the West. The records in those two countries and elsewhere in the Arab world show that in a variety of different national settings, Islamist groups accommodated to liberalized political environments with considerable success, although not always with results that Western governments and publics welcomed.

The Islamist wave in the Arab world won its greatest recent successes when authoritarian, military regimes moved toward liberalization, and important groups of Islamists opted to work within the system. Governments that undertook at least some liberalization saw Islamist political movements move rapidly into the mainstream of political life via the democratic route, contesting elections and winning cabinet positions.[35]

Bloody anti-government riots in Algeria resulted in a move to political pluralism by one of the most authoritarian of Arab regimes. In 1988, large-scale riots occurred protesting austerity measures ordered by President Chadli Benjedid. The army cracked down harshly and hundreds were killed. Chadli responded unexpectedly with a program to turn Algeria into a multiparty democracy. Toleration of opposition parties saw a proliferation of Islamic groupings and the eventual emergence of the Islamic Salvation Front (FIS) led by Shaikh Madani. The Front gained recognition as North Africa's first legal Islamic party and one of the strongest opposition parties in Algeria; it won a stunning 54 percent of the vote in the June 1990 municipal elections. Tense relations with the government did not prevent the FIS from entering and doing extremely well in legislative elections held in December 1991. The Islamists took 188 of the 430 parliamentary seats in the first round. They needed to pick up only twenty-eight seats in the second round of voting in January 1992 to win a majority in Parliament. Despite widespread fears among the secular elite (reinforced by the French), Chadli appeared confident that he could work with the FIS. The army disagreed and the military coup in January 1992 forced Chadli to resign, canceled the second round, and thereby blocked the Islamists—for the moment.[36]

Although not as dramatic, Jordan's experience was also notable. Riots over food prices in the spring of 1989 precipitated a call for the first parliamentary elections in twenty-two years. The Muslim Brotherhood and Islamic independents won a combination of thirty-four of the eighty parliamentary seats and registered even more impressive gains in subsequent municipal elections.

Developments in Tunisia were more checkered from the Islamist perspective. The seizure of power from Habib Bourguiba in 1987 by Zine al-Abidine Ben Ali came with a promise of democratization. The previously banned Islamic Tendency Movement re-emerged as the al-Nahda Party (Renaissance) and under Rashid al-Ghannushi's leadership applied for legal status. The government responded with a ban and a hardline policy that included imprisonment of al-Nahda leaders and closure of the party paper. Despite the repression, independents won an unprecedented thirty-four contests in the June 1990 local elections.

These state-level political gains made travel and communication easier for activists and movement leaders. As a result, transnational links among important Islamist groupings improved. Today, Islamist political actions often have their most important meaning in contexts that reach beyond national boundaries. Certain key political events can only be understood when the constraints and opportunities of the larger Islamist arena are considered.

Certainly, one unanticipated and ironic consequence of the democratization trend was to facilitate the popular expression of anger and then revulsion at the Western intervention in the Gulf and the subsequent massive scale of death and destruction in Iraq wrought by the U.S. bombing. In Egypt, the loudest and most effective voice expressing the anti-Western position was that of Adel Hussein, the editor in chief of *al-Sha'ab*, the Islamist-inclined Labor Party paper. The amplification of Hussein's voice, threatening to drown out the more moderate positions, owed a great deal not only to the relative openness of the Egyptian arena, but also to his ability to forge important transnational linkages.

At first glance, it would seem that its impressive organizational and electoral strength should have guaranteed the Muslim Brotherhood the leadership position in the Islamist reaction. Yet, in one of the more surprising developments as the crisis unfolded, the Labor

Party's Islamist faction, associated with Adel Hussein and distinct from the Brotherhood, eclipsed such Brotherhood figures as Hudaiby as spokesman for the Islamist trend. During the course of the crisis, Adel Hussein emerged as the most active, vocal, and effective critic of government policy from an Islamist perspective. Together with Shukry, Hussein argued that Iraq's invasion of Kuwait was not unprovoked. Although not directly supporting the invasion, the pair did argue that resolution of the Gulf crisis was an Islamic affair that should be handled within an Islamic framework and without Western intervention. Reacting to such arguments, government supporters labeled al-Sha'ab "an Iraqi publication in Egypt."[37]

Clearly, Adel Hussein's powerful public presence owed a great deal to the impressive and unrivaled institutional resources he controlled in the purely Egyptian context. As a major figure, along with Labor leader Ibrahim Shukry, Adel Hussein had the advantages of legal recognition and legitimacy and symbolized the distinctive Islamist orientation of the Labor Party. These connections meant that Hussein could count on support in key syndicates, student unions, and faculty clubs where support for the Muslim Brotherhood was consistently strong. From the critical bases, Adel Hussein easily projected himself as a major player in the domestic debate over the war.

But these Egyptian factors tell only part of the story. To comprehend Hussein's role and the reactions of others to him, one must also take into account the context of the Islamist ummamiyya, or transnational Islamist community in which Hussein became an important political actor. Naturally, the divisions over the Gulf War were felt in the larger Islamist community. The Muslim Brotherhood, for example, was pulled in a number of contradictory directions by its various national branches. In Jordan, the Brotherhood cooperated smoothly with King Hussein in his strong opposition to the intervention and not so tacit support for Iraq. As noted, the Egyptian Brotherhood took a more equivocal position, criticizing both the Iraqi invasion and the foreign intervention. The pro-Saudi wing of the Brotherhood, which dominated the Islamic weekly al-Nur, leaned heavily against the pro-Iraqi stance of the Labor party, regularly publishing denunciations of Saddam Hussein.[38] For the Kuwaiti Brotherhood, however, even the clear tilt of this segment of the Brotherhood was not enough, and serious tensions developed between the Egyptian and Kuwaiti wings of the movement, eventually producing an open break.[39]

The splits and the resulting equivocations of the Muslim Brotherhood left the Islamist field open to rival leadership. In addition to the question of the Islamist stance on the Gulf War, events in Algeria and intense debate over the issue of the strategy for the Islamists in Algeria, where the most important Islamist breakthrough occurred, provided a second and related issue for the leadership struggle. Turabi of the Sudan, in particular, became a forceful spokesman for the powerful mass anger at the Western intervention and assault on Iraq that found particular resonance in North Africa where Madani of Algeria and, to a lesser extent, Ghannushi of Tunisia responded to Turabi's calls for militant action. Madani and Ghannushi also advanced claims to speak for Islamists outside their respective national borders. But Turabi took the lead during the crisis in expressing the need to coordinate Islamist reactions on a transnational plane, implicitly criticizing the Muslim Brotherhood for its failure to do so.

Adel Hussein of Egypt cooperated with the transnational company of Turabi, Madani, and Ghannushi and, as a result, he clashed with his allies in the Egyptian Muslim Brotherhood who adopted a more moderate stance on both the Gulf War and on the tactics appropriate in the Algerian arena. The most important indicator of Adel Hussein's bid for a distinctive leadership role in the transnational arena came with the failed Islamist mediation attempt that occurred before the launching of the ground war. Although one might have expected the Muslim Brotherhood leadership to represent Egypt in the Islamists delegation that attempted to mediate the conflict, Adel Hussein and Ibrahim Shukry appeared instead. Thus, not only did Hussein take the most vociferous stand within Egypt against the government, he also spoke for Egyptian Islamists in the transnational environment on both the Gulf and the promising developments in Algeria.[40] In this context Adel Hussein emerged not simply as an Egyptian Islamist, but rather as an advocate of a certain transnational faction and perspective, the militant view associated with al-Turabi. The political fallout for Adel Hussein from these developments included dissent within the Labor party, strains with the Brotherhood in the Islamic Alliance, and a brush with government repression.[41]

Not all members of the Labor Party agreed with the militant stand adopted by Shukry and Hussein. When the reports of atrocities in occupied Kuwait reached Cairo, rank and file members, and even some activists, left the party to speak out publicly against the leadership's stand.[42] The close identification of Hussein with the militant Turabi wing of the transnational Islamist current also embarrassed the Brotherhood, which had no choice but to respond to moderating pressures that the Hussein-Shukry leadership wing could ignore. Having prospered by acting carefully within the liberalized Egyptian political system, the Brotherhood was not inclined to push its opposition beyond a certain limit. This same experience encouraged the organization to urge the Algerian Islamists to work with rather than against the liberalizing military regime. In addition, the Egyptians could not be completely unresponsive to the stance of the Kuwaiti wing of the Brotherhood. Although the Brotherhood clearly lined up with the opposition, a gap opened for all to see between it and the militant editorial positions taken in *al-Sha'ab*. The Brotherhood's caution proved warranted; once the ground war was underway, the government tried to rein in Hussein and Shukry by blocking demonstrations, arresting leadership cadres, and interfering with the publication of *al-Sha'ab*.[43]

With the crushing defeat of Iraq in February, the political impact of the crisis on the Islamic Alliance took a new turn. The old socialist wing of the party that had left when the coalition with the Brotherhood was formed attempted a comeback, aimed at ousting the Brotherhood or moderating the increasingly shrill Islamist tone that Hussein had given *al-Sha'ab*. In addition, some Islamist elements previously associated with Hussein also announced their disagreement with the militant line that Hussein had taken. At the same time, rumors circulated that the Muslim Brothers were bolting from the Alliance entirely. At the time of writing, the Islamic Alliance appears to have survived all these immensely complicated strains.[44]

Conclusion

The struggle over Islam that took place against the backdrop of the Gulf War is a powerful reminder that the meaning of Islam, in the context of events of our time, involves a complex and contested process of interpretation. In determining how their faith speaks to the events that shape their lives, Muslims respond to a political logic that is at once local and transnational, national, and international. Islamic political expressions and entanglements reverberate, sometimes in quite controlled ways, as parts of the deliberate political strategies of individuals and groups in an interconnected though not unified world. Islam should be recognized as a powerful force in history, but one whose meaning eludes any singular, explanatory formula derived from the dogma of the inherited faith. As a force in human life, Islam is undergoing profound and unanticipated changes as Muslims struggle to determine the meaning of their faith for their own times and places. Specific human communities can hope to shape these changes through contested processes of interpretation and attendant political struggles in these multiple worlds of Islam. These struggles remain open-ended and indeterminate, however, as the contest over the democratic idea shows. The events surrounding the Gulf crisis made it clear that the political future of Muslims is no more automatic nor predictable than our own.

Acknowledgments

I am grateful for the help I received in researching and writing this article from Nevine Mounir Tewfih, Manar Shorbagy, and Kamel Ahmed Attia, my friends and colleagues at the American University in Cairo. Paul Schemm and Norman Spaulding, my research assistants at Williams, assisted in editing the manuscript.

Notes

1. See Peter W. Rodman, "Middle East Diplomacy After the Gulf War," *Foreign Affairs* (Spring 1991): 1–18.

2. For an astute assessment of the reasons for the response to Iraq in Islamist terms despite the implausibility of Hussein's religious posturing, see Fahmy Huwaidy, "Arab Irrationalism," *al-Ahram* (5 February 1991). Huwaidy explains that "there is a logical explanation for this phenomenon; with the overwhelming frustrations, consciousness has been separated from truth. We have to admit that people lack hope and feel depressed and humiliated. As a result, they await a savior so eagerly that they are capable of responding to a mirage." Huwaidy, an eloquent moderate Islamist, scathingly remarks on the transparency of Saddam Hussein's manipulation of religious feelings: "In his last visit to Kuwait, Saddam was keen to perform the moon prayers on the seashore. When the visit was broadcast by British Television, I and others noticed that Saddam was not praying in the right direction. . . . And since the correct direction was certainly known to everybody accompanying him, it is most likely that the prayers were simply a display for television." In a similar vein, Ma'mun Hudaiby, the counsellor of the Egyptian Muslim Brotherhood, explained, "We were not fooled by him or by his Islamic call or his talk of holy war." Hussein's record on Islam was well-known, and still the Islamist response came.

3. Interview with Hudaiby by Abdullah Kamal, "Ma'mun Hudaiby: I Say Good-bye to the Brotherhood of Kuwait!" *Rose al Yusuf* (29 July 1991).

4. "Islam Divided: Purse Strings and Prayer," *The Economist* (22 September 1990).

5. "Islam: Bitterness Rules," *The Economist* (2 February 1991).

6. Daniel C. Diller, ed., *The Middle East*, 7th ed. (Washington, DC: Congressional Quarterly, 1991): 409.

7. Ann Mosely Lesch, "Contrasting Reactions to the Persian Gulf Crisis: Egypt, Syria, Jordan, and the Palestinians," *Middle East Journal* 45 (Winter 1991): 30–50.

8. "Islam Divided."

9. The large corps of Sudanese teachers in the Yemen provided one important vehicle for this influence. See the discussion of Tarek Hassan in *Rose al-Yusuf* (24 June 1991).

10. "Islam Divided."

11. "Islam: Bitterness Rules."

12. The most comprehensive and reliable survey of the Islamist current in the Arab world appears in the yearly *Arab Strategic Report* (Cairo, Egypt: al-Ahram Center for Political and Strategic Studies). The *Report* notes: "No political current, whether official or oppositional, can ignore the Islamist discourse."

13. Bernard Lewis, "The Roots of Muslim Rage," *The Atlantic Monthly* (September 1990): 47–60.

14. William Pfaff, "Reflections: Islam and the West," *The New Yorker* (28 January 1991): 83–88.

15. The notion of Muslim "rage" comes from Lewis, "The Roots of Muslim Rage," that of "uneasiness" from Pfaff, "Reflections."

16. For a clear example of such thinking during the Gulf crisis, see Krauthammer on "The Weapon State" (Charles Krauthammer, "The Unipolar Moment," *Foreign Affairs* 70, 1990–1991: 23–33).

17. Samir Khalil, the Iraqi exile and critic of the Hussein regime, has explained this apparent contradiction best:

> Francis Fukayama, the former U.S. State Department analyst whose much discussed essay "The End of History" posited the triumph of Western democratic government throughout the world, said in a speech in London: "My liberal democracy and your liberal democracy are in the process of piling up a mighty military machine in Saudi Arabia to confront Iraq, trying in effect to oust a bunch of 16th century Italian condottieri in order to protect the domains of a 14th-century ecclesiastical family."

Khalil refuses this characterization of the Kuwaiti and Iraqi regimes, arguing that both are, in fact, the product of modern influences such as the international oil and arms market, and dominated by the great powers. Khalil concludes with the observation that "in the recent weeks of war preparation, I have found the view all too often expressed that the Arab world stands outside modern civilization—that it is a part of the world congenitally hostile to liberal democracy" (Samir Khalil, "In the Middle East; Does Democracy Have a Chance?")

18. Edward Said, "Arabesque," *New Statesman & Society* (24 August 1990).

19. Of the various experts called on by the U.S. national media, none surpassed Judith Kipper in overall visibility. Kipper's credentials and her orientation are instructive. David Segal points out that "she has no political, academic, diplomatic, or military experience in the Middle East. Her graduate studies consist of a master's degree in clinical psychology. She doesn't speak Hebrew or Arabic, and has never written anything on the region much longer than an op-ed. . . . Having a poor grasp of the cultural, economic, and religious complexities of the region, she clings to the idea that the Middle East conflict would be over later tonight if everyone in the region just sat down, held hands, and talked out their angst." Although Segal's own political biases are obvious in his rather brutal criticisms of Kipper, the more general points he makes about the psychologizing expert remain valid (see David Segal, *The New Republic*, 25 March 1991). For an Egyptian critique that registers many of the same objections to psychological approaches to political and strategic issues, see my assessment of the thinking of Sayyid Yassine, Director of the Al-Ahram Center for Political and Strategic Studies in *Sadat and After: Struggles for Egypt's Political Soul*, ed. Raymond Baker (Cambridge, MA: Harvard University Press, 1990): 189–90, 202–3.

20. Julius Jacobson, "Gulf Crisis: Villains and Victims," *New Politics* (Winter 1991): 5–19.

21. Examples of such contradictions are easily found. An Egyptian opposition newspaper appeared at the height of the bombing of Baghdad with a banner headline announcing, "Muslims! Your brothers are being annihilated. Hurry to aid Iraq in its heroic steadfastness!"; to the consternation of the government, all copies sold out within hours (see *The Economist*, 26 January 1991). More than one Arab family had sons on both sides of the fighting; undoubtedly, their parents prayed for both.

22. The internationally known economist Galal Amin remarked that "the history of political Islam, as everyone knows, since the murder of Osman is the history of political struggle where every group fights the other in the name of religion. But the struggle did not stem in the beginning because of differences in the interpretation of religion. On the contrary, disagreement stemmed from political issues and interpretations were made for the sake of the struggle" (see Galal Amin, "Religion and the Gulf War," *al-Yassar*, March 1991).

23. For a discussion of the local political logic of the Jordanian and the Sudanese positions, see Mahmud al Maraghi, Yusuf al Sharif, Tarek Hassan and Abdul Qader Shoheib, "Top Secret—The Islamic Squads in the Gulf War," *Rose al Yusuf* (18 February 1991). Despite a pronounced anti-Islamist bias, the article provides helpful clarification of the national political circumstances that affect the various Islamist currents.

24. John L. Esposito and James P. Piscatori, "Democratization and Islam," *Middle East Journal* 45 (Summer 1991): 427–40.

25. Raymond William Baker, *Sadat and After Struggles for Egypt's Political Soul* (Cambridge, MA: Harvard University Press, 1990): 365.

26. For a helpful clarification of the attempt by the Labor Party to accommodate both strong Arab nationalist and Islamist elements, see Ibrahim al-Ja'fary, "Let the Party Project Prevail," *al-Sha'ab* (7 November 1989). Ja'fary stresses that the party has an Arab nationalist history, including connections to the 1952 revolution, while at the same time having a clear Islamist emphasis. Accommodation is possible, al-Ja'fary concludes, because the party represents an "Islamic political project and not a religious theological one."

27. Esposito and Piscatori, "Democratization and Islam."

28. For a discussion of the background of the ruling, see *al Ahram* (28 October 1990).

29. The most complete statement of Sha'rawy's position, stated with the simple eloquence for which he is celebrated, can be found in *October* (16 September 1990).

30. The quotations from all party statements in this section are taken from "A Rapprochement Between the NPUP, Communists, Labor, and the Muslim Brotherhood and a Complete Agreement Between the Government and the New World," *al-Yassar* (September 1990).

31. For Baghat's thinking, see "The Hooligan," *al-Ahram* (21 July 1990) and "Dialogue," *al-Ahram* (6 August 1990); for Khaled Muhammad Khaled, see "Khaled Muhammad Khaled to al-Musawwar: We Stand Before a Legitimation War and Not a War of the Crusaders. . . ," *al-Musawwar* (1 February 1991).

32. See especially the editorials of Al-Hamza De'ibis in *al-Nur* during the crisis period.

33. "Intellectuals, Writers, and Artists Express their Shock at the American Aggression and their Disapproval of Egypt Media Coverage," *al-Ahaly* (23 January 1991).

34. The statement was published in *al-Ahram* (21 August 1990). The moderates issued a second statement that was published in *al-Ahram* on 29 January 1991.

35. Esposito and Piscatori, "Democratization and Islam."

36. See *The Economist* (15 February 1992).

37. Marwan Fouad, "Time to get Their House in Order," *The Middle East* (July 1991).

38. Ahmed Abdullah, "Mubarak's Gamble," *Middle East Report* (January-February 1991): 18-21.

39. The Egyptian Counsellor of the Muslim Brotherhood, Ma'mun al Hudaiby, explained that the Egyptian Brotherhood position in the Gulf was never pro-Iraqi although it did stand against foreign interference and distinguished between an anti-foreign presence and a pro-Iraqi stand: "But actually did they want us to side with the U.S.A.? If that's what they wanted, I say good-bye." Interview with Hudaiby by Abdullah Kamal, "Ma'mum al Hudaiby."

40. Magdy Hussain (on Algeria) and Adel Hussein (on the Sudan) took positions that supported developments in those countries in contrast to the critical stance adopted by the mainstream Muslim Brotherhood. See Magdy Hussain in *al-Sha'ab* (26 July 1991) and Adel Hussein in *al-Sha'ab* (16 July 1991); for the Brotherhood position, see *Rose al Yusuf* (29 July 1991).

41. An assessment of the international Islamist reaction to the Gulf crisis in *Rose al-Yusuf* documents the Turabi-Hussein link and speculates plausibly that it caused the strains in the Labor Party-Muslim Brotherhood coalition. "Currently al-Turabi talks about [the unified international Islamic movement]. This is totally new talk. This might be what is bothering the Muslim Brotherhood's leadership in Egypt now" (*Rose al-Yusuf*, 18 February 1991). Adel Hussein gives his version of government harassment in *al-Sha'ab* (18 February 1991).

42. See Muhammad Hassan Dura, "I Was Expecting More Courage from the Labor Party and its Leadership in Admitting Its Mistakes" *October* (17 March 1991). This disagreement compounded the difficulties that the party experienced early when socialist elements objected to the party's increased Islamist coloration.

43. One important example of the repression is covered in "The Chief Prosecutor Decides to Jail Magdy Hussain for 15 days," *al-Akhbar* (28 January 1991).

44. *The Middle East* reported in July 1991 that the Brotherhood had quit the Alliance. See Marwan Fouad, "Time to get Their House in Order," *The Middle East* (July 1991).

21
Islam at War and Communism in Retreat

===============

What Is the Connection?

Ali A. Mazrui

In the last quarter of the twentieth century, the three most momentous events in the Muslim world were the 1979 Islamic revolution in Iran, the crusade in Afghanistan after the Soviet invasion of 1979, and the 1990–1991 Gulf crisis. Each of these had major global and historic repercussions.

In 1973, when the monarchy was overthrown in Afghanistan and was succeeded by a leftist regime, few people realized the global consequences. The stage was set for two decisive processes in world history that went far beyond the borders of Afghanistan. One was the disroyalization of Islam, of which the fall of the Afghan monarchy was only a minor illustration; the other was the de-Leninization of Marxism that soon engulfed much of Eastern Europe and profoundly affected the Soviet Union. Afghanistan played a surprisingly important role globally in the events that led to this latter process.

Islam: Royalist and Republican

The distinction between royalist Islam (based on hereditary leadership) and republican Islam (based on leadership chosen by an electoral college) dates back to the earliest days of the religion. Royalist Islam was consolidated with the advent of the Umayyad Dynasty (A.D. 661–750) headquartered in Damascus. It was later succeeded by the Abbasid Dynasty (A.D. 750–1258) based in Baghdad.

In doctrine, there was a quasi-hereditary factor in Shi'ite Islam. According to a well-known tradition, the Prophet Muhammad said on his deathbed, "I am leaving with you [the Muslim community] the two weights onto which if you hold fast, you shall never go astray: the Book of God and my family, the people of my household. They shall never be separated until they come to me at the spring."[1]

Although the hereditary principle of the Prophet's family is not the same as the royal principle of a sultanate, the issue of hereditary versus nonhereditary Muslim leadership had been debated from the earliest days of the faith. In doctrine, Shi'ite Islam was closer to the hereditary principle, but in the twentieth century, it was still possible for a revolutionary theocratic republic in Iran to be the defiant successor to a hereditary secular monarchy. Contradictions continue to be part of the dynamics of Muslim history.

By the twentieth century, royalist Islam acquired certain unique characteristics both doctrinally and politically. Under Muslim monarchies in the twentieth century, Islam tended to be ritually pious as well as socially and politically conservative. This configuration of piety and conservatism included Afghanistan under a monarchy as well as the Arab royal houses in the Near East.

The political conservatism of royalist Islam gave it a pro-Western orientation. Most Muslim kings in the second half of the twentieth century were great political friends of the West. This pro-Western tilt was strengthened by a royal distrust of communism. Saudi Arabia did not establish diplomatic relations with the Soviet Union until the eve of its disintegration in 1990. Communism was feared by Muslim kings because of its anti-royalist tendency as well as its atheistic posture.

By extension, royalist Islam distrusted socialism—democratic, atheistic, or otherwise. Left-wing domestic opinion in monarchical Muslim countries was regarded as potentially subversive and anti-royalist. When royalist Islam was strengthened by oil wealth in the last third of the twentieth century, the feudal conservatism of royalty combined with the bourgeois conservatism of capitalist wealth. The pro-Western orientation of Muslim kings now found additional economic foundations.

Whereas royalist Islam in the second half of the twentieth century was invariably conservative, republican Islam could be either conservative or militant. Republican Islam could also become politically radical, and at times regarded Western culture as a threat to Islamic values. When radicalized, republican Islam could be strongly anti-imperialist and profoundly suspicious of the West. At times, inspired by revolutionary nostalgia, republican Islam wished to recreate the glorious Islam of yesteryears. Motivated by these desires, it could be a profoundly frustrated force and, therefore, prone to political anger and cultural indignation.

Libya is illustrative of the preceding scenario. King Idris was a royalist conservative Muslim; he was pious and very pro-Western. In 1969, he was overthrown by the radically republican Muslim, Mu'ammar Qaddafy. Libya then rapidly moved toward political radicalism and anti-imperialism with a militant distrust of the West.

Twenty years earlier, King Farouk of Egypt had been a decadent, pro-Western monarch of a Muslim society. In 1952, Farouk was deposed by the Free Officers of the Egyptian revolution led by Gamal Abdel Nasser. After some hesitation, Nasser moved toward republicanism at home and radicalism in his relations with the West. He saw Egypt as the center of three concentric circles—the Arab, the Muslim, and the African worlds. Nasser was more radical than either his predecessors in modern Egypt or his successors, Sadat and Mubarak.

The shah of Iran also opted for pro-Western secularism in a Muslim society. In the 1950s he had been challenged by Prime Minister Muhammad Moussadeq, a secular Iranian republican. Partly because of U.S. Central Intelligence Agency (CIA) actions, Moussadeq was ousted, and the shah was restored to his throne. But the shah lived to be overthrown on another day and was succeeded by a radical Islamic republic defined by Ayatollah Khoumeini.

King Feisal of Iraq was a pro-Western young Hashemite monarch. He got a little too close to the West and was destroyed in the revolution of 1958 in Baghdad. The assassinated monarch was succeeded by one revolutionary republican regime after another, culminating in Saddam Hussein's.

The other Hashemite monarch was King Hussein of Jordan. Like most Muslim monarchs, Hussein was a loyal friend of the West. Hussein's allegiance to his Western friends extended over more than a quarter of a century. The first half of the 1990s may see Hussein destroyed by a combination of the Gulf crisis and the insensitivity of his Western friends. He could be succeeded by radical republicanism, either Islamic, Arab nationalist, or Palestinian in nature, although Israel may temporarily interrupt the process by military intervention.

It is one of the ironies of history that most Muslim monarchs have been close friends of the United States—the abode of the first successful and permanent anti-royalist revolution in Western history. The English in the Cromwellian era staged the first anti-royalist revolution, but it did not last. The monarchy was restored in England in 1660. The 1789 French revolution was more destructive of the old order than the American revolution, but France temporarily restored its emperors in the nineteenth century. Only the United States was consistent in its internal republican arrangements from 1776 onward.

Yet, in the twentieth century, the United States has been a supreme friend of foreign kings including Islamic monarchies. The political chemistry has, however, seen U.S. republicanism destroy Muslim royalty; the U.S. embrace of foreign kings, when it has become too close, has turned into a kiss of death. It is as if the founding fathers of the United States were playing a supreme game of historical irony. The United States was intended as a beacon of opposition to royal privileges; yet, its twentieth-century leaders have instead tried to safeguard and strengthen Muslim kings. The additional irony arises when this embrace has helped to create revolutionary conditions in those monarchies that subsequently destroyed the royal houses.

King Feisal of Iraq was destroyed partly because of British-U.S. attempts to create a Muslim extension of the North Atlantic Treaty Organization (NATO); this NATO extension was called the Baghdad Pact. Widespread Arab opposition to the pact finally ignited a revolution in Baghdad, and Iraq's royal house was convincingly destroyed in a major upheaval.

The shah of Iran was also too close to the United States. President Jimmy Carter was the last U.S. president to pay the shah inordinate compliments in the presence of his subjects—Jimmy Carter's equivalent of the kiss of death. Within months, the Iranian revolution started and destroyed both the shah and Carter's chances for reelection in the United States. The monarchy in Iran was succeeded by the most Islamic of all modern revolutions and the most revolutionary of all Islamic regimes. The shah's political conservatism was succeeded by political radicalism; the shah's pro-Western orientation was replaced by militant anti-Westernism. The stage was set for a decade of confrontation between Iran and the West.

The most intriguing revolution took place in Afghanistan, not Iran. The overthrow of royalist Islam in Kabul in 1973 did not initiate republican Islam; it set the stage for republican Marxism. Although initially the Afghan left-wingers reaffirmed their Islamic sympathies in Kabul, the trend was toward Marxist rather than Islamic radicalization. This double-jump was too strong for Afghan society. It is one thing to leap from conservative royalist Islam to radical republican Islam; it is another to turn from the piety of rural Afghanistan to the Marxist ideology borrowed from a more industrialized Eastern Europe.

The Brezhnev regime in Moscow sensed the vulnerability of a Marxist republic in a Muslim society such as Afghanistan. Without trying to understand the sensibilities of this highly religious society, Moscow decided to safeguard the Marxist regime in Kabul with Soviet troops and tanks. In the short run, the world witnessed the triumph of Marxist republicanism in a society that, until 1973, had been a pro-Western Islamic monarchy. In time, Soviet interventionism was to boomerang in Moscow's face, with global implications. It is to these complexities of international causation that we must turn.

Between Iran and Afghanistan

To what extent was the global resurgence of Islam in the 1970s a contributory factor to the Gorbachev revolution of the 1980s and 1990s? What part did Muslims play in the ending of the Cold War? What price will Muslims pay for the rapprochement between the East and West?

Two Muslim countries played an important role in creating the chain of events that produced the world of *glasnost, perestroika,* and the superpower accord. Afghanistan was one player that seriously affected the former Soviet Union's will to hold onto its empire. The other was Iran; it fatally weakened the presidency of Jimmy Carter and produced the tough militarism of the first Reagan administration. Whereas Afghanistan succeeded in weakening the Soviet Union's imperial resolve, the U.S. hostage crisis in Teheran toughened U.S. military resolve after Carter was ousted. The combined circumstances of a Moscow humbled by Afghanistan and a Washington newly emboldened by Iran set the stage for the dramatic transformation in the relationship between the two superpowers in the second Reagan administration.

Soviet frustrations in Afghanistan dealt a fatal blow to pax Sovietica and to future Soviet interventionism. To the surprise of much of the world, the people of Afghanistan put up a far greater resistance to Soviet occupation than had the people of Hungary in 1956, the people of Czechoslovakia in 1968, or the people of Poland at any time since World War II. Afghan resistance was a sobering experience for Soviet military and imperial calculations. If the Kremlin's machinery could not subdue the Afghans, could the Soviets cope with any future rebellions in their empire? Would the tenacity of Afghan resistance impact on future militants of Charter 77, or upon the underground militants of Solidarity in Poland?

The fiasco in Afghanistan convinced the USSR of the risks of future military intervention in Eastern Europe. The Soviet defeat in Afghanistan was substantially due to an alliance between Islam and Afghan nationalism. It was that synthesis of religious fervor and militant Afghan patriotism that produced the *mujahiddin* (the Afghan Liberation crusaders).

More specifically, how did the Afghan resistance set the stage for the era of *glasnost* and *perestroika*? There was first the high human cost to Soviet soldiers in the hills, valleys, and townships of Afghanistan; estimates of dead Soviet troops exceeded 20,000. Many more were injured or maimed, and some were damaged psychologically by the war. These human costs were accompanied by a sharp decline in the morale of Soviet armed forces. Many young soldiers lost their sense of purpose and patriotic commitment; they were fighting a war in which they no longer believed.

Moreover, far from Soviet intervention in Afghanistan preventing the radicalization of the Soviet Union's own Muslims, there was a serious danger that prolongation of the war might trigger off precisely the radicalization it sought to prevent. Also, Soviet military occupation of Afghanistan strained the Soviet Union's relations with the rest of the Muslim world and became a general diplomatic embarrassment to global Soviet prestige.

Leonid Brezhnev did not adequately consult with the appropriate bodies in the Soviet hierarchy before he invaded Afghanistan in December 1979. This arbitrary decision by Brezhnev was one of the main factors behind pressures for *glasnost* within the Soviet system. From December 1979, the story of Afghanistan can be seen as part of the old Soviet Union's distorted military, political, and economic priorities. The war in Afghanistan was another unbearable drain on Soviet resources as well as a debilitating factor on military morale. A superpower was faltering. Resistance by the *mujahiddin* in Afghanistan further weakened the country and set the stage for Eastern Europe's pro-democracy revolutions in 1989.

The factors that weakened the Soviet Union and its will to intervene in Eastern Europe were not the same as those that strengthened Eastern Europe's will to assert itself in 1989 and 1990. Certainly, Afghanistan, the only successful case of satellite resistance to Soviet power, profoundly encouraged Eastern Europe in its self-assertion.[2]

The USSR's invasion of Afghanistan was partly motivated by fear of "Islamic fundamentalist contagion" from revolutionary Iran to Afghanistan and into Soviet Asia. The spectacular growth of the Soviet Union's Muslim population at that crucial time added to the Kremlin's anxieties. The 1979 census showed that this sector had grown five times faster than the rest of the population; in January 1979, the Soviet Muslim population was forty-three million, up from thirty-five million in 1970. The Uzbeks, situated on both sides of the border between the USSR and Afghanistan, had increased in number by 36 percent between the two censuses and were the largest Soviet Muslim group. In the 1979 census, they numbered 12,456,000. The Muslims of central Asia also showed the least inclination to cultural Russianization or to migration to other parts of the Soviet Union.

Partly because of the great increase in Muslim population, the proportion of ethnic Russians in the union dropped "dangerously" close to the psychologically important dividing line of 50 percent of the population. In 1970, ethnic Russians accounted for 53.4 percent of the population. By 1972, they comprised 52.4 percent, and this downward trend continues.[3]

It was the combination of internal demographic concerns and anxiety about the effect of external Islamic radicalism that provided part of the background to Brezhnev's decision to intervene in Afghanistan in December 1979. In the end, however, Islam in Afghanistan was radicalized more by the Soviet invasion than by the revolution in Iran. It was not just the Soviet Asian republics that were affected when Afghani resistance forced the USSR to withdraw. The reverberations were felt by the entire Soviet empire, to the relief of Eastern Europe, and led to the transformation of the world.

The importance of Iran in this venture was dual; its Islamic revolution alarmed the Soviet Union and caused it to intervene in Afghanistan. Iran's subsequent capture and detention of U.S. hostages denied incumbent Jimmy Carter a second term. U.S. humiliation under Carter produced another type of president—Ronald Reagan—one who was prepared to send marines to Lebanon, invade Grenada, denounce the Soviet Union as an "evil empire," proclaim a Strategic Defense Initiative (Star Wars), bomb Tripoli and Benghazi in Libya, send a naval armada to the Gulf to defend Kuwaiti ships against Iran, and (inadvertently?) shoot down an Iranian civilian aircraft.

At the very time that Soviet losses in Afghanistan were creating a "kinder, gentler" Kremlin, Ronald Reagan, recoiling from the Carter years, demonstrated U.S. military weight around the world. The Soviet Union was humbled by the setbacks in Afghanistan under Brezhnev; the United States was enraged by its setbacks in Iran under Carter. A more modest Kremlin and a more arrogant Washington provided the setting for Gorbachev's determination to sue for peace under the second Reagan administration.

Gorbachev Revolution Versus Islam?

Although revolutionary Islam in Iran and liberation Islam in Afghanistan played important roles in ending the Cold War between the East and West, Muslims found themselves to be among the major casualties. The issue began with the question: If communism is no longer feared, will the Western policymakers look for another adversary in world politics? Is Islam the leading candidate? The signs are inconclusive, but already ominous.

In 1990, the Soviet Union abdicated its countervailing role as a balancing superpower to the United States. Because of Soviet economic difficulties, it sometimes appeared that Soviet foreign policy was held hostage to its own domestic financial needs. Was Soviet foreign policy toward the Muslim world for sale? Could radical Muslims afford the price?

Certainly Soviet support for the Palestinian cause declined in the wake of *perestroika*, and Soviet interest in cultivating Israel increased. Soviet Jews were permitted to emigrate in large numbers to Israel, and the Soviet Union made no credible effort to negotiate with Israel for the protection of Palestinian rights in the wake of this Jewish influx. Further, no effort was made to ensure that Soviet Jews would not settle in the Occupied Territories of the West Bank or East Jerusalem.

It would not have mattered if the emigration of Soviet Jews was just a trickle. But Jewish emigration became a flood, partly because *glasnost* in the Soviet Union had released pent-up popular anti-Semitism that made many Jews feel unwelcome in the land of their birth. Both *glasnost* and the East-West reconciliation hurt Palestinian rights and will continue to do so, unless the aftermath of Saddam Hussein's invasion of Kuwait reverses the marginalization of the Palestinian issue.

The end of the Cold War also witnessed Eastern European countries mending their fences with Israel. President Václav Havel of Czechoslovakia lost no time in paying an official visit to the Jewish state in 1990. Such a high-powered visit from an East European country, other than Romania, would have been inconceivable before the Gorbachev era.

Another cost paid by the Muslim world for the end of the Cold War was the reduced strategic value of Pakistan. Now that Soviet troops had withdrawn from Afghanistan, Pakistan's proximity to the Soviet Union was no longer militarily valuable to the West. This made it easier for the United States to withhold aid to Pakistan unless it submitted to an inspection of its nuclear facilities.

This clearly illustrates a double standard in U.S. policy. Certainly, Israel possesses a more advanced nuclear program than Pakistan and is in possession of a significant number of nuclear bombs. Israel has consistently refused to have its nuclear facilities at Dimona inspected by either the United States or the International Atomic Energy Agency (IAEA). Yet there has not been even a Congressional whisper of the United States withholding its annual largesse of billions of dollars to force Israel to submit to international inspection. Now that the Cold War is over, the United States will be able to indulge its nuclear double-standard policy with greater impunity and seek to prevent "the nuclearization of Islam." The United States bought off Sadat's Egypt by bribing it to sign the Nuclear Non-Proliferation Treaty (NPT). The United States is now in favor of ending any Iraqi nuclear program; even if it means bombing Baghdad again. And Washington is now attempting to bully Islamabad into nuclear abstinence while Israel remains unharassed by U.S. power on that nuclear issue.

An additional cost paid by the Muslim world was its declining influence in the United Nations. In 1974, Yassir Arafat, chairman of the Palestine Liberation Organization (PLO), came to New York and addressed the UN General Assembly in the face of Western disapproval. In 1975, the General Assembly, in opposition to the United States and Israel, even passed a resolution describing Zionism as a form of racism. This has since been repealed by the UN General Assembly by an overwhelming vote.

For some twelve years, a Muslim, Amadou-Mahtar M'Bow of Senegal, headed UNESCO as its director general, and in 1980 a Muslim, Salim Ahmed Salim of Tanzania, nearly became secretary general of the UN, until his candidacy was sabotaged by the United States. The 1970s and the early 1980s witnessed Muslim influence in the UN system and Muslim leverage in alliance with Africa and other parts of the Third World. This was also the period when the

UN added Arabic as one of its official languages. The former Soviet Union helped the Third World whenever a clear Third World consensus emerged. Socialist votes in the UN usually sided with the Third World consensus. In 1989, however, the Soviet decision to abdicate its countervailing role as a balancing superpower no longer guaranteed its support for Third World causes. Also, Eastern Europe could no longer be relied on as a supporter of those causes. Both Islam and the Third World were the losers in the UN.

Another area in which Islam lost out after the Cold War concerned the declining strategic value of Turkey. Its proximity to the Soviet Union was its paramount asset when the NATO confronted the old Warsaw Pact. With the disintegration of the Warsaw Pact, NATO no longer focused against the old USSR, and with the former Soviet republics asserting their independence from Moscow, Turkey became less and less important to the West.

The possibility of Turkey being admitted as the first Muslim member of the European Community (EC) is remote. Also, in future Turkish confrontations with Greece, Western support for Athens may become more frequent. In the Gulf crisis, Saddam Hussein temporarily helped to restore Turkey's strategic value to the West, but the longer-term strategic prospects for Turkey are likely to entail greater marginalization. Thus, the end of the Cold War dealt one more blow against the Muslim world.

Marxism De-Leninized

Marxism-Leninism was an earlier casualty of this changed atmosphere in world politics. Marxists throughout the world often spoke about "the crisis of international capitalism." What emerged from 1989 onward was a crisis of international socialism. The credibility of the entire Marxist paradigm was at stake.

Since the October Revolution in Russia in 1917, Marxism influenced the world in three distinct capacities: first as an ethic of distribution, second as an ideology of development, and third as a methodology of analysis. As an ethic of distribution, Marxism was concerned with economic equality, social justice, and minimization of exploitation. As an ideology of development, Marxism placed special emphasis on the role of the state in the economy and the centralized role of the Communist party in both the formulation and implementation of policy. As a methodology of analysis, Marxism emphasized class analysis and the study of economic determinants of social change and advancement.

Of these three roles, it was the development ideology that was decisively discredited in Eastern Europe, the former Soviet Union, and much of the remaining old socialist world. In developmental terms, if Marxism constituted the emperor's new clothes, the emperor was naked. In one socialist country after another, it was revealed that Marxism could not deliver the goods to develop the country.

The evidence clearly demonstrated that the genius of capitalism was production. No mode of production in human history has achieved greater results in terms of sheer productivity than capitalism. The genius of socialism, on the other hand, may be distribution rather than production. No ideology in history aspired to greater distributive justice. No system of values showed a greater distrust of inequalities of income and economic power than socialism.

Marxism was a special school of socialism and by far the most influential in the twentieth century. Marxism, as an ethic of distribution, was not discredited by the upheavals in Eastern Europe and the former Soviet Union. On the contrary, many East Germans are nostalgic for the "fairer" pricing system of consumer goods in the old German Democratic Republic, or the fairer rents for apartments, or the fairer access to jobs and employment. Other Eastern and Central European countries that moved toward the market economy since 1989 are discovering similar stresses of social maldistribution and economic maladjustment in the 1990s. Many will miss socialism as an ethic of distribution.

Unlikely to be missed, however, are the developmental and centralizing pretensions of Marxism. When one looks more closely at these pretensions, the main culprit was V.I. Lenin, not Karl Marx. Lenin's concept of a vanguard party resulted in the monopoly of power by the Communist party as the sole representative of the working class. Lenin's principle of democratic centralism created a situation in which there was too little "democracy" and too much "centralism." Lenin also laid the foundations for an excessively interventionist state in the economy. The worst features of Soviet statism were not consolidated until the era of Joseph Stalin and continued to distort economic development and political democracy in the Soviet Union for several decades after his reign of terror.

In recent years, the Leninist additions to the Marxist heritage—the statist focus, the single-party obsession, the centralization of the economy, and the polity—have been disgraced. These are part of the ideology of development. Marxism, as an ethic of distribution and a methodology of class analysis, is not factually discredited by events either in the socialist world or in Afghanistan. There is no justification yet for throwing out the Marxist baby with the Leninist bathwater.

Yet, even before the war in Afghanistan, the Leninist side of the Marxist heritage was viewed with skepticism, even by Marxist believers. The movement in favor of "Eurocommunism" in Western Europe in the 1970s was an affirmation of political pluralism by political parties that had once been Stalinist. More and more, Western European Marxists accepted the principle of pluralism as a desired condition in their countries and not merely as a capitalist evil to be tolerated. The de-Sovietization of Western European Communist parties was underway, the de-Leninization of Western European Marxism had begun. The Socialist party in France gained strength while the Communist party declined. The Communist parties of Italy and Spain emphasized their independence of Moscow. Trade union newspapers throughout Western Europe were ominously declining in circulation and in political impact. Communist leaders of trade unions in Britain were losing their grip on union command.

Although the 1970s witnessed the de-Sovietization and decline of communism in Western Europe, the 1980s saw this trend spread to Eastern Europe. Only one power, the Soviet Union, could stem the tide of de-Sovietization in Europe as a whole. The will of the USSR to intervene "in defense of socialism" was dealt a severe blow by the Afghanistan military stalemate, however, and the stage was set for the rapid shrinkage of Soviet power and influence in the world.

The stage was also set for a long-delayed ideological experimentation. Did Marxism have a chance of finding revolutionary fulfillment without Leninism? It may take some time before history provides an adequate answer to that question but it appears that the de-Leninization of Marxism has begun.

There is one aspect of Leninism that most of the Muslim world will miss—Leninist anti-imperialism. It was Lenin, rather than Marx, who made the Marxist legacy an anti-imperialist force in world politics. In the nineteenth century, Friedrich Engels applauded French colonization of the Muslims of Algeria, and Marx approved of British imperialism in India as a historically progressive force. It was Lenin, half a century later, who wedded Marxist thought more firmly to the theory that imperialism was the highest stage of capitalism.

Lenin's book launched the whole Marxist legacy into its momentous anti-imperialist role.

There is much in Lenin's contribution to Marxism that deserves to die, but his critique of imperialism is not one of them. For now, the process of de-Leninization is quite comprehensive. Those who were once comrades in arms against colonialism have become collaborators with apartheid. To some extent this has narrowed the gap between Eastern Europe and the Muslim monarchies, and between the former Soviet Union and royalist Islam. But while Marxism is becoming de-Leninized, how much can Islam be dethroned? Is the royalist tradition in Islam, dating back to the Umayyads, about to decline as sharply as Leninism?

The final historic moment for royalist Islam came with the Iraqi invasion of Kuwait rather than the overthrow of the Afghan shah in Kabul. Although the overthrow of the Afghan monarchy made a decisive contribution to the decline of Leninism, if not its demise, it was not particularly significant in the annals of royalist Islam except as one more collapse of a Muslim throne. What put the entire future of royalist Islam in jeopardy was the Iraqi invasion of Kuwait on 2 August 1990 and the massive international aftermath. After the Iranian revolution and the Afghan crusade, the Gulf crisis was the third most momentous event in recent Muslim history.

The Contradictions of the Gulf

In a chapter drafted in 1988 for my book, *Cultural Forces in World Politics*,[4] I described the United States as an "indirect custodian of the Islamic Holy cities of Mecca and Medina." This was written in 1988, well before the Iraqi invasion of Kuwait in August 1990. In 1989 (with the book still in draft), my publishers persuaded me that my description of the U.S. role would offend not only the Saudis but also many other Muslims. Although I still regarded my remark as valid, it was not fundamental enough to my argument to insist on its inclusion. I agreed to its deletion from the book.

When the Gulf crisis led to the literal U.S. military presence in Saudi Arabia in defense of His Majesty King Fahd, the Saudi custodian of Mecca and Medina, I wired my publishers in London, asking them to reinstate my prophetic description of the United States as "indirect custodians of Mecca and Medina" (custodians of the custodians). The book was already in press but there was a chance. Or was there?

In population, the United States is the largest Christian country in the world; it is also numerically the largest Jewish country. In 1991, this large Judeo-Christian country was "defending" the holiest soil in Islam against a presumed threat from a Muslim country. Many Muslims were worried by this contradiction.

Of course, constitutionally, the United States was a secular state whereas Saudi Arabia was a theocracy. This was a second contradiction. The most secular of all the states of the Gulf was, in fact, Iraq under the Ba'ath Party. The United States was the first thoroughly secular state in modern Western history; Iraq was arguably the first thoroughly secular state in modern Arab history. Lebanon had been an ecumenical state—sharing power among denominations—rather than a secular regime that separated the church from the state. Egypt, under Nasser, combined pan-Arabism with pan-Islamism. Since the revolution in 1958 and more so since the new Ba'athist takeover in 1968, Iraq has been the most clearly secular of all Arab regimes and certainly of all the Gulf states. The Gulf crisis put the United States in defense of a theocracy against the forces of secularism.

On the seventieth anniversary of the nineteenth amendment to the U.S. Constitution, which gave women the right to vote, the U.S. armed forces were in Saudi Arabia defending a regime that would not even allow a woman to drive a car. Ironically, Margaret Thatcher—until November 1990 the most politically powerful woman in the world—joined forces with the United States in defense of the most chauvinist male rulers of the period—the King of Saudi Arabia and the Emir of Kuwait.

In contrast, Iraq, although still far behind in gender justice, was far ahead of Saudi Arabia and the Gulf monarchies in extending rights to women. In Baghdad, little more than a decade after the Ba'athists captured power, many women were employed in the industrial sector, a phenomenon not seen in other Muslim societies. The further expansion of the Iraqi army in the 1980s (as a result of the war with Iran) aided the economic liberation of Iraqi women; wives obtained work partly because their husbands were at war. Because of the manpower enlisted into the army, Iraq hired more Iraqi women and also employed immigrant labor of both genders. Although Saddam Hussein was a brutal dictator, his regime was far less oppressive to women than the Saudi system. Men are better off under the Saudis than under the Iraqis.

The United States, as mentioned earlier, was arguably the first successful and permanent anti-Royalist revolution in western history.

(Oliver Cromwell, in seventeenth century England, was only temporarily successful.) In the twentieth century, Iraq was the first Gulf state to overthrow its monarchy. The U.S. embrace of the Iraqi monarchy in the 1950s, and the creation of the Baghdad Pact as a Middle Eastern extension of the NATO, were among the causes of the Iraqi revolution of 1958. Closeness to the United States and Britain constituted the kiss of death for the Hashemite Kingdom of Iraq. Young King Feisal was killed in revolutionary Baghdad.

Iran was the second Gulf state to overthrow its monarchy. As already mentioned, in the 1950s, the CIA helped to save the shah of Iran from the secular nationalism of Muhammad Moussadeq. By the 1970s, the U.S. embrace of the shah partially caused his subsequent downfall. This time, it was not secular Iranian nationalism that threatened the Shah; it was a combination of Iranian nationalism and Islamic fundamentalism. A more militantly anti-Western force than Moussadeq finally overthrew the Pahlavi dynasty in 1979. The dynasty's friendship with the United States was part of its undoing.

We have argued that this is the double paradox of the republican legacy of the American revolution. By the twentieth century, U.S. administrations tended to befriend kings and enemies of revolutions— pro-Czar and anti-Lenin, pro-Farouk and anti-Nasser, pro-Idris and anti-Qaddafy, pro-Shah and anti-Khoumeini. Yet in an ironic twist of historic destiny, the United States inadvertently promoted republicanism by fatally befriending kings. The republican legacy of the U.S. revolution is indeed being implemented by the United States, but through an unintended kiss of death.

The question now is whether the new U.S. military presence in the Gulf endangers the remaining royal houses in the region. Is President Bush's Gulf policy the latest U.S. kiss of death on foreign monarchies? Is the republican legacy of the American revolution about to be promoted by default as Uncle Sam seeks to protect alien kings? Is the Saudi royal house at risk as a result? The possibilities are many. Some Gulf monarchies may become constitutional and democratic. One or two may be completely abolished by the twenty-first century. The United States will have contributed to their demise by straining too hard to protect them.

If the United States is, indeed, "the indirect custodian of Mecca and Medina," a central part of the explanation lies beneath the sacred soil rather than above it. The United States is the largest Christian consumer of petroleum, Saudi Arabia is the largest Muslim producer. Petroleum has created its own paradoxical ecumenicalism.

The Gulf crisis is sometimes perceived as a confrontation between the world of Islam and the Western world. In fact, the Muslim kingdoms of the Gulf are among the most pro-Western countries in the Third World. What is more, the Gulf kingdoms are also among the most ritually pious of all Muslim societies. This involves yet another contradiction; the more pious Muslim regimes of the Gulf have also been the most pro-Western.

Part of the explanation for this is feudal conservatism. Monarchical Muslim regimes in the twentieth century tended to be conservative across the board—socially, religiously, and politically. Their social and religious conservatism favored a pious form of nonconfrontational Islam. The political conservatism of Muslim monarchies favored good relations with the West; especially in a world that, until recently, included the threat of atheistic communism. Saudi Arabia did not even have diplomatic relations with the Soviet Union until 1990, after the Cold War.

In addition to neo-feudal conservatism, the Gulf monarchies also developed bourgeois forms of conservatism. After all, those monarchies and emirates were also petro-rich and had a vested interest in Western capitalism. In the summer and fall of 1990, Arab monarchical faith in Western capitalist friends seemed to be vindicated. The United States, the largest and richest country in the world, rose to the defense of Kuwait, a rich but small country. Capitalist petro-consumers joined forces to protect feudal petro-producers.

There were certainly obvious contradictions during the Gulf crisis. On one side was the precedent set by the United States: Military intervention could occur without military occupation, as exemplified by U.S. military interventions in Grenada, Panama, and the blockade of Nicaragua. On the other side of the Atlantic were the precedents set by Israel: Military intervention accompanied military occupation. These included Israel's territorial expansion after most Arab-Israeli wars until the Camp David Accords granted Israel continued occupation of the West Bank and Gaza, its annexation of East Jerusalem and the Golan Heights, and its partial occupation of southern Lebanon.

The U.S. precedents of aggression against small neighbors never resulted in any UN Security Council resolutions; the United States veto saw to that. Israeli war games in intervention and occupation did result in Security Council resolutions, none of which gave rise to an international show of force that would compel Israel to comply. In October 1990, the Israeli cabinet added another insult to its list against the Security Council. The government refused to cooperate with UN enquiries into the killing of twenty-one Palestinians and the wounding of over one hundred others by Israeli police in Jerusalem. The question arose: Would Israeli rejection of this latest UN resolution result in international sanctions against Israel?

There is an old adage that is worn down by repetition, yet is still valid. "Justice must not only be done; it must be seen to be done." Double standards in dealing with international offenders do not help the cause of international justice or strengthen respect for international law. They will not save the royal houses of the Gulf either. Contradictions in world affairs are sometimes a dialectic in search of a synthesis, but contradictions may also be a negation of the positive. Where are the Gulf contradictions taking us? Where are they taking the human race? The region that proclaimed "In the beginning was the word" is silent about the end.

Conclusion

In this chapter I have attempted to demonstrate how three explosive events in the Muslim world changed the course of global history— the Iranian revolution, the war in Afghanistan, and the Gulf crisis. Their impact ranged from undermining the Soviet empire to the slow erosion of royalist Islam.

I noted that the resurgence of Islam in Iran and Afghanistan were major contributory factors to the Soviet decision to intervene militarily in Afghanistan in December 1979. Soviet military losses and political setbacks in Afghanistan helped to erode Moscow's imperial will to intervene elsewhere. If the Afghans could fight Soviet troops to a stalemate, why not the militants of Charter 77 and of Solidarity in Europe? The Soviet empire was dealt a severe and eventually fatal blow by its defeat in Afghanistan. On the other hand, U.S. humiliation in Iran under the Carter administration resulted in the triumph of Ronald Reagan's militarism in his first years in office. It was the combination of a humbled USSR and an emboldened United States that helped Gorbachev in his quest for a "gentler, kinder" East-West relationship. The end of the Cold War included among its origins the Iranian revolution and the war in Afghanistan.

Although resurgent Islam was among the causes of East-West reconciliation, that reconciliation exacted a price from the Muslim world, ranging from large-scale emigration of Soviet Jews to Israel to the decline of Pakistan's strategic value. The big question for the future hinges on the long-term outcome of the Gulf War as the third most momentous Muslim crisis. Will the inconclusive Gulf crisis further damage the interests of the Muslim world or help to moderate the anti-Islamic tendencies of the post-Gorbachev revolution?

It is too early to tell. The aftermath of the Gulf crisis exhibits too many contradictions—the dialectic between monarchies and republics, wealth and power, piety and "unbelief," and ultimately concerning Islam, the West and Zionism. There is a causal interrelationship between the resurgence of Islam and the decline of communism, but the full ramifications of this encounter still hang ominously in the balance.

In terms of normative revolutions, we identified two global processes of wide-ranging implications. One process concerned the de-Leninization of Marxism as Lenin's developmental and centralizing additions to Marxism were discredited in practice. Marxism, as an ethic of distribution and a methodology of analysis, remains part and parcel of the ancestral legacy of Marx and Engels. But ideas such as a vanguard party, democratic centralism, and socialist statism are part of the revisions of Leninist and Soviet experience. "Eurocommunism" in Western Europe in the 1970s showed signs of disenchantment with the Soviet ideological leadership; Eastern Europe followed with more fundamental disillusions in the 1980s and 1990s. It was primarily the Afghan war that crippled the Soviet will to save its own empire. De-Leninization continued relentlessly in Europe, socialist Africa, and elsewhere. Unfortunately, the decline of Leninism included the decline of Leninist anti-imperialism, with significant costs to the Palestinians, South Africans, and other oppressed peoples.

Will the world also witness the dis-royalization of Islam? When Saddam Hussein invaded Kuwait in August 1990, he initiated a process that may eventually weaken what is left of royalist Islam in world affairs. The seeds of anti-royalist revolutions were sown in Operations Desert Shield and Desert Storm. The monarchies could become democratic or be fatally wounded.

The fall of the Afghan shah in Kabul in 1973 was a larger reason for the decline of Leninism than of royalist Islam. The invasion of Kuwait by Iraq may have tolled the knell of parting royalty from the entire span of Muslim history although some republics have suffered more than some monarchies. What the twenty-first century has in store for humankind has probably been profoundly affected by these last few years of the twentieth century. It began with the convulsions in the streets of Teheran in 1979 and implicated the world of Islam and the universe of neighboring communism. The momentous aftermath ranged from Afghanistan to glasnost—the miraculous synthesis of "Afghlasnost" in history. The Gulf crisis and its aftermath completed the triad of dramatic Muslim experiences of the last quarter of the twentieth century. As a result of that Islamic triad, the nature of the twenty-first century will be remarkably altered for better or for worse.

Acknowledgments

This paper is greatly indebted to my lecture, "The Resurgence of Islam and the Decline of Communism: Are They Causally Connected?" Second Calamus Distinguished Annual Lecture delivered on 17 November 1990, London and sponsored by the Calamus Foundation, London, England.

Notes

1. See Abu Jafar al-Saduq Ibn Babawyh al Quammi, *Ikmal al-Din* (Najaf: al-Matbach al Haydariyyah, 1389/1970): 62. Mahmoud M. Ayoub, "Martyrdom in Christianity and Islam," in *Religious Resurgence: Contemporary Cases in Islam, Christianity and Judaism*, ed. Richard T. Antoun and Mary E. Hegland (Syracuse, NY: Syracuse University Press, 1987): 73.

2. Eastern Europe's self-assertion in the 1980s and 1990s also has to be seen as part of wider civil rights and anticolonial movements that have occurred in other parts of the world since the end of World War II. Eastern Europe was catching up with the politics of self-determination typical of the second half of the twentieth century worldwide. See, for example, Ali A. Mazrui, "Eastern European Revolutions: African Origins?" *TransAfrica Forum* 7(2) (Summer 1990): 3–10.

3. Consult Theodore Shabad, "Moslems in Soviet Show Big Increases," *The New York Times* (28 February 1980). By 1990, the Muslim population of the USSR had topped fifty million and was expected to top seventy million before the end of the 1990s.

4. Ali Mazrui, *Cultural Forces in World Politics* (Portsmouth, NH, and London: Heinemann and James Currey, 1990).

22

Global Apartheid?

Race and Religion in the New World Order

Ali A. Mazrui

Now that secular ideological divisions between the East and West have declined in relevance, are we witnessing the re-emergence of primordial allegiances? Are we witnessing new forms of *retribalization* on the global arena—from Natal in South Africa to Bosnia and Herzegovina, from Los Angeles to Slovakia? In Europe, two levels of retribalization are discernible. In Eastern Europe, *microretribalization* is particularly strong. Microretribalization is concerned with microethnicity, involving such conflicts as Serbians versus Croats, Russians versus Ukrainians, and Czechs versus Slovaks.

On the other hand, Western Europe shows strides in regional integration despite hiccups as the 1992 referendum in Denmark against the Maastricht Treaty. Regional integration can be *macroretribalization* if it is race-conscious. Macroretribalization can be the solidarity of white people, an arrogant pan-Europeanism greater in ambition than anything seen since the Holy Roman Empire.

Is the white world closing ranks in Eastern Europe and the West? Will we see a more united, and potentially more prosperous, white world presiding over the fate of a fragmented and persistently indigent black world in the twenty-first century? Put in another way, now that apartheid in South Africa is disintegrating, is there a global apartheid in the process of formation? With the end of the Cold War, is the white world closing ranks at the global level—in spite of current divisions within individual countries such as Yugoslavia? Is the danger particularly acute between black and white people?

In addition to the black-white divide in the world, Muslim countries, in particular, may have reason to worry in the era after the Cold War. Will Islam replace communism as the West's perceived adversary? Did the West exploit the Gulf War of 1991 to put Islam and its holiest places under the umbrella of Pax Americana? It is to these issues that we turn.

Between Ideology and Race

There was a time when the white people of the Soviet Union colonized fellow white people of Eastern Europe while at the same time Soviet weapons and money aided black liberation. In other words, Moscow was an imperial power in Europe and a liberating force in Africa. At the global level, alliances for or against imperialism did not coincide with racial differences. Indeed, the liberation of black people from white minority governments in Africa would probably have been delayed by at least a generation without the support of white socialist governments during the days of the Cold War.

The end of the Cold War ended inter-white rivalries in the Third World. On the positive side, this meant an earlier end to African civil wars. The war in Eritrea would not have lasted thirty years had there been no external material support and encouragement. The war in Angola would not have lasted a decade and a half if the Cold War had ended sooner. Similar things can be said of the war in Mozambique, which was a child of external racist manipulation.

On the negative side, former members of the Warsaw Pact lost all interest in supporting Third World causes. Leninist anti-imperialism seems to be as dead as other aspects of Leninism. V. I. Lenin added to Marxism some elements that are responsible for the present crisis of socialism worldwide. These factors included a vanguard party; democratic centralism; statism; and Marxism as an ideology of development, which in the end failed to deliver economic goods.

But Lenin also rescued Marxism from ethnocentrism and racism. Karl Marx's historical materialism once applauded British imperialism in India as a force that was destroying older precapitalist Hindu forms, propelling the country towards capitalism as a higher phase. Friedrich Engels also applauded French colonization of Algeria as two steps forward in the social evolutionary process. In other words, Engels and Marx were so Eurocentric that their paradigm legitimated European imperialism.

It was Lenin, however, who put European imperialism on trial with his book, *Imperialism: The Highest Stage of Capitalism.*[1] From then on, Marxism-Leninism became one of the major anti-imperialist forces of twentieth century history. Now that even Marxists in Eastern Europe are de-Leninized, socialist anti-imperialism has declined. White socialists are far less likely to support black liberation today than they were two or three decades ago. De-Leninization strengthened the bonds between white socialists and white imperialists. For now, the process of de-Leninization is quite comprehensive. What were once Africa's comrades in arms against colonialism are now collaborators with apartheid in South Africa.

The demise of Leninism in Eastern Europe resulted in the decline of antiracism and anti-imperialism as well. Some Eastern European countries in 1990 moved almost obscenely toward full resumption of relations with the apartheid regime in South Africa before the racist structure had begun to be dismantled. Some newly democratized Eastern European countries started to violate international sanctions against Pretoria even before they held their first multiparty elections. The Soviet Union in 1990 used a subsidiary of a South African company, DeBeers, to market diamonds for Moscow—something that would have been unthinkable before *glasnost* and *perestroika*. Liberalization among the former Warsaw Pact members meant their greater readiness to do business with the world's leading racist regime, Pretoria.

Between Ideology and Religion

Meanwhile, another tilt was taking place—not a shift from ideology to race, but a transition from anticommunism to anti-Islamism. Western fears of Islam are centuries older than Western fears of communism. But in recent times, Western anti-Islamic tendencies were ameliorated by the indisputable superiority in technological and military power held by the West. Western nervousness about Islam was also ameliorated by the West's need for Muslim allies in its confrontation with the Soviet Union and the Warsaw Pact.

Three things occurred in the last quarter century to affect this shift. First, some elements in the Muslim world learned that those who are militarily weak have one strategy of last resort against the mighty—terrorism. They became convinced that terrorism was no worse than any other kind of warfare; if anything, it killed far fewer civilians than conventional, let alone nuclear, warfare.

As the fear of communism receded in the 1980s, however, the West felt freer to be tough about terrorism from the Muslim world. Libya was bombed. Syria was put into diplomatic cold storage. U.S. ships went to the Persian Gulf in the midst of the Iran-Iraq War to intimidate Iran and protect Kuwaiti ships. In the process, the United States shot down an Iranian civilian airliner and killed all—over 300 passengers—on board.

Second, if terrorism becomes the weapon of the militarily weak, nuclear weapons are for the technologically sophisticated. While some elements of the Muslim world were experimenting with terrorism and guerrilla warfare, others explored the nuclear option and other weapons of mass destruction. Ancient Western worries about Islam were rekindled. Egypt must be bribed to sign the Nuclear Nonproliferation Treaty whether or not Israel complied. Pakistan must be stopped from acquiring a nuclear capability. And Iraq must be given enough rope to hang itself over Kuwait so that all Iraqi weapons of mass destruction could then be destroyed.

The third reason for Western anxiety about Islam was the importance of Muslim oil for Western industry. Although Western technological power was still preeminent and undisputed, its dependence on Middle Eastern oil made it vulnerable to political changes in the Muslim world—changes of the magnitude of the revolution in Iran or of Iraq's annexation of Kuwait.

It seems almost certain that Muslims became the frontline military victims of the new world order while Blacks became the frontline economic victims of this emerging global apartheid. Muslims, especially in the Middle East, felt the firing power of U.S. guns and U.S.-subsidized Israeli planes. Blacks felt the deprivations of economic exploitation and neglect.

The military victimization of Muslims took either the direct form of Western bombing, as in the war against Iraq, or the surrogate Western aggression of heavily subsidizing Israel without adequately criticizing its repressive and military policies. There have also been Western double standards of crying "foul" when Muslim killed Muslim (as when Arab Iraqis repressed Kurds), but remaining apathetic when the Indian army committed atrocities in Kashmir.

Was the Gulf War against Iraq part of global apartheid? Aspects of the war were certainly ominous including Soviet submissiveness to the United States, Western hegemony in the United Nations, the attempted recolonization of Iraq after the war, and Western insensitivity to the killing of over two hundred thousand Iraqis. It was not a war; it was a massacre. Admittedly, it was triggered by Iraq's unforgivable aggression against Kuwait. But Bush, in turn, was more keen on saving time than saving lives. He refused to give sanctions enough time, even if it meant killing hundreds of thousands of Iraqis.

The coalition against Iraq was multiracial. Its leadership was decidedly and unmistakably white. Bush regarded the war against Iraq as the first major war of the new world order. Perhaps one day we will also lament the Gulf War as the first major war of the era of global apartheid. Just when we thought apartheid in South Africa was over, apartheid on a global scale reared its ugly head.

The apparent demise of Soviet and East European anti-imperialism hurt the Muslim world in other ways. When a U.S. ship shot down an Iranian civilian airliner over international airspace, the new Soviet Union under Gorbachev did not attempt to rally the world against this act of manslaughter committed by Americans. Would the Iranian airliner have been shot down if there was a chance that European passengers were on board? Would Soviets have been silent if Soviet citizens were aboard? Moscow said it was deliberately not going to follow the accusatory precedent set by the United States in 1983 when Washington led the world in vigorously denouncing the Soviet Union's shooting down of a Korean civilian airliner. When the Soviets shot down South Korea's Flight 007, the Cold War was still on. Many of the passengers killed were Westerners, including a U.S. Congressman. The United States served as the conscience of the world. But when a U.S. battleship shot down the Iranian airliner, the Cold War was ending, there was no reason to believe that any Westerners or Soviet citizens were on board, and the USSR refused to serve as the conscience of the world and to denounce this fatal "accident."

If there is global apartheid in formation, how will it affect the European Soviet Union in relation to the Asian Soviet Union? One out of five citizens of the former USSR was a Muslim, and the Muslim pace of natural reproduction was much faster than that of non-Muslims. One future scenario could be an alliance between the Russian Federation and the Muslim Republics. Indeed, the possibility of a Muslim president of the USSR was already in the cards, although with much reduced power. Gorbachev even considered appointing a Muslim vice president.

No less likely a scenario is one in which the European parts of what used to be the Soviet Union would align more closely to the newly integrated Western Europe, while the Muslim parts of the former USSR developed relationships with the rest of the Muslim world and Third World. Pakistan is now seeking new markets in places such as Uzbekistan and may open a consulate there. Turkey is seeking a new role in that part of the Muslim world. Such a trend would once again reinforce global apartheid. There is even a risk that the former Muslim republics would become Russian Bantustans, "backyards" with even less power than they had before.

But not all aspects of the newly emerging global apartheid may be detrimental to Muslim interests globally. After all, the new world order is predicated on the foundation of Pax Americana. An imperial system values stability and peace (hence the "pax"), but on its own imperial terms. Objectively, the main obstacle to peace in the Middle East since the 1970s is Israel. Will Pax Americana not only force Israel and the Arabs to the negotiating table, but compel them to consider exchanging land for peace as well? Indeed, will the Gulf War against Iraq turn out to be the undoing of Israel as we have so far known it?

Before he went to war against Iraq, George Bush vowed that there was no linkage between the Gulf crisis and the wider Arab-Israeli conflict. Almost as soon as the war was over, Secretary of State James Baker started a series of diplomatic trips in order to start a peace process in the Arab-Israeli conflict. There was de facto linkage.

The Gulf War that Bush and his allies launched was not really a war; it was a massacre. On the other hand, Desert Storm temporarily made Bush so strong in domestic politics that he was able to stand up to the pro-Israeli lobby and defy the Israeli prime minister. George Bush may turn out to be the toughest president on Israel since Eisenhower. Are there signs that the Gulf War may turn out to be the beginning of the political undoing of the old, defiant Israel after all?

Israel's political decline in Washington, although modest, may be due to two very different factors: the end of the Cold War and the new U.S.-Arab realignments following the Gulf War. The end of the Cold War, as indicated, reduced the strategic value of Israel to the United States. It also increased Syria's desire to be friends with the United States. Israel may become a less intimate friend to the United States; Syria has already become less objectionable as an adversary to the United States. The Gulf War provided a test for U.S.-Syrian realignment. Damascus and Washington moved closer as a result of the Gulf War.

Most commentators focused on the political and economic losses the Palestinians sustained as a result of the Gulf War. Few noted that this was balanced, at least to some degree, by the political losses sustained by Israel as a result of a new U.S.-Arab realignment and by the popularity of George Bush in the aftermath of the war. The popularity was great enough to withstand the criticism of the pro-Israeli lobby, at least for one year.

On the other hand, the end of the Cold War also reduced the strategic value of Pakistan to the Western world. Pressures on Pakistan to conform to Western prescriptions have already increased and its nuclear credentials have become even more of an issue in its relations with the United States. As far as the West is concerned, Islam must on no account be nuclearized. This means (1) stopping Pakistan from developing nuclear capability, (2) destroying Iraq's capacity in weapons of mass destruction, (3) neutralizing Egypt by getting it to sign the Nuclear Non-Proliferation Treaty, (4) coopting Syria into pro-Western respectability, and (5) preventing Qaddafy from buying nuclear credentials.

On the other hand, the United States' conventional capability—although originally targeted at the Second World of Socialist countries—in reality tended to be used against the Third World. There were disproportionate numbers of Muslim victims. Under the Reagan and Bush administrations the United States (1) bombed Beirut from the sea, (2) invaded Grenada, (3) bombed Tripoli and Bengazi in Libya, (4) hijacked an Egyptian plane in international airspace, (5) shot down an Iranian civilian aircraft in the Gulf and killed all on board, (6) invaded Panama and kidnapped General Manuel Noriega, and (7) bombed Iraqi cities as part of an anti-Saddam coalition. More than two-thirds of the casualties of U.S. military activity since the Vietnam War were Muslims, amounting to at least a quarter of a million, and possibly half a million, Muslim deaths.

Between Ideology and Economics

If the first military victims of global apartheid were disproportionately Muslims, the first economic victims of global apartheid may be Blacks. The good news is that Europe, in spite of Yugoslavia and the fragmentation of the Soviet Union, is carrying forward the torch of continental unification and regional integration. The bad news is that countries such as France, often "champions of African interests" in world affairs, are beginning to turn their eyes away from Africa toward Europe.

In the struggle against old style narrow nationalism and the nation-state, Western Europe led the way. The Treaties of Rome created the European Economic Community (EEC) in March 1957 and set the stage for wider regional integration. In 1992, an enlarged European Community achieved even deeper integration as more walls between

members disappeared (or came down). The former German Democratic Republic was reunited with the Federal Republic of Germany
as part of this wider Europe. And the newly liberated Eastern European countries are seeking new links with the European Community,
further eroding narrow nationalism and enlarging regional integration.
Yugoslavia and the Soviet Union, torn by ethnic separatism, still
manifest in the European areas an eagerness to be accepted into the
wider European fraternity. The decline of socialist ideology throughout Eastern Europe is accompanied by a resurgence of primordial
culture. Marxism has either died or been de-Leninized, but a pan-
European identity is reasserting itself on a scale greater than the Holy
Roman Empire.

Marxism-Leninism, while it lasted, was transracial. It made European Marxists seek allies and converts among people of color. But
European identity is, by definition, Eurocentric. It increases the
chances of pan-Europeanism. The bad news is that pan-Europeanism
can carry the danger of cultural chauvinism and even racism.

Anti-Semitism has been on the rise in Eastern Europe as an aspect
of this cultural chauvinism. And racism and xenophobia in the re-
unified Germany have reached new levels. Racism in France took its
highest toll among North Africans. And all over Europe, there is a
new sense of insecurity among immigrants who are of a darker hue
than the local populations; some of the immigrants farther north may
even be Portuguese mistaken for Turks or North Africans. Where
does xenophobia end and racism begin? An old dilemma once again
rears its head.

Then there is the racial situation in the United States with all its
contradictions. On the one hand, the country produced the first black
governor of a state (Virginia) and the first black mayor of New
York City. On the other hand, in 1991 the state of Louisiana produced a startling level of electoral support for David Duke, a former
member of the Ku Klux Klan and former advocate of Nazi policies.
Duke got a majority of the white votes that were cast, but lost the
election because of the other votes. In April 1992, a mainly white
jury in California found that beating and kicking of a black suspect
(Rodney King) while he was down was not excessive use of force.
The verdict sparked some of the worst riots in U.S. history in Los
Angeles in which nearly sixty people were killed.

George Bush exploited white racial fears in the presidential electoral campaign of 1988. A television commercial of the Bush campaign exploited to the utmost the image of a black convict, Willie

Horton, who had been prematurely "furloughed" in Massachusetts and who killed again. The television commercial was probably a significant factor behind George Bush's victory in the 1988 presidential election.

Meanwhile, the Supreme Court of the United States moves farther and farther to the right, endangering some of the interracial constitutional gains of yesteryear. The new right wing Supreme Court legalized atrocities, ranging from violence by prison wardens to kidnapping by U.S. agents in countries such as Mexico. The economic conditions of the black underclass in the United States are as bad as ever. Poverty, drug abuse, crime, broken homes, unemployment, infant mortality, and now the disproportionate affliction by AIDS are a stubborn part of the black condition in the United States.

The holocausts of the Western hemisphere continue to inflict pain and humiliation on native Americans and descendants of enslaved Africans. Approximately 40 percent of the prisoners on death row in the United States are African Americans. The jails, mortuaries, and police cells still bear anguished testimony to the disproportionate and continuing suffering of U.S. holocausts. In the United States today, there are possibly more male descendants of enslaved Africans in prison than in college.

Equally ominous on a continental scale is the economic condition of Africa. The continent still produces what it does not consume, and consumes what it does not produce. Agriculturally, many African countries have evolved dessert and beverage economies, producing cocoa, coffee, tea, and other incidentals for Northern dining tables. In contrast, Africa imports the fundamentals of its existence from basic equipment to staple foods. In addition, Africa is liable to environmental hazards that lead to drought and famine in certain areas. The Horn of Africa and the Sahel were particularly prone to these ecological deprivations.

The external factors that retarded Africa's economic development included price fluctuations and uncertainties about primary commodities, issues over which Africa had very little say. The debt crisis in Africa is also a major shackle on the pace of development. Although the debts of African countries are modest compared with countries such as Brazil and Mexico, it is important to remember that African economies are not only smaller, but also more fragile than those of the major Latin U.S. states. The West demonstrated more flexibility in recent times about Africa's debt crisis, and some Western countries extended debt forgiveness. Speedy action toward resolving the debt problem would be a contribution in the fight against the forces of global apartheid.

Just as African societies are becoming more democratic, African states exert less influence on the global scene than ever. African people are increasing their influence on their governments just when African countries are losing leverage on the world system. As the African electorate is empowered, the African countries are enfeebled.

Africa's international marginalization does include among its causes the absence of the Soviet bloc as a countervailing force in the global equation. A world with only one superpower is a world with less leverage for the smaller countries in the global system. Africa's marginalization is also a result of the re-emergence of Eastern European countries as rivals for Western attention and Western largesse.

Africa is also being marginalized in a world of such mega-economies as an increasingly unified North America, an increasingly unified European Community, an expanding Japanese economy, and some of the achievements of the member states of the Association of South East Asian Nations (ASEAN). In the economic domain, global apartheid is a starker and sharper reality between white nations and black nations than between white nations and some of the countries of Asia.

In the United Nations and its agencies, Africa is also marginalized, partly because Third World causes have lost the almost automatic support of former members of the Warsaw Pact. On the contrary, former members of the Socialist bloc are now more likely to follow the U.S. lead than to join forces with the Third World. Moreover, the African percentage of the total membership of the UN system is declining. In 1991, five new members were admitted to the UN, none of them African (the two Koreas and three Baltic states). The disintegration of Yugoslavia and the Soviet Union has resulted in at least ten more members. The numerical marginalization of Africa within the world body is likely to continue.

In the financial world, the power of the World Bank and the International Monetary Fund (IMF) not only remains intact, but is bound to increase in the era of global apartheid. It was once said of a British monarch that the power of the king has increased, is increasing and ought to diminish. This philosophy is especially applicable to the power of the World Bank in Africa. Unfortunately, all indications continue to point in the direction of greater escalation of Africa's dependence upon such international financial institutions.

On the other hand, the World Bank sometimes acts as an ambassador on behalf of Africa, coaxing Japan, for example, to allocate more money for African aid. The World Bank may help to persuade Western countries to bear African needs in mind even as the West remains mesmerized by the continuing drama in the former Soviet Union and Eastern Europe. At its best, the World Bank can be a force against the drift towards global apartheid. But at its worst, the World Bank is an extension of the power of the white races over the darker peoples of the globe.

It is virtually certain that German money is already being diverted from Tanzania and Bangladesh toward the newly integrated East Germany, to compensate the Soviet Union for its cooperation with German reunification. Before long, larger amounts of Western money will be going to Poland, Hungary, the Czech and Slovak republics, and the newly independent republics of Lithuania, Latvia, and Estonia.

Western investment in former Warsaw Pact countries may also be at the expense of investment in Africa. Western trade may also be redirected to some extent. Now that white Westerners and Easterners no longer have an ideological reason for mutual hostility, are their shared culture and race acquiring more primary salience? Are we witnessing the emergence of a new Northern solidarity as the hatchets of the Cold War are at last buried? Are Blacks the first economic victims of this global apartheid?

Conclusion

Are we witnessing new forms of retribalization and race consciousness just as the more localized apartheid of South Africa is coming to an end? I argued that if there is a new world order, its first economic victims will be black people of Africa, the Americas, Europe, and elsewhere. I also argued that the new world order's first military victims are Muslims; about half a million have been killed by the West or Western-subsidized initiatives since the Vietnam War. Palestinians, Libyans, Iraqis, and Lebanese are among the casualties. Since World War II, far more Muslims have been killed by the West than have citizens of the former Warsaw Pact, from the Suez War of 1956 to the Gulf War of 1991.

One advantage of the old East-West divide was that is was trans-racial and interracial. White socialist countries supported black liber-ation fighters militarily against white minority governments in Africa. But now the former Socialist countries are among the least suppor-tive of Third World causes. In the UN, the former communist ad-versaries are often more cooperative with Washington than are some Western allies. In reality, Paris is more independent of Washington than is Moscow since the Gorbachev revolution.

With regard to this new world order, are there racial and racist dif-ferences between the Western response to Iraqi aggression against Kuwait in 1990 and to Serbia's aggression against Bosnia and Her-zegovina in 1992? Both Bosnia and Kuwait had prior international recognition as sovereign states. Both had prior historical links with the countries that committed aggression against them, Serbia and Iraq respectively. Bosnia and Serbia had once been part of Yugosla-via; Kuwait and Iraq had once been part of the same province of the Ottoman Empire. Iraq in 1990 had territorial appetites masquer-ading as a dispute over oil wells between Iraq and Kuwait; Serbia had territorial appetites masquerading as protection of ethnic Serbs in Bosnia.

The West, under the leadership of the Bush administration, said to Iraqi aggression: "This will not stand!" To end Iraqi aggression in Kuwait, the West and its allies bombed Baghdad and Basra. To end Serbian aggression in Bosnia, was the West in 1992 prepared to bomb Belgrade? If not, why not? Did the reasons include racism? Was it all right to bomb Arab populations thousands of miles away, but insupportable to bomb fellow Europeans next door?

The new idea of creating a European army answerable to the Eu-ropean Community, as well as to NATO, also seemed to draw a sharp distinction between "military intervention" *outside* Europe and "peacekeeping" within Europe.

According to Joseph Fitchett, writing for the *International Herald Tribune*:

> Braving Bush administration objections, France and Germany are proceeding . . . to establish a substantial joint military force that could assume functions previously reserved for NATO.
>
> Conceived as the core for a future European army, the pro-posed Euro-corps is supposed to ready the equivalent of two divisions by 1995 for military intervention outside Europe and

for peacekeeping and other, as yet undefined, operations within Europe.[2]

Is there a clear reluctance to shed European blood among some nations, such as France and Britain, which have very recently shed Arab and Muslim blood?

Regarding the war in Bosnia, Anthony Lewis of *The New York Times* said in 1992:

> The Americans and Europeans have plenty of warplanes, based near enough . . . to take command of the air. . . . We could have said to Mr. Milosovic, and still could: Stop your aggression at once, or our military aircraft will control your skies. Not just over Dubrovnik or Sarajevo, but over Belgrade. . . . The failure of nerve and imagination in the face of Serbian aggression is Europe's as well as America's. But Mr. Bush raised expectations so high in the Gulf War that disappointment naturally focussed on him. What happened to the man who three days after Iraq grabbed Kuwait said, "This will not stand?"[3]

Was it a "failure of nerve" on the part of the United States or Europe? Or was it a triumph of macroracial empathy? It was easier to remember British planes bombing Baghdad in 1991 than to imagine British planes bombing Belgrade in 1992. And U.S. planes bombing Sarajevo or Dubrovnik in the 1990s in order to save them seems distasteful. It was easier to bomb parts of Kuwait in 1991 and would be easier to rebomb Tripoli and Baghdad in 1992 and 1993.

Long before the end of the Cold War, I had occasion to worry publicly about a "global caste system" in the making. I argued in a book published in 1977 that the international stratification did not have the flexibility and social mobility of a class structure, but had some of the rigidities of caste:

> If the international system was, in the first half of the twentieth century a class system, it is now moving in the direction of rigidity. We may be witnessing the consolidation of a global caste structure. . . . Just as there are hereditary factors in domestic castes, so there are hereditary elements in international castes. Pre-eminent among those factors is the issue of *race*. . . . If people of European extraction are the Brahmins of the international caste system, the Black people belong disproportionately

to the caste of the untouchables. Between the highest international caste [Whites] and the lowest [Blacks] are other ranks
and estates such as Asians].[4]

What prevented this global caste system from becoming global
apartheid at that time was, ironically, the Cold War, which divided
the white world ideologically. Rivalry between the two white power
blocs averted the risk of racial solidarity among the more prosperous
whites. The white world was armed to the teeth against each other.
This was unlike apartheid in South Africa. At the global level, we
had Brahmins at dagger point.[5]

But there is now a closing of ranks among the white peoples of
the world. The ethnic hiccups of Yugoslavia and the Soviet Union
notwithstanding, and after allowing for Denmark's caution and Britain's relative insularity, the mood in Europe is still toward greater
continental union. Pan-Europeanism is reaching levels greater than
anything experienced since the Holy Roman Empire. The question
that arises is whether this new pan-European force, combined with
the economic trend towards a mega-North America, will produce a
human race more than ever divided between prosperous white races
and poverty-stricken Blacks. Is a global macroretribalization in the
making?

The era of global apartheid coincided with the era of a unipolar
world—a global system with only one superpower. The declining
fear of communism may reactivate an older Western fear of Islam.
The location of petroleum disproportionately in Muslim lands, combined with the tensions of the Arab-Israeli conflict, cost the Muslim
world upward of half a million lives as a result of military actions by
the United States and its allies during the Reagan and Bush administrations. The main victims were Libyans, Iranians, Lebanese, Palestinians, and, most recently, Iraqis.

Race and religion remain potent forces in global affairs. Historically, race has been the fundamental divisive factor between Westerners and people of African descent almost everywhere. Religion has
been the fundamental divisive factor between Westerners and people
of Muslim culture almost everywhere. Was the collapse of the Berlin
Wall in 1989 the beginning of the racial reunification of the white
world? Did the Gulf War of 1991 put the holiest places of Islam under the imperial umbrella of Pax Americana? Is the twentieth century
getting ready to hand over to the twenty-first century a new legacy of
global apartheid? The trends are ominous, but let us hope that they
are not irreversible.

Acknowledgments

An earlier version of this paper was originally presented at the 90th Anniversary Nobel Jubilee Symposium, on the panel on "The Changing Pattern of Global Conflict: From East-West to North-South Conflicts?" sponsored by the Norwegian Nobel Committee and the Norwegian Nobel Institute, Oslo, Norway, 6-8 December 1991. I am especially indebted for stimulation to Professor Darryl Thomas of State University of New York, Binghamton.

Notes

1. V. I. Lenin, *Imperialism: The Highest Stage of Capitalism* (New York: International Publishers, 1939).

2. Joseph Fitchett, "Paris and Bonn to Form the Nucleus of a 'Euro-corps,'" *International Herald Tribune* (14 May 1992).

3. Anthony Lewis, "What was that About a New World Order?" *International Herald Tribune* (18 May 1992).

4. Ali A. Mazrui, *Africa's International Relations: The Diplomacy of Dependency and Change* (Boulder, CO: Westview Press, 1977): 7-8.

5. Gernot Köhler used the concept of "global apartheid" in a working paper published for the World Order Models Project (Gernot Köhler, *Global Apartheid*, New York: World Order Models Project, Institute for World Order, Working Paper No. 7, 1978). His definition of apartheid did not require a fundamental solidarity within the privileged race. My definition does.

23
Democracy Died at the Gulf

Richard Falk

Those states with long and deep traditions of democracy seemed all too ready to rush headlong into the cruel, merciless, and vengeful war in the Gulf; to deploy massive force to maintain resource hegemony and satisfy geopolitical ambitions. Despite the rhetoric that legitimized the war in the name of democracy, this was a war about pricing oil and the U.S. capacity to establish itself as the leader of post-cold war global security arrangements or, as George Bush expressed it, the new world order.

The relevance of democracy to the behavior of belligerent states in such a conflict is always overdetermined. There were differences, for example, between the U.S. intervention in Indochina and the Soviet intervention in Afghanistan, and some of these could be linked to the presence or absence of a democratic political culture. The role of public opinion and domestic opposition was more significant in the United States, but it was easier to reverse official policy in the Soviet Union. Yet from the perspective of target societies, the similarities undoubtedly outweighed the differences. In both cases, the political life of a Third World country was manipulated to validate military intervention against its civilian society. In both, the battle confined to the Third World arena was characterized by unequal combatants—a superpower pitted against an underdeveloped, yet stubborn, nationalist adversary. Both wars could be classified as imperialist expressions of East-West geopolitical rivalry. Although military superiority and decisive technological advantage were on the intervening side in both instances, the U.S. style of intervention emphasized techno-war more than did its Soviet counterpart. This is not surprising given the U.S. role as the leader of militarist aspects of modern industrial society. In fact, it could be argued that this capacity for techno-war is itself a reflection of the degree of innovation that can be sustained only by a democratically constituted polity, although the evidence for such a position is scant.

The most ardent belligerents in the Gulf War—the United States and Great Britain—possessed the best credentials among the coalition states for democratic governance, having sustained political moderation and the rule of law without rupture for centuries. It was ironic that Germany and Japan, whose democratic allegiance was imposed after 1945, and then only as the outcome of military defeat, were the most troubled among the coalition partners by the war, both among their leaders and public. Furthermore, and for a variety of motives, it was nondemocratic states such as the Soviet Union, Iran, Yemen, and Algeria that struggled valiantly to restore peace. Along the same lines, the most severe societal resistance within the coalition occurred in the least democratic states, especially Syria, Egypt, and Morocco. Those governing elites that most closely reflected popular mass sentiments (for example, Jordan and the Palestinian Liberation Organization) sided in the war with Iraq and were "punished" by the victors for their alignment, despite its democratic backing, implying far better treatment by the "democratic" victors if their leaders had ignored, or even repressed, the will of the people.

Of course, the situation was complex. Iraq, and especially Saddam Hussein, were easily cast in the role of the evil Other. Saddam was guilty of bloody crimes against his own people and against nature. His Iraq continuously worshipped at the altar of the war gods, distorting priorities to build an extravagant war machine, embarking on aggressive war-making against Iran before the conquest of Kuwait, and mindlessly allowing the encounter with Kuwait's mighty protectors to drift from crisis to war. Saddam Hussein was likened in some circles to Hitler. This analogy provided a useful tool to mobilize support for a military response by the citizenry in liberal democracies. These same democracies held themselves partially accountable for failing to stop Hitler earlier, a failure interpreted as a direct cause of World War II. Leaving aside the questionable accuracy of this premise, "the lesson of Munich" has been influential in recent decades: to guard the global order against aggressive challenges at their earliest manifestations. This lesson was reinforced by the conviction that the cold war was won by a democratic West because it was willing and ready to engage in warfare to contain the Soviet-led communist challenge. Such readings of the past partly explain why democratic countries so easily embraced a militarist conception of their own security and even succumbed to the seductive illusion that war-making could be the keystone in the arch of a peaceful world.

There is a reinforcing factor that operates in a democratic political culture of the sort that emerged in the West, especially in the United States, namely the simplifying impact of the political energy required to mobilize the citizenry on behalf of the war effort. War is presented as a polar struggle in which compromise is unthinkable: slow to war, but even slower to peace had been the U.S. experience. Walter Lippmann eloquently criticized this tendency to absolutize the enemy as making more disruptive adjustments among states on the basis of shifting power relationships.[1]

Historically, the U.S. disposition toward isolationism in relation to European warfare raised the threshold of persuasion and became associated with the sense that war is justifiable only if the enemy can be absolutely destroyed. When it comes to war, the U.S. orientation is that of the crusader, not the merchant looking for a decent bargain, or the diplomat seeking a dignified compromise.

To some extent, the emergence of nuclear weaponry eroded this crusader mentality. The prospect of mutual annihilation aroused apocalyptic fears and generated a managerial approach premised on cost-benefit calculations. The cold war produced a maximal mobilization for war, but also an imperative to avoid a direct encounter. Thus, the awakened crusader sought combat on more remote battlefields. The U.S. frustrations in Korea and Vietnam—wars in which military superiority could not be translated into victory—generated deep disappointment. In the Gulf crisis, the conditions for victory seemed apparent: an encounter in which one-sided military tactics could not be neutralized by the terrain and the struggle could not be shifted to a political arena shared with the Soviet Union. From this perspective, providing Iraq with modern armaments had to be accomplished before Iraq could be defeated. The Pentagon's enthusiasm for "mid-intensity" warfare was finally tested and vindicated, showing how technological differences could dominate battlefield outcomes and produce military victory while avoiding the catastrophic effects of "high-intensity" warfare, that is, wars in which weapons of mass destruction could devastate the homelands of both sides. As long as only one side was vulnerable, threats and the use of nuclear weapons could sustain the mid-intensity character and keep victory within the range of acceptable cost-benefit ratios. The limits of war under modern conditions have been the subject of continuous debate among strategic planners, raising questions about the rationality of war as an instrument of foreign policy.

Relevant here, also, is the proclaimed enthusiasm for overcoming the Vietnam syndrome. George Bush's 89 percent or better approval rating among the American people after the Gulf War confirmed what seemed only a suspicion in the aftermath of the 1983 Grenada invasion, the 1986 Libyan bombing, and the 1989 Panama intervention. That is, the Vietnam syndrome proved a political inhibition only to unsuccessful and prolonged war. The American people demonstrated, as the post-Vietnam political leadership in the United States believed, that war can be successfully prosecuted under a variety of conditions in the Third World, and that if it ends in a quick victory, the public will adore the experience and celebrate the outcome. The Gulf War inscribed a bellicose message in the U.S. political consciousness of citizenry and leadership alike—military intervention in the Third World is effective abroad and good politics at home.

Taking on Iraq was further encouraged by a variety of situational factors. Most Arab governments in the region, each acting in response to diverse interests but converging on the desirability of restoring Kuwaiti sovereignty and containing Iraq, were ultimately favorable to war. These regional supporters of the war policy regarded the political risks of participating in the U.S.-led military campaign as real, but as less dangerous than an unchecked Saddam Hussein. This Arab participation at the governmental level helped obscure the North-South and the inter-religious characteristics of the conflict.

Further, Israel, regarded by the West as an island of Western values including adherence to the principles of liberal democracy, keenly supported war as a response to the Gulf crisis and regarded as unacceptable anything less than the destruction of Iraq's war machine. This was a further mobilizing influence in the United States, particularly in building support for the Bush approach in a closely divided Congress. There were no comparable countervailing forces active in the political arena of the United States to build the case for diplomacy and sanctions as a better alternative. This absence of a peace constituency tells us more about the militarist configuration of social forces in democracies at present than about the structures of political democracies in general, or in the United States in particular.

Such a militarist temptation was reinforced by the post-cold war availability of the UN for such purposes. The initial Security Council resolutions after the Iraqi conquest of Kuwait, which imposed extensive sanctions to achieve the goal of unconditional Iraqi withdrawal, seemed consistent with the Charter commitment to protect the victims of aggression while searching for a peaceful resolution of international disputes. Even the early post-August 1990 deployment of the U.S. military forces in the region was consistent with an effort to contain Iraq during a period of increasing pressure through sanctions and diplomacy. In retrospect, there were serious flaws in this use of the UN: Washington exercised too large a degree of control over the language and rituals of the UN Security Council. George Bush insisted, and no one challenged him, that the friends of Kuwait had the authority to act militarily on their own even if the United Nation withheld its endorsement from recourse to force. Events of the period and features of the UN colluded to provide such a climate. These were the willingness of the Soviet Union and China to bargain away an independent international voice because of their domestic troubles and the over-representation of Europe and the under-representation of the Third World in the Security Council. The UN appeared deficient from a democratic standpoint, relying on representation by way of rich states and thereby excluding important social forces in the world, lending itself on this occasion to the geopolitical maneuverings of a single member state. From the outset, it was evident that only the United States, aside possibly from Israel, had the resolve and capabilities to check Iraq's ambitions in the region, and thus the world found itself dependent on Washington's priorities and outlook.

In effect, the presence and absence of democratic forms and substance worked in tandem to help produce the Gulf War. Democratic dispositions in the United States encouraged its citizenry to heed a presidential summons to war whereas democratic deficiencies in the UN removed obstacles in the path of the United States and its allies to turn the organization, by stages, into an instrument legitimizing a war that could and should have been avoided. The sanctions alternative was abandoned despite the evidence of its remarkable effectiveness in cutting Iraq's gross national product by more than half in its first six months of operation.

Abandoning sanctions also meant diminishing the prospect of a more democratic regime in Iraq. Journalists and opposition leaders in exile noted the rising tide of anti-Hussein sentiment in Iraq before the outbreak of war. Sanctions might have exerted sufficient pressure on the Iraqi regime to have enabled a successful challenge by more moderate political forces in Iraq. Such a possibility remains no more than informed conjecture, but the onset of war unified Iraqi society, gave Saddam Hussein considerable street support throughout the region, and undermined whatever hope existed for the emergence of an indigenous democratic process. In the aftermath of the Gulf War, the tragic circumstances of the Iraqi people were reinforced, combining a degree of Lebanonization by way of persistent civil strife with external strangulation, even insisting that their ruined country pay the cost of rebuilding Kuwait.

Coalition forces, especially the United States, let it be known that late in the period of combat Saddam Hussein was to be treated as the lesser evil. The organized opposition to Saddam Hussein was not supported: Shi'a resistance in the South aroused concern because its success could strengthen Iran's regional influence and Kurdish resistance in the North was feared because it could destabilize Turkey and Syria (both had large and restive Kurdish minority populations). The reemergence of old geopolitical games in the region was not surprising, but the blatant repudiation of the idealistic claims being made by the victors in the Gulf War might have put off such behavior for a decent interval.

In the last decade, the U.S. government had been intent on giving the process of democratization a capitalist coloring. In the 1980s, the Reagan doctrine identified adherence to a market economy as the crucial defining feature of a democratic polity. The wider dynamics of the market included a green light for arms sales, especially as an aspect of the cold war game of projecting influence overseas and diminishing negative trade balances. The militarization of Iraq in the 1970s and 1980s was facilitated by both of these factors; the Soviets supplied arms to gain influence and earn some hard currency—the West later gained a piece of this profitable market. The revealed character of Saddam's criminality—launching an aggressive war against Iran, introducing poison gas on the battlefield, and using poison gas and chemical weapons against Kurdish villages in Iraq—did nothing to impair Iraq's status as a privileged customer for Western technology. Bush, who claimed to be appalled by Saddam in August 1990, was the same man who only weeks earlier had intervened with the U.S. Congress to discourage terminating a U.S. $200 million credit in Iraq's favor. At that time Bush had reminded lawmakers that Saddam Hussein was a fact of life, better to befriend than to alienate. Other disclosures about U.S.-Iraq relationships reinforced the impression of a U.S. government eager to appease Saddam's regime. To the extent, then, that Iraq became the monster of the region, it did so as a direct result of the way the existing international capitalist and political order worked—no anomaly here.

Democratic orientations toward governance were consistently subordinated to racist dispositions embodied within political cultures. There had long been tension between the humanistic aspirations associated with democracy and the racist practices of specific democracies, but, internally at least, some progress had been made in several countries toward overcoming racial discrimination. Such internal progress was fragile, however, as the recent backlash against refugees and Third World immigration in Europe illustrates. But externally, democracies were quick to associate the evil other with non-white, non-Christian peoples, and with support from their biblical heritage of divine backing, they easily assumed a religious self-righteous posture to justify an exterminist ethos. This cruel side of democratic attitudes expressed itself most crudely in the United States and Britain during the Gulf War in the form of popular support for nuking Baghdad. More generally, there seemed little or no sympathy in the West for the Iraqi civilian population victimized by the indirect but massive effects of the most sustained and intensive bombing campaign in human history.

This indifference to the suffering of innocent civilians has many sources and cannot be properly associated with any particular political or cultural form. Yet the moral pretensions of democratic societies in the West made their enthusiasm for destructive warfare somewhat surprising. The modernist democratic sensibility had been shaped by the commercialization of violence, an addiction to entertainment built around grotesque encounters between various idioms of violence, and a culture shaped by rising crime, official corruption, and pervasive fear even at the neighborhood level. A culture immersed in violence can easily shift gears into displays of flag-waving support for a merciless war against a society that cannot retaliate, especially if victory is achieved and the outcome can be celebrated. An unacknowledged part of the enthusiasm was undoubtedly racist in character—a recovered confidence that the tools of white supremacy were again working well and encouraging the belief that the privileged order favoring the North could be maintained for the indefinite future. Such a reading of the war also affected the domestic "text," suggesting the fate that awaited those nonwhite hordes if they dared to challenge directly the domestic status quo that during the 1980s had deliberately shifted income from poor to rich and offered little opportunity to the mass of minority poor, especially among the urban young.

Even here there are twists and turns of historical memory. The flags that waved so furiously to support the U.S. troops in the Gulf expressed a belated acknowledgment that the citizenry had deserted their own soldiers during the last stages of the Vietnam war. In a sense, U.S. society refused to participate in the failure of the Vietnam War, and this distancing embittered those who had fought there,

more than two million of whom returned from Indochina to tor-
ment family and neighbors, as much by their depression and withdrawal as by their anger. The poison of embitterment was exchanged
for the poison of jingoism. More significantly, in both Vietnam and
the Gulf, and countless other places as well, U.S. political identity
was defined and redefined at the expense of distant peoples of a different race and religion on Third World killing fields that diverted
energies from the anguish on street corners at home, a reality temporarily brought home by the Los Angeles riots in the spring of 1992.

One chilling dimension of the Gulf War was disclosed during the
televised debates in Congress between the Bush forces that obtained
their mandate to wage unrestricted warfare after 15 January and the
liberal critics who favored sanctions because they did not want U.S.
boys coming home in body bags. These critics were reluctant opponents, often suggesting that if there were some kind of assurance
that the war could be waged from air and sea, without a ground
fight, they would support it. The ideal war would be conducted by
high-tech weaponry that could inflict damage and pain at will and
face no threat in return. What was called war in these debates and
what unfolded after 15 January is more accurately described as a
massacre. This is the latest version of the sort of unequal war characteristic of the settler conquests of indigenous peoples in the "age
of discovery" and of colonial warfare ever since. The mixture of democracy, capitalism, and technology has generated a powerful war
machine. There is little resistance except at the margins. The meta-
phors of victory are overpowering. The assumption that God is on
the side of the better technology is deeply engrained in the pretensions of Western civilization.

Discussions of the failures of modernity are so familiar by now as
to seem rather tedious. The extent to which modernity offers a mandate for unequal war remains obscure. The inner logic of modernity
helps explain the evolution of warfare over the centuries, the progressive shift from fighting prowess to relative technological capability and what Anthony Giddens calls the displacement of "the traditional warrior ethic that flourished when warfare was associated with
spectacle and display."[2]

The technologizing of war proceeded in two directions: the delit-
eralization of war or what Mary Kaldor identified as "the imaginary
war"[3]—too awful to fight as a matter of intention, but a persuasive
dark cloud dominating the political landscape—and the Nintendo
war in which money inserted at one end would generate techno-

power that inflicted one-sided destruction at the other end and which depended for its reality on denying the weaker side the technological and political means to fight back. The cold war was an imaginary war; the Gulf War is better understood as a Nintendo war.

In order to make the world safe for Nintendo war, the adversary must be denied the capacity to leap over the technology gap. The nonproliferation of nuclear weapons is crucial in this respect as is the denial of other weapons of mass destruction and the effective means of long range missile delivery. Iraq was an important enemy because it challenged this technology gap. It possessed chemical weapons and was evidently pursuing both nuclear and biological capabilities with vigor. Moreover, the SCUD missiles, although largely ineffective, indicated an ability to expand the scope of the battlefield beyond the target society, a capacity that neither Vietnam nor Afghanistan possessed. Terrorism against Western targets was an additional means of carrying the war beyond Iraq and Kuwait, and even the dumping of oil in the Gulf could be understood as a futile attempt by Iraq to inflict pain in retaliation.

The new world order will attempt to deepen the vulnerability of the entire non-Western world to Nintendo war by widening the technological gap through a process of continuous innovations that improves the effectiveness of electronic warfare and increases the control and surveillance over Third World acquisitions of weapons that threaten the relative invulnerability of the West. The sinister underlying drive is now, metaphorically and potentially, to turn the entire Third World into "a desert," giving night vision and precision munitions the capacity to do in jungle and mountain terrain what they achieved in the receptive settings of the Gulf War. At the same time, every attempt will be made to keep the scenarios of an imaginary war in the North as latent as possible, retaining much of the weaponry but, in light of the pro-Western outlook of Russia, seeking to redirect political energy toward a more collaborative framework.

The Gulf War both embodied and prefigured high-tech, North-South warfare. The military commander, General Norman Schwarzkopf, summarized the war with a hunting image: "It's been like a beagle chasing a rabbit. It's been all pleasant surprises."[4] The image captured the essence of Nintendo—the hunter pursuing the hunted with no self-risk. But the abandonment of a high intensity imaginary war was also relevant because of Soviet diplomatic support for the war and the consequent mantle of UN legitimacy. This new world order was threatened on the one side by the SCUD missiles and on the other by the Soviet peace initiatives that almost ended the war prior to its ground phase. The Bush administration made no secret of its resentment of this initiative; leaks indicated that Bush was "biting his lip" to refrain from lashing out at the Soviets and spoiling the illusion of consensus; more discreetly, U.S. government officials let it be known to the press that Mikhail Gorbachev's strenuous last-minute efforts to avert the Gulf War, even while achieving the stated UN goal of unconditional withdrawal, had done more harm to Soviet-U.S. relations than "all the head-knocking in the Baltics."[5]

It is evident that the new world order as conceived in Washington is about control and surveillance, not about values or a better life. Whether this geo-strategy for the next phase of U.S.-led world capitalism can be successfully maintained is highly uncertain. Even the victory in the Gulf may be seen in retrospect as a crucial step in the final unraveling of Western hegemony. The oil wells aflame in Kuwait for more than a year may be seen not only as an ecological disaster and an economic waste, but also as a beacon that Islamic masses will eventually follow in a spirit of militant anti-Western fundamentalism. The U.S. war machine may in the end imperil control over Gulf oil to a greater extent than Saddam Hussein's expansionism. Already units of the Republican Guard were permitted by coalition forces to escape to the North so that they could turn their guns on the Iraqi resistance in Basra and thereby deny Iran political gains from the outcome of the Gulf War. Recall that earlier during the 1980s Saddam was less threatening to Western regional interests than Ayatollah Khomeini's Islamic Revolution. Still earlier, the Islamic fundamentalists were viewed as an ally against leftist threats to the stability of the shah's rule, and even earlier in 1953, a constitutional form of nationalism under Muhammad Mossadegh in Iran was displaced with the help of the U.S. Central Intelligence Agency to make way for the shah. The opportunism of Western diplomatic influence in the region has been consistently guided by considerations of oil and regional hegemony.

The Gulf War also promises new life for Star Wars, but now adapted to a North-South axis of conflict as well as a more generalized and intensified effort to extend the technologies of Nintendo war into space. Similarly, there will be some restrictions on arms suppliers in the North to prevent future acquisitions by countries in the South of weaponry and technologies that threaten the military invulnerability of the North. Whether even these restrictions will be maintained is questionable. One can expect formidable market pressures to be mounted, especially by the U.S. arms exporters, to lift restrictions. This will enable the suppliers to cash in on the performance of their weaponry in the Gulf War and contribute their earnings to the reduction of U.S. trade deficits. The U.S. government may even tempt Third World countries to aspire after some form of regional invulnerability, thereby increasing the demand for expensive items and building the case at home for a bigger research and development effort to retain a decisive military edge in the North.

More broadly, there are other problematic aspects of the Bush redesign of world order: can the United States continue to offset its economic and societal weaknesses by military muscle? Will not West-West economic rivalry induce the formation of security alternatives to continued dependence an the United States? Will the Commonwealth of Independent States avert chaos or reversion to a pre-Gorbachev anti-Western stance? Will economic distress in the Third World generate an array of political challenges to current arrangements? Will a new North-South split, anchored in the hostility between Islam and the West, produce a variant of the cold war although without the constraint of mutual deterrence? Is there the will and capability on the part of political leaders to address the various aspects of ecological decay?

Modernity also has a normative dimension that can be associated with the UN Charter as a visionary instrument pointing the way to a less violent global order rather than the UN as a political actor (in tension with its own Charter) mainly responsive to the power structure of the state system. The Gulf War dramatized the tension between visionaries and geopoliticians and confirmed that the latter are in firm control of the UN and enjoy widespread popularity even in constitutional democracies. The miles of yellow ribbon festooning American residential and commercial areas in celebration of victory in a one-sided war is as depressing as the devastation of Iraq by what came to be called World War III weaponry. Indeed, one crucial feature of the U.S. triumph was the degree to which it relied on battlefield experience in the Gulf War to insist anew on its superior technological prowess over Europe and Japan, implying that military technology was the real test of "civilization," temporally displacing anxiety among Americans about economic overextension and the prospects of decline.

Visionaries and progressive forces were effectively marginalized in this war. To varying degrees, they were disoriented in the wake of the collapse of socialist thinking at the end of the cold war, confused by the demonic persona of Saddam Hussein, distracted by the apparent recourse of the United States to internationalism in response to aggression, and quickly swayed in the main by the intoxicating thrill of a painless victory that included the decimation of an aggressive Islamic society. Antiwar efforts were widespread during 1990 and 1991 but were incoherent and lacked an alternative conception of a new world order. They were, therefore, caught between an outdated and arid "anti-imperialism" and a predisposition toward "pacifism" that lacked any credible response to aggression. The complexities of a sophisticated view of peace-oriented collective security did not lend itself to political mobilization. Peace politics included support for sanctions; an emphasis on containment and defensive deployments; a reliance on diplomacy, especially in relation to a long deferred and overdue Middle Eastern peace conference with Palestinian self-determination at the top of the agenda; encouragement of regional security arrangements; and a scrupulous attitude of respect for the UN Charter and the autonomy of the Security Council as imposing real constraints on superpower discretion.

At this stage of reflection upon the reality of the Gulf War, those of us associated with struggles for peace and justice are confronted by a master project under U.S. auspices to lead the world. This project is still being constituted. It is, in many respects, a resumption of what seemed successful to power wielders in the nineteenth century, "a long peace" at the geopolitical core of techno-financial power and one-sided mastery over the non-Western world. The Gulf War revived the plausibility of aspiring to master geopolitics and, with almost religious finality and patriarchal zeal, associated this vision of renewed Northern domination of the South with the militarization of space. Such a conception of order is content to witness the spread of Lebanonization in countries of the South, reserving an interventionary option for exceptional cases where crucial resources or strategic chokepoints are threatened by hostile forces or where a country in the South seems on the verge of acquiring the sort of military capability and political will that endangers the sense of Northern invulnerability.

Such a geopolitical project, while menacing, is but the latest stage in a long struggle that has gone on for several centuries in a variety of settings. Although it is necessary to acknowledge this latest set of moves connected with weapons innovations, it is also imperative to realize that military superiority rarely controls political change for very long, although it may influence shifts in tactics and perceived opportunities by those whose struggle is against oppression on behalf of greater equity and solidarity. The ebb and flow of history has proceeded with great force during the past decade, raising hopes here, dashing them there, suggesting above all that the present casts a short shadow. What seems definite beyond ambiguity at this juncture is predictably likely to be superseded in significance within a period of months or, at most, a few years. Amid all of these contradictory tendencies, there exist many opportunities to reestablish confidence that the struggles for a just world order will not be long frustrated by the temporary post-Gulf War triumphal proclamation of a new world order.

The revealed roots of war in the political culture of the West suggest that analysis, action, and hope must be recast along more radical lines touching directly on the deep structures of political life. It is necessary to confront the unpleasant truth that militarism can be democratic and that so long as beliefs, myths, and glory are bound to the traditions and imagination of patriarchy, there can be no fundamental challenge mounted against the war system. Perhaps, most depressing, is the degree to which multitudes of women as well as men seem to be still patriarchally entrapped.

Notes

1. See Walter Lippmann, *The Public Philosophy* (Boston: Little, Brown, 1955): especially 16–27.

2. Anthony Giddens, *Violence and the Nation State* (Cambridge: Polity Press, 1985): 230.

3. Mary Kaldor, *The Imaginary War* (Oxford: Basil Blackwell, 1980).

4. David Lamb, "Schwarzkopf Says Iraqi Forces Are on Verge of Collapse,'" *International Herald Tribune* (21 February 1991): 3.

5. Jack Nelson, "Gorbachev Plan Risks Ties With U.S., Analysts Say," *International Herald Tribune* (22 February 1991): 3.

Contributors

KAMEL S. ABU JABER was appointed Minister of Foreign Affairs for the Hashemite Kingdom of Jordan in September 1990. A professor of political science at the University of Jordan, he is the author and editor of numerous authoritative works on Middle Eastern Politics, including *The Arab Ba'ath Socialist Party* (1966), *The Jordanians and the People of Jordan* (1980), and *Major Issues in the Development of Jordan* (1983) and is a contributor to books including *Government and Politics of the Contemporary Middle East* (1970) and *Regional Security in the Third World* (1986). He also served as editor of the *Journal of the Arab Political Science Association* and *al-Reem (Journal of the Royal Society for the Conservation of Nature in Jordan)*.

TOZUN BAHCHELI has taught international and Middle Eastern politics at the University of Western Ontario since 1971. He has conducted research and published many articles on Cyprus, Greek-Turkish relations, and other aspects of Turkish foreign policy. His book, *Greek-Turkish Relations Since 1955*, was published by Westview Press in 1990.

RAYMOND W. BAKER divides his time between Williamstown, Massachusetts, where he is the Fred Greene Third Century Professor of International Relations and Chair of the African and Middle East Studies Program at Williams College, and Cairo, Egypt, where he holds an appointment as Adjunct Professor of Political Science at the American University in Cairo. Professor Baker is author of *Egypt's Uncertain Revolution Under Nasser and Sadat* and *Sadat and After: Struggles for Egypt's Political Soul*, both published by Harvard University Press. He is currently completing a book on Islamist moderates to be called *Islam, Democracy, and the Arab Future*.

FRIEDEMANN BUETTNER is Professor of Politics and Contemporary History of the Middle East at the Free University of Berlin and coordinator of the Interdisciplinary Research Unit "Ethnicity and Society" at the same university. He has completed numerous publications (mostly in German) on Islam and politics, authoritarianism and social change, state and society in Egypt, the Arab-Israeli conflict and Germany's Middle Eastern policy.

LOUIS J. CANTORI is Professor of Political Science, University of Maryland, Baltimore County and Adjunct Professor, Center of Contemporary Arab

Studies, Georgetown University. He is preparing for publication the edited volumes *Democratization in Egypt* (Middle East Institute and Indiana University Press) and *Development Theory Reconsidered: Political Change in the Middle East.*

SCHEHERAZADE DANESHKHU is on the staff of the *Financial Times* and is their writer on Iran. She has made contributions to various publications, including *Strategic Survey* (International Institute of Strategic Studies, London) and *Middle East International and the Middle East* (magazine), and to BBC Radio.

RICHARD FALK is Albert G. Milbank Professor of International Law and Practice at Princeton University. He is the author of *Revolutionaries and Functionaries: The Dual Face of Terrorism* (E. P. Dutton, 1988) and *Explorations at the Edge of Time* (Temple University Press, 1992). His concerns with the Middle East include being vice chairman of the MacBride Commission, which investigated Israeli violations of international law during the 1982 invasion of Lebanon, and serving as a member of the International Peace Research Association's Commission on a Peace Process for the Middle East.

MARION FAROUK-SLUGLETT teaches development politics and Middle Eastern politics at the University College of Wales, Swansea. She is co-editor and translator with Peter Sluglett of Bassam Tibi, *Arab Nationalism: A Critical Enquiry* (London, 1981), co-author, with Peter Sluglett, of *Iraq since 1958: From Revolution to Dictatorship* (London, 1987, 1990), and co-editor, with Peter Sluglett, of the *Times Guide to the Middle East* (London and Boston, 1992).

MALCOLM HAYWARD is Professor of English at Indiana University of Pennsylvania, teaching in its graduate program in literature. He is director of the Center of Research in Written Communication and Translation at IUP. He is also director of media relations for the American-Arab Institute for Strategic Studies and editor of its publication, the *Middle East Policy Review.*

ENID HILL is Professor of Political Science at the American University in Cairo, Egypt where she has lived and taught for over two decades. She obtained a Ph.D. from the University of Chicago in 1967 and is the author of *Mahkamal Studies in the Egyptian Legal System* (1979), *Al-Sanhuri and Islamic Law* (1989), and numerous articles on law, courts, contemporary politics and political economy in Egypt and the Middle East. She is presently working on studies of the Egyptian laws of "opening" (*infitah*) and liberalization, of the history and development of the Egyptian judiciary, and of the Islamic political philosophers.

JACQUELINE S. ISMAEL is a Professor of Social Work at the University of Calgary. She has published a number of articles and monographs on social change in the Middle East, as well as several works on Canadian social policy. She is co-author with Tareq Y. Ismael of *The People's Democratic Republic of Yemen: The Politics of Socialist Transformation* (1986), *Government and Politics in Islam* (1986), and *Politics and Government in the Middle East and North Africa* (1991). Her most recent work is *Kuwait: Dependency and Class in a Rentier State* (1993).

TAREQ Y. ISMAEL is a Professor of Political Science at the University of Calgary. He has written extensively on Middle East politics, the international relations of the Middle East, and ideology in the Arab world. His recent publications include *International Relations of the Contemporary Middle East* (1986), *Middle East Studies: International Perspectives on the State of the Art* (1990), *The Communist Movement in Egypt* (1990), and *Politics and Government in the Middle East and North Africa* (1991).

EBERHARD KIENLE is lecturer in politics of the Middle East at the School of Oriental and African Studies, University of London. He previously taught at the Free University of Berlin and held a research fellowship at St. Antony's College, Oxford. He is the author of *Ba'th v. Ba'th: The Conflict between Syria and Iraq 1968-1988* (London, I.B. Tauris, 1990) and is currently preparing another book on inter-Arab politics.

YASUMASA KURODA is Professor of Political Science at the University of Hawaii. He has authored and co-authored over 100 scholarly articles, seven monographs, and five books. His articles and reviews of his work have appeared in Arabic, English, Hebrew, Italian, and Japanese. He has served as a member of the editorial board of the *Journal of Arab Affairs* since its inception in 1982.

MARTIN LANDGRAF studied political science at the Free University of Berlin (Dipl. Pol. 1991) and completed postgraduate studies at the College of Europe, Bruges, Belgium (Diplome de Hautes Etudes Europénnes 1992). He is presently working on a Ph.D. thesis at the Free University of Berlin on *Europe and the Gulf: The Middle Eastern Policy of the European Community.*

ALI A. MAZRUI is Albert Schweitzer Professor in the Humanities and Director of the Institute of Global Cultural Studies at the State University of New York at Binghamton. He is also Albert Luthuli Professor-at-Large in the Humanities and Development Studies at the University of Jos in Nigeria, Senior Scholar at Cornell University, and was (1986-1992) Andrew D. White Professor-at-Large at Cornell University. His research interests include African politics, international political culture and North-South relations. He has published numerous works on African politics, including *African's International Relations* (Heinemann, 1977, reprinted a number of times), *A World Federation of Cultures: An African Perspective* (Free Press, 1976) and *Cultural Forces in World Politics* (James Currey and Heinemann, 1990), and he has served as special advisor to the World Bank, Washington, D.C.

TIMOTHY NIBLOCK is senior lecturer in Middle Eastern Politics and Director of the Graduate School of Political and Administrative Studies, University of Exeter. Between 1969 and 1977 he was Associate Professor of Political Science at the University of Khartoum. His publications include *Social and Economic Development in the Arab Gulf*; *State, Society and Economy in Saudi Arabia*; *Iraq: The Contemporary State*; and *Class and Power in Sudan: The Dynamics of Sudanese Politics, 1898–1985*. He has recently been working on democratization and economic liberalization in the Middle East, and with Emma Murphy has edited *Economic and Political Liberalization in the Middle East* (British Academic Press, 1992).

ANDREW T. PARASILITI is a doctoral candidate in international relations at the Johns Hopkins University School of Advanced International Studies.

MEIR PORAT is a practising lawyer and private scholar. A student of international politics, he has taught at the University of Calgary.

CHERYL A. RUBENBERG is Associate Professor of International Relations in the Political Science Department at Florida International University. She is the author of numerous books, articles, and book chapters on the Palestine Liberation Organization, the Israeli-Palestinian conflict, and U.S.-Israeli relations including *Israel and the American National Interest: A Critical Examination* (University of Illinois Press, 1986); *The Palestine Liberation Organization: Its Institutional Infrastructure* (Institute of Arab Studies, 1983); and "Sovereignty, Inequality, and Conflict: The Conflict over Palestine as a Case Study of the Dysfunctionalism of the Existing International System" in *Research in Inequality and Social Conflict*, vol. 2 (JAI Press, 1992).

PETER SLUGLETT teaches Middle Eastern history at the University of Durham, England. He is the author of *Britain in Iraq, 1914–1932* (1976), co-editor and translator, with Marion Farouk-Sluglett, of Bassam Tibi, *Arab Nationalism: A Critical Enquiry* (1981), and joint editor and co-author of several books on Middle East politics.

ROBERT SPRINGBORG is Associate Professor of Middle East Politics at Macquarie University. He is the author of *Family, Power and Politics in Egypt* and *Mubarak's Egypt* and co-author of *Politics in the Middle East*. He formerly taught at the University of California, Berkeley, and at the University of Pennsylvania.

SHIBLEY TELHAMI is Associate Professor of Government at Cornell University. He is author of *Power and Leadership in International Bargaining: The Path to the Camp David Accords* (Columbia, 1990) and numerous articles on international affairs. During the Gulf crisis, he served as Council on Foreign Relations Fellow advising the United States Mission at the UN. He also served as adviser to Representative Lee. H. Hamilton, Chairman of the House Subcommittee on Europe and the Middle East. He has taught at Ohio State University, the University of Southern California, Princeton, Swarthmore, and the University of California at Berkeley, where he received his doctorate in political science.

Index